A Comprehensive Review, and Self-assessment

NOT JUST QUESTION
KCET Series

Dr. Ankur Rustagi (AIIMS)
Dept of Oral and Maxillo-facial Surgery
All India Institute of Medial Science, New Delhi
Dr. Akansha Gupta (AIIMS)
Dept of Conservative Dentistry and Endodontics
All India Institute of Medial Science, New Delhi

CBS PUBLISHERS & DISTRIBUTORS PVT. LTD.
NEW DELHI • BANGALORE • PUNE • COCHIN • CHENNAI (INDIA)

ISBN : 978-81-239-1589-0

First Edition : 2008
Reprint : 2012

Published by Satish Kumar Jain and produced by V.K. Jain for
CBS Publishers & Distributors Pvt. Ltd.,
CBS Plaza, 4819/XI Prahlad Street, 24 Ansari Road, Daryaganj,
New Delhi - 110002, India. • Website: www.cbspd.com
e-mail: delhi@cbspd.com, cbspubs@airtelmail.in
Ph.: 23289259, 23266861, 23266867 • Fax: 011-23243014

Branches:

- ***Bengaluru:*** Seema House, 2975, 17th Cross, K.R. Road,
  Bansankari 2nd Stage, Bengaluru - 560070 Ph.: +91-80-26771678/79
  • E-mail: cbsbng@gmail.com, bangalore@cbspd.com
- ***Pune:*** Bhuruk Prestige, Sr. No. 52/12/2+1+3/2,
  Narhe, Haveli (Near Katraj-Dehu Road By-pass), Pune - 411051
  Ph.: +91-20-64704058/59, 32342277 • E-mail: pune@cbspd.com
- ***Kochi:*** 36/14, Kalluvilakam, Lissie Hospital Road,
  Kochi - 682018, Kerala • Ph.: +91-484-4059061-65
  Fax: +91-484-4059065 • E-mail: cochin@cbspd.com
- ***Chennai:*** 20, West Park Road, Shenoy Nagar, Chennai - 600030
  Ph.: +91-44-26260666, 26208620 E-mail: chennai@cbspd.com

Printed at :
India Binding House, Noida (UP)

DEDICATED TO

OUR PARENTS

Sh Narender and Anita Rustagi and

Dr Rajendra and Madhu Gupta

For their unlimited Love and Sacrifice

and our Siblings

Aayush and Dr Anupama

for their continuous encouragement and love

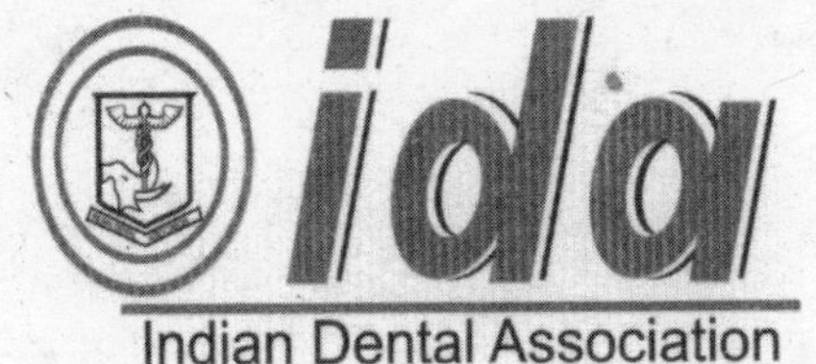

Indian Dental Association

President
Dr. M. C. Mohan
Tellicherry Dental Clinic
Logans Road
Tellicherry - 670101
Kerala State
Tel: 0490 - 2322406
Email: drmohanmc@yahoo.co.in
drmcmohan@hotmail.com

Hon. Secretary General
Dr. Ashok Dhoble
Bombay Mutual Terrace, 2nd floor,
534, Sandhurst Bridge, Opera house,
Mumbai 400 007.
Tel: 91-22-2364 3344/ 2363 6655
ashokdhoble@ida.org.in

Head Office
Bombay Mutual Terrace, 2nd floor, 534, Sandhurst Bridge, Opera House, Mumbai 400 007. India.
Phone : 91-22-23696655 / 23671515. Fax : 91-22-23685613. Email : ho@ida.org.in Website: www.ida.org.in

Committed to Dental Excellence

It gives me great pleasure in writing this foreword to **NJQ KCET- MDS series by TARGET EDUCARE** compiled by Dr Ankur Rustagi and Dr Akanksha Gupta.

Multiple Choice questions test the basic knowledge of the candidates in the most intriguing way. Limited time and opportunities poses hurdle even for the brightest of the student, and herein lies the importance of a comprehensively written and at the same time a "user-friendly" book.

By virtue of this effort, the authors, am sure, would enable students, of not only Karnataka, but all over India to successfully crack various MDS entrances.

I, highly recommend NJQ series to all those, who are looking for a successful career ahead in various specialties in dentistry.

Dr. Ashok Dhoble
Hon. Secretary General,
Indian Dental Association, Head Office

Preface

In modern India, MDS is becoming a necessity and the ever growing competition leaves no quarter for error or lapse. In this cut-throat competition for little over 1000 MDS seats across the nation, recognized by the DCI, over 10,000 aspirants appear every year. So effectively every single lapse pushes you back by approximately 10 ranks! So, its clear that ***EVERY SINGLE QUESTION MATTERS,*** and its not the answer only that matters, the aspirant should have an attitude to "crack" the question by knowing the "how" and "why" aspects of the answer.

By the medium of this book, the authors have utilized their own experiences and knowledge to deliver to you a thorough, and comprehensive review of the KCET MDS-Entrance Examinations.

One may wonder, as to why you need to practice Karnataka papers if you are not eligible for them at the first place. Well, dear friends, the point is to expose yourselves to the diverse world of MCQ's and by our personal experience we feel, the questions add to the "so needed" extra dimension to any candidate's preparation. The questions are basic, testing the candidate's theoretical and clinical application of his knowledge. Topics on the new horizon like Distraction Osteogenesis, Implants, and other medical developments have been dealt in depth catering to the needs of modern examination pattern.

By virtue of this book, and its succeeding volumes, we hope to combine the best from us with the best in you.

" If you have the will to succeed, you have achieved half your success
If you don't, you have achieved half of your failures...... "

David Ambrose

SUBJECT WISE CLASSIFICATION

Contents

2007

Questions & Answers

1

KCET 2007

QUESTIONS

ANATOMY AND HISTOLOGY

1. **The Preganglionic parasympathetic fibers for otic ganglion commence at**
   (a) Superior Salivatory nucleus (b) Inferior Salivatory nucleus
   (c) Nucleus of tractus solitarius (d) Lacrimatory nucleus
2. **Medial pterygoid muscle is supplied by**
   (a) Branch from trunk of mandibular nerve
   (b) Branch from anterior division of mandibular nerve
   (c) Branch from posterior division of mandibular nerve
   (d) Branch from maxillary nerve
3. **Facial vein communicates with the cavernous sinus through**
   (a) Retromolar vein and internal jugular vein
   (b) External jugular vein and internal jugular vein
   (c) Internal jugular vein and retromandibular vein
   (d) Superior ophthalmic vein and pterygoid venous plexus
4. **The maxillary air sinus opens into middle meatus at**
   (a) Infundibulum (b) Summit of Infundibulum
   (c) Bulla ethmoidalis (d) Hiatus semilunaris
5. **'Wry neck' deformity is due to the damage 'of:**
   (a) Platysma (b) Sternohyoid
   (c) Sternocleidomastoid (d) Omohyoid
6. **Schwann cells are derived from:**
   (a) Neural crest cells (b) Mesoderm
   (c) Endoderm (d) Ectoderm

DENTAL ANATOMY AND HISTOLOGY

7. Roots of the permanent mandibular 1st molar are
(a) Mesio buccal, Distobuccal & Lingual (b) Mesiolingual, Distolingual & Buccal
(c) Mesial & Distal (d) Buccal & Lingual

8. Mixed dentition period lasts from
(a) 6-9 years (b) 8-9 years
(c) 6-12 years (d) 2-12 years

9. Longest root in the permanent maxillary molar is:
(a) Buccal (b) Lingual
(c) Mesio buccal (d) Distobuccal

10. Eruption of maxillary permanent canine takes place at the age of:
(a) 9 to 10 years (b) 11 to 12 years
(c) 13 to 14 years (d) 8 to 9 years

PHYSIOLOGY

11. Cephalic phase of gastric secretion can be demonstrated by the following experiment:
(a) Heidenhan's pouch (b) Condition reflex
(c) Pavlov's pouch (d) None of the above

12. 'P' wave in ECG recording is caused due to
(a) Atrial depolarization (b) Atrial repolarization
(c) Ventricular depolarization (d) Ventricular repolarization

13. Factor V is
(a) Stable factor (b) Christmas factor
(c) Hageman's factor (d) Labile factor

14. Trypsin is an activator of all of the following enzymes EXCEPT
(a) Chymotrypsinogen (b) Pepsinogen
(c) Proelastase (d) Procolipase

15. Delta waves of Electroencephalogram have frequency of:
(a) More than 14 cycles per second (b) Between 8 and 13 cycles per second
(c) Less than 3.5 cycles per second (d) Between 4 and 7 cycles per second

16. Parathyroid hormone increases the blood level of
(a) Copper (b) Calcium
(c) Iron (d) Sodium

17. Glycosylated haemoglobin assay is helpful in the monitoring of patients with
(a) Addison's disease (b) Diabetes Mellitus
(c) Cushing's disease (d) Graves' disease

18. The tissue macrophages are derived from the

(a) Neutrophil (b) Eosinophil
(c) Monocyte (d) All of the above

MICROBIOLOGY

19. Sterilization by moist heat is used in

(a) Autoclave (b) Hot air oven
(c) Filters (d) Incineration

20. The small non-particulate protein leading to enhanced replication of HBV as well as HIV is

(a) HBc Ag (b) HBs Ag
(c) Hbe Ag (d) HBx Ag

21. The Gram negative bacteria most numerous in the oral cavity are

(a) Streptococci (b) Veillonellae
(c) Selenomonas (d) Eikenella

22. Antiseptic technique in surgery was first introduced by

(a) Joseph Lister (b) Louis Pastuer
(c) Robert Koch (d) Antony Van Leeuwenhoek

23 Which component of the cell wall is responsible for endotoxic activity:

(a) Region I (b) Region II
(c) Region III (d) Boivin antigen

24. Immunoglobin molecule which mediates in anaphylaxis is

(a) Ig-M (b) Ig G
(c) Ig E (d) IgA

25. Which of the following viruses appears to be involved in the pathogenesis of Kaposi's sarcoma?

(a) Human Herpes Virus 3 (b) Human Herpes Virus 1
(c) Human Herpes Virus 8 (d) Human Herpes Virus 4

26. Candidal hyphae can be stained using

(a) Van Gieson's stain (b) Periodic acid Schiff stain
(c) Masson Trichrome stain (d) Toluidine blue stain

27. Infection mononucleosis is caused by the virus:

(a) CMV (b) EB
(c) HIV (d) Herpes simplex

BIOCHEMISTRY

28. Enzymes increase reaction rates by
(a) Altering the free energy of the action
(b) Decreasing the energy of activation
(c) Enhancing the forward reaction
(d) Inhibiting the backward reaction

29. Von Gierkes disease is associated with a deficiency of
(a) Glucose-6-phosphate dehydrogenase
(b) Glucose -6-phosphatase in liver
(c) Phosphorylase in muscle
(d) Hexokinase

30. Ammonia produced by brain is trapped as
(a) Urea
(b) Uric acid
(c) Creatinine
(d) Glutamine

31. Dietary fiber is rich in:
(a) Starch
(b) Cellulose
(c) Collagen
(d) inulin

GENERAL PATHOLOGY

32. An increase in the number of cells in an organ or tissue is
(a) Hypertrophy
(b) Hyperplasia
(c) Aplasia
(d) Metaplasia

33. Severe generalized edema is called as
(a) Myxoedema
(b) Pitting edema
(c) Anasarca
(d) Dependent edema

34. Transfusion transmitted diseases are all EXCEPT:
(a) HIV
(b) Hepatitis C
(c) CMV
(d) Tuberculosis

DENTAL MATERIALS

35. Steel is an alloy of iron in which the carbon content is
(a) less than 18%
(b) less than 2%
(c) more than 8%
(d) none of the above

36. The % of free monomer in a heat-cured acrylic resin is
(a) 3% to 5%
(b) 8% to 10%
(c) 0.2% to 0.5%
(d) 0.600 to 0.8%

37. Liquid used in polycarboxylate cement is
(a) Poly acrylic acid
(b) Phosphoric acid
(c) Eugenol
(d) Methacrylic acid

38. The total copper content in admixed alloy ranges from approximately

(a) 1 to 6 weight percent
(b) 9 to 20 weight percent
(c) 30 to 40 weight percent
(d) 45 to 55 weight percent

39. For Dental Amalgam, the elastic modulus and tensile strength is

(a) 40 Gpa and 60 - 100 MPa
(b) 21 Gpa and 27- 55 MPa
(c) 350 Gpa and 110 -120 MPa
(d) 360 Gpa and 125-130 MPa

40. The Knoop Hardness Number of Microfilled Composite Restorative material ranges from

(a) 50-60KHN
(b) 25-35KHN
(c) 15-20KHN
(d) 40-48KHN

41. The biting force at molar region during mastication is

(a) 20 to 55 N
(b) 30 to 75 N
(c) 50 to 75 N
(d) 90 to 200 N

42. In air-abrasive technology the abrasive particles used are

(a) Iron oxide
(b) Tin oxide
(c) Aluminium oxide
(d) Silicon oxide

43. Finer particle size of silica:

(a) Slower the hygroscopic expansion
(b) Greater the hygroscopic expansion
(c) Normal setting expansion
(d) No setting expansion

44. The minimum film thickness for luting a single crown:

(a) 20 μm
(b) 25 μm
(c) 35 μm
(d) 45 μm

45. Putty wash technique (two stage) :

(a) Light body and Putty used at the same time
(b) Putty used first and light body used second
(c) Light body first and putty later
(d) None of the above

PHARMACOLOGY

46. Following administration, nitrous oxide will become saturated in blood and dissolved in serum fraction of blood within?

(a) 3-5 mins
(b) 10 mins
(c) 10-15 mins
(d) 6-8 min

47. Which of these is not a Glycoside?

(a) Digoxin
(b) Digitoxin
(c) Ergotoxine
(d) Gitoxin

48. Immune mediated qualitative drug intolerance is called

(a) Super sensitivity
(b) Idiosyncrasy
(c) Hyper sensitivity
(d) Hyper acidity

49. The statement, NOT true of Selective Cox-2 inhibitor is:

(a) The analgesic and anti-inflammatory effects identical to that of Non-selective NSAID
(b) They do not offer the cardio-protective effect
(c) Safe in patients with renal insufficiency
(d) Fewer incidence of gastrointestinal side effect

GENERAL MEDICINE

50. Rotten apple smell of breath is associated with

(a) Liver insufficiency
(b) Kidney insufficiency
(c) Unbalanced insulin dependent diabetes
(d) Respiratory problems

51. Outright or full-blown AIDS is characterized by

(a) CD4 T-cells 800 cells/ mm^3
(b) CD4 T-cells 400 cells/ mm^3
(c) CD4 T-cells 600 cells/ mm^3
(d) CD4 T-cells<200 cells/ mm^3

52. For Arsenic poisoning Antidote is

(a) Penicillamine
(b) Des ferrixamine
(c) E.D.T.A
(d) B.A.L

53. A hemophiliac patient has rheumatoid arthritis. Which drug might be prescribed to relieve the pain?

(a) Acetaminophen
(b) Acetylsalicylic acid
(c) Phenylbutazone
(d) Naproxen

54. In hemophilia, abnormality is found in

(a) Total leukocyte count
(b) Platelet count
(c) Red blood Cell count
(d) Activated partial thromboplastin time

55. The treatment of choice for trigeminal neuralgia is

(a) Carbamezepine
(b) Morphine
(c) Aspirin
(d) Ibuprofen

56. Most specific histological lesion in diabetic nephropathy is

(a) Widening of glomerular basement membrane
(b) Generalized mesangial thickening
(c) Occlusion of glomeruli with fibrin caps
(d) Hyalinization of afferent arterioles and Kimmelstein-Wilson bodies

57. Infectious disease causing cirrhosis of the liver are

(a) Viral hepatitis
(b) Toxoplasmosis
(c) E.B.Virus
(d) All of the above

58. Portal hypertension is characterized by all of the following EXCEPT:

(a) Splenomegaly
(b) Variceal bleeding
(c) Dilated veins over the abdomen
(d) Gynecomastia

59. The peripheral smear picture in Iron deficiency anaemia will be:

(a) Macrocytic, Hypochromic
(b) Leukoerythroblastic
(c) Normocytic, Normochromic
(d) Microcytic, Hypochromic

60. The drug of choice in Trigeminal neuralgia is:

(a) Phenytoin sodium
(b) Carbamazepine
(c) Gabapentin
(d) Sodium Valproate

61. Causes of a Transudate Ascites include all the following EXCEPT:

(a) Tuberculosis
(b) Nephrotic syndrome
(c) Hypoproteinaemia
(d) Congestive cardiac failure

62. Gas gangrene infection is caused by ¬

(a) Staphylococcus aureus
(b) Pseudomonas
(c) Clostridium perfringes
(d) E.Coli

GENERAL SURGERY

63. Specimens for a biopsy should be taken from

(a) necrotic area
(b) subdermal layer
(c) border of an ulcerated area
(d) center of an ulcerated area

64. A Branchial cyst develops from vestigial remnants of

(a) Fourth branchial cleft
(b) 2nd branchial cleft
(c) 3rd branchial cleft
(d) 1st branchial cleft

65. Gut suturing material is absorbed by

(a) Oxidation
(b) Hydrolysis
(c) Fibrinolysis
(d) Proteolysis

66. In modified radical neck dissection following structure is preserved-

(a) Submandibular gland
(b) Internal jugular vein
(c) Fat tissue
(d) Great auricular nerve

67. Following ONE is not true of carcinoma of lip-

(a) Most common on vermilion of lower lip
(b) A 90% cure rate is possible with surgery or radiotherapy
(c) Initially tumor spreads laterally rather than infiltrating deeply
(d) Up to one third of the lip can not be removed

68. The common site of glomangioma is

(a) Head and Neck
(b) Nail bed
(c) Chest wall
(d) Retroperitoneal

69. Commonest cause of cellulites is:

(a) Staphylococcus (b) Pseudomonas
(c) Streptococcus (d) Pneumococcus

70. Marjolin's ulcer is :

(a) Squamous cell carcinoma from scar (b) Trophic ulcer
(c) Tuberculous ulcer (d) Rodent ulcer

71. Commonest site for ectopic salivary gland tumor is:

(a) Tongue (b) Cheek
(c) Palate (d) Neck

72. In 3rd degree burns, all are seen EXCEPT:

(a) Vesicles are absent (b) Painful
(c) Leathergy skin (d) Charred & black

73. Which of the following statements is true for MEN type 1

(a) There is hyperplasia of parathyroid gland
(b) Chromophobe adenoma of pituitary gland may result in acromegaly
(c) Pancreatic tumours may produce gastrin, insulin, glucogon, somatostatin
(d) All the above

74. Rule of 9 to estimate surface area of burnt patient was introduced by:

(a) Mortiz Kaposi (b) Alexander & Wallace
(c) Lister (d) Barclag

75. Squamous cell carcinoma has tendency to metastasize through

(a) Blood stream (b) Lymphatic system
(c) Direct contact (d) None of the above

76. The benign neoplasm of 'brown fat' noted in oral/pharyngeal region is

(a) Lipoma (b) Hibernoma
(c) Teratoma (d) Brown tumor

ORAL PATHOLOGY

77. Monro's abscess is seen in the histological picture of

(a) Darriers disease (b) Psoriasis
(c) Systemic lupus erythematosus (d) Behcets disease

78. 'Canker sore' is otherwise commonly known as

(a) Recurrent apthous ulcer (b) Recurrent herpetic gingivitis
(c) Acute necrotizing ulcerative gingivitis (d) Recurrent herpes labialis

79. Generalized microdontia is often associated with

(a) Pituitary dwarfism (b) Pituitary gigantism
(c) Herediatary ectodermal dysplasia (d) All the above

80. Which of the following is not a feature of Hutchinsons triad

(a) Gumma
(b) Hypoplasia of incisors and molars
(c) Eighth nerve deafness
(d) Intestinal keratitis

81. Venous malformations involving the leptomeninges of the cerebral cortex is a salient feature of

(a) Rendu-Osler-Weber disease
(b) Maffuci's syndrome
(c) Angio-osteohypertrophy syndrome
(d) Sturge Weber Syndrome

82. The manifestation of congenital syphilis include

(a) Lympadenopathy
(b) Condyloma Lata
(c) Hepatosplenomegaly
(d) All of the above

83. Peripheral giant cell granuloma occurs most commonly on the

(a) Gingiva
(b) Alveolar ridge
(c) Palate
(d) Floor of the mouth

84. The term 'pulse granuloma' suggests reaction towards the fragments of foreign material like

(a) Cotton fibers
(b) Black silk
(c) Silver amalgam
(d) Legumes

85. A patient 18 years of age with sebaceous cysts on the scalp and back of the neck, an osteoma on the right mandible; Radiographs reveal multiple impacted supernumerary teeth in both jaws. These findings suggest

(a) Cleidocranial dysostois
(b) Ectodermal dysplasia
(c) Gardner's syndrome
(d) Osteogenesis imperfecta

86. Of the following syndromes, taurodontism is associated with

(a) Rubinstein - Taybi Syndrome
(b) Klinefelter Syndrome
(c) Ascher's Syndrome
(d) Gardner's Syndrome

87. Absence of cementum is a feature of

(a) Vitamin D resistant rickets
(b) Hypocalcaemia
(c) Hypophosphatasia
(d) Osteoporosis

88. Phycomycete causing infection in man

(a) Rhizopus
(b) Mucor
(c) Absidia
(d) All

89. 'Chemical mumps' is synonymous with

(a) Epidemic parotitis
(b) Nutritional mumps
(c) Iodine mumps
(d) Nonspecific mumps

90. Epstein Barr virus is believed to cause

(a) Burkitt's Lymphoma
(c) Nasopharyngeal carcinoma
(b) Oral hairy leukplakia
(d) All of the above

ORAL MEDICINE AND RADIOLOGY

91. The most common neoplasm among HIV positive homosexual males
(a) Non-Hodgkin's lymphoma
(b) Glomus tumor
(c) Kaposi's sarcoma
(d) None of the above

92. Hair-on-end appearance of skull is seen in
(a) Sickle cell anemia
(b) Fibrous dysplasia
(c) Iron deficiency anemia
(d) Megaloblastic anemia

93. The Sialogogues used in Xerostomia is
(a) Hyoscine
(b) Pilocarpine
(c) Hyaluronidase
(d) Vitamin C

94. Topical Antifungal agent in candidiasis is
(a) Clotrimazole
(b) Clotrimoxazole
(c) Ornidazol
(d) Propronolol

95. One of the following lesions has extremely high rate of malignant transformation
(a) verrucous leukoplakia
(b) White spongy nevus
(c) Nodular leukoplakia
(d) Target or iris lesion

96. The oral lesion called mucous patches is usually multiple, grayish white plaque associated with
(a) Pain
(b) No pain
(c) Itching
(d) Burning sensation

97. Antinuclear Antibodies are seen in
(a) Systemic Lupus Erythematous
(b) Recurrent Apthous Stomatitis
(c) Leukoplakia
(d) NOMA

98. Bleeding time and Prothrombin time is prolonged in
(a) DIC
(b) Thrombocytopenia
(c) Hemophilia
(d) Von Willebrand's Disease

99. Ground Glass appearance is seen in
(a) Fibrous Epulis
(b) Fibrous dysplasia
(c) Ossifying Fibroma
(d) Crouzon Syndrome

100. The optical density of gross film for typically is:
(a) 0.6 to 3.0
(b) 0.2 to 0.3
(c) 0.2 to 0.4
(d) 0.6 to 4.0

101. Fixed post mitotic cells are
(a) Spermatocytes
(b) Fibroblasts
(c) Endothelial Cells
(d) Muscle

102. Clearing agent in fixer solution is
(a) Ammonium chloride
(b) Ammonium Thio Sulfate
(c) Ammonium sulfate
(d) Ammonium oxalate

103. Phleboliths are seen in
(a) Dental Pulp
(b) Salivary Gland duct
(c) Cavernous Haemangioma
(d) Subepithelial Bulla

104. Units of radiation exposure is
(a) Rad
(b) Roentgen
(c) Rem
(d) Seivert

PERIODONTICS

105. Bacterial plaque can effectively induce bone loss (Radius of action) is about
(a) 1 mm
(b) 1.5 - 2.5 mm
(c) 3 - 5 mm
(d) 6 mm - 8 mm

106. ANUG is frequently associated with deficiency of
(a) Thiamine
(b) Riboflavin
(c) Niacin
(d) Pyridoxine

107. Which of the following is a root-conditioning agent?
(a) Hydrogen peroxide
(b) Citric acid
(c) Benzoic acid
(d) Sodium hypochlorite

108. After curettage how long does it take re-epitheliazation to occur?
(a) 2-7 days
(b) 4-5 weeks
(c) 1-3 days
(d) 1-2 weeks

109. When occlusal forces exceed the adaptive capacity of the tissue injury results. The resultant injury is called
(a) Traumatic occlusion
(b) Bruxism
(c) Trauma from occlusion
(d) Tissue injury

110. Splitting of two rooted tooth into two separate portions is called
(a) Root resection
(b) Hemisection
(c) Furcation
(d) Recession

111. Current concepts of evaluating health care require a scientific basis for treatment referred as
(a) Evidence based therapy
(b) Periodontal maintenance
(c) Tooth mortality
(d) Prevention of loss of attachment

112. Periodontitis is caused by
(a) Malnutrition
(b) Supra gingival plaque
(c) Bio-film
(d) Faulty tooth brushing

113. Dental floss is used to prevent

(a) Discoloration of teeth
(b) Caries in teeth
(c) Sensitivity in teeth
(d) Inter proximal plaque formation

114. Regeneration in periodontal therapy aims at

(a) Bone refill
(b) Repair of the bony defect
(c) Reconstitution of the lost periodontium
(d) Removal of the diseased bone

115. Pellicle formation on enamel starts with

(a) Absorption of glycoprotein from saliva
(b) Focal areas of mineralization
(c) Bacterial colonization
(d) Absorption of endotoxins

116. An enzyme present in saliva which causes cell wall lysis

(a) Lysozyme
(b) Peroxidase
(c) Lactoferin
(d) Hyaluronidase

117. Post extraction bleeding in a leukemic patient is due to:

(a) increase in leukocytes
(b) low calcium level
(c) platelet disorder
(d) deficiency of clotting factors

118. In the concept of biological width, the value of biological width is

(a) 1 mm
(b) 2 mm
(c) 3 mm
(d) 4 mm

CONSERVATIVE DENTISTRY AND ENDODONTICS

119. The matrix retainer where in anatomy adaptation is possible without wedges is

(a) Tofflemire
(b) Steele's siqveland
(c) Ivory no. 1
(d) Ivory no. 8

120. R.C Prep is

(a) EDTA
(b) EDTA and urea peroxide
(c) EDTA and carbamide peroxide
(d) EDTA and Cetavlon

121. Self etching primers

(a) simultaneously etches and prime dentin and enamel
(b) Etches enamel only
(c) Only bonds to enamel
(d) Only removes smear layer

122. The most practical method to disinfect gutta percha prior to obturation is

(a) Submerge in 5% solution of NaOC1
(b) Submerge in Ethyl Alcohol
(c) Submerge in 5% NaOC1 and rinse with ethyl alcohol
(d) Rinse with 3% Hydrogen peroxide

123. A ferrule is

(a) A rule governing gold inlay cavity preparation
(b) A mechanical rapid tooth separator
(c) An encircling band of metal that increases fracture resistance of the tooth
(d) An electronic measuring device for determination of the length of tooth during root canal treatment

124. The compressive strength of dentine is approximately

(a) 468 Mpa (b) 162 Mpa
(c) 350 Mpa (d) 266 Mpa

125. The bleaching material used in night guard vital tooth bleaching is

(a) Superoxol (b) Anesthetic ether and hydrochloric acid
(c) Sodium bicarbonate (d) Carbamide peroxide

126. Powdered gold is

(a) Made by a combination of chemical precipitation and atomization
(b) Made by electrolytic precipitation
(c) Made by beating pure gold at high temperatures
(d) Made by milling pure gold ingots

127. Stieglitz pliers is

(a) Used to contour matrix bands
(b) Used to hold the silver point
(c) Used to remove roots during hemisection
(d) Used to place rubber dam clamp on the tooth

128. Which among the following Root Canal irrigant removes the smear layer:

(a) Sodium hypochloride (b) EDTA
(c) Hydrogen peroxide (d) Chlorhexidine

129. Currently available composites undergo polymerization at a wavelength of:

(a) 474 nm (b) 470 nm
(c) 460 nm (d) 464 nm

130. The ideal marginal metal for cast inlay restoration should be:

(a) 20 - 30 degree (b) 30 - 40 degree
(c) 40 - 50 degree (d) More than 50 degree

131. All the following criteria contribute to a successful direct pulp capping procedure except:

(a) Hemorrhage from the exposure site is easily controlled
(b) The exposure site is small, less than 0.5 mm in diameter
(c) Exposure site is the consequence of infected dentin extending into the pulp
(d) Exposure occurred in a clean uncontaminated filed

132. The maximum head diameter of ISO Gatesglidden drill # 1 is equivalent to

(a) No 50 file at Do (b) No 40 file at Do
(c) No 60 file at Do (d) No 80 file at Do

133. The instrument that has four unit formula
(a) Gingival margin trimmer
(b) Enamel hatchet
(c) Hoe
(d) Chisel

134. Rubber dam was introduced by
(a) Tomy Hanks
(b) S.(C) Barnum
(c) Hedstorm
(d) G.V.Black

135. The simplest form of pulp therapy is
(a) Apicoectomy
(b) Pulp capping
(c) Pulpectomy
(d) Pulpotomy

ORAL AND MAXILLO-FACIAL SURGERY

136. The maximum dosage of local anesthetic agent like lidocaine must be reduced when used in combination with a CNS and/respiratory depressant because, it may result in
(a) Seizures
(b) Coma
(c) Death
(d) All of the above

137. The most common reason for removal of impacted mandibular third molars:
(a) referred pain
(b) orthodontic treatment
(c) recurrent pericoronitis
(d) chronic periodontal disease

138. Enbloc resection of the segment of the bone
(a) Complete resection of the jaw bone
(b) Resection of half of the affected jaw
(c) Resection of the tumor only
(d) The entire tumor is removed intact with a rim of uninvolved bone while maintaining continuity of jaw

139. The intercanthal distance suggestive of traumatic telecanthus is
(a) 30 mm
(b) 32 mm
(c) 25 mm
(d) 40 mm

140. Which of the following is used for 'Figure of eight' wiring for stabilization of subluxated teeth in alveolar injuries
(a) 0.23 mm stainless steel wire
(b) 0.35 mm stainless steel wire
(c) 0.45 mm stainless steel wire
(d) 0.55 mm stainless steel wire

141. Carnoys solution is used in the treatment of
(a) Odontogenic Keratocyst
(b) Ameloblastome
(c) Dentigerous cyst
(d) Mucocele

142. Frey's syndrome can occur following
(a) Saggital split osteotomy
(b) Cald-wel-Iuc operation
(c) Parotidectomy
(d) Marsupilization

143. Which of the following infection is the cause for multiple sites of osteomyelitis of the jaw

(a) peritonsillar abscess (b) local trauma
(c) hematogenous infection (d) buccal space infection

144. The oral cleft problem occurs between the period of

(a) 1st and 2nd week of embryo-fetal life (b) 6th and 10th week of embryo-fetal life
(c) 3rd week of embryo-fetal life (d) None of the above

145 Cavernous sinus thrombosis can occur due to spread of odontogenic infection via

(a) Tissue spaces (b) Lymphatic route
(c) Hematogenous route (d) All of the above

146. The least difficult impaction to remove surgically is

(a) Vertical (b) Mesioangular
(c) Distoangular (d) Horizontal

147. The distance from the apical end of the implant and superior aspect of Inferior alveolar CEI should be minimum of

(a) 2 mm (b) 4 mm
(c) 6 mm (d) 5 mm

PEDODONTICS

148. Which of the following is not a type of cerebral palsy?

(a) Spasticity (b) Autism
(c) Ataxia (d) Athetosis

149. Tell-show-do technique was introduced by

(a) Addelston (b) Craig
(c) Christopher (d) Keith moore

150. According to Stanford -Binet, non-trainable type of mental retardation has IQ of

(a) Below 20 (b) between 36-51
(c) Above 51 (d) 130

151. Which of the following molar relationship is the most common in primary

(a) Mesial step (b) Distal step
(c) Flush terminal plane (d) Can't say

152. The type of space maintainer advised when there is bilateral loss of teeth same arch

(a) Distal shoe (b) Band & Loop
(c) Band & Bar (d) Lingual arch holding app

ORTHODONTICS

153. Adenoid facies is seen in

(a) Mouth breathing habit
(b) Bruxism
(c) Sub mandibular lymphadenitis
(d) Thumb sucking habit

154. Distal shoe guiding appliance is

(a) Habit Breaking Appliance
(b) Space regainer
(c) Helps in eruption of first permanent molar
(d) It is a type of pulpectomy procedure

155. Anterior open bite & maxillary constriction is caused by

(a) Thumb sucking
(b) Nail biting
(c) Bruxism
(d) None

156. Site at which ossification stops in the mandible

(a) Mandibular lingula
(b) Coronoid process
(c) Symphysis
(d) Angle of the mandible

157. Adams clasps for premolar is made using the following diameter wire:

(a) 0.8 mm
(b) 0.7 mm
(c) 0.6 mm
(d) 0.5 mm

158. Transposition of teeth is most commonly seen in the region of

(a) Maxillary central and lateral incisors
(b) Mandibular canine and first premolar
(c) Maxillary lateral incisor, canine and premolar
(d) Mandibular first and second premolars

159. An expansion appliance made with an expansion screw is an example

(a) Simple anchorage
(b) Reciprocal anchorage
(c) Multiple anchorage
(d) Reinforced anchorage

160. The Optimal orthodontic force per square centimeter of the root surface area is held to be

(a) 18-22 gms
(b) 18-26 gms
(c) 20-26 gms
(d) 26-30 gms

161. All of the following are considered micro-skeletal units of the mandible as per the matrix theory EXCEPT

(a) Chin
(b) Glenoid fossa
(c) Coronoid process
(d) Angle of the mandible

162. An example of a Tissue-borne appliance among the following is

(a) Activator
(b) Bionator
(c) Frankel's Functional Regulator
(d) Twin Block

163. The three main vertical pillars of trajectories of force arising from the alveolar process and ending in the base of the skull are all except

(a) Canine pillar
(b) Zygomatic pillar
(c) Pterygoid pillar
(d) Condylar pillar

164. The Activator appliance was introduced by,

(a) Robin
(b) Andresen
(c) Clark
(d) Andrews

165. "Baker's anchorage" refers to the use of

(a) Intramaxillary elastics
(b) Intermaxillary elastics
(c) Anterior Vertical elastics
(d) Cross elastics

166. The kind of force that is best suited for orthodontic tooth movement

(a) Light continuous forces
(b) Intermittent forces
(c) Interrupted continuous forces
(d) Heavy continuous forces

167. Functional matrix theory suggests that the determinant growth of skeletal tissues resides in

(a) Skeletal
(b) Sutures
(c) Cartilages
(d) Non-skeletal tissues

168. The SCAN index is generally used as a

(a) Malocclusion index
(b) Treatment need index
(c) Treatment change index
(d) Treatment of priority index

169. Gingivectomy of which of the fibers can reduce the relapse of orthodontically moved teeth

(a) Gingival fibers
(b) Alveolar crest fibers
(c) Transseptal
(d) None

PROSTHODONTICS

170. The theory of matching teeth to face forms was advanced by

(a) Hanau
(b) Frush and Fisher
(c) J.Leon Williams
(d) Schiffman

171. Common indication for a hygienic pontic is in

(a) Maxillary anteriors
(b) Mandibular anteriors
(c) Mandibular posteriors
(d) Maxillary premolars

172. The I-Bar RPD was introduced by

(a) Berg and caputo
(b) Kratochvil
(c) McDowell
(d) Krol

173. Thickness of the dies spacer should be:

(a) 10 - 20 μm
(b) 20 - 40 μm
(c) 30 - 60 μm
(d) 25-50 μm

174. Anatomic teeth should have a cusp angle of
(a) 30°
(b) 31°
(c) 32°
(d) 33°

175. Ovate pontics are used in :
(a) Well rounded ridges
(b) Knife edged ridges
(c) Recently extracted tooth sockets
(d) Flat ridges

176. A High Tracing Device is used for :
(a) Extra oral graphic tracings
(b) Intra oral graphic tracings
(c) Cephalometric tracings
(d) Determining focal forms

177. Functional Cusp Bevel is given for:
(a) Marginal integrity
(b) Structural durability
(c) Retention and resistance form
(d) To improve the geometry of tooth surface

178. Osseointegration was first defined by:
(a) Bothe and Coworkers
(b) Greenfield
(c) Strock
(d) Branemark

179. The average intercondylar distance which is adequate for complete dentures is:
(a) 110 mm
(b) 120mm
(c) 115mm
(d) 140mm

180. Name the muscle group which opposes the buccinator mechanism
(a) Medial pterygoid
(b) Lateral pterygoid
(c) Masseter
(d) Tongue muscles

181. The superior border of lingual bar major connector should be located below the gingival margin by a minimum of
(a) 2 mm
(b) 4 mm
(c) 5 mm
(d) 1 mm

182. Two or more parallel vertical surfaces of abutment teeth shaped to direct the prosthesis during placement and removal, are known as
(a) Orientation plane
(b) Parallel block out
(c) Survey lines
(d) Guiding planes

183. The relationship of mandible to the maxilla when the teeth are in maximum occlusal contact irrespective of the position or alignment of the condyle dist assemblies is known as
(a) Centric occlusion
(b) Centric relation
(c) Plane of occlusion
(d) Curve of Spee

184. Vibrating line is present on
(a) Hard palate
(b) Junction of hard and soft palate
(c) Soft palate
(d) Junction of muscularis mucosae & palatine muscle

COMMUNITY DENTISTRY

185. Fluoride in any form is contraindicated in:
(a) Chronic renal failure
(b) Osteoporosis
(c) Hypertension
(d) Thyrotoxicosis

186. 'Crippling Fluorosis' is characterized by:
(a) Blockage of blood vessels
(b) Chipping of teeth
(c) Rigid spine
(d) Calcification of blood vessels

187. Interruption of transmission of disease
(a) Disease control
(b) Disease elimination
(c) Disease eradication
(d) Disability limitation

188. Which is the first study on water fluoridation?
(a) Grand rapids (Michigan) & Muskegon
(b) Newberg &Kingston
(c) Brantferd & Sarnia
(d) Evanston & park

189. The lethal dose of fluoride for 70 kg adult is:
(a) 32 - 64 mg of fluoride/kg body weight
(b) 50 - 60 mg of fluoride/kg body weight
(c) 30 - 70 mg of fluoride/kg body weight
(d) 60 - 80 mg of fluoride/kg body weight

190. Who introduced APF?
(a) Muhler
(b) Bibby
(c) Brudevold
(d) More

191. In which year was 1st F dentifrice accepted by ADA?
(a) 1920
(b) 1984
(c) 1994
(d) 1964

192. What is the percentage of F present in APF?
(a) 1.23%
(b) 2 %
(c) 1.85%
(d) 0.2%

193. Where was the atraumatic restorative treatment first introduced?
(a) Tanzania
(b) China
(c) U.S.A
(d) New Zealand

194. What is the function of humectants in dentifrices?
(a) Liquefies the dentifrice
(b) Prevents water loss and hardening on exposure to air
(c) Flavors the tooth paste
(d) Cleans tooth surface effectively

195. The model of web of causation of diseases was first suggested by
(a) Pettenkofer
(b) Mac Mohan & Pugh
(c) John M. Last
(d) C.E.A Winslow

196. DMFT Index in 1938 was not developed by:

(a) Dean H.T.
(b) Henry T. Klein .
(c) Knutson.J.W
(d) Carole E. Palmer

197. "Disability limitation" is a mode of intervention in

(a) Primary level of prevention
(b) Secondary level of prevention
(c) Tertiary level of prevention(d) Primordial prevention

198. The personal involved in Integrated Child Development Services (ICDS) scheme initiated by Government of India is

(a) Dhai
(b) Anganwadi worker
(c) Village health volunteers
(d) School health teacher

199. The caking (drying) of dentifrice is prevented by adding

(a) Cellulose
(b) $CaCO_3$
(c) Water
(d) Silica

200. Opaque white areas covering more than 25% but less than 50% of the tooth surface is given the Dean's score of

(a) 1
(b) 2
(c) 3
(d) 4

2007
ANSWERS & EXPLANATIONS

ANATOMY AND HISTOLOGY

Ans.1. (b) Inferior Salivatory nucleus

Ref B.D.C, textbook of anatomy, 4th ed, vol 3, pg 156

The otic ganglion is a peripheral parasympathetic ganglion which relays secreto-motor fibers to the ***parotid gland***.

- The **motor root** is formed by the lesser petrosal nerve. The preganglionic fibers are derived from the inferior salivatory nucleus- the 9th nerve-tympanic branch-tympanic plexus- lesser petrosal nerve to reach the ganglion. From here the Auriculotemporal nerves supply the parotid gland.
- The **sympathetic root** is derived from the plexus on the middle meningeal artery. It contains postganglionic fibers arising in the superior cervical ganglion.

Ans.2. (a) Branch from trunk of mandibular nerve

Ref B.D.C, textbook of anatomy, 4th ed , vol 3,pg 145

The muscles of mastication arise from first branchial arch and are supplied by the Mandibular nerve. All muscles of mastication except medial pterygoid are supplied by branches from the anterior division of the Mandibular nerve. The medial pterygoid muscle is supplied by nerve to medial pterygoid, which is a branch of the ***main trunk*** of Mandibular nerve.

Ans.3. (d) Superior ophthalmic vein and pterygoid venous plexus

Ref Neelima Malik , pg 591

Formation of a thrombus in cavernous sinus or its communicating branch may be a result of infection of head and face spreading by two mechanisms:

(a) **External route:** from face and lip carried by facial and angular veins and nasofrontal veins(danger area of face) to the superior ophthalmic vein

(b) **Internal route:** dental infections to the pterygoid plexus of veins from post. maxillary regions to the inferior ophthalmic veins and subsequently the cavernous sinus.

Ans.4. (d) Hiatus semilunaris

Ref B.D.C, textbook of anatomy, 4th ed , vol 3 , pg 231

Lateral wall of nose: Chonchae and meatuses.

1. **Inferior concha:** independent bone. The meatus is the largest of all 3 and receives the opening of nasolicrimal duct. This opening is guarded by the ***Hasner's valve***.

2. **Middle concha:** part of ethmoid bone. The meatus presents with
   (a) ethmoidal bulla –middle ethmoidal sinus
   (b) hiatus semilunaris – anteriorly-frontal air sinus; posteriorly- maxillary sinus
   (c) infundibulum- at the anterior end of hiatus.
3. **Superior concha:** also a projection of ethmoid. The meatus is short and shallowest. Receives the opening of posterior ethmoidal air sinuses. Just above this is the sphenoethmoidal recess where the sphenoidal air sinus opens.

Ans.5. (c) Sternocleidomastoid

Ref B.D.C, textbook of anatomy, 4th ed , vol 3 , pg 74

Torticollis: or wry neck is a deformity in which the head is bent to one side and the chin points to another. This results a s a result of spasms of muscles supplied by spinal accessory nerve i.e. sternocleidomastoid and trapezius. The causes may be-

(a) Rheumatoid torticollis –exposure to cold
(b) congenital
(c) reflex torticollis - due to suppurating cervical nodes

Ans.6. (a). Neural crest cells

Ref <u>*http://en.wikipedia.org/wiki/Ectoderm*</u>

Named after the *German* physiologist *Theodor Schwann,* **Schwann cells** are a variety of *neuroglia* that mainly provide *myelin* insulation to *axons* in the *peripheral nervous system* of jawed vertebrates. The vertebrate nervous system relies on this myelin sheath for insulation and as a method of decreasing membrane capacitance in the axon, thus allowing for ***saltatory conduction*** to occur and for an increase in impulse speed, without an increase in axonal diameter. Non-myelinating Schwann cells are involved in maintenance of axons and are crucial for neuronal survival. Some group around smaller axons and form Remak bundles. Schwann cells are the peripheral nervous system's analogues of the *central nervous system oligodendrocytes.*

The **ectoderm** is the start of a tissue that covers the body surfaces. It emerges first and forms from the outermost of the *germ layers*

In *vertebrates,* the ectoderm has three parts: external ectoderm, the *neural crest,* and *neural tube.*

- **External Ectoderm**
  - *skin* (along with *glands, hair, nail* (*anatomy*))
  - *epithelium* of the *mouth* and *nasal cavity* salivary glands, and glands of mouth and nasal cavity
  - *enamel* (in teeth) - as a side note *dentin* and *dental pulp* is formed from mesoderm
  - Epithelium of pineal and *pituitary* glands
  - *lens* and *cornea* of the *eye*
  - *Apical Ectodermal Ridge* inducing development of the limb buds of the embryo.
  - *Sensory receptors* in epidermis

- **Neural crest**
  - *pigment cells in the skin*
  - *ganglia* of the *autonomic nervous system*
  - *dorsal root ganglia.*
  - ***Schwann cells***
  - facial *cartilage*
  - *spiral septum* of developing *heart*
  - *ciliary body* of the eye.
- **Neural Tube**
  - *brain* (*rhombencephalon, mesencephalon* and *prosencephalon*)
  - *spinal cord* and *motor neurons*
  - *retina*
  - *posterior pituitary*
- **Adrenal Medulla**

DENTAL ANATOMY AND HISTOLOGY

Ans.7. (c). Mesial & Distal

Ref Wheelers, 6th ed, pg 245

The permanent Mandibular first molar has two roots namely mesial and distal.

Features of permanent mandibular first molar-

- Largest tooth in mandibular arch
- Five well developed cusps- 2 buccal, 2 lingual and 1 distal
- Meslo-dlstal dimension(11mm) is greater than bucco-lingual dimension by 1 mm
- The two roots are wider bucally than lingually providing high anchorage (due to I-beam principle)
- Bifurcation distance- 3mm (bucally) , 4mm (lingually)
- Occlusal form- hexagonal
- Mesio-lingual and disto-lingual ridges at 100°

EXTRA EDGE

Sometimes a third supernumerary root may be present lingually, known as **'radix entomolaris'**

Ans.8. (c) 6-12 years

Ref bhalajhi, pg 54

Mixed dentition period starts with the transitional phase (emergence of first permanent molar) at the age of 6 yrs until the shedding of last deciduous teeth (maxillary canine) at 11yrs of age. So the mixed dentition period usually ranges from **6-12yrs** of age.

Ans.9. (b). Lingual

Ref Wheelers, 6th ed , pg 216

"The palatal root in the maxillary first molar is the largest of all 3 roots."

Features of permanent maxillary 1st molar-

- 4 well formed cusps and three roots(2 buccal and 1 lingual)
- Largest tooth in maxillary arch
- Labio-lingual dimension (1mm) greater than bucco-lingual by 1 mm
- All 4 cusps can be seen in the buccal aspect
- Bifurcation area – 4mm(bucally), 3mm (mesially) and 5mm (distally)
- Lingual root is longest, banana shaped (smooth tapered)
- Occlusal aspect – rhomboidal.

Ans.10. (b) 11 to 12 years

Ref Wheelers, 6th ed , pg 24

Eruption of maxillary canine – 11-12yrs

eruption of Mandibular canine- 9-10yrs

Primary Teeth Development Chart				
Upper Teeth	**Eruption**	**Exfoliation**	**Crown completed**	**Root completed**
Central incisor	8 to 12 months	6 to 7 years	4 months	1 ½ - 2 years
Lateral incisor	9 to 13 months	7 to 8 years	5 months	1 ½ - 2 years
Canine (cuspid)	16 to 22 months	10 to 12 years	9 months	2 ½ - 3 years
First molar	13 to 19 months	9 to 11 years	6 months	2 – 2 ½ years
Second molar	25 to 33 months	10 to 12 years	10-12months	3 years
Lower Teeth				
Second molar	23 to 31 months	10 to 12 years	10-12 months	3 years
First molar	14 to 18 months	9 to 11 years	6 months	2 – 2 ½ years
Canine (cuspid)	17 to 23 months	9 to 12 years	9 months	2 ½ - 3 years
Lateral incisor	10 to 16 months	7 to 8 years	4 ½ months	1 ½ - 2 years
Central incisor	6 to 10 months	6 to 7 years	4 months	1 ½ - 2 years

Permanent Teeth Development Chart			
Upper Teeth	**Eruption**	**Crown completed**	**Root completed**
Central incisor	7 to 8 years	4-5 years	10 years
Lateral incisor	8 to 9 years	4-5 years	11 years
Canine (cuspid)	11 to 12 years	6-7 years	13-15 years
First premolar (first bicuspid)	10 to 11 years	5-6 years	12-13 years
Second premolar (second bicuspid)	10 to 12 years	6-7 years	12-14 years

First molar	6 to 7 years	2 ½ - 3 years	9-10 years
Second molar	12 to 13 years	7-8 years	14-16 years
Third molar (wisdom teeth)	17 to 21 years	12-16 years	18-25 years
Lower Teeth			
Third molar (wisdom tooth)	17 to 21 years	12-16 years	18-25 years
Second molar	11 to 13 years	7-8 years	15-16 years
First molar 6 to 7 years	17 to 21 years	2 ½ - 3 years	9-10 years
Second premolar (second bicuspid)	11 to 12 years	6-7 years	13-14 years
First premolar (first bicuspid)	10 to 12 years	5-6 years	12-13 years
Canine (cuspid)	9 to 10 years	6-7 years	12-14 years
Lateral incisor	7 to 8 years	4-5 years	10 years
Central incisor	6 to 7 years	4-5 years	9 years

PHYSIOLOGY

Ans.11. (c) Pavlov's pouch

Ref http://physiologyonline.physiology.org/cgi/content/full/19/6/326

The traditional teaching of the "cephalic phase" of gastric and pancreatic secretion originated with Pavlov. The stimulation of gastric (acid and pepsin) and the pancreatic secretion of digestive enzymes starts with the anticipation of the ingestion of a desirable meal and is mediated by input from efferent nerves of the Vagus.

Pavlov's cephalic phase was a brilliant demonstration of a brain-gut interaction. The stimulation of secretion evoked by linking environmental stimuli (*e.g.*, lights and sounds) with presentation of appetizing food was discovered by Pavlov in his dogs and was called by what is now a classic term: a "conditioned reflex."

His development of the "**Pavlov pouch**" enabled the discovery of the cephalic phase of secretion and its role in the anticipatory preparation of the upper digestive tract for the ingestion of a meal. The pouch is surgically prepared with a fistula formed by a segment of small intestine with stoma at the surface of the abdominal wall

The Pavlov gastric pouch is essentially the same as the pouch developed by **Rudolph Heidenhain** in Germany, with the ***exception*** that *the vagal innervations remains intact.* Pavlov's discovery that severing the vagal innervation eliminated the cephalic phase for both gastric and pancreatic secretion underlies the discovery of acetylcholine as the neurotransmitter and the muscarinic subtype as the involved receptor.

Ans.12. (a) Atrial depolarization

Ref Ganong, 22nd ed , pg 551

Intervals	Duration (s)	Events
PR	0.18	Atrial depolarization and conduction through AV node
QRS	0.08	Ventricular depolarization and atrial repolarization
QT	0.40	Ventricular depolarization plus repolarization
ST (QT – QRS)	0.32	Ventricular repolarization

Ans.13. (d). Labile factor

Ref Ganong, 22nd ed , pg 540

Factor	Names	Clinical syndrome (def)
I	fibrinogen	afibrinogenemia
II	prothrombin	Hypoprothombinemia
III	thromboplastin	
IV	calcium	
V	Proaccelerin , labile factor	Para hemophilia
VII	Proconvertin,stabile factor	hypoconvertinemia
VIII	Antihemophilic factor A	Hemophilia A
IX	Christmas factor (AHF B) Plasma thrmboplastin component (PTC)	Hemophilia B
X	Stuart-Prower factor	SP factor deficiency
XI	Plasma thromboplastin antecedent(PTA) (AHF C)	Hemophilia C
XII	Hageman / glass factor	Hageman trait
XIII	Fibrin stabilizing factor, Laki-Lorand factor	
HMW-K	Fitzgerald factor	
Pre-Ka	Prekallikrein, Fletcher factr	

Ans.14. (b). Pepsinogen

Ref Ganong, 22nd ed , pg 491-495

Enzyme enterokinase converts trypsinogen to active form trypsin in the duodenum. Form here, trypsin converts chymotrypsinogen and other pro-enzymes into active form. Once activated trypsin is self-regulatory. However, pepsinogen is a gastric enzyme secreted by chief (peptic) cells and has no relation to trypsin.

Ans.15. (c) Less than 3.5 cycles per second

Ref Ganong, 22nd ed , pg 195

EEG recordings of human brain

Rhythms	Occurrence	Frequency	Amplitude
Alpha rhythm	Adults who are awake with eyes closed and minds wandering. Emitted from parietooccipital area	8-12 Hz	50 – 100 μV
Beta rhythm	Frontal regions, REM sleep	18-30 Hz	<25 μV
Gamma rhythm	When attentive and aroused	30-80 Hz	<10 μV
Theta rhythm	Seen in children, hippocampus area	4-7 Hz	>100 μV
Delta rhythm	Large slow waves, deep sleep (III,IV) surgical anesthesia,	<4 Hz	>100 μV

EXTRA EDGE

Stages of sleep- NREM

- Stage I – lightest stage, predominantly theta waves
- Stage II- sleep spindles and K complexes (14-16/sec, 50 μv)
- Stage IV- predominantly delta waves

Features

- sleep walking (Somnanbulism),
- night terror (pevor Nocturnus)
- Bruxism
- Sleep talking (Somniloqui)

REM sleep – or paradoxical sleep,

- beta waves predominate
- light sleep but difficult arousal
- active dreaming and body movements
- reduced tone of neck muscles
- rapid eye movement
- night mares, narcolepsy (apnea during sleep)

Remember, friends while *night terror* occurs in NREM, *night mares* seen in REM sleep.

Ans.16. (b) Calcium

Ref Ganong, 22nd ed , pg 391

Parathyroid hormones play an important role in calcium equilibrium. It acts directly on bone to increase resorption and mobilize **Calcium.** It also increases phosphate excretion in the urine. Calcium absorption is also increased by Vit D (1, 25 dihydroxy cholecalciferol)

EXTRA EDGE

Remember, Calcitonin the major site of action is on osteoclasts (by inhibiting bone resorption) while PTH, although acts on both osteoclasts and blasts, on a longer time scale has a net anabolic effect. So unlike the general conception, PTH acts mainly on osteoblasts.

Ans.17. (b) Diabetes Mellitus

REF; Ganong, 22nd ed , pg 534

http://en.wikipedia.org/wiki/Diabetes_mellitus#Diagnostic_approach

- The quantity increases in poorly controlled diabetes mellitus.
- While not used for diagnosis, an elevated level of glucose irreversibly bound to **hemoglobin** (termed **glycosylated hemoglobin** or *HbA1c*) of 6.0% or higher (the 2003 revised U.S. standard) is considered abnormal by most labs.
- HbA_{tc} has a glucose attached to the terminal ***valine*** in each beta chain and is of special interest because it can help clinician in assessing average blood glucose levels over the preceding ***90 days*** (approximately).
- The current recommended goal for HbA1c in patients with diabetes is <7.0%, which as defined as "good **glycemic control**", although some guidelines are stricter (<6.5%). People with diabetes who have HbA1c levels within this range have a significantly lower incidence of complications from diabetes, including **retinopathy** and **diabetic nephropathy.**

Ans.18. (c) Monocyte

Ganong, 22nd ed , pg 519

The monocytes enter the blood from the bone marrow and circulate for about 72 hours. They then enter the tissues and become tissue macrophages. They have a life span of approx. 3 months.

MICROBIOLOGY

Ans.19. (a) Autoclave

Ref Ananthnarayana, 6th ed

Sterilization is the process by which an article or medium is freed of all microorganism either in vegetative or spore state.

Sterilization using ***moist heat*** – steam autoclave-121^{0}C at 15lbs/15 min or 134^{0}C/30lbs/3min ; test spore- **Bacillus stearothermophilus.**

Sterilization using ***dry heat*** - hot air oven; 160^{0}C /2hrs or 120^{0}C/ 6hrs. Test spore- ***C tetani***

AGENTS IN STERILIZATION

I. PHYSICAL AGENTS

- **Sunlight:** natural bactericidal agent by its UV rays.
- **Drying:** does not affect spores and is unreliable method.
- **Dry heat:** denatures + oxidative damage. Includes flaming, incineration and hot air oven. Used for materials like glassware, forceps, scissors, oils, greases, dry powder.
- **Moist heat:** coagulates + denatures protein. Steam condenses on spores, transmits latent energy and cause hydrolysis of protein. Used for dressings, instruments, laboratory ware, media. Not suitable for bottled fluids.

- **Filtration:** candle filters, earthenware, asbestos, glass filters for antibiotic solutions, sera and carbohydrate solutions used in culture media.
- **Radiation:** (cold sterilization) ionizing radiations like X-ray, gamma rays for plastic tubes, catheters, culture plates, syringes, and non-ionizing rays for wards, OTs, and bulk sterilizations.

2. CHEMICAL AGENTS

- **Alcohols:** 60-70% alcohol effectively kills bacteria (TB bacilli) , isopropyl alcohol for thermometers.
- **Aldehydes:** bactericidal and sporicidal. Formaldehyde used to preserve anatomic specimens and fumigation of wards. Glutaraldehyde is used for tubes and scopes (heat-sensitive instruments) it does not affect the lenses of instruments
- **Dyes:** aniline and acridine dyes used as disinfectant on skin.
- **Phenols:** introduced by Lister are bactericidal at 1%. CHX used as skin disinfectant
- **Gases:** ethylene oxide gas highly lethal to all microbes including spores. Used for catheters, clothing, and plastics, but is highly inflammable. Formaldehyde is used for fumigating rooms after septic case.
- **Halogens:** like iodine, chlorine are bactericidal with moderate activity on spores.
- **Metallic salts:** like silver, copper, mercury are disinfectants and fungicides in the management of ulcers.

Ans.20. (d) HBx Ag.

- HBx, the protein encoded by the X open reading frame, is a transcriptional activator that has been implicated in hepatocarcinogenesis.
- HBx inhibits the function of the tumor suppressor protein p53 in what is thought to be an early event in hepatocyte transformation before the later accumulation of inactivating p53 point mutations.
- HBx ***inhibits apoptosis*** but also exerts pro-apoptotic effects. The effects of HBx on apoptosis may be important not only for the development of HCC but also for the establishment of HBV infection.
- Further implication of HBx in hepatocyte transformation has been the demonstration that it inhibits the repair of damaged hepatocyte DNA. This effect may be mediated by interaction with p53 or through binding to the damaged DNA binding protein (DDB), which plays an accessory role in nucleotide excision repair.
- In addition, HBx activates cell signaling cascades involving mitogen-activated protein kinase (MAPK) and Janus family tyrosine kinases (JAK)/signal transducer and activators of transcription (STAT) pathways. The implications of these modulating effects of HBx are not fully understood, but they are likely to have wide-ranging effects on hepatocyte proliferation, apoptosis and the regulation of cell growth checkpoints.
- The cellular functions ascribed to HBx are unusually diverse, and defining the *biologically important role of HBx during HBV replication* will go some way to understanding the sequel of chronic HBV infection.

EXTRA EDGE

Also remember,

Condition	Serum HBV Ag or Ab present
Acute HBV	HBsAg, IgM anti-HBc, HBV DNA
Chronic HBV	HBsAg, HBeAg, IgG anti-HBc, HBV DNA (HBeAg to anti-HBe seroconversion may occur at some point)
Convalescent HBV infection (immune patient)	anti-HBs, IgG anti-HBc
Vaccinated subject	anti-HBs

Ans.21. (b). Veillonellae

Ref http://www.medscape.com/viewarticle/449821_4

Common oral flora

Aerobic and Facultative Anaerobic Bacteria	Anaerobic Bacteria
Gram-positive cocci	**Gram-positive cocci**
Streptococcus spp	*Peptostreptococcus* spp
Beta-hemolytic streptococci	*Peptostreptococcus micros*
Streptococcus milleri group (viridans)	**Gram-negative bacilli**
Streptococcus mutans group*	*Veillonella* spp
Gram-positive bacilli	**Gram-positive bacilli**
Rothia dentocariosa	*Actinomyces* spp
Lactobacillus spp*	*Eubacterium* spp
Gram-negative cocco-bacilli	*Propionibacterium* spp
Actinobacillus spp	*Lactobacillus* spp.
Actinobacillus actinomycetemcomitans†	**Spirochetes**
Campylobacter spp	*Treponema denticola*
Campylobacter rectus	*Treponema sokranskii*
Capno cytophaga spp	**Gram-negative bacilli**
Eikenella spp	*Prevotella* spp
Gram-negative rods	*Prevotella intermedia*
Pseudomonas spp‡	*Prevotella nigrescens*
Enterobacteriaceae‡	*Porphyromonas* spp
	Porphyromonas gingivalis†
	Bacteroides spp
	Bacteroides forsythus
	Fusobacterium spp
	Fusobacterium nucleatum
	Selenomonas sputigena

Ans.22 (a) Joseph Lister

Ref http://en.wikipedia.org/wiki/Joseph_Lister

Joseph Lister, 1st Baron Lister, (5 April 1827 – 10 February 1912) was an English surgeon who promoted the idea of sterile surgery while working at the Glasgow Royal Infirmary. He successfully introduced carbolic acid (phenol) to sterilize surgical instruments and to clean wounds; as a result of his work in sterilization, *Listerine* mouthwash was named after him.

Ans.23 (b). Region II

Ref http://en.wikipedia.org/wiki/endotoxin

Region II refers to core on the LPS molecule while Region III is the O antigen. LPS contributes to the structural and functional properties of the OM and is present in almost all Gram Negative Bacteria.

- There is **conservation of architecture and structure** in the Lipid A and inner core regions. Lipid A and immediately-adjacent core units are **essential for viability**. Mutants defective in their biosynthesis do not survive.
- LPS is an **endotoxin** [cell-bound]. The **Lipid A** portion of LPS is responsible for the endotoxic activities (numerous, including *fever, low blood pressure, septicaemia, toxic shock, death*). There are ~500k cases of septic shock per annum with ~50% mortality

Ans.24. (c). Ig E

Ref Ganong, 22nd ed , pg 529

Immunoglobulin	Function	Plasma conc(mg/dL)
Ig G	Complement activation, crosses placenta, secondary response	1000
Ig A (secretory Ig)	Localized protection in secretions	200
Ig M	Complement activation(most potent) primary response	120
Ig D	Antigen recognition by B cells	3
Ig E	*Reagin* activity, allergic response	0.05

Ans.25. (c) Human Herpes Virus 8

Ref Shafer 5th ed , pg 231.

Kaposi sarcoma is a multicentric proliferative vascular and spindle cell malignancy first described by *Moritz Kaposi in 1872*. Human herpes virus 8 (**HHV8**) has been linked as a causative agent of the malignancy (Moore, 1995) in other cases histocompatibilty factor HLA-DR5 has been associated. AIDS related Kaposi sarcoma is a very aggressive variant seen in 40% of the homosexuals male.

Ans.26. (b) Periodic acid Schiff stain

Ref http://crobm.iadrjournals.org/cgi/content/full/

Candidal hyphae tend to be poorly stained by the routine hematoxylin/eosin stain; there is a risk that they may not be adequately visualized. Therefore, special staining techniques may be required to demonstrate their presence.

- **The periodic acid-Schiff** (PAS)- the aldehydes react with the Schiff reagent, and the fungi then appear a pinkish red.
- **Gridley's or Grocott's methenamine silver** (GMS) - the aldehydes reduce the methenamine silver nitrate complex, producing a brown-black staining as a result of the deposition of reduced silver.

Ans.27. (b). EB

Ref http://en.wikipedia.org/wiki/Epstein_Barr_virus

The **Epstein-Barr virus (EBV)**, also called *Human herpesvirus 4* (HHV-4), is a virus of the herpes family (which includes *Herpes simplex virus* and *Cytomegalovirus*), and is one of the most common viruses in humans.

Most people become infected with EBV, which is often asymptomatic but commonly causes infectious mononucleosis.

It is named after Michael Epstein and Yvonne Barr, who together with Bert Achong discovered the virus in 1964.

- **Infectious mononucleosis**

Epstein-Barr can cause infectious mononucleosis, also known as 'glandular fever', 'Mono' and 'Pfeiffer's disease'. Infectious mononucleosis is caused when a person is first exposed to the virus during or after adolescence. It is therefore predominantly found in the developed world,.

EBV-associated malignancies

The strongest evidence linking EBV and cancer formation is found in Burkitt's lymphoma and nasopharyngeal carcinoma. It has been postulated to be a trigger for a subset of Chronic Fatigue Syndrome patients as well as Multiple Sclerosis and other autoimmune diseases.

- **Burkitt's lymphoma** is a type of Non-Hodgkin's lymphoma and is most common in equatorial Africa and is co-existent with the presence of malaria. Malaria infection causes reduced immune surveillance of EBV immortalized B cells, so allowing their proliferation. This proliferation increases the chance of a mutation to occur. Repeated mutations can lead to the B cells escaping the body's cell-cycle control, so allowing the cells to proliferate unchecked, resulting in the formation of Burkitt's lymphoma. Burkitt's lymphoma commonly affects the jaw bone, forming a huge tumor mass. It responds quickly to chemotherapy treatment, namely cyclophosphamide, but recurrence is common.
- Other B cell lymphomas arise in immunocompromised patients such as those with AIDS or who have undergone organ transplantation with associated immunosuppression (Post-Transplant Lymphoproliferative Disorder (PTLPD)). Smooth muscle tumors are also associated with the virus in malignent patients.
- **Nasopharyngeal carcinoma** is a cancer found in the upper respiratory tract, most commonly in the nasopharynx, and is linked to the EBV virus. It is found predominantly in Southern China and Africa, due to both genetic and environmental factors linked to the Chinese diet of a high amount of smoked fish, which contain nitrosamines, well known carcinogens (environmental).

- **Chronic fatigue syndrome**

  Other diseases associated with EBV
- Stevens-Johnson syndrome
- Hepatitis
- Herpes
- Alice in Wonderland syndrome
- Several Non-Hodgkin's lymphomas, including primary cerebral lymphoma
- Hodgkin's disease
- Posttransplant lymphoproliferative disorder
- Herpangina
- Multiple Sclerosis
- Hairy leukoplakia
- Common variable immunodeficiency (CVID)
- Kikuchi's disease

BIOCHEMISTRY

Ans.28. (b) Decreasing the energy of activation

Ref http://en.wikipedia.org/wiki/Enzymes

Essentials of Biochemistry, Satyanarayana 1st ed, pg 41

Enzymes are proteins that catalyze (*i.e.* accelerate) chemical reactions. In enzymatic reactions, the molecules at the beginning of the process are called substrates, and the enzyme converts them into different molecules, the products. Although all enzymes are proteins, not all biochemical catalysts are enzymes, since some RNA molecules called ribozymes also catalyze reactions. Other synthetic molecules called artificial enzymes, can also display enzyme-like catalysis

In 1878 German physiologist Wilhelm Kühne (1837–1900) coined the term *enzyme*,

Enzymes can act in several ways, all of which lower ÄG‡:

- **Lowering the activation energy** by creating an environment in which the transition state is stabilized (e.g. straining the shape of a substrate - by binding the transition-state conformation of the substrate/product molecules, the enzyme distorts the bound substrate(s) into their transition state form, thereby reducing the amount of energy required to complete the transition).
- Providing an alternative pathway (*e.g.*, temporarily reacting with the substrate to form an intermediate ES Complex which would be impossible in the absence of the enzyme).
- Reducing the reaction entropy change by bringing substrates together in the correct orientation to react. Considering ÄH‡ alone overlooks this effect

Cofactors can be either inorganic (*e.g.*, metal ions and iron-sulfur clusters) or organic compounds, (*e.g.*, flavin and heme). Organic cofactors (coenzymes) are usually *prosthetic* groups, which are tightly bound to the enzymes that they assist.

Enzymes that require a cofactor but do not have one bound are called **apoenzymes**. An apoenzyme together with its cofactor(s) is called a **holoenzyme** (*i.e.*, the active form). Most cofactors are not covalently attached to an enzyme, but are very tightly bound.

Coenzymes are small molecules that transport chemical groups from one enzyme to another. Some of these chemicals such as riboflavin, thiamine and folic acid are vitamins.

Ans.29. (b). Glucose -6-phosphatase in liver

Ref Essentials of Biochemistry, Satyanarayana 1st ed , pg145

Glycogen storage disorders	Enzyme deficient
Type I (Von Gierke's)	Glucose-6-phosphatase
Type II (Pompe's)	Acid maltase
Type III	Debranching enzyme, limit dextrinase
Type IV	Branching enzyme (Amylopectinase)
Type V (Mc Ardles syndrome)	Muscle phosphorylase
Type VI (Her's disease)	Liver phosphorylase

Ans.30. (d). Glutamine

Ref Lippincott 3rd ed , pg 250

Most tissues like brain use amino acid glutamine for the transport of ammonia to liver. However, in muscle amino-acid ***alanine*** is used for this purpose.

Ans.31. (b). Cellulose

Ref Ganong, 22nd ed , pg 510

Humans do not digest much of the vegetable products like cellulose, hemicellulose and lignin in the diet which are important constituent of the dietary fibre various gums, algal polysaccharides, and pectin substances also constitute dietary fiber. The role of such fibers is to increase the bulk and easy defecation.

GENERAL PATHOLOGY

Ans.32. (b). Hyperplasia

Ref Robin, Basic pathology, 6th ed pg 21

- **Hypertrophy** means an increase in the ***size of a cell***, tissue, or organ. Since hypertrophic cells are synthesizing more cytoplasm (*i.e.,* more protein) they have more structural components, appear larger and may stain more basophilic than normal cells.
- **Hyperplasia** means an increase in the size of a tissue or organ concomitant with an ***increase in the numbers*** of cells. Hyperplastic cells are often more basophilic than ordinary cells. Hyperplasia may appear in the form of compact cell growth (nodular hyperplasia) or form the lining of multiple cysts (cystic hyperplasia). Persistent hyperplasia may serve as a site for development of cancer.
- **Dysplasia** is an imprecise term applied to cellular changes that fit in between hyperplasia and cancer.

- **Atrophy** is an acquired decrease in size of cells, tissues and organs. Atrophy can occur via programmed deletion of cells (**apoptosis**) or via cell shrinkage.
- **Hypoplasia** If a tissue or organ is congenitally underdeveloped.
- **Aplasia** implies that an organ has never developed or that its cells have ceased to multiply (*e.g.*, aplasia of the bone marrow).
- **Involution** overlaps atrophy; it applies to normal programmed shrinkage of certain organs (*e.g.*, the thymus in early life; the uterus after giving birth).
- **Metaplasia** is a microscopic change whereby one type of mature cell is replaced by another type of mature cell.

Ans.33. (c). Anasarca

Ref Robin, Basic pathology, 6th ed , pg 61

Anasarca is a severe and generalized edema with profound subcutaneous tissue swelling. Common causes are congestive heart failure, nephritic syndrome.

Ans.34. (d) Tuberculosis

Ref Burket, 10th ed, pg 534

It is well known that viral infections like HIV, Hepatitis B and C (but not A or E), CMV etc are highly infectious diseases having a primary blood borne mode of transmission. While TB spreads primarily by inhalation of contaminated air.
For further details please refer KCET-05 A50

DENTAL MATERIALS

Ans.35. (b). less than 2%

Ref Philips, ch: Wrought Base metal alloys, pg 538

Steels are iron-based alloys that contain *less* than **1.2 %** carbon. When Chromium in the range of 12-30% is added to steel it becomes stainless steel (SS). The iron content of SS differs from carbon steel. (SS has carbon content as low as ***0.15-0.2 %***)

Also remember, Carbon steel exists in three forms-

1. **Ferrite** – at room temp. has a BCC(Body Centered Cubic) structure. This phase is stable up to 912 ^{0}C (1674 ^{0}F). max carbon solubility- 0.02% wt.
2. **Austenite** – exists at temp between 912 – 1394 ^{0}C (2541 ^{0}F). Austenite has a FCC structure (Face centered cubic) which have larger interstitial spaces in the lattice as compared to BCC form and hence more stable. Max carbon solubility – 2.11 % by wt.
3. **Martensite** – when the austenite phase is cooled rapidly (quenched) the FCC phase undergoes diffusion less transformation to a BCT (Body centered tetragonal) structure. The lattice is highly distorted and strained and hence the resultant alloy is very hard, brittle but strong. This property of martensite is utilized in the cutting edges of carbon steel instruments.

Ans.36. (c) 0.2% to 0.5%

Ref Philip's science of dental materials, ch Denture base resins, pg 192

Polymerization in self cure resin is never as complete as that of a heat cure type. In the former 3-5 % of the resin is composed of free monomer, while in heat cure it is only 0.2 -0.5 % free monomer.

Ans.37. (a) Poly acrylic acid

Ref Philips, pg 453

The powder composition of Zn-polycarboxylate Is similar to Zn-phosphate cement while the liquid is same as that of Glass ionomer cement, *i.e.* polyacrylic acid with a copolymer of itaconic, maliec acid.

EXTRA EDGE

Remember, tartaric acid present functions to improve handling characteristics, ***increase working time and shortens the setting time.***

Ans.38. (b) 9 to 20 weight percent

Ref:Philips, pg 311.

Admixed alloy usually contain 30-55 % spherical high copper by weight. The total copper content usually ranges from 9 – 20 %.

Single composition high copper – 13-30 %

Lowcopper - <6 %

Ans.39. (b) 21 Gpa and 27- 55 MPa

Ref Skinner's, pg 319; http://www.ucsf.edu/ocsci/pdf/jms2005.pdf

Compressive strength of amalgam should be a minimum of 310 Mpa and ideal tensile strength in between 48-70 Mpa.

Now, ***what is elastic modulus***? A variable often tested when evaluating dental materials is the elastic modulus. The elastic modulus describes the relative stiffness of the material within the elastic range. Natural hard tissues have a range of intrinsic stiffness or modulus values and the addition of restorative materials of different moduli can affect the overall stiffness of the restored tooth and the interfacial stresses that are generated.

According to Combe et al (1999) and Martinez-Insua, et al (2002) ***the modulus of elasticity of amalgam is closer to that of dentin.*** (Elastic modulus of Dentin = 10-25 GPa)
So, narrowing on to two choices, A and B, -'*B*' seems to be more appropriate.

Ans.40. (b) 25-35KHN

Ref Vimal Sikri , pg 377

Property	Conventional	Microfilled	Hybrid
Compressive strength	36-43,000 psi	50,000 psi	60,000 psi
Tensile strength	7000	7500	10-13,000
Water sorption	0.5 %	1.4%	0.5 %
Shrinkage	1.2-1.3 %	1.5-2.0 %	1.0-1.5 %
KHN	50-60	20-30	50-60
COTE	25 x 10^{-6}/C	50 x 10^{-6}/C	30-40 x 10^{-6}/C

Ans.41. (d) 90 to 200 N

Ref Boucher, 10th ed ; http://www.womenlargejaw.com/biteforce.php

Average biting force in males – 533 N; females – 393 N

Avg bite force in first molar	59.61kg, (90-200 N)
premolar	45.38kg
central incisor	17.10kg
Biting force with complete dentures	6-8kgs or 13-16lbs, 110N

The bite force is negatively correlated to genial angle, mandibular plane angle, the angle between occlusal plane and mandibular plane, the angle between palatal plane and mandibular plane, and positively correlated to posterior height of face, length of mandibular body, length of ramus, facial depth in craniofacial structure.

Ans.42. (c) Aluminium oxide

Ref Sturdevant, 4th ed pg 328

Air abrasive system is helpful in stain removal, debriding pit and fissures and micro-mechanical roughening. It relies on transfer of kinetic energy from a stream of powder particles (usually aluminium oxide) on the tooth surface or restoration.

EXTRA EDGE

Properties

distance between tip and surface	3-5mm
angle of hand piece	60-90 degrees
air pressure	20-55 psi
motion	12 mm/s scanning motion
particle size	25-250 um
duration	2-20 sec

Ans.43. (b) Greater the hygroscopic expansion

Ref Philips pg 398, Investments for small castings

Silica is added to investment to increase refractive ness during heating and to regulate the thermal expansion. Gypsum shrinks considerably when heated. If the proper amount of silica is used this can be overcome. As it changes from alpha to beta form, density decreases and there is rapid increase in linear expansion.

Normal setting expansion: 0.6 % (ADA)

Normal Hygroscopic expansion: 1.2 – 2.2%

The magnitude of HSE is proportional to the silica content of investment. ***The finer the particles size of the silica, the greater the expansion***. Similarly higher the W: P lower the HSE.

Ans.44. (b) 25 µm

Refer Philip's pg 481

ADA specification no.8 prescribes the thickness for luting cement to be ***25μm***

Ans.45. (b) Putty used first and light body used second

Ref Philip's, ch: elastomeric impression material, pg 151

Putty wash technique refers to use of a heavy filled elastomer which is used as a tray material and later the "wash" impression is made by either cutting away some putty material or providing a relief using a resin, rubber or wax sheet spacer and use of light body material

There are essentially three ways of recording a putty-wash impression:

- *One stage impression* - putty and wash are recorded simultaneously (also called twin mix or laminate technique)
- *Two stage unspaced* - putty is recorded first and after setting relined with a thin layer of wash
- *Two stage spaced* - as for two stage unspaced except a space is created for the wash. This space may be made by:
  (*i*) Polythene spacer over the teeth prior to making the putty impression.
  (*ii*) Recording the putty impression before tooth preparation.
  (*iii*) Gouging away the putty and providing escape channels for the wash.

PHARMACOLOGY

Ans.46. (a) 3-5 mins

Ref http://www.aapd.org/media/Policies_Guidelines/G_Nitrous.pdf

Nitrous oxide

- Colorless and virtually odorless gas with a faint, sweet smell.
- It is an effective analgesic/anxiolytic agent causing central nervous system (CNS) depression and euphoria with little effect on the respiratory system.
- It has rapid uptake, being absorbed quickly from the alveoli and held in a simple solution in the serum.
- As nitrous oxide is 34 times more soluble than nitrogen in blood, diffusion hypoxia may occur.
- Studies have shown that children become desaturated more rapidly than adolescents; administering 100% oxygen to the patient for ***3 to 5 minutes*** once the nitrous oxide has been terminated is important.
- Nitrous oxide is absorbed rapidly, allowing for both rapid onset and recovery (2-3 min).

Ans.47. (c) Ergotoxine

Ref K.D.Tripathy, 4th ed pg 487

Glycosides are drugs having cardiac inotropic activity. Main use is in congestive heart failure and cardiac arrhythmias Examples are digitoxin, digoxin, gitoxin, gitalin, bufotoxin, thevetin etc.

Ergotoxine is a white, crystalline, water-insoluble alkaloid, $C_{35}H_{41}N_5O_6$, obtained from ergot, used chiefly in obstetrics as a uterine stimulant.

Ans.48. (c) Hyper sensitivity

Ref K.D.Tripathy , 4th ed , pg 72

Hypersensitivity is an immunologically mediated reaction producing stereotype symptoms unrelated to pharmacodyanamic response or dosage.

Super sensitivity refers to an increased response of a drug at a particular drug dosage.

Idiosyncrasy is a genetically determined abnormal reactivity to a chemical *e.g.*, barbiturates causes excitement or mental confusion in some.

Ans.49. (c) Safe in patients with renal insufficiency

Ref K.D.Tripathy , 4th ed , pg 464

Selective COX-2 inhibitors like celecoxib, offer advantage that they are not associated with common side effects, associated with inhibition of protective COX-1 enzyme like gastric irritation. However, they do not affect platelet function and hence are not considered cardio-protective. (The anti-coagulant effect, as seen with aspirin). Also COX-2 inhibitors like nimusilide may be associated with renal complications.

GENERAL MEDICINE

Ans.50. (c) Unbalanced insulin dependent diabetes

Ref Carranza 9th ed , pg 209; http://www.enlmedical.com/article/003058.htm

Diabetes mellitus, is characterized by a fruity odour/ breath due to excess ketone bodies in blood. A fruity odor to the breath occurs as the body attempts to get rid of excess acetone through the breathing. This is a characteristic sign of ketoacidosis (such as diabetic ketoacidosis), a potentially life-threatening condition.

A fecal odor to the breath (the breath smells like feces) can occur with prolonged vomiting , especially when there is a bowel obstruction. It can also occur temporarily if the person has a nasogastric tube in place (a tube placed through the nose or mouth to the stomach to drain the stomach contents).

The breath may have an ammonia-like odour (also described as urine-like or "fishy") in people with chronic kidney failure

Ans.51. (d) CD4 T-cells<200 cells/ mm^3

Ref: Carranza , 9th ed , pg 416

According to CDC case classification, severe form is described as CD4- T4 countless than ***200/ mm^3*** or percentage less than ***14 %*** of total lymphocytes.

Ans.52. (d) B.A.L

Ref http://en.wikipedia.org/wiki/Dimercaprol

Dimercaprol (INN) or **British anti-Lewisite** (abbreviated **BAL**),

- Developed by British biochemists at Oxford University during World War II. It was developed secretly as an antidote for Lewisite, the now-obsolete arsenic-based chemical warfare agent.
- Used medically in treatment of arsenic, mercury and lead, and other heavy metal poisoning.
- In addition, it is used for the treatment of Wilson's disease, a genetic disorder in which the body tends to retain copper.
- Although treatments with BAL will increases the excretion of cadmium, there is a concomitant increase in renal cadmium concentration, so that its use in case of ***cadmium toxicity is to be avoided***.
- It does, however, remove inorganic mercury from the kidneys; but is not useful in the treatment of alkyl-mercury or phenyl mercury toxicity.
- BAL also enhances the toxicity of *selenium and tellurium*, so it is not to be used to remove these metals from the body.

Ans.53. (a) Acetaminophen

Ref K.D.Tripathy,4th ed pg 465

Although aspirin is the drug of choice for the management of rheumatoid arthritis, the patient in this case is also suffering from hemophilia. Bleeding and clotting disorders are an absolute contraindication for aspirin. In such cases a milder NSAID like acetaminophen (Paracetamol) is preferred which has no effect on CVS or platelets.

Ans.54. (d) Activated partial thromboplastin time

Ref Burket's oral medicine, 10th ed , pg 459

Disorder	Platelet count	PT	aPTT	BT
Thrombocyto -penia	decreased	N	N	increased
Hemophilia	N	N	increased	N
Von Willebrand	N/decreased	N	N/increased	increased
DIC	decreased	increased	increased	increased
Factor XIII def	N	N	N	N

Hence we see from the table that in DIC both bleeding time (BT) and prothrombin time (PT) are increased.

Ans.55. (a) Carbamezepine

Ref Burket 10th ed , pg 329

Trigeminal neuralgia, also known as ***tic douloureux***, chiefly affects women over 50yrs of age.

Etiology

- may be due to tumor of cerebellar pontine (meningioma),
- demyelinating plaque of multiple sclerosis,
- vascular malformations,
- idiopathic.

- Diagnosis is by history and presence of trigger zones in the distribution of trigeminal (most commonly maxillary) nerve.

Management

- *Pharmacological* includes carbamazepine(DOC), baclofen, gabapentin, phenytoin,
- *Surgical* – percutaneous radiofrequency thermo-coagulation (gasserion ganglion) microvascular decompression of the nerve root at brainstem.

Ans.56. (d) Hyalinization of afferent arterioles and Kimmelstein-Wilson bodies

Ref Davidson, principles of Medicine, 19th ed, pg 673

Diabetic nephropathy features-

1. first changes are thickening of glomerular basement membrane and accumulation of matrix material in mesangium.
2. nodular deposits, ***Kimmelstein-Wilson bodies***, are characteristic feature.
3. micro-albuminuria accompanied by hypertension is a ominous sign for developing renal failure.
4. Other lesions include papillary necrosis, ischemia and chronic nephritis.

Ans.57. (d) All of the above

Ref Davidson, 19th ed pg 840

Causes of liver cirrhosis-

1. Any cause of chronic hepatitis- Hepatitis A,B,E or C infection, CMV, toxoplasmosis, EBV. etc.
2. Alcohol
3. Primary sclerosing colangitis
4. hemochromatosis, Wilson's disease, cystic fibrosis.

Ans.58. (d) Gynecomastia

Ref: Davidson, 9th ed pg 852

Portal hypertension is characterized by:

1. Splenomegaly which is the cardinal sign.
2. Collateral vessels are dilated and visible on abdominal wall.
3. Variceal bleeding-oesophageal, gastric, etc.
4. Fetor hepaticus- results from portosystemic shunting of blood,whichallows mercaptans to pass directly to the lungs.
5. Ascites, renal failure and encephalopathy.

Choice'd' gynecomastia is usually seen in cirrhosis and not portal hypertension.

Ans.59. (d). Microcytic, Hypochromic

Ref http://en.wikipedia.org/wiki/Iron_deficiency_anemia

Anemia will be diagnosed on the basis of suggestive symptoms, or found on the basis of routine testing, which includes a complete blood count (CBC). A sufficiently *low hemoglobin or hematocrit value* is diagnostic of anemia. One of the first abnormal values to be noted on a CBC will be a high red blood cell distribution width (RDW), reflecting a varied size distribution of red blood cells. A low MCV, MCH or MCHC, and the appearance of the RBCs on visual examination of a peripheral blood smear will narrow the diagnosis to a ***microcytic anemia***.

The diagnosis of iron deficiency anemia will be suggested by appropriate history (e.g., anemia in a menstruating woman), and by such diagnostic tests as a low serum ferritin, a low serum iron level, an elevated serum transferrin and a high total iron binding capacity (TIBC). **Serum ferritin is the most sensitive lab test for iron deficiency anemia.**

Change in lab values in iron deficiency anemia

Change	Parameter
Decrease	ferritin, hemoglobin, MCV
Increase	TIBC, transferrin, RDW

GOLD STANDARD

A definitive diagnosis requires a demonstration of depleted body iron stores by performing a bone marrow aspiration, with the marrow stained for iron. Because this is invasive and painful, while a clinical trial of iron supplementation is inexpensive and non-traumatic, patients are often treated without a definitive diagnosis.

Ans.60. REPEAT, Please refer answer 55.

Ans.61. (a) Tuberculosis

Ref Davidson 9th ed , pg 855

Tuberculosis is an important cause of 'exudative' ascites and not transudative ascites. Other conditions producing similar lesions are malignant diseases, immunologic diseases like SLE, Rheumatic heart disease etc.

Ans.62. (c) Clostridium perfringes

Ref Davidson, 9th ed pg 27.

Gas gangrene or myonecrosis is defined as acute invasion of healthy muscle mot commonly by Cl perfringes. It is usually seen after a deep penetrating injury which favors anaerobic environment for the bacteria to grow over next 18-24hrs.

GENERAL SURGERY

Ans.63. (c) Border of an ulcerated area

Ref Neelima Malik, pg 16

When there is a large diffuse lesion. A 'representative' section from the border of the lesion along with the normal tissue and sent for histological examination. The depth of the biopsy should be enough to obtain an elliptical, wedge-shaped tissue with the "v" of the wedge converging into the deeper tissues.

Ans.64. (b) 2nd branchial cleft

Ref http://www.emedicine.com/derm/topic61.htm

Branchial cleft cysts are congenital epithelial cysts, which arise on the lateral part of the neck from a failure of obliteration of the ***second branchial cleft*** in embryonic development.

Phylogenetically, the branchial apparatus is related to gill slits. In fish and amphibians, these structures are responsible for the development of the gills, hence the name branchial (*branchia* is Greek for gills).

Pathophysiology: At the fourth week of embryonic life, the development of 4 branchial (or pharyngeal) clefts results in 5 ridges known as the branchial (or pharyngeal) arches, which contribute to the formation of various structures of the head, the neck, and the thorax. The second arch grows caudally and, ultimately, covers the third and fourth arches. The buried clefts become ectoderm-lined cavities, which normally involute around week 7 of development. If a portion of the cleft fails to involute completely, the entrapped remnant forms an epithelium-lined cyst with or without a sinus tract to the overlying skin.

- A branchial cyst commonly presents as a solitary, painless mass in the neck of a child or a young adult. A history of intermittent swelling and tenderness of the lesion during upper respiratory tract infection may exist. Discharge may be reported if the lesion is associated with a sinus tract.
- In some instances, patients may present with locally compressive symptoms.

Most branchial cleft cysts are lined with stratified squamous epithelium with keratinous debris within the cyst. In a small number, the cyst is lined with respiratory (ciliated columnar) epithelium. Lymphoid tissue is often present outside the epithelial lining. Germinal centre formation may be seen in the lymphoid component, but true lymph node architecture is not seen. In infected or ruptured lesions, inflammatory cells are seen within the cyst cavity or the surrounding stroma

- Surgical excision is definitive treatment for this condition.
- A series of horizontal incisions, known as a stair step or stepladder incision, is made to fully dissect out the occasionally tortuous path of the cyst.

Ans.65. (d) Proteolysis

Ref Neelima Malik , pg 59, suturing materials and technique
Ref http://en.wikipedia.org/wiki/Suture_material

Surgical gut is an absorbable suture material used for suturing subcutaneous tissues, ophthalmic surgery and oral surgery. These are hydrolyzed by the tissue enzymes, with approximate absorption time of *70 days*.

Absorbable suture materials-

Property	Plain catgut	Chromic gut	Polyglycolic acid (PGA)	Poly dioxanone (PDS)
Composition	Plain catgut	Natural purified collagen treated with chromic acid	Polyglycolic acid treated with Mg-stearate	Polyester and poly (p-dioxanone)
Tensile strength	Strength for 7 days	Strength decrease after 18-21 days	Excellent	Excellent
Structure	Monofilament	Monofilament	Braided	Monofilament
Absorption	Proteolytic enzymatic absorption within 70 days	Proteolytic enzymatic absorption within 90 days	Absorption by hydrolysis complete between 60 and 90 days	Absorption by hydrolysis
Origin	Bovine serosa	Bovine serosa	Synthetic	Synthetic
Sterilization	Ethylene oxide	Ethylene oxide	Ethylene oxide	Ethylene oxide
Indications	Ophthalmic, GIT, general	Ophthalmic, GIT, general	Subcutaneous, intracutaneous closures,	pediatric cardiovascular, ophthalmic
Advantages	↑ handling properties, ↑ knot pull tensile strength	↑ handling properties ↑ knot pull tensile strength	High initial tensile strength easy hand ling excellent knotting ability secure knot	Tensile strength reetention, guaranteed holding power

Ans.66. (b) Internal jugular vein

Ref http://en.wikipedia.org/wiki/Neck_dissection

The **neck dissection** is a surgical procedure for control of neck lymph node metastasis from squamous cell carcinoma (**SCC**) of the head and neck. The aim of the procedure is to remove lymph nodes from one side of the neck into which cancer cells may have migrated. Metastasis of squamous cell carcinoma into the lymph nodes of the neck reduces survival and is the most important factor in the spread of the disease. The metastases may originate from SCC of the upper aerodigestive tract, including the oral cavity, tongue, nasopharynx, oropharynx, hypopharynx, and larynx, as well as the thyroid, parotid and posterior scalp.

History of Neck Dissections

- 1906 - **George W. Crile** describes the radical neck dissection. The operation encompasses removal of all the lymph nodes on one side of the neck, and includes removal of the spinal accessory nerve (**SAN**), internal jugular vein (**IJV**) and sternocleidomastoid muscle (**SCM**).
- 1957 - Hayes Martin describes routine use of the radical neck dissection for control of neck metastases.
- 1967 - Oscar Suarez and E. Bocca describe a more conservative operation which preserves ***SAN, IJV and SCM***.
- Last 3 decades - Further operations have been described to selectively remove the involved regional lymph groups.

EXTRA EDGE

Division of the Neck into Levels and Sublevels

To describe the lymph nodes of the neck for neck dissection, the neck is divided into 6 areas called *Levels*. The levels are identified by roman numeral, increasing towards the chest. A further Level VII to denote lymph node groups in the superior mediastinum is no longer used. Instead, lymph nodes in other non-neck regions are referred to by the name of their specific nodal groups.

- **Level I -** This includes the submental and submandibular lymph nodes.
  The submental triangle (sublevel IA) is bounded by the anterior belly of the digastric muscles (laterally) and the hyoid (inferiorly). The submandibular triangle (sublevel IB) is bounded by the body of the mandible (superiorly), the stylohyoid (posteriorly), and the anterior belly of the digastric (anteriorly).
- **Level II** - This includes lymph nodes of the upper jugular group and is divided into sublevels IIA and IIB.
  Level II is bounded by the inferior border of the hyoid (inferiorly), the base of skull (superiorly), the stylohyoid muscle (anteriorly) and the posterior border of the SCM (posteriorly). Sublevel IIA nodes lie anterior to the SAN. Sublevel IIB nodes lie posterior to the SAN.
- **Level III** - This includes lymph nodes of the middle jugular group.
  This level is bounded by the inferior border of the hyoid (superiorly) and the inferior border of the cricoid (inferiorly), the posterior border of the sternohyoid (anteriorly) and the posterior border of the SCM (posteriorly).
- **Level IV** - This includes lymph nodes of the lower juglar group.
  This level is bounded by the inferior border of the cricoid (superiorly), the clavicle / sternal notch (inferiorly), the posterior border of the sternohyoid (anteriorly) and the posterior border of the SCM (posteriorly).
- **Level V** - This includes posterior compartment lymph nodes.
  This compartment is bounded by the clavicle (inferiorly), the anterior border of the trapezius (posteriorly), the posterior border of the SCM (anteriorly). It is divided into sublevels VA (lying above a transverse plane marking the inferior border of the anterior cricoid arch) and VB (below the aforementioned plane).
- **Level VI** - This includes the anterior compartment lymph nodes.
  This compartment is bounded by the common carotid arteries (laterally), the hyoid (superiorly), the suprasternal notch (inferiorly).

Classification of Neck Dissections

The 2001 revisions proposed by the American Head and Neck Society (AHNS) and the American Academy of Otolaryngology-Head and Neck Surgery (AAO-HNS) are as follows.

1. **Radical Neck Dissection (RND)** - removal of all ipsilateral cervical lymph node groups from levels I through V, together with SAN, SCM and IJV.
2. **Modified Radical Neck Dissection (MRND)** - removal of all lymph node groups routinely removed in a RND, but with preservation of one or more nonlymphatic structures (SAN, SCM and IJV).

3. **Selective Neck Dissection** (**SND**) (together with the use of parentheses to denote the levels or sublevels removed) - cervical lymphadenectomy with preservation of one or more lymph node groups that are routinely removed in a RND. Thus for oral cavity cancers, SND (I-III) is commonly performed. For oropharyngeal, hypopharyngeal and laryngeal cancers, SND (II-IV) is the procedure of choice.
4. **Extended Neck Dissection** - This refers to removal of one or more additional lymph node groups or nonlymphatic structures, or both, not encompassed by the RND.

Ans.67. (d) Up to one third of the lip can not be removed

Ref Manual of surgery, pg 192

Carcinoma of lip is common in the western, elderly, white people, especially those exposed to sunlight. It is commonly called as Countryman's lip. Non-healing ulcers are the common presentation. They generally are not aggressive, deeper invasion is seen later stage.

Treatment includes excision of small lesions with direct suturing. ***When more than 1/3rd*** of the lip is removed, flap reconstruction may be necessary. These are:-

1. *Abbe flap*: based on upper labial artery.
2. *Estlanders flap* : wedge shaped flap for lesions at the angle of mouth.

So we see, option 4 is absolutely wrong , and hence the answer here.

Ans.68. (c) Nail bed

Ref http://www.diagnosis.com/medical/glomangioma

Glomangioma: A blue-red, extremely painful vascular neoplasm involving a glomeriform arteriovenous anastomosis (glomus body), which may be found anywhere in the skin, most often in the distal portion of the fingers and toes, ***especially beneath the nail***. It is composed of specialized pericytes (sometimes termed glomus cells), usually in single encapsulated nodular masses which may be several millimeters in diameter (From Stedman, 27th ed).

CHEMODECTOMA, a tumor of NEURAL CREST origin, is also sometimes called a glomus tumor.

Ans.69. (b).Streptococcus

Shafer 5th ed pg 697

Cellulitis is defined as a deep acute spreading infection of subcutaneous tissues commonly caused by group A streptococci and Staph aureus. These organisms produce various factors like streptokinase, hyaluronidase (spreading factor of Duran-Reynals), and fibrinolysins, which act to break down or dissolve hyaluronic acid and fibrin.

Ans.70. (a) Squamous cell carcinoma from scar

Ref Manipal manual of surgery, pg 97

- Squamous cell carcinoma which develops in a scar tissue is called as Marjolin's ulcer.
- Burn scar is the commonest cause followed by varicose ulcer, snake bite scar, chronic osteomyelitis scar, lupus vulgaris (TB of face).
- The lesion grows very slowly and is clinically painless.

- Metastasis by lymphatic does not occur as the lymphatic are destroyed.
- Surgery cures the disease; *however* radiotherapy is not very useful.

Ans.71. (c) Palate

Ref http://famona.erbak.com/pathology/cawson2

Ectopic salivary tissue can form within the developmental areas of the first and second branchial arches, in the lateral part of the neck, pharynx or middle ear.

- Aberrant salivary tissue is frequently found intra-orally in palate, buccal mucosa, floor of mouth etc.

  - Ref Shafer 5th ed pg 51
- Salivary tissue is frequently present in lymph nodes or extranodal lymphoid tissue particularly in the parotid and adjacent regions and this is more important from the practical viewpoint as the appearances may be mistaken for nodal metastases.
- More rarely, ectopic salivary tissue may be found in a variety of sites within the head and neck region, ranging from the gingiva to the brain.
- An uncommon anomaly known as a ***Stafne bone cyst*** as a result of its radiological appearance, is formed by invagination into the bone of the lingual aspect of the angle of the mandible, by a lobe of the submandibular gland.
- More rarely, normal salivary tissue may be found within the anterior mandible. They are seen radiographically as round, sharply defined cyst-like areas of radiolucency. Intraosseous salivary gland tumors of the jaw are a recognized but rare entity and presumably arise from these foci of ectopic tissue.
- Even more rarely, tumors may develop in any other sites of ectopic salivary gland tissue. Ectopic salivary tissue lacking an excretory duct can rarely give rise to salivary fistulas.

Ans.72. (b) Painful

Ref Manual of Dental surgery , pg 121
http://en.wikipedia.org/wiki/Burn_(injury)

BURNS

1. **partial thickness burns (I degree)** – superficial layers of skin are destroyed exposing the nerve endings an hence are extremely painful. Heals in 3-5 days without any scar.
2. **II degree burn –** here the dermis is involved .pain is extreme with blister formation and skin appearing soft waxy. It heals in 10-20 days with hypertrophic scar.
3. **full thickness burn (III degree)** – the subcutaneous tissue is exposed . since the nerves are damaged there is little/no pain. Sensations are lost and *eschar* develops. An eschar is a scab that has separated from the unaffected part of the body. Heals in 3-5 weeks with grafting.

Burns that injure the tissues underlying the skin, such as the muscles or bones, are sometimes categorized as **fourth-degree burns**. These burns are additionally broken down into three additional degrees: fourth-degree burns result in the skin being irretrievably lost, fifth-degree burns result in muscle being irretrievably lost, and sixth-degree burns result in bone being charred.

Ans.73. (d) All the above

Ref http://www.emedicine.com/med/byname/Wermer-Syndrome-(MEN-Type-1).htm

Multiple endocrine neoplasia (MEN) syndromes consist of 2 categories,

- MEN 1(Wermer syndrome) and
- MEN 2. Since 1975, MEN 2 (Sipple syndrome) has been subcategorized into MEN 2a and MEN 2b.

The combination of parathyroid tumors, pancreatic islet cell tumors, and pituitary hyperplasia or tumor formation is called MEN 1. It is an autosomal dominant disorder, but it may also occur sporadically as a result of new mutations.

In 1954, Wermer was the first to describe the syndrome as a distinct clinical entity.

PATHOPHYSIOLOGY

Parathyroid tumors

Hyperparathyroidism is the most common manifestation of MEN 1, caused by hyperplasia of multiple parathyroid glands. Penetrance is almost 100% by age 50 years.

Clinical manifestations include urolithiasis, bone abnormalities, and, in severe cases, generalized weakness and mental or cognitive dysfunction.

Hyperparathyroidism in MEN 1 differs from sporadic cases by earlier age at presentation, involvement of multiple glands, and high recurrence rate postoperatively (50% by 8-12 y after surgery).

ENTEROPANCREATIC TUMORS

- Pancreatic islet cell tumors represent the second most common manifestation of MEN 1 and occur in 80% of patients. Tumors are often multicentric and may undergo malignant transformation. Often, they produce multiple peptides and biogenic amines.
- Nonfunctioning pancreatic endocrine tumors are the most common pancreatic tumors, occurring in 80-100% of cases. However, the name is a misnomer because most of them produce pancreatic polypeptide. The tumor mass, even at an advanced stage, may not cause a clinical syndrome outside of its mass effect. They may be malignant; however tumors less than 2 cm in size have low risk of metastasis or death. Average life expectancy of patients with nonfunctioning pacreatic endocrine tumors is decreased when compared to MEN 1 patients who do not have them.
- Gastrinomas are the most common cause of symptomatic disease and are found in approximately 60% of patients with MEN 1. Compared to the sporadic form of gastrinomas in Zollinger-Ellison syndrome (ZES), tumors in MEN 1 are more often duodenal, small, and multicentric, thus diminishing the probability of surgical cure. The features predictive of poor prognosis include pancreatic location of lesions, metastases, ectopic cushing syndrome, and height of gastrin levels. Development of gastrinomas is preceded by multifocal hyperplasia of the gastrin-producing cells. Long-standing MEN 1/ZES may lead to development of gastric carcinoid tumors that might be aggressive.

- Insulinomas account for approximately 20-35% of functional pancreatic islet cell tumors. Similar to gastrinomas, they can be multicentric (10-20%), where 25% metastasize either to regional lymph nodes or to the liver.
- Glucagonomas occur in 3% of patients with MEN 1 and are silent or present with hyperglycemia. Only a few patients show the typical skin lesions known as necrolytic migratory erythema.
- The occurrence of the watery diarrhea, hypokalemia, hypochlorhydria, and acidosis (WDHA) syndrome (incidence approximately 1%) may be due either to either a pancreatic islet cell or to a carcinoid tumor.

Pituitary tumors

- These often-multicentric tumors occur in more than 50% of patients and are clinically apparent in up to 20% of patients. These tumors tend to be larger and more aggressive than those not associated with MEN 1.
- Prolactinomas are the most common pituitary tumor in patients with MEN 1.
- Growth hormone–producing tumors account for 25% of these adenomas. Growth hormone levels rise due to autonomous secretion from the pituitary tumor or, less commonly, by production of growth hormone–releasing factor by a pancreatic or other endocrine tumor.
- A pituitary tumor or carcinoid tumor that produces corticotropin can cause Cushing syndrome in patients with MEN 1.

Other tumors associated with MEN 1

- Carcinoid tumors usually in the foregut (*e.g,* thymus, lungs, stomach, duodenum). In men, (thymus) they are often nonfunctional and aggressive. In women, the lung is affected most often. Carcinoids may release ectopic adrenocorticotropic hormone.
- Cutaneous tumors include angiofibromas (occurring in 40-80% of patients) and collagenomas. *They are often multifocal. Finding of more than 3 angiofibromas and any collagenomas has a sensitivity of 75% and specificity of 95% for diagnosis of MEN 1.* This criterion has greater sensitivity than pituitary or adrenal disease and comparable to hyperparathyroidism in some studies.
- Lipomas, subcutaneous and visceral, are found in one third of patients. They have loss of heterozygosity for chromosome band 11q12-12 and are associated with defective globular (G) protein function.
- Adrenal tumors are most often benign and consist of nonfunctional cortical adenomas or diffuse or nodular hyperplasia.
- Thyroid adenomas (5-30% of patients).

Ans.74. (b). Alexander & Wallace

Ref Manual of Dental surgery, 121

Assessment of degree of burns is done by 'Rule of 9' given by Alexander and Wallace.

Head and neck	9 %
upper limbs	9 x 2 = 18 %

thorax	9 x 2 = 18 % (front and back)
abdomen	9 x 2 = 18 %
lower limbs	18 x 2 = 36 %
Genitals	1 %

Curling's ulcers are acute peptic ulcers seen in burns patient.

Ans.75. (b). Lymphatic system

Ref Robbins, 6th ed pg 140

Direct - basal cell carcinoma
Blood - sarcomas and renal cell carcinoma
Lymphatics - squamous cell carcinoma, malignant melanoma.
Liver and Lungs are the most commonly involved in metastasis.

Ans.76. (b). Hibernoma

Ref http://www.ispub.com/ostia/index.php?xmlFilePath=journals/ijs/vol7n2/hibernoma.xml

Hibernoma denotes a tumor derived from brown fat.

- It is an uncommon tumor has been described only in a few case reports and small series.
- The distribution of this tumor follows the sites of persistence of brown fat.
- Although it is usually found in the inter-scapular region, it has also been reported in sites where brown fat is less common.
- Only a few cases have been described in the head and neck region.
- Hibernomas are usually asymptomatic and slow growing.
- Adequate treatment consists of complete excision.

ORAL PATHOLOGY

Ans .77. (b). Psoriasis

Ref Shafer 5th ed , pg 1108

Munro's abscess is seen as a histological feature of Psoriasis. Psoriasis is a non-contagious skin disorder that presents with silvery white scaly lesions of skin.

Salient features:

1. the mitotic rate is found to be very high in this lesion at 2-3 days(normal 23 days)
2. **Auspitz's sign** : characteristic sign where multiple bleeding spots are seen when the scales are removed form the lesion. Clinically, lesions are seldom pruritc and painless.
3. it is at times associated with the condition- benign migratory glossitis
4. histological findings include absence of stratum granulosum, presence of intra-epithelial micro abscesses (Monroe's abscess).

Ans.78. (a). Recurrent apthous ulcer

Ref: Shafer's 5th ed , allergic and immune disease of oral cavity , pg 915

Recurrent Apthous Stomatitis also known as apthous ulcers or *canker sores* is characterized by the development of painful, recurring solitary or multiple ulcerations of oral mucosa.

Ans79. (a). Pituitary dwarfism

Ref Shafer's , development disturbance of oral structures, 5th ed pg 52

Tuc generalized microdontia all the teeth are smaller than normal as in pituitary dwarfism. The teeth are well formed but smaller in size.

Ans.80. (a). Gumma

Ref Shafer's, bacterial infection of oral cavity , 5th ed , pg 453

Hutchinson's triad is seen in congenital syphilis and includes:

- Interstitial keratitis,
- eight nerve deafness and
- Hypoplastic incisors/molars (Moon's, Fournier's molars).

Other features: frontal bossing, mandibular protrusion, saber shin, rhagades.

Higoumenaki's sign: irregular thickening of clavicle.

Ans81. (d). Sturge Weber Syndrome

Ref Shafer, 5th ed , Benign and Malignant tumours of oral cavity , pg 204

Sturge- weber syndrome (Encephalotrigeminal Hemangiomatosis) is an uncommon congintal condition affecting eye, skin and CNS at different times, characterized by venous malformations of the leptomeninges over the cerebral cortex with ipsilateral angiomataous lesions of the face and sometimes skull and oral tissues. It is a group of disease known as ***Phakomatoses*** (mother- spot disease) as it is generally first spotted by mother during feeding.

Osler-Weber-Rendu syndrome (Herediatry hemorrhagic telangiectasis) is an autosomal dominant disorder. There is a multi-system arteriovenous malformations with episodes of recurrent epistaxis and haemorrhage.

EXTRA EDGE

Maffuci syndrome- Maffucci syndrome is a rare dysembryoplasia associating cartilage tumors similar to enchondromas in Ollier's disease and vessel tumors. The patient may have capillary hemangiomas, cavernous angiomas, and lymphangiomas facing the cartilage tumefactions. Regular clinical surveillance is required for such patients due to the risk of degeneration of the enchondromas and the angiomas, but also due to the possible occurrence of other malignant tumors besides the cartilage and vessel tumors.

Ans.82. (a). Lympadenopathy AND (c) Hepatosplenomegaly

Ref http://en.wikipedia.org/wiki/Congenital_syphilis

Friends, this was one of the most controversial questions of this paper. Although Condyloma lata is seen in the second stage of syphilis, the answer given was 4.All the above. Well little can be done in this regard, but you should know the features of congenital syphilis:-

Notched incisors known as Hutchinson's teeth which are characteristic of congenital syphilis

·abnormal x-rays

- ***Hutchinson's Triad***, a set of symptoms consisting of deafness, Hutchinson's teeth (centrally notched, widely-spaced peg-shaped upper central incisors), and interstitial keratitis (IK), an inflamation of the cornea which can lead to corneal scarring and potentially blindness
- mulberry molars (sixth year molars with multiple poorly developed cusps)
- frontal bossing
- poorly developed maxillae
- enlarged liver and jaundice
- enlarged spleen (***hepato-splenomegaly***)
- petechiae and other skin rash
- sabre shins
- anemia
- *lymph node enlargement*
- pseudoparalysis
- Snuffles, the name given to rhinitis in this situation. When chronic, this can lead to saddle nose deformity.
- rhagades, linear scars at the angles of the mouth and nose result from bacterial infection of skin lesions.

Death from congenital syphilis is usually through pulmonary hemorrhage.

Ans 83. (a) Gingiva

Ref Shafer 5th ed , pg 185

Peripheral giant cell granuloma –

- is considered a reactive lesion.
- F>M ,4th -6th decade of life, mandible >maxilla.
- Common site is gingiva anterior to molars.
- Radiographically, peripheral cuffing is the pathognomonic feature.

Ans 84. (d) Legumes

REF with text

Pulse granuloma or giant-cell hyaline angiopathy was first described by *Dunlop* and Barker. This consists of inflammatory cell infiltration, collection of foreign material type giant cells, and the presence of ring like structures known as Rushton's bodies, composed of an eosinophilic material resembling hyalinized collagen. Fragments of ***foreign materials*** (legumes etc), may resemble vegetable matter (and hence the term ''pulse granuloma'') this may be seen in variety of conditions such as Periapical granuloma, nasopalatine cysts etc.

Ref Shafer 5th ed , pg 674

Hyaline ring (pulse granuloma) is a rare benign lesion of the oral cavity soft tissues characterized by round or oval structures with scalloped borders composed by a collagenous matrix variable associated with inflammatory and foreign bogy giant cells. Vegetable fragments are variably identified. Whereas most cases occur in the oral cavity, it has also been described in other sites such as the lung and rectum. It is thought by most to represent a reaction to foreign materials. We report two incidentally discovered cases of colonic hyaline rings associated with perforated diverticulitis. Vegetable residues were seen in both cases.

Ref http://www.sciencedirect.com/science?_ob=ArticleURL

Ans 85. (c) Gardner's syndrome

Ref Shafer 5th ed, pg 65

While both Gardener and Cleidocranial dysostosis present with multiple impacted teeth. The following features differentiate the two.

Gardener syndrome has the following characteristics:-

1. occurrence of multiple impacted supernumerary teeth.
2. multiple polyposis of large intestine.
3. osteomas of long bones,skulls and jaws.
4. multiple epidermoid /sebaceous cysts and desmoids tumors.

Ans 86. (b) Klinefelter Syndrome

Ref Shafer 5th ed , pg 56-57

Taurodontism was first described by Sir Arthur Keith in 1913 where the tooth is enlarged at the expense of the roots. The pulp chamber is extremely large and the bifurcation area of roots approaches the apical third. This condition may be associated with Klinefelter syndrome (extra X chromosome), Amelogenesis imperfecta, was seen in Neanderthal man, or may be genetic.

Remember,

- Rubinstein-Taybi syndrome is associated with Talon cusp (Eagle's cusp) seen in cingulum area of maxillary or mandiibular permanent incisors.
- Aschers syndrome is associated with acquired double lip , blepharochalasis (drooping of upper eye lid) and non-toxic thyroid enlargement.

Ans 87. (c) Hypophosphatasia

Ref Shafer 5th ed , pg 881

Hypophosphatasia

- Described by Rathbun (1948) is a disorder of deficiency of enzyme alkaline phosphatase in serum or tissue and excess secretion of phospho-ethanolamine in urine.
- The characteristic features include premature loosing and loss of deciduous teeth chiefly the incisors.
- Radiographically, the long bones show 'spotty or streaky' ossification and absence of any cementum with loss of alveolar bone.
- The teeth are hypocalcified with large pulp chamber.

EXTRA EDGE

Remember, Vitamin D resistant rickets is associated with *abnormal* cementum but cementum is still present. Other features include hypocalcified teeth with globular dentin, multiple gingival fistulas and ABSENCE of lamina dura.

Ans 88. (d). All

Ref Shafer, 5th ed , pg 510

- Phycomycosis is a fungal infection caused by the order mucorales.
- The three most important types causing infection in man are Rhizopus, Mucor, and Absidia.
- Infections by these are characterized by classical syndrome of uncontrolled DM, cellulitis, opthalmoplegia, and meningoencephalitis.
- Mode of transmission is via nose and paranasal sinus.

Ans.89. (b). Iodine mumps

Ref Shafer 5th ed , pg 486

Chemical mumps refers to a condition with bilateral swelling of the parotid gland seen after administration of either organic or inorganic iodine. This condition may be seen even after administration of other drugs such as isoproterenol etc.

Ans.90. (d) All the above

Explained Earlier. Please refer A27

ORAL MEDICINE AND RADIOLOGY

Ans.91. (c) Kaposi's sarcoma

Ref Shafer, 5th ed , pg 232

Approximately 40% of homosexual AIDS patient develops Kaposi's sarcoma, often as an early sign of the disease. Individuals (young adults or early middle-aged males) may develop as cutaneous locations, especially along lines of cleavage and on tip of the nose. Commonly found on palatal and gingival areas.

Ans.92. (a). Sickle cell anemia

Ref Oral radiology, White and Pharoah, 5th ed, Systemic disease manifested in Jaws pg 533

http://radiology.rsnajnls.org/cgi/content/full/221/2/347

Hair on end appearance

- seen in lateral skull projections is a radiographic appearance attributed to widening of the diploic space and thinning of the outer and inner tables of the skull to the extent, that they may not be visible at all.
- The skull alterations are due to over activity of the red marrow in response to anemia. This marrow hyperplasia widens the diploic space and thins the outer table.
- There is trabecular destruction with thickening of the residual trabeculae. The trabecular pattern within the diploë may sometimes be arranged perpendicular to the curvature of the cranial vault.

- There is alternating opaque, thickened trabeculae and radiolucent marrow hyperplasia and has the appearance of long, thin vertical striations that look like ***hair standing on end***.
- This pattern of bone changes is seen in patients suffering from sickle cell anemia, and sometimes thalessemia.

Remember, chipmunk or rodent facies is seen in thalessemia (Cooley's anemia) due to prominent cheekbones and protrusive premaxilla.

Ans 93. (b). Pilocarpine

Ref http://www.nci.nih.gov/cancertopics/pdq/supportivecare/oralcomplications HealthProfessional/page13 Burket's Oral medicine,10th ed

Xerostomia alters the mouth's buffering capacity and mechanical cleansing ability, thereby contributing to dental caries and progressive periodontal disease. Development of dental caries also is accelerated in the presence of xerostomia due to reduction in delivery to the dentition of antimicrobial proteins normally contained in saliva.

Saliva is necessary for the normal execution of oral functions such as taste, swallowing, and speech. Unstimulated whole salivary flow rates less than 0.1 mL/minute are considered indicative of xerostomia (normal salivary flow rate **= 0.3–0.5 mL/minute**)

Oral and Dental Management of the Xerostomic Patient

- Plaque removal:
  - Tooth brushing.
  - Flossing.
  - Other oral hygiene aids.
- Remineralizing solutions:
  - Fluoride and calcium/phosphates.
  - Topical high concentration fluorides.
  - Children: topical and systemic.
  - Adults: topical.
- Topical antimicrobial rinses:
  - Chlorhexidine solutions/rinses (Peridex).
  - Povidone iodine oral rinses.
  - Tetracycline oral rinses.
- Sialogogues:
  - pilocarpine (Salagen)
  - cevimeline (Evoxac)
  - bethanechol
  - antholetrithione (Sialor)

Management of xerostomia also includes use of saliva substitutes or sialagogues. Saliva substitutes or artificial saliva preparations (oral rinses containing hydroxyethylcellulose, hydroxypropylcellulose, or carboxymethylcellulose) are palliative agents that relieve the discomfort of xerostomia by temporarily wetting the oral mucosa. Sialagogues pharmacologically stimulate saliva production from intact salivary glandular tissues. Submandibular gland transfer has been used for xerostomia.

EXTRA EDGE

Pilocarpine

- Only drug approved by the U.S. Food and Drug Administration for use as a sialogogue (5 mg tablets of pilocarpine hydrochloride) for radiation xerostomia.
- Treatment is initiated at 5 mg by mouth 3 times a day; dose is then titrated to achieve optimal clinical response and minimize adverse effects. The patient's evening dose may be increased to 10 mg within 1 week after starting pilocarpine. Subsequently, morning and afternoon doses may also be increased to a maximum 10 mg/dose (30 mg/day). Patient tolerance is confirmed by allowing 7 days between increments.
- The most common adverse effect at clinically useful doses of pilocarpine is hyperhidrosis (excessive sweating); its incidence and severity are proportional to dosage. Nausea, chills, rhinorrhea, vasodilation, increased lacrimation, bladder pressure (urinary urgency and frequency), dizziness, asthenia, headache, diarrhea, and dyspepsia are also reported, typically at doses >5 mg 3 times a day.
- Pilocarpine usually increases salivary flow within 30 minutes after ingestion. Maximal response may occur only after continual use.

Cevimeline (30 mg three times a day) also appears anecdotally to have efficacy in managing radiation-induced xerostomia. Although to date cevimeline is only approved for use in the management of Sjogren's syndrome, appropriate clinical trials are underway and its efficacy should soon be established. While cevimeline has greater selective affinity for M_3 muscarinic receptors than pilocarpine, whether this can prove advantageous for treating radiation xerostomia remains unclear.

Ans.94. (a). Clotrimazole

Ref K.D tripathy, textbook of pharmacology

Anti-fungal agents

1. Antibiotics-
   (*a*) Polyenes- Amphotericin B , Nystatin, Natamycin
   (*b*) Heterocyclic benzofuran – Griseofulvin
2. Antimetabolites : Flucytosine (5-FC)
3. Azoles :
   (*a*) Imidazoles (topical) Clotrimazole, Econazole, Miconazole
   (systemic) Ketoconozole
   (*b*) Trazoles : (systemic) Fluconazole,itraconazole
4. Allyamine : terbinafine
5. Other : Gentian Violet , Haloprogin, Tolnaftate Undecylenic acid

Looking at other choices

- Cotrimoxazole is a combination of trimethoprim and sulfamethoxazole in the ratio of 1 : 20 to achieve a plasma level of 1:5.
- Ornidazole is a congener of metronidazole used for amoebiasis, giardiasis, vaginosis etc.
- Propronolol is a well known beta blocker used in treating hypertension.

Ans.95. (c) Nodular leukoplakia

Ref Burket's oral medicine, 10th ed. pg 102

Leukoplakia is a white patch or plaque that can't be characterized clinically or pathologically as any other disease.

Subtypes:-

1. Homogenous – well, defined, localized , slightly elevated dry patch.
2. Verrucous leukoplakia – thick white papillary lesion usually heavily keratinized exophytic.
3. Nodular – granular or non-homogenous, mixed red and white lesion with atrophic background. Has a higher malignant transformation rate (>60%).
4. Proliferative verrucous leukoplakia- involves multiple sites and invariably transforms into squamous cell carcinoma.

So, among the options given, nodular variety is the answer of choice.

Ans.96. (b). No pain

Ref Burket's oral medicine, 10th ed , pg 101, ch Red and white lesions of oral cavity

A mucous patch is a superficial grayish area of mucosal necrosis associated with secondary syphilis. They develop within 6 weeks of primary lesion and inside oral cavity exists as ***multiple painless*** grayish white plaques covered by necrotic surface. Although they may resolve within a few weeks, these lesions are highly infectious as they contain large amounts of spirochetes.

Ans.97. (a). Systemic Lupus Erythematous

Ref Burket's oral medicine, 10th ed , pg 488

SLE diagnosis and lab investigation

The most important diagnostic test for SLE is the Anti-nuclear antibody (ANA) test in the serum which is positive for 96-100% of patients with SLE. Other conditions with ANA positive- scleroderma, rheumatoid arthritis. In addition to ANA, other antibodies present in SLE are abs to Smith (Sm) antigen, abs to Ro (SS-A) and abs to La(SS-B) antigen.

EXTRA EDGE

LE'cell test is positive in SLE and not DLE. This test advocated by *Hargraves* et al consists of addition of patient's serum to a buffy coat of normal blood. The ''LE'' cells is a rosette of neutrophils surrounding a pale nuclear mass apparently derived from lymphocytes.

Ans.98. (a). DIC

Ref Burket's oral medicine.10th ed , pg 459

Disorder	Platelet count	PT	aPTT	BT
Thrombocyto-penia	decreased	N	N	increased
Hemophilia	N	N	increased	N
Von Willebrand	N/decreased	N	N/increased	increased
DIC	decreased	increased	increased	increased
Factor XIII def	N	N	N	N

Hence, we see from the table that in DIC both bleeding time (BT) and prothrombin time (PT) are increased.

Ans 99. (b). Fibrous dysplasia

Ref White and Pharoah, 5th ed pg 487

Fibrous Dysplasia, is characterized by presence of abnormal trabeculae which are shorter, thinner, irregularly shaped and more numerous than normal. This creates a radio-opaque pattern having a granular appearance or the "*ground glass appearance*".

Other condition with ground glass appearance of bone is Primary hyperparathyroidism.

Pagets disease – characterized by 'cotton-wool appearance'.

Ans.100. (b) 0.2 to 0.3

Ref White and Pharoah , 5th ed , pg 78

An unexposed film, when processed, shows some density. This is due to the inherent density of the base and added units, as well as the development of unexposed silver halide crystals. This minimum density is called as gross fog or base plus fog. The optical density of gross fog typically is 0.2 to 0.3

Ans.101. (d). Muscle

Ref White and Pharoah, 5th ed, pg 30

Mammalian cells may be divided into five categories of radio sensitivity on basis of histologic evaluation:-

1. Vegetative inter-mitotic cells- are the most radiosensitive. *e.g.,* early precursor cells of spermatogenic or erythroblastic series, basal cells of mucosa.
2. Differentiating inter-mitotic cells- less sensitive as lower mitotic potential. *e.g.,*cells of inner enamel epithelium, intermediate erythrogenic and spermatocytes, oocytes
3. Multipotent connective tissue cells- have intermediate sensitivity *e.g.,* vascular endothelial cells, fibroblasts, mesenchymal cells.
4. Reverting postmitotic cells- generally radioresistant *e.g.,* ductal cells of salivary gland, liver, kidney, thyroid.
5. Fixed postmitotic cells- are resistant to direct actions of radiation. Highly differentiated such as neurons, muscle cells, squamous epithelial cells.

Ans.102. (b). Ammonium Thio Sulfate

Ref White and Pharoah, 5th ed, pg 97

Composition of Dental developing solution

1. Developer- phenidone (primary electron donor) and hydroquinone.
2. Activator – sodium or potassium hydrozide makes pH alkaline (10) and increases the diffusion of developer into emulsion.
3. Preservative – sodium sulfite acts as an anti-oxidant/preservative.
4. Restrainer – bromide,like potassium bromide or benzotriazole, are added to the developing solutions to restrain development of unexposed particles. Hence they also act as anti-fog agent and increase film contrast.

Composition of Fixing Solution

1. Clearing agent – ammonium thiosulfate (hypo) forms a stable, water soluble complex with silver ion. This gives the exposed area its white color in radiograph.
2. Acidifier – Acetic acid (pH 4) keeps the fixer acidic so essential for clearing agent, besides it also helps in inhibiting any developer accidentally left on the film.
3. Preservative ammonium sulfite performs the same function as it does in the developing solution
4. Hardener – aluminium sulfite is the most commonly used, it complexes with gelatin making it hard and resistant to damage and also limits water absorption by the emulsion.

Ans.103. (c). Cavernous Haemangioma

Ref White and Pharoah, 5th ed , pg 605

Phleboliths

- Are intravascular thrombi, which arise secondary to venous stagnation and later organize and mineralize.
- They are usually found in veins, venules or sinusoidal vessels of hemangiomas (especially the cavernous type).
- The involved soft tissue may be swollen, painful or discolored.
- In radiographs they resemble straight or slightly curved sausages.
- The internal structure may give an appearance of bull's eye due to laminations. They should be differentiated from sialoliths.

Ans.104. (b). Roentgen

Ref White and Pharoah , 5th ed, pg 21

Exposure- A measure of radiation quantity, or the capacity to ionize air.

S.I. unit – air kerma. ***earlier used*** -Roentgen, R

Absorbed Dose- energy absorbed by any type of ionizing radiation per unit mass.

S.I unit – Gray (Gy) ***earlier used*** rad (radiation absorbed dose)

1 gray = 100 rads

1 rads = 100 ergs/g

Equivalent Dose- compares the biologic effect of different type of radiation on a living tissue.

S.I. unit – Sieverts (Sv), ***earlier used***- rem(roentgen equivalent mass)

1 Sv = 100 rem

Effective dose (E) –is used to calculate the risk in humans.

Unit again is Sv.

Radioactivity – measures the decay rate of a sample of radioactive material.

S.I. unit – Becquerel (Bq) ***earlier used*** – curie (Ci)

1 Bq = 2.7 x 10^{-11} Ci

PERIODONTICS

Ans.105. (b). 1.5 - 2.5 mm

Ref Carranza clinical periodontology, 9th ed pg 358

Garant et al suggested that locally producing bone resorption factors may have to be present in the proximity of bone surface to be able to exert their effect. The range of effectiveness has been postulated to be about **1.5 – 2.5 mm** within which bacterial plaque can induce loss of bone.

Ans.106. (c). Niacin

Ref Shafer, oral aspects of metabolic disease, 5th ed pg 890; Carranza, 9th ed pg 302

Deficiency of niacin manifests as ***pellagra.***

- In prodormal stage loss of appetite and vague GI symptoms manifests.
- In the acute stages , entire oral mucosa becomes fiery red and painful. Salivation is profuse.
- The epithelium desquamates along with tenderness, and ulceration of interdental papillae, superimposed necrotizing ulcerative gingivostomatitis or Vincent's infection is a common sequel.

Carranza mentions the role of riboflavin deficiency BUT this increases the severity of existing infection and not results in such infection. (The original key had niacin as the answer but latter revised it to riboflavin. I would suggest readers to follow niacin, rest is up to you!)

Ans.107. (b).Citric acid

Ref Carranza, 9th ed pg 812

In regenerative procedures, the root surface is usually conditioned with ***citric acid*** pH 1 for 3 min or with 24 % EDTA pH 6.7 for 15 sec. This removes the smear layer and favors the adhesion of grafting material.

Ans.108. (a). 2-7 days

Ref Carranza, 9th ed pg 747

After gingival curettage, restoration and re-epithelialization of the sulcus generally require **2-7 days**. While the junctional epithelium gets restored in about 5 days, immature collagen fibrils appear within 21 days of treatment.

Ans. 109. (c). Trauma from occlusion

Ref Carranza 9th ed, periodontal response to External forces pg 371.

Friends, please make these two terms very clear in your mind.

Traumatic occlusion is reference to the occlusion which causes an injury while ***trauma from occlusion*** is a reference to the trauma caused by such occlusion.

Ans. 110. (b). Hemisection

Ref Carranza, 9th ed, furcation and its management, pg 832

- Splitting of a two rooted tooth into separate portions is called <u>hemi-section</u>.
- If the two parts are separated and preserved then the procedure is referred as <u>bicuspidization</u>
- However, if one of the roots is removed after hemisection the procedure is known as <u>root resection</u>.

Ans. 111. (a). Evidence based therapy

Ref Carranza, 9th ed, pg 978

Current concepts of evaluating health care require a scientific basis for treatment and is known as *evidence based therapy*. Evidence is now overwhelming that periodontal therapy is effective in preventing periodontal disease, slowing the destruction of periodontium and reducing tooth loss.

Ans. 112. (c). Bio-film

Ref Carranza, 9th ed , Periodontal microbiology pg 104

Dental Plaque acts as **biofilm,** wherein bacteria and their products, exist and proliferate within the intracellular matrix through which channels course. The association of Plaque with periodontal disease is well documented by the specific and non-specific plaque hypothesis by *Walter Loesche* in 1976.

Ans. 113. (d). Inter proximal plaque formation

Ref Carranza, 9th ed , pg 660 Plaque control for the perio patient

Dental floss is the most commonly used tool for removing plaque from proximal tooth surfaces.

Please remember, that it is not used for removing impacted food material or calculus from the interdental area. The prime indication is to improve the interproximal gingival health.

Ans. 114. (c). Reconstitution of the lost periodontium

Ref Carranza, 9th ed ,pg 509

Regeneration is the growth and differentiation of new cells and intercellular substances to form new tissues or parts. Regeneration of periodontium is a continuous physiological process.

<u>New attachment</u>: is the embedding of new fibers into new cementum and attachment of gingival epithelium to tooth surface previously denuded by disease.

While adaptation refers to close apposition without complete obliteration of the pocket.

Ans. 115. (a) Absorption of glycoprotein from saliva

Ref Carranza 9th ed , Periodontal microbiology, pg 99

Formation of dental pellicle is the initial phase of plaque formation. All surfaces of oral cavity are coated with a glycoprotein pellicle. This pellicle is derived from components of ***saliva*** and crevicular fluid as well as bacterial and host cell products and debris. Pellicle functions as a protective barrier and prevents tissue desiccation but also acts as a substrate for plaque formation.

Ans. 116. (a) Lysozyme

Ref Carranza, 9th ed , pg 259

Saliva contains numerous organic and inorganic factors which influence bacteria and their products.

- **Lysozyme** is a hydrolytic enzyme that cleaves the linkage between glycopeptide-containing region of the cell wall of certain bacteria like *Veillonella* and *Actinobacillus actinomycetum comitans*.
- Lactoperxidase-thiocyanate systems is bactericidal to lactobacilli and streptococci.
- Similarly, lactoferrin and myeloperoxidase are effective against AA.

Ans. 117. (c). platelet disorder

Ref Carranza 9th ed , pg 216.influence of systemic disease of periodontium

Gingival hemorrhage is a common finding in leukemic patients, this is due to the ensuing ***thrombocytopenia*** that results from replacement of the bone marrow cells by leukemic cells and also inhibition of normal stem cells. Similarly other minor surgical procedures like tooth extraction are accompanied with massive bleeding and hence great care should be prescribed in handling such cases.

Ans. 118. (b). 2 mm

Ref Carranza, 9th ed , pg 945

The biological width is composed of junctional epithelium and the connective tissue attachment.

In effect,

Biologic Width (2.04mm) = JE (0.97 mm) + CT (1.07mm)

Also remember, that it is essential that there be at least 3 mm between the most apical end of restoration and the alveolar bone crest.

CONSERVATIVE DENTISTRY AND ENDODONTICS

Ans. 119. (b). Steele's siqveland

Ref Vimal Sikri , pg 162

MATRIX RETAINERS

Steele's Siqveland Self-adjusting –

- So built so as to form two diameters of the band the larger for occlusal and other for gingival area.
- Anatomic adaptation is possible without wedges.
- The band follows the tooth contour without impinging the gingival tissue.
- Works on a principle of a movable slide which holds and tightens the band in required position.

The Ivory Matrix No. 1 and 8 are suitable for MOD, Class II amalgam restorations as the band encircles the entire crown of the tooth.

Ans. 120. (b). EDTA and urea peroxide

Ref: Endodontic practice. Grossman, 11th ed pg 225

A combination of EDTA and urea peroxide (R-C Prep) was developed by Stewart, which is an effective lubricating and cleaning agent for root canals and also allowed deeper penetration of the medicaments into the dentin.

Also,

- EDTA-C = EDTA + Cetavlon
- EDTA concentration 15% at pH 7.3

Ans. 121 (a) simultaneously etches and prime dentin and enamel

Ref textbook of operative dentistry, Vimal Sikri, pg361-62

The three steps – conditioning, priming and bonding may be done separately or combined to two steps. The third generation of dentin bonding agents aim primarily to combine the conditioner and primer to form the ***"self-etching primers"***. The acidic conditioner removes the smear layer while the primer consists of an adhesion promoter in a solvent like water, ethanol or acetone. These when dried, expose the hydrophobic ends of dentin and create a favorable surface for the bonding agent.

The initial systems consisted of acidic ferric oxalate on the enamel and dentine as a conditioner nowadays, Scotch bond 2 Prisma universal are used which provide bond strength of up to 9-18 MPa.

Ans. 122. (a). Submerge in 5% solution of NaOC1

Ref Grossman, 11th ed , pg 140

Gutta percha cones may be kept sterile in screw capped vials containing alcohol. To sterilize a GP cone before use, one should immerse it in 5.2% NaOCl for 1 min then rinse the cone with hydrogen peroxide and dry between two layers of gauze.

- So friends, the answer here is A) as it is the most appropriate here. Choice 'C' is wrong as GP cones are stored in alcohol and latter treated with NaOCl and not vice-versa.

Ans. 123. (c). An encircling band of metal that increases fracture resistance of the tooth

Ref Nallaswamy textbook of Prosthodontics, pg 556

While preparing a dowel core the coronal portion of the dowel should be encircled by at ***least 1-2mm*** of tooth structure to obtain a ferrule effect and protect the tooth from fracture.

Ans. 124. (d). 266 Mpa

Ref Sturdevant, 4th ed ,pg26

Tooth dentin features:-

Modulus of elasticity	1.67×10^6 PSI
Compressive strength	266 MPa
Tensile strength	40 MPa

Ans. 125. (d) Carbamide peroxide

Ref Sturdevant, 4th ed, pg 610-611

Night guard bleaching also known as ***dentist –prescribed –home*** applied bleaching utilizes a custom made vacuum formed soft vinyl night guard to deliver a 10-15%. Carbamide peroxide bleaching material to the affected area. Carbamide peroxide degrades into 3% hydrogen peroxide and 7 % urea. It is recommended that only one arch is treated at a time preferably maxillary arch.

Ans. 126. (a). Made by a combination of chemical precipitation and atomization

Ref Vimal Sikri, pg 328

Powdered gold is in the form of minute particles. It can be obtained by atomization from a molten state or by chemical precipitation using *aquaregia* and precipitated by oxalic acid sulphur dioxide or sodium nitrate. Average particle size is **15μm**. Because powdered gold produces very less porosity compared to mat gold, veneering with gold foil is not necessary.

Ans. 127. (b) Used to hold the silver point

Ref Grossman, pg 252

Steiglitz forceps are useful for carrying silver cones into root canals and for bending over the butt ends of the silver cones prior to cementing them into the root canals. The forceps are also useful for conveying instruments into root canals that are not readily accessible.

Ans. 128. (b) EDTA

Ref Grossman, pg 225

The chelating agent EDTA was introduced by Nygaard-Ostby . the effects of EDTA have been studied both in-vitro and in-vivo as:-

1. EDTA is effective in softening dentin.
2. has a distinct anti-microbial property.
3. is capable of moderate degree of irritation.
4. is biologically compatible when used as a irrigation media.
5. Irrigation with EDTA removes the smear layer.

Ans. 129. (a). 474 nm

Ref Vimal Sikri, pg 376

- Light cure composites were introduced which utilizes Benzoin methyl ether (UV light activated) or camphorquinone (visible-light activated).
- The U-V light works in the range at 360-400 nm. While current light activated composites utilize wavelengths of **474nm** (range 400-480 nm).

Ans. 130. (b) 30 - 40 degree

Ref Sturdevant pg 812

Flame shaped, fine grit diamond instrument is used to bevel the occlusal and gingival margins and to apply secondary flare on the distolingual and distofacial walls. This should result in a ***30 – 40*** degree marginal metal on the inlay. This cavsurface design helps seal and protects the margins and result in a string enamel margins of 140-150 degree. An angle of more than 150 results in less defined enamel margin and a thin marginal cast metal alloy. Similarly an angle of less than 140 results in the metal being too bulky and difficult to burnish. Hence the marginal metal is generally kept between 30 to 40 degrees.

Ans. 131. (c) Exposure site is the consequence of infected dentin extending into the pulp

Refer Ingle 5th ed, pg 870

The salient features of a clinically successful direct pulp capping treatment are:

1. Pinpoint pulp exposures (less than 1 mm) surrounded by normal dentine.
2. No history of spontaneous pain, exudates.
3. minimum/no tooth mobility and pulp inflammatory response.
4. Hemorrhage, if any, be easily controlled.
4. Absence of radiographic signs of dystrophic changes.

Evidence, has it that this procedure cannot be successful in the presence of pulpal inflammation and such a condition is generally regarded as a contra-indication for direct pulp capping.

Ans. 132.(a) No 50 file at Do

Ref http://jada.ada.org/cgi/content/full/135/7/903

Gates Glidden drills are used in endodontics for preparation of root canals. They are engine driven drills that come in 6 sizes. Their primary purpose is to enlarge the canal space for proper access. The various drill diameters are as following:

Size #1- 0.50 mm
Size #2- 0.70 mm
Size #3- 0.90 mm
Size #4- 1.10 mm
Size #5- 1.30 mm
Size #6- 1.50 mm

So friends, we see that Size #1 GG drills correspond to *Size #50 K-files* (with diameter 0.50 mm, yellow color)

[K-file color coding is explained in details in KCET-03 A133]

Ans. 133. (a) Gingival margin trimmer

Ref Sturdevent, pg 311

Instrument formulae

3 number	4 number
1. width of blade in tenths of mm 2. blade length in mm	1. width of blade in tenths of mm 2. Primary cutting edge angle. Angle is expressed as a % of 360, instrument is so positioned that this is always ***greater than 50***
3. Blade angle relative to long axis of the handle in clockwise centigrade instrument is positioned such that this no. is ***always 50 or less.*** E.g. Hoe , enamel hatchet , straight chisel;	3. blade length in mm 4. Blade angle.*e.g.*, GMT, angle former

Ans. 134 (b) S.C. Barnum

Ref Sturdevent, pg 445-450

Rubber dam, usually made of latex rubber, was first developed by ***Barnum*** (1864)

Remember,

Thickness of dam

- Thin : 0.006 inch (0.15 mm)
- Medium : 0.008 inch (0.2 mm)
- Heavy : 0.010 inch (0.25 mm)
- Extra heavy : 0.012 inch (0.30 mm)
- Special heavy : 0.014 inch (0.35 mm)

Winged retainers, although provides extra retention, interfere with placement of bands, retainers and wedges.

The distance between punched holes is generally **¼ inch or 6.3** mm.

Ans.135. (b) Pulp capping

Ref Ingle, pg 864

The goal in managing deep caries lesion is preservation of pulp vitality before instituting endodontic therapy. Pediatric pulp therapy for primary and young permanent teeth involves the following techniques:

1. Pulp capping – indirect and direct
2. Coronal pulpotomy
3. Pulpectomy

The first two methods are vital techniques that involve conservative management of portions of inflamed pulp tissue.

ORAL AND MAXILLO-FACIAL SURGERY

Ans. 136. (d) All of the above

Ref http://www.rxmed.com/b.main/b2.pharmaceutical/b2.1.monographs/CPS-%20Monographs/CPS-%20(General%20Monographs-%20X)/XYLOCAINE.html

Precautions while using LA -

- Lidocaine should be used with caution in patients receiving other local anesthetics or agents structurally related to amide-type local anesthetics, since the toxic effects are additive.
- Lidocaine with epinephrine or other vasopressors should not be used concomitantly with ergot-type oxytocic drugs, because a severe persistent hypertension may occur and cerebrovascular and cardiac accidents are possible.
- Likewise, lidocaine with epinephrine or another vasoconstrictor should be used with extreme caution in patients receiving MAO inhibitors or antidepressants of the triptyline or imipramine types, because severe prolonged hypertension may result.

- In situations when concurrent therapy is necessary, careful patient monitoring is essential. Phenothiazines and butyrophenones may reduce or reverse the pressor effect of epinephrine.
- If **sedatives** are employed to reduce patient apprehension, they should be used in reduced doses, since local anesthetic agents, like sedatives, are CNS depressants which in combination may have an ***additive effect***.
- Solutions containing epinephrine should be used with caution in patients undergoing general anesthesia with inhalation agents such as halothane, due to the risk of serious cardiac arrhythmias.
- Acidosis increases the systemic toxicity of lidocaine while the use of CNS depressants may increase the levels of lidocaine required to produce overt CNS effects. Objective adverse manifestations become increasingly apparent with increasing venous plasma levels above 6.0 μg free base.

CNS toxicity is a graded response, with symptoms and signs of escalating severity. The first symptoms are circumoral paresthesia, numbness of the tongue, lightheadedness, hyperacusis and tinnitus. Visual disturbance and muscular tremors are more serious and precede the onset of generalized convulsions. Unconsciousness and grand mal convulsions may follow, which may last from a few seconds to several minutes. ***Hypoxia and hypercarbia*** occur rapidly following convulsions due to the increased muscular activity, together with the interference with normal respiration. In severe cases apnea and death may occur.

Ans. 137. (c) Recurrent pericoronitis

Ref Neelima malik, textbook of oral surgery,pg 114

Indications for removal of impacted teeth

1. Recurrent pericoronitis/pain/infection/caries.
2. Deep periodontal pocket associated with partially erupted teeth.
3. Prior to orthodontic treatment.
4. Prevention of root resorption and caries of adjacent tooth.
5. Management of cysts and tumours.
6. Prevention of pathological fracture.

Ans. 138. (d) The entire tumor is removed intact with a rim of uninvolved bone while maintaining continuity of jaw

Ref Neelima Malik, benign tumors of the jaw bone, pg 436

En block or marginal resection is indicated in benign lesions with a known propensity for recurrence (Ameloblastoma, CEOT, myxoma, hemagioma etc) . The procedure involves complete excision of tumor while maintaining the continuity of the jaw bone which prevents the need for a second surgery for rehabilitation.

Ans. 139. (d) 40 mm

Ref http://www.maxfaxsho.co.uk/index_files/Page8040.htm

Naso-ethmoidal fractures

Clinical features of a naso-ethmoidal fracture:

- Flattened nasal bridge with splaying of nasal complex
- Saddle-shaped deformity of nose from side
- Traumatic telecanthus
- Circumorbital oedema and ecchymosis
- Subconjunctival haemorrhage
- Epistaxis
- CSF rhinorrhoea
- Possible supra-orbital / supra-trochlear nerve paraesthesia
- Tenderness, crepitus and mobility of nasal complex
- Overlying laceration

With naso-ethmoidal fractures a CSF leak should be assumed to be present even if it is not clinically demonstrable, and appropriate chemoprophylaxis should be commenced. An intercanthal distance of greater than **35mm** is suggestive of traumatic telecanthus, and measurement approaching **40mm** are almost diagnostic.

Closed manipulations of these injuries give a poor result, with a high incidence of persistent telecanthus and residual nasal deformity postoperatively. The results of secondary surgery of these abnormalities are not always satisfactory.

The principles of treatment are the same as for any other fractures, namely:

1. Reduction
2. Immobilisation
3. Rehabilitation

The naso-ethmoidal region can be accessed through the existing laceration, or through modification to a H-shaped or W-shaped incision. A bicoronal flap may be required for access to the frontal bone or orbital walls.

The naso-ethmoidal fracture often shows extensive comminution, although the nasal bridge may be intact, but depressed. This can be elevated back into position and stabilized by direct wiring, or using mini-plates to the frontal bone. Any individual fragments can be reduced, aligned and directly wired both to each other and to the surrounding intact bony skeleton.

The medial canthal ligament must be identified and repositioned into its position in the frontal process of the maxilla, and stabilized by wiring to the opposite anterior lacrimal crest (transnasal canthopexy). If both canthal ligaments are detached then the telecanthus can be repaired by means of wiring the two medial canthal ligaments to each other (transnasally).

Ans. 140. (b) 0.35 mm stainless steel wire

Ref Ingle's book of Endodontics, 5th ed , pg 822

When a tooth, as a result of trauma, is sensitive to percussion and has increased mobility, it is classified as subluxated. Pulp test may be positive or may elicit no response.

Treatment initially may be none, or it may become necessary to stabilize the tooth for minimal period *(2-3 weeks*). This may be done using unfilled resin bonded to small etched labial areas, or with the help of a thin ***0.3mm*** orthodontic SS wire, etched to the labial areas.

Definitive treatment for teeth not responding to EPT includes root canal therapy for fully developed teeth.

Ans. 141. (a). Odontogenic Keratocyst

Ref http://www.ndsu.nodak.edu/ndsu/lreynold/fixation.htm

Carnoy's solution is a commonly used fixative. It is sometimes used as an adjunct with enucleation and chemical curettage in management of lesions that have a predisposition towards recurrence such as OKC. Ameloblastoma and other aggressive lesions should not be treated with this technique.

EXTRA EDGE

Fixatives:

Carnoy's Solution

6 parts ethanol (absolute or 95%)
3 parts chloroform
1 part glacial acetic acid

10% Neutral Buffered Formalin

100 ml 37-40% formalin (formaldehyde)
900 ml distilled water
4.0 gm sodium phosphate monobasic
6.5 gm sodium phosphate dibasic (anhydrous)

Bouin's

750 ml Picric acid, saturated aqueous solution
250 ml 37-40% formalin (formaldehyde)
50 ml Glacial acetic acid

Ans. 142 .(c). Parotidectomy

Ref Neelima Malik, Diseases of salivary gland, pg 503

Auriculotemporal nerve palsy or **Frey's syndrome** (gustatory sweating) – condition wherein sweating and sometimes flushing of the skin in the area of distribution of the Auriculotemporal nerve occurs. This may occur after injury, wherein the fibers of postganglionic parasympathetic arising form superior cervical ganglion become united and supply the seat glands of skin.

The syndrome may be due to – surgery of parotid gland. TMJ joint, injury to face or an infection in the area.

Ans. 143. (c). hematogenous infection

Ref Neelima Malik, pg 595, osteomyelitis and Osteoradionecrosis of jaw bones.

Diffuse and multiple cases of osteomyelitis may be attributed to infections derived by hematogenous route for *e.g.,* furuncle on face, URTI, systemic tuberculosis.

Ans. 144. (b) 6th and 10th week of embryo-fetal life

Ref Neelima Malik , cleft lip and palate management , pg 509

The embryological development of face takes place between ***4th and 8th*** week of gestation. The median nasal process coalesces during the ***6th*** week. While anteriorly, the secondary palate fuses with triangular primary palate and the incisive foramen is formed at this junction between ***7th and 10th*** week of development.

Any failure of inter-contact or fusion between the various process may arise to a cleft deformity.

Ans. 145. (c) hematogenous spread

Explained earlier, please refer A 3

Ans. 146. (b) Mesioangular

Ref Neelima Malik, minor oral surgical procedures, pg 115

Most probably, the question refers to Mandibular third molars.

- In mandible, the *mesio-angular impaction is the easiest* while distoangular impaction is the most difficult of all (the fact that it is embedded in the ramus).
- While in the maxilla reverse is true, where the *mesioangular is the most difficult* for the fact that there is lack of space and visibility.

Ans. 147. (a) 2 mm

Ref Peterson textbook of oral surgery, 4th ed

Implants – facts

- Time required in maxilla : 6 months
- Time required in mandible : 4 months
- Distance between two implants – 3 mm
- Distance between implant and inferior alveolar nerve- 2 mm
- Implants and mental foramen – 5 mm
- Implant and PDL of adjacent tooth – 1mm
- Success of implant if bone loss <0.002 mm/annum
- Temp during placement should not exceed 47 degree C
- Placement should be done at high torque and low speed of 1500-2000 rpm

PEDODONTICS

Ans. 148. (b) Autism

Ref Shobha tandon, pg 541

Cerebral palsy manifests itself as a number of neuromuscular dysfunctions involving muscle weakness, stiffness, paralysis etc.

Classification

1. Based on *anatomical* involvement
   (*a*) Monoplegia: involvement of one limb.
   (*b*) hemiplagia: one side of body.
   (*c*) paraplegia : both legs.
   (*d*) quadriplegia : all the four limbs are involved.
2. Based on *neuro-muscular* involvement
   (*a*) Spasticity: hyper-reflexia, drooling ,stiffness and difficulty in moving limbs.
   (*b*) Athetosis: uncontrolled slow, twisting voluntary movements, bruxism.
   (*c*) Ataxia: lack of balance, stiffness.
   (*d*) Mixed: combination of above.

Ans. 149. (a). Addelston

Ref textbook of pedodontics, Shobha tandon pg 148

Addleston, 1959, introduced the - tell, show, do technique. This is a popular method used nowadays for modifying the behavior by desensitization in children. By having various verbal and non-verbal interactions, one can overcome the many dental related anxieties of any child

(This technique is explained in detail in *KCET-04*)

Ans. 150 (a) Below 20

Ref Shobha tandon, Ch management of developmentally disabled child pg 540

I.Q classification guide (Stanford –Binet)

IQ range	Grade
Above 140	Very superior
120 - 139	Superior
110 - 119	High average
90 - 109	Average
80 - 89	Low average
70 - 79	Borderline impaired
< 69	Mentally retarded
52 - 68	Mild , educable in special classes
36 - 51	Moderate, trainable
20 - 35	Severe, ability limited to simple language
< 20	Profound, non-trainable

Ans. 151. (c). Flush terminal plane

Ref Shobha tandon, ch developing dentition and its disturbances. Pg 110

Ideally, the eruption of the permanent molars into a class I relationship is desired. Since the flush terminal plane is more common in deciduous dentition, it is common for the permanent first molar to erupt in an end-end relation relationship. This is established by early shift, late shift or primary molar guidance of permanent dentition.

Prevalence of terminal planes- Flush terminal (59.1%), Mesial (19.1 %) Distal (4.8 %) – bilaterally; and FTP (9.1%) distal step (8.1%) unilaterally.

[According to RGUHS key, the answer is mesial step. However, we have no reference as yet for this. So we would prefer option 'c', till proved otherwise!]

Ans. 152. (d) Lingual arch holding app

Ref Shobha tandon, Developing malocclusion and its management, pg 394.

Of the given choices, only Lingual arch appliance is a bilateral space maintainer

- It is a fixed, non-functional, passive Mandibular arch appliance.
- They can control not only the antero-poterior movements but also are capable of controlling and preventing an arch perimeter distortion, by controlling the lingual collapse of a single tooth or segments of the arch.
- By adding features like loops mesial to molars, they can act as ***space regainers.***

ORTHODONTICS

Ans. 153. (a). Mouth breathing habit

Ref textbook of orthodontics bhalajhi, pg 112

The type of malocclusion most often seen with mouth breathing is long face syndrome or the classic adenoid facies. These patients exhibit the following:

- Long and narrow facies
- Narrow nose and nasal passage
- Short and flaccid upper lip
- Constricted upper arch with posterior cross bite
- Expressionless or blank face
- Anterior open bite with flaring of upper anteriors

Ans. 154. (c) Helps in eruption of first permanent molar

Ref bhalajhi pg 229

The distal show appliance first given by **Willet** is also known as intra-alveolar appliance. The distal surface of second primary molar *guides the unerupted permanent first molar*. When the second primary molar is extracted prior to eruption of permanent first molar, the distal shoe provides greater control of path of eruption and provides undesirable mesial migration. The current modification by Roche is the commonly used appliance.

Ans. 155. (a) Thumb sucking

Ref bhalajhi, Habits , pg 108

Effects of thumb sucking:

1. Labial tipping of the maxillary anterior teeth and resulting increase in over jet.
2. Anterior open bite as a result of restriction of incisor eruption and supra eruption of buccal teeth.

3. The cheek muscles contract during thumb sucking resulting in a narrow maxillary arch which predisposes to posterior cross bite.
4. Tongue thrust may develop as a result of open bite.
5. The upper lip is generally hypotonic while the lower part of face exhibits hyperactive mentalis activity.

Ans. 156. (a) Mandibular lingula

Ref bhalajhi, 2nd ed, Pre-natal growth and development, pg 33

- The ossifying membrane is located lateral to the Meckel's cartilage and its accompanying neuro-vascular bundle.
- As ossification, continues, the cartilage becomes surrounded and invaded by bone.
- Ossification stops at the site that will later become the Mandibular lingula form where the Meckel's cartilage continues into the middle ear and develops into auditory ossicles, malleus and incus.

Ans. 157. (b) 0.7 mm

Ref Textbook of removable appliances, Philip Adams

Adams clasp also known as Liverpool clasp, universal clasp is usually constructed form 0.7mm or 28 mil or 22 gauge SS wire on posterior teeth. However, on canine and anterior teeth, usually 0.6 mm SS wire is used.

Ans. 158. (c). Maxillary lateral incisor, canine and premolar

Ref http://ejo.oxfordjournals.org/cgi/content/full/28/2/145

Dental transposition is the positional interchange of two adjacent teeth, or the development or eruption of a tooth in a position normally occupied by a non-adjacent tooth (Peck *et al.*, 1993✦). In the general population the prevalence of this anomaly varies according to sample, but remains under 1 per cent in most investigations. Dental transposition can affect the maxillary or mandibular dentition, either unilaterally or bilaterally however, the canine tooth is almost always affected, with the majority of cases involving the ***canine/first premolar in the maxilla*** (Peck *et al.*, 1993✦) and canine/lateral incisor in the mandible (Peck *et al.*, 1998✦).

Transposition affected the maxillary dentition (76 per cent) more frequently than the mandibular dentition (24 per cent). Unilateral transposition accounted for 88 per cent of cases, with the maxilla being involved more commonly than the mandible. Overall, the most common transposition involved the maxillary canine and first premolar (58 per cent)

The canine tooth has a long path of eruption, is theoretically more susceptible to deflection during its long eruptive descent, and is frequently associated with transposition.

Ans. 159. (b). Reciprocal anchorage

Ref bhalajhi, 2nd ed , Anchorage in orthodontics, pg 212

Reciprocal anchorage refers to the resistance offered by two malposed units when the dissipation of equal and opposite forces tends to move each other towards a more normal occlusion. Correction of midline diastema, the use of crossbite elastics and dental arch expansion are examples of such an anchorage.

Ans. 160. (c). 20-26 gms

Ref bhalajhi, biology of tooth movement, pg 193

Optimum orthodontic force is one which moves the teeth rapidly in desired position with minimum damage to the periodontium and least discomfort to the patient.

Oppenhiem *et al* following extensive studies state that the optimum orthodontic force is equivalent to the capillary pulse pressure at ***20-26 gm/sq.cm*** of root surface area. It is generally recommended that a *light, continuous orthodontic force* producing frontal type of resorption should be applied whenever possible. Extreme force produces hyalinization of PDL and an undermining pattern of resorption which is both deleterious to the supporting tissues and unpleasing for the patient. Also remember, hyalinization is an irreversible process except in PDL where it is slowly resorbed.

EXTRA EDGE

Theories of tooth movement:-

1. pressure tension theory – Schwartz (1932)
2. fluid dynamic theory - Bein (postulated the 'squeeze film effect ')
3. Bone bending piezoelectric theory – first observed by Farrar (1876)

Ans. 161. (b) Glenoid fossa

Ref bhalajhi, Growth and development, pg 19

Functional matrix theory of growth was given by Melvin Moss. This theory attempts to comprehend the relationship between form and function.

According to Moss, the functional cranial component is divided into:

1. **Functional matrix:** tissues, organs, spaces which influence the growth of skeletal unit. This includes the:
   (*a*) **Periosteal matrix** –act ***directly*** and ***actively*** on skeletal units. Comprises muscles, blood vessels, nerves, glands etc. brings out a transformation in the skeletal counterpart by resorption and deposition.
   (*b*) **Capsular matrix**: - neuro-cranial (skin, dura mater) and oro-facial capsule (skin, oral mucosa). Act ***indirectly*** and ***passively*** on their counterparts. Growth is brought about by expansion of capsule and secondary movement of skeletal unit within.
2. **Skeletal unit:** bone, cartilage and tendinous tissue. This comprises:
   (*a*) **Macro-skeleton** – when multiple adjoining bones unite to function as a single skeletal unit. For eg the entire endocranial surface of calvarium. Even the maxilla and mandible bone function as macro-skeletal bones.
   (*b*) **Micro-skeletal** – when a bone is comprised of several contiguous units in:
   Maxilla – orbital, pneumatic, palatal and basal units.
   Mandible – alveolar, condylar, angular, gonial, mental , coronoid and basal.

Now, since glenoid fossa is a part of temporal bone and not mandible, it is the answer here.

Ans. 162. (c) Frankel's Functional Regulator

Ref bhalajhi, ch: Myofunctional appliance, pg 316

Classification of Functional appliance

A.

1. Tooth borne passive appliances- activator, bionator, Herbst's.
2. Tooth borne active - when above mentioned appliances are fitted with springs, expansion screws to provide intrinsic force.
3. Tissue borne passive- Frankel's functional regulator.

B.

1. Myotonic appliances – those which depend upon muscle mass for their function. *e.g.,* vestibular screen
2. Myodynamic - those which depend upon the muscle activity for their action. *e.g.,* Lip bumper.

C.

1. Removable appliance – activator, bionator, Frankel's.
2. Fixed appliances – Herbst's, Twin block.

D.

1. Group 1 appliances – those that transmit the muscle force directly on the teeth *e.g.,*oral screen, inclined plane
2. Group 2 appliances – those that reposition the mandible and the resultant force is transmitted to teeth. *e.g.,* activator, bionator.
3. Group 3 appliances – those that reposition the mandible but their area of action is beyond the dental arch (Vestibule) *e.g.,* Frankel's regulator.

Ans. 163. (d) Condylar pillar

Ref bhalajhi, Functional development, pg 62

The concept of force trajectories was first given by Benninghoff. He stated that the bony trabeculae orients themselves to the lines of maximal pressure/tension and the trabeculae in such a zone are thicker when compared to other areas.

Trajectories of Maxilla:-

Vertical: fronto-nasal buttress , malar-zygomatic buttress and the pterygoid buttress in order passing from incisors/canines, buccal teeth and second/third molars respectively and ending until the base of the skull .

Horizontal: Hard palate, orbital ridge, zygomatic arches, palatal bones, lesser wing of sphenoid.

Trajectories of Mandible:

Vertical: a line of stress passes from one condyle to the condyle of other side. Other includes vertical lines radiating down the roots of Mandibular teeth.

Horizontal: lower border (basal), mylohyoid ridge.

So we see, that condylar pillar is a Mandibular trajectory and hence is the answer here.

Ans. 164. (b) Andresen

Ref bhalajhi, Myofunctional appliance, pg 326

Although the first reference to the use of an activator like device is credited to Kingsley in 1879, it was merely a vulcanite palatal plate with an anterior incline. The current form was first developed by ***Viggo Andresen in 1908 in Denmark*** and called it the 'biomechanical working retainer'. Later it was called the Norwegian appliance and finally "activator" for the fact that it has ability to activate muscle force.

EXTRA EDGE

Also remember, the term "*visco-elasticity*" refers to the ability of muscles, soft tissues etc to induce bone formation, when under passive tension, after being stretched.

Activator modifications-

- Cybernator of Schmuth- resembles a bionator
- The propulsor –added features of oral screen. This appliance is *devoid* of any wire component.

Ans. 165. (b). Intermaxillary elastics

Ref bhalajhi, Anchorage in orthodontics, pg 214

Baker's anchorage is a type of anchorage in which the resistance units situated in one jaw are used to effect tooth movement in opposing jaw. This is an example of ***inter-maxillary anchorage***.

e.g.,

- Class II elastics between upper anteriors and lower molars ;
- Class III elastics between lower anteriors and upper molar.

EXTRA EDGE

Also remember, Sved appliance is a type of reinforced ***upper*** anterior inclined plane. (And not lower inclined plane). Students generally confuse this. Another common error that occurs is the difference between an inclined plane and a bite plane.

Please remember, that a bite plane is a flat block of acrylic and cannot be used to effect crossbite correction. The basic purpose of a bite plane is to either intrude or effect such a vertical movement of teeth. For transverse and saggital movements, an inclined plane is utilized.

Ans. 166. (a) Light continuous forces

Explained earlier, Please refer A160.

Ans. 167. (d) Non-skeletal tissues

Explained earlier, Please refer A161 for details.

Ans. 168. (b) Treatment need index

Ref http://ejo.oxfordjournals.org/cgi/reprint/25/1/57.pdf

Occlusal indices have been widely used as a method of achieving a more uniform evaluation of orthodontic treatment need for many years. Several indices have been developed to categorize malocclusion into groups according to the level of treatment need. Some examples of these indices are:

- Grainger's Treatment-Priority Index (1967) serves as a guide for epidemiological surveys. Also estimates severity of malocclusion.
- Salzmann's Handicapping Malocclusion Assessment Record (1968)
- HLD (Handicapping Labio-lingual deviation index)– Draker 1960 which is applicable to permanent dentition only.
- Summer's Occlusal Index (1971).
- The Index of Orthodontic Treatment Need (IOTN), described by Brook and Shaw (1989) and Shaw *et al.*, (1991) and modified by Richmond (1990)
- the Peer Assessment Rating : measures the treatment outcome.

The Index of Orthodontic Treatment Need has been gaining national and international recognition as a method of objectively *assessing treatment need*. This index ranks malocclusion in terms of the significance of various occlusal traits for the person's dental health and perceived aesthetic impairment with the intention of identifying those persons who would be most likely to benefit from orthodontic treatment.

The IOTN was introduced as a combination of the SCAN scale (Standardized Continuum of Aesthetic Need; Evans and Shaw, 1987) and the index used by Swedish Dental Health Board (Linder-Aronson, 1974). This was subsequently modified by Richmond et al. hence the index comprises 2 parts:

1. Dental Health Component (DHC) – ranks malocclusions in terms of the significance of tooth irregularities for a person's health.
2. SCAN – take into account the aesthetic impairment. The AC consists of a 10-grade scale illustrated by numbered color intra-oral photographs. The photographs represent three treatment categories; "no-treatment need" (grade 1-4), borderline need (grade 5-7) and great treatment needs (grade 8-10).

Ans. 169. (a) Gingival fibers

Ref bhalajhi, pg 436

Pericision or circumferential supra-crestal fibrotomy is undertaken to counter the relapse tendency of the stretched gingival fibers. The transseptal and alveolar crest groups of gingival fibers are responsible for relapses in orthodontics

PROSTHODONTICS

Ans. 170. (c) J.Leon Williams

Ref Textbook of prosthodontics, Nallaswamy , pg 174

Typal form theory: L.Williams (1917) this theory helps to determine the size and form of anterior teeth . According to him the shape of teeth should be inverse the shape of the face.

Remember Frush and Fisher gave the *Dentogenic concept* (SPA concept) where, according to them, the sex, personality and age of patient determine the form of anterior teeth.

Ans. 171. (c) Mandibular posteriors

Ref: Rosenstiel S, Land M, Fujimoto J. Contemporary fixed prosthodontics, ed. 3. 520-527.

• Shillingburg H, Hobo S, Whitsett L. Fundamentals of fixed prosthodontics, ed. 3.488-491.

Pontic design and selection directly impact periodontal health.

- Pontics should contact keratinized attached tissue and rest passively, free of pressure, to prevent ulcerations and plaque buildup.
- Pontic designs with concavities (such as the saddle-shaped pontic) are difficult to clean because the hollow or depression on their inner surface is inaccessible to conventional methodsof oral hygiene.
- Egg- or bullet-shaped pontics are easiest to clean because they are convex in all aspects and contact the residual ridge at a single point. This design is acceptable for replacing ***posterior mandibular teeth***.
- Modified ridge lap pontic is preferred for esthetically demanding areas.
- Cleaning devices can pass easily beneath hygienic or sanitary pontics; however, this design is unsuitable for regions where limited space exists because they must be positioned ***at least 3.0 mm*** above the residual ridge to be properly maintained.

Ans. 172. (b) Kratochvil

Ref http://www.harcourt-international.com/e-books/viewbook.cfm?ID=483

Textbook of prosthodontics, Nallaswamy, pg 456

Precision attachments

According to *The Glossary of Prosthodontic Terms*(Academy of Prosthodontics, 1999), a precision attachment is: 'a device which comprises of two or more components which is machined or fabricated for the purposes of providing retention to a prosthesis'.

The suitable guide plane is achieved by modification of tooth contour or by planned contour of fixed restorations. This is the basis of the RPI system advocated by Kratochvil (1963), and modified by Krol in1973, as a solution to the problems of free-end saddles.

R stands for the occlusal rest, which is placed on the mesial of the terminal abutment tooth. P stands for the guide plane (proximal plate), which enhances retention and ought to reduce rotating movements on the tooth. I stand for the I-bar, which is the principal direct retainer. Krol's modification aimed primarily in reducing the excessive tooth contact that the original I-bar system had. Reciprocation for this I-bar, which should be on the distobuccal aspect of the tooth, is achieved via the mesially placed occlusal rest. A more sophisticated philosophy concerns a rotational path of insertion.

Ans. 173. (b) 20 - 40 μm

Ref multiple net references

Casting relief is required for proper seating of castings to allow for luting agent thickness.

- The application of die spacer to the die is the most common method of obtaining casting relief.
- Die spacer film thicknesses that are outside the ideal range of **25 to 40 μm** can cause clinical problems. Thickness can be affected by the separation of die spacer constituents, which may not be reconstituted by mixing, in the bottle and by the evaporation of volatile components while the bottle is open.
- Incomplete seating may result in occlusal interference after cementation, loss of proximal contact, reduced crown retention, discrepancy of marginal fit, secondary caries, plaque accumulation, periodontal problems, rapid dissolution of luting agents, and/or hypersensitivity.
- Internal relief, or venting of the casting, can overcome the effects of luting agent hydraulic pressure. The use of venting requires drilling holes in the casting. The casting is cemented in place and the vent holes filled.
- Although venting is an effective technique to improve the seating of the restoration, it has several disadvantages: An extra visit is necessary to fill the vent hole; the materials used to fill the vent hole may cause microleakage and/or discoloration; and, in the case of ceramometal restorations, occlusal venting may weaken the strength of the porcelain.
- Internal relief avoids the limitations of venting. The most popular method to achieve adequate internal relief is die spacing.
- Die spacer is a solution that consist of metal-oxide powders and adhesives dispersed in an organic liquid such as a ketone, and is painted on the die before the fabrication of the pattern. The presence of the spacer provides space for the luting agent. The use of die spacer reduces elevation of the casting restorations, decreases seating time, improves outflow of excess cement, and lowers seating forces. The reported ideal die spacer thickness ranges from *25 to 40 μm.*

Ans.174. (d)33°

Ref Boucher CO J Prosthet Dent 1953; 3(5):633-656

Anatomic teeth artificial teeth which duplicate the anatomic forms of natural teeth 2: teeth which have prominent cusps on the masticating surfaces and which are designed to articulate with the teeth of the opposing natural or prosthetic dentition 3: anatomic teeth have cuspal inclinations greater than 0° and tend to replica natural tooth anatomy usage cusp teeth **33^0**(30-45^0) are considered anatomic teeth. Modified occlusal forms are those with a 20^0 cusp incline or less called also semi-anatomical teeth.

Nonanatomic teeth artificial teeth with occlusal surfaces which are not anatomically formed. The term nonanatomic as applied to artificial posterior teeth, and especially their occlusal forms, means that such teeth are designed in accordance with mechanical principles rather than from the anatomic standpoint. Nonanatomic teeth with flat occlusal surfaces (0^0) set to a flat occlusal plane were first introduced by IR. Hardy,

J Prosthet Dent 1953; 3(5):596-617. Hardy IR. Technique for use of non-anatomic acrylic posterior teeth. D Digest 1942; 48(12): 562-566

Ans.175. (c) Recently extracted tooth sockets

Ref: Spears, F. Maintenance interdental papilla following anterior tooth removal. Aesth ; Miller, MB. Ovate Pontics: The natural tooth replacement. 1996 etic dentistry 1999

- The ovate pontic is a technique, first used in early 1933, used to create the illusion that the tooth is growing out of the gum.
- The ovate pontic can also help to create or maintain the presence of interdental papilla, plus an ovate pontic contour is an effective design for cleansibility.
- Unfortunately, an ovate pontic design is not usually utilized by clinicians, One of the most challenging issues in a dental treatment plan is to preserve interproximal tissue after the removal of a tooth.
- To avoid alveolar bone collapse is highly desirable in restorative dentistry. It is important to preserve the socket size, shape, and the space of the gingival tissue in order to preserve the tissue height.
- When a tooth is extracted the recession of the interproximal papilla and the collapse of the buccal bone must be prevented and this means that the extracted socket must be preserved in the same shape and location.
- It is highly important to preserve the papilla during the extraction procedure and to fill the extraction site with the provisional pontic as soon as possible. The form of the teeth is not the only important matter to take into account for a nice outcome, the control of the gingival contours is just as important. The ovate pontic eliminates "black triangle" spaces.

Ans.176. (a) Extra oral graphic tracings

Ref textbook of prosthodontics, Nallaswamy, pg 148-150

Centric relation may be recorded by intra-oral or extra-oral tracing devices. The intra-oral device is a small metal styli and plate attached to the occlusal rims. The main disadvantage is that the recordings cannot be viewed while tracing. To overcome this high or extra-oral tracer is used. Apart from ability to view the movements, the apex (corresponding to the centric relation) can also be made out more accurately.

Amore complicated and accurate variant of extra-oral tracers are the, pantograph. This device can record even eccentric movements with much accuracy.

Gothic arch tracings are graphs or tracings used to record the centric relation (horizontal relation of maxilla to mandible). They may be either arrow point tracings or pantographs. The apex of the tracing gives the centric relation.

Remember, in extra-oral tracings the Central bearing plate is attached to the mandible rim while the centric bearing point (stylus) is attached to the maxillary rim. It is generally the opposite in the intra-oral tracings.

Other methods to record centric relations:

- *Physiologic methods* – tactile or interocclusal check record, pressure/ pressure less (nick and notch method).

- *Functional methods* – Needlehouse (metal styli attached to rim) , Patterson (a trough filled with 1:1carborundum + plaster).
- Radiographic methods.

Ans.177. (b) Structural durability

Ref Nallaswamy textbook of prosthodontics, pg 576-577

The functional cusp bevel is:

- Usually placed using a round-end tapered diamond bus on buccal inclines of Mandibular buccal cusps and palatal inclines of maxillary palatal cusps.
- The angulation of this bevel should be parallel to the inner inclination of the opposing cusps.
- The occlusal clearance should be verified. the main function of this bevel is to provide ***structural durability*** to the prepared tooth.

Ans.178. (d) Branemark

Ref http://en.wikipedia.org/wiki/Osseointegration

Osseointegration is the direct structural and functional connection between living bone and the surface of a load-bearing artificial implant, typically made of titanium. It is a property virtually unique to titanium, and has enhanced the science of medical bone, and joint replacement techniques.

THEORIES

Two theories regarding the chemical mechanism by which endo-steel implants integrate with bone have been proposed:

- Osseointegration by Dr. Per-Ingvar Brånemark (Sweden)
- Fibro-osseous integration by Dr. A. Weiss
- Functional ankylosis by Dr Shroeder (Switzerland)

Branemark's theory of osseointegration

Branemark proposed that implants integrate such that the bone is laid very close to the implant without any intervening connective tissue. The titanium oxide permanently fuses with the bone, as Branemark showed in 1950s. *Osseointegration* can be defined as,

- The apparent direct attachment or connection of osseous tissue to an inert alloplastic material without intervening connective tissue.
- The process and resultant apparent direct connection of the endogenous material surface and the host bone tissues without intervening connective tissue.
- The interface between alloplastic material and bone.

Branemark also stated that the implant should not be loaded and left out of function during the healing period for osseous integration to occur.

Weiss' theory of fibro-osseous integration

Weiss' theory states that there is a fibro-osseous ligament formed between the implant and the bone and this ligament can be considered as the equivalent of the periodontal ligament found in the gomphosis. He defends the presence of collagen fibers at the bone-implant interface. He interpreted it as the peri-implantal ligament with an osteogenic effect. He advocates the early loading of the implant.

Osseointegration versus Biointegration

In 1985, Dr. C. de Putter proposed two ways of implant anchorage or retention as mechanical and bioactive. Mechanical retention can be achieved in cases where the implant material is a metal, for example, commercially pure titanium and titanium alloys. In these cases, topological features like vents, slots, dimples, threads (screws), etc. aid in the retention of the implant. There is no chemical bonding and the retention depends on the surface area: the greater the surface area, the greater the contact.

Bioactive retention can be achieved in cases where the implant is coated with bioactive materials such as hydroxyapatite. These bioactive materials stimulate bone formation leading to a physico-chemical bond. The implant is ankylosed with the bone.

Ans.179. (a) 110 mm

In semi-adjustable articulators the average inter-condylar distance adequate in edentulous patients is about 110 mm.

Ans.180. (d) Tongue muscles

Ref Nallaswamy , textbook of prosthodontics

The neutral zone , advocated by Fish, exist where the inward forces of buccinators muscle exerted on the buccal teeth or denture are equally opposed or counter acted by the musculature of the tongue. When this balance is disrupted, the retention of denture is greatly affected.

Ans. 181. (b) 4 mm

Ref Nallaswamy, pg 337

In maxillary major connectors, the border should be about *6-8 mm* away from the gingival margin. Whereas in mandible, there is a need for about *3 mm* clearance from marginal gingiva to avoid any soft tissue reaction.

Ans. 182. (d) Guiding planes

Ref Nallaswamy, pg 321

During surveying procedure for a removal partial denture the proximal surface of abutment teeth which contacts the body of clasps during insertion and removal on the wax pattern are trimmed until they are parallel. These "***guiding planes'*** facilitate proper positioning of the rigid and flexible parts of the clasp. Whenever possible, a single path of insertion should be achieved by preparing additional guiding planes on the lingual surfaces of remaining teeth.

Ans. 183. (a) Centric occlusion,

Ref Nallaswamy, pg 759

The relationship of mandible to the maxilla when the teeth are in maximum occlusal contact irrespective of the position or alignment of the condyle disk assemblies.

When the teeth are fully occluded, the condyle is forced into a specific position within the glenoid fossa. Note that the term centric occlusion does not take joint configuration into account. A patient's centric occlusion may be physiologic, meaning that the joint is placed into a comfort-

able position, or pathologic, meaning that the joint is forced into an eccentric position which may produce organic joint dysfunction.

Ans. 184. (c). Soft palate

Ref Nallaswamy, pg 52

Vibrating line is an imaginary line across the posterior aspect of palate making the division between the movable and non-movable portions of soft palate. The vibrating lines should always be in the area of soft palate. It passes 2 mm in front of the fovea palatinae. The distal end of denture should lie 1-2 mm beyond this line.

The patient head is tilted to an angle of 30 degrees while recording this line

COMMUNITY DENTISTRY

Ans. 185. (a) Chronic renal failure

Ref Shobha tandon, ch preventive approach to caries control pg 249

Spencer *et al* (1978) reported that kidney is the main pathway of fluoride excretion with an average fluoride intake of **3.9mg/kg**. Urinary fluoride is 30% of fluoride intake in renal patients while it is about 50-60% in normal patients. Hence, fluoride in any form is absolutely contraindicated in patients suffering from chronic renal failure.

Ans. 186. (c). Rigid spine

Ref Soben Peter, 2nd ed , pg 345

- Safely Tolerated Dose: 8 -16 mgF/kg
- Certainly Lethal Dose: 32-64 mgF/kg

At higher concentration of fluoride, osteosclerosis become denser, progressing to marked thickening of cortical bone, numerous exostoses throughout the skeleton and calcification of ligaments and tendons. The spine becomes rigid and the joints stiffen, virtually immobilizing the patient. This ***crippling type*** of fluorosis is generally seen in exposure in the range of 10-25mgF/day for 10-20 yrs

Ans. 187. (c). Disease elimination

Ref Park 17th ed , pg 33Please refer answer 178

- **Disease control** refers to operations that reduce the incidence, duration and consequently the risk of transmission of a disease. Here the disease agent is permitted to persist but at a level where it ceases to be a public health problem.
- **Disease elimination:** is used to describe interruption of transmission of disease. *e.g.,* elimination of measles, polio.
- **Disease eradication:** refers to "to tear out by roots" *e.g.,* termination of transmission by extermination of infectious agent. *e.g.,* small pox Is the only disease to be eradicated to date.

Ans. 188. (a) Grand rapids (Michigan) & Muskegon

Ref Soben Peter, 2nd ed , pg 348

Water fluoridation history;-

Test city	Control city	Date
Grand Rapids	Muskegon	25th jan ,1945(U.S.A)
Newburgh	Kingston	2nd May , 1945
Evanston	Oak Park	Jan 1946
Tiel	Culemborg	March, 1953

Ans. 189.(a) 32 - 64 mg of fluoride/kg body weight

Please refer A186

Ans. 190. (c). Brudevold

Ref Soben Peter, 2nd ed , pg 313.

- Acidulated phosphate fluoride (APF) was introduced by Brudevold (1960's) the general formulation has 1.23% F as NaF, pH 3-4, in 0.1 M phosphoric acid.
- Stannous fluoride was popularized by Muhler as 10% solution for adults and 8% for children.
- Sodium fluoride on other hand, was first applied by Bibby, Knutson and co-workers.

Remember, while SnF etches silicate restorations, APF is detrimental to Porcelain.

Ans. 191. (d) 1964

Ref Soben Peter, 2nd ed , pg 322

- The first clinical trial of a fluoride dentifrice was initiated by Bibby in 1942.
- In 1955, a stannous fluoride dentifrice became the first dentifrice recognized by FDA.
- However, it was only in **1964** that the ADA accepted fluoride dentifrices.
- Sodium monofluorophosphates are the most widely used in modern dentifrices.

Ans. 192. (a) 1.23%

Please refer answer 190

Ans. 193. (a) Tanzania

Ref Soben Peter, 2nd ed , pg 402

- ART or atraumatic restorative treatment is a procedure based on removing carious tooth material using hand instruments alone and restoring the cavity with adhesive material with minimum patient trauma.
- The material most frequently used is glass ionomer cement (Fuji IX).
- ART was pioneered in Tanzania in mid 1980's and latter in Thailand (1991) where the first clinical trial began.

Ans. 194. (b) Prevents water loss and hardening on exposure to air

Ref Soben Peter, 2nd ed, pg 463

Composition of Dentifrices

1. Polishing agent- calcium carbonate, alumina etc. have mild abrasive action.

2. Binding /thickening agent: alginates, carrageenates – controls consistency of paste and eases dispersion in mouth.
3. Detergents: sodium lauryl sulfate- produces foam, antimicrobial property.
4. Humectants: sorbitol, glycerin, polyglycol, cellulose- retains moisture and prevents desiccation of paste.
5. Flavoring agent: peppermint, spearmint Sweeteners like saccharin.
6. Antibacterial like triclosan, anticaries like NaF, anti-calculus like pyrophosphates zinc citrate, zinc chloride and Gantrez (copolymer of methyl vinyl ether and malcic anhydrate).

Ans. 195. (b) Mac Mohan & Pugh

Ref Park , 17th ed , pg 28

- The model of **Web of Causation** was proposed by MacMahon and Pugh which suited best the occurrence of chronic disease. This concept considers all the predisposing factors of any type and their complex inter-relationship with each other.
- **Multifactorial causation**: this concept was given by Pettenkofer and Munich which stressed on the modern diseases of human civilization like blood pressure, and cancer. This concept provides multiple approaches to prevention of diseases.
- Winslow gave the definition for Public Health.

Ans. 196. (a) Dean H.T

Ref Soben Peter, 2nd ed , pg 183

- The DMFT index was given by Henry Klien , Carrole Palmer and Knutson in 1938 to determine the prevalence of coronal caries.
- The 'def' was described by Gruebbel in 1944.

Ans. 197. (c) Tertiary level of prevention

Ref Soben Peter, 2nd ed , pg 262

Levels of Prevention:

1. Primordial - measures undertaken prior to development of risk factors.
2. Primary - includes health promotion and specific protection.
3. Secondary - includes early diagnosis and prompt treatment.
4. Tertiary - Disability limitation and Rehabilitation.

Ans. 198. (b). Anganwadi worker

Ref Park, 17th ed , pg 455

ICDS program was started in 1975 with a strong nutrition component in it. Supplementary nutrition like Vitamin A, iron and folic acid are distributed amongst children below 6 yrs of age. The workers who deliver the service at village levels are the Anganwadi workers. Each of them covers a population of 1000 and help in providing health and nutrition.

Ans. 199. (a) Cellulose

Please refer A194

Ans. 200. (b). 2

Ref Soben Peter, 2nd ed , pg 212

Dean's Fluorosis Index:

Classification	Criteria
Normal (0)	Smooth, glossy surface, pale creamy white color of enamel
Questionable (0.5)	Slight aberrations, few white flecks no definite diagnosis possible
Very mild (1)	Small opaque, paper white areas affecting 25% of tooth surface. Also included are bicuspids/second molars with1-2 mm of opacity at tips
Mild (2)	White opaque areas covering more than 25 but less than 50 %
Moderate (3)	All enamel surfaces are affected. Brown stain
Severe (4)	Marked hypoplasia affecting the general form of tooth. Characteristic pitting and brown stains giving a corroded app.

So friends we see, that the answer should be B. "2". However the key gave the answer as 3. Now, a recent revised Dean's scale proposes questionable to be scale 1 instead of 0.5. So according to that scale answer is 3 **BUT** the question nowhere mentions the word 'revised'. The question clearly refers to the original index given by Dean in 1942. Here, I would suggest you to follow the original index unless the question specifies a 'revised' version.

2006

Questions & Answers

2

KCET 2006

QUESTIONS

ANATOMY

1. The nerve which lies in association to Wharton duct is

(a) Facial
(b) Spinal accessory
(c) Hypoglossal
(d) Lingual

2. Inferior meatus of nasal cavity contains the opening of

(a) Maxillary sinus
(b) Middle ethmoidal sinus
(c) Nasolacrimal duct
(d) Frontal sinus

3. The artery that passes forwards through cavernous sinus is

(a) Supra trochlear artery
(b) Supra orbital artery
(c) Internal carotid artery
(d) Anterior ethmoidal artery

4. Accessory meningeal artery enters cranial cavity through

(a) Foramen lacerum
(b) Foramen rotundum
(c) Foramen spinosum
(d) Foramen ovale

5. Basic metabolic unit of bone is

(a) Osteon
(b) Osteoblast
(c) Osteocyte
(d) Osteoclast

6. The following muscles are supplied by Mandibular Nerve except

(a) Tensor Tympani
(b) Tensor Veli Palatini
(c) Levator Veli Palatini
(d) Mylohyoid

7. Mastoid air sinus is posteriorly related to

(a) Cavernous sinus
(b) Sigmoid sinus
(c) Straight sinus
(d) Spheno Parietal sinus

8. **The medial surface of the neck of the mandible is related to the**
(a) Inferior alveolar nerve (b) Lingual nerve
(c) Auriculo temporal nerve (d) Chorda tympani nerve

9. **The epithelial lining of the maxillary air sinus is**
(a) Simple squamous (b) Simple cuboidal
(c) Ciliated columnar (d) Stratified squamous non keratinized

DENTAL ANATOMY AND HISTOLOGY

10. **Band of fibrous tissue which slings the tooth between the walls of the crypt according to Sicher is**
(a) Hammock ligament (b) Gomphosis
(c) Dento alveolar ligament (d) Fibrosis

11. **To protrude the mandible the following muscles will contract in conjunction with controlled stabilizing of the opening muscles**
(a) Outer and inner layers of temporalis
(b) Contraction of posterior fibers of temporalis and geniohyoid
(c) Lateral and medial pterygoid muscles
(d) Mylohyoid and temporalis

12. **Mesial developmental depression is the characteristic feature of**
(a) Maxillary first premolar (b) Maxillary second premolar
(c) Mandibular first premolar (d) Mandibular second premolar

PHYSIOLOGY

13. **The Chief cation in extra cellular fluid**
(a) Sodium (b) Potassium
(c) Calcium (d) Magnesium

14. **The feature of slow pain is**
(a) No projection to reticular nucleus (b) Carried by Aë fibers
(c) Poor localization (d) Glutamate is the neuro transmitter

15. **Cyanosis is bluish discoloration of skin due to more than ....gms/100 ml in blood of deoxygenated hemoglobin**
(a) 2 (b) 5
(c) 8 (d) 10

16. **Normal blood flow pattern is**
(a) Predominantly stream line (b) Predominandy turbulent
(c) Streamline and turbulent in equal ratio (d) none of the above

17. Coronary blood flow to the left ventricle is predominantly from

(a) Right coronary artery and during diastole (b) Right coronary artery and during systole
(c) Left coronal artery and during systole (d) Left coronal artery and during diastole

18. Secretions of the parafollicular cells of the thyroid gland are stimulated by

(a) Increase in serum calcium (b) increase in serum thyroxin
(c) Decrease in serum calcium (c) decrease in serum thyroxin

19. Platelets adhere to the subendothelial collagen through one of the following

(a) Platelet factor 4 (b) Fibro nectin
(c) Von wille brands factor (d) None of the above

BIOCHEMISTRY

20. The following Carbohydrate is called Animal Starch

(a) Glucose (b) Fructose
(c) Sucrose (d) Glycogen

21. Lesch Nyhan Syndrome is due to deficiency of

(a) HGPRTase (Total). (b) PRPP Glutamine Amino Transferase
(c) CTP Synthetase (d) OMP Decarboxylase

22. Thyroxine is derived from

(a) Tyrosine (b) Tyramine
(c) Taurine (d) Tryptophan

23. The storage form of Carbohydrates in our body is

(a) Starch (b) Glycogen
(c) Sucrose (d) Cellulose

MICROBIOLOGY

24. Gas gangrene is not caused by

(a) Clostridium welchii (b) Clostridium septicum
(c) Clostridium emotines (d) Clostridium tetani

25. Lophotrichous flagella are seen in

(a) Spirilla (b) Vibrio
(c) Pseudomonas (d) Kliebsiella

26. The efficacy of moist heat sterilization is tested by using spores of

(a) Bacillus anthracis (b) Bacillus cereus
(c) Bacillus subtilis (d) Bacillius stearothermophilus

27. Microscope was invented by
(a) Louis Pasteur
(b) Hippocrates
(c) Robert Koch
(d) Leeuwen Hoeck

28. Plasmid is transmitted to other bacteria in
(a) Transformation
(b) Transduction
(c) Conjugation
(d) All of the above

29. The immunoglobulin which crosses placenta is
(a) Ig G
(b) Ig M
(c) Ig A
(d) Ig D

30. Diphtheria toxin acts by
(a) Increasing levels of cramps
(b) Inhibiting protein synthesis
(c) Inhibiting acetyl choline release
(c) Inhibiting glucose transport

PATHOLOGY

31. One of the following is not capable of replication
(a) Neuron
(b) Liver
(c) Kidney
(d) None of the above

DENTAL MATERIALS

32. The process of heating a cast alloy to eliminate composition difference is
(a) Hardening heat treatment
(b) Softening heat treatment
(c) Homogenisation
(d) Crystallisation

33. Type IV gold alloy contains
(a) 2% gold
(b) 13% gold
(c) 75% gold
(d) 80% gold

34. Galvanism is
(a) Tarnishing
(b) Electrolytic corrosion
(c) Chemical corrosion
(d) Annealing

35. Shape memory exhibited by
(a) Beta titanium
(b) Nickel titanium
(c) Cobalt chromium
(d) Nickel chromium

36. Non gamma 2 alloy is
(a) Resistant to marginal leakage
(b) Resistant to discoloration
(c) Resistant to sensitization
(d) Resistant to corrosion

37. The irreversible hydrocolloid impression material used in removal partial denture prosthesis construction -
(a) Agar Agar
(b) Alginate
(c) Silicone
(d) Thiobal

38. How much minimum amount of alloy percentage by weight of noble elements in high noble metals
(a) 60% by weight of noble elements
(b) 30% Gold
(c) 40% by weight of noble elements
(d) Less than 40% by weight of noble elements

39. How much fraction of methyl mercury is absorbed from the gut?
(a) 20%
(b) 50%
(c) 80%
(d) 100%

40. The average particle size of powdered gold is
(a) 10 um
(b) 15 um
(c) 30 um
(d) 0.1 mm

41. Loss of gloss test in gypsum product is an indication for
(a) Adequate mixing time
(b) Adequate working time
(c) Initial set
(d) Final set

42. Stabilization of stainless steel is achieved by addition of
(a) Carbon
(b) Chromium
(c) Nickel
(d) Titanium

43. The best method to control gelation time while mixing alginate material is
(a) Alter the temperature of water
(b) Alter the water/powder ratio
(c) Increase the mixing time
(d) Reduce the percentage of retarder

44. The modulus of elasticity of an alloy refers to
(a) Flexibility
(b) Ductility
(c) Stiffness
(d) Malleability

PHARMACOLOGY

45. Optic neuritis is the side effect of
(a) Rifampicin
(b) isoniazid
(c) Ethambutol
(d) Pyrazinamide

46. Following are the prodrugs except one
(a) Levodopa
(b) Enalapil
(c) Epinephrine
(d) Proguanil

47. Which one of the following drugs is not a cardio selective (â1) beta blocker?
(a) Metoprolol
(b) Alprenolol
(c) Atenolol
(d) Esmolol

48. Which one of the following drugs is not an aminoglycoside?
(a) Kanamycin
(b) Tobramycin
(c) Erythromycin
(d) Streptomycin

49. 'Second gas effect' is exerted by the following gas when co-administered with halothane
(a) Nitrogen
(b) Cyclopropane
(c) Nitrous oxide
(d) Helium

50. Amphotericin B is not effective in the following fungal disease
(a) Cryptococcosis
(b) Histoplasmosis
(c) Blastomycosis
(d) Dermatophytosis

51. Tachyphylaxis during local anesthesia is brought about through the following factors except
(a) Increased PH of the tissues
(b) Hypernatremia
(c) Transudation
(d) Localised hemorrhage

52. Antispastic drug used in treating trigeminal neuralgia is
(a) Gabapentin
(b) Nortriptyline
(c) Clonazepam
(d) Baclofen

53. Among the following drugs which is not an immunosuppressive agent
(a) Levamizole
(b) Azathioprine
(c) Cyclosporin
(d) Corticosteroid

GENERAL MEDICINE

54. Exudative pleural effusion is seen in all except
(a) Tuberculosis
(b) Rheumatoid disease
(c) SLE
(d) Cardiac failure

55. Acromegaly is due to increased
(a) Growth harmone
(b) Thyroid harmone
(c) Adrenalin
(d) Parathyroid harmone

56. Serum amylase is elevated in
(a) Pancreatitis
(b) Intestinal ischemia
(c) Ruptured ovarian cyst
(d) All of the above

57. Asterixis is caused by all except
(a) Hepatic failure
(b) Renal failure
(c) Hypo capnia
(d) Phenytoin toxicity

58. The most common cause of mitral regurgitation in a patient who has no evidence of mitral stenosisz
(a) Congenital
(b) Mitral valve prolapse
(c) Rheumatic heart disease
(d) Secondary to aortic valve disease

59. A patient with hypertension
(a) Will always have symptoms
(b) Will not be able to reduce blood pressure without drug treatment

(c) Will usually not have an underlying identifiable cause or condition
(d) Can always have the blood pressure controlled by single drug

60. If a patient presents with generalized pruritis the following condition should be considered as a possibility
(a) Cholestatic jaundice (b) Addison's disease
(c) Acromegaly (d) Myxedema

61. Diseases typically acquired by man from animals include
(a) Hepatitis A (b) Cholera
(c) Tuberculosis (d) Leptospirosis

62. Flask shaped ulcer is a feature of
(a) Cholera (b) Amoebiasis
(c) Sac moneccosis (d) Bacillary dysentery

63. Antibiotic recommended for prophylaxis of bacterial endocarditis in patients who are allergic to penicillin
(a) Clindamycin (b) Azithromycin
(c) Clarithromycin (d) All the above

64. Diseases of the liver can produce bleeding tendencies because
(a) Synthesis of Vit K is decreased (b) Production of prothrombin is low
(c) Plasma protein levels are low (d) All of the above

65. In which of the following condition immune mediated damage is implicated
(a) Hemophilia (b) Congenital heart disease
(c) Rheumatic fever (d) All the above

66. Presence of Bence-Jones proteins is a characteristic feature of
(a) Infectious mononucleosis (b) Multiple myeloma
(c) Malignant melanoma (d) Paget's disease

GENERAL SURGERY

67. The following thyroid diseases are diagnosed by FNAC except
(a) Follicular carcinoma (b) Papillary carcinoma
(c) Medullary carcinoma (d) Malignant lymphoma

68. Cause of persistence of a sinus and fistulas
(a) Foreign body (b) Unrelieved distal obstruction
(c) Presence of malignancy (d) All of the above

69. Carcinoma lip commonly occurs in
(a) Upper lip skin surface (b) Vermillion border of lower lip
(C) Commisures (d) Mucosal surface of upper lip

70. Level V nodes in neck lymph nodes refer to

(a) Anterior compartment nodes
(b) Posterior triangle nodes
(C) Sub mandibular nodes
(d) Sub lingual nodes

71. The most common thyroid cancer is

(a) Anaplastic
(b) Medullary
(c) Papillary
(d) Fàllicular

72. The statement which is false regarding thyroglossal cyst

(a) Almost always arises in the midline
(b) Vestigeal remnant of second branchial cleft
(c) Sistrunk's operation is indicated
(d) Moves upwards on protrusion of the tongue

73. Branchial cyst is located at

(a) The junction of middle third & lower third of sternomastoid at anterior border
(b) The junction of upper third & middle third of sternomastoid at its posterior border
(c) The junction of middle third & lower third of sternomastoid at its posterior border
(d) The junction of upper third and middle third of sternomastoid at its anterior border

ORAL PATHOLOGY/ MEDICINE

74. Sjogrens syndrome refers to disease of

(a) Thyroid glands
(b) Parotid glands
(c) Parathyroid glands
(d) Multiple endocrine glands

75. Abtropfung (or) dropping off effect is seen in

(a) Intradermal nevus
(b) Junctional nevus
(c) Compound nevus
(d) Blue nevus

76. Physiologic wearing of a tooth as a result of tooth to tooth contact is

(a) Attrition
(b) Abrasion
(c) Erosion
(d) All the above

77. "Triangular frontal defect" occurs in

(a) Crouzon disease
(b) Crouzon syndrome
(c) Cranio facial dysostosis
(d) All the above

78. Difference between ranula and mucous cyst is presence of

(a) Epithelial lining in ranula
(b) Mucous glands in mucocele
(c) Extra vasation of mucous in mucocele
(d) Transparency of ranula

79. In hypoplastic amelogenesis imperfecta

(a) Shape normal, enamel soft
(b) Shape abnormal, enamel brown
(C) Shape abnormal, enamel normal
(d) Shape abnormal, enamel soft

80. On inspection of mouths of patients with malabsorption following may be observed

(a) Leucoplakia
(b) Aphthous Ulcers
(c) Black tongue
(d) Macroglossia

81. Hutchinson triad-Notched central incisors, blindness and deafness are seen in
(a) Primary syphilis (b) Secondary syphilis
(c) Tertiary syphilis (d) Congenital syphilis

82. Squamous cell carcinoma most common in mouth is in
(a) Upper lip (b) Lower lip
(c) Tongue (d) Floor of mouth

83. The fundamental defect in Down syndrome is the presence of an extra chromosome in the affected individual karyotype this was proven by
(a) Le Jeune (b) Turpin
(c) Gautier (d) All of the above

84. Usually the natal teeth are
(a) Supernumerary primary incisors (b) Prematurely erupted primary teeth
(c) Variations of Epstein pearls (d) Variations of Bohn's nodules

85. Condition like Treacher Collin syndrome and hemifacial microsomia, the defect is primarily in:
(a) Origin and migration of neural crest cell (b) Germ layer formation
(c) Differentiation of tissues (d) Neural tube formation

86. Radiographic image of Botryoid odontogenic cyst has an
(a) Multilocular Radiolucent appearance (b) Unilocular Radiolucent appearance
(c) Solitary Radio-opaque appearance (c) Salt and pepper appearance

87. In hemolytic Anemia the Radiographic appearance of lamina dura is
(a) Normal (b) Lost
(c) Less Radio-opaque (d) More Radio-opaque

88. Dilaceration of a permanent incisor is resulted due to
(a) Extrusion of deciduous predecessor (b) Intrusion of deciduous predecessor
(c) Avulsion of deciduous predecessor (d) none of the above

89. Leukodema has a characteristic sign that it
(a) Disappears on stretching (b) Remains fluctuant throughout
(c) Is not fluctuant (d) Has a malignant potential

90. Sialosis is
(a) Non-inflammatory non-neoplastic swelling of major salivary glands
(b) Disease associated with sailors
(c) Stone in salivary gland
(d) Sialorrhea

91. Oral pathogonomonic sign of measles
(a) Fordyce's spots (b) Koplick's spots
(c) Cafè-Au-lait spots (d) Purpuric spots

92. Osteomyelitis is defined as an inflammation of
(a) Periosteum of the bone (b) Haversian system of the bone
(c) Medullary portion of the bone (d) Cortical bone

93. Ludwigs angina begins usually in

(a) Sub-lingual space
(b) Sub-mental space
(c) Sub-maxillary space
(d) Sub-massetric space

94. Acute lymphonodular pharyingitis is caused by

(a) Coxsaskie virus A-I6
(b) Coxsaskie virus A-10
(c) Coxsaskie virus A-6
(d) Coxsaskie virus A-22

95. Pathogonomic feature of cervicofacial actinomycosis is

(a) Involvement of submandibular region
(b) Presence of multiple discharging sinuses
(c) Presence of sulphur granules in the pus
(d) Presence of non healing tooth socket

96. Salivary calculi are most commonly discovered in

(a) Parotid gland duct
(b) Stenson's duct
(c) Maxillary sinus
(d) Submandibular duct

97. In AIDS, Hairy leukoplakia is found most commonly in which location

(a) Hard palate
(b) Buccal mucosa
(c) Lateral borders of tongue
(d) Soft palate

98. Malignancy in pleomorphic adenoma is indicated by

(a) Rapid enlargement
(b) Pain
(c) Fascial nerve paralysis
(d) All of the above

99. Patients with Sjogren's syndrome have higher incidence of

(a) Papillary carcinoma thyroid
(b) Pleomorphic adenoma
(c) Malignant lymphoma
(d) None of the above

100. Boggy gums seen in

(a) Scurvy
(b) Leukemia
(c) Polycythemia
(d) Only a & b

101. Which type of ameloblastoma appears to be aggressive with a marked activity for recurrence

(a) Follicular ameloblastoma
(b) Plexiform ameloblastoma
(C) Granular cell ameloblastoma
(d) Acanthomatous-ameloblastoma

ORAL RADIOLOGY

102. Radiation causes the following biological effects in younger tissues and organs

(a) Carcinogenesis
(b) Teratogenesis
(c) Mutagenesis
(d) All the above

103. The x-ray tube is evacuated to facilitate

(a) The movement of electrons
(b) The oxidation of filament
(c) The production of electrons
(d) The collision of electrons

104. The energy of resultant photon is numerically

(a) Double the energy of electron that hits the nucleus of target atom
(b) More than the energy of electron that hits the nucleus target atom
(c) Less than the energy of electron that hits the nucleus of a target atom
(d) Equal to the energy of electron that hits the nucleus of a target atom

105. The use of intensifying screens results in

(a) Greater clarity in a Radiograph
(b) Recording of minute details
(c) Reduction of dose to the patient
(d) Reduction of the speed of the film

CONSERVATIVE DENTISTRY AND ENDODONTICS

106. Gingival retraction cord impregnated with epinephrine is contraindicated in

(a) Cardiovascular diseases
(b) Diabetes
(c) Hyperthyroidism
(d) All of the above

107. An example of exploring instrument

(a) Reamer
(b) Smooth broach
(c) File
(d) Barbed broach

108. Lining cement used is

(a) Zinc-Oxide Eugeno
(b) Zinc-phosophate cement
(c) Calcium Hydroxide
(d) Alginate

109. The most common cause of flap injury is

(a) Insufficient extension of releasing incisions
(b) Excessive extension of releasing incision
(c) Using undermining elevation
(d) Improper reactor positioning

110. The most important aspect of irrigation of canal is

(a) Aspiration of solution
(b) The irrigating needle use
(C) Chelating action of solution
(d) Volume of solution

111. The bleaching agent prescribed for night guard bleaching technique is

(a) Hydrogen peroxide — 2%
(b) Sodium hypochlorite — 5.25%
(c) Hydrochloric acid
(d) Carbamide peroxide 15%

112. Fourth canal is a maxillary first molar is most commonly present in

(a) Palatal root
(b) Mesio buccal root
(c) Mesio lingual root
(d) Disto buccal root

113. Tip angle of an endodontic instrument should be

(a) 70 + 10°
(b) 75 + 15°
(c) 70 ± 50
(d) 70 ± 150

114. K flex files are manufactured from

(a) Diamond shaped blank
(b) Cylindrical blank
(c) Square blank
(d) Triangular blank

115. Zone of irritation is characterized by

(a) Polymorpho nuclear leucocytes
(b) Round cells infiltration
(c) Macrophages and osteoclasts
(d) Fibroblasts & osteoblasts

116. When a calcified root canal cannot be located or instrumented

(a) Extraction is the treatment of choice
(b) Retrograde and re-plantation procedures should be considered
(c) The dentist must proceed with the understanding that an unexplored or unfilled canals is worse than perforations
(d) It is no longer accessible to bacterial infection

117. When the spread of caries along DEJ exceeds the caries in the contiguous enamel it is termed as

(a) Forward caries
(b) Residual caries
(c) Rampant caries
(d) Backward caries

118. Which of the following is not present in original G.V. Block's classification of caries

(a) Class IV lesion
(b) Class II lesion
(c) Class III lesion
(d) Class VI lesion

119. The second number in the instrument formula of a gingival marginal trimmer indicates

(a) Length of the blade
(b) Width of the blade
(c) Primary cutting edge angle
(d) Blade angle

120. Smear layer debris in root canal is best removed by

(a) Citric acid
(b) 17% EDA+25% NaOCI
(c) 5.25% NaOCI only
(d) 17% EDTA only

121. Most common organism causing caries

(a) Streptococcus faecalis
(b) Streptococcus viridans
(c) Streptococcus mutans
(d) Staphylococcus albus

122. On an average in the saliva of an adult man the lactobacilli count is

(a) 50,000 ml
(b) 75,000 ml
(c) 70,000 ml
(d) 30,000 ml

123. The most important organism to initiate dental caries is

(a) Streptococcus pyogenes
(b) Streptococcus viridans
(c) Streptococcus mutans
(d) Streptococcus pneumoniae

124. Samples from root canal can be collected by

(a) Swab
(b) Syringe and needle
(C) Trocar
(d) Sterile paper points

ORAL AND MAXILLOFACIAL SURGERY

125. LE fort I fracture is also known as

(a) Pyramidal fracture (b) Suprazygomatic fracture
(c) Guerin fracture (d) Guardman's fracture

126. The nerve most likely to get injured during incision placement in wisdom tooth surgery is

(a) Lingual nerve (b) Inferior dental nerve
(c) Mylohyoid nerve (d) Mental nerve

127. Role of sodium metabisulfite in local anesthetic solution is

(a) To main isotonicity of solution (b) Antioxidant for vasoconstrictor
(c) Preservative (d) Antioxidant for local anesthetic agent

128. The new immature bone that forms during distraction osteogenesis is known as

(a) Regenerate (b) Osteoid
(c) Callus (d) Osteointegrate

129. In bilateral parasymphyseal fractures of the mandible the fractured segment is displaced posteriorly under the influence of

(a) Mylohyoid and geniohyoid
(b) Masseter and medial pterygoid
(c) Buccinator and post belly of digastric
(d) Genioglossus, geniohyod and posterior belly of digastric

130. Abducent nerve paralysis is the earliest finding in the case of

(a) Lefort III fracture (b) Nao orbito ethmoid fracture
(c) Zygomatic fracture (d) Cavernous sinus thrombosis

131. Dental extraction when indicated in controlled hemophiliacs can be done with

(a) Nerve block like inferior alveolar (b) Endotracheal general anesthesia
(c) Field block (d) Periodontal ligament injection of LA

132. The technique of doing the incision and drainage of an abscess is known as

(a) Andrew's method (b) Hilton's method
(c) Nilaton's method (d) Killey's method

133. In children fracture mandible which has not been perfectly reduced but has become firm with slight imperfection the choice of the management would be

(a) Arch bar and elastic traction
(b) Accept the slight imperfection and allow for later remodeling
(c) Refracture and plating
(d) Refracture and interosseous wiring

134. The minimum required distance recommended between implant and superior aspect of inferior alveolar canal is

(a) 1mm (b) 2mm
(c) 4mm (d) 6mm

135. Wand' is the name of equipment used for

(a) Jet injection (b) Electron dental anesthesia
(c) Computer controlled local anesthesia (d) General anesthesia

136. Sodium bisulphate used in dental local anesthetic acts as

(a) Antibacterial for lignocaine (b) Antibacterial for adrenaline
(c) Antioxidant for methylparaben (d) Antioxidant for adrenaline

PERIODONTICS

137. During scaling and root planning procedures optional angulation is between

(a) 35 and 45 degrees (b) 45 and 90 degrees
(c) 10 and 20 degrees (d) More than 90 degrees

138. The operator position to perform scaling in mandibular right posterior extent on lingual aspect is

(a) Front position (b) Left side of the patient
(c) Right side of the patient (d) Back position

139. Langer technique is used in

(a) Sub epithelial connective tissue grafts (b) Free soft tissue autografts
(c) Fenestration operation (d) Vestibular extension operation

140. For interproximal areas of diastema or for wide proximal spaces to properly adapt the proximal papilla against the bone, the recommended technique of suturing method is

(a) Interdental ligation (b) Horizontal mattress suture
(c) Continuous, independent slight suture (d) Closed anchor suture

141. When osseous defects amenable to regeneration are present, the technique of choice in order of first preference is

(a) Modified Wildman flap (b) Apically displaced flap
(c) Scaling & root plan1iing (d) Papilla preservation flap

142. Specific and non specific hypothesis was delineated by

(a) Walter Loesche (b) William Hunter
(c) Socransky (d) Slot

143. Electronic transducer used to measure gingival crevicular fluid is

(a) Periotron (b) Perio Test
(c) Perio Scan (d) Perio Scope

144. Furcation defects are often diagnosed by
(a) Naber's probe
(b) DNA probe
(c) William probe
(d) Michigan probe

145. Frenectomy is a surgical procedure where in
(a) Gingiva is removed
(b) Bone is removed
(c) Frenum is only incised
(d) Frenum is completely removed

146. Transfer of the patient from active treatment status to a maintenance program for total patient care is a
(a) Step forward
(b) Step backward
(c) Definitive step
(d) Premature step

147. The pH at which citric acid should be applied for root biomodification
(a) 1
(b) 2
(c) 2.5
(d) 3

148. The brushing technique that can be recommended for the routine patient with or without periodontal involvement
(a) Bass method
(b) Modified Stillman method
(c) Charter's method
(d) Leonard technique

149. Periodontal therapy should not be performed in patients who are seen after a stroke
(a) For 3 months
(b) For 6 months
(c) For 9 months
(d) For 12 months

150. Peripheral buttressing bone formation is called as
(a) Ledging
(b) Hemisepta
(c) Crater
(d) Lipping

151. Periostat is
(a) 20mg capsule of doxycycline hyclate
(b) 40mg capsule of doxycycline hyclate
(c) 100mg capsule of doxycycline hyclate
(d) 200mg capsule of doxycycline hyclate

152. The prime etiological candidate for dental plaque is
(a) Streptococcus sanguis
(b) Streptococcus milleri
(c) Streptococcus mutansci
(d) Streptococcus mitis

PEDODONTICS

153. Technique considered as the 'Corner stone of behaviour management' is
(a) Voice control
(b) Tell-show-do
(c) Hand over mouth exercise
(d) Reinforcement

154. 'Window of Infectivity' in children is possibly seen in the age group of
(a) 6 — 18 months
(b) 19 — 33 months
(c) 34 — 48 months
(d) 36 — 60 months

155. Most of the cerebral palsy children are
(a) Spastic
(b) Dyskinetic
(c) Ataxic
(d) Mixed

156. A Time period usually required for erupting premolar tooth to move through one 1 mm of bone is
(a) 1-2 months
(b) 4-5 months
(c) 6-9 months
(d) 10-12 months

157. Prophylactic restoration (Odontotomy) was introduced by
(a) Hyatt
(b) Bodecker
(c) Buonocore
(d) Herman

158. Place of the child in the pedodontic treatment triangle is
(a) At the base
(b) In the centre
(c) At the apex
(d) None of the above

159. Complete pulpectomy technique for primary molars is developed by
(a) Garcia-Godoy
(b) Buckley
(c) Starkey
(d) Sweet

160. The deciduous molar relation indicative of a developing angles class II malocclusion
(a) Flush terminal plane
(b) Mesial step
(c) Distal step
(d) None of the above

ORTHODONTICS

161. Severe crowding is
(a) Crowding of more than 2 mm
(b) Crowding of more than 5 mm
(c) Crowding of more than 8 mm
(d) Crowding of more than 10 mm

162. South end clasp by Stephens is more effective on
(a) Upper central incisors
(b) Canines
(c) First molars
(d) on any tooth

163. RESPOND is a
(a) Invisible retainer
(b) Braided wire used in pea for alignment
(c) Adhesive-pre coated (APC) bracket system
(d) Clear bracket

164. Myofunctional exercises were first advocated by
(a) Robin 1902
(b) Moyers 1925
(c) Rogers 1918
(d) Kingsly 1930

165. The main aim of Frankel appliance is to influence
(a) Function of tongue
(b) Temporomandibular joint
(c) Outer neuro muscular envelop
(d) Control of vertical dimension

166. Implant studies on jaw rotations were conducted by

(a) Moss (b) Balchier
(c) Bjork (d) Sicher

167. Child has a flush terminal plane early in mixed dentition, movement of the lower molar forward relative to the upper molar by

(a) 1 mm (b) 1.5 mm
(c) 2 mm (d) 3.5 mm

168. When the twin block appliances is enlarged in full closure the upper and lower bite blocks interlock at

(a) 45° Angle (b) 60° Angle
(c) 70° Angle (d) 90° Angle

169. The sequence in which growth of jaw occurs is

(a) Width- Length- Height (b) Height - Width -Length
(c) Length - Height -Width (d) Width - Height -Length

170. Patient friendly functional appliance

(a) Bionator (b) Activator
(c) Twin block (d) Frankel

171. In Catalan's appliance (inclined plane) the plane should be at approximately 45 degrees to

(a) Occlusal plane (b) Long axis of the tooth
(c) Curve of Spee (d) To facial plane

172. Imbrication denotes

(a) Teeth which irregularity arranged within the arch due to lack of space for them
(b) Lack of space due extra teeth
(c) Spacing of teeth
(d) Crowding in the posterior of segment of arch

173. The combined width of deciduous canines and first and second molar is greater than that of the permanent canine and premolars in the lower is by

(a) 3mm (b) 1.7mm
(c) 1mm (d) Equal

174. Distal shoe appliance is contra indicated in

(a) Hemophilia (b) Congenital heart disease
(c) Rheumatic fever (d) All the above

PROSTHODONTICS

175. Trubyte tooth indicator is

(a) Reinforced tooth for posterior
(b) Determine the size of the maxillary lateral incisor

(c) To measure the length of the lip
(d) To determine the size of maxillary central incisor

176. The maximum bite force for persons wearing complete denture when compared to persons with natural teeth appears to be less by how many times
(a) 5 — 6 times
(b) 4 — 5 times
(c) 3 — 4 times
(d) 2 — 3 times

177. Which of the following is not a mouth temperature wax
(a) Adaptol
(b) Korecta type I
(c) HL physiologic paste
(d) Iowa wax

178. Posterior palatal seal is recorded when the head is bent at
(a) 150°
(b) 30°
(c) 60°
(d) 45°

179. Size of the bur for preparing lingual rest seat for an RPD is
(a) ¼ th of an inch
(b) ¾ th of an inch
(c) ½ an inch
(d) 1 inch

180. When the ceramic crown is contra indicated
(a) More conservative restoration
(b) Less conservative restoration
(c) Rampant caries
(d) Root canal treated tooth

181. Conservative alternative to full coverage for improving the appearance of an anterior tooth is
(a) Full veneer metal crown
(b) Porcelain jacket
(c) Three-quarter crown
(d) Laminate veneer

182. The apico-occlusal taper of the preparation for a cast restoration should be
(a) 15° - 30°
(b) 40° - 45°
(c) 2° - 5°
(d) 70 – 100°

183. The angle between occlusal rest and the vertical minor connector from which it originates is
(a) 90°
(b) 100°
(c) 120°
(d) Less than 90°

184. 'Fishbelly' design refers to which type of pontic in fixed partial denture?
(a) Saddle
(b) Hygienic
(c) Ovate
(d) Modified ridge lap

185. Continuous clasp is a type of
(a) Kennedy's multiple circumferential clasps
(b) Embrasure clasp
(c) Combination clasp
(d) None of the above

COMMUNITY DENTISTRY

186. 'The Cigarette Act of 1975' was introduced by the Government of India on
(a) 1st April 1976
(b) 15th May 1975
(c) 1st June 1976
(d) 18th January 1975

187. April 7th is observed as
(a) World Anti-AIDS day
(b) Doctors day
(c) World Health day
(d) Anti-Tobacco day

188. The 'Swish and Swallow' technique is
(a) Water fluoridation program
(b) Salt fluoridation program
(c) Milk fluoridation program
(d) Class-room based fluoride tablet program

189. Case control study is
(a) Prospective study
(b) Retrospective study
(c) Longitudinal study
(d) None of the above

190. The prevention of emergence or development of risk factors in countries where they have not appeared is what type of prevention?
(a) Primary
(b) Secondary
(c) Tertiary
(d) Primordial

191. The earliest phase in public health is
(a) Disease control
(b) Health promotion
(c) Social engineering
(d) Health for all

192. The dental auxiliary who fabricate dentures directly to patients is called
(a) Dental lab technician
(b) Expanded function dental auxiliary
(c) Denturist
(d) Dental assistant

193. Beneficence is
(a) To do no harm
(b) To do good
(c) Justice
(d) Respect for persons

194. The ideal physical quality of life index score for any country should be
(a) 0
(b) 50
(c) 100
(d) Infinity

195. The Consumer Protection Act was passed by the Parliament in the year
(a) 1996
(b) 1976
(c) 1986
(d) 2000

196. The test used to evaluate the caries activity in very young children is
(a) Calorimetric Snyder test
(b) The swab test
(c) Susceptibility test
(d) Alban test

197. The study that attempts to do no more than describe the pattern of occurrence of a disease or a condition relative to other characteristics of the population is

(a) Descriptive epidemiology
(b) Specific epidemiology
(c) Clinical epidemiology
(d) General epidemiology

198. Duraphat is a

(a) Fluoride mouth wash
(b) Fluoride varnish
(c) Fluoride tooth paste
(d) Fluoride gum paint

199. Fluorspar used in water fluoridation is

(a) Sodium fluoride
(b) Calcium fluoride
(c) Sodium silico fluoride
(d) Silico fluorides

200. Histogram is

(a) Areas of segments in circle compound
(b) Pictorial representation
(c) Series of blocks
(d) Bars separated by appropriate spaces

2006
ANSWERS & EXPLANATIONS

ANATOMY

Ans. 1. (d) Lingual

Ref BDC, 4th ed, vol3, pg 161

The submandibular duct (Wharton's duct) is thin and about 5cm long. At the anterior border of the hyoglossus muscle the duct is crossed by the lingual nerve. It opens in the floor of mouth, at the summit of sublingual papillae.

Ans. 2. (c) Nasolacrimal duct

Explained earlier, please refer K-CET 07, A4

Ans. 3. (c) Internal carotid artery

Ref www.wikipedia.com/cavernous sinus/

The **cavernous sinus** (or **lateral sellar compartment**) is a large collection of thin-walled ***veins*** creating a cavity bordered by the ***sphenoid bone*** and the ***temporal bone*** of the ***skull.***

Contents

Each cavernous sinus (one for each hemisphere of the brain) contains the following:

- **vertically**, from superior to inferior
  - ***Oculomotor nerve*** (CN III)
  - ***Trochlear nerve*** (CN IV)
  - ***Ophthalmic nerve***, the V_1 branch of the ***trigeminal nerve*** (CN V)
  - ***Maxillary nerve***, the V_2 branch of CN V
- **horizontally [through the sinus]**
  - ***Internal carotid artery*** (and ***sympathetic plexus***)
  - ***abducens nerve*** (CN VI)

One mnemonic for remembering the contents is "O-TOM CAT"

Ans. 4. (d) Foramen ovale

Ref BDC, 4th ed , vol 3 , pg 17

Structures passing through ***F.ovale***

M- mandibular nerve
A- accessory meningeal artery
L- lesser petrosal nerve
E- emissary veins

F.spinosum middle meningeal artery, nevus spinosum, middle meningeal vein

Ans. 5. (a) Osteon

Ref http://www.britannica.com/ebc/article-9057598

In compact bones, nutrients are supplied via Haversian canal which contains blood vessels. Around each Haversian canal, collagen is arranged in concentric layers, forming cylinders called osteons or haversian systems.

More about osteons

- Osteons are formations characteristic of mature bone and take shape during the process of bone remodeling, or renewal.
- New bone may also take this structure as it forms, in which case the structure is called a primary osteon.
- The process of the formation of osteons and their accompanying haversian canals begins when immature, woven bone and primary osteons are destroyed by large cells called osteoclasts, which hollow out a channel through the bone, usually following existing blood vessels.
- Layers of bone-forming cells, or osteoblasts, follow the osteoclasts, laying down new bone on the sides of the channel; the layers of bone built up in this way slowly narrow the channel until a tunnel not much larger than the central blood vessel remains.
- The blood supply for the bone cells, or osteocytes, then passes through these channels, which are the haversian canals.
- The spaces between adjacent osteons are filled with interstitial lamellae, layers of bone that are often remnants of previous haversian systems.
- Transverse pathways called ***Volkmann's canals*** connect adjacent osteons and also connect the blood vessels of the haversian canals with the periosteum, the tissue covering the bone's outer surface.

Ans. 6. (c) Levator Veli Palatini

Ref BDC, 4th ed , vol3 , pg 152,211

Remember some common exceptions:

(1) All muscles of soft palate (levator palate) are supplied by pharyngeal plexus (from cranial part of accessory nerve through Vagus) ***except*** tensor veli palate supplied by mandibular nerve.

(2) All muscles of tongue are supplied by hyoglossus (motor) ***except*** palatoglossus supplied by pharyngeal plexus.

(3) All the infra-hyoid muscles are supplied by ansa cervicalis ***except*** thyrohyoid supplied by C1 though hypoglossal nerve.

(4) All muscles of larynx are supplied by recurrent laryngeal ***except*** cricothyroid supplied by external laryngeal nerve (this is also the only intrinsic muscle of larynx lying on external aspect).

(5) All muscles of pharynx are supplied by cranial accessory nerve ***except*** the stylopharyngeus supplied by glossopharyngeal nerve.

(6) All muscles of eye are supplied by occulomotor (III) nerve ***except*** superior oblique by trochlear (SO4) and lateral rectus by abducent nerve (LR 6).

Ans. 7. (b) Sigmoid sinus

Ref BDC,4th ed ,vol3, pg 264

Mastoid air cells are series of intercommunicating spaces of variable size present within the mastoid process. Infection from the mastoid antrum and air cells can spread to any structure related to them including the temporal lobe of cerebrum, cerebellum, and the sigmoid sinus.

Ans. 8. (c) Auriculotemporal nerve

Ref pg BDC,4th ed, vol3 pg 155

Auriculotemporal nerves arise by two roots which run backwards, encircle the middle meningeal artery and unite to form a single trunk. It continues backwards between the neck of condyle and the sphenomandibular ligaments. Its two roots:

(1) **Auricular:** supplies upper parts of pinna, skin of tragus, external acoustic meatus, tympanic membrane.

(2) **Temporal:** branch supplies skin of the temple.

Remember, the nerve supplies postganglionic secretomotor fibers from otic ganglion to the parotid gland.

Ans. 9. (d) Stratified squamous non keratinized

Ref http://www.emedicine.com/ent/topic340.htm

Maxillary sinus

- The maxillary sinus begins developing in the *third month of gestation*. It arises as an ectodermal invagination in the middle meatal groove and develops laterally, measuring $7 \times 4 \times 4$ mm at birth.
- After birth it continues to grow at a rate of 2 mm vertically and 3 mm anteroposteriorly until early adulthood.
- The sinus grows rapidly for the first 3 years of life and then grows at a slower rate until age 7 years. A second rapid growth phase takes place from age 7-12 years; growth then slows until early adulthood, when the sinus has reached its final adult proportions. The floor of the sinus is level with the floor of the nose at age 12 years and then descends inferiorly into the alveolus as adult teeth begin to erupt.
- The paranasal sinuses are air-filled bony cavities extending from the skull base to the alveolar process and laterally from the nasal cavity to the inferomedial aspect of the orbit and the zygoma.
- They are lined with a ***pseudostratified columnar epithelium***, which is continuous with the lining of the nasal cavity via the ostia. This epithelium contains a number of mucus-producing goblet cells.

- Branches of the internal and external carotid arteries provide arterial supply to the sinuses, while the venous and lymphatic drainage is through the sinus ostia into the nasal cavity plexi. Venous drainage occurs through valveless vessels corresponding to the arterial supply.

DENTAL ANATOMY AND HISTOLOGY

Ans. 10. (a) Hammock ligament

Ref Orban's oral histology, 10th ed, pg 369

The bone at the base of the socket cannot act as a fixed base because pressure on bone results in resorption. Advocates of the ***root growth theory*** of tooth eruption postulated the existence of a ligament- **"the hammock ligament"** that acts as cushion, straddling the base of the socket form one bony wall to the other like a ***"sling"***. Its purpose was to act as a fixed base for the growing root to rcact against.

Ans. 11. (c) Lateral and medial pterygoid muscles

Ref Wheeler's, pg 372

Type of movement	Muscles participating
Mandibular opening	L D My G
Mandibular closing	T M Mp
Retrusion	Tp S
Protrusion	L + contra lateral Mp, also, (M + Ta)

Where,

T = Temporalis muscle (Tp – posterior fibers, Ta – anterior fibers)
L = Lateral pterygoid muscle
Mp = Medial Pterygoid muscle
M = Masseter; D = Digastric ; G = Geniohyoid ; SI = Supra+ Infra hyoid muscles

Ans. 12. (a) Maxillary first premolar

Ref Wheeler's, 6th ed , pg 185

Lingual development groove - Mandibular II premolar
Mesio-lingual development groove - Mandibular I premolar
Mesial developmental groove - Maxillary I premolar

PHYSIOLOGY

Ans. 13. (a) Sodium

Ref Ganong, 22nd ed, pg 30

The principle cation of ECF is Na^+ followed by K^+. while the anion is Cl^- followed by HCO_3. The situation is ***reverse*** in intracellular fluid.

Remember, ICF = 60% of total body water while ECF = 40%

ECF = 25% plasma + 75% interstitial fluid.

Ans. 14. (c) Poor localization

Ref Ganong, 22nd ed, pg142

PAIN

Property	Fast pain	Slow pain
Character	Bright, sharp and well localized	Dull, intense, diffuse and unpleasant
Fibers transmitting	A λ	C
Neuro transmitter	Glutamate	Substance P
Rate of conduction	12-30m/s	0.5-2 m/s
Projection	Lamina I and V	Lamina I and II
Diameter of nerve fiber	2-5μm	0.4-1.2μm

Ans. 15. (b) 5

Ref Ganong, 22nd ed, pg 684

Cyanosis is a bluish discoloration of tissues when the amount of reduced hemoglobin exceeds **5mg/dL.**

EXTRA EDGE

Remember, cyanosis is not seen in

(1) **Anemic hypoxia:** as total Hb is less in the first place.(while for cyanosis to occur, at least 5mg/dL of Hb should be present).

(2) **Hypoxic hypoxia:** as the blood gas content is normal.

(3) **carbon-monoxide poisoning:** the cherry red color obscure the signs of cyanosis.

Ans. 16. (a) Predominantly stream line

Ref Ganong, 22nd ed, pg 583

The flow of blood in straight vessels is usually laminar (streamline). The velocity of each layer increases from outwards to inwards. Laminar flow occurs up till certain velocities (critical velocity), above which the flow is turbulent.

Ans. 17. (a) Right coronary artery and during diastole

Ref Ganong, 22nd ed, pg 620-22

The 2 coronary arteries (CA) that supply the myocardium arise from behind the aortic valve at the root of aorta. The ***right CA has a higher flow*** in 50% cases and the left in 20%, while both have an equal flow in 30% of the cases.

The pressure inside the left ventricle is slightly higher than the aorta during systole, consequently, flow through the sub-endocardial portions of left ventricle occur only during diastole. This is significant as, in conditions like tachycardia, the left ventricle (due to prolonged systole) virtually remains without blood supply and there are chances of development of ischemia.

EXTRA EDGE

Also remember,.

Coronary flow (rest)	= 250mL/min (5% of cardiac output)
Oxygen consumption by heart (rest)	= 2mL/100g/min
Oxygen consumption by heart (work)	= 9mL/100g/min

Ans. 18.(a) Increase in serum calcium

Ref Ganong, 22nd ed, pg 393

Parafollicular cells of thyroid secrete the hormone Calcitonin. Calcitonin has its primary effect on osteoclasts by inhibiting them. This occurs in response to increase in serum calcium level (normal 9-11mg)

Ans. 19. (c) Von Willebrand's factor

Ref http://en.wikipedia.org/wiki/Von_willebrand_factor ; Robbin , pg 638.

Von Willebrand factor is a blood glycoprotein involved in coagulation. It is deficient or defective in von Willebrand disease and is involved in a large number of other diseases, including thrombotic thrombocytopenic purpura, Heyde's syndrome, and possibly hemolytic-uremic syndrome

- vWF is a large multimeric glycoprotein present in blood plasma and produced constitutively in endothelium (in the Weibel-Palade bodies), megakaryocytes (á-granules of platelets), and subendothelial connective tissue.
- vWF is named after *Dr. Erik von Willebrand*, a Finnish doctor who in 1924 first described a hereditary bleeding disorder in families from the Åland islands who had a tendency for cutaneous and mucosal bleeding, including menorrhagia.
- Von Willebrand factor is *not an enzyme* and therefore has no catalytic activity. Its primary function is binding to other proteins, particularly Factor VIII and it is important in platelet adhesion to wound sites.

vWF binds to a number of cells and molecules. The most important ones are:

- Factor VIII is bound to vWF while inactive in circulation; Factor VIII degrades rapidly when not bound to vWF. Factor VIII is released from vWF by the action of thrombin.
- vWF binds to ***sub-endothelial collagen***, *e.g.,* when it is exposed in endothelial cells due to damage occurring to the blood vessel.
- vWF binds to platelet gpIb when it forms a complex with gpIX and gpV; this binding occurs under all circumstances, but is most efficient under high shear stress (*i.e.,* rapid blood flow in narrow blood vessels, see below).
- vWF binds to other platelet receptors when they are activated, *e.g.,* by thrombin (*i.e.,* when coagulation has been stimulated).

BIOCHEMISTRY

Ans. 20. (d) Glycogen

Ref Ganong, 22nd ed, pg 467

Starches (glucose polymers) are the only polysaccharides that are digested to any degree in the human GIT. In glycogen, the glucose molecules are mostly long chains(1:4á and to some extent 1:6 á linkages). Amylopectins, which constitute 80-90% of dietary starch is similar to glycogen but less branched.

Glycogen is found in animals, whereas amylase and amylopectin are of plant origin.
It is the principle storage form of carbohydrates in human body. The liver and muscle glycogen provide the bulk of the store.

Ans. 21. (a) HGPRTase (Total).

Ref http://en.wikipedia.org/wiki/Lesch-Nyhan_syndrome

Lesch-Nyhan syndrome (LNS), also known as **Nyhan's syndrome**, is a rare, inherited disorder. It was first described in 1964 by Dr. Michael Lesch and Dr. William Nyhan.

- caused by a deficiency of the enzyme ***hypoxanthine-guanine phosphoribosyltransferase (HGPRT)***.
- LNS is an X-linked recessive disease: the gene is carried by the mother and passed on to her son. LNS is present at birth in baby boys.
- Patients have severe mental and physical problems throughout life. A striking feature of LNS is self-mutilating behaviors, characterized by lip and finger biting, that begin in the second year of life.
- The lack of HPRT causes a build-up of uric acid in all body fluids, and leads to problems such as severe gout, poor muscle control, and moderate mental retardation, which appear in the first year of life. Abnormally high uric acid levels can cause sodium urate crystals to form in the joints, kidneys, central nervous system and other tissues of the body, leading to gout-like swelling in the joints and severe kidney problems.
- Neurological symptoms include facial grimacing, involuntary writhing, and repetitive movements of the arms and legs similar to those seen in Huntington's disease. The direct cause of the neurological abnormalities remains unknown.
- Because a lack of HPRT causes the body to poorly utilize vitamin B12, some boys may develop a rare disorder called megaloblastic anemia.

The symptoms caused by the buildup of uric acid (arthritis and renal symptoms) respond well to treatment with drugs such as *allopurinol* that reduce the levels of uric acid in the blood. The mental deficits and self-mutilating behavior do not respond to treatment. There is no cure, but many patients live to adulthood. LNS is rare, affecting about one in 380,000 live births.

Ans. 22. (a) Tyrosine

Ref Lippincott , 3rd ed, pg 260

Derivatives of Tyrosine/phenyl alanine-

- Melanin
- Catecholamine (Epinephrine, nor epinephrine, dopamine)
- Thyroid hormones

Remember, *Melatonin* is derived from Tryptophan

Ans. 23. (b) Glycogen

Explained above, please refer A20

MICROBIOLOGY

Ans. 24. (a) Clostridium welchii

Please refer KCET 07, A62

Ans. 25. (a) Spirilla

Ref http://wiki.cotch.net/wiki.phtml?title=Flagellum

The **flagellum** (plural: **flagella**) is a propulsive structure used by many single-celled organisms to move through a liquid medium. There are three main varieties of flagellum;

- the bacterial flagellum (a helical filament that rotates like a screw)
- archaeal flagellum (similar but non-homologous to the bacterial flagellum), and
- the eukaryotic flagellum (a whip-like structure that lashes back and forth).

The filament is composed of the protein ***flagellin*** and is a hollow tube 20 nanometers thick. It is helical, and has a sharp bend just outside the outer membrane called the "hook" which allows the helix to point directly away from the cell. A shaft runs between the hook and the basal structure, passing through protein rings in the cell's membranes that act as bearings. Gram-positive organisms have 2 rings, one in the cell wall and one in the cell membrane. Gram-negative organisms have 4 rings, 2 in the cell wall and 2 in the cell membrane.

EXTRA EDGE

Different species of bacteria have different numbers and arrangements of flagella.

- Monotrichous bacteria have a single flagellum *e.g., Vibrio cholera*
- Lophotrichous bacteria have multiple flagella located at the same spot on the bacteria's surface which act in concert to drive the bacteria in a single direction. *e.g., spirillium*
- Amphitrichous bacteria have a single flagellum each on two opposite ends (only one end's flagellum operates at a time, allowing the bacteria to reverse course rapidly by switching which flagellum is active).
- Peritrichous bacteria have flagella projecting in all directions. *e.g., E.coli*
- Some species of bacteria (those of *Spirochete* body form) have internal flagella that lie between their inner and outer membranes, the rotation of which causes the entire bacterium to corkscrew through its medium.

Ans. 26. (d) Bacillius stearothermophilus

Explained Earlier, Please Refer KCET-07 A19

Ans. 27. (d) Leeuwen Hoeck

Ref http://inventors.about.com/library/inventors/blleeuwenhoek.htm

The father of microscopy, Anton Van Leeuwenhock of Holland (1632-1723), started as an apprentice in a dry goods store where magnifying glasses were used to count the threads in cloth. He taught himself new methods for grinding and polishing tiny lenses of great curvature which gave magnifications up to 270x diameters, the finest known at that time.

These lenses led to the building of Anton Van Leeuwenhoek's microscopes considered the first practical microscopes, and the biological discoveries for which he is famous. Anton Van Leeuwenhoek was the first to see and describe bacteria (1674), yeast plants, the teeming life in a drop of water, and the circulation of blood corpuscles in capillaries.

Ans. 28.(c) Conjugation

Ref http://www.answers.com/topic/plasmid?cat=health

A ***circular extra-chromosomal*** genetic element that is ubiquitous in prokaryotes and has also been identified in a number of eukaryotes. In general, bacterial plasmids can be classified into two groups on the basis of the number of genes and functions they carry.

The larger plasmids are deoxyribonucleic acid (DNA) molecules of around 100 kilobase (kb) pairs, which is sufficient to code for approximately 100 genes. There is usually a small number of copies of these plasmids per host chromosome, so that their replication must be precisely coordinated with the cell division cycle.

The plasmids in the second group are smaller in size, about 6–10 kb. These plasmids may harbor 6–10 genes and are usually present in multiple copies (10–20 per chromosome).

The functions specified by different bacterial plasmids are usually quite specialized in nature. Moreover, they are not essential for cell growth since the host bacteria are viable without a plasmid when the cells are cultured under conditions that do not select for plasmid-specified gene products. Plasmids thus introduce specialized functions to host cells which provide versatility and adaptability for growth and survival. Plasmids which confer *antibiotic resistance (R plasmids)* have been extensively characterized because of their medical importance. Plasmids have played a seminal role in the spectacular advances in the area of genetic engineering. Individual genes can be inserted into specific sites on plasmids in cell cultures and the recombinant plasmid thus formed introduced into a living cell by the process of bacterial transformation.

Ans. 29. (a) Ig G

Explained earlier, please refer KCET07 A24.

Ans. 30. (c) Inhibiting glucose transport

Ref http://en.wikipedia.org/wiki/Diptheria_toxin

Diphtheria toxin

- Diphtheria toxin was discovered in 1890 by Emil Adolf von Bering
- The exotoxin is secreted by *Corynebacterium diphtheriae*, the pathogen bacterium that causes diphtheria.
- Diphtheria toxin is a single polypeptide chain of 535 amino acids consisting of two subunits linked by disulfide bridges. Binding to the cell surface of the less stable of these two subunits allows the more stable part of the protein to penetrate the host cell.
- It catalyzes the ADP-ribosylation eucaryotic ***elongation factor-2 (eEF2),*** inactivating this protein. It does so by ADP-ribosylating the unusual aminoacid diphthamide. Thus, it inhibits the G-protein coupled receptor.
- The enzyme adenylate cyclase is activated by $G_{ás}$-GTP and synthesizes the second messenger cyclic adenosine monophosphate (cAMP) from ATP .
- However in absence of this second messenger, glucose uptake by intestinal mucosa is affected. Thus, large amounts of water are lost as a result of ***osmotic gradient*** created along with glucose that accounts for the severe diarrhea associated with diphtheria.
- In this way, it acts as a DNA translational inhibitor.
- The exotoxin A of Pseudomonas aeruginosa uses a similar mechanism of action.
- Diphtheria toxin is extraordinarily potent. The lethal dose for humans is about 0.1 ìg/kg of pure protein. A massive release of toxin into the body will likely cause lethal necrosis of the heart and liver.

GENERAL PATHOLOGY

Ans. 31. (a) Neuron

Ref: Robbins,6th ed, pg 49

Non-dividing cells (permanent cells) cannot undergo postnatal mitotic division. These include nerve cells and cardiac myocytes, where irreversible injury results in only scarring. Although skeletal tissues are also placed in this category, but they have limited regenerative capacity (largely because of their immature stem cells associated with endomysial sheaths.)

DENTAL MATERIALS

Ans. 32. (c) Homogenization

Ref Skinner's, pg 336 10th ed

If an alloy is cooled rapidly from its liquidus temperature, the stress can be relieved by heat treatment. The alloy is held at temperature near solidus temperature so that solid state atomic diffusion can occur. NO grain growth occurs when casting is heat treated. The process of heating a casting alloy to eliminate composition difference caused by cooling is called ***Homogenization***.

EXTRA EDGE

Remember,

Liquidus temp: is the temp at which the first solid begins to form for any given composition as determined from the cooling curves.

Solidus temp: is the temp at which the last liquid solidifies.

Hence, all metals exist as liquids above the liquidus line and as solids below the solidus line. In the equilibrium phase, both states co-exist.

Ans. 33. (c) 75% gold

Ref Skinners, pg 361

http://jdr.iadrjournals.org/cgi/reprint/48/6/1284

Remember,

Only Type III and IV gold alloys can be age-hardened (and not Type I or II)

Type	Noble alloy % (ADA)	VHN	BHN	Uses
I (soft)	83	50-90	40 -75	Small inlays- very low stress
II (medium)	78	90-120	70-100	Inlays, ¾ crowns, ponticmoderate stress
III (hard)	78	120-150	90 – 140	High stress areas of Type II
IV (extra hard)	75	150+	130 – 200	Denture base, long span FPD, full crowns

Ans. 34.(b) Electrolytic corrosion

Galvanism is an important example of electrochemical corrosion occurring when dissimilar metals are in direct physical contact with each other.

Ref Skinner's pg 353

Dental galvanism refers to production of galvanic current in the oral cavity due to the presence of two or more dissimilar metals in dental restorations that are bathed in saliva, or a single metal restoration and two electrolytes, saliva and pulp tissue fluid, thus producing an electrolytic cell and an electric current. When such restorations touch each other, the current may be high enough to irritate the dental pulp and cause sharp pain. The anodic restoration or areas of a restoration are subject to electrolytic corrosion.

Ref http://medical-dictionary.thefreedictionary.com/Galvinism

Ans. 35. (b) Nickel titanium

Ref http://en.wikipedia.org/wiki/Shape_memory_alloy

A **shape memory alloy** (SMA, also known as a **smart alloy** or **memory metal**) is an alloy that "remembers" its geometry. After a sample of SMA has been deformed from its original crystallographic configuration, it regains its original geometry by itself during heating (one-way effect) or, at higher ambient temperatures, simply during unloading (pseudo-elasticity or superelasticity). These extraordinary properties are due to a ***temperature-dependent martensitic phase transformation*** from a low-symmetry to a highly symmetric crystallographic structure. Those crystal structures are known as martensite (at lower temperatures) and austenite (at higher temperatures).

The four main types of SMA are the copper-zinc-aluminium-nickel, copper-aluminium-nickel, and nickel-titanium (NiTi) alloys. NiTi alloys are generally more expensive and possess superior mechanical properties when compared to copper-based SMAs. The temperatures at which the SMA changes its crystallographic structure, called *transformation temperature*, is characteristic of the alloy, and can be tuned by varying the elemental ratios in the alloy.

The nickel-titanium alloys were first developed in 1962–1963 by the Naval Ordnance Laboratory and commercialized under the trade name Nitinol (an acronym for Nickel Titanium Naval Ordnance Laboratories).

Under the transition temperature, Nitinol is in the martensite phase and can be bent into various shapes. To set the "parent shape" the metal must be held in position and heated to about 500° C. (varies for different SMAs). The high temperature causes the atoms to arrange themselves into a high symmetry, often cubic arrangement known as the austenite phase. In the low temperature martensite each atom "remembers" which should be its neighbors in austenite, even when the metal is deformed by crystal twinning deformation.

Ans. 36. (d) Resistant to corrosion

REF with text

Friends, the options are slightly misframed here. Read the following lines:

"High copper amalgams set in a similar fashion as low copper amalgams except that Sn-Hg molecules are suppressed by the Cu-Sn molecules, which are preferentially formed. ***The Cu-Sn molecules are much less corrosion-prone when compared to Sn-Hg they replace.***

Now, the Cu-Sn phase is still susceptible to corrosion, however, when they corrode penetration corrosion does not occur"

Ref Sturdevant, pg 154

Corrosion products of high-Cu include copper and tin-oxides and oxy-chlorides but no mercury is involved.

This means that, ***although high copper are more resistant than compared to low-copper, they are still very much susceptible to it***.

As for other options, "During electro-chemical corrosion of low-Cu , the Sn-Hg phase is oxidized into SnO and or SnOCl. While the oxy-chlorides are soluble compounds, the oxides precipitate as crystals and helps seal the space along margins against microleakage. This phenomenon, however, is not seen with the High-Cu amalgams."

Ref Sturdevant, pg 156

Amalgams are also susceptible to chemical corrosion which forms a surface layer of oxides over the restoration. Low-copper forms a black Ag-S tarnish film while even very high Cu amalgams produce a ***copper oxide platina***. Although it does not affect the mechanical properties, esthetics is compromised.

Ref Sturdevant, pg 154

Ans. 37. (b) Alginate

Ref Nallaswamy, pg 413

In Functional Dual impressions like McLean's or Hindle's occlusal rims are attached over the custom tray and then used for compressing the tissues in functional form. An alginate (irreversible hydro-colloid) *over-impression* is made using a large stock-tray. Since the alginate over impression carries the functional impression along with it, it is called a **pick-up impression.**

Ans. 38. (a) 60% by weight of noble elements

Ref. Sturdevant Pg 215

Noble metal alloys are very resistant to tarnish and corrosion. These systems are based on gold, platinum, palladium, rhodium, iridium etc. Precious metal alloys are all noble plus silver. Approximately, 75% by weight of noble metals are advised for adequate corrosion resistance.

Low – gold alloys contain only 3-50 % gold or other noble metal elements.

Since option A is the closest, it is the answer here.

Ans. 39. (d) 100%

Ref Sturdevent, pg 160

Mercury facts

- Elemental Hg absorption from lungs - 80% ; GIT – 0.01%
- Inorganic Hg absorption form lungs – 80% ; GIT - 7%
- Organic Hg absorption from GIT - 95-98 %
- Average half-life in body = 55 days
- Threshold limit value (TLV) for exposure = 50 μg/m^3
- Average level in humans = 25 μg/ kg

Ans. 40. (b) 15 μm

Ref Vimal Sikri, pg 324

Powdered gold avg particle size 15μm

- Density of pure gold = 19-19.3 (14-15 actual) g/cm^2
- Coefficient of thermal expansion – 14.4 x 10^{-6} / ^{0}C
- Thermal conductivity -0.710 cal/sec/cm^2/ C/ cm
- BHN = 25-60
- Tensile strength = 19,000 – 32,000 psi
- Fusion temp – 1063 C ; boiling temp 2200 C

Percentage elongation = 12.8

Ans. 41. (c) Initial set

Ref Philips, 9th ed , pg 74.

First the definitions:

- **Setting Time:** time elapsed from the beginning of mixing until the material hardens. This is further studied as initial and final ST.
- **Mixing time:** the time form the addition of powder to the water until mixing is completed. Mixing may be achieved using mechanical (20-30 s) or hand (1min)
- **Working time:** time available to use a workable mix *i.e.* from the time mixing s completed until the mass begins to set. Ideally, 3 min WT is adequate for gypsum.
- **Loss of Gloss:** as the reaction proceeds, some of the excess water is taken up for forming the dihydrate while other evaporates, which causes the mix to loose its gloss. This is about 9min, the material doesn't develop mechanical properties at this point.
- **Gillmore test:** Two Gillmore needles are generally employed to test the ST of dental cements and gypsum compounds. The smaller needle gives the ***initial set*** wherein it no longer leaves an impression over the spread material. At this point (13 min), there is definite increase in strength.
- **Vicat test:** this is a needle with a weighted plunger rod. The needle is released from the plunger just after the gloss is lost. The time elapsed until the needle no longer penetrates the bottom of the mix is known as the ***Setting time*** (ST). mostly the Initial Gillmore and Vicat measurements coincide.
- **Final Gillmore:** the heavier Gillmore needle is used for testing the next stage in setting. The elapsed time when it leaves only a barely perceptible mark on the surface is called the ***final setting time***.

Ans. 42. (d) Titanium

Ref Philips, 9th ed , pg 540.

Stabilization of Stainless Steel: involves addition of some metal that precipitates as a carbide in preference to chromium. **Titanium** is often used for this purpose. In an amount nearly 6 times the carbon content, the precipitation of chromium carbide can be inhibited for a short time at the temperatures encountered during soldering procedures. (Remember, during soldering the high temperatures cause the ppt of CrC_3 and results in decrease in the corrosion resistance of SS). Thus stabilization is a procedure to improve the corrosion resistance of SS wire.

Ans. 43. (a) Alter the temperature of water

Ref Philip's, 9th ed , pg 128

Gelation time: time elapsed from the beginning of mixing until the gelation begins to occur. Ideally, this should be sufficient to allow dentist to mix, load and place the tray. Too short would result in premature gelation and distortion of the impression. Too long would be tedious for both the patient and the dentist. Hence optimal time is considered in between **3 -4 min** at room temp (20 ^{0}C).

Gelation of alginate is a <u>*chemical*</u> reaction and various methods can be used to modify it:-

- Gelation is best regulated by addition of small amounts of retarder like sodium or potassium phosphate, oxalate, or carbonate. These compete with calcium sulfate of the alginate and prevent reaction within. HOWEVER, the addition of these retarders is best regulated by the **manufacturer.**

- The clinician may alter the GT by changing the W:P ratio and the mixing time. The higher the W: P, the longer is the GT. HOWEVER; this may impair certain characteristics of the gel and is not recommended routinely.
- The **BEST** method to control the GT is to alter the temp of water for mixing the alginate. The higher the temp of water , lower is the GT (and hence a faster gelation process) . Some material have shown a ***20sec change with every degree Celsius change in temperature***

Ans. 44. (c) Stiffness

Ref Philip's, pg 33

Please remember, MOE refers to the rigidity or stiffness of a material. (***And not flexibility***: strain that occurs when a material is stressed to its proportional limit.)

MOE is represented by Young's Modulus (E) = Stress/Strain

Unit: MPa/ psi /force per unit area

Remember, Proportional limit is the stress level where the curve deviates first from the straight line. Hence, the material is elastic below and plastic above this point.

Yield strength, on the other hand, is the stress required to produce a particular deviation. Hence, yield strength is always greater or equal to proportional limit but never less.

PHARMACOLOGY

Ans.45. (c) Ethambutol

Ref http://en.wikipedia.org/wiki/Ethambutol

Ethambutol is a bacteriostatic anti-mycobacterial drug prescribed to treat tuberculosis (*Mycobacterium tuberculosis*). It is usually given in combination with other tuberculosis drugs, such as isoniazid, pyrazinamide and rifampicin.

Bacteriostatic against actively growing TB bacilli, it works by obstructing the formation of cell wall. Mycolic acids attach to the 5'-hydroxyl groups of D-arabinose residues of arabinogalactan and form mycolyl-arabinogalactan-peptidoglycan complex in the cell wall. Disruption of the arabinogalactan synthesis inhibits the formation of this complex and leads to increased permeability of the cell wall.

Side effect

- Rash
- Itching (pruritis)
- Visual disturbances
- "Pins and needles" sensation in hands and feet (peripheral neuritis)
- Decrease in the number of platelets in the blood (thrombocytopenia)
- Inflammation of the optic nerve (the nerve connecting the eye to the brain) which results in blurring of vision (optic neuritis)
- Color blindness

Ans. 46. (c) Epinephrine

Ref "http://en.wikipedia.org/wiki/Prodrug"

A **prodrug** is a pharmacological substance (drug) which is administered in an inactive (or significantly less active) form. Once administered, the prodrug is metabolised in vivo into the active compound.

- The rationale behind the use of a prodrug is generally for Absorption, Distribution, Metabolism, and Excretion (ADME) optimization.
- Prodrugs are usually designed to improve oral bioavailability - poor absorption from the gastrointestinal tract is usually the limiting factor, and is often due to the chemical properties of the drug.
- Equally, the use of a prodrug strategy increases the selectivity of the drug for its intended target. An example of this can be seen in many anti-cancer treatments, in which the reduction of adverse effects is always of paramount importance. Drugs used to target hypoxic cancer cells, through the use of redox-activation, utilise the large quantities of reductase enzyme present in the hypoxic cell to convert the drug into its cytotoxic form, essentially activating it. As the prodrug has low cytotoxicity prior to this activation, there is a markedly lower chance of it "attacking" healthy, non-cancerous cells which reduces the side-effects associated with these chemotherapeutic agents.

EXAMPLES

- Enalapril is converted by esterase to the active enalaprilat.
- Valaciclovir is converted by esterase to the active aciclovir.
- Levodopa is converted by DOPA decarboxylase to the active dopamine.
- Chloramphenicol succinate ester is used as intravenous prodrug of chloramphenicol, because pure chloramphenicol does not dissolve in water.
- Psilocybin is dephosphorylated to the active psilocin.
- Heroin is deacetylated by esterase to the active morphine.
- Codeine is demethylated by the liver enzyme CYP2D6 to the active morphine.
- gamma-Butyrolactone (GBL) is dehydrolysed form of gamma-Hydroxybutyric acid (GHB)

Remember, Epinephrine is not a prodrug.

Ans.47. (b) Alprenolol

Ref http://en.wikipedia.org/wiki/Beta blocker

Beta blockers block the action of endogenous catecholamines (epinephrine (adrenaline) and norepinephrine (noradrenaline) in particular), on â-adrenergic receptors, part of the sympathetic nervous system which mediates the "fight or flight" response.

Remember

There are three known types of beta receptor, designated β_1, β_2 and β_3.

Receptor type	Location	Effects - Agonists
β_1-Adrenergic receptors	heart and in the kidneys	Positive chronotropic and inotropic effect on the heart and increases cardiac conduction velocity and automaticity. In the kidney causes renin release.
β_2-Adrenergic receptors	lungs, GIT, liver, uterus, vascular smooth muscle, and skeletal muscle	receptors induces smooth muscle relaxation (resulting in vasodilatation and bronohodilation amongst other actions), induces tremor in skeletal muscle, and increases glycogenolysis in the liver and skeletal muscle
β_3-receptors	fat cells	induces lipolysis

Beta blockers inhibit these normal epinephrine-mediated sympathetic actions, but have minimal effect on resting subjects. That is, they reduce the effect of excitement /physical exertion on heart rate and force of contraction, dilation of blood vessels and opening of bronchi, and also reduce tremor and breakdown of glycogen.

It is therefore somewhat unexpected that non-selective beta blockers have an antihypertensive effect, since they appear to cause vasoconstriction.

- The **antihypertensive mechanism** appears to involve: reduction in cardiac output (due to negative chronotropic and inotropic effects), reduction in renin release from the kidneys, and a central nervous system effect to reduce sympathetic activity.
- **Antianginal** effects result from negative chronotropic and inotropic effects, which decrease cardiac workload and oxygen demand.
- The **antiarrhythmic** effects of beta blockers arise from sympathetic nervous system blockade – resulting in depression of sinus node function and atrioventricular node conduction, and prolonged atrial refractory periods. Sotalol, in particular, has additional antiarrhythmic properties and prolongs action potential duration through potassium channel blockade.

CLASSIFICATION

Non-selective agents

Sotalol
Oxprenolol
Alprenolol - (SOAP)
Propranolol

Carteolol
Levobunolol
Mepindolol
Metipranolol
Nadolol

Penbutolol
Pindolol
Timolol

β_1-Selective agents

Metoprolol
Acebutolol - (MAA)
Atenolol

Betaxolol
Bisoprolol - (BhEN)
Esmolol
Nebivolol

Mixed β_1/β-adrenergic antagonists

Carvedilol
Celiprolol
Labetalol

β_2-Selective agents

Butaxamine (weak α-adrenergic agonist activity)

Ans. 48. (c) Erythromycin

Ref http://en.wikipedia.org/wiki/Aminoglycoside

- **Aminoglycosides** are a group of antibiotics that are effective against certain types of bacteria. They include amikacin, gentamicin, kanamycin, neomycin, netilmicin, paromomycin, streptomycin, tobramycin and apramycin.
- Aminoglycosides that are derived from *Streptomyces* genus are named with the suffix *-mycin*, while those which are derived from *Micromonospora* are named with the suffix *-micin*.
- Aminoglycosides work by binding to the bacterial 30S ribosomal subunit (some work by binding to the 50s subunit), inhibiting the translocation of the peptidyl-tRNA from the A-site to the P-site and also causing misreading of mRNA, leaving the bacterium unable to synthesize proteins vital to its growth
- Aminoglycosides are useful primarily in infections involving aerobic, gram-negative bacteria, such as *Pseudomonas*, *Acinetobacter*, and *Enterobacter*. In addition, some *Mycobacteria*, including the bacteria that cause tuberculosis, are susceptible to aminoglycosides.
- The most frequent use of aminoglycosides is empiric therapy for serious infections such as septicemia, complicated intraabdominal infections, complicated urinary tract infections, and nosocomial respiratory tract infections.

EXTRA EDGE

Please remember: The nomenclature system '*-mycin*' is not specific for aminoglycosides, as **vancomycin** is a glycopeptide antibiotic with a different mechanism of action than aminoglycosides. Similarly, **Erythromycin** is a macrolide antibiotic.

Ans. 49. (c) Nitrous oxide

Ref http://www.cja-jca.org/cgi/content/full/47/6/506

THE concentration and second gas effects were first demonstrated in dogs. Increasing the inspired concentration of N_2O concentrated both N_2O and any gas delivered concurrently (the second gas) due to a difference of the blood/gas partition coefficient between N_2 and N_2O. Thus, rapid and massive initial uptake of N_2O during the induction of anesthesia increased the delivery of both gases to the lung.

Halothane is a less soluble gas, which means that it does not cross membranes easily.

As nitrous oxide is additionally inspired along with the anesthetic agent, the Fa /Fi ratio will quickly rise to near one. In addition, nitrous oxide is more soluble than other gases, which allows it to cross into the tissues more rapidly. Nitrous oxide is taken up into the blood more readily than other gases. This leaves a higher concentration of the second gas in the alveoli, causing a concentration gradient between the alveoli and blood. The higher the gradient, the more quickly the gas crosses into the blood, despite a low solubility. Any anesthetic agent inspired along with nitrous oxide will reach equilibrium more quickly than it would have been if inspired alone.

Ans. 50. (d) Dermatophytosis

Ref http://en.wikipedia.org/wiki/Amphotericin_B

Amphotericin B is a polyene antifungal drug, often used intravenously for systemic fungal infections. As with other polyene antifungals, amphotericin B associates with ergosterol, a membrane chemical of fungi, forming a pore that leads to K^+ leakage and fungal cell death.

Oral preparations of amphotericin B are used to treat oral thrush; these are virtually nontoxic. The main i.v. use is in systemic fungal infections (*e.g.,* in immunocompromised patients), and in visceral leishmaniasis. Aspergillosis, cryptococcus infections (*e.g.,* meningitis) and candidiasis are treated with amphotericin B. It is also used empirically in febrile immunocompromised patients who do not respond to broad-spectrum antibiotics

Remember, although Dermatophytes are inhibited **invitro** , the concentration of amphotericin attained in infected skin is low and ineffective and hence advocated only in serious systemic infections.

EXTRA EDGE

Important Interactions

- **Flucytosine:** Toxicity of Flucytosine increased and vice versa.
- **Diuretics or Cisplatin:** Increased renal toxicity and incrised risk of hypokalemia.
- **Corticosterioids:** Increased risk of hypokalemia.
- **Cytostatic drugs:** Increased risk of kidney damage, hypotension and bronchospasms.
- **Other nephrotoxic drugs:** Increased risk of serious renal damage. Monitor patients closely.
- **Foscarnet, Ganciclovir, Tenofovir, Adefovir:** Risk of hematological and renal side-effects of Amphotericin B increased.
- **Transfusion of Leukocytes:** Risk of pulmonal (lung) damage. Space intervals between the

application of Amphotericin B and the transfusion and monitor pulmonal.

Ans. 51. (a) Increased PH of the tissues

Ref http://www.ionchannels.org/showabstract.php?pmid=10665308

- Tachyphylaxis to local anesthetics is defined as a decrease in duration, segmental spread or intensity of a regional block despite repeated constant dosages.
- In contrast to tachyphylaxis, pseudotachyphylaxis denotes time dependent variations in pain or circadian changes in the duration of local anesthetic action.
- Tachyphylaxis appears neither to be linked to structural or pharmacological properties of the local anesthetics nor to the technique or mode of their administration.
- The mechanisms underlying tachyphylaxis include changes in pharmacokinetics or pharmacodynamics
- Considering pharmacokinetics, *local edema, an increased epidural protein concentration, changes in local anesthetic distribution in the epidural space or a* ***decrease of perineural pH*** could result in decreased diffusion of the local anesthetics from the epidural space to their binding sites at the sodium channel. Increased clearance of local anesthetics from the epidural space may be caused both by increased epidural blood flow or increased local metabolism.
- Considering pharmacodynamics, antagonistic effects of nucleotides or increased sodium concentration, increased afferent input from nociceptors or receptor down regulation of the sodium channels have been implicated.
- A new possibility to maintain for a longer time neural blockade is the design of new ultra long-acting local anesthetics. Liposomal formulations of local anesthetics also appear suitable to provide longer lasting regional anesthesia. The recent observation that NMDA-antagonists as well as NO-synthase-inhibitors prevent the development of tachyphylaxis suggests involvement of the nitric oxide pathway in the development of tachyphylaxis. Accordingly, NMDA-antagonists or NO-synthase-inhibitors may prevent tachyphylaxis.

Thus we see, that a decrease (and not increase) in tissue pH causes tachyphylaxis. (Option 1)

Ans.52. (d) Baclofen

Explained Earlier Please refer KCET-07 A55

Remember, although both baclofen and gabapentin may be used, the ***anti-spastic*** drug is baclofen

Baclofen is selective $GABA_B$ receptor agonist, acting primarily on spinal cord and is a potent anti-spastic drug.

Ans.53. (a) Levamizole

Ref http://en.wikipedia.org/wiki/Levamisole

Levamisole (Ergamisol, HCl salt) is an antibiotic belonging to a class of synthetic imidazothiazole derivatives, and was originally used as an *antihelminthic* to treat worm infestations in both humans and animals.

It is also used infrequently to treat melanoma and head and neck cancer. It is unclear from its mechanism of action why it would have an effect in treating colon cancer, although it has been shown to have **"immune-stimulating"** properties in some situations. A 1984 study on complicated viral influenza had found levamisole to be an effective interferon inducer and had recommended its use in combination therapy for influenza. It is also used routinely in India to treat steroid dependent childhood nephrotic syndrome cases.

Levamisole reversibly but uncompetitively inhibits (independent from presence or absence of Mg^{2+}) most alkaline phosphatase isoforms (*e.g.*, human liver, bone, kidney, and spleen) except the intestinal and placental isoform.

GENERAL MEDICINE

Ans. 54. (d) Cardiac failure

Explained earlier, please refer KCET-O7 A61

Ans. 55. (a) Growth hormone

Ref http://en.wikipedia.org/wiki/Acromegaly

Acromegaly is a hormonal disorder that results when the pituitary gland produces excess growth hormone (hGH). Most commonly it is a benign hGH producing tumor derived from a distinct type of cells (somatotrophs) and called **pituitary adenoma**.

- Acromegaly most commonly affects middle-aged adults and can result in serious illness premature death.
- Soft tissue swelling of the hands and feet.
- Brow and lower jaw protrusion.
- Enlarging hands ; Enlarging feet.
- Arthritis and carpal tunnel syndrome.
- Teeth spacing increase and Macroglossia [enlarged tongue].
- Heart failure.
- Compression of the optic chiasm leading to loss of vision in the outer visual fields (typically bitemporal hemianopia).
- Headache.
- Diabetes mellitus and Hypertension.
- Increased palmar sweating and sebum production over the face (seborrhea) are clinical indicators of active growth hormone (GH) producing pituitary tumours.

The distinction between gigantism (occurring in children) and acromegaly (occurring in adults) can be made by the occurrence of the adenoma in relation to the closure of the epiphyses. If elevated growth hormone levels occur before the closure of the epiphyses (*i.e.* in prepubertal children), then gigantism ensues. If it occurs after the closure of the epiphyses (*i.e.*, in adults) then acromegaly ensues

Ans. 56. (d) All of the above

Ref http://en.wikipedia.org/wiki/Alpha-Amylase

α-Amylase is the major form of amylase found in humans and other mammals. Although found in many tissues, amylase is most prominent in *pancreatic juice* and *urine* which each have their own isoform of human α-amylase. Amylase is found in saliva and breaks starch down into maltose and dextrin. This form is also called ***ptyalin***. Ptyalin breaks large, insoluble starch molecules into soluble starches (amylodextrin, erythrodextrin, achrodextrin) producing successively smaller starches and ultimately maltose

Increased plasma levels in humans are found in:

- Salivary trauma (including anesthetic intubations).
- Mumps — due to inflammation of the salivary glands.
- Pancreatitis — because of damage to the cells that produce amylase.
- Renal failure — due to reduced excretion.

EXTRA EDGE

Remember, Total amylase readings of over **10X** the upper limit of normal (ULN) are suggestive of pancreatitis. **5-10x** times the ULN may indicate ileus or duodenal disease or renal failure, and lower elevations are commonly found in salivary gland disease

Ans. 57. (c) Hypo capnia

Ref http://en.wikipedia.org/wiki/Asterixis

Asterixis (Greek *a*, not + *stçrixis*, fixed position) is a *flapping tremor* of the wrist upon extension (dorsiflexion), sometimes said to resemble a "bird flapping its wings". Also called "liver flap", it can be a sign of **hepatic encephalopathy** (damage to brain cells due to inability of the liver to metabolize ammonia to urea). The exact cause is not known but it is thought to be related to *abnormal ammonia metabolism*.

Adams and Foley first described asterixis in 1949 in patients with severe liver failure and encephalopathy. Typically there are brief, arrhythmic interruptions of sustained voluntary muscle contraction causing brief lapses of posture, with a frequency of 3-5 Hz. It is bilateral, but may be asymmetrical.

Asterixis is seen most often in drowsy or stuporous patients with metabolic encephalopathies, especially in decompensated cirrhosis or *acute hepatic failure.* It is also seen in some patients with *renal failure* and azotemia, and in *carbon dioxide toxicity*. Asterixis can also be a feature of Wilson's disease, and *drug toxicity*.

Thus, friends we see that asterixis may be associated with hypercapnia (CO^2 toxicity) and not HYPOcapnia as the choice 'c' states.

Ans. 58. (b) Mitral valve prolapse

Ref http://en.wikipedia.org/wiki/Mitral_valve_prolapse

Common cause of M.R. with no evidence of Mitral Stenosis(MS) is Mitral valve prolapse (MVP).

Ref Davidson pg 456

Mitral valve prolapse (**MVP**) is a heart valve condition marked by the displacement of an abnormally thickened mitral valve leaflet into the left atrium during systole. In its non-classic form, MVP carries α low risk of complications. In severe cases of classic MVP, complications include mitral regurgitation, infective endocarditis, and — in rare circumstances — cardiac arrest usually resulting in sudden death.

- MVP is a common occurrence in individuals with the Marfans syndrome.

Ans. 59. (c) Will usually not have an underlying identifiable cause or condition

Ref http://en.wikipedia.org/wiki/Hypertension

Hypertension can be classified as either **essential** (primary) or **secondary**. Essential hypertension indicates that no specific medical cause can be found to explain a patient's condition. Secondary hypertension indicates that the high blood pressure is a result of (*i.e.* secondary to) another condition, such as kidney disease or certain tumors (especially of the adrenal gland).

Remember, Over 90% of adult hypertension has no clear cause and is therefore called **essential/ primary hypertension**. Often, it is part of the metabolic "syndrome X" in patients with insulin resistance: it occurs in combination with diabetes mellitus (type 2), combined hyperlipidemia and central obesity.

In hypertensive children most cases are **secondary hypertension**, and the cause should be pursued diligently

Ans.60. (a) Cholestatic jaundice

Ref http://en.wikipedia.org/wiki/jaundice

- Post-hepatic (or obstructive) jaundice, also called ***cholestasis***, is caused by an interruption to the drainage of bile in the biliary system.
- The most common causes are gallstones in the common bile duct, and pancreatic cancer in the head of the pancreas.
- Also, a group of parasites known as "liver flukes" live in the common bile duct, causing obstructive jaundice.
- Other causes include strictures of the common bile duct, ductal carcinoma, pancreatitis and pancreatic pseudocysts. A rare cause of obstructive jaundice is Mirizzi's syndrome.
- The presence of pale stools and dark urine suggests an obstructive or post-hepatic cause as normal feces get their color from bile pigments.
- Patients often complain of severe itching

Ans. 61. (d) Leptospirosis

Ref http://en.wikipedia.org/wiki/Leptospirosis

Leptospirosis (**Weil's disease**, **canicola fever**, **canefield fever**, **nanukayami fever**, **7-day fever** and many more)- is a bacterial ***zoonotic*** disease caused by spirochaetes of the genus *Leptospira* that affects humans and a wide range of animals, including mammals, birds, amphibians, and reptiles. It was first described by *Adolf Weil* in 1886

The infection is commonly transmitted to humans by allowing fresh water that has been contaminated by animal urine to come in contact with unhealed breaks in the skin, eyes or with the mucous membranes. Leptospiral infection causes a wide range of symptoms, and some infected persons may have no symptoms at all.

- Leptospirosis is a **biphasic disease** that begins with flu-like symptoms (fever, chills, myalgias, intense headache). The first phase resolves and the patient is asymptomatic briefly before the second phase begins.
- that is characterized by meningitis, liver damage (causing jaundice), and renal failure. Because of the wide range of symptoms the infection is often wrongly diagnosed. This leads to a lower registered number of cases than there really are.
- Symptoms of leptospirosis include high fever, severe headache, chills, muscle aches, and vomiting, and may include jaundice, red eyes, abdominal pain, diarrhea, and/or a rash.
- The symptoms in humans appear after 4-14 day incubation period

Diagnosis of leptospirosis is confirmed with tests such as Enzyme-Linked Immunosorbent Assay (ELISA) and PCR. Serological testing, the **MAT** (microscopic agglutination test), is considered the *gold standard* in diagnosing leptospirosis.

Aetiotropic drugs are **antibiotics,** such as **doxycycline**, penicillin, ampicillin, and amoxicillin (doxycycline can also be used as a prophylaxis*). There are no human vaccines*; animal vaccines are only for a few strains, and are only effective for a few months. Human therapeutic dosage of drugs is as follows: doxycycline 100 mg orally every 12 hours for 1 week or penicillin 1-1.5 MU every 4 hours for 1 week.

* Doxycycline 200-250 mg once a week is administered as a prophylaxis.

Ans. 62. (b) Amoebiasis

Ref http://www.health-disease.org/digestive-disorders/amoebiasis.htm

Amoebiasis: is an infection of the large intestine produced by a parasite *Entamoeba histolytica*. In a country like India almost 75% of the population suffers from this condition in view of the poor hygienic status of the population, flies, open hawking of cooked food. The common mode of spread is the fecal-oral route as also common food borne and water borne transmission. Infection can then spread from the intestines to other organs, e.g. liver, lungs and brain, via the venous system.

The E histolytica is present in **two forms** viz the amoebic motile form and the cyst form. The cyst is commonly spread through the oral route. In the small intestine the cyst wall disintegrates. Immature amoebae pass into the large intestine where they live in the lumen of the gut feeding on bacteria and debris.

About 9 out of 10 of those who have E. histolytica in their intestines do not develop any symptoms. However, sometimes the amoebas can start eating away at the wall of the intestine, causing diarrhoea and other symptoms. Amoebiasis, a type of gastro, is a cause of diarrhoea among travellers to developing countries. The cysts of Entamoeba Histolytica enter the small intestine and release active amoebic parasites (trophozoites), which invade the epithelial cells of the large intestines, causing ***flask-shaped ulcers***.

Some are common Symptoms of Amoebiasis :

- Abdominal (stomach) cramps.
- Blood-stained stools.
- Tenesmus (painful passage of stools).
- Tenderness in the lower abdominal region.
- High grade fever, severe abdominal pain and profuse diarrhoea occurs in children and in patients receiving steroids.
- Severe diarrhoea that contains blood or mucus.
- Sometimes allergic reactions can occur throughout the body, due to release of toxic substances or dead parasites inside the intestines.

Treatment

For amebic dysentery a multi-prong approach must be used, starting with one of:

- Metronidazole 500-750mg three times a day for 5-10 days.
- Tinidazole 2g once a day for 3 days is an alternative to metronidazole.

In addition to the above, to destroy *E. histolytica* in the colon:

- Paromomycin 500mg three times a day for 10 days.
- Diloxanide Furoate 500mg three times a day for 10 days.
- Iodoquinol 650mg three times a day for 20 days.

For amebic liver abscess:

- Metronidazole 400mg three times a day for 10 days
- Tinidazole 2g once a day for 6 days is an alternative to metronidazole.
- Diloxanide furoate 500mg three times a day for 10 days must always be given afterwards.

Ans. 63. (d) All the above

Ref http://clevelandclinicmeded.com/diseasemanagement/infectiousdisease/prophylaxis/prophylaxis.htm

First it is important to identify the situations where prophylaxis is indicated . The patients may be categorized into three categories:-

- High-Risk Category
  - Prosthetic cardiac valves, including bioprosthetic and homograft valves.
  - Previous bacterial endocarditis.
  - Complex cyanotic congenital heart disease (*e.g.,* single ventricle states, transposition of the great arteries, tetralogy of Fallot).
  - Surgically constructed systemic-pulmonary shunts or conduits.
- Moderate-Risk Category
  - Congenital cardiac malformations other than those listed in the high-risk and negligiblerisk categories.
  - Acquired valvular dysfunction (*e.g.,* rheumatic heart disease).

  - Hypertrophic cardiomyopathy.
  - Mitral valve prolapse with valvular regurgitation and/or thickened leaflets[1]
- Negligible-risk category (no greater risk than the general population)
  - Isolated secundum atrial septal defect.
  - Surgical repair of atrial septal defect, ventricular septal defect or patent ductus arteriosus (without residua beyond six months).
  - Previous coronary artery bypass graft surgery.
  - Mitral valve prolapse without valvular regurgitation or thickened leaflets.[1]
  - Physiologic, functional or innocent heart murmur.
  - Previous Kawasaki disease without valvular dysfunction.
  - Previous rheumatic fever without valvular dysfunction.
  - Cardiac pacemakers (intravascular and epicardial) and implanted defibrillators.

Now, we shall see the current guidelines by American Heart Association,1997

Endocarditis Prophylactic Regimens for Dental, Oral,Respiratory Tract, and Esophageal Procedures		
Situation	**Agent**	**Regimen**
Standard general prophylaxis	Amoxicillin	Adults: 2.0 g; children 50 mg/kg,orally 1 h before procedure
Unable to take oral medications	Ampicillin	Adults: 2.0 g IM or IV; children 50 mg/kg IM or IV within 30 min before procedure
Patient is allergic to penicillin	Clindamycin or	Adults: 600 mg; children 20 mg/kgorally 1 h before procedure
	or Cefadroxil[2] or cephalexin[2] or Azithromycin	Adults: 2 g; children 50 mg/kgorally 1 h before procedure
	or clarithromycin	Adults: 500 mg; children 15 mg/kgorally 1 h before procedure
Allergic to penicillin and unable to take oral medications	Clindamycin	Adults: 600 mg; children 20 mg/kgIV within 30 minutes before procedure
	or Cefazolin[2]	Adults: 1.0 g; children 25 mg/kg IM or IV within 30 min before procedure

Ans.64. (d) All of the above

Ref Ganong, 22nd ed, pg 500

To know the deficiencies associated with liver diseases, it is important to know the various functions of liver in body.

Principal functions of liver:

(1) Formation and secretion of bile.

(2) Metabolism of – glucose, amino acids, cholesterol, water soluble vitamins.

(3) Inactivation of toxins and hormones.

(4) Synthesis of plasma proteins, clotting factors, albumins, and immune cells.

Therefore, all the conditions mentioned in the question can be expected in a patient with liver disease.

Ans. 65. (c) Rheumatic fever

Ref http://www.nlm.nih.gov/medlineplus/ency/article/003940.htm

Rheumatic fever

Rheumatic fever is an *inflammatory disease* that may develop after an infection with streptococcus bacteria (such as strep throat or scarlet fever) and can involve the heart, joints, skin, and brain. Rheumatic fever primarily affects children between ages 6 and 15 and occurs approximately 20 days after strep throat or scarlet fever. In up to a third of cases, the underlying strep infection may not have caused any symptoms.

Symptoms

- Fever
- Joint pain, migratory arthritis — involving primarily knees, elbows, ankles, and wrists
- Joint swelling; redness or warmth.
- Abdominal pain.
- Skin rash (erythema marginatum).
  - Skin eruption on the trunk and upper part of arms or legs.
  - Eruptions that are ring-shaped or snake-like in appearance.
- Skin nodules.
- Sydenham's chorea — emotional instability, muscular weakness and rapid, uncoordinated jerky movements affecting primarily the face, feet and hands
- Epistaxis (nosebleeds)
- Cardiac (heart) involvement which may be asymptomatic or may result in shortness of breath, chest pain.

While Hemophilia is an inherited bleeding disorder, congenital heart diseases may be due to mutations in the NOTCH1 gene.

Ans. 66. (b) Multiple myeloma

Ref http://en.wikipedia.org/wiki/Multiple_myeloma

Investigations: in patient with multiple myeloma:

- The presence of unexplained anemia, kidney dysfunction, a high erythrocyte sedimentation rate (ESR) and a high serum protein (especially raised immunoglobulin) may prompt further testing.
- **Protein electrophoresis** of the blood and urine, which might show the presence of a *paraprotein* (monoclonal protein, or M protein) band, with or without reduction of the other (normal) immunoglobulins (known as immune paresis). One type of paraprotein is the **Bence Jones protein** which is a urinary paraprotein composed of free light chains. Light chains

precipitate when heated to 50 - 60 degrees C and re-dissolve at 90 -100 degrees C. These tests are essential in patients suspected of having Bence Jones proteins in their urine as these proteins don't react with the reagents normally utilized in urinalysis dipsticks. This leads to false negative results in people with Bence Jones proteins in their urine undergoing standard urinalysis.

- There are various rarer conditions which can produce Bence Jones proteins, such as Waldenström's macroglobulinemia and other malignanices. Quantitative measurements of the paraprotein are necessary to establish a diagnosis and to monitor the disease. The paraprotein is an abnormal immunoglobulin produced by the tumor clone. Very rarely, the myeloma is *nonsecretory* (not producing immunoglobulins).

In theory, multiple myeloma can produce all classes of immunoglobulin, but **IgG** paraproteins are most common, followed by IgA and IgM. IgD and IgE myeloma are very rare. In addition, light and or heavy chains (the building blocks of antibodies) may be secreted in isolation: κ- or λ-light chains or any of the five types of heavy chains (α-, γ-, ε-, μ- or δ-heavy chains).

- Additional findings include: a raised calcium (when osteoclasts are breaking down bone, releasing calcium into the bloodstream).
- raised serum creatinine due to reduced renal function, which may be due to paraprotein deposition in the kidney.

GENERAL SURGERY

Ans. 67. (a) Follicular carcinoma

Ref Manipal manual of surgery, pg234

FNAC is the investigation of choice in all carcinoma thyroid, except the Follicular variant. It should be remembered that FNAC cannot differentiate between a follicular adenoma and carcinoma. Hence if a patient presents with a solitary nodule, frozen section biopsy is the investigation of choice.

Ans. 68. (d) All of the above

Ref Manipal manual of surgery, pg 12

Causes of persistence of sinus and fistulae-

(a) Foreign bodies
(b) Persistent infection
(c) Distal obstruction
(d) Mobility/ absence of rest
(e) Epithelialization of the tract
(f) Malignancy
(g) Non-dependent drainage

Ans. 69. (b) Vermillion border of lower lip

Explained earlier, please refer KCET 07 A67

Ans. 70. (b) Posterior triangle nodes

Explained earlier, Please refer KCET 07 A66

Ans. 71. (c) Papillary carcinoma

Ref Manipal manual of surgery, pg

- May be due to irradiation to the neck or a complication of Hashimoto's thyroiditis.
- Contains colloid filled follicles (***psammoma bodies***).
- Pale, empty, nuclei- Orphan eyed nuclei Annie.
- May present as solitary nodule.
- Most common malignancy affecting thyroid.

Ans.72. (b) Vestigeal remnant of second branchial cleft

Ref Manipal manual of surgery, pg 166

Thyroglossal cyst is an example of ***tubulo-embryonic dermoid cyst***. It arises from thyroglossal tract (from foramen caecum to the isthmus of thyroid gland) lined by pseudostratified columnar ciliated epithelium.

Subhyoid is the most common site. The cyst is attached to the hyoid bone hence moves with tongue protrusion and deglutition movements.

Surgical management includes Sistrunk's operation wherein the entire thyroglossal tract is removed along with central portion of hyoid bone up to foramen caecum.

Ans. 73. (d) The junction of upper third and middle third of sternomastoid at its anterior border.

Explained earlier, please refer KCET-07 A64

ORAL PATHOLOGY

Ans. 74. (b) Parotid glands

Ref Shafer's, 5th ed, pg 347; Ref http://en.wikipedia.org/wiki/Sj%C3%B6gren's_syndrome

Sjögren's syndrome is an autoimmune disorder in which immune cells attack and destroy the exocrine glands that produce tears and saliva. It is named after Swedish ophthalmologist Henrik Sjögren (1899-1986), who first described it. Sjögren's syndrome is also associated with rheumatic disorders such as rheumatoid arthritis, and it is rheumatoid factor positive in 90 percent of cases.

The hallmark symptoms of the disorder are dry mouth and dry eyes (part of what are known as ***sicca symptoms***). In addition, Sjögren's syndrome may cause skin, nose, and vaginal dryness, and may affect other organs of the body, including the kidneys, blood vessels, lungs, liver, pancreas, and brain. Nine out of ten Sjögren's patients are women and the average age of onset is late 40s, although Sjögren's occurs in all age groups in both women and men 80% of the patients with Sjögren's syndrome have parotid enlargement.

EXTRA EDGE

DIAGNOSIS: apart from clinical evaluation, common tests employed are:

- Blood tests can be done to determine if a patient has high levels of antibodies that are indicative of the condition, such as *anti-nuclear antibody* (ANA) and rheumatoid factor, which are associated with autoimmune diseases. Typical Sjögren syndrome ANA patterns are SSA/Ro and SSB/La, of which SSB/La is far more specific; SSA/Ro is associated with numerous other autoimmune conditions but are often present in Sjögren's.
- The ***Schirmer test*** measures the production of tears: a strip of filter paper is held inside the lower eyelid for five minutes, and its wetness is then measured with a ruler.
- A slit-lamp examination is done to look for dryness on the surface of the eye. Salivary gland function can be tested by collecting saliva and determining the amount produced.
- A lip biopsy can reveal lymphocytes clustered around salivary glands, and damage to these glands due to inflammation.
- A sialography is an important tool wherein the gland gives a branchless fruit laden tree appearance.

Ans. 75. (b) Junctional nevus

Ref Shafer, 5th ed pg 120

In junctional nevus, the zone of demarcation is absent and nevus cells contact and seen to blend into surface epithelium. This overlying epithelium is thin and irregular and shows cells apparently crossing the junction and growing down into the connective tissue – ***abtropfung phenomenon*** or 'dropping off' effect. This junctional activity has serious implications as junctional nevi have been known to undergo malignant transformation.

Ans. 76. (a) Attrition

Ref Shafer, 5th ed pg 788

Attrition: is the physiologic wearing seen during a tooth to tooth contact. This occurs only on the occlusal and incisal, proximal surfaces of teeth. This is associated with aging process. This may be seen in deciduous teeth or permanent but severe attrition is generally not seen in deciduous dentition as they are not retained for a great period of time.

Ans. 77. (d) All the above

Ref http://en.wikipedia.org/wiki/Crouzon_syndrome

Crouzon Syndrome or Crouzon disease is a genetic disorder known as a branchial arch syndrome. Specifically, this syndrome affects the first branchial (or pharyngeal) arch, which is the precursor of the maxilla and mandible.

This syndrome is named after Octave Crouzon, a French physician who first described this disorder. He noted the affected patients were a mother and her daughter, implying a genetic basis. First called **"craniofacial dysostosis'.**

What occurs in the disease is that an infant's skull and facial bones, while in development, fuse early or are unable to expand. Thus, normal bone growth cannot occur. Fusion of different sutures lead to different patterns of growth of the skull. The most common involved are the coronal and Saggital sutures. As a result, the antero-posterior diameter is smaller than the transverse diameter giving a ***triangular frontal defect***.

Typical features

- The most notable characteristic of Crouzon Syndrome is cranial synostosis, as described above, but it usually presents as brachycephaly, which results in the appearance of a short and broad head.
- Exophthalmos (bulging eyes due to shallow eye sockets after early fusion of surrounding bones).
- hypertelorism (greater than normal distance between the eyes).
- psittichorhina (beak-like nose).
- A common occurrence is external strabismus, which can be thought of as opposite from the eye position found in Down Syndrome.
- Lastly, hypoplastic maxilla (insufficient growth of the midface) results in relative mandibular prognathism (chin appears to protrude despite normal growth of mandible) and gives the effect of the patient having a concave face.

EXTRA EDGE

Remember,

- **Trigonocephaly:** premature fusion of the ***metopic*** suture (part of the frontal suture which joins the two halves of the frontal bone of the skull) in which a V-shaped abnormality occurs at the front of the skull. It is characterized by the triangular prominence of the forehead and closely set eyes.
- **Brachycephaly:** also known as flat-head syndrome, occurs when ***coronal*** suture fuses prematurely, causing a shortened front-to-back diameter of the skull. The coronal suture is the fibrous joint that unites the frontal bone with the two parietal bones of the skull.
- **Plagiocephaly:** is a condition characterized by an ***asymmetrical distortion*** (flattening of one side) of the skull. It is a common finding at birth and may be the result of a restrictive intrauterine environment giving a "diamond" shaped head when seen from above.
- **Oxycephaly:** also known as *turricephaly* and high-head syndrome, is a term sometimes used to describe the premature closure of the ***coronal suture plus*** any other suture (lamboidal), or it may be used to describe the premature fusing of ***all sutures***. Oxycephaly is the most severe of the craniostenoses.
- **Dolichocephaly:** refers to fusion of the Saggital suture.
- Kleeblattschaedel - premature closure of all sutures.

Ans. 78. (a) Epithelial lining in ranula

Ref Shafer, 5th ed pg 750

Ranula generally arise form the sublingual gland but sometimes also form submandibular duct/ floor of mouth. It is a dome shaped, fluctuant swelling in the floor of the mouth with translucent blue color. It develops into slowly enlarging, painless swelling located lateral to midline of the floor of mouth.'

Ans. 79. (b) Shape abnormal, enamel brown

Ref Shafer's, 5th ed, pg, 67

Amelogenesis Imperfecta may be differentiated into three types:

- Hypolastic
- Hypocalcified
- Hypomature

Hypoplastic AI

- represent almost 60-73 percent of all cases.
- Both primary and permanent dentitions are involved in hereditary types.
- A mutation in *enamelin* gene has been identified as the etiology.
- The various types are – pitted, smooth, or rough.
- In mild types there are few small pit , grooves or fissures.
- These defects occur only before enamel calcification is complete. These are stained brown.
- The teeth lack normal enamel thickness in severe types.

Remember, the enamel is soft in hypomaturation types.

Ans. 80. (b) Aphthous Ulcers

Ref http://en.wikipedia.org/wiki/Apthous_ulcer ; Shafer 5th ed , pg 1044

An **ulcer** or **canker sore** is a type of mouth ulcer which presents as a painful open sore inside the mouth caused by a break in the mucous membrane. The condition is also called **aphthous stomatitis,** also known as "Sutton's Disease", especially if there are multiple or recurring mouth ulcers.

The exact cause of aphthous ulcers is unknown. Factors that provoke them include

- stress, fatigue, illness, injury from accidental biting, hormonal changes, menstruation, sudden weight loss, food allergies, the foaming agent in toothpaste (SLS), and
- ***deficiencies in vitamin B12, iron, and folic acid (malabsorption or inadequate intake)***
- Some drugs, such as nicorandil, also have been linked with mouth ulcers.
- Thought to be caused by an overreaction by the body's own immune system.
- There is a commonly held belief that another cause of apthous ulcers is gluten intolerance (***Coeliac disease***), whereby consumption of wheat, rye, barley and sometimes oats can result in chronic mouth ulcers. The oral manifestation includes severe glossitis, atrophy of filiform papillae, burning sensation in addition to the recurrent apthous ulcerations. These patients may experience benefit in eliminating breads, pastas, cakes, pies, cookies, scones, biscuits, beers and so on from their diet and substituting gluten-free varieties where available

Ans. 81. (d) Congenital syphilis

Explained Earlier Please Refer A82

Ans. 82. (c) Tongue

Ref Shafer, 5th ed, pg 155

Friends the key word in intra-oral. Consider the following points-

- SCC is the most common malignancy of oral cavity.
- SCC is frequently seen in pre-existent leukoplakia, OSMF.
- Affects tongue and buccal mucosa with more frequency.
- CA tongue accounts for 25-50 % of all intraoral cancers.
- M>F (except Scandinavian women with Plummer-Vinson syn).
- Lateral border lesions are highly metastatic.

Ans. 83. (d) All of the above

Ref http://en.wikipedia.org/wiki/Cytogenetics# note-1

- **Cytogenetics** is the study of the structure of chromosome material.
- It includes routine analysis of G-Banded chromosomes, other cytogenetic banding techniques, as well as molecular cytogenetics such as fluorescent in situ hybridization (FISH) and comparative genomic hybridization (CGH).
- Modern cytogenetics is generally said to have begun in 1956 with the discovery that normal human cells contain 46 chromosomes by Tjio and Levan.
- With the advent of harvest procedures which allowed easy enumeration of chromosomes, discoveries were quickly made in abnormalities arising from nondysjunction events which cause cells with aneusomy (additions or deletions of entire chromosomes).
- In 1959 ***Lejeune,Gautier M, Turpin MR*** discovered patients with Down syndrome had an extra copy of chromosome 21. Down syndrome is also referred to as trisomy 21. In 1960 Nowell[3] discovered a small chromosome, dubbed the Philadelphia chromosome, which was shown to be the cause of Chronic myelogenous leukemia. 13 years later this was shown by Janet Rowley to be a translocation of chromosomes 9 and 22.

Ans. 84. (b) Prematurely erupted primary teeth

Ref Shafer, 5th ed , pg 67

The pre-deciduous dentition usually represents hornified epithelial structures without roots occurring on the gingiva over the crest of the ridge that are easily removed. However, they should be distinguished from the so-called '***natal***' teeth which are prematurely erupted true deciduous teeth and are not to be extracted.

Ans. 85. (a) Origin and migration of neural crest cell

Ref http://en.wikipedia.org/wiki/Treacher Collins Syndrome

Treacher Collins syndrome (also known as **Franceschetti-Zwahlen-Klein syndrome** or **mandibulofacial dysostosis**) is a rare genetic disorder characterized by craniofacial deformities.

Treacher Collins syndrome is found in 1 in 10,000 births. The typical physical features include downward slanting eyes, a small lower jaw, and malformed or absent ears. It is named after Edward Treacher Collins (1862–1932), the English surgeon and ophthalmologist who described its essential traits in 1900.

Treacher Collins syndrome is inherited in an ***autosomal-dominant pattern***.

One known cause of this syndrome is a mutation in the *TCOF1* gene, at chromosome 5-q32-q33.1. The protein coded by this gene is called ***treacle*** . Even though the genetic alterations causing TCS have been uncovered, the mechanism underlying its pathogenesis and the function of treacle remain unknown. *It has been hypothesized to assist in protein sorting and cell migration during particular stages in embryonic development, particularly that of the structures of the head and face.*

So friends, option 'a' is the most appropriate answer here.

Ans. 86. (a) Multilocular Radiolucent appearance

Ref Shafer's textbook of oral pathology, 5th ed, pg 371

Botryoid odontogenic cyst is a polycystic variant of lateral periodontal cyst developing through cystic transformation of multiple islands of dental lamina rests. It is an unusual form of cyst reported in 1973 by Weathers and Waldron. They described two cases of cysts which had multilocular pattern apparent radiographically, histologically and even clinically at the time of surgical removal.

Ans. 87. (d) More Radio-opaque

Reference with text

Friends this was a tough one. The incomplete nature of the question hasn't helped the cause either. Now hemolytic anemia, constitute a diverse set of conditions including infections, hereditary spherocytosis, G6PD deficiency, sickle cell disease, hemophilia etc.

Usually, the erythroid elements of the bone marrow are hyperplastic in an attempt to compensate for the anemia. This creates a characteristic radiolucency in the radiographs. However, contrary to this the lamina dura appears ***dense and distinct***.

Ref Burket, pg 434

However, *White and Pharoah Pg 536* states that the lamina dura appears ***thinned out*** in patients with Thalassemia.

If the question is referring to the congenital type (Erythroblastosis fetalis) there may be deposition of blood pigment in the enamel and dentin of the developing teeth, giving them a green, brown or blue hue, ***but,*** it does not involve teeth or portions of teeth developing after cessation of hemolysis, shortly after birth. Hence the lamina dura is essentially ***normal*** in such conditions.

Ref Shafer's textbook of oral pathology, 5th ed, pg 1053

So friends, all you can do is hope for a complete question next time. Personally, we feel that Burket is more specific and hence we recommend option 'D' as the answer.

Ans. 88. (b) Intrusion of deciduous predecessor

Ref Shafer, 5th ed, pg 56

Dilacerations refers to a sharp bend or curve, in the root or crown of a formed tooth. The condition is thought to be due to trauma to the developing tooth bud as a result the position of calcified tooth is changed.

Thus of the given choices, 'b' indicates a traumatic condition which may affect the underlying permanent tooth.

Ans.89. (a) Disappears on stretching

Ref Burket, 10th ed ,pg 86

Leukoedema is a common mucosal alteration that appears faint white and wrinkled. Although it can not be scrapped off, *it disappears upon stretching*. No malignant change has ever been reported.

Ans. 90. (a) Non-inflammatory non-neoplastic swelling of major salivary glands

Ref White and Pharoah,5th ed pg 670.

Sialosis/ Sialadenosis is a non-specific, non-neoplastic, non-inflammatory enlargement of salivary glands mainly the parotid glands. It is generally not associated with any etiological agent however metabolic and secretory disorders have been implicated.

Ans. 91. (b) Koplick's spots

Ref Shafer 5th ed, ph 476

Oral lesions of Measles (Rubeola) are prodromal frequently occurring 2-3 days before the cutaneous rashand are pathognomonic of the disease. These are known as **Koplik's spots**. Immune reactions to the virus in the endothelial cells of dermal capillaries play an important role in development of these spots. They are usually found on the buccal mucosa and appear as small irregularly shaped bluish white flecks surrounded by a bright red margin.

Ans. 92. (c) Medullary portion of the bone

Ref Shafer, 5th ed , pg 682

Osteomyelitis is defined as an inflammation of the medullary bone. Changes in the calcified tissue are secondary to the soft tissue content.

Most commonly caused by – Staphylococcus aureus. Dental infections are the prime source for osteomyelitis of jaws.

Ans. 93. (c) Sub-maxillary space

Ref Shafer 5th ed , pg 706

Ludwig's angina refers to bilateral severe cellulites beginning usually in the submandibular (sub-maxillary) space and secondarily involving the submental and sublingual spaces. The most common cause is spread of infection from infected root apices of second and third mandibular molars. The infection from this area drains into submandibular space which then spreads to other spaces.

Ans. 94. (b) Coxsackie virus A-10

Ref Shafer, 5th ed, pg 473

Infections by Coxsackie group of viruses:

(*i*) **herpangina:** groupA type 6,8,10,16,22. clinically, presents with mild symptoms resembling herpes but the lesions are located more posteriorly.

(*ii*) **ALP (Acute Lymphonodular Pharyngitis):** A10; lesions include papules but **not** vesicles and ulcers.

(*iii*) **Hand, Foot and Mouth disease:** A16 ; lesions are severe and numerous.

Ans. 95. (c) Presence of sulphur granules in the pus

Ref Shafer, 5th ed, pg 446

Actinomycosis: chronic granulomatous suppurating and fibrosing disease.

- Caudative agent: *Actinomyces israelii, naeslundi,viscosus*, etc.
- Cervicofacial is the most common of the 3 types present
- indurations ('woody'), discoloration, swelling with multiple abscesses draining with liberation of characteristic "sulphur granules".
- The granules consist primarily of microorganisms. This is better demonstrated by the dye methinamine silver.
- Other types- abdominal and pulmonary.
- Treatment includes penicillin and tetracycline.

Ans. 96. (d) Submandibular duct

Ref Shafer, 5th ed , pg 754

Sialolithiasis commonly affects middle-aged adults. The submandibular gland is the most frequently involved because of the long, narrow and torturous nature of the duct, the high mucin content of secretion and the fact that drainage occurs against the gravity.

Ans. 97. (c) Lateral borders of tongue

Ref Shafer, 5th ed, pg 493

OHL frequently appears bilaterally on the lateral borders of the tongue as painless, faint white vertical streaks or thickened and furrowed areas with shaggy keratotic surface giving a corrugated appearance. Other areas where it may occur are floor of mouth, buccal mucosa, etc. EB virus is associated with the etiology.

Ans.98. (d) All of the above

Ref Manipal Manual of Surgery, pg 210

Pleomorphic adenoma – F>M (6:4), 4th – 6th decade.

Ominous signs of malignancy-

(1) Fixation to surrounding and deeper tissues.

(2) Sudden rapid growth.

(3) Presence of red, dilated veins over the surface.

(4) Facial nerve paralysis, sudden pain.
(5) Stony hard consistency and enlarged lymph nodes.

Ans. 99. (c) Malignant lymphoma

Ref Shafer.5th ed, pg 349

Sjogren's syndrome or *Sicca* syndrome – F>M (10x) ; >40yrs.

The major complicating factor is the development of pseudo and malignant lymphoma. The risk is estimated at 6.4 per 100 cases/year, mainly Non-Hodgkin's types and other B-cell origin.

Ans. 100. (d) Only a & b

Reference with text

Scurvy or Vitamin C def manifests chiefly in gingival and periodontal tissue.

(1) Inflamed marginal gingiva. In later stages the gingiva becomes 'boggy', ulcerates and bleeds.
(2) Dental findings include irregular dentin with a heavy, basophilic staining line between pulp and dentin.
(3) peri-follicular hemorrhages.

HISTOLOGICAL FINDINGS

- ***epiphyseal plate is calcified but non-ossified***
- The Lattice increase in width developing more fragile zones which when later freacture and this creates the particular Trummerfeld-zone.
- The area beneath this zone is free of any hematopoietic cells and made up of Connective Tissue cells, called the Gerustmark.

Remember, in absence of Vit C there is absence of hydroxylation of proline.

And humans can't synthesize Vit C due to absence of an enzyme, L-gulonolactone.

Because of this there is endothelial dysintegrity due to immature collagen.

Ref Shafer, 5th ed, pg 885

Leukemia- Often the patient with leukemia presents with gingival hyperplasia, hemorrhage, petechiae and ulceration of the mucosa. This 'boggy' gingiva is the most constant feature of leukemia except in edentulous patients. In severe cases the teeth may be almost completely hidden. This swelling is due to leukemic infiltration in areas of mild chronic irritation. Rapid loosening of teeth due to periodontal destruction is also a common feature.

Ref Shafer, 5th ed, pg 1071

Ans. 101. (C) Granular cell ameloblastoma

Ref Shafer, 5th ed , pg 387

Ameloblastom subtypes:

(1) Follicular: most common variant. Cyst formation is very common in this type.
(2) Plexiform : double rows of columnar cells, and cystic degeneration.
(3) Acanthomatous : squamous metaplasia with keratin formation, usually occur in the follicular variant.

(4) Granular : coarse granules, eosinophilic cytoplasm with marked aggressiveness and high propensity for recurrence.
(5) Basal cell : resembles basal cell carcinoma and is the rarest of the variant.
(6) Desmoplastic : dense collagen stroma, hyalinized and hypocellular with classic islands of follicular ameloblastoma.

ORAL MEDICINE AND RADIOLOGY

Ans. 102. (d) All the above

Ref *http://en.wikipedia.org/wiki/Ionizing_radiation*

The biological effects of radiation are thought of in terms of their effect on living cells. For low levels of radiation exposure, the biological effects are so small they may not be detected in epidemiological studies. The body repairs many types of radiation and chemical damage. Biological effects of radiation on living cells may result in a variety of outcomes, including:

- Cells experience DNA damage and are able to detect and repair the damage.
- Cells experience DNA damage and are unable to repair the damage **(teratogenesis)**. These cells may go through the process of programmed cell death, or apoptosis, thus eliminating the potential genetic damage from the larger tissue.
- Cells experience a non-lethal DNA mutation that is passed on to subsequent cell divisions. This mutation may contribute to the formation of a **cancer**.

Other observations at the tissue level are more complicated. These include:

- In some cases, a small radiation dose reduces the impact of a subsequent, larger radiation dose. This has been termed an 'adaptive response' and is related to hypothetical mechanisms of ***hormesis.***
- Cells that are not 'hit' by a radiation track but are located nearby may express damage or alterations in normal function, presumably after communication between the 'hit' cell and neighboring cells occurs. This has been termed the 'bystander effect'.

The progeny of a cell that survives radiation exposure may have increased probabilities for **mutation**. This has been termed 'genomic instability'.

Ans. 103. (a) The movement of electrons

Ref. White and Pharaoh; oral radiology, principles and interpretation, 5th edition, pg8

The movement of electrons: The electrons emitted by the incandescent filament into a narrow beam in x-ray tube are directed at a small rectangular area on the anode called the *focal spot*. The electrons move in this direction because they are repelled by the negatively charged cathode and attracted by positively charged anode. The x-ray tube is evacuated to prevent collision of the moving electrons with gas molecules, which would significantly reduce their speed. This also prevents oxidation and burn out of the filament.

Ans. 104. (d) Equal to the energy of electron that hits the nucleus of a target atom

Ref White and Pharoah, pg 12

Bremsstrahlung interactions

- Are the primary sources of x-ray photons from an x-ray tube.
- Produced when a high-speed electron is suddenly stopped/slowed at target.
- If the high speed electron hits the nucleus of target atom, all its kinetic energy is transforms into a single x-ray photon.
- ***E (incident e) = E (photon) = kVp across the tube***
- When , it misses the nucleus, it interacts with the positively charged nuclei, the closer the high speed e^- approaches, the greater is the generation of photons.

Ans. 105. (c) Reduction of dose to the patient

Ref. White and Pharaoh, textbook of oral radiology, 5th ed, pg 75

The presence of intensifying screens creates an image receptor that is 10-60 times more sensitive to x-rays than the film alone. Thus, use of intensifying screens means a substantial reduction in the dose of x radiation to which the patient is exposed. Intensifying screens are used with films for virtually all extra oral radiography, including panoramic, cephalometric and skull projections.

CONSERVATIVE DENTISTRY AND ENDODONTICS

Ans.106. (d) All of the above

Reference with text

Retraction cords provide a unique method of isolation wherein a retraction cord (plain or impregnated) is used to reflect the marginal gingiva away from tooth without damaging the supporting structure.

However carefully done, there is some absorption of epinephrine into the systemic circulation through the gingival sulcus. Hence to understand the question, we should know the various absolute and relative contraindications of the use of epinephrine:

(1) **Hyperthyroidism:** absolute C/I for the use of epinephrine. Thyroxine sensitizes the myocardium to epinephrine.

Ref KDT, pg125

(2) **Diabetes mellitus:** epinephrine by virtue of its â agonistic actions, worsens the sugar profile of the patient (induces glycogenolysis, rise in serum free fatty acids).

Ref KDT, pg124

(3) ***CVS disorders:*** conditions like ischemic events, stroke, etc are common C/I to the use of epinephrine. In fact, any elective treatment is postponed until next 6 months.

Ref Carranza, pg 533

Ans. 107. (b) Smooth broach

Ref Grossman, 11th ed, pg 191

Grossman has classified endodontic instruments according too their use as:

(1) Exploring: to locate the canal orifice and assist in obtaining patency *e.g.,* smooth broaches and endodontic explorer.

(2) Debridement: to extirpate the pulp and remove debris , *e.g.,* barbed broach.

(3) Shaping: to shape the canal laterally and apically *e.g.,* reamers and files.

(4) Obturating: to cement and pack GP into root canals e.g. plugger, spreaders, lentulospirals.

Ans. 108. (c) Calcium Hydroxide

Ref Sturdevent,4th ed pg 170-171

Liners are relatively thin layers of materials used primarily to provide a barrier to protect the dentin from residual reactants diffusing out of a restoration or oral fluids that may leak from defective restorations. They provide some thermal and electrical insulation as well. Some may even provide pulpal treatment.

Liners may be thin (1-50μm), or thick liners (0.2-1 mm) .thin liners may further be: solution liners (2-5 μm) or suspension liners (20 – 25 μm). Light cured calcium hydroxide cement is the material of choice for the use as a liner.

Ans. 109. (d) Improper reactor positioning

Ref Grossman, 11th ed, pg 296-300

Cardinal principles for all flap design:

(1) Base wider than free end to ensure good circulation.

(2) Incisions should be made with firm, continuous motion and perpendicular to cortical bone, to avoid ragged margins that may retard healing.

(3) The flap should be retracted properly using passive pressure.

(4) Releasing incisions should be made to prevent stretching and tearing during suturing.

Retraction is achieved using a periosteal elevator. The flap can be held passively in this position using periosteal or Senn retractor. Post surgical swelling is mainly due to flap injury caused during retraction and keeping the trauma to minimum reduces the post-operative sequels.

Ans. 110. (d) Volume of solution

Ref Grossman, 11th ed, pg 188

Several investigators have shown that unless adequate irrigation is part of the canal process, debris will be left behind regardless of the irrigant used. The clearance of debris from the canal was proportional to the amount of irrigant used.

- **NaOCl 5.2%:** is the most effective irrigant for removing loose debris.
- **Hydrogen peroxide 3%:** via its effervescent action forces debris out of canal and kills anaerobic microorganisms.
- **EDTA 14%:** removes the smear layer and other debris due to its chelating action.

Hence alternating use of irrigating solutions are advocated for complete debridement.

Ans.111. (d) Carbamide peroxide 15%

Please refer KCET 07 Answer 125

Ans.112. (b) Mesio buccal root

Ref Grossman, 11th ed, pg161

The mesio-buccal root of Maxillary first molar has 1 root and 1 canal in 64% of cases. In 22% of the cases the MB canal is often divided to form a second canal. Only 14 % of these are well separated.

Ans.113. (b) 75 + 15°

Ref Grossman, 11th ed, pg194

The tip angle of an instrument should be standardized at <u>75+/- 15^0</u>

Other specifications include instrument size should increase by 0.05mm at D_1 between No's 10 and 60 and later by 0.1mm from No.60-150

Ans.114. (a) Diamond shaped blank

Ref Grossman, 11th ed, pg 196

K-flex files are prepared from <u>rhomboidal or diamond shaped</u> blanks that has been twisted .This improves the flexibility and cutting efficiency of the instrument. The rhomboidal blank produces alternating high and low flutes that are supposed to make the instrument more efficient.

Ans.115. (d) Fibroblasts & osteoblasts

Ref Grossman, 11th ed , pg 122

Fish described 4 zones in peri-radicular infection and reaction:

(1) **Zone of infection:** characterized by PML's,+ microorganism in the center.
(2) **Zone of Contamination:** round cell infiltration+ destruction by toxins from bacteria+ bony lacunae appear empty+ Lymphocytes predominate.
(3) **Zone of Irritation:** Macrophages+ osteoclasts, toxins get diluted, live bone cells.
(4) **Zone of Stimulation:** Fibroblasts + osteoblasts, mild toxin acts as stimulant, collagen and new bone laid down in irregular fashion.

Ans.116. (c) The dentist must proceed with the understanding that an unexplored or unfilled canals is worse than perforations

Ref Grossman, 11th ed, pg 219

Read the following lines from Grossman:

"When a pulp stone seems to occlude the entire root canal, one should patiently explore the canal with a fine instrument, and with a rotary motion try to bypass the obstruction."

A close scrutiny of the radiograph should be made for any sign of a root canal. If none is apparent, and if no area of rarefaction is present and the tooth is asymptomatic, no attempt should be made to create an opening through the apical foramen. In such cases, it must be assumed that the foramen has become sealed with secondary cementum. However if the tooth is symptomatic, access should be obtained either with EDTA or root resection/retrograde filling. "

So, from the above lines, we shall conclude that although calcified canals may be left with provisional prognosis, treatment may be required at a later date. So the dentists should always keep in mind that an unexplored or unfilled canals has worse prognosis than perforations.

Ans.117. (d) Backward caries

Ref Sturdevant 4th ed, pg 275

- **Forward caries**: when the caries cone in enamel is greater or at least equal to that of dentin.
- **Backward caries:** When the spread of caries along DEJ exceeds the caries in the contiguous enamel.
- **Residual caries:** caries remaining after excavation and tooth preparation.
- **Recurrent caries:** caries that occur at junction of restoration and tooth and progresses under the restoration.

Ans.118. (d) Class VI lesion

Ref Vimal Sikri, pg 128

G.V.Black in his original classification gave five classes based on cavity location. Later ***Simon*** added a sixth class which included incisal edges and cusp tips of all the teeth.

Ans.119. (c) Primary cutting edge angle

Explained Earlier, Please Refer KCET-07 A133.

Ans.120. (b) 17% EDA+25% NaOCl

Ref Ingle 5th ed, pg 505.

17% EDTA (pH 7.3) is a potent chelating agent which removes only calcified tissue while NaOCl removes organic material. Hence it is advised to use an alternating regime of EDTA and NaOCl to remove the smear layer efficiently.

Ans.121. (c) Streptococcus mutans

Ref Sturdevant, pg 74

Habitat	Predominant species
Mucosa	S. mitis, S. salivarius, S. sanguis
Tongue	S. salivarius ; S. sanguis
Teeth (non-carious)	S. sanguis
Gingival crevice	Fusobacterium, Speirochaeta, Veillonella
Enamel caries	Streptococcus mutans
Dentinal caries	S. mutans ; Lactobacilli
Root caries	Actinomyces species

Ans.122. Sorry friends, we just could not make out what the exact choices are. But remember that in normal caries immune persons Lactobacilli count is below <u>1000 CFUmL</u>

Ans.123. (c) Streptococcus mutans

Explained earlier, Refer Answer 121

Ans.124. (d) Sterile paper points

Ref Grossman, 11th ed, pg 238

Samples from the root canal may be easily collected using sterile paper point. A fresh, sterile absorbent point is inserted into the canal and kept for atleast1min. It is then removed by sterile cotton plier and dropped into test tube containing medium.

Sampling for anaerobes is more complicates and involves the use of *Luer-Lok* syringe and Anaport vial. With chopped meat glucose broth as medium.

ORAL AND MAXILLO-FACIAL SURGERY

Ans.125. (c) Guerin fracture

Ref Manipal manual of surgery, pg 280

Rene Le Fort in 1901 gave the classification as:

Le Fort I – Guerin's fracture

Le Fort II- Pyramidal fracture

Le Fort III – Transverse/high/craniofacial disjunction

Ans.126. (a) Lingual nerve

Ref http://www.oralhealthjournal.com/issues/ISarticle.asp

Different surgical techniques for mandibular third molar removal have been felt to potentially affect the frequency of lingual nerve damage and as well the IAN. The "Lingual Split-Bone Technique" is considered to result in a higher frequency of nerve disturbances than the "Buccal Approach."

The lingual Split-bone technique was first developed in the United Kingdom (UK), where practices were largely hospital based and the use of chisels and osteotomes predominated. A purely lingual approach had been described by Warwick James.

Sir William Kelsey Fry: as later described by Ward in 1956,4 developed the buccal approach in conjunction with the lingual split. This technique involves the reflection of tissues buccally, distally and lingually in order to expose the bone and tooth from all aspects.

A periosteal elevator, usually a Howarth's, is placed between the lingual periosteum and the lingual plate of bone. Chisels are used for socket saucerization and the tooth delivered distolingually. Ward has stated the advantages of this technique when the tooth is in lingual version, are "speed, elimination of dead space and better healing." The primary goal of using a lingual flap retractor is to protect the lingual nerve during bone removal and tooth elevation.

Bone and tooth are removed using a drill from a buccal direction. The goal in both techniques is the same, namely, to minimize the incidence of ***lingual nerve injury*** during mandibular third molar removal.

Ans.127. (b) Antioxidant for vasoconstrictor

Ref Shobha tandon, pg 462

Composition of LA solution

(1) **LA agent:** Lignocaine 2% with 1:1,00,000 epinephrine.

(2) **Vasoconstrictor:** to counteract the dilating property of LA agent. Reduces the systemic absorption, prolongs the duration and reduces bleeding.

(3) **Reducing agent:** vasoconstrictors are unstable and oxidize, in exposure of sunlight. To prevent this, a small amount of sodium metabisulphite is added.

(4) **Preservative:** methylparaben are now replaced by caprylhydrocuprinotoxin as preservatives of LA solution.

(5) **Fungicide:** thymol serves as anti-fungal agent.

(6) Vehicle: as modified Ringer Lactate solution.

Ans.128 (c) Callus

Ref http://www.emedicine.com/ent/topic765.htm

Distraction osteogenesis,

- also called callus distraction, callotasis, osteodistraction, is a surgical process used for the reconstruction of skeletal deformities and for the lengthening of bones (as limb lengthening or particularly leg lengthening when referred to the lower limbs).
- The bone is surgically (with a corticotomy) split in two segments (therefore creating a bone fracture) and the two ends of the bone are gradually moved apart (distraction phase) slowly enough that new bone can form in the gap.
- When the aimed length has been reached, a consolidation phase follows. The uniqueness and value of distraction osteogenesis lie in its ability to simultaneously expand both the bone volume and the surrounding soft tissues.

Ilizarov is the father of modern distraction osteogenesis. In 1951, Ilizarov developed a technique for repairing complex fractures or nonunions of the long bones. Later research by Ilizarov demonstrated that the tension-stress effect caused an increase in metabolic activity, an increase in cellular proliferation, and a neovascular ingrowth similar to normal endochondral ossification.

Mandibular retrognathia is one of the most common craniofacial deformities; approximately 10% of the populations have significant dental overjet. Mandibular retrognathia can be congenital or acquired. Congenital causes include hemifacial microsomia, Treacher Collins syndrome, Pierre Robin syndrome, and mandibular hypoplasia. Acquired causes of mandibular retrognathia include trauma (ie, condylar fractures occurring at an early age and resulting in bony ankylosis or disrupted growth) and previous surgery for developmental cysts or tumors.

Although less common than retrognathia, the mandible can also exhibit a transverse deficiency, resulting in a severe malocclusion and anterior dental crowding. This condition is difficult to correct with traditional osteotomies, and multiple extractions are often necessary. Distraction osteogenesis of the mandible has become a commonplace procedure with the flexibility to allow the surgeon to address a wide variety of mandibular defects.

Pathophysiology

- After osteotomy is performed, a hematoma begins to organize in the latency period.
- Pluripotential mesenchymal cells are activated into fibroblasts and osteoblasts, and type I collagen is laid down parallel to the vector of distraction.
- Bony trabeculae grow into the fibrous area from the periphery, parallel to the line of tension that occurs during the distraction phase.
- A bridge of immature bone forms across the distraction gap.
- During the consolidation phase, bony remodeling begins.
- The regenerate eventually matures into osseous tissue similar to the native bone.

Soft tissue also has the ability to grow linearly along lines of tension. This is referred to as *distraction histogenesis*. Skin, muscle, nerves, and vascular tissue are generated, not stretched. The advantage is obvious, especially for severe retrognathia, in which the stretched soft tissue envelope can contribute to relapse when a traditional mandibular osteotomy is performed for a large (>10 mm) advancement.

Distraction osteogenesis is **indicated** in the following cases:

- Severe retrognathia associated with a syndrome (*e.g.*, Pierre Robin syndrome, Treacher Collins syndrome), especially in infants and children who are not candidates for traditional osteotomies.
- Unilateral hypoplasia of the mandible (*e.g.*, hemifacial microsomia).
- Nonsyndromic mandibular hypoplasia associated with a dental malocclusion (especially if the advancement exceeds the capabilities of a traditional osteotomy or if the patient is hesitant to undergo a bone graft harvest with the associated morbidity).
- Mandibular transverse deficiency associated with a dental malocclusion and dental crowding.
- Severe OSA (respiratory disturbance index [RDI] >60) and in patients who are obese (body mass index [BMI] >28).
- Mandibular hypoplasia due to trauma and/or ankylosis of the temporomandibular joint.
- Mandibular continuity defects resulting from excision of tumors and/or aggressive developmental cysts.
- Shortened vertical height of the alveolar bone (Distraction of the alveolar segment can be performed to increase the vertical height in preparation for osteointegrated dental implant placement. In patients that have had a mandibular reconstruction with a free fibular bone graft, the fibular segment can be distracted vertically to facilitate dental implant placement.

No absolute **contraindications** to treatment exist. However, relative contraindications are as follows:

- Patients who are unable or unwilling to comply with the distraction schedule are not ideal candidates for this procedure.
- Mandibular distraction osteogenesis has been performed on infants as young as nine days old (Tibesar, 2006), but more difficulty is encountered when dealing with small fragile bones in the placement of the distraction device.

- Adequate bone stock must be available to accept the device and to provide adequate surface area of the osteotomy sites for regeneration.
- Distraction osteogenesis of the mandible may be used on patients who have received prior radiation treatment. However, this procedure must be performed with caution because these patients are more likely to develop complications and to experience delays in wound healing.
- In older patients, the decreased number of mesenchymal stem cells may impair bone healing at the distraction site.

Postoperative details

The traditional latency period is **5-7 days**. Young children have an increased bone metabolism and may have a latency period as short as 24-48 hours, without affecting ultimate consolidation. Waiting too long increases the risk of bony union; waiting 7 days is advised if the periosteum is excessively traumatized. In addition, if both hard tissue and soft tissue are less than ideal in quality or quantity, increasing the latency period may be considered.

According to most study results, the recommended rate of distraction is **1 mm/d**. A slower rate could result in premature bony union, whereas a faster rate could result in a fibrous union. The inferior alveolar nerve seems to tolerate a distraction rate of 1 mm/d. Ilizarov recommended a continuous rhythm for distraction; however, this is not feasible in the clinical setting, so a rhythm of 1-2 times per day is recommended. The surgeon or a responsible adult should activate the appliance. During a bilateral mandibular advancement, an anterior open bite tends to develop; this can be corrected at the end of advancement with orthodontic elastics.

The consolidation phase is typically **8 weeks**, although some adults may require up to 12 weeks of consolidation. During this phase, the fixation must be rigid enough to prevent the formation of fibrous tissue but not too rigid to prevent physiologic loading of the new bone. The formation of the regenerate can be monitored with serial radiographs or CT scans.

Distraction osteogenesis has many advantages over traditional mandibular osteotomies, as delineated below.

(1) Distraction osteogenesis decreases the need for bone grafting for large (>10 mm) mandibular advancements; one can achieve 20 mm or more of advancement without a bone graft and the associated donor site morbidity, scarring, and potential for infection.

(2) The procedure can be performed in infants and children, who would otherwise not be candidates for mandibular osteotomy because of the interference with the developing tooth buds and/or insufficient bone to safely perform a traditional osteotomy. In addition, distraction osteogenesis often has obviated the need for a tracheotomy in newborns and infants with micrognathia and airway obstruction.

(3) Distraction osteogenesis results in less distortion and loading of the temporomandibular joint than sagittal split osteotomy.

(4) Distraction osteogenesis can be performed in 3 dimensions, that is, advancing, widening, and increasing vertical height of the basal mandibular bone. In addition, the vector and the amount of movement can be tailored to each patient, especially in those with significant facial asymmetry.

(5) Distraction osteogenesis can be used to increase ramus height.

(6) Greater patient acceptance exists with this procedure, especially with the development of low-profile intraoral devices.

(7) Distraction osteogenesis appears to have a decreased potential for relapse, especially with large advancements.

(8) Distraction osteogenesis seems to limit the likelihood of damaging the inferior alveolar nerve.

(9) Widening the mandible, which is difficult to do with traditional osteotomies, is possible.

(10) Due to the process of distraction histogenesis, resistance to advancement by the soft tissue envelope is decreased.

Ans.129. (d) Genioglossus, geniohyoid and posterior belly of digastric

Ref Killey's , 4th ed , pg 13

When a bilateral parasymphyseal fracture occurs it is usually displaced posteriorly under the influence of genioglossus, and to lesser extent geniohyoid and digastric muscles.

Contrary to the common belief, tongue doesn't always fall back and obstruct the oropharynx because it is still firmly attached to the hyoid bone. Also, the intrinsic muscles of tongue keep it in a forward position. Only when the consciousness is lost, the tongue control is lost.

Ans.130. (d) Cavernous sinus thrombosis

Ref BDC, 4th ed , pg 116.

ABDUCENT nerve

- The sixth cranial nerve supplies the lateral rectus muscle of the eyeball. One nerve fiber supplies only 6 muscle fibers.
- The nerve is attached to the lower border of *pons* opposite the upper end of pyramid of medulla.
- It enters the cavernous sinus at its *posterior wall* lateral to dorsum sellae and superior to apex of petrous temporal bone. In the cavernous sinus , it lies lateral to ICA and then infero-lateral.
- Sixth nerve paralysis is one of the most *common* localizing signs with raised intra cranial pressure (as a result of infection, etc). Its susceptibility is due to its long course and a sharp bend over the petrous temporal bone.
- Paralysis of 6th nerve results in medial /convergent squint and diplopia.

Ans.131. (a) Nerve block like inferior alveolar

Ref Burket, pg 471

Oral surgical procedures have the greatest potential of hemorrhage amongst all dental procedures. Appropriate precautionary measure allows surgery to be performed safely. A single bolus injection of factors assures a pre-operative level of 40-50%.

Canadian guidelines

- Factor VIII- 40-50% (20-25 U/kg)
- Factor IX- - 40-50 U/kg

PAIN control: intra-pulpal anesthesia are the safest and effective. Even periodontal ligament injection and gingival papillary injections can be given with little risk.

Block injections including inferior alveolar nerve, infra-orbital etc can be given at concentration level around 20-30% ***although***; risk is still there for hematoma formation.

Oral endotracheal intubations are preferred in major surgeries over nasal as it avoids trauma to nasal mucosa.

Ans.132. (b) Hilton's method

Ref http://www.meb.uni-bonn.de/dtc/primsurg/docbook/html/x1167.html

HILTON'S METHOD

- **ANAESTHESIA:** If an abscess is already pointing, infiltrate the site of the incision with a local anesthetic solution or Intravenous thiopentone with pethidine /Morphine. Ethyl chloride local spray is the least satisfactory, but can use it for very superficial abscesses. It makes the tissues hard and difficult to incise.
- **INCISION:** Drain the abscess at the site of maximum tenderness and try to follow Lange's lines. This is safer than following any set rule. If an abscess is superficial, use a **pointed (No. 11) blade,**

(1) If the abscess is deep, try to incise parallel to any nerves or vessels, not across them. (2) The common mistake is not to make the incision large enough.

- **HILTON'S METHOD:** should always be used if there is anything near the abscess which might possibly get injured. Incise the tissues down to the deep fascia, and then push blunt scissors or a hemostat into the softest or most prominent part of the swelling. Open them out inside the abscess. If necessary, enlarge the wound by blunt dissection inside the tissues.
- **DRAIN THE PUS:** by putting a finger into the abscess, and breaking down all loculi, so that there is only one cavity.If there is much pus, suck it out or clean out the cavity with a swab.
- **PROVIDE FREE DRAINAGE:** Make sure that any more pus which forms can drain from the bottom of the cavity.

Ans.133. (b) Accept the slight imperfection and allow for later remodeling

Ref Killey's , pg 125.

Late complications of fractures:

MALUNION

- When mild discrepancy are found after fracture reduction or when the patient has had no treatment at all, the occlusion will often correct itself, as the patient starts to use the jaw again. The process of readjustment may be helped by selective occlusal grinding.
- When due to inadequate reduction, there is gross deformity of face and occlusal derangement. The mandible has good capacity to heal itself and unattended patients, thus, present a greater chance of malunion than non-union.

- Such gross imperfections generally require formal planned osteotomy or ostectomy with autogenous bone chips fill.

So, we see that mild derangements are self correcting and generally require little/no treatment.

Delayed Union: due to foreign bodies, fibrous union, healing prolonged by 12 months.

Non-Union: no sign of any contact, 'eburnation' of fracture ends.

Ans.134. (b) 2mm

Explained earlier please refer KCET-07 A147

Ans.135. (c) Computer controlled local anesthesia

Ref Shobha tendon, pg 467

The Computer Controlled injection system: *e.g.,* Wand LA System consists of a conventional local anesthetic cartridge that is linked by micro tubing to a disposable, light weight, pen like handle with a Luer-Lok attached. A foot control allows precise control over rate, volume ratio of solution dispensed. The patients report virtually no perception of needle penetration.

Jet injections a technique in which a small anesthetic solution is propelled by a jet into the submucosa. The fine jet of solution is particularly useful in palatal injections.

- EDA (Electronic Dental Anesthesia) based on the principal of TENS (trans Electrical nerve stimulation) . Can be used as a supplement to LA.
- Lignocaine patch- patches of lignocaine upto concentration of 10-20% can be applied to the mucosa near premolar region.

Ans.136. (d) Antioxidant for adrenaline

REPEAT refer answer 127

PERIODONTICS

Ans.137. (b) 45 and 90 degrees

Ref Carranza, pg 600

During scaling and root planning optimal angulations is 45-90 degrees. The exact blasé angulation depends on the amount and nature of calculus, the procedure being performed and the overall condition of the tissues.

If blade angle is <45 or >90, then, instead of biting into the calculus, the scaler would burnish and smoothen the calculus.

Ans.138. (c) Right side of the patient

Ref Carranza, pg 598.

Working Area	Operator position	Finger rest type
Maxillary anterior	Behind the patient's head using a combination of direct/indirect vision	Intra-oral, palm up ; fourth finger on incisal edges of adjacent teeth.
Mandibular anterior	Back position direct/indirect illumination/visibility.	Intra-oral palm down, ; fourth finger on incisal edges of adjacent teeth.
Maxillary posterior - left	At Right side/back of the patient; direct/indirect	Intra-oral palm downopposite arch where fourth finger rests on mandibular teeth (L), extra-oral palm down (F)
	At Right side/back of the patient; direct/indirect	Intra-oral palm up finger on finger rest (L) and extra-oral palm up fulcrum for (F)
Mandibular posterior	At right side/front of the patient; direct/indirect	Intra-oral palm down, ; fourth finger on occlusal edges of adjacent teeth (L) and cross arch/Intra-oral palm down, (F)
-right	In front/right side of the patient	-do-

L- lingual surface
B-buccal surface

Ans.139. (a) Sub epithelial connective tissue grafts

Ref Carranza, pg 866

Langer's sub epithelial connective tissue graft is a procedure indicated for larger and multiple defects with good vestibular depth and gingival thickness to allow a split-thickness flap to be elevated. Adjacent to denuded root surface, the donor C.T. is sandwiched between the split flaps. It was described by Langer and Langer in 1985.

EXTRA EDGE

Also remember,

- Coronally displaced – Semilunar flap by **Tarnow** (for maxillary cases only).
- Pouch and Tunnel technique – highly esthetic ; shows ***'creeping attachment'***.
- Lateral pedicle graft – by *Gruppe* 1956 for isolated tooth.

Ans.140. (b) Horizontal mattress suture

Ref Carranza, pg 772

Types of sutures in periodontal surgery:

- **Horizontal Mattress Suture:** for interproximal areas or for wide diastema to properly adapt the papilla against the bone. Two sutures are often necessary.
- **Continuous independent sling suture:** when there is both a facial and lingual flap involving many teeth. The suture is initiated on the papilla closest to the midline.
- **Anchor suture:** used best for closing a flap, mesial or distal to a tooth as in wedge procedures.
- **Closed anchor sutures:** used to close a flap located in the edentulous area mesial or distal to a tooth. This suture encircles the tooth (hence, 'closed').

- **Periosteal suture:** used to hold in place an apically repositioned flap. These may be either holding or closing sutures.

Ans.141. (d) Papilla preservation flap

Ref Carranza, pg 781

In current, regenerative therapy, either bone grafts, membranes or a combination of these with or without other agents are used for successful outcome. The flap design should therefore, set up so that maximum amount of gingival tissue and papilla are retained to cover the regenerative material placed in the pocket. Two flap designs are available:

- **Papilla preservation flaps (PPF):** the preserved papilla are incorporated either in the facial or lingual flaps and returned back into original positions later on.
- **Conventional flap with only crevicular incision:** the papilla is split below the contact point. A thick flap is necessary to protect the graft.

The flap design of ***choice*** is the PPF which retains the entire papilla covering the lesion. However when there very narrow interdental space, it is impossible to use PPF and hence a conventional flap is utilized.

Ans.142. (a) Walter Loesche

Explained earlier Please Ref KCET-O7 A112

Ans.143. (a) Periotron

Ref Carranza , pg 255.

Methods of collecting GCF

- Brill's method- Absorbing paper strips within the sulcus until resistance is observed. Not reliable method.
- Loe modified this method by placing the strip just at the entrance of the pocket.
- Pre-weighed twisted beads/threads.
- Micro-pipettes help in collecting sample by their capillary action.
- The GCF collected on paper strip is then stained with ninhydrin and studied with a microscope.
- Electronic method – measures the fluid collected on a 'blotter' (Periopaper) employing an electronic transducer (Periotron). The wetness affects the flow of current through the appliance which then gives out a digital read-out of same.

Remember, GCF is now considered as an exudate. The daily average is **0.43 – 1.56 μl.**

Ans.144. (a) Naber's probe

Ref Carranza, pg 568, 826

Careful probing is required for determining the presence and extent of furcation involvement. Clinically, the furcation defects are best diagnosed with the help of curved narrow probes – **Naber Probe**.

Trans-gingival probing under LA may further define the anatomy of furcation defect,

Ans.145. (d) Frenum is completely removed

Ref Carranza, pg 870.

Frenectomy is the complete removal of frenum including the attachment to underlying bone, may be required for correction of diastema between the maxillary incisors.

Remember, **Frenotomy** is only an incision of the frenum. This procedure is more commonly used for periodontal purposes (relocating the frenum to increase the width of attached gingiva).

Ans.146. (c) Definitive step

Ref Carranza, pg 966

Transfer of a patient from active phase to maintenance phase is a '***definitive***' step in total patient care that requires time and effort on part of dentist and staff. The patient must be made to understand the purpose of maintenance program and the dentist must emphasize that the preservation of teeth is dependent on it.

The maintenance phase of periodontal treatment starts immediately after the completion of phase I therapy and continues till the end of treatment.

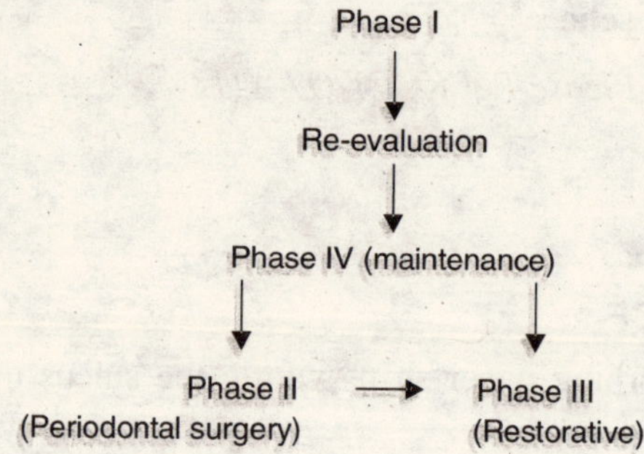

Ans.147. For biomodification of root surface citric acid has shown:

Ref. Carranza, pg 811

(a) accelerated healing and new cementum formation after demineralization of the root surface by means of citric acid.
(b) after root planning, the acid produces a 4mm deep demineralized zone with exposed collagen fibers.
(c) citric acid removes smear layer, exposing the dentinal tubules, but also makes the tubules appear wider and with funnel shaped orifices.
(d) it has shown invitro to eliminate endotoxin and bacteria from diseased root surface.
(e) early fibrin linkage to collagen exposed to citric acid treatment prevents the epithelium from migrating over treated roots.

Thus using citric acid with ph 1 is recommended for biomodification of root surface.

Ans.148. (a) Bass method

Ref Carranza, pg 657

Bass method is a vibratory method of brushing. It is efficient method and can be recommended for any patient with or without periodontal involvement.

The short back and forth stroke is easily mastered. It concentrates on cleaning the cervical and interproximal portions of teeth, where microbial plaque is most likely to have accumulated. The head of brush is placed is placed parallel to occlusal plane, with brush head covering three or four teeth beginning at the most distal tooth in the arch. The bristles are placed 45 degrees to the long axis of the teeth on the gingival margin. Using short back and forth movement without dislodging the tips of the bristles, the motion forces the bristles into gingival sulcus area.

Ans.149. (b) For 6 months

Explained Earlier, Ref A106

Ans.150. (d) Lipping

Ref Carranza, pg 373

When bone is resorbed by excessive occlusal forces, the body attempts to reinforce the thinned bony trabeculae with new bone. This attempt to compensate for lost bone is called ***buttressing bone formation*** and is an important feature of the reparative process associated with trauma form occlusion. It may also occur when bone is destroyed by inflammation or osteolytic tumors.

- Buttressing bone formation may occur at two locations-
- **Central:** the endosteal cell deposit new bone, which restores the bony trabeculae and reduces the size of the bone marrow.
- **Peripheral:** occurs on the facial and lingual surfaces of the alveolar plate. Sometimes a shelf- like thickening of the alveolar margin may be produced , known as '***lipping***'.

Ans.151. (a) 20mg capsule of doxycycline hyclate

Ref http://www.drugs.com/cons/periostat.html

DOXYCYCLINE (Doryx®, Doxy®, ***Periostat***®, Vibramycin®) is a tetracycline-type antibiotic. Doxycycline kills certain bacteria that cause infection, or stops their growth. It treats many kinds of infections of the skin, bone, stomach, respiratory tract, sinuses, ear, and urinary tract. It also treats Lyme disease and certain sexually transmitted diseases. For travelers to certain areas doxycycline can be given to suppress malaria. Periostat® is a specific capsule and tablet form of doxycycline which helps to treat periodontitis.

For *oral* dosage form (tablets):

For periodontitis (gum disease):

- Adults— 20 mg twice a day.
- Children—Use in children up to 8 years of age is not recommended.

Tetracycline, such as doxycycline, can permanently discolor teeth.

Ans.152. (a) Streptococcus sanguis

Ref Carranza, 9th ed, pg 100,

The following lines from Carranza are self-explanatory-

Initial colonization on the dental pellicle occurs within few hours of its formation. The initial bacteria colonizing the pellicle-coated tooth surface are predominantly gram-positive facultative microorganism such as A.viscosus and S sanguis. The plaque then matures through the growth of these attached species and the secondary colonizers.

Co-aggregation is seen between F.nucleatum and S.sanguis;, P.loeschii with A.viscosus '

PEDODONTICS

Ans.153. (b) Tell-show-do

Ref http://www.rcseng.ac.uk/fds/docs/non pharm behaviour.pdf

BEHAVIOR MANAGEMENT – NON PHARMACOLOGICAL

- **Non verbal communications**
  This form of communication occurs continuously and may reinforce or contradict verbal signals. Such communication includes - having a child friendly environment and a happy, smiling team. Reassurance has been shown to be ineffective as a method of controlling distress. In contrast, reinforcement, which is enquiring how the child is feeling or gentle pats and squeezes has been found to minimize distress. These verbal cues and signs are used to give positive encouragement and enhance other management techniques and may be useful with all patients.
- **Voice control**
  Young children often respond to the tone of voice rather than the actual words. Voice control techniques use a controlled alteration of voice, volume, tone or pace to influence and direct a patients behavior. Such techniques aim to improve attention and compliance as well as to establish authority. For example, an abrupt change from soft to loud, to gain attention of a child who is not complying. Voice control has been shown to decrease disruptive behaviors without producing long-term negative effects. However, while reported as widely used by dentists-it may not be acceptable to all parents-or clinicians.
  The technique is useful for inattentive but communicative children. However, it is not appropriate for children too young to understand or with intellectual or emotional impairment.
- **Enhancing control**
  Here the patient is given a degree of control over their dentists' behavior through the use of a stop signal. Such signals have been shown to reduce pain during routine dental treatment and during injection. The stop signal, usually raising an arm, should be rehearsed and the dentist should respond quickly when it is used.

The technique is useful for all patients who can communicate. There are no contraindications.

- **Behavior shaping and positive reinforcement**

  Many dental procedures require quite complex behaviors and actions from our patients which need to be explained and learned. For children this requires small clear steps. This process is termed behavior shaping. It consists of a defined series of steps towards ideal behavior. This is most easily achieved by selective reinforcement. Reinforcement is the strengthening of a pattern of behavior, increasing the probability of that behavior being displayed again in the future. Anything that the child finds pleasant or gratifying can act as a positive reinforcer, stickers or badges are often used at the end of a successful appointment. However, the most powerful rein forcers are social stimuli, such as, facial expression, positive voice modulation, verbal praise, approval by hugging. A child centered, empathic response giving specific praise, for example, "I like the way you keep your mouth open" has been shown to be more effective than a general comment such as "Good girl. As with TSD the use of age specific language is important.

  The technique is useful for all patients who can communicate. There are no contraindications.

- **Modeling**

  The technique is based on the psychological principle that people learn about their environment by observing others' behavior, using a model, either live or by video to exhibit appropriate behavior in the dental environment. This may demonstrate appropriate behavior via a third party, decrease anxiety by showing a positive outcome to a procedure a child requires themselves, and illustrate the rewards for performing appropriately. For best effects models should be the same age as the target child, should exhibit appropriate behavior and be praised. They should also be shown entering and leaving the surgery.

  The technique is useful where an appropriate model is available.

- **Distraction**

  This approach aims to shift the patient's attention from the dental setting to some other situation or from a potentially unpleasant procedure to some other action. Cartoons have been shown to reduce disruptive behaviors in children when combined with reinforcement, that is when children knew the cartoon would be switched off if they did not behave. Later studies suggest that audio tapes may be even more effective. Short term distractors such as diverting the attention by pulling the lip as a local anesthetic is given or having patients raise their legs to stop them gagging during radiography may also be useful. The dentist who talks while applying topical paste and administering local anesthetic is also using distraction with words.

  The technique is useful for all patients who can verbally communicate. There are no contraindications.

- **Systematic desensitization (SD)**

  This technique helps individuals with specific fears or phobias overcome them by repeated contacts. A hierarchy of fear-producing stimuli is constructed, and the patient is exposed to them in an ordered manner, starting with the stimulus posing the lowest threat. In dental terms, fears are usually related to a specific procedure such as use of local anesthetic. First, the patient is taught to relax, and in this state exposed to each of the stimuli in the hierarchy in turn, only progressing to the next when they feel able. The technique is useful for a child who can clearly identify their fear and who can verbally communicate.

- **Negative reinforcement**
  The powerful effect of positive reinforcement has been discussed already. Negative reinforcement has also been used in dental practice. It is the strengthening of a pattern of behavior by the removal of a stimulus which the individual perceives as unpleasant (a negative reinforcer) as soon as the required behavior is exhibited. The stimulus is applied to all actions except the required one, thus reinforcing it by removal of a negative stimulus. It should not be confused with punishment, which is the application of an unpleasant stimulus to inappropriate behavior.
  Well known examples in dental practice are Hand over mouth (HOM) and selective
- **Exclusion of the parent (SEP). :**
  HOM involves restraining the child in the dental chair, placing a hand over the mouth (to allow the child to hear). The nose must not be covered. The dentist then talks quietly to the child explaining that the hand will be removed as soon as crying stops. As soon as this happens the hand is removed and the child praised. If protests start again the hand is replaced. The technique aims to gain the child's attention and enable communication, reinforce good behavior and establish that avoidance is futile. Those who advocate the technique recommend it for children aged 4-9 years when communication is lost or during temper tantrums. Parental consent is important and the technique should never be used on children too young to understand or with intellectual or emotional impairment.
  Selective exclusion of the parent (SEP) is less controversial but uses similar principals. The indications for SEP are the same as for HOM. Parental consent is required. When inappropriate behavior is exhibited the parent is asked to leave. Ideally, the parent should be able to hear, but be out of sight of the child. When appropriate behavior is exhibited the parent is asked to return, thus reinforcing that behavior.

Methods commonly used now-days for modifying the behavior in children is TSD. By having verbal (tell) and non-verbal (show + do) communications, a dentist can overcome the many small dental related anxieties of any child.

Ref- Shobha tandon, pg 148

Ans.154. (a) 6 — 18 months

Ref Shobha tendon, pg 189

Carfield(1993), noted the initial acquisition of S mutans from birth till 5 years and designated the time period as 'window of infectivity''. As the teeth erupt into oral cavity, they provide ideal atmosphere for the MS to colonize and overcome competition from other organisms. This period ranges from **7-24 months** (First *Window Infectivity*) . Later on the "*Second Window Infectivity*" is present in permanent dentition between **6-12 yrs** of age.

Ans.155. (a) Spastic

Explained earlier , Please refer KCET 07 A148

Ans.156. (b) 4-5 months

Ref Bhalajhi, chap: Preventive Othodontics, pg 231

Factors influencing space maintainer application-

* Amount of bone covering the unerupted teeth: the more the bone covering the unerupted teeth, longer it would take to erupt. Generally a premolar takes 4-5months to erupt through a bone covering of about 1 mm

Ans.157. (a) Hyatt

Ref Shobha tendon, pg 233

- Hyatt: (1923) proposed prophylactic odontomy – filling the fissures of newly erupted teeth with oxy-phosphate cement and later preparing a cavity filled amalgam.
- Bodecker (1929) proposed the fissure eradication by mechanically converting deep fissures into shallow self-cleaning one.
- Bunocore (1955) advocated filling the pit n fissures with bonded resin using conc phosphoric acid.
- Bowen (1965) reported BIS-GMA (modern composite material).

Ans.158. (c) At the apex

Ref Textbook of Pedodontic, Shobha tendon, pg4

The pedodontic triangle places the child at the apex while the dentist and the parent occupy left and right corners respectively. The purpose of this triangle is to suggest the importance of child as a individual patient requiring the attention of both dentist and the parent. The dentist and the parent work in close association for the better health of the child.

Ans.159 (c) Starkey

Ref Ingle, 5th ed pg 891

Sweet developed a 4-5 appointment technique using Formocresol.for necrotic teeth but without fistulae.

Hobson then gave a technique using beachwood cresolate.

Starkey introduced one and multi-appointment pulpectomy for cariously involved primary pulp. He also gave a partial pulpectomy technique involving removal of some portion of coronal pulp.

Ans.160. (c) Distal step

Ref Bhalajhi , pg 55

The flush terminal plane is used as guide to predict the status of occlusion in deciduous dentition.

- When in flush terminal plane, the permanent molars erupts in an end- end relation which may revert to Class 1 by either early shift or late shift of mandibular I molar.
- When the distal surface of deciduous maxillary second molar is mesial to the mandibular (Distal step), development of a Class II relationship of the permanent first molars is eminent.
- When there is a mesial step, (i.e. distal surface of Mand dec. II molar mesial to that of maxillary), the final relation may be a Class III or Class I.

ORTHODONTICS

Ans.161. (b) Crowding of more than 5 mm

Ref Bhalajhi pg 180

Severe crowding refers to space discrepancy of more than 5 mm.

Ans.162. (a) Upper central incisors

Ref Bhalajhi, 2nd ed, pg 278

Southend clasp

- Used when retention is required in the anterior region.
- The wire is adapted along the cervical margins of both the central incisors.

Crozat clasp

- Resembles full clasp with additional piece of wire soldered into mesial and distal undercut.
- Provides better retention than full clasp.

Schwartz clasp

- Or arrowhead clasp is modified Adam's clasp
- Number of arrowheads engrave the inter-proximal undercuts between molars and premolars.

Ans.163. (b) Braided wire used in pea for alignment

Sorry friends, in spite of the best of efforts, we could not gather information about this. Need, your help for a reference!

Ans.164. (c) Rogers 1918

Ref http://www.jisppd.com/article.asp?issn=0Chawla

A definition of tongue thrust: 'The forward movement of the tongue tip between the teeth to meet the lower lip, in deglutition and in sounds of speech so that the tongue becomes interdental. This does not include consideration of forward tongue posture, which has a more important role.

Tulley proposed a working clinical classification of tongue thrust. According to him, the main types are: tongue thrusting as a habit; tongue thrusting which is possibly endogenous or innate; tongue thrust as an adaptive behavior; and pathologic and grossly abnormal tongue problems. Of these, tongue thrust habit and tongue thrust as an adaptive behavior are amenable to correction with orthodontic treatment or natural growth placing the labial segments in good relationship

Interceptive attempts to contain tongue thrust have conventionally involved suggestions to the patient, *myofunctional exercises* and a gamut of appliances such as cribs, rakes, overlay bite plates, interocclusal elastics, maxillary expanders and loose fitting training appliances. ***Rogers*** first, advocated myofunctional for harnessing muscle forces to treat malocclusions.

Ans.165. (c) Outer neuro muscular envelop

Explained Earlier, Please refer KCET-O7 Answer 162

Ans.166. (c) Bjork

Ref Bhalajhi , pg 14

The use of implant to study the bone growth was first introduced by **Bjork** in 1969. It involves implanting small bits of biologically inert alloys into growing bone. This serves as radiographic reference points for further serial analysis.

Ans.167. (d) 3.5 mm

Ref Bhalajhi , pg 54

When in the distal surfaces of deciduous second molars are in a Flush-terminal plane the permanent first molars too, may erupt in such a vertical relation. For transition of such end-on relation to Angle's Class I. The lower molar has to move forward by **3-5** mm relative to the upper. This occurs by the utilization of the physiologic and the leeway spaces and by the differential forward growth of mandible.

Ans.168. (c) 70° Angle

Ref http://www.aurumgroup.com/usa/spacemaintainers/twinblock.stm

Unlike bulky, one-piece functional appliances, the Twin Block has a separate, unattached upper and lower bite block components - actually two appliances which work together as one. In function, these two appliances interlock at the ***70 degree angle*** set into the bite blocks and posture the mandible forward into the ideal Class I position preset by your wax registration.

The Twin Block Appliance has been described as "***the most comfortable and the most esthetic of all the functional appliances.***" The Twin Block does not contain anterior wires or cheek and lip pads. Lingual extensions are eliminated ensuring patient comfort. The patient can eat and speak normally - movements of the tongue, lip and mandible are not restricted. The high comfort level allows the appliance to be worn 24 hours a day. This harnesses the forces of occlusion and mastication, leading to faster results and shorter treatment times. Patient appearance and profile are improved immediately:

Indicated for following malocclusions:

- Class II Division I; Class II Division 2;
- Class I open bites; Class I closed bites
- Class III
- Lateral arch constriction and anterior/posterior arch length discrepancies (can also be used effectively in TMJ therapy).

Ans.169. (a) Width- Length- Height

Ref Shobha tendon, ch: normal growing child, pg 73

During post-natal development, growth in jaw width is completed first, followed by growth in length and the in height. The growth in width is accomplished before the adolescent growth curve.

Ans.170. (c) Twin block

Explained earlier, please refer A168

Ans.171. (a) Occlusal plane

Re Bhalajhi, pg 406.

Catalan's appliance is an inclined plane constructed on the lower anterior teeth that can be used to treat maxillary cross-bites.

- Made either of acrylic or cast metal having ***45 degree*** angulation to the occlusal plane , which forces maxillary teeth in an anterior direction.
- Can only be used in cases where adequate space exists and the cause of cross-bite is maxillary teeth in retroclination (and not due to proclined mandibular teeth).
- Is used more than 6 months can cause anterior pen bite due to supra-eruption of posterior teeth.
- Dietary restrictions and speech problems make this appliance uncomfortable.

Ans.172. (a) Teeth which irregularity arranged within the arch due to lack of space for them

Ref http://www.braces.org/healthcareprofessionals/dentists/glossary/I.cfm

Imbrication refers to An overlap of incisors and canines due to crowding.

Remember, Imbrication lines of von Ebner are:- Incremental lines in the dentin and cementum of the tooth that reflect variations in mineralization during dentin formation.

Ans.173. (b) 1.7mm

Ref Bhalajhi , pg 56

Lee way spaces

- Maxilla - 1.8 mm (0.9 x 2)
- Mandible – 3.4 mm(1.7 x 2)

Incisal Liability: (difference in space requirement for deciduous and permanent incisors)

- Maxilla - 7 mm
- Mandible - 5 mm

Ans.174. (d) All the above

Ref Shobha tandon , pg 396

- The fixed distal shoe space maintainer was first reported by Willet (1932) and later modified by Roche.
- The appliance finds its use when the deciduous second molars are prematurely lost before the eruption of first permanent molar.
- A sub gingival extension of metal (bar in Willet's and V-shaped in Roche's) guides the eruption of first molar.
- Hence, due to its sub-epithelial location, they may act as reservoir of infection and are considered risk factors in patients who are predisposed to systemic conditions like leukemia, Rheumatic fever, SABE, hemophiliacs, congenital heart diseased etc.
- Although, antibiotic prophylaxis can keep infection level to minimum, their use over such long periods (months) are not recommended and hence, contraindicates the use of fixed distal shoe space maintainers.

PROSTHODONTICS

Ans.175. (d) To determine the size of maxillary central incisor

Ref http://iadr.confex.com/iadr/2002SanDiego/techprogram/abstract 18112.htm

Trubyte Tooth Indicator

- Is an incolor ruler – like appliance, with cavities that fit the nose and eyes and a central line to fit above the midline of the face.
- This appliance measures the width of the face between the ***zygoma,*** and the length of the face from the hairline to the ***gnathion*** when the lips are in light contact. The width and length of the upper central incisor are measured with one drawing compass.
- The width was measured from mesial contact to distal contact, and the length from gingival edge to incisal edge.
- This tooth indicator is designed for calibration of the 16 to 1 ratio between facial dimension and maxillary central incisors
- It has been found that the use of Trubyte Tooth Indicator for anterior teeth selection could result in prostheses with narrower and longer teeth.

Ans.176. (a) 5 — 6 times

Explained earlier, please refer KCET 07 A41

Ans.177. (b) Korecta type I

Ref Skinner's, Nallaswamy, pg 87.

Common mouth temp waxes used for recording PPS

Iowa wax (white)	Smith
Korrecta wax no. 4 (orange)	O.C. Applegate
Adaptol wax (green)	Nathan, Kaye
H-L physiological paste (yellow-white).	CS Harkins

EXTRA EDGE

Also remember, common constituents of waxes, their functions:

Paraffin (10-60 %)	Main ingredient-'bulk'. Tends to produce flaking when trimmed. Lacks gloss.
Gum Dammar	Improves smoothness + luster , prevents flaking +cracking. ! toughness.
Carnauba wax	Hard + high melting point. Together with Paraffin *reduces* the flow at mouth temp. Greatly improves the *glossiness* of wax.
Candelilla wax	Can replace carnauba but properties are !
Ceresin wax	Can replace paraffin.

According to ADA specification 4 , inlay waxes are of 2 types:-

(1) Type I wax – medium wax employed for ***direct*** procedure.

(2) Type II wax- soft wax used for ***indirect*** technique.

Inlay wax	30⁰ C	37⁰ C	40⁰ C		45⁰ C	
	max	max	min	max	min	max
Type I	-	1%	-	20%	70%	90%
Type II	1%	-	50%	-	70%	90%

Ans.178. (b) 30°

Explained earlier, please refer KCET 07 A184

Ans.179. (a) ¼ th of an inch

Ref Nallaswamy, pg 406

The lingual rest seat should be half moon shaped located above the cingulum. The rest seat should be gingival to the contact point with the adjacent teeth. A flat, ¼ th inch diamond bur/disc is usually used for this purpose.

Ans.180. (a) More conservative restoration

Ref Nallaswamy, pg 521

Ceramic crowns offer the best esthetics but the worst marginal finish. Also, they require large amount of tooth reduction as it requires good bulk to overcome its brittleness. Hence they are contraindicated in cases requiring conservation of tooth structure

Ans.181. (d) Laminate veneer

Ref Nallaswamy , pg 490

Laminate veneers are usually made of ceramic and cover the facial surface of anterior teeth mainly to improve the esthetics. They are very conservative and afford good esthetics and patient compliance.

Ans.182. (c) 2° - 5°

Ref Nallaswamy, pg 567

The degree of taper is inversely proportional to the retention form. Zero degree taper is the most retentive but almost impossible to attain. For optimum retention a degree of **4-10** is sufficient. Usually a tapering fissure diamond bur is used for such purpose. When an operator aligns the bur parallel to the long axis of the tooth, a ***6 degree*** convergence will be produced.

Ans.183. (d) Less than 90°

Ref Nallaswamy, pg 347

The occlusal rest seat is a triangular-shaped depression, with its base at the marginal ridge and apex at the center of the tooth. Its margins should be smooth and gently curved. The angle between the line drawn along the proximal surface of tooth and the floor of rest seat ***should be less than 90.***

If it is more than or equal to 90 then forces acting on the prosthesis will not be transmitted along the long axis but an inclined plane of abutment tooth.It will have a tendency to slip away whenever loaded.

Ans.184. (b) Hygienic

Ref Nallaswamy, pg 511

Sanitary pontics: they have zero tissue contact and are easy to maintain but are highly unaesthetic. Hence are used only for posterior teeth. A clearance of 3 mm is ideal. Also known as 'hygienic' pontic.

3 common designs are employed in fabricating sanitary pontics:

(1) **Bar sanitary:** they have flat gingival surface with adequate clearance.

(2) **Conventional or ''fish-belly'' pontics:** the gingival surface is convex both B-L and M-D resembling the belly of a fish. The main disadvantages are – reduced strength of prosthesis due to decreased size and difficulty in contouring the proximal surfaces.

(3) **Modified sanitary/ perel / arc fixed pontics:** gingival surface is hyperparaboloid The proximal surfaces are concave and hence overcome the limitations of the fish-belly type.

Ans.185. (a) Kennedy's multiple circumferential clasps

Ref Nallaswamy, pg 360

Kennedy's multiple circlet clasp (Continuous clasp) is a combination of two clasps joined at the terminal end of the reciprocal arms. Prime indication is abutments with poor periodontal support that need extra retention. Hence it also act as a splint.

COMMUNITY AND PREVENTIVE DENTISTRY

Ans.186. (a) 1st April 1976

Ref Soben Peter, 2nd ed , pg 497

The government of India passed the Cigarette Act of 1975 on 1st April 1976., which requires all manufacturers to display a warning sign on their products.

Ans.187. (c) World Health day

EXTRA EDGE

Some important dates:

- 30th Jan – Anti-leprosy
- 7th April – World health day
- 31st May – World no-tobacco day
- 1st July – Doctor's day
- 11th July - World Population day
- 2nd Oct - Anti-drug addiction day
- 1st Dec – Anti – AIDS day
- 11th Dec – UNICEF day

Ans.188. (d) Class-room based fluoride tablet program

Ref Soben Peter, 2nd ed , pg 578

Fluoride tablets are easier to dispense. Each tablet is chewed, swished and then swallowed for 1 min. this 'swish and swallow technique provides topical as well as systemic benefits.

Remember, 2.2 mg NaF = 1 mg fluoride.

Daily tablet is more effective than weekly rinse.

Ans.189. (b) Retrospective study

Ref Park's, pg 69

Case control studies are often called as retrospective studies are common first approach to test the causal hypothesis.

Main differences between case control and cohort studies.

Ans.190. (d) Primordial

Explained earlier, please refer KCET07 A197

Ans.191. (a) Disease control

Ref Soben Peter, 2nd ed, pg 3-4

Concept	Time period	Aims
I. Disease control phase	1880 - 1920	To control man's physical environment by sanitary legislations and reforms
II. Health Promotion phase	1920-1960	Personalized health care like mother and child care, school health services. The concept of 'health center' by Lord Dawson (1920) and latter by Bhore committee in India
III. Social Engineering phase	1960 - 1980	Focus on ''chronic diseases'' and Risk Factors. Social and behavioral aspects of disease were given priority
IV. Health For ALL phase	1981 – 2000 A.D	The basic amenities of health, sanitation, education, and drinking water to all. Focus on preventive, therapeutic and rehabilitative aspects.

Ans.192. (c) Denturist

Ref Soben Peter, 2nd ed, pg 827, 664

Denturists is a term applied to those dental lab technicians who are permitted in some states in USA, Canada to fabricate and dispense dentures directly to the patients without dentist's prescription.

EFDA are basically dental assistants or hygienists with additional training in reversible procedures only. The are also referred as technotherapist. They play an impporatnt role in the practice of Four handed dentistry.

Ans.193. (b) To do good

Ref Soben Peter, 2nd ed, pg 697

- **Beneficence** is to do good, a concept advocated even by Hippocrates. In the process of treating a patient one should weigh the consequence of treatment with no treatment at all.
- **Ethics :** is a branch of philosophy concerned with moral duties and obligations of health professional towards the patient, colleagues and to the society.
- **Jurisprudence :** is the philosophy of law or the science that deals with the principles of law and legal relations.

	Case control study	Cohort study
1.	Starts from 'effect' to 'cause' (***retrospective***), starts with the disease	Proceeds from 'cause' to 'effect' (***prospective***), starts with 'at risk' people
2.	Tests whether the suspected cause occurs more frequently in those with the disease than among those without the disease	Tests whether disease occurs more frequently in those exposed than in those not similarly exposed
3.	Usually the first approach for testing the hypothesis, also for exploratory studies	Usually reserved for testing precisely formulated hypothesis.
4.	Involves fewer subjects ; inexpensive Larger number of subjects ; more expense	Larger number of subjects ; more expense
5.	Results are drawn quickly	Long follow-ups ; delayed results
6.	Suitable for study of '***rare***' diseases	Inappropriate
7.	Yields only estimate RR (relative risk)	Incidence rate, RR as well as AR
8.	Suitable for only 1 disease at a time	Can yield information about more than 1 disease outcome.

Ans.194. (c) 100

Ref Park, 17th ed, pg 15

PQL or Physical Quality of Life Index is an important concept in quality of life which comprises in three indicators *i.e.*

(i) infant mortality, (ii) life expectancy at age one (iii) literacy

For each component the performance of the individual countries is placed on a scale of **0 -100**. (0-worst and 100 is best performance). After taking an average of three indices the score is scaled. The ultimate objective is to attain a PQL of 100.

EXTRA EDGE

Remember, PQL **does not** measure economic growth. This aspect is taken care of by the *Human Development Index (HDI)*

- Sullivan's index- is one of the most advanced indicators of disability.
- **Daly index** gives a measure of the ''burden'' of disease in a defined population.

Ans.195. (c) 1986

Ref Soben Peter, 2nd ed, pg 804.

CPA or Consumer Protection Act 1986, came into force on 15th April,1987. The Act aims to protect the interests of the consumer (patient) and for settlement of consumer disputes. Doctors and Hospitals offering free treatment are not liable under this Act.

Ans.196. (b) The swab test

Ref Soben Peter, 2nd ed, pg 375

Grainger et al in 1965 devised the Swab test, where no collection of saliva is necessary. so, it is extremely valuable in assessing the caries activity in very young children. It is based on the same principles as Snyder's sample is collected by swabbing the buccal surface of teeth with cotton and later incubated in medium after 48hrs of incubation the pH change is read using a pH meter:

pH 4.1 to <4. 1 – Marked activity

pH 4.2 to 4.4 – Active

pH 4.5 to 4.6 – Slightly active

pH 4.6 and over – Caries active

Also remember, color in Snyder's test changes from green to yellow (Bromocresol green)

Ans.197. (a) Descriptive epidemiology

Ref Park, 17th ed , pg 54

Descriptive epidemiologies are usually the first phase of an investigation. They are concerned with observing the distribution of diseases and identifying characteristics with which the disease in question seems to be associated.

Whereas, in analytical study, the objective is not to formulate, but to **test** the hypothesis.

Ans.198. (b) Fluoride varnish

Ref Soben Peter, 2nd ed, pg 304

Fluoride varnish:

- **Duraphat**: developed in Germany, as a viscous yellow material containing 22,600 ppm fluoride (2.26% F) in a neutral colophonium base. High levels are deposited in all layers of enamel after 6-12 hrs of application.
- **Fluor Protector**: is a clear polyurethane based containing 7,000ppm fluoride (0.7% F) from a compound difluorosilane. It is dispensed in 1mL ampoules each containing 6.21mgF. A total of 0.3-0.5 mL solution (6.9-11.5 mgF) is required to cover full dentition.
- **Carex**-contains 1.8% F (18,600 ppm F).

Ans199. (b) Calcium fluoride

Ref Soben Peter, 2nd ed, pg 354

- Fluorspar is a mineral containing varying amount ***calcium fluoride.(85-98%)***
- Sodium fluoride: is a white, odorless compound manufactured from HF. It is the most expensive source of fluoride.
- Sodium silicofluoride: it is the cheapest of all but is corrosive.
- Ammonium silicofluoride: is primarily used to manufacture chloramines for water disinfection.

Ans.200. (d) Bars separated by appropriate spaces

Ref Park 17th ed , pg 610

- **Histogram**: is a pictorial diagram of frequency distribution. It consists of a series of blocks where the class interval is given along the x-axis and frequencies along y-axis. The area of each block corresponds to the frequency at that interval.
- **Frequency polygon**: is obtained by joining the mid-points of histogram blocks.
- **Line diagrams** – represent trends of events with the passage of time.
- **Scatter diagrams**: are prepared after cross-tabulation in which frequencies of at least 2 variables have been classified, one variable being dependent and te other independent. This is used to show correlation between 2 variables *e.g.,* height and weight, chronological age and growth age, etc.

2005

Questions & Answers

3

KCET 2005

QUESTIONS

ANATOMY

1. **Nerve passing through the center of cavernous sinus is:**
   (a) Occulomotor nerve.
   (b) Trochlear nerve.
   (c) Abducent nerve.
   (d) Maxillary nerve.
2. **Structure passing through superior constrictor muscle and base of skull are:**
   (a) Stylopharageus and glossopharyngeal nerve.
   (b) Auditory tube and levator palati muscle.
   (c) Internal laryngeal Nerve & Superior laryngeal vessels.
   (d) Recurrent laryngeal nerve and inferior laryngeal vessels.
3. **Inferior salivary nucleus supplies:**
   (a) Lacrimal gland.
   (b) Parotid gland.
   (c) Submandibular Salivary gland.
   (d) Sub lingual salivary gland.
4. **Hassalls corpuscles are seen in:**
   (a) Prostate.
   (b) Spleen.
   (c) Thymus.
   (d) Liver.
5. **Which of the following paranasal sinuses is formed before birth?**
   (a) Maxillary sinus.
   (b) Frontal sinus.
   (c) Ethmoid sinus
   (d) Mastoid air sinus.

DENTAL ANATOMY AND HISTOLOGY

6. The Oblique ridge runs from the distobuccal cusp to

(a) Mesiobuccal. (b) Mesiolingual.
(c) Distolingual Cusp (d) None of the above

7. The Human Teeth are:

(a) Haplodont. (b) triconodont
(c) Bunodont. (d) All the above

8. Sharp momentary pain elicited by pulp is caused by:

(a) A delta fibers. (b) C Fibers .
(c) A alpha fibers (d) None of the above

9. The formation of hard tissue initiates in the:

(a) Bud Stage: (b) Cap Stage.
(c) Advanced Bell Stage. (d) Early Bell Stage.

10. The most accepted dentine sensitivity theory is:

(a) Transudation Theory (b) Hydrodynamic theory.
(c) Direct Neuronal Theory (d) None of the above.

PHYSIOLOGY

11. Renin is secreted by

(a) Cells in proximal tubules. (b) Cells in distal tubules.
(c) Macula Densa (d) Juxtaglomerular Cells.

12. Calcium absorption is increased by:

(a) Increased Na+ absorption. (b) Hypercalcemia.
(c) Iron over load. (d) 1, 25 dyhydroxycholecalciferol.

13. When the radius of the resistance vessels is increased, which of the following in increased?

(a) Capillary blood flow. (b) Systolic Blood pressure.
(c) Diastolic Blood pressure (d) hematocrit.

14. Which of the following has the greatest effect on the ability of blood to transport oxygen?

(a) $C0_2$ content of red blood cells. (b) PH of Plasma.
(c) Amount of Hemoglobin in the blood. (d) Capacity of the blood to dissolve oxygen.

15. In infants, defecation often follows a meal. The cause of colonic contraction in this situation is:

(a) The Gastroileal reflex. (b) The Enterogastric reflex.
(c) Gastrocolic reflex. (d) Increased circulatory levels of C.C.K.

16. Principle cation require for absorption of D-Glucose is:

(a) K+ (b) Na+
(c) Ca++ (d) Mg++

BIOCHEMISTRY

17. Mucopolysaccharide which function as a lubricant and shock absorber in synovial fluid is:

(a) Heparin. (b) Hyaluronic Acid
(c) Keratin Sulphate. (d) Chondroitin - 4- Sulphate.

18. Figlu excretion test is used to detect:

(a) Folic acid deficiency. (b) Biotin deficiency.
(c) Pantothenic Acid Deficiency. (d) Vit-B 12 deficiency.

19. Biological value (fuel value) of fat is:

(a) 4.0 kc/g. (b) 5.4 kc/g.
(c) 7.0 kc/g. (d) 9.0 kc/g.

20. Electron transport chain (ETC) and ATP synthesizing structures are located in:

(a) Outer membrane of Mitochondria. (b) Mitochondrial matrix.
(c) Inner membrane of Mitochondria (d) Microsomes

MICROBIOLOGY

21. The temperature and pressure at which spores are killed during sterilization by autoclave are:

(a) 102^0 C. temp and pressure is 8 lb/sq. inch for 10 min
(b) 105° C. temp and pressure is 15lb/sq. inch for 12 min
(c) 110^0 C. temp and pressure is 4 lb/sq. inch for 5 min
(d) 121^0C. temp and pressure is 15lb/sq. inch for 12 min

22. Rice water stools are seen in infections with:

(a) Proteus (b) Shigella
(c) vibrio cholera (d) Salmonella

23. Donavan bodies are seen in bone marrow and splenic aspiration smears in infection with:

(a) Leishmania donovani (b) Lymphogranuloma venereum
(c) Klebsiella pneumonia (d) Heamophilis ducreyi

24. Hydatid cysts are due to infection with:

(a) Hymenilepis nana (b) Diphyllobothrium latum
(c) Echinococcus granulosus (d) Ascaris Lumbricoides

25. The Commonly done screening test for HIV infection is:

(a) Radio immune assay. (b) ELISA.
(c) Fluorescent antibody technique (d) Electrophoresis .

GENERAL PATHOLOGY

26. Enzymatic digestion is the predominant event in the following type of necrosis

(a) Coagulative necrosis (b) Caseous necrosis
(c) Liquefactive necrosis (d) Fibrinoid necrosis

27. Sago spleen is found in:

(a) Chronic inflammation (b) Amyloidosis
(c) Tuberculosis (d) Syphilis

28. Langhan's type of giant. cell is found in:

(a) Fat necrosis (b) Malignancy
(c) Tuberculosis (d) Acute inflammation

29. Transudate differs from exudates in having the following except:

(a) Few inflammatory cells (b) Glucose content
(c) Low protein content (d) Low specific gravity

30. Nutmeg liver is seen in :

(a) Thrombosis (b) Embolism
(c) CVC liver (d) Alcoholism

DENTAL MATERIALS

31. Which of the following impression material is most biocompatible ?

(a) Polysulphide. (b) Condensation Silicone.
(c) Addition Silicone. (d) Polyether.

32. According to ADA specification No.3 Type I Impression Compound, at 45° C, should have a minimum flow

(a) More than 65 % (b) More than 75 %
(c) More than 85% (d) More than 95 %

33. Which of the following impression material is most biocompatible?

(a) Polysulphide. (b) Condensation Silicone.
(c) Addition Silicone. (d) Polyether.

34. Which of the following is not a direct restorative material?

(a) Dentin bonding agent (b) Composite resin
(c) dental amalgam (d) Dental Ceramic

35. Loss of gloss test in gypsum product is an indication for:
(a) Adequate mixing time
(b) Adequate working time
(c) Initial set
(d) Final set

36. Rouge, used as dental abrasive, is chemically known as:
(a) Tin oxide
(b) Iron oxide
(c) Ethyl silicate
(d) Zirconium silicate

37. Casting porosity, which is caused by the inability of air to escape through the pores in thc investment, is
(a) Localized shrinkage porosity
(b) Suck-back porosity
(c) Back pressure porosity
(d) Micro porosity

38. Particle size of Micro filled Composite Restorative Resin. is in the following range:
(a) 0.04-0.4 micrometer
(b) 0.4-1 micro meter
(c) 0.5 - 3 micrometer
(d) 8 -12 micro meter

39. Which of the following is a castable dental ceramic?
(a) Aluminous porcelain
(b) IPS - Empress - 2
(c) In-ceram
(d) Dicor

40. Invisible light cured denture base resin, Camphorquinone serves as the:
(a) Activator
(b) Initiator
(c) Retarded
(d) Filler

PHARMACOLOGY

41. Therapeutic Index is a measure of :
(a) Safety of a drug
(b) Toxicity of a drug.
(c) Efficacy of drug
(d) All of the above

42. Dissociative anesthesia is produced by :
(a) Lignocaine.
(b) Nitrous Oxide.
(c) Diazepam.
(d) Ketamine.

43. Contra indications for the use of corticosteroids are the following except:
(a) Peptic ulcer.
(b) Herpes simplex Infection.
(c) Diabetes Mellitus
(d) severe acute Bronchial asthma

44. Obtundents are:
(a) Abrasives
(b) Mummifying agents.
(c) Sweetening agents
(d) Dentine desensitizers.

45. Malignant hyperthermia is caused by :
(a) Atropine.
(b) Aspirin.
(c) Succinyl choline
(d) None of the above

GENERAL MEDICINE

46. The invasion of living tissues by larvae of certain species of flies is called

(a) Helminthiasis (b) Myiasis
(c) Myelofibrosis (d) Moniliasis

47. Which of the following is indicative of left ventricular failure?

(a) Neck Vein distension. (b) Ascitis.
(c) Anorexia. (d) Generalized edema

48. Lobar pneumonia is usually caused by :

(a) Klebsiella pnemoniae. (b) Streptococcus pyogenes.
(c) Pneumococci. (d) Staphylococcus aureus

49. All of the following contribute to hepatic encephalopathy except:

(a) Antibiotic Therapy. (b) Hypokalemia
(c) Gastro-Intestinal Bleeding. (d) Cirrhosis

50. Intravenous drug abusers have following diseases except:

(a) Hepatitis B. (b) Polyneuritis
(c) Endocarditis (d) None

51. Blood borne Hepatitis are all except:

(a) Hepatitis B. (b) Hepatitis C.
(c) Hepatitis D. (d) Hepatitis E.

52. Massive splenomegaly is seen in :

(a) Typhoid. (b) Infective endocarditis.
(c) Acute Leukemia (d) Portal hypertension

53. Drug of choice for dermatitis herpetiform is :

(a) Rifampicin. (b) Corticosteroid.
(c) Acyclovir. (d) Dapsone.

54. All of the following are clinical features of Infective endocarditis except:

(a) Anemia (b) Pyrexia.
(c) Hepatomegaly. (d) Splenomegaly

55. The Commonest cause of Jaundice in India is:

(a) Anti-tubercular Drugs. (b) Viral Hepatitis
(c) Liver Cancer. (d) Stone in common Bile duct.

56. Commonest mode of death in patients of Hypertension is :

(a) Epistaxis. (b) Gastro-intestinal bleeding.
(c) Heart failure. (d) Kidney failure

57. Vasovagal shock is precipitated due to activation of :

(a) Parasympathetic system (b) Sympathetic System.
(c) Dilation of all vessels. (d) None of the above.

58. In cerebral concussion the pupils are:

(a) Constricted and reacting to light.
(b) Dilated and not reacting to light.
(c) Dilated and reacting to light.
(d) Constricted and not reacting to light.

59. Mannitol is given in head injury patients to :

(a) Decrease hematoma formation
(b) Decrease intracranial pressure
(c) To differentiate cerebral edema and hematoma formation.
(d) To decrease osmolarity of blood.

GENERAL SURGERY

60. Primary closure of wounds fail if there is :

(a) Tight closure.
(b) Haematoma formation
(c) When no drainage is present
(d) All of the above

61. Cystic Hygroma is a :

(a) Haemangioma
(b) Lymphangioma.
(c) Lung abscess
(d) Liver cirrhosis manifestation

62. Marjolin's ulcer is a:

(a) Malignant"ulcer found on skin of face
(b) Malignant ulcer found on the scar of burn
(c) Trophic ulcer
(d) Tropical ulcer characterized by absence of pain

63. Positive Murphy's signs is indicative of :

(a) Peritonitis
(b) Perforation of peptic ulcer
(c) Acute Appendicitis
(d) Tender gallbladder

64. Pyelography is a method by which dye is injected to visualize:

(a) Parotid Gland.
(b) Liver.
(c) Kidneys
(d) Spleen

65. Colles' fracture is associated with:

(a) Mandible
(b) Knee
(c) Ankle
(d) Wrist

66. Cold abscess formation is due to :

(a) Presence of acute inflammation.
(b) Formation of casseous pus with signs of acute inflammation.
(c) Formation of casseous pus without signs of acute inflammation
(d) Infected cyst.

67. The term poikilokaryosis refer to

(a) Alteration of nuclear-cytoplasmic ratio.
(b) Division of nuclei without division of cytoplasm.

(c) Large, prominent nuclei
(d) Loss of polarity and disorientation of cells

68. Phlegmon is a :
(a) Sexually transmitted disease.
(b) Type of cellulitis.
(c) Type of osteomyelitis.
(d) Venereal disease

ORAL PATHOLOGY

69. Which type of Odontogenic Keratocyst is more aggressive, more common & more likely to recur
(a) Orthokeratinised
(b) Parakeratinised
(c) Nonkeratinised
(d) Dekeratinised

70. The epithelium of a dentigerous cyst it :
(a) 15-20 cell thick
(b) 6-10 cell thick
(c) 2-4 cell thick
(d) 1-2 cell thick

71 . The' Swiss cheese Appearance is seen in microscopic picture or :
(a) Lichen Planus
(b) Adenoid Cystic Carcinoma
(c) Ameloblastoma
(d) Pleomorphic adenoma

72. Candidiasis associated with Dentures is :
(a) Acute Pseudo Membranous
(b) Acute Atrophic
(c) Chronic Hyperplasic
(d) Chronic Atrophic

73. Munro's abscess is seen in :
(a) Leukoplakia
(b) White spongy Nevus
(c) Psoriasis
(d) Lichen Planus

74. Serum alkaline phosphatase is raised in all of the following except:
(a) Paget's disease.
(b) Fibrous dysplasia
(c) Osteomyelitis
(d) Hyperparathyroidism

75. Mask - like appearance 0;- race with narrowing of oral aperture and rigidity of the mucosa is characteristic of:
(a) Progressive systemic sclerosis
(b) Tetanus
(c) Multiple sclerosis
(d) Osteomalacia

76. Intraepithelial vesicle is the feature found in :
(a) Lichen planus
(b) Pemphigus
(c) Bullous pemphigoid
(d) All of the above

77. Double lip is one of the features of :
(a) Albright's syndrome.
(b) Frey's syndrome
(c) Aldrich syndrome.
(d) Ascher's syndrome

78. The Capacity to reproduce skin lesions at sites of injury in psoriasis is called:
(a) Koebner's phenomenon:
(b) Nikolsky's sign
(c) Chvostek sign
(d) Raynaud's phenomenon

79. Chloromas are a feature of :
(a) Lymphomas.
(b) Leukemia.
(c) Leukodema.
(d) Leukoplakia

80. Swelling of the nasolabial fold with no radiographic findings is suggestive of :
(a) Median palatine cyst.
(b) Periapical cyst.
(c) Nasopalatine cyst.
(d) Nasoalveolar cyst

81. Abnormality in morphodifferentiation stage of tooth development results in :
(a) Mottled enamel.
(b) Mesiodens.
(c) Dens in dente.
(d) Dentinogenesis imperfecta

82. Gustatory sweating is seen in : ,
(a) Auriculotemporal syndrome.
(b) Facial palsy
(c) Myofacial pain dysfunction syndrome
(d) Mickluicz's disease.

83. Complete obliteration of pulp is seen in all the following except:
(a) Type I dentinogenesis imperfecta.
(b) Type II dentinogenesis imperfecta.
(c) Type III dentinogenesis imperfecta.
(d) Dentinal dysplasia.

84. Epstein pearls are cysts that arise from:
(a) Squamous tissue of the mucosa.
(b) Connective tissue of the mucosa
(c) Rests of Malassez
(d) Papilloma virus

85. Which of the following viruses are not implicated in human malignancies?
(a) Epstein - Barr Virus.
(b) Herpes simplex virus type I.
(c) HTLV I.
(d) Papilloma virus.

86. Secretary immunoglobulin is:
(a) IgA.
(b) IgE
(c) IgG
(d) IgM

87. Paul-Bunnel test is positive in :
(a) Infectious mononucleosis
(b) Multiple myeloma
(c) Malignant nerves
(d) Rubella

88. The Cell body seen in microscopic picture of Lichen planus is :
(a) Lipshultz Bodies.
(b) Barr Bodies.
(c) Civatte Bodies
(d) Koilocyte body.

ORAL MEDICINE AND RADIOLOGY

89. A disease that only affects formation and eruption of tooth but does not cause hypoplasia is:
(a) Hypoparathyroidism
(b) Hyperparathyroidism
(c) Rickets.
(d) Syphilis

90. The overall degree of darkening of exposed film is known as:
(a) Contrast. (b) Density
(c) Sharpness (d) Fog

91. The Filter in an X-Ray apparatus is made up of:
(a) Aluminum (b) Lead.
(c) Molybdenum. (d) Tungsten.

92. Choose the false statement among the four:
(a) X-rays are ionizing rays (b) X-rays can be focused
(c) X-rays cannot be seen or touched. (d) X-rays can cause mutation

93. Juvenile rheumatoid arthritis is called:
(a) Still's disease. (b) Cushing's syndrome.
(c) Addison's disease (d) Van recklinghausen's syndrome.

94. Injecting radio-opaque dye into the joint space to visualize the joint is referred to as:
(a) Arthorscopy (b) Arthrography
(c) Orthropantomography (d) Arthroplasty.

95. Target lesions are seen in:
(a) Erythroplakia (b) Pemphigus.
(c) Erythema Multiforme (d) Lichen planus

96. The Compton Effect is seen when:
(a) X-rays strike on Film.
(b) X-rays strike on skin
(c) X-rays interact with matter
(d) X-rays interact with emulsion coating on film.

PERIODONTICS

97. Gingival fluid is a :
(a) Transudate
(b) Exudate
(c) Can be either of the two (Transudate & Exudate)
(d) neither of the two (Transudate & Exudate)

98. Burtonian line is a linear pigmentation gingival margin due to overexposure to :
(a) Bismuth (b) Silver
(c) Lead (d) Arsenic

99. The flap technique for pocket elimination which also increase the which of attached gingiva is :
(a) Coronally repositioned flap (b) Apically repositioned flap
(c) Laterally displaced flap (d) Modified Widman flap

100. In modified Widman flap:

(a) Internal bevel incision is the last incision
(b) Interdental papilla is eliminated
(c) Posterior areas are difficult to access the bone
(d) Crevicular incision is made from base of the pocket

101. For root planning and sub gingival scaling of mesial surface in posterior teeth, Gracey curettes

(a) No 7-8 are used
(b) No.9-10 are used
(c) No.11-12 are used
(d) No.13-14 are used

102. Coronoplasty should be carried out in patients with:

(a) Occlusal prematurities
(b) Parafunctional habits
(c) Signs of trauma from occlusion
(d) All of the above feature

103. Presence of ammonia in the saliva will

(a) Increase plaque formation
(b) Decrease plaque formation
(c) Have no effect on plaque formation
(d) Increase calculus formation

104. The periodontal fibers which are more resistant to forces along the long axis are:

(a) Apical
(b) Oblique
(c) Alveolar crest
(d) Horizontal

105. Electro-Surgery or surgical diathermy uses controlled high frequency electrical current in the range of :

(a) 1.5-7.5 million cycles / second
(b) 7.5-10.0 million cycles / second
(c) 15-20 million cycles / second
(d) 25-30 million cycles / second

106. A glycoprotein that promotes new attachment and increased cell proliferation is :

(a) Fibronectin
(b) Fibro pectin
(c) Glycogen
(d) Glycoaminologlycan

107. Healing of a graft of intermediate thickness is completed by

(a) 3 Weeks
(b) 5 Weeks
(c) 10 Weeks
(d) 16 Weeks

108. The offset angle of Gracey curette between the blade and shank is

(a) 70 degrees
(b) 60 degrees
(c) 80 degrees
(d) 90 Degrees

109. CADIA is used to assess:

(a) Occlusal trauma
(b) Furcation involvement
(c) Gingival enlargement.
(d) Periodontal disease progression

110. DNA Probe

(a) Measures periodontal pocket depth
(b) Identifies a particular micro-organism
(c) Calculate the length of gingival epithelial attachment
(d) Is not useful in all the above three

111. The graft with maximum osteogenic potential is :

(a) Allograft
(b) Xenograft
(c) Auto-Cortical
(d) Auto – cancellous

CONSERVATIVE DENTISTRY AND ENDODONTICS

112. Most of the routinely used burs in Conservation Dentistry have:

(a) Positive rake
(b) Negative rake.
(c) Neutral rake
(d) None of the above

113. In a class V preparation, during application of rubber dam the punch of the tooth to be restored should be made:

(a) According to the template supplied
(b) According to the existing arch form
(c) Labial to the position of the tooth to be operated
(d) Lingual to the position of the tooth to be operated

114. Lentulospirals are used for:

(a) Locating canal orifice
(b) Pulp extirpation
(c) Enlarging coronal third root canal
(d) Application of root canal sealer

115. Penetrating corrosion in an amalgam restoration is caused by:

(a) Ag-Hg phase
(b) Sn-Hg phase
(c) Cu-Sn phase
(d) All the above

116. Which among the following statements is true:

(a) file have more flutes than reamers
(b) reamers have more flutes than files
(c) both have the same number of flutes.
(d) files and reamers have no flutes

117. According to ISO standardization, root canal files and reamers should have a taper of :

(a) 0.02 mm per em
(b) 0.02 mm per mm
(c) 0.03 mm per cm
(d) 0.03mm per mm

118. One of the purpose of etching beveled enamel surface is to :

(a) increase surface energy
(b) produce macro under cut
(c) to increase convenience
(d) to prevent caries

119. The Massermann Kit technique for removing solid objects :

(a) is very short procedure
(b) is more successful in posterior teeth than in anterior ones
(c) requires frequent radiographic monitoring
(d) is better than the ultrasonic technique

120. The angle of the beveled resected root:

(a) should be sufficient to provide access to perform the retro preparation.
(b) should be at 45 degrees to the facial surface.

(c) shall enable the removal 1 to 2 mm of apex to ensure that apical ramifications are not present.
(d) should be at 60 degrees to the facial surfaces.

121. A pulp is inflamed as a result of deep caries and cavity preparation, which of the following helps the best to resolve the inflammation:
(a) Calcium Hydroxide
(b) No medication / material available presently which can promote pulp healing
(c) Mineral trioxide aggregate
(d) Poly antibiotic preparation

122. The blue light used to polymerize composite resin is harmful to eye if one looks at it, which portion of the eye is affected
(a) Cornea
(b) Retina
(c) Lens
(d) None of the above

123. Once triturated, the Dental amalgam should be condensed with in
(a) 5 minutes
(b) 6 minutes
(c) 3 minutes
(d) 15 minutes

124. Which of the following Principles of the cavity preparation is not considered much in modern methods of restorative dentistry :
(a) extension of prevention
(b) convenient form
(c) removal of the undermined enamel
(d) removal of the carious enamel

125. Rounding of the axio - pulpal line angle in a proximo-occlusal preparation is considered as a part of :
(a) refining the line form
(b) retention form
(c) resistance form
(d) convenient form

126. As far as the raise of fractional heat, in using various rotary cutting instruments, is concerned which one of the following is the most kind to the pulp.
(a) stainless steel bur
(b) diamond bur
(c) carbide bur
(d) carbon steel bur

127. Which of the following is least likely to be used as a pit and fissure sealant?
(a) Cyanocrylates
(b) Urethane
(c) Gold alloy
(d) BIS-GMA

ORAL AND MAXILLO-FACIAL SURGERY

128. The proximal segment of horizontally unfavorable mandibular angle fracture is displaced
(a) Inferiorly
(b) Posteriorly and medially
(c) Anteriorly and superiorly
(d) Anteriorly and laterally

129. Surgical management of Ludwig's Angina includes:
(a) Application of heat
(b) Incision and decompression
(c) Drainage through closed dwelling catheter
(d) both b and c

130. Gunning splints are used when the patient is :
(a) Dentulous
(b) Edentulous
(c) Children
(d) Young Adults

131. Ecchymosis in the mastoid region seen after a fracture of the petrous bone is known as :
(a) Chvostek's sign
(b) Battle sign
(c) Guerin's sign
(d) Tinel's sign

132. Direct interdental wiring is also known is :
(a) Risdon's wiring
(b) Gilmer's wiring
(c) Stout's wiring
(d) Eyelet wiring

133. Paresis means:
(a) Total loss of sensory function.
(b) Total loss of motor function
(c) Incomplete paralysis
(d) None of the above

134. The following structures are divided when the angle of the mandible is exposed through the submandibular incision
(a) Skin and superficial fascia, platysma, deep cervical fascia and medial pterygoid muscle.
(b) Skin, superficial fascia, deep cervical fascia and masseter muscle.
(c) Skin, platysma, deep cervical, fascia and masseter muscle.
(d) Skin, superficial fascia, platysma, deep cervical fascia and masseter muscle.

135. The "Red Line" in Winter's classification of impacted teeth represents:
(a) The depth at which the impacted tooth is located.
(b) The angulations of the second molar.
(c) The summit of the alveolar bone covering the impacted.
(d) The level of the occlusal plane.

136. Apicoectomy is:
(a) Periapical curettage
(b) Retrograde restoration
(c) Surgical removal of root
(d) surgical removal of root tip of an endodontically treated tooth

137. Hyperbaric oxygen therapy is indicated in :
(a) Pulmonary hypertension
(b) Myocardial Infarction
(c) Syncope
(d) Osteoradionecrosis

138. "Kelsey Fry technique" refer to the removal in :
(a) Impacted maxillary 3rd molars
(b) Impacted mandibular 3rd molars'
(c) Impacted mandibular canines
(d) Impacted maxillary canines

139. "Dumb-bell" shaped swelling is characteristic of which type of odontogenic space infections:

(a) Submandibular space
(b) Buccal space infection
(c) Submassetric space infection
(d) Temporal space infection

140. Infection from the dangerous area of the face spreads to the cavernous sinus via the:

(a) Neural sheath.
(b) Emissary veins
(c) Orbital fissure.
(d) Ethmoidal air sinuses

141. B.P. blade used for the "Hilton method" is :

(a) No. 10
(b) No. 11
(c) No. 12
(d) No. 15

142. Visor osteotomy is a :

(a) in orthognathic surgical procedure.
(b) a cancer resection procedure
(c) a fracture reduction and fixation procedure
(d) a preprosthetic procedure

PEDODONTICS

143. The ugly ducking stage of dentition in a child is corrected by the eruption of which tooth

(a) Central incisor
(b) Lateral incisor
(c) Canine
(d) First molar

144. In the absence of a second premolar the roots of the primary second molar will most likely

(a) Resorb at normal site
(b) Resorb more slowly than Normal
(c) Resorb more rapidly than normal
(d) Show no resorption as the initiator force is absent

145. Which of the following procedure is replaced by the use of occlusal sealants

(a) Occlusal amalgam restoration
(b) Topical fluoride restoration
(c) Prophylactic odontomy
(d) All

146. The Green stains frequently seen in children's teeth are caused by :

(a) Chromogenic bacteria
(b) Acute necrotizing gingivitis
(c) Enamel defects
(d) Vitamin B deficiency

147. Most common cause of acute generalized gingival inflammation in a preschool child

(a) Acute herpetic gingivostomatitis
(b) Acute necrotizing gingivitis
(c) Apthous stomatitis
(d) Vitamin B deficiency

148. On the first dental visit, basic fear of a child under the age of 2 is related to:
(a) Fear of injection.
(b) Anxiety over being separated from parent.
(c) Anxiety regarding instruments used to perform dental treatment.
(d) Not understanding the reason for dental treatment.

149. The success of calcium hydroxide pulpotomy is determined by the
(a) Formation of calcified
(b) Formation of hard base to support the restoration.
(c) Continuation of root formation and apexogenesis.
(d) All of the above.

150. Teeth usually emerge when:
(a) ¼ of their roots are complete
(b) ½ of roots are complete
(c) ¾ of roots are complete
(d) After completion of root formation

151. In primary molars when proximal portion of Class II cavity preparation extends deep gingivally, a satisfactory gingival seat is not obtained because:
(a) Enamel rods extend occlusally in gingival third.
(b) Buccal and lingual surface converge occlusally.
(c) Primary teeth have marked cervical constriction.
(d) All of the above.

ORTHODONTICS

152. The best age for giving a functional appliance for correcting skeletal dysplasia in girls is :
(a) 6-8years
(b) 10-11 years
(c) 13-15 years
(d) After 18 years

153. The optimal time to employ an orthodontic appliance that takes advantage of growth is during
(a) Late primary dentition
(b) Early mixed dentition
(c) Late mixed dentition
(d) Early permanent dentition

154. A retained lower deciduous incisors will usually:
(a) Deflect the permanent tooth labially.
(b) Deflect the permanent tooth lingually.
(c) Causes ankylosis of the underlying permanent tooth.
(d) Causes impaction of underlying permanent tooth.

155. The difference between the amount of space needed for the permanent incisors to erupt and the space available for them is called
(a) Primate space
(b) Leeway space
(c) Interdental space
(d) Incisor liability

156. Rotation of the teeth around its long axis is known as :

(a) Axioversion
(b) Transversion
(c) Perversion
(d) Torsiversion

157. The most common tooth to get impacted (excluding the third molars) is :

(a) Maxillary canine
(b) Mandibular canine
(c) Maxillary II premolar
(d) Mandibular II premolar

158. The face that is long and narrow is said to be :

(a) Mesoprosopic
(b) Leptoprosopic
(c) Euryprosopic.
(d) Brachyprosopic

159. Lisping is associated commonly with which of the following malocclusions:

(a) Anterior deep bite
(b) Anterior crowding
(c) Anterior open bite
(d) Anterior retroclination

160. The average angle of convexity as in Down's Cephalometric analysis is :

(a) 0 degree
(b) 25 degree
(c) 82 degree
(d) 84 degrees

161. Fishman's SMI is a method of evaluation of:

(a) Symmetry of the dental arch
(b) Skeletal maturity
(c) Arch length discrepancy
(d) Prognathism of maxilla

162. Which of following analysis is used to asses the tooth size discrepancy between the upper and lower teeth

(a) Wits analysis.
(b) Korkhaus analysis.
(c) Bolton analysis.
(d) Moyers analysis.

163. The type of tooth movement most notorious for relapse is:

(a) Tipping
(b) Translation
(c) Torquing
(d) Rotation

164. Rapid palatal expansion using a Hyrax screw is an example for:

(a) Extra-oral anchorage.
(b) Intermaxillary anchorage
(c) Muscular anchorage.
(d) Reciprocal anchorage

165. The most important disadvantage of removable appliances is :

(a) They are dependent .on patient co-operation
(b) They are not hygienic
(c) They are ineffective in treating deep bite
(d) Fabrication is cumbersome

166. Shape memory is a characteristic of which of the following wires:

(a) Beta - Titanium
(b) Alpha - Titanium
(c) Nickel - Titanium
(d) Chrome - Cobalt

167. The force exerted by wire is:

(a) Directly proportional to the cube of the length of the wire.
(b) Inversely proportional to the cube of the length of the wire.

(c) Directly proportional to the fourth power of the length of the wire.
(d) Inversely proportional to the fourth power of the length of the wire.

168. Delaire's Facemask is used in the treatment of :
(a) Mandibular retrognathism
(b) Maxillary retrognathism
(c) Mandibular ankylosis
(d) Maxillary prognathism

169. Which of the following is a fixed functional appliance:
(a) Bionator
(b) Bow activator
(c) Herbst appliance
(d) Kinetor

170. In classical Begg Mechano therapy, bite opening is primarily effected in :
(a) Stage I
(b) Stage II
(c) Stage III
(d) Stage IV

PROSTHODONTICS

171. Fovea palatine are formed:
(a) Behind the vibrating line.
(b) In front of vibrating line.
(c) On the vibrating line.
(d) has no relation to the vibrating line.

172. The stability of denture refer to :
(a) Resistance against vertical forces
(b) Resistance against horizontal forces.
(c) Resistance to removal in the opposite direction.
(d) Mobility of Dentures.

173. The Gothic arch tracing device is used to record:
(a) The vertical dimension of occlusion.
(b) The centric relation
(c) Centric occlusion
(d) Orientation relation

174. Reduced interocclusal distance in complete dentures
(a) Reduces biting forces
(b) Increases biting force
(c) Is not related to biting force
(d) Causes increased soreness

175. Difficulty in use of metallic denture bases is :
(a) Less margin of error in posterior palatal seal.
(b) Lack of tissue tolerance.
(c) Increased weight of dentures.
(d) Difficulty in getting accuracy of fit.

176. Antes law states that:
(a) Combined periodontal ligament area of the abutment tooth should equal or exceed that of tooth or teeth to be replaced.
(b) Combined periodontal ligament area of the abutment tooth should be less than that of tooth or teeth to be replaced.
(c) Combined periodontal ligament area of the abutment tooth should be at least double that of tooth or teeth to be replaced.
(d) Ante's law has now been proved to be obsolete

177. The Pontic of maxillary posterior region should be :

(a) Sanitary (b) Point contact
(c) Bullet nose (d) Saddle

178. A full veneer crown is one that.

(a) Fully veneers one surface of a tooth.
(b) Covers whole of the clinical crown of a tooth.
(c) Is basically a porcelain veneer.'
(d) Covers more than 7/8th of the tooth.

179. Time taken for osseo integration of implants in the maxilla is :

(a) 4 months (b) 2 months
(c) 6 months (d) 8 months

180. The recommended time interval between surgery and placing load in the posterior mandible is :

(a) 2 months (b) 3 months
(c) 4 months (d) 3 months

181. Margin for all ceramic crowns should be:

(a) Feather edge (b) Shoulder
(c) Shoulder with bevel (d) Chamfer

182. The Ideal occlusal clearance for a complete cast crown is:

(a) 0.5 mm (b) 1.5 mm
(c) 2mm (d) 2.5mm

183. Indirect retainers in bilateral distal extension base removable partial dentures are based on :

(a) Class I lever principle (b) Class II lever principle.
(c) Class III lever principle. (d) Combination of more than one of the above

184. Least preferred maxillary major connector is:

(a) Single palatal strap (b) Anterior-posterior palatal bar
(c) Horse shoe shaped major connector (d) Complete palatal coverage

185. Back action clasp is a modification of :

(a) Embrasure clasp. (b) Half & half clasp
(c) Reverse action clasp (d) Ring clasp

COMMUNITY AND PREVENTIVE DENTISTRY

186. Bias is any systematic error in the determination of association between:

(a) Relative risk and attributable risk (b) incidence and prevalence
(c) Exposure and disease (d) Disease and environmental factors

187. Salt fluoridation was pioneered' by

(a) U.S. Public Health commission
(b) Switzerland
(c) New Zealand
(d) Singapore

188. "Loss of head" in water purification is related to :

(a) Filtration capacity
(b) Disinfections of water
(c) Fluoridation of water
(d) Chlorination of water

189. Estimated lethal dose of body in adults:

(a) 1-2 Gm/kg of body weight
(b) 2.5-3.5 Gm/kg of body weight
(c) 3.5-4 Fm/ kg of body weight
(d) 5-10 Gm/kg of body weight.

190. DMF score for anyone individual can range from:

(a) 0-28
(b) 0-32
(c) 0-48
(d) 0-64

191. Revised Deans Fluorosis Index has

(a) Five Point scale
(b) Six point scale
(c) Seven point scale
(d) Nine point scale

192. Which of the following in not an indicator for nutritional status:

(a) Vital signs.
(b) Weight and height
(c) Mid arm circumference
(d) Prevalence of low birth weight

193. Primordial prevention, a new concept receiving special attention in the prevention of :

(a) Acute disease.
(b) Chronic disease.
(c) Epidemics
(d) Pandemics

194. Repeated topical application of a fluoride agent will not produce tooth mottling because:

(a) the concentration in topical agent is not as high as required for mottling.
(b) the saliva neutralizes the excess fluoride delivered by topical agent.
(c) it is not fluoride that produces the mottling seen in Fluorosis.
(d) the tooth is already calcified and cannot be altered in this fashion.

195. Select the false principal for DMF Score:

(a) Last permanent molars are included in scoring.
(b) Naturally exfoliated teeth should not be taken into consideration.
(c) Teeth extracted due to orthodontic treatment or periodontal disease or Impaction should not be considered.
(d) Endodontically treated tooth should be considered.

196. Which of the followings is the wrong statement?

(a) 2% NaF Solution is recommended as caries preventive agent.
(b) 2% NaF Solution can be prepared by dissolving 0.2 gm of NaF powder in 10 ml of distilled water in plastic bottle.
(c) If NaF aqueous solution is stored in glass bottle, then the fluoride ions of solution can react with silica of glass forming Si F2, thus reducing the availability of free active fluorides to anticaries activity.

2005
ANSWERS & EXPLANATIONS

ANATOMY

Ans.1. (c) Abducent nerve

Explained earlier, Please refer KCET-06 A3

Ans.2. (b) Auditory tube and levator palati muscle

Ref B D CHAURASIA; PG NO-223

The large gap between the superior constrictor muscle and base of the skull is known as the ***Sinus of Morgagni***. Structures passing through this gap are –

- auditory tube
- levator veli palate muscle
- ascending palatine artery

Structures passing through gaps between *superior and middle constrictor* are-

- stylopharyngeus
- glossopharyngeal nerve

Structures passing through gap between *middle and inferior* are-

- internal laryngeal nerve
- superior laryngeal nerve

Passing between *inferior constrictor and esophagus* are-

- recurrent laryngeal
- inferior laryngeal nerve

Ans.3. (b) Parotid gland

Explained earlier, please refer KCET-07 A1

Ans.4. (c) Thymus

Ref B D CHAURASIA PG 172; http://en.wikipedia.org/wiki/Hassall's_corpuscles

- **Hassall's corpuscles** (or **thymic corpuscles**) are structures in the human thymus, composed of epithelial reticular cells.
- They are named for Arthur Hill Hassall, who discovered them in 1849.
- The function of Hassall's corpuscles is currently unclear, and the absence of this structure in the murine thymus has restricted mechanistic dissection.
- It is known that Hassall's corpuscles are a potent source of the cytokine TSLP. *In vitro*, TSLP directs the maturation of dendritic cells, and increases the ability of dendritic cells to convert naive thymocytes to a Foxp3+ regulatory T cell lineage.

- The cortical lymphocytes of the thymus arises form the stem cells of the bone marrow origin. Most (95%) are auto-allergic and hence short lived. They never make it out of the thymus. Their remnants are seen in Hassalls corpuscles.

Ans.5. (a) Maxillary sinus

Explained earlier, please refer KCET-06 A9

DENTAL ANATOMY AND HISTOLOGY

Ans.6. (b) Mesiolingual

Ref wheelers 228 pg 6th ed)

It is formed by the union of the triangular ridge of the distobuccal cusp and the distal ridge of the mesiolingual cusp.

Ans.7. (c) Bunodont

Ref Wheelers, pg-82, 83, 6th ed)

Tooth forms and development

1. **haplodont** : the reptilian stage is represented by the simplest form of tooth, the single cone. The single pattern is found in both jaws which in effect limits the jaw movement. There is no occlusion of teeth in this class with procurement of food as their main function.
2. **triconodont** : the early mammalian stage exhibits three cusps in line in posterior teeth. The largest cusp is centered with the smaller cusps anteriorly and posteriorly. This pattern may still be found in some breed of dogs.
3. **tritubercular** : the three in line stage evolved to the three cornered shape which later developed into the quadritubercular stage wherein the occlusion was finally established.

Deuterocone: one of the cusps of a premolar tooth of a mammal corresponding in position (anteromedial) to the protocone of a true molar.

Bunodont: refers to the tooth bearing conical cusps seen primarily in primates. The cone shaped cusps are low and rounded and allow only simple opening and closing movements of the mandible with little/no lateral excursions; the humans present this type of dentition.

EXTRA EDGE

Selenodont: denoting an animal, or man, having teeth, as the human molars, with longitudinal crescent-shaped ridges. The simple bunodont dentition of dogs,cats etc evolved into complex morphological characteristics like enamel foldings,ridges and crests which together with increased anisognathism , greatly increased the amount of lateral excursion possible . in camel, giraffe and other cattles.

Lophodont: teeth having elongated ridges called lophs that run between cusps.

Dilambdodont: molars with a W-shaped outer ridge.

Zalambdodont: Molars having a lateral, V-shaped ridge.

Incisiform: chisel-like; used to describe teeth which are flattened and truncate with sharp edges like the front teeth of some mammals such as humans, also compressed and wedge-shaped; said of teeth with a cutting edge resembling incisors of higher vertebrates, such as ungulates (deer

Acrodont: in this type of dentition, the teeth are directly attached to the jaw bone.

Pleurodont dentition: the teeth arise from a one-sided groove. (inner margins of bone) Lizards have either pleurodont or acrodont dentition..

Monophyodont: presence of only one set of teeth during entire lifetime.

Diphyodont: presence of two sets of teeth.

Polyphyodont: more than two sets of teeth in lifetime.

Ans.8. (a) A delta fibers

Explained earlier please refer KCET-06 A14

Ans.9. (d) Early Bell Stage

Ref Orbans, 10th ed , pg30-35

Friends, another controversial question!

Consider the following lines from Orban-

"Cap stage- *the dental papilla shows active budding of capillaries and mitotic figures nd its peripheral cells adjacent to the inner enamel epithelium enlarge and later differentiate into odontoblast.*"

So, one thing is clear, hard tissue formation is not initiated in Cap stage

"Bell-stage – *before formation of dental tissues begin, the dental sac shows a circular arrangement of fibers and resembles a capsular structure. The peripheral cells of dental lamina differentiate into odontoblast under the organizing influence of the epithelium, and assume a columnar form"*

So we see that hard tissue formation actually begins in the' Bell stage'. Now whether this is indeed 'early Bell' is a question.

In Advance Bell stage- '' *the boundary between inner epithelium and odontoblasts outlines the future DEJ and the enamel organ gives rise to the epithelial root sheath of Hertwig.*' HERS develops after enamel completion.

I guess, we have no choice but to go with 'Early Bell' as the answer of exclusion.

Ans.10. (b) Hydrodynamic theory

Orbans 11th ed, pg123

- **DIRECT NEURAL THEORY**

It is the1st theory which states that stimulus reaches directly the dentinal inner nerve ending…but it lacks any scientific proof .

- **HYDRODYNAMICS THEORY:** it is 2nd and ***most popular*** theory, it states that alteration of fluid and cellular content of the dentinal tubules causes stimulation of the nerve ending closely associated with the odontoblast.

- **TRANSDUCTION THEORY:** it presumes that the odontoblast process is the primary structure excited by the stimulus and the impulse is transmitted to the nerve ending in the inner dentine. Not popular as there is no neurotransmitter vesicle within the odontoblast.

PHYSIOLOGY

Ans.11. (d) Juxtaglomerular Cells

Ref Ganong 22nd edition, pg 457 ; pg482 Chaudhari 2nd Ed

Renin in kidney extract and the blood stream is produced by the juxtaglomerular cell (JG cell). These epitheloid cells are located in the media of the afferent arterioles as they enter the glomeruli. Renin is also found in agranular ***lacis cells*** located at the junction between afferent and efferent arterioles, however it is less significant.

JG apparatus = JG cells + lacis cells + macula densa

EXTRA EDGE

Remember, ***Rennin*** (chymosin) is a proteolytic enzyme present in young animals and probably absent in humans acting upon milk casein. *Ref, Ganong 22nd edition pg 471*

Ans.12. (d) 1, 25 dyhydroxycholecalciferol.

Explained earlier, please refer KCET-07 A16

Ans.13. (a) Capillary blood flow

Ref Ganong 12th ed pg-586; pg235, chaudhary

According to **Hagen poiseuillie** equation.

$$F = (Pa - Pb) \times (\pi / 8) \times (1/\eta) \times (r^4/L)$$

Where,

F = flow

(Pa-Pb) = pressure difference between two ends

h = viscosity

r = radius

L = length

Also,

$R = 8 \eta L/\pi r^4$ R = resistance

So we see, F œ r^4 ;   and

R œ 1 / r^4

Ans.14. (c) Amount of Hemoglobin in the blood

Ref Ganong 22nd edition, pg 666

The oxygen delivery system in the body consists of the lung and the CVS. The mount of oxygen in the blood is determined by the ***amount of hemoglobin*** in the blood and the affinity of the Hb for oxygen.

Also remember,

- Hb is a protein made up of 4 sub units each with a heme moiety. Heme is a complex made of porphyrin and 1 atom ferrous ion.
- Fully saturated 1 gm of Hb contains 1.39 mL of oxygen.(total Hb 14-16 g/dL).

Ans.15. (c) Gastrocolic reflex

Ref Ganong 22nd edition, pg 511

Distention of the stomach by food initiates contraction of the rectum and frequently a desire to defecate. This response is termed as the gastro-colic reflex. There is some evidence that this may be due to action of *gastrin* on the colon and not only neurally mediated. Because of this response, ***defecation after meal*** is the RULE in children. In adults, habit and cultural factors play a large role in determining when defecation occurs.

Ans.16. (b) Na^+

Ref Ganong 22nd edition, pg 471

- The transport of most hexoses is uniquely affected by the amounts of Na^+ in the intestinal lumen.
- This is because glucose and Na^+ share the same co-transporter or ***symport***, the sodium-dependent glucose transporter (SGLT 1 and 2)
- The Na^+ moves into cell along with its concentration gradient and the glucose follows via the GLUT 2 receptors, hence,
- the energy for glucose transport is provided indirectly by the active transport of Na^+ out of the cell.(an example of secondary active transport)

BIOCHEMISTRY

Ans.17. (b) Hyaluronic Acid

Ref Lippincott's ; 2nd ed , pg 149

Glycosaminoglycans (GAGs) are large complexes of negatively charged heteropolysaccharide chains generally associated with a small amount of protein. These have special property to bind large amounts of water, thereby producing a gel – like matrix (ground substance), due to their viscous properties they are also known as mucopolysaccharides.

Types :-

Name	Features
Chondroitin sulfates	Most abundant GAG. Found in cartilage, tendons, ligament aorta
Keratan Sulfate	Most hetrogenoous GAG, found in cartilages and cornea
Hyaluronic acid	Unsulfated , only GAG found also in bacteria. *Serves as a lubricant and shock absorber.* Found in synovial fluid of joints, loose CT and vitreous humor of eye
Dermatan Sulfate	Found in skin , blood vessels and heart valves
Heparin	Unlike other GAGs that are extracellular compounds, heparin is an intracellular component of mast cells and line arteries. Serves as an anticoagulant
Heparan Sulfate	Extracellular GAGs found in basement membrane and as a ubiquitous component of cell surfaces.

Ans.18. (a) Folic acid deficiency

Ref Lippincott , 2nd ed , pg 246

Histidine is deaminated and hydrolyzed to form N-*formiminoglutamate* (FIGlu) which donates its formimino group to tetrahydrofolate , leaving glutamate. Individuals deficient in folic acid excrete increased amounts of FIGlu n the urine, particularly after ingestion of large amounts of histidine. The **FIGlu excretion test** has been used in diagnosing a deficiency of folic acid.

EXTRA EDGE

Remember, Folic acid plays an important role in 1-C metabolism, and is essential for bio-synthesis of the purines and the pyrimidine, thymine.

Ans.19. (d) 9.0 kc/g.

Ref Lippincott, 2nd ed , pg 304

Energy content of food is calculated form the heat released by the total combustion of food in a calorimeter. It is expressed in kilo calories (kcal). The ***standard conversion factors*** are:

- Carbohydrates – 4 kcal/g
- Proteins - 4 kcal/g
- Fat - 9 kcal/g
- Alcohol - 7 kcal/g

Remember, the term Biological value refers to quality of a dietary protein. That is its ability to provide the essential amino acids required for tissue maintenance. Biological values are measured on a relative scale, with whole egg protein scored at 100.

Ans.20. (c) Inner membrane of Mitochondria

Ref Lippincott pg 66

First, **What is electron transport chain?**

Energy rich molecules such as glucose or fatty acids are metabolized by a series of oxidation reactions ultimately yielding CO_2 and water involving various intermediates (coenzymes, FAD, NAD). Part of this energy can be stored and used for production of ATP from AMP (oxidative phosphorylation).

ETC and the Inner mitochondrial membrane

The electron transport chain is present in the ***inner mitochondrial membrane*** and is the final common pathway by which electrons derived flow to oxygen. The inner membrane is specialized structure that is impermeable to many small molecules including H^+, Na^+ and K^+ important to mitochondrial function. This membrane is unusually ***rich in protein***. It is also highly convulated (cristae)

Matrix of the mitochondrion

The gel-like solution houses various enzymes for oxidation of pyruvate, fatty acids (beta oxidation). TCA cycle, the synthesis of urea and heme also occur partially here.

The ETC

Remember, with the exception of Coenzyme Q , all other members are proteins:

- CoQ is also known as ubiquinone . it is a H^+ acceptor.
- Cytochromes contains a heme group with bound $Fe2^+$.
- Cy a+a3 is the only member which has free ligand that can react directly with the oxygen molecule. They contain bound **copper.**
- **Inhibitors** – *oligomycin* binds to the stalk of ATP synthetase; uncouplers ***like 2,4- dinitrophenol*** which causes ETC to proceed at a rapid rate without establishing proton gradient(as a result energy produced is released as heat without ATP formation).

MICROBIOLOGY

Ans.21. (d) 121°C. temp and pressure is 15lb/sq. inch for 12 min

Explained Earlier, please refer KCET- 07 A19

Ans.22. (c) Vibrio cholera

Ref http://en.wikipedia.org/wiki/Vibrio cholerae

Vibrio cholerae is a gram negative bacterium with a curved-rod shape that causes cholera in humans. *V. cholerae* and other species of the genus *Vibrio* belong to the gamma subdivision of the Proteobacteria. There are two major strains of *V. cholerae*, classic and El Tor, and numerous other serogroups.

V. cholerae occurs naturally in the plankton of fresh, brackish, and salt water, attached primarily to copepods in the zooplankton. Coastal cholera outbreaks typically follow zooplankton blooms. This makes cholera a typical ***zoonosis***.

Pathogenesis

V. cholerae colonizes the gastrointestinal tract, where it adheres to villous absorptive cells via pili, and secretes a Binary toxin, called ***cholera toxin*** (CT). The two CT subunits are named A and B, and are synthesized in a 1:5 ratio. B subunits bind and internalize A subunits, which are processed to A1. The A1 form catalyses ADP ribosylation from NAD to the regulatory component of adenylate cyclase, thereby activating it. Increased adenylate cyclase activity ***increases*** cyclic AMP (cAMP) synthesis causing massive fluid and electrolyte efflux, resulting in diarrhea .

With serious cases of cholera, there is a rapid onset of symptoms, which include weakness, malaise (feeling rotten), and torrents of watery diarrhea with flecks of mucous — called **rice water stools**.

Water and electrolyte replacement are necessary in treating cholera. In some cases, tetracycline may be used. A vaccine is available outside the US, but it is short-lived and not currently recommended by the CDC. Fluoroquinolones such as norfloxacin are used, but resistance has been reported.

Ans.23. (a) Leishmania donovani

Ref http://www.earlham.edu/~jonesst2/leishmania.htm

The genus Leishmania is a member of the phylum *Sarcomastigophora* of the kingdom ***protista***. It is a diploid, intracellular parasite with a single flagellate.

- Leishmania is a parasite that affects vertebrates with the disease called Leishmaniasis. It has a complex life cycle.
- When an infected *Phlebotomid* **sand fly** (Phlebotomus) takes a blood meal it infects the vertebrate host with promastigote metacyclic forms.
- Within a short time the promastigotes are taken up by macrophages, the first line of defense of the immune system.
- The promastigote then loses its flagella and transforms into the amastigote form. Once internalized in a phagosome the macrophage lysosome fuses with the phagosome to from a phagolysosome containing the parasite.

Leishmania can be present in the human in three different types:

1. **Visceral Leishmaniasis:** (VL) is the most severe form of the disease. It is characterized by irregular bouts of fever, substantial weight loss, swelling of the spleen and liver, and anemia. This form is caused by *L.donovani.*
2. **Mucocutaneous Leishmaniasis:** (MCL) produces lesions, which can lead to extensive and disfiguring destruction of mucous membranes of the nose, mouth and throat cavities. This form is caused by *L. braziliensis* and *L. mexicana.*
3. **Cutaneous leishmaniasis:** (CL) There are two different species that cause this; they are L. tropica and L. major. They both have the same symptoms and life cycles but differ in their geographic distribution. Both species can produce large numbers of skin ulcers on the exposed parts of the body, such as the face, arms and legs, causing serious disability and leav-

ing the patient permanently scarred. The infection site is usually localized to the site in which the sand fly bite occurs. This form is caused by *L. tropica* and *L. major*.

The Visceral (VL) is the most severe of the three types of disease, in this form the parasite becomes systemic (spread through out the entire body) by infecting macrophages (immune cells) that in turn carry it to the spleen, liver and bone marrow. The typical symptoms for this form of the disease are fever, night sweats, fatigue, weakness, anorexia (appetite loss), weight loss, vomiting, diarrhea, cough, skin lesions and hair loss. If visceral leishmaniasis goes untreated it will usually result in death of the host do to liver damage, fever, weight loss and often secondary infection do to the fact that the macrophages are killed there by compromising the immune system. Visceral leishmaniasis is extremely dangerous to people already infected with HIV as the already compromised immune system is damaged even more so by the loss of macrophages.

Testing for Leishmania

- For cutaneous mucocutaneous infections skin biopsy fallowed by culturing of biopsy material is the most common way to check for Leishmania infections.
- For visceral infections spleen or bone marrow biopsies are possible, and are the most accurate tests, but are also very expensive and require invasive surgery. The presence of ***Donovanan*** bodies is the hallmark for this disease.
- The more common test is to draw blood, and test the blood with florescent antibodies to check for the presence of Leishmania. Complementary tests that can be performed include CBC (shows decreased cellularity of blood), hemoglobin (shows signs of anemia), serum protein (decreased), serum albumin (decreased) and immunoglobulins (increased).

The most commonly used cheapest and most effective chemotherapies for Leishmania infections are antimony-containing compounds such as ***Meglumine or Amphotericin B***

Another option in the case of allergy to the antimony compounds is Sodium stibogluconate, however this drug is less effective and has been shown to more often result in drug immune Leishmania. In the case of cutaneous Leishmania infections Paromomycin that is an antimony topical ointment is an option.

Ans.24. (c) Echinococcus granulosus

Ref http://en.wikipedia.org/wiki/Echinococcus_granulosus

Echinococcus granulosus, also called the **Hydatid worm**, is a cyclophyllid cestode that parasitizes the small intestine of canids as an adult, but which has important intermediate hosts such as livestock and *humans*, where it causes hydatid disease.

- The adult tapeworm is about 5 mm long and has three proglottids ("segments") when intact. Like all cyclophyllideans, *E. granulosus* has four suckers on its scolex ("head"), and *E. granulosus* also has a rostellum with hooks.
- In canids, *E. granulosus* causes a typical tapeworm infection, and produces eggs that are passed with the dog's feces.
- In the Intermediate hosts (including humans) that ingest dog feces, eggs hatch into oncosphere larvae that travel through the blood and form **hydatid cysts** in the host's tissues.

- These cysts can grow to be the size of a softball or basketball, and may contain several smaller "balloons" inside the main cyst.
- In the related worm *Echinococcus multilocularis*, the outer cyst is not present. If the outer cyst ruptures, new cysts can form at a different location in the body.
- Each smaller section contains several juvenile worms, and dogs may eat millions of them, resulting in very heavy infections.
- Hydatid cysts occur in organs like the liver, brain and lungs, not in subcutaneous tissue..
- Symptoms can include liver enlargement, hooklets in sputum and possible anaphylactic shock when the immune system reacts to ruptured cysts.
- A cyst is diagnosed with ultrasound, MRI, or immunoelectrophoresis.

Hydatid disease is treated with surgery, taking special care to leave the cyst intact so new cysts do not form, and ***mebendazole*** over a long period of time at low dosages.

Ans.25. (b) ELISA

Ref http://en.wikipedia.org/wiki/HIV#HIV test

HIV-1 testing consists of *initial screening* with an enzyme-linked immuno-sorbent assay (ELISA) to detect antibodies to HIV-1. Specimens with a non-reactive result from the initial ELISA are considered HIV-negative unless new exposure to an infected partner or partner of unknown HIV status has occurred.

Specimens with a reactive ELISA result are retested in duplicate. If the result of either duplicate test is reactive, the specimen is reported as repeatedly reactive and undergoes confirmatory testing with a more specific supplemental test (*e.g.,* Western blot or, less commonly, an immuno-fluorescence assay (IFA)).

Only specimens that are repeatedly reactive by ELISA and positive by IFA or reactive by Western blot are considered HIV-positive and indicative of HIV infection.

GENERAL PATHOLOGY

Ans.151. (c) Liquefactive necrosis

Ref (pg 35 dental harsh mohan 2nd Ed) ; Robbin's 6th ed , pg 12

Liquefactive necrosis

- due to degradation of tissue by hydrolytic enzyme.
- due to ischemic injury and bacterial and fungal infection and white cell infiltration
- *e.g.,* -infarct brain and abscess cavity.

Coagulative necrosis

- Most common form.
- Preservation of basic structural outline.
- By sudden cessation of blood (ischemia) in all tissues except brain.

Caseous necrosis

- It is a type of coagulative necrosis where in the tissue structure is completely lost.
- Necrotic area surrounded by granulomatous inflammation.
- Most typically seen in TB.

Fibrinoid necrosis

- Characterized by the deposition of the fibrin like material.
- *e.g.,* -immune complex autoimmune disease Arthus reaction.

Fat necrosis

- Focal areas of fat destruction following pancreatic injury (acute Pancreatitis).
- The released fatty acids combine with calcium to form chalky white areas (fat saponification).

Ans.27. (b) Amyloidosis

Ref http://en.wikipedia.org/wiki/Amyloidosis

Amyloidosis refers to a variety of rare conditions which result in pathological aggregation of extra cellular amyloid deposition. Amyloidosis may be inherited or acquired. Acquired amyloidosis is generally more common than inherited

Amyloid deposits can be identified histologically by Congo red staining and viewing under polarized light where amyloid deposits produce an ***'apple green birefringence'***. However, this is not a sensitive test for amyloidosis. Amyloid deposits can best be characterised by their cross â-core structure. In addition, all amyloid deposits contain serum amyloid P component (SAP), α circulating protein of the pentraxin family. Dermatan and heparan sulfate are also associated with amyloid deposits.

With amyloidosis involving the spleen and resulting in splenomegaly, large hyaline masses are seen as lesions occupying the white pulp space. Two forms exist, including the "***sago spleen***," in which amyloid deposits are limited to follicles (White pulp), and the "***lardaceous spleen***," in which amyloid is deposited in the walls of the splenic sinusoids (Red pulp).

Ans.28. (c) Tuberculosis

Ref dental harsh mohan pg 102, 2nd Ed; http://en.wikipedia.org/wiki/Langhans_giant_cell

Langhans giant cells are large cells found in granulomatous conditions. They are formed by the fusion of epithelioid cells (macrophages), and contain nuclei arranged in a horseshoe-shaped pattern in the cell periphery. Their presence could indicate tuberculosis, sarcoidosis, etc.

Remember, they should not be confused with **Langerhans** cell. While, Langhans giant cells are macrophages, Langerhans cells are dendritic cells.

Ans.29. (b) Glucose content

Ref dental harsh Mohan 2nd ed pg-175

Remember, glucose is same as in blood, in transudate and in exudates, it is decreased.

Ans.30. (c) CVC liver

EXUDATE	TRANSUDATE
An **exudate** is any fluid that filters from the circulatory system into lesions or areas of inflammation	**Transudate** are caused by disturbances of hydrostatic or colloid osmotic pressure, not by inflammation
Its composition varies but generally includes water and the dissolved solutes of the blood, some or all plasma proteins, white blood cells, platelets and (in the case of local vascular damage) red blood cells	Poor in protein content basically extra-vascular fluids collection
Exudate has a specific gravity greater than 1.020	the specific gravity of the transudate is usually less than 1.012.
Pus is an example of exudate found in infected wounds	e.g. edema fluid following lymphatic obstruction

Ref http://en.wikipedia.org/wiki/Nutmeg_liver

Nutmeg liver is the pathological appearance of the liver caused by ***chronic passive congestion*** of the liver secondary to right heart failure. The liver appears "speckled" like a nutmeg, from the dilated, congested central veins (dark spots) and paler, unaffected surrounding liver tissue.

Etiology

Increased pressure in the sublobular branches of the hepatic veins causes an engorgement of venous blood, and is most frequently due to chronic cardiac lesions, especially those affecting the right heart, the blood being dammed back in the inferior vena cava and hepatic veins. This retardation of the blood also occurs in pulmonary lesions, such as chronic interstitial pneumonia, pleural effusions, and intrathoracic tumors.

Symptoms

These depend largely upon the primary lesions giving rise to it. In addition to the cardiac or pulmonary symptoms, there will be a sense of fullness and tenderness in the right hypochondriac region. Gastro-intestinal catarrh is usually present, and hematemesis may occur. There is usually more or less jaundice. Owing to portal obstruction, ascites occurs, followed later by general dropsy. The stools are light or clay colored, and the urine is colored by bile. On palpation, the liver is found enlarged and tender, sometimes extending several inches below the costal margin.

DENTAL MATERIALS

Ans.31. (a) Polysulphide

Anusavice, 11th ed, Pg 229

The ADA specification for testing bio-compatibility includes- dental impression materials, despite the fact that the probability for toxic reaction form these materials or their components is small. Comparing the cell cytotoxicity for diff impression materials reveals that, ***polysulphide results in lowest cell death count and the set polyether produces the highest cell cytotoxicity*** core.

Elastic impression materials

	Advantages	Disadvantages	Recommended	Precautions
Polysulfide polymer	High tear strength Easier to pour than elastomers	Messy Unpleasant odor Long setting time Stability only fair	Most impressions	Pour with in 1 hour Allow 10 minutes to set
Addition Silicone	Dimensional stability Pleasant to use Short setting time	Hydrophobic Poor wetting Expensive Some materials release H_2	Most	Delay pour of some Materials care to avoid bubbles Care to avoid bubbles
Condensation silicone	Pleasnat to use Short setting time	Hydropobic Poor wetting Low Stability	Most impressions	Pour immediately Care to avoid bubbles
Polyether	Dimensional stability Accuracy Short setting time	Set material very stiff Imbibition short working time time imbibition	Most impressions	Care not to break teeth when separating cast

Similar results are also observed in multiple exposure test. Perhaps the most elastomer induced bio-compatibility problem occurs when a segment of impression material is lodged in the patients gingival sulcus causing sever inflammation, which can be misdiagnosed to have been caused by the tooth prep or cementation.

Contact dermatitis and hypersensitivity are common with polyether.

Ans.32. (c) More than 85%

Ref Skinner's, 9th ed , pg 97

Properties of Impression compound Type I

- FLOW – a max flow of 6 % at mouth temp. and at 45 ^{0}C , a ***minimum of 85 %***
- Average linear contraction at 25 ^{0}C = 0.3-0.4 %
- Volume of expansion at 25 ^{0}C = 1.38 – 2.29 %
- Fusion temperature = 43.5 ^{0}C (110.3 ^{0}F)
- Glass transition temp = 39 ^{0}C (102 ^{0}F)

Ans.33. (a) Polysulphide

Repeat, Refer A31

Ans.34. (d) Dental Ceramic

Ref Sturdevant, 4th ed pg 148

Direct restorative dentistry is a process where the restorative material can be applied and contoured directly in the intra-oral environment. Although , they save time and money , the use of direct materials may require compromise on the mechanical properties.

e.g., amalgam, liners and base materials, dental adhesive materials (bonding agents), pit and fissure sealants, composites, direct filling gold.

If the materials cannot be made fluid for direct use, they are fabricated into a restoration outside the mouth and later cemented or bonded in place. This process is known as indirect restorative dentistry.

e.g., cast metal restorations, porcelain restorations, etc

Ans.35. (c) Initial set

Please refer, KCET 06 A41

Ans.36. (b) Iron oxide

Ref Skinner's 9th ed, pg 562

Commonly used dental abrasives and polishing agents -

- Iron oxide (rouge) –is used to polish high noble metal alloy like gold.
- Tin oxide (putty powder) -for polishing teeth and metallic restoration in mouth.
- Zirconium silicate-as a component of prophylaxis paste, strips and disks.
- Emery – *corundum*, a natural oxide of Aluminium.
- Aluminium Oxide – (from bauxite), *levigated alumina* obtained by water floatation process is used for polishing metallographic specimens.
- Garnet – denotes silicates of any combination of Al, Co, Mg, Fe, and Mn. Coated on paper/ cloth, it is commonly used as denture abrasive disks.
- Pumice – highly siliceous material of volcanic origin. Polishing of denture, teeth.
- Kieselguhr – siliceous remains of diatoms, excellent mild abrasive.
- Tripoli – mild abrasive originating form certain porous rocks in North Africa.
- Chromic oxide – relatively hard material used for polishing SS (Stainless Steel).

Ans.37. (c) Back pressure porosity

Ref Skinner's 9th ed , pg 441

POROSITY	CAUSES	REMEDY
Localized Shirinkage	1. Incomplete feeding of molten metal during solidification. 2. sprue freezes in corss section due to narrow dimensions 3. Creation of a 'hot-spot' and resultant suck-back	1. Sufficient feed of molten metal to compensate for the shrinkage (1.25%). the use of a reservoir is advocated. 2. Adjust sprue diameter(?) and length (?) to prevent metal freezing 3. Flare the point of sprue attachment (45 degree) and reduce mold-metal temp difference (lowering the casting temp by 300°C)
Micro porosity	1. Too rapid solidification preventing the micro-voids to segregate to liquid pool. 2. Casting temp too low.	1. Avoid a rapid influx and solidification of metal. Adjust the casting temp

Pinhole	Due to entrapment of gases during solidification. Metals like Cu and Ag trap O_2 while Pt and Pd trap H_2 gas when in molten state, which are expelled during solidification forming blebs	Premelting the noble alloy on a charcoal block and correctly adjusting the blowpipe flame during melting of the alloy.
Gas inclusion porosity	Due to entrapment of gases during solidification. These are *larger* of the two defects. Use of flame zone other than the reducing zone can also result in these.	Premelting the noble alloy on a charcoal block and correctly adjusting the blowpipe flame during melting of the alloy.
Sub surface porosity	Due to simultaneous nucleation of solid grains and gas bubbles at the first moment the metal freezes at the mold walls.	Control the rate at which the molten metal enters the mould
Back-pressure porisity	Entrapped air on the inner surface of the casting and their inability to escape from the pores of the investment, or by the pressure gradient pushing the air pocket out via the molten sprue and button.	It is eliminated by— * Proper burn out * An adequate mold and melting temperature * A sufficient high casting pressure * A proper W:P ratio
	* It is increased by an increase in mold density produced by the vaccum investing * use of low heat technique producing excess residual carbon, clogging the pores of investment	It is best to make sure that the thickness of investment form the tip of pattern and the end of the ring is not greater than 6.5 mm (¼ **in**)

EXTRA EDGE

Type of porosity	**↑ sprue width**	**↑ sprue length**	**↑ melt temp**	**↑ mould temp**
LSP	↓	↑	↓	↓
Sub surface	↑	↓	↑	↑
Micro porosity	-	-	↓	↓

Composite	**Properties**
1. Conventional	• Filler size 8-12 um • Filler content – 75 % by wt • High strength and hardness • Less water sorption and COTE • Rough surface, polishing difficult
2. Micro filled	• Filler size – 0.04 – 0.4 um • Lowest filler (colloidal silica) content at 50 % wt

3. Small particle	• Lowest strength and hardness • Highest water sorption and COTE • Excellent esthetics • Filler size 1-5 um • Good surface smoothness • Highest compressive strength of all
4. Hybrid composites	• Mechanical prop of conventional + esthetics of micro filled • Filler size 0.6 – 1 um • Filler content 70-80 % • Better esthetics than small particle but physical properties are same

Ans.39. (d) Dicor

Ref Skinner 10th Ed pg609

The use of glass ceramics in dentistry was first proposed by W.T MacCulloch in 1968

Castable glass ceramics

- **DICOR:** it was the first commercially available castable ceramic formed into inlay, facial veneer or full crown investment by lost wax casting procedure. It was developed by Corning Glass Works (Dentsply). After heat treatment the matrix assumes a crystalline *mica-like* appearance. The superior esthetics of this product was attributed to its ''chameleon effect" where part of color is picked from the adjacent teeth and from the tinted luting cements as well.
- Another product , in Japan, had similar fabrication procedure as Dicor , however the ceramming process produces a *hydroxyapatite crystals* in matrix.
- **CERESTORE:** by Coors company, involved a specialized technique for fabrication of all ceramic restorations, where in , a special non-shrinking epoxy resin die of the prepared tooth is constructed. Aluminium oxide is the principle component (70%) . the á-alumina and magnesium aluminate spinel are the strengthening phases.

EXTRA EDGE

Other ceramic systems

IPS –EMPRESS—(INJECTED MOLDED GLASS CERAMICS)

it is a pre-cerammed glass ceramics that is heated in a cylinder form and injected under pressure and temperature

Advantages

- lack of metal or ceramic core
- excellent fit
- moderate flexure
- Excellent esthetics

Disadvantage

- Potential to fracture in posterior area
- need special lab equipment

IN- CERAM (GLASS INFILITERATED ALUMINA CORE)

Indication

- single anterior and posterior teeth
- anterior 3 unit bridge
- Pts allergy to metal
- when aesthetics of PFMs would not be acceptable

Advantage

- its very high flexure strength
- excellent fit
- lack of metal

Disadvantage

- opacity of the core
- unsuitability of for conventional acid etching
- need for special equipment

IN -CERAM SPINELL—with low flexure stre

- more aesthetics

Ans.40. (b) Initiator

Ref Skinner 10th ed pg253

Remember,

Activator-visible light
Filler-acrylic resin beads

PHARMACOLOGY

Ans.41. (a) Safety of a drug'

Ref KDT 5th ed pg 48

The gap b/w the therapeutic effect of DRC and the adverse effect of the DRC (dose response curve) defines the ***safety margin*** OR therapeutic margin of the drug.

It is calculated as- $\dfrac{\text{Median lethal dose } (LD_{50})}{\text{Median effective dose } (ED_{50})}$

But this is irrelevant where therapeutic range is bounded by the dose which produces minimal therapeutic effect and maximal acceptable adverse effect. That is, a drug may be capable of inducing a higher therapeutic response (higher efficacy) but development of adverse effects may preclude their use at higher doses. E.g. Reserpine as hypertensive

Ans.42. (d) Ketamine

KDT 5TH ED Pg344; http://en.wikipedia.org/wiki/Ketamine

Ketamine is a dissociative anesthetic for human and veterinary use.

- Pharmacologically, ketamine is classified as an NMDA receptor antagonist, and, like other drugs of this class such as tiletamine, memantine, and phencyclidine (PCP), induces a state referred to as "***dissociative anesthesia***."
- Ketamine has a wide range of effects in humans, including analgesia, anesthesia, hallucinations, arterial hypertension, and bronchodilation.
- It is primarily used for the induction and maintenance of general anesthesia, usually in combination with some sedative drug.
- Other uses include sedation in intensive care, analgesia (particularly in emergency medicine), and treatment of bronchospasm.
- Ketamine is a chiral compound. Most pharmaceutical preparations of ketamine are *racemic*,
- Ketamine may be used in small doses (0.1–0.5 mg/kg/h) as a local anesthetic, particularly for the treatment of pain associated with movement and neuropathic pain. It has the added benefit of counter-acting spinal sensitization or wind-up phenomena experienced with chronic pain.
- The effect of Ketamine on the respiratory and circulatory systems is different from that of other anesthetics. When used at anesthetic doses, it will usually ***stimulate*** rather than depress the circulatory system. It is sometimes possible to perform ketamine anesthesia without protective measures to the airways. Ketamine is also a potent analgesic and can be used in sub-anesthetic doses to relieve acute pain; however, its psychotropic properties must be taken into account. Patients have reported vivid hallucinations.
- It is best avoided in patients with H/O raised intra-cranial and intra-ocular pressure and CVS disturbances like hypertension.

Ans.43. (d) severe acute Bronchial asthma

KDT 5th ed pg 265

Synthetic glucocorticoids are used in the treatment

- Of joint pain or inflammation (arthritis)
- Temporal arteritis,
- Dermatitis, allergic reactions,
- Asthma
- Hepatitis, systemic lupus erythematosus, inflammatory bowel disease (ulcerative colitis and Crohn's disease), sarcoidosis and for glucocorticoid replacement in Addison's disease or other forms of adrenal insufficiency.
- Topical formulations for treatment of skin, eye diseases (uveitis) or inflammatory bowel disease are available.
- Corticosteroids are also used supportively to prevent nausea, often in combination with 5-HT3 antagonists (*e.g.*, ondansetron)

Contraindication of corticosteriod are

- Peptic ulcers
- Diabetes mellitus
- Hypertension
- Osteoporosis
- Viral. fungal. tuberculosis and other infection
- Epilepsy
- CHF and renal failure

Ans.44. (d) Dentine desensitizers

Ref Oxford Medical Dictionary

Obtundents: drugs/materials having the capacity to dull the sensibilities or produce a soothing effect.

Mummifying agent: drugs that have an ability to induce drying and shriveling of a living tissue (as in dry gangrene)

So friends, from the above definitions, we came to conclusion that, dentin desensitizers like (Zno Eugenol) are an example of obtundents.

Ans.45. (c) Succinyl choline

Ref http://en.wikipedia.org/wiki/Malignant_hyperthermia

Malignant hyperthermia (**MH** or **MHS** for "malignant hyperthermia syndrome", or "malignant hyperpyrexia due to anesthesia")

- Is a rare life-threatening condition that is triggered by exposure to drugs used for general anesthesia, such as volatile anesthetics or the depolarizing muscle relaxant suxamethonium chloride.
- In susceptible individuals, these drugs can induce a drastic and uncontrolled increase in skeletal muscle oxidative metabolism which overwhelms the body's capacity to supply oxygen, remove carbon dioxide, and regulate body temperature, eventually leading to circulatory collapse and death if untreated.
- MH is often inherited as an Autosomal dominant disorder, MH is sometimes confused with the ***neuroleptic malignant syndrome***, but the two syndromes are distinct,.

The phenomenon presents with muscular rigidity, followed by a hyper metabolic state with increased oxygen consumption, increased carbon dioxide production (hypercarbia), metabolic acidosis, tachycardia, and an increase in body temperature (hyperthermia) at a rate of up ***to ~2°C per hour***. This is followed by a breakdown of muscle cells (rhabdomyolysis), which release their contents such as myoglobin, creatine kinase (CK/CPK) and potassium, into the bloodstream.

Triggers

- Halothane, (60%), a once popular but now rarely used volatile anesthetic, has been linked to a large proportion of cases, however, *all* halogenated volatile anesthetics are potential triggers of malignant hyperthermia.

- Succinylcholine, (77%), a neuromuscular blocking agent, is also a trigger for MH.
- Lidocaine, mepivacaine..

Malignant hyperthermia is caused in a large proportion (50-70%) of cases by a mutation of the ***ryanodine receptor (type 1)***, located on the sarcoplasmic reticulum (SR), the organelle within skeletal muscle cells that stores calcium. RYR1 opens in response to increases in intracellular Ca^{2+} level mediated by L-type calcium channels, thereby resulting in a drastic increase in intracellular calcium levels and muscle contraction In contrast, the neuroleptic malignant syndrome consists of a defect in the central nervous system manifesting in altered responses to dopamine antagonist drugs. Rigidity and hyperthermia can result, but the mechanisms do not involve altered calcium regulation as in MH.

The current treatment of choice is the intravenous administration of **dantrolene,** discontinuation of triggering agents, and supportive therapy directed at correcting hyperthermia, acidosis, and organ dysfunction

GENERAL MEDICINE

Ans.46. (b) Myiasis

Ref http://en.wikipedia.org/wiki/Myiasis

Myiasis is an animal or human disease caused by parasitic dipterous fly larvae feeding on the host's necrotic or living tissue. Colloquialisms for Myiasis include "fly-strike" and "fly-blow."

- The classical classification describes the myiasis by the infected area of the host: dermal, sub-dermal, cutaneous nasopharyngeal, ocular ,intestinal/enteric or urogenital.
- Another classification is based on the relationship between the host and the parasite and provides insight into the biology of the fly species causing the myiasis and its likely effect. Thus the myiasis is described as either obligatory or facultative or accidental.

Flies responsible for Myiasis

There are three main fly families causing economically important myiasis in livestock and also, occasionally, in humans:

- Oestroidea (botflies)
- Calliphoridae (blowflies)
- Sarcophagidae (fleshflies)

Other families occasionally involved are:

- Anisopodidae
- Piophilidae
- Stratiomyidae
- Syrphidae

The adult flies are not parasitic, but when they lay their eggs in open wounds and these hatch into their larval stage (also known as maggots or grubs), the larvae feed on live and/or necrotic tissue, causing myiasis to develop. They may also be ingested or enter through other body apertures

Ans.47. (a) Neck Vein distension

Ref *http://en.wikipedia.org/wiki/Left_ventricular_failure*

Left Heart Failure: Symptoms of decompensated heart failure include:

- Dyspnea (shortness of breath) on exertion.
- Orthopnea (dyspnea that increases upon lying down).
- Fatigue and paroxysmal nocturnal dyspnea ("cardiac asthma", shortness of breath that occurs hours or minutes after lying down).
- Nocturnal cough, confusion and memory impairment (in advanced stages).
- Diaphoresis and cool extremities at rest.

Signs of decompensated left heart failure include: Displaced apex beat (usually to left due to cardiomegaly), Pathologic S3 Gallop, S4, crackles at the lung bases due to pulmonary edema (fluid accumulation in the lungs), dullness to percussion and tactile fremitus of lower lung fields. Increased intensity of pulmonic component of 2nd heart sound.

EXTRA EDGE

Right Heart Failure: symptoms and signs include:

- peripheral edema (fluid build-up in dependent portions of the body),
- ascites (fluid in the abdominal cavity),
- nocturia (due to increased venous return with leg elevation), jugular venous distention, epistaxis (due to an increase in venous pressure), Hepatomegaly, hepatojugular reflux, and right ventricular heave.

Individuals with heart failure are sensitive to small shifts in their intravascular volume status (the amount of fluid in their circulatory system). Increasing the volume in their circulatory system can cause symptoms and signs of decompensated heart failure, while decreasing the volume in the circulatory system can cause hypotension.

Chest X-rays (CXRs) are frequently used to aid in the diagnosis of CHF. Signs of CHF on CXR are

- Vascular redistribution
- Peribronchial cuffing/interstitial edema (bat-shaped)
- Kerley B lines
- Consolidation of lower lung fields
- Cardiomegaly

Diagnostic Lab Values

***B-type natriuretic peptide*, (BNP)** is found to be elevated in people suffering from CHF. Measurement of BNP along with other clinical information can be used to differentiate between causes of dyspnea due to congestive heart failure (CHF) from that of other causes of dyspnea.

Ans.48. (c) Pneumococci

Ref *http://en.wikipedia.org/wiki/Lobar_pneumonia*

Pneumonia is an illness of the lungs and respiratory system in which the alveoli (microscopic air-filled sacs of the lung responsible for absorbing oxygen from the atmosphere) become inflamed and flooded with fluid. Pneumonia can result from a variety of causes, including infection with bacteria, viruses, fungi, or parasites. Pneumonia may also occur from chemical or physical injury to the lungs.

- **VIRAL PNEUMONIA** is commonly caused by viruses such as influenza virus, respiratory syncytial virus (RSV), adenovirus, and metapneumovirus. Herpes simplex virus is a rare cause of pneumonia except in newborns. People with immune system problems are also at risk for pneumonia caused by cytomegalovirus (CMV).
- **BACTERIAL PNEUMONIA:** *Streptococcus pneumoniae*, often called "pneumococcus", is the **most common** bacterial cause of pneumonia in all age groups except newborn infants. Other *e.g., Staphylococcus aureus*.
- Some of the gram-negative bacteria that cause pneumonia include *Haemophilus influenzae, Klebsiella pneumoniae, Escherichia coli, Pseudomonas aeruginosa* and *Moraxella catarrhalis*. These bacteria often live in the stomach or intestines and may enter the lungs if vomit is inhaled.
- "***Atypical***" bacteria which cause pneumonia include *Chlamydophila pneumoniae, Mycoplasma pneumoniae*, and *Legionella pneumophila*
- **FUNGAL PNEUMONIA** is most often caused by *Histoplasma capsulatum, Cryptococcus neoformans, Pneumocystis jiroveci*, and *Coccidioides immitis*.
- **PARASITES** causing pneumonia are *Toxoplasma gondii, Strongyloides stercoralis*, and *Ascariasis*.

A ***lobar*** pneumonia is an infection that only involves a single lobe, or section, of a lung. Lobar pneumonia is often due to ***Streptococcus pneumoniae***. *Multilobar* pneumonia involves more than one lobe, and it often is a more severe illness than lobar pneumonia. *Interstitial* pneumonia involves the areas in between the alveoli, and it may be called "interstitial pneumonitis." Interstitial pneumonia is more likely to be caused by viruses or by atypical bacteria.

Ans.49. (d) Cirrhosis

Ref http://en.wikipedia.org/wiki/Hepatic_encephalopathy

Hepatic encephalopathy is a complication of liver failure, whether chronic (as in cirrhosis), or acutely. With severe liver impairment, toxic substances normally removed by the liver accumulate in the blood and impair the function of brain cells. Signs can include impaired cognition, a flapping tremor (asterixis), and a decreased level of consciousness including coma and, ultimately, death.

PRECIPITANTS

Although the onset of hepatic encephalopathy may simply reflect worsening of underlying liver disease, it may also be due to a number of independent factors, each treatable in its own right.

- **Hyponatremia** (often arising as a result of diuretic treatment or simply as a complication of the edema typically found in advanced cirrhosis),

- Hypokalemia (again, often as a result of diuretic use), alkalosis, dehydration, hypoglycemia (a condition to which people with cirrhosis are susceptible), and renal failure of even mild degree.
- Medications like benzodiazepines (*e.g.*, diazepam, lorazepam), narcotics, and diuretics.
- Alcohol ingestion, whether or not it was the cause of the patient's liver disease, may also precipitate hepatic encephalopathy.
- Infection is an important precipitant of hepatic encephalopathy. In some cases, the *only* clinical manifestation of the infection is the development of the encephalopathy *e.g.*, spontaneous bacterial peritonitis).
- Non compliance with dietary protein restriction.
- **Bleeding** into the stomach or small intestine (both of which occur with increased frequency in people with liver disease and/or portal hypertension) may also lead to hepatic encephalopathy as blood contains large quantities of protein in the form of hemoglobin. Hence, the presence of blood in the stomach or small intestine represents a protein load which, as a result of bacterial metabolism in the lumen of the gut, is converted to potentially toxic products such as ammonia.
- Certain surgical procedures employed to treat portal hypertension commonly lead to the development of hepatic encephalopathy. For example, operations to relieve pressure in the portal vein by connecting it to the splenic vein or, the more recently developed "TIPS" procedure (transjugular intrahepatic portosystemic shunt).

The toxic substances which accumulate in the setting of liver failure and affect the brain have been thought to include ***ammonia*** (***NH_3***) and ***mercaptans.*** Ammonia is normally converted to urea by the liver and, as with mercaptans, is produced by the bacterial breakdown of protein in the intestines.

Ammonia can cross the blood-brain barrier, where it causes the support cells of the brain (astrocytes) to swell. The swelling of the brain tissue increases intracranial pressure, and can lead to coma or death via herniation of the brainstem.

Ans.50. (b) Polyneuritis

http://en.wikipedia.org/wiki/Intravenous_drug_use_%28recreational%29

Increased chance of blood-borne infection: this is generally a two-fold problem.

- One is needle sharing which transmits blood-borne diseases (one that can be spread by contamination by blood, most common examples are HIV, hepatitis B, hepatitis C and viral hemorrhagic fevers) between users.
- The other is secondary infection of injection sites caused by lack of hygiene and failure to rotate the injection site (local and systemic infection *e.g.*, endocarditis).
- In addition, the use of cotton to filter some drugs can lead to cotton fever (**Cotton fever** is a syndrome that is often associated with intravenous drug use, specifically the use of cotton to filter drugs like heroin. The cause of the condition is believed to be endotoxin shed by the bacteria *Enterobacter agglomerans* which colonizes cotton plants. cotton fever, if left alone, will usually resolve itself spontaneously within 12-24 hours. Symptoms usually appear with

10-20 minutes after injection and in addition to fever may include headaches, malaise, chills, nausea and tachycardia. The fever itself usually reaches 38.5 - 40.3°C (101 - 105°F) within the first hour.

Thus we see that while both Hepatitis and SABE can be found in such patients, polyneuritis is not a complication of IV drug abuse.

EXTRA EDGE

Causes of Polyneuritis include: [*http://en.wikipedia.org/wiki/Polyneuritis*]

- Infection:
  - Herpes simplex
  - Shingles
  - Leprosy
  - Guillain-Barre syndrome
- Chemical injury
- Physical injury
- Radiation
- Underlying conditions causing localized neuritis (affecting a single nerve):
  - Diphtheria
  - Localized injury
  - Diabetes
- Underlying conditions causing polyneuritis:
  - Beriberi
  - Vitamin B12 deficiency
  - Metabolic diseases
  - Diabetes
  - Hypothyroidism
  - Porphyria
  - Infections, bacterial and/or viral
  - Autoimmune disease, especially Multiple Sclerosis
  - Cancer
  - Alcoholism

Ans.51. (d) Hepatitis E.

Ref http://en.wikipedia.org/wiki/Hepatitis

Hepatitis A: Hepatitis A or infectious jaundice is caused by a picornavirus. It is transmitted by the *orofecal* route, transmitted to humans through methods such as contaminated food. It causes an acute form of hepatitis and does not have a chronic stage.

Hepatitis B: Hepatitis B is caused by a hepadnavirus, which can cause both acute and chronic hepatitis. Chronic hepatitis develops in the 15% of patients who are unable to eliminate the virus after an initial infection. Identified methods of transmission include *blood* (blood transfusion, now rare), tattoos (both amateur and professionally done), sexually (through sexual intercourse or through contact with blood or bodily fluids), or in utero (from mother to her unborn child, as the virus can cross the placenta).

Hepatitis C : Hepatitis C (originally "non-A non-B hepatitis") is caused by a Flavivirus. It can be transmitted through contact with blood (including through sexual contact where the two parties' blood is mixed). Hepatitis C may lead to a chronic form of hepatitis, culminating in cirrhosis.

Hepatitis D: is a disease caused by a small circular RNA virus (Hepatitis delta virus or hepatitis D virus, HDV). HDV is considered to be a *subviral* satellite because it can propagate only in the presence of another virus, the hepatitis B virus (HBV)

Hepatitis E: Hepatitis E produces symptoms similar to hepatitis A, although it can take a fulminant course in some patients, particularly ***pregnant*** women; it is more prevalent in ***the Indian subcontinent***. Hepatitis F (existence unknown).

Hepatitis G: Another type of hepatitis, hepatitis G, has been identified and is probably spread by blood and sexual contact.

Ans.52. (d) Portal hypertension

Ref http://en.wikipedia.org/wiki/Splenomegaly#Causes

Causes of splenomegaly

Splenomegaly grouped on the basis of the pathogenic mechanism

Increased	Abnormal blood flow	Infiltration
Removal of defective RBCs		
Spherocytosis		
Thalassemia	**Organ Failure**	
Hemoglobinopathies		**Metablolic diseases**
Nutritional anemia	Cirrhosis	Gauchers disease
Early sickle cell anemia	congestive heart	Niemann-Pick disease
	failure	Hurler syndrome and other
		mucopolysaccharidoses
Immune Hypcrplasia		Amyloidosis
Response to infection (viral,	**Vascular**	Tangier disease
bacterial, funga, parasitic)	hepatic vein	
Mononucleosis, AIDS,	obstruction	**Benign and malignant**
viral hepatitis	portal vein	**infiltrations**
sub acute bacterial endocarditis,		
bacterial septicemia	obstruction	Leukemia (acute, chronic,
splenic abscess, typhoid fever	Budd-chiari	lymphoid and myeloid)
brucellosis, leptospirosis, tuberculosis	syndrome	lymphomas(hodgkin's and
histoplasmosis	splenic vein	non-Hodgkin's)
malaria, leishmaniasis, trypanosomiasis	obstruction	myeloproliferative disorder
ehrlichiosis		Metastatic tumors (commo-
Disordered immunogregulation		nly melanoma)

Rheumatoid arthritis SLE Serum sickness Autoimmune hemolytic anemia Immune thrombocytopenia sarcoidosis drug reactions ***Extramedullary hematopoiesis*** Myelofibrosis Marrow infiltration by tumors, leukemia marrow damage by radiation, toxins	**Infections** hepatic hepatic echinococcosis	histiocytosis X Haemangioma, lymphan- gioma splenic cysts Hamartoma eosinophillic granuloma

The causes of massive splenomegaly (>1000gms) are much fewer and include:

- Chronic myelogenous leukemia
- lymphomas
- hairy cell leukemia
- myelofibrosis
- polycythemia vera
- portal hypertension
- Gauchers disease
- chronic lymphocytic leukemia
- sarcoidosis/ amyloidosis
- autoimmune hemolytic anemia
- Malaria

Ans.53. (d) Dapsone

Ref http://www.emedicine.com/derm/byname/dermatitis-herpetiformis.htm

Dermatitis herpetiformis (DH)

- is an *autoimmune* blistering disorder associated with a gluten-sensitive enteropathy (GSE).
- The disease was described and named in 1984 by Dr. Louis Duhring at the University of Pennsylvania.
- It is characterized by grouped excoriations; erythematous, urticarial plaques; and papules with vesicles.
- These are located on the extensor surfaces of the elbows, knees, buttocks, and back.
- It is exquisitely pruritic, and the vesicles are often excoriated to erosions by the time of physical examination.
- Diagnosis requires direct immunofluorescence of a skin biopsy specimen showing deposition of immunoglobulin A (IgA) in a granular pattern in the upper papillary dermis.
- Although most patients are asymptomatic, more than 90% have an associated GSE upon endoscopic examination. Among patients with celiac disease, 15-25% develop DH.

- The mainstays of treatment are dapsone and a gluten-free diet.

Ans.54. (c) Hepatomegaly

Ref http://www.helenacardiology.com/infective_endocarditis.htm

Clinical and pathological features

- Fever (often spiking).
- Continuous presence of micro-organisms in the bloodstream determined by serial collection of blood cultures.
- Vegetations on valves on echocardiography, which sometimes can cause a new or changing heart murmur, particularly murmurs suggestive of valvular regurgitation.
- Vascular phenomena: Septic emboli (causing circulatory problems such as stroke in the parietal lobe of the brain or gangrene of fingers), Janeway lesions (painless hemorrhagic cutaneous lesions on the palms and soles), intracranial hemorrhage, conjunctival hemorrhage, splinter hemorrhages.
- Immunologic phenomena: Glomerulonephritis, Osler's nodes (painful subcutaneous lesions in the distal fingers), Roth's spots on the retina, positive serum rheumatoid factor.

Less Specific (Possible) features

- Heart Disease
- Weight Loss
- Splenomegaly

Thus, friends, while all other are mentioned as clinical findings, Hepatomegaly is the answer by exclusion.

Ans.55. (b) Viral Hepatitis

Commonest cause of Jaundice in India is infection by Hepatitis E virus.

EXPLAINED ABOVE, Pleases refer A51

Ans.56. (c) Heart failure

Ref http://www.bmj.com/cgi/content/full/320/7227/104

- Coronary artery disease and hypertension (either alone or in combination) were implicated as the cause in over 90% of cases of heart failure.
- Hypertension has been associated with an increased risk of heart failure in several epidemiological studies. In the Framingham heart study, hypertension was reported as the cause of heart failure—either alone or in association with other factorsin over 70% of cases.
- Hypertension predisposes to the development of heart failure via a number of pathological mechanisms, including left ventricular hypertrophy. Left ventricular hypertrophy is associated with left ventricular systolic and diastolic dysfunction and an increased risk of myocardial infarction, and it predisposes to both atrial and ventricular arrhythmias.
- Electrocardiographic left ventricular hypertrophy is strongly correlated with the development of heart failure, as it is associated with a 14-fold increase in the risk of heart failure in those aged 65 years or under.

Ans.57. (a) Parasympathetic system

Ref http://en.wikipedia.org/wiki/Vasovagal_syncope

Friends, please take time and understand the following mechanism of syncope-

Regardless of the trigger, the mechanism of syncope is similar in the various vasovagal syncope syndromes. In it, the nucleus tractus solitarius of the brainstem is activated directly or indirectly by the triggering stimulus, resulting in simultaneous enhancement of parasympathetic nervous system (vagal) tone and withdrawal of sympathetic nervous system tone.

This results in a spectrum of hemodynamic responses:

- On one end of the spectrum is the **cardioinhibitory** response, characterized by a drop in heart rate. The drop in heart rate leads to a drop in blood pressure that is so severe that consciousness is lost. It is thought that this response results primarily from enhancement in parasympathetic tone.
- On the other end of the spectrum is the **vasodepressor** response, caused by a drop in blood pressure without much change in heart rate. This phenomenon occurs due to vasodilatation, probably as a result of withdrawal of sympathetic nervous system tone.
- The majority of people with vasovagal syncope have a **mixed** response somewhere between these two ends of the spectrum.

One account for these physiological responses is the **Bezold-Jarisch Reflex.** This reflex involves a variety of cardiovascular and neurological processes, which can be summarized as follows: Prolonged upright posture results in some degree of pooling of blood in the lower extremities that can lead to diminished intracardiac volume. This phenomenon is accentuated if the individual is dehydrated. The resultant arterial hypotension is sensed in the carotid body baroreceptors, and afferent fibers from these receptors trigger autonomic signals that increase cardiac rate and contractility. However, pressure receptors in the wall and trabeculae of the underfilled left ventricle may then sense stimuli, indicating high-pressure C-fiber afferent nerves from these receptors. They may respond by sending signals that trigger paradoxical bradycardia and decreased contractility, resulting in additional and relatively sudden arterial hypotension.

So friends, it is clear from the above explanation that vasodilatation in skeletal muscles and stimulation of parasympathetic fibers lead to vasovagal syncope. Thus answer here is '**a**' and not 'c' as vasodilatation is seen in vessels of skeletal muscles and ***not all vessels***.

Ans.58. (c) Dilated and reacting to light

Ref http://www.answers.com/topic/concussion?cat=health

Definition

Concussion is a trauma-induced change in mental status, with confusion and amnesia, and with or without a brief loss of consciousness.

Description

A concussion occurs when the head hits or is hit by an object, or when the brain is jarred against the skull, with sufficient force to cause temporary loss of function in the higher centers of the brain. The injured person may remain conscious or lose consciousness briefly, and is disoriented for some minutes after the blow.

While concussion usually resolves on its own without lasting effect, it can set the stage for a much more serious condition. "Second impact syndrome" occurs when a person with a concussion, even a very mild one, suffers a second blow before fully recovering from the first. The brain swelling and increased intracranial pressure that can result is potentially fatal.

Causes and symptoms

Causes

Most concussions are caused by motor vehicle accidents and sports injuries. Young children are likely to suffer concussions from falls or collisions on the playground or around the home. Child abuse is, unfortunately, another common cause of concussion.

Symptoms

Headache, nausea or vomiting.

Disorientation as to time, date, or place.

Confusion, dizziness.

Vacant stare or confused expression.

Incoherent or incomprehensible speech.

Incoordination or weakness.

Amnesia for the events immediately preceding the blow.

Double vision.

Ringing in the ears.

These symptoms may last from several minutes to several hours. More severe or longer-lasting symptoms may indicate more severe brain injury. The person with a concussion may or may not lose consciousness from the blow; if so, it will be for several minutes at the most. More prolonged unconsciousness indicates more severe brain injury.

The severity of concussion is graded on a **three-point scale**, used as a basis for treatment decisions.

- **Grade 1:** no loss of consciousness, transient confusion, and other symptoms that resolve within 15 minutes.
- **Grade 2:** no loss of consciousness, transient confusion, and other symptoms that require more than 15 minutes to resolve.
- **Grade 3:** loss of consciousness for any period.

Days or weeks after the accident, the person may show signs of:

- Headache
- Poor attention and concentration
- Memory difficulties
- Anxiety
- Depression
- Sleep disturbances
- Light and noise intolerance

The occurrence of such symptoms is called "post-concussion syndrome."

Diagnosis

The duration of unconsciousness and degree of confusion are very important indicators of the severity of the injury and help guide the diagnostic process and treatment decisions.

- A **neurologic exam** of the pupils(CN III, IV, and VI: These nerves examine the pupillary (the circular center structure of the eye that light rays enter) reaction. *The pupils get smaller, **normally** when exposed to the light*. The eyelids are also examined for drooping or retraction.)
- The eyeball is also checked for abnormalities in movement, coordination, and sensation; and brief tests of orientation, memory, and concentration.
- Questionable or more severe cases may require computed tomography scan (CT) or magnetic resonance imaging (MRI) scans to look for brain injury.

Treatment

The symptoms of concussion usually clear quickly and without lasting effect, if no further injury is sustained during the healing process.

So friends, we have seen that simple concussion injuries do not present with neurological deficit and symptoms may range from headache to blurring of vision (dilation of pupil). So, the answer here is *dilated and reacting to light*.

In contrast to this, ***Contusions***, which are frequently associated with edema, are especially likely to cause increases in intracranial pressure (ICP) and concomitant crushing of delicate brain tissue. Contusions are also more likely to result in hemorrhage than is diffuse axonal injury because they occur more often in the cortex, an area with more blood vessels. Hence, the pupils in contusion injuries are fixed, dilated and unresponsive to light stimuli.

Ans.59. (b) Decrease intracranial pressure

Ref http://en.wikipedia.org/wiki/Mannitol

Mannitol or **hexan-1,2,3,4,5,6-hexol** ($C_6H_8(OH)_6$) is an osmotic diuretic agent and a weak renal vasodilator. It is a sorbitol isomer, originally isolated from manna, and may also be referred to as **Mannite** and **Manna Sugar.**

USES

- Mannitol is used clinically to reduce *acutely raised intracranial pressure*, until more definitive treatment can be given, *e.g.* after head trauma.
- to treat patients with *oliguric renal failure*. It is administered intravenously, and is filtered by the glomerulus of the kidney, but is incapable of being reabsorbed from the renal tubule, resulting in decreased water and Na^+ reabsorption via its osmotic effect. Consequently, mannitol increases water and Na^+ excretion, thereby decreasing extra cellular fluid volume.
- To open the blood-brain barrier by temporarily shrinking the tightly coupled endothelial cells that makes up the barrier. This makes mannitol indispensable for delivering various drugs directly to the brain (*e.g.* in the ***treatment of Alzheimer's disease***).

- Mannitol is also used as a *sweetener* for people with diabetes. Since mannitol has a negative heat of solution, it is used as a sweetener in "breath-freshening" candies, the cooling effect adding to the fresh feel. In doses larger than 20g, mannitol acts as a laxative, and is sometimes sold as a laxative for children.
- It is sometimes used as an adulterant or cutting agent for heroin, methamphetamines or other illicit drugs.
- it is often referred to as *baby laxative*.
- Mannitol can also be used to temporarily encapsulate a sharp object (such as a helix on a lead for an artificial pacemaker).
- Mannitol may be administered in cases of severe Ciguatera poisoning. Severe ciguatoxin, or "*tropical fish poisoning*" can produce stroke-like symptoms.
- Mannitol is a non-permeating molecule *i.e.* it cannot cross biological membranes.
- Mannitol is commonly used in the circuit prime of a heart lung machine during cardiopulmonary bypass (CPB).
- Mannitol is also being developed as a treatment for cystic fibrosis and bronchiectasis and as a diagnostic test for airway hyper responsiveness.

GENERAL SURGERY

Ans.60. (d) All of the above

Ref Shenoy Manipal manual of Surgery, pg 9,

General factor affecting wound healing

- Age
- Nutritional deficiency, Vit C ,zinc,
- Immuno-compromised patient, diabetics
- Cytotoxic drug, malignancy

Local factor

- Poor blood supply
- Local infection
- Haematoma formation
- Tension while suturing
- Corticosteroid, cortisol

Ans.61. (b) Lymphangioma

Ref http://www.emedicine.com/ped/topic536.htm

First described by Wernher in 1843, **Cystic hygroma** (CH) is a cystic lymphatic lesion that can affect any anatomic subsite in the human body. CH usually affects the head and neck (approximately 75%), with a left-sided predilection. Within the neck, the posterior triangle tends to be affected most frequently. Approximately 20% of CHs occur in the axilla; more infrequent subsites include the mediastinum, groin, and retroperitoneum. CH is synonymous with *cystic lymphangioma*, which is also known as a macrocystic lymphatic malformation.

Pathophysiology

Lymphangiomas are thought to arise from a combination of the following:

- A failure of lymphatics to connect to the venous system.
- Abnormal budding of lymphatic tissue, and sequestered lymphatic rests that retain their embryonic growth potential.
- These lymphatic rests can penetrate adjacent structures or dissect along fascial planes and eventually become canalized. These spaces retain their secretions and develop cystic components because of the lack of a venous outflow tract.
- The nature of the surrounding tissue determines whether the lymphangioma is capillary, cavernous, or cystic.
- CHs tend to form in loose areolar tissue, whereas capillary and cavernous forms of lymphangioma tend to form in muscle.
- Molecular studies suggest that vascular endothelial growth factor C (VEGF-C) and its receptors may play an important role in the development of lymphatic malformations.
- In addition to congenital development, lymphangioma can be acquired. They can arise from trauma (including surgery), inflammation, or obstruction of a lymphatic drainage pathway.

These are soft, compbressible and show trans-illumination.

Ans.62. (b) Malignant ulcer found on the scar of burn

Explained earlier Please refer KCET-O7 A70

Ans.63. (d) Tender gallbladder

Ref http://en.wikipedia.org/wiki/Murphy_sign

Murphy's sign

- Refers to a physical examination maneuver that is part of the abdominal examination and a finding elicited in ultrasonography.
- It is useful for differentiating right upper quadrant abdominal pain.
- Typically, it is positive in ***cholecystitis***, but negative in choledocholithiasis and ascending cholangitis.
- The sign is named for the American physician John Benjamin Murphy (1857-1916) who described it.

Murphy's sign has a high sensitivity and Positive Predictive Value. However, specificity is of moderate value.

- *Classically*, it is performed by asking the patient to breathe out and then gently placing the hand below the costal margin on the right side at the mid-clavicular line (the approximate location of the gallbladder). The patient is then instructed to inspire (breathe in).
- Normally, during inspiration, the abdominal contents are pushed downward as the diaphragm moves down (and lungs expand).

- If the patient stops breathing in (as the gallbladder is tender and, in moving downward, comes in contact with the examiner's fingers) the test is considered positive. A positive test also requires no pain on performing the maneuver on the patient's left hand side.

Ans.64. (c) Kidneys

Ref http://en.wikipedia.org/wiki/Pyelography

An **intravenous pyelogram** (also known as **IVP**, **pyelography**, **intravenous urogram** or **IVU**)

- is a radiological procedure used to visualize disturbances of the urinary system, including the kidneys, ureters, and bladder. Among other uses, IVP can detect kidney stones.
- It is done as a series of X-rays before and after a contrast agent (dye) is injected into a vein. This contrast is removed from the blood by the kidneys at a predictable time, where they initially appear opaque on X-ray film early after injection, followed by the appearance of iodinated contrast in the urine which outlines the renal calyces, ureters and bladder in the later X-rays in the series. Finally, the bladder is imaged while filled and then after emptying, allowing assessment of any unseen abnormalities and completeness of voiding.
- Metformin should be stopped some time prior to the procedure as it causes a reaction with the contrast agent.

Ans.65. (d) Wrist

Ref http://en.wikipedia.org/wiki/Colles_fracture

Colles' fracture, is a fracture of the *distal radius bone.*

It is named after Abraham Colles (1773-1843), an Irish surgeon who first described this in 1814 before the advent of X-rays.

The term Colles fracture is classically used to describe a fracture through the distal metaphysis no further than 4 centimeters proximal to the distal articular surface of the radius.

The fracture is most commonly caused by people falling forward onto a hard surface and breaking their fall with extended, outstretched hands - falling with wrists flexed would lead to a ***Smith's fracture***. It can also be caused by overuse. It usually occurs about an inch or two proximal to the radio-carpal joint with posterior and lateral displacement of the distal fragment resulting in the characteristic ***dinner fork*** like deformity.

Colles fracture is a common fracture in people with osteoporosis, second only to vertebral fractures.

Ans.66. (c) Formation of casseous pus without signs of acute inflammation

Ref dental Shenoy Manipal manual pg 169,22

It is the commonest cystic swelling in the carotid triangle. **Features**:-

- Cold abscess means a abscess with *no sign of inflammation.*
- Cold abscess result due to caseous necrosis in the lymph node.
- It form a soft ,cystic, fluctuant swelling with negative transillumination.
- Usually it is due to tuberculosis, however other chronic disease like leprosy, Actinomycosis, madura foot also produces abscess which are cold in nature.
- Cold abscess is seen in 3rd stage of tuberculosis lymphadenitis.

STAGES OF TUBERCULOSIS LYMPHADENITIS

- stage of lymphadenitis
- stage of periadenitis / stage of matting
- stage of cold abscess
- stage of collar stud abscess
- stage of sinus formation

Ans.67. (b) Division of nuclei without division of cytoplasm

Ref Oxford Medical Dictionary

'poikilo' refers to irregular, varied; while karyolysis is nuclear dissolution

So poikilo-karyolysis refers to irregular division of nucleus.

Friends at this point I don't have any other reference besides Shafer's who mentions that this is seen in lesions of Erythroplakia.

But, you can definitely go with choice 'b' without any doubts.

Ans.68. (b) Type of cellulites

Ref SHAFERS 5th ed pg 697

- Cellulites or *Phlegmon* is a diffuse inflammation of soft tissue not circumscribed to one area.
- It occurs as a result of infection by microorganism that produces significant amount of hyaluronidase (Spreading factor of Duran-Renyles) and fibrinolysis which act to break down or dissolve.
- Streptococci are potent producer of hyaluronidase.

ORAL PATHOLOGY

Ans.69. (b) Parakeratinised

Ref Shafer,5th ed pg364,

In follow up study it has been found that Parakeratinized has high recurrence rate and are aggressive in nature. The variant of OKC that produces only orthokeratin are frequently associated with Dentigerous cysts, usually around mandibular 3rd molar, and are considerably less aggressive. They ***do not*** have a hyper chromatic basal layer which is flattened. They are ***not*** associated with basal cell nevus syndrome.

Ans.70. (c) 2-4 cell thick

Ref http://www.uscap.org/newindex.htm?iap2006/symp29-6.htm

Well friends, this was a hard one. Shafer's states that the primordial cysts and the OKC are characterized by a uniform thickness of 6-10 cells without rete peg formation now, Shafer doesn't mention clearly the exact thickness for Dentigerous cyst but a reference has been made with this regard.

Brannon reviewed 1,850 cases of Dentigerous cysts and found characteristics of OKC in 8.5 % cases. These included a thickness of 6-10 cells, and a polarized palisaded basal layer of cells.

Ref Shafer's. 5th Ed, pg 359

But, finally I have found at least one, non-text ref. citing the thickness of Dentigerous cysts. Read the following statement-

"A **dentigerous cyst** surrounds the crown of an unerupted tooth, mostly the maxillary canine or the mandibular third molar tooth. The cyst wall has a thin epithelial lining that may be **only two to three** cells thick. In case of inflammation, the epithelium becomes thicker and will show features similar to the lining of a radicular cyst. Also, mucous producing cells as well as ciliated cells may be observed. The cyst wall may also contain varying amounts of epithelial nests representing remnants of the dental lamina."

Hence, the answer more appropriate here, is 'c' 2-4 cell thick

Ans.71. (b) Adenoid Cystic Carcinoma

Ref Shafers,5th ed 330,

- Swiss cheese pattern, Cribriform, honey comb are see in histological section.
- Deeply staining basaloid epithelial cell nests resembling small cell that are commonly arranged in anastomosing cord or a duct like pattern, the centre of which portion may contain a mucoid material.
- Slow growing but aggressive tumor.
- Most commonly in parotid , 5th -6th decade, F>M.
- Tendency to spread perineural spaces and extend beyond clinically apparent border.

Ans.72. (d) Chronic Atrophic

Shafers,5th ed pg 394

Chronic atrophic candidiasis is considered as synonymous with the condition better known as "denture sore mouth", a diffuse inflammation of denture bearing area often occurring with angular chelitis

—acute pseudomembranous is commonly known as "thrush"

—acute atrophic it appear erythematous rather than white, and its only painful candidiasis

—chronic hyperplastic candidiasis often known as "leukoplakia" type of candidiasis.

Ans.73. (c) Psoriasis

Explained earlier please refer KCET-07 A77

Ans.74. (c) Osteomyelitis

Ref http://en.wikipedia.org/wiki/Alkaline_phosphatase

Alkaline phosphatase (ALP) is a hydrolase enzyme responsible for removing phosphate groups from many types of molecules, including nucleotides, proteins and alkaloids.

In humans, alkaline phosphatase is present in all tissues throughout the entire body, but is particularly concentrated in ***liver, bile duct, kidney, bone, and the placenta***. The optimal pH for the enzyme activity is pH=10.

Concentrations blood plasma (serum) levels of ALP are typically 3-15 Units per liter, depending on the assay and local normal guidelines.

Elevated levels (hyperphosphatasemia)

If it is unclear why alkaline phosphatase is elevated, isoenzyme studies using electrophoresis can confirm the source of the ALP. Heat stability also distinguishes bone and liver isoenzymes ("bone burns, liver lasts").

- **Liver** (Liver ALP):
  - Cholestasis, cholecystitis, cholangitis, cirrhosis, hepatitis, fatty liver, liver tumor, liver metastases, drug intoxication.
  - N.B. concurrently elevated GGT (gamma glutamyl transpeptidase) helps rule in favor of liver metastasis (rather than bone, kidney, etc.) when assessing spread of cancer.
  - Drugs: *e.g.* verapamil, carbamazepine, phenytoin, erythromycin, allopurinol, ranitidine
- **Bone** disease (Bone ALP):
  - **Paget's disease,** osteosarcoma, bone metastases of prostatic cancer (High / very high ALP values) 250 Bodansky unit.
  - Other bone metastases.
  - Fractured bone.
  - Multiple myeloma (***only when associated with fractures***)
- **Skeletal** involvement of other primary diseases:
  - Osteomalacia, rickets, vitamin D deficiency, (Moderate rise).
  - Malignant tumors (ALP originating from tumor).
  - Primary hyperparathyroidism.
  - Renal disease (secondary hyperparathyroidism).
  - Primary hypothyroidism.
- Polycythemia vera .
- Myelofibrosis.
- Leukemoid reaction to infection.
- Women on oral contraceptives.
- Pregnancy.
- Biliary obstruction.
- Transient hyperphosphatasaemia of infancy: benign, often associated with infection.

Lowered levels (hypophosphatasemia)

- Hypophosphatasia, an autosomal recessive disease.
- Postmenopausal women receiving estrogen therapy because of osteoporosis.
- Men with recent heart surgery, malnutrition, magnesium deficiency, hypothyroidism or severe anemia.
- Children with achondroplasia and cretinism.
- Children after a severe enteritis.

- Pernicious anemia.
- Aplastic anemia.
- Chronic myelogenous leukemia.

Remember,

Leukocyte alkaline phosphatase (LAP) is found within white blood cells.

It is decreased in CML and PNH (paroxysmal nocturnal hemoglobinuria).

Ans.75. (a)Progressive systemic sclerosis

Ref http://en.wikipedia.org/wiki/Systemic_sclerosis

Scleroderma is a rare, chronic disease characterized by excessive deposits of collagen in the skin or other organs. The localized type of the disease tends not to be fatal. **Diffuse scleroderma** or **systemic sclerosis**, the generalized type of the disease, can be fatal as a result of heart, kidney, lung or intestinal damage.

- It is seen 3 to 4 times more predominant in female occurring between 25-50 yrs.
- Scleroderma affects the skin, and in more serious cases it can affect the blood vessels and internal organs. The most evident symptom is the hardening of the skin and associated scarring.
- Typically, the skin appears reddish or scaly in appearance. The contracture of the skin gives a ***mask-like appearance*** of the face and a ***claw like appearance*** of hand. Blood vessels may also be more visible.
- Where large areas are affected, fat and muscle wastage will weaken limbs and affect appearance.
- There is discoloration of the hands and feet in response to cold. Most patients (over 80%) have Raynaud's phenomenon, a vascular symptom that can affect the fingers and toes.
- Systemic scleroderma and Raynaud's can cause painful ulcers on the fingers or toes which are known as digital ulcers.
- Calcinosis is also common in systemic scleroderma, and is often seen near the elbows, knees or other joints.

The limited form is often referred to as CREST syndrome. "CREST" is an acronym for:

- Calcinosis
- Raynaud's syndrome
- Esophageal dysmotility
- Sclerodactyly
- Telangiectasia

Ans.76. (b) Pemphigus

Shafer's, 5th ed, 828.

INTRAEPITHELIAL VESICLE

- herpes, pox,

- pemphigus,
- familial benign pemphigus,
- oral lesion of erythemia multiforme

SUBEPITHELIAL VESICLE

- pemphigoid,
- bullous pemphigoid,
- dermatitis herpiformis,
- skin lesion of erythemia multiforme

Ans.77. (d) Ascher's syndrome

Explained earlier please refer KCET-07 A86

Remember,

Aldrich syndrome: Wiskot Aldrich syndrome, disease involving the platelets, characterized by thrombocytopenia purpura, eczema, increased susceptibility of infection—these pts are unable to form antibody against the polysaccharide containing organism such as pneumococcoi, Haemophillius influenza, coliforms bacilli.

Ans.78. (a) Koebner's phenomenon

Ref http://www.nutripharm.net/Medical%20Conditions/psoriasis_skinconditions.htm

Psoriasis is a hyper-proliferative skin disorder affecting also possibly the joints. It is hypothesized to be an immune-mediated disease.

Types of Psoriasis

- **Psoriasis Vulgaris**: The most common form (80% of cases). Sharply edged, reddened scaly patches, typically on the scalp, elbows, knees and between the buttocks.
- **Guttate Psoriasis**: Often occurs after streptococcal infection. Numerous reddened, slightly raised small lesions appear on the trunk. Often reappears if strep reinfection occurs.
- **Inverse Psoriasis**: The inner aspect of joints is involved rather than the usual outer areas. Armpits and creases of the knees and elbows are often affected with reddened scaly patches.
- **Von Zumbusch Psoriasis**: Sterile pustules (raised lesions containing pus) cover large portions of the trunk and extremities. The skin's protective function can be impaired, making patients susceptible to infection. Severe cases require hospitalization.
- **Palmoplantar Pustular Psoriasis:** (hand and foot psoriasis) - Pus containing lesions are limited to the hands and feet. This condition can restrict walking and use of hands.
- **Koebners Phenomenon**: Psoriasis lesions formed in response to local trauma such as scratching.

People with psoriasis often notice new lesions 10 to 14 days after the skin is cut, scratched, rubbed, or severely sunburned.

This is called the "***Koebner phenomenon***" and is named after Dr. Koebner who in the 19th century observed that a patient developed new lesions in areas where his horse bit him. This relationship between skin injury and developing new psoriatic lesions has been observed in many patients. A wide range of traumas are known to trigger Koebners phenomenon: Skin Trauma, Acupuncture, Bites, Bruises, Burns, Chemical irritation Pressure against the skin, Shaving, Sunburn and peeling, vaccinations Research shows that about 50% of people with psoriasis experience the Koebner phenomenon developing a psoriatic lesion at the site of a skin injury or in the same place as another skin condition. About 10% of psoriasis patients develop a new psoriatic lesion each time the skin is injured. The likelihood of developing the Koebner phenomenon may increase when psoriasis lesions are already present.

Histologic features

- Uniform parakeratosis, absence of stratum granulosun, elongation and clubbing of rete pegs.
- Epithelium over connective tissue are thin and from these point bleeding occurs when scales are peeled off (Auspitz's sign).
- Dilated, tortuous capillaries extending high in the papillae are prominent.
- Monoro's abscess or intraepithelial micro-abscess is a common histologic feature.

Ans.79. (b) Leukemia

Ref http://en.wikipedia.org/wiki/Chloroma

- A **chloroma**, or **granulocytic sarcoma**, or most appropriately, **extramedullary myeloid tumor**, is a solid tumor composed of immature malignant white blood cells called myeloblasts.
- A chloroma is an extramedullary manifestion of ***acute myeloid leukemia***; in other words, it is a solid collection of leukemic cells occurring outside of the bone marrow. This name is derived from the Greek word *chloros* (green), as these tumors often have a green tint due to the presence of myeloperoxidase.
- Chloromas may occur in virtually any organ or tissue. The most common areas of involvement are the skin (also known as *leukemia cutis*) and the gums. Skin involvement typically appears as violaceous, raised, nontender plaques or nodules, which on biopsy are found to be infiltrated with myeloblasts.
- Note that leukemia cutis differs from Sweet's syndrome, in which the skin is infiltrated by mature neutrophils in a paraneoplastic process. Gum involvement (gingival hypertrophy) leads to swollen, sometimes painful gums which bleed easily with tooth brushing and other minor trauma.

Ans.80. (d) Nasoalveolar cyst

Ref Shafer's, 5th ed , pg 92

Nasoalveolar cyst (Nasolabial / Klestadt's cyst)

- Is a rare fissural cyst that not usually found in bone.
- Arise at junction of globular, the lateral nasal and maxillary process.
- Presents as a swelling in the naso-labial fold.
- Mean age of occurrence – 41-46yrs.
- Since it is extra-osseous it presents with ***no*** radiographic features.

Ans.81. (c) Dens in dente

Ref Shafers,4th ed pg 41, Orbans textbook of histology

Anomaly	Stage
Initiation	Anodontia, supernumerary teeth, fusion, germination.
Histo differentiation	Dentinogenesis imperfecta, corresponds to bell stage.
Morpho differentiation	Talon's cusp, dens in dente, macrodontia, Hutchinson's incisor, peg lateral.
Apposition	Enamel hypoplasia, concrescence, intrinsic staining, hypo calcification.

Ans.82. (a) Auriculotemporal syndrome

Explained earlier please refer KCET-07 A142

Ans.83. (c) Type III dentinogenesis imperfecta

Shafer, 4th ed pg60,

- In type 1 and type 2 there is partial or total precocious obliteration of the pulp chamber and root canal by continued formation of dentine.
- In type 3 -enamel appears normal, dentin is thin and the pulp chambers are enormous. In X-ray, it appears as SHELLS of enamel and dentine surrounding extremely large pulp chamber and root canal.

Ans.84. (c) Rests of Malassez

- Dental lamina cyst of the newborn/ Gingival cyst/ Epstein's pearls, Bohn's).
- They are multiple/solitary superficial raised nodules on edentulous ridges of infants that resolve without treatment.
- They are usually derived from the ***rests of dental lamina*** consisting of keratin-producing epithelial lining.
- **Epstein's pearls** are cystic, keratin filled nodules found along the mid-palatine raphe, formed due to entrapment of epithelial cells along the line of fusion.
- **Bohn's nodules** are keratin-filled nodules scattered over the palate, commonly at the junction of hard and soft palate.

Ans.85. (b) Herpes simplex virus type I

Ref http://www.medscape.com/viewarticle/417716_4; Shafer, 4th ed pg 115

Epstein Barr virus

- Nasopharyngeal carcinoma
- Infectious mononucleosis
- Burkitt's lymphoma
- Hodgkin and NHL

HTLV (human T-cell leukemic viruses), includes HTLV-I and HTLV-II.

- HTLV-I encodes for the oncogene termed *Tox*, which promotes a transforming function by up regulating growth genes More than 90% of those with adult T-cell leukemia (ATLV) are HTLV-I antibody positive.
- HTLV-II has been linked to hairy-cell leukemia.

Papilloma virus

- More than 90 types of HPV are known to infect genital and non-genital skin and mucosa.
- HPV is type-specific for carcinomas and for stage of carcinoma intraepithelial neoplasia (CIN) lesions. Although there is a geographic variation in the frequency of HPV types, 16 and 18 are most often linked to malignancy.
- Type 16 is frequently seen in CIN II and III and in cervical cancer. Type 16 also has been seen in Bowen's disease and has been linked to anal carcinomas.
- A variety of types are common in high-grade CIN lesions: 16, 18, 31, 33, 35, 45, 51, 52, 56, 58, and 61.
- The most common types seen in *oral carcinomas* are 6, 11,16, and 18, with 6 and 11 strongly linked to papillomas. HPV has also been encountered in Verrucous and conjunctival carcinomas.
- HPV types 16 and 18 are found in penile carcinoma.

While HSV-1 has ***not*** been implicated in any malignancy, HSV 2 is associated with carcinoma of uterine cervix.

Ans.86. (a) IgA

Explained earlier, please refer KCET-07 A24

Ans.87. (a) Infectious mononucleosis

Ref http://en.wikipedia.org/wiki/Infectious_mononucleosis#Laboratory_tests

- ***Infectious mononucleosis***, (also known as **the kissing disease**, or **Pfeiffer's disease**, in North America as **mono**, and more commonly known as **glandular fever** in other English-speaking countries),.
- Disease seen most commonly in adolescents and young adults, characterized by fever, sore throat, muscle soreness, and fatigue. White patches on the tonsils or in the back of the throat may also be seen, (resembling strep throat). Mononucleosis is usually caused by the Epstein-Barr virus (EBV).
- The laboratory hallmark of the disease is the presence of so-called ***atypical lymphocytes*** (a type of mononuclear cell, see image) on the peripheral blood smear. In addition, the overall white blood cell count is almost invariably increased, particularly the number of lymphocytes.
- Mononucleosis causes so-called ***heterophile*** **antibodies**, which cause agglutination (sticking together) of non-human red blood cells, to appear in the patient's blood.
- The ***monospot*** is a non-specific test that screens for mono by looking for these antibodies. Confirmation of the exact etiology can be obtained through tests to detect specific antibodies

to the causative viruses. The spot test may be negative in the first week, so negative tests are often repeated at a later date. Since the spot test is usually negative in children *less than 6-8 years* old, an EBV serology test should be done on them if mononucleosis is suspected.

- An older test for heterophile antibodies is the ***Paul Bunnell test***, in which the patient's serum is mixed with sheep red blood cells and checked for agglutination of these cells. In positive Paul Bunnell test titer of agglutinins and haemolysin in human blood rise to **1:4096**....(normal is 1:8).

Ans.88. (c) Civatte Bodies

Ref Shafer,4th ed pg 813,

Civatte bodies: also known as—colloid bodies, hyaline bodies, fibrillar bodies, cytoid bodies. They are mostly present in spinous and basal layers appearing as round, eosinophilic globules representing degenerated epithelium or keratinocyte or phagocytosed epithelial cell remnants within macrophages. This is seen as a histologic feature of oral lichen planus (OLP). Other features include:

- liquefactive degeneration of the basement membrane,
- focal inflammatory cell infiltration
- saw-tooth rete pegs
- hyperparakeratosis

Looking at other options

- lipshultz body –herpetic stomatitis
- Barr- bodies—is present in one X chromosome of female, characteristic of feminine

ORAL MEDICINE AND RADIOLOGY

Ans.89. (b) Hyperparathyroidism.

EFFECTS ON TEETH AND SUPPORTING STRUCTURES

Hyperparathyroidism

- Loss of lamina dura in 10% cases
- Root appears tapered n such cases
- Mature teeth are immune to demineralizing effect of PTH

Hypoparathyroidism

- Enamel hypoplasia
- External root resorption
- Delayed eruption
- Root dilacerations

Hyperthyroidism

- Premature development of teeth
- Early eruption
- Premature loss of deciduous teeth
- Loss of alveolar bone structure

Hypothyroidism (cretinism/ myxedema)

- Delayed eruption
- Short roots
- Thinning of lamina dura
- Small sized jaws
- Adults experience increased periodontal diseases
- Enlarged tongue
- External root resorption
- Loss/migration of teeth

Rickets

- Hypoplasia of developing enamel
- Unerupted teeth
- Lamina dura thin or missing in some areas

Congenital syphilis is known to cause enamel hypoplasia. (Congenital syphilis has been explained in detail earlier KCET-07 A82).

Ans.90. (b) Density

Ref White and Pharoah, 5th ed, pg 80-82

- **DENSITY:** the overall degree of darkening of an exposed film.
- **CONTRAST:** difference between the light and dark regions of a X-ray film.
- **SPEED:** amount of radiation required to produce an image of standard density. Expressed as reciprocal of exposure required to produce an optical density of 1 above gross fog.
- **NOISE:** appearance of uneven density in a uniformly exposed film.
- **SHARPNESS:** the ability of a radiograph to define an edge precisely.
- **RESOLUTION:** ability of a radiograph to separate structures that are close to each other. Usually OPG – 5 lines/mm and IOPA- 20 lines/mm.

Ans.91. (a) Aluminum

Ref White and Pharoah, 5th ed , pg14

Filtration is a procedure of removing the low energy (long wavelength) photons that contribute to patient exposure but do not have enough energy to reach the film. This can be accomplished by placing an ***aluminium filter*** in the path of beam. The aluminium preferentially removes the lower energy photons with minimal effect on the higher energy photons.

EXTRA EDGE

Remember, inherent filtration consists of materials (glass wall of tube) that the x-ray photons encounter on their path. Mostly the value ranges from 0.5 – 2mm of Aluminium.

Total filtration = inherent + external (Al filters)

Recommended values at 70kVp = 1.5mm; and 2.5mm at higher voltages.

Ans.92. (b) X-rays can be focused

Ref White and Pharoah, 5th ed , pg 5

X-rays are electromagnetic radiations that travel in a wave form at the speed of light. X-rays always travel in a straight line and can't be focused but can deflect from a surface.

Ans.93. (a) Still's disease

Ref http://en.wikipedia.org/wiki/Still%27s_disease

Still's disease is a form of juvenile idiopathic arthritis, characterized by high spiking fevers and transient rashes, named after the English physician *Sir George Frederic Still* (1861-1941). The disease was first discovered in children, but now it is also known to occur, less commonly, in adults in whom it is referred to as adult-onset Still's disease described by another English physician, Bywaters on 1971 (the same author is famous for the crush syndrome).

There are several theories about the cause of Still's disease. It has been suggested it may be caused by a micro-bacterial infection. However, the cause of Still's disease remains unknown. The pathogenesis of the disease is more secure to be autoimmune.

Patients with Still's disease usually have systemic symptoms. Usual symptoms include:

- waves of high fevers that rise to 40 °C (104 °F) which may be accompanied by extreme fatigue.
- A faint transient non-itching salmon-colored skin rash can also be observed.
- Flu like pain throughout the body.
- muscle pain.

DIAGNOSIS

- Persistent arthritis (lasting at least 6 weeks) is frequently a symptom.
- A rash is frequently visible on the body, and the patients usually suffer from high, spiking fevers.
- Blood tests frequently indicate elevated white blood cell counts, suggesting there is serious inflammation.
- Also, low red blood cell counts (anemia) are common. Typically, elevated blood tests indicate in high sedimentation rates, an indicator of inflammation.
- Other indicators of inflammation may also be elevated, including CRP (c-reactive protein) and ferritin levels.
- *However, the classic blood tests for rheumatoid arthritis and systemic lupus erythematosus are usually negative.*

- A new important marker of AOSD is the glicosilated ferritin: the percentage of this form of the protein is often below the 50% of the total during the flare of the disease and often during the intercritic phases.

Ans.94. (b) Arthrography

Arthrograhy is a technique in which indirect image of the disk is obtained by injecting a radio opaque contrast agent into one or both joint spaces under fluoroscopic guidance. It is indicated when information regarding disk position, function, morphology and integrity is required. A perforation may be detected if the dye injected in one compartment is found to be present in other as well.

Ref White and Pharoah, 5th ed , pg 548

Arthroscopy on the other hand is the direct visualization of the joint space by insertion of a specially designed fiber optic endoscope into a joint compartment for observation and therapeutic purpose. Ohnishi, in 1975 used a 1.7mm needle for this purpose.

This technique is used for biopsy, lavage (arthrocentesis), sclerotherapy, and for treating disk mobility disorders.

Ref Neelima Malik, pg 231

Other options are very clear; OPG is an extra-oral projection while arthroplasty is a surgical procedure for correction of disk disorders.

Ans.95. (c) Erythema Multiforme

Ref Shafers,5th ed 1111,

FEATURES

- Occurs chiefly in young adults, in 2nd to 4th decade. M>F.
- Concentric ring like erythematous macule, papule or vesicle occurring in some case has been termed target, iris, or bull's eye lesion.
- Steven Johnson syndrome is a severe bullous form affecting skin, oral cavity, eyes and genitilia.
- Both sub-dermal and intra-epithelial vesicle formation may occur.

Ans.96. (c) X-rays interact with matter

Ref White and Pharoah, 5th ed, pg 16

Interaction of X-rays with matter: - 3 means of beam attenuation:

(1) **COHERENT SCATTERING:** (classic, elastic or *Thompson* scattering) when a low-energy incident photon passes near an outer electron of an atom causing it to get temporarily excited at the same frequency. Contributes little to film fog, as energy is too low.

(2) **PHOTO ELECTRIC ABSORPTION: critical** in diagnostic imaging. Occurs when an incident photon collides with a bound electron.

Kinetic energy (recoiled e^-) = E of incident photon – binding energy of electron.

Although it is essential for high quality radiographs , it also ***increases*** the patient's exposure because of increased absorption.

(3) **COMPTON SCATTERING:** occurs when a photon interacts with an outer orbital electron. This is the ***major*** (62%) type of scattering in dental x-ray. This type of interaction results in loss of an outer electron and ionization of the atom. The probability to Compton is directly proportional to the electron density of the absorber. These scattering cause ***unwanted darkening*** of the film but are advantageous to the patient due to ***lower exposure***.(the deflection cause them to exit via the patient's head without absorption by the tissues).

PERIODONTICS

Ans.97. (b) Exudate

Explained earlier Please refer KCET-06 A143

Ans.98. (c) Lead

Ref Shafer, 5th ed , pg 774

Heavy metals absorbed systemically from therapeutic use or occupational environments may discolor the gingiva and other areas of the oral mucosa. Bismuth, arsenic, and mercury produce a black line in the gingiva which follows the contour of the margin.

Lead results in a bluish red or deep blue linear pigmentation of the gingival margin (**Burtonian line or *halo saturninus***). Exposure to silver causes a violet marginal line, often accompanied by a diffuse bluish-grey discoloration throughout the oral mucosa.

Ans.99. (b) Apically repositioned flap

Ref Carranza, 9th ed, pg 775

FLAP TECHNIQUE	FEATURES
Modified Widman Flap	• Ramfjord and Nissle 1974 • Facilitates instrumentation • Pocket depth maintained
Undisplaced flap	• Internal bevel gingivectomy • Removes the pocket lining • Improves accessibility • Most common procedure
Apically displaced flap	• Apically positioning of pocket • Eliminates pocket wall • Improves accessibility • Preserves/ increases the width of attached gingiva by converting the soft tissue wall of pocket into it

Incisions

- **Internal bevel:** first incision, directed to alveolar crest starting 0.5-1.0mm from the gingival margin. Surgical scalpel #11 or #15.
- **Crevicular incision:** made from the bottom of pocket to the bone wedge shaped tissue separates. Blade #12D(beak shaped).
- **Interdental incision:** last incision removes the gingival collar coronal to bone. Orbans knife is used.

Ans.100. (d) Crevicular incision is made from base of the pocket

EXPLAINED ABOVE

Ans.101. (*c*) No.11-12 are used

Ref Carranza 9th ed , pg 573

Gracey curettes are area-specific double ended paired instruments as :-

- #1-2 and #3-4 : Anterior teeth
- #5-6 : Anterior teeth and premolars
- #7-8 and 9-10 : Posterior teeth: facial and lingual
- #11-12 : Posterior teeth : mesial
- # 13-14 : posterior teeth : distal
- # 15-16 : modified 11-12, for Posterior mesial
- #17-18 : modified 13-14 , for posterior distal

EXTRA EDGE

GRACEY curette	UNIVERSAL curette
Designed for specific area and surface	Designed for all surfaces
One cutting edge (outer)	Two cutting edges (either is used)
Blade curved in 2 planes: up and to side	Blade curved in 1 plane ; up only
Offset blade at 60° to shank	Not Offset : 90°

Ans.102. (d) All of the above feature

Ref Carranza,9th ed pg 701

Occlusal adjustment or ***coronoplasty***, is the selective reshaping of occlusal surfaces with the goal of establishing a stable, non-traumatic occlusion. The resulting occlusion is termed as therapeutic occlusion.

Indications

- Signs of occlusal trauma
- TMJ symptoms
- Bruxism
- Frequent headaches
- Tooth mobility due to underlying periodontal disease

However, the main aim is to promote healing after inflammation has subsided.

Ans.103. (b)Decrease plaque formation

Ref Shafer's 5th ed, pg 591.

Read the following lines from Shafer

"Turkheim noted that the *saliva of caries immune persons have a higher urea and ammonia content. The ammonia nitrogen level ranged from 0-8mg/100ml.* ***They also suggested that high ammonia concentration retarded plaque formation and neutralized acid to some extent.*** *Urea may be further hydrolyzed by urease to ammonium carbonate increasing the neutralizing power of saliva.*"

Ans.104. (b) Oblique

Ref Carranza, pg 37

The principal fibers of PDL are arranged in 6 groups:-

- **Transseptal fibers:** extended interproximally over the alveolar crest and embed in the cementum of adjacent tooth. Reconstructed even after destruction by a PDL disease. As they do not have any osseous attachment, they are regarded as gingival fibers.
- **Alveolar crest group:** extends obliquely from cementum (jus below junctional epithelium) to the alveolar crest. They prevent extrusion of the tooth and resist lateral tooth movement.
- **Horizontal group:** extend at right angles to the long axis of the tooth from cementum to alveolar bone.
- **Oblique group:** they are the largest group, extends from cementum (coronally) down into the alveolar bone. They transfer vertical masticatory forces to the alveolar bone along the long axis of tooth.
- **Apical group:** radiate in irregular fashion at apical region of tooth socket. They are not seen in incompletely formed roots.
- **Inter-radicular fibers:** these fan out from the cementum to the tooth in the furcation areas of multi-rooted tooth.

Ans.105. (a) 1.5-7.5 million cycles / second

Ref http://www.valleylab.com/education/poes/poes_04.html

Electrosurgery is the application of a high-frequency electric current to human (or other animal) tissue as a means to remove lesions, staunch bleeding, or cut tissue. Electrosurgery can be used to cut, coagulate, desiccate, or fulgurate tissue.

Often "electrocautery" is used to describe electrosurgery. This is incorrect. Electrocautery refers to direct current (electrons flowing in one direction) whereas electrosurgery uses alternating current. During electrocautery, current does not enter the patient's body. Only the heated wire comes in contact with tissue. In electrosurgery, the patient is included in the circuit and current enters the patient's body.

Standard electrical current alternates at a frequency of 60 cycles per second (Hz). Electrosurgical systems could function at this frequency, but because current would be transmitted through body tissue at 60 cycles, excessive neuromuscular stimulation and perhaps electrocution would result.

Because nerve and muscle stimulation cease at 100,000 cycles/second (100 kHz), electrosurgery can be performed safely at "radio" frequencies above 100 kHz. An electrosurgical generator takes 60 cycles current and increases the frequency to over 200,000 (200 kHz) cycles per second. To avoid electric shock, electrosurgical equipment operates in the frequency range of ***200 kHz to 5 MHz (5 million)***. At this frequency electrosurgical energy can pass through the patient with minimal neuromuscular stimulation and no risk of electrocution.

Option 'a' is the closest and hence, the answer here.

Ans.106. (a) Fibronectin

Ref Carranza , pg 811

Fibronectin is a high-molecular-weight glycoprotein containing about 5% carbohydrate that binds to receptor proteins that span the cell's membrane, called integrins. In addition to integrins, they also bind extra cellular matrix components such as collagen, fibrin and heparin. The addition of fibronectin to the root surface ***may promote new attachment.***

Ans.107. (c) 10 Weeks

Ref Carranza, 9th ed, pg 858.

Microscopically, healing of graft:

- Intermediate thickness (0.75mm) – 10.5 weeks.
- Thicker grafts (1.75 mm) – 16 weeks or more.

Greatest shrinkage in grafts occurs within first 6 weeks.

EXTRA EDGE

Healing of grafts:

- *First day* – the CT swells and is disorganized. Imbibed tissue fluid is the chief source of nutrition.
- Revascularization takes place by 2nd -3rd day.
- The epithelium undergoes degeneration and necrosis. By 4th day a thin new epithelium develops. rete pegs by 7th day.
- The new epithelium gives a grey, veil-like appearance.

Ans.108. (b) 60 degrees

Explained above, please refer A101

Ans.109. (d)Periodontal disease progression

Ref Carranza, pg 494

CADIA (Computer Assisted Densitometric Image Analysis System)

- An objective method for following alveolar bone density changes quantitatively over time.
- It has shown higher sensitivity, and higher degree of reproducibility and accuracy.
- Consists of a video camera that measures the light transmitted through a radiograph that are converted into grey-scale images.

- This method may also be utilized for assessing attachment levels.

Ans.110. (b) Identifies a particular micro-organism

Ref Carranza, pg 498

DNA probes entail segments of single-stranded nucleic acid, labeled with an enzyme or radio-isotope. DNA probes may target whole genomic DNA or individual genes. Genomic probes carry greater risk for cross-reactivity, however, specific genes like 16S rRNA are specific to organisms of same species. The sample is subjected to lysis and denaturation.

The assay can rapidly test for multiple bacteria, including AA, P gingivalis, B intermedius etc. the probe are able to detect as few as 10^2 to 10^4 bacteria.

Ans.111. (d) Auto – cancellous

Ref Carranza, pg 812

Grafts are classified on their ability of osteogenesis, osteoinductive or osteoconductive potential. While auto-cancellous grafts like ileac-grafts are osteogenic others like allografts, xenografts and alloplast are either osteo-inductive or conductive in nature.

CONSERVATIVE DENTISTRY AND ENDODONTICS

Ans.112. (b) Negative rake angle.

Ref. Sturdevant, pg 336

The actual cutting action of a bur (or diamond) takes place in a *very small* region at the edge of the blade (or at the point of a diamond chip).

- In the high speed range, this effective portion of the individual blade is limited to no more than a few thousandths of a centimeter adjacent to blade edge.
- Each blade has two sides, the ***rake face*** (towards the direction of cutting) and the ***clearance face*** and three important angles, the rake angle edge angle, clearance angle.
- The optimal angle are dependant on such factors as the mechanical property of blade material, the mechanical property of the material being cut , the rotational speed and diameter of the bur and lateral force applied by operator to hand piece, thus the bur.
- The **rake angle** is the most important design characteristics of bur blade. For cutting hard, brittle materials, a ***negative rake angle*** minimizes fractures of the cutting edges, thereby increasing tool life.
- A rake angle is said to be negative when the rake face is ahead of radius (from cutting edge to axis of bur). Increasing the edge angle reinforces the cutting edge and reduces the likelihood for the blade to fracture.
- Carbide bur blades have higher hardness and more wear resistance, but they are more ***brittle*** than steel blades, require greater edge angles to minimize fracture.

The three angles cannot be varied independently for each other. An increase in clearance angle, for example, eliminates rubbing friction of the clearance face, provides a stop to prevent the bur edge from digging into tooth structure excessively, and reduces the radius of blade back of the cutting edge to provide sufficient flute space or clearance space for chips formed ahead of following blade. Carbide burs normally have blades with slight negative rake angle and edge angles of approximately 90 degrees. Their clearance faces either are curved or have two surfaces to provide a low clearance angle near the edge and a greater clearance space ahead of the following blade.

Ans.113. (c) labial to the position of tooth to be prepared.

Ref. Sturdevant, pg 452

When a cervical retainer is to be placed to isolate a class V lesion, heavier rubber dam is usually recommended for better tissue retraction, and hole for the tooth should be punched ***slightly facial*** to the arch form to compensate for the extension of the dam to cervical area. The farther gingivally the lesion extends, the further the hole must be positioned from the arch form. In addition, the hole should be slightly larger, and distance between it and holes for the adjacent teeth should be slightly increased.

Ans.114. (d) Lentulospirals

Ref httphttp://en.wikipedia.org/wiki/Lentulo_spiral

- Are twisted drills used for the application of the sealer inside the root canal.
- After bio-mechanical preparation, the canal is dried and the sealer cement (like $Ca(OH)_2$ is introduced into the canals using these instruments.
- They may be hand operated or engine driven.
- Reverse spiral forces the sealer apically.
- Flexible shaft. Durable. Stainless steel.
- Right angle. Color coded sizes: 25, 30, 35 and 40.
- Maillefer's Lentulo spiral, produced by Dentsply®, happens to be the only one licensed to use the Lentulo name.

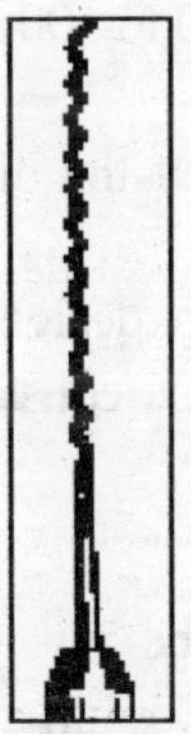

Ans.115. (b) Sn-Hg phase.

Ref. Sturdevant, pg 154

Sn-Hg reaction product crystals are long and blade like, penetrating through out the matrix. Although they constitute less than 10% of the final composition, they form a penetrating matrix because of inter-crystalline contacts between the blades. That image is reinforced by scanning electron microscope. This phase is prone to corrosion in clinical restorations, a process that proceeds from the outside of amalgam, along crystals, connecting to new crystals at the inter-crystalline contacts. This produces ***penetrating corrosion*** that generates a porous and spongy amalgam with minimal mechanical resistance. Two key features of this degradation are: the corrosion prone character of Sn-Hg phase and the connecting path formed by the blade like geometry of the crystals. Both of these are eliminated by the use of ***more*** copper in the initial composition.

Ans.116. (b) Files have more flutes than reamers

Ref Grossman , 11th ed, pg 195

K-FILES	REAMERS
Manufactured from a square blank	Manufactured form a triangular blank
Blanks are twisted t produce tighter flutes (1.93-0.88 mm)	Reamers have looser flutes (0.8 – 0.28 mm)
Motion used – rasping/pulling	Motion used- pushing-rotating (torque)
Number of flutes are more	Number of flutes is less.
Square blank offers more fracture resistance	Triangular blanks are susceptible to fracture at
(used for small, fragile instruments)	Lower diameter

Ans.117. (b) 0.02mm per mm.

Ref. Grossman pg 193- 194

Ingle and Levine, using an electronic micro-coparator, found variations in diameter and taper for the same size of instruments. They then suggested a definite increase in diameter as the size progressed while maintaining a constant taper of all blades regardless of size. Essentially their recommendations were as follows:

- Instruments shall be numbered from 10 to 100, the numbers to advance by 5 units to size 60, then by 10 units to size 100.
- Each number shall be representative of the diameter of the instrument in hundredths of a millimeter at the tip.
- The working blade shall begin at the tip, designated site D1 and the diameter of 0.2 plus 0.32 or 0.52mm at D2. This sizing ensures a constant increase in taper of ***0.02mm per mm*** for every instrument regardless of size.

Other specifications were added later:

- The tip angle of an instrument should be 75 +/- 15 degrees,
- Instrument sizes should increase by 0.05 mm at D1 between no's 10 and 60 and increase by 0.1mm from no's 60 to 150.
- In addition instrument handles are color coded for easier recognition.

Ans.118. (a) Increase surface energy.

Ref . Sturdevant's pg 238

Inspired by the industrial use of 85% phosphoric acid to facilitate adhesion of paints and resins to metallic surfaces, Bunocore envisioned the use of acids to etch enamel for sealing pits and fissures. Since Bunocore's introduction of the acid etch technique many dental researchers have attempted to achieve methods for reliable and durable adhesion between resin and tooth structure.

Acid etching transforms the smooth enamel into very irregular surface and also ***increases its surface energy.*** When a fluid resin based material is applied to the etched surface, the resin penetrates aided by capillary action. Monomer in the material polymerizes and material becomes interlocked with the enamel surface. The formation of resin micro tags within enamel is the fundamental mechanism of adhesion of resin to enamel. Enamel etching results in 3 different micro morphologic pattern.

- Type I – dissolution of prism core without dissolution of prism periphery.
- Type II- opposite of type I.
- Type III- less distinct than other two. Includes areas that resemble other patterns and area where topography is not related to enamel prism morphology."

EXTRA EDGE

Remember, while acid etching increases the surface energy in enamel, it reduces the energy when applied to dentin. This is due to the fact that when dentin is etched, more negatively charged collagen fibrils are exposed when compared to enamel.

Ans.119. (c) Requires frequent radiographic monitoring

Ref Ingle, 5th ed, pg647

Johnson and Beatty developed a commercial version of cyanoacrylate device. It may be used to remove silver points, broken files, cemented cores and metal carrier of thermofills, the endo-extractor consists of tubular tripan end-cutting burs, described by **Masseram**, along with a variety of sizes of tube to which a handle is attached. The different size trepan burs sit as over the point and are use to cut a trench around it. Thus freeing a few mm of point that may be grasped and appropriate size hollow tube extractor is chosen that will snuggly fit the extruding point. The extractor is then cemented to at least 2 mm of point with cyanoacrylate glue and 5min are allowed to set. The handle of tube is then used to twist and lift the point from its feet.

Ans.120. (a) Should be sufficient to provide access to perform the retro preparation

Ref Grossman, 11th ed pg 300

Apicoectomy or root resection/amputation is the most common form of peri-apical surgery. The root tip is resected when:

- The canals cannot be adequately obturated due to internal obstruction.
- Apical root fracture.
- Root perforation, calcified canals, lateral or accessory canals.
- To convert a inadequately sealed canal into a well sealed one without the need for retrograde sealing.

Ans.121. (b) No medication/ material available presently which promote pulp healing.

Ref Sturdevant, pg 100; Grossman pg 120

Friends, lets first see what exactly the question means.

Inflamed pulp – due to deep caries/cavity prep-

Now, we all know the pulp repairing capacity of Ca $(OH)_2$ by virtue of its capability to induce dentin bridge formation. This technique involves either *indirect/direct pulp capping.*

But friends, a major indication for such procedure is a healthy pulp without any signs of inflammation.

So, if the pulp is inflamed we can either do conventional RCT or a pulpotomy procedure. However, no agent till date can reverse a pulp inflammation.

A pulpotomy followed by application of dycal paste helps maintain the radicular pulp vitality. The rationale behind this is that pulp has arterio-venous anastomoses and 'U-turn' loops that reduce the flow to areas of inflammation and thereby decease the vascular pressure. This prevents inflammation to spread rapidly into the radicular pulp which can be saved by timely measures.

Ans.122. (b) Retina.

Ref. Phillip's pg 297-298

The light emitted by curing units can cause <u>*retinal damage*</u> if one looks directly at the beam for an extended period. To avoid this, never look directly into the light tip and minimize observation of the reflected light for longer periods. Protective eyeglasses and various types of shields that further filter the light, is available for increased protection.

Light activated material afford a number of advantages over chemical activated resin.

1. They are single component pastes, thus require no mixing.
2. Working time is chosen by the clinician.
3. Material hardens rapidly once exposed to curing light.
4. But, depth of curing is limited and depends on the color of material, location of light source, quality of light source.

Ans.123. (c) 3 minutes.

The objective of trituration of amalgam is to provide a proper amalgamation of the mercury and alloy. The alloy particles are coated with a film of oxide that is difficult for mercury to penetrate. This film must be rubbed off in some manner so as a clean surface of alloy can come in contact with mercury. This oxide layer is removed by abrasion when alloy particles and mercury are triturated.

Ref Phillip's pg 390

The goal of condensation is to compact the alloy into the prepared cavity so that the greatest possible density is attained with sufficient mercury present to ensure continuity of matrix phase. After the mix is made, condensation of the amalgam should be promptly initiated. Longer the time lapse, weaker the amalgam. Also, mercury content and creep of amalgam increases. Condensation of partially set material probably fractures and breaks up the matrix that has already formed. Also, if the alloy has lost certain amount of plasticity, it is difficult to condense without producing voids. Most alloys mixed with minimal mercury harden with considerable rapidity. The working time is short, thus, condensation should be done ***within 3-4 minutes*** after trituration.

Ref. Phillip's pg 394

Ans.124. (a) Extension for prevention.

Ref. Sturdevant pg 277

Black noted that in tooth preparation for smooth surface caries, restoration should be extended to areas that are normally self cleansing to prevent recurrence of caries. This principle was known as <u>*extension for prevention*</u> and was broadened to include the extensions necessary to remove remaining enamel defects, such as pits and fissures. But this has been virtually eliminated because of relative caries immunity provided by preventive measures such as fluoride, improved oral hygiene and proper diet. This has fostered a more conservative approach defining the factors that dictate extension on smooth surface to be the extent of caries or injury and the restorative material used.

Ans.125. (c) Resistance form.

Ref Sturdevant pg. 290

Primary resistance form is a part of initial cavity preparation. It is defined as that shape and placement of the preparation walls that best enable both restoration and the tooth to withstand, without fracture, masticatory forces delivered principally in the long axis of the tooth.

Principles

1. Use the box shape with a relatively flat floor, which helps the tooth resist occlusal loading by the virtue of being at right angles to those forces of mastication that are directed in the long axis of the tooth.
2. To restrict the extension of the external walls to allow strong cusps, ridges to remain with sufficient dentin support.
3. To have slight rounding of internal line angles to reduce stress concentration in the tooth structure. *e.g.* Axiopulpal line angle in class II cavity preparation.
4. In the extensive preparation, cap the weak cusp and envelope or include enough of the weakened tooth structure within restoration to prevent fracture of the tooth by forces both long axis and obliquely directed.
5. To provide thickness of restorative material to prevent fracture under load.
6. To bond the material to tooth structure when appropriate.

Ans.126. (c) carbide bur.

Carbide bur was introduced in 1947, have replaced steel burs for tooth preparation as they perform better at all speed and superiority greatest at high speed. Carbide is much harder, less subjected to dulling during cutting so is less damaging to pulp.

Ref Sturtevant's pg 330

Vickers's hardness number for carbide is 1650-1700 whereas for steel is 800. However, carbide is also more brittle and susceptible to fracture when sudden blow is subjected.

But steel burs perform well only at low speed and dull rapidly at high speed or when cutting enamel. Once dulled, their cutting efficiency is reduced thereby increasing heat production and vibration.

Ref. Vimal k Sikri pg 144

Ans.127. (c) gold alloy.

Ref. Sturdevant's pg 541

Pit and fissures occur due to incomplete coalescence of the enamel and are particularly prone to caries. By using low viscosity fluid resin, these can be sealed, following acid- etching of the walls of the pits and fissures and a few millimeter of surface enamel bordering these faults. First used were cyanoacrylates which are now replaced by sealants materials like self cured and light cured are based on urethane dimetha-acrylate or Bis-GMA resins. Tints are usually added to sealant to give color contrast for visual assessment.

So we see that while all others are used as Pit and Fissure sealants, gold alloys are not feasible to be used in these situations.

ORAL AND MAXILLO-FACIAL SURGERY

Ans.128. (c) Anteriorly and superiorly

Ref Killey's 4th ed , pg 12

Fractures at the angle of mandible are under the prime influence of medial-pterygoid masseter sling.

Horizontally unfavorable fracture: the medial pterygoid displaces the posterior fragment ***upwards.***

Vertically unfavorable fractures: the posterior fragment is pulled ***lingually*** .

Hence, the option 'c' is correct.

EXTRA EDGE

Also remember,

- Symphysis area is under the influence of massater and geniohyoid muscle which may displace the segment ***posteriorly*** after fracture.
- In edentulous mandible, the fracture segment is pulled ***downward*** and ***backward*** under the influence of digastric and mylohyoid muscles, producing a typical '*bucket-handle*' fracture.

Ans.129. (d) Both 'B' and 'C"

Ref Neelima Malik, pg 586

Ludwig angina is, in fact cellulites and its management is accordingly both pharmacological and surgical.

Management of Ludwig Angina

- Ensure a patent airway, if the edema is large enough to restrict airway, perform a tracheostomy with a cuffed endo-tracheal tube.

- Antibiotics play a vital role in management and have significantly reduced the mortality associated previously with Ludwig angina.
- IV penicillin/Ampicillin with metronidazole are usually indicated. In patients allergic to penicillin, clindamycin is preferred.
- Surgical management includes bilateral submandibular incisions followed be aseptically placing a drain to relieve the pressure.
- The catheter is secured by suturing it to the margins. This allows post-operative drainage of any residual pus not seen initially
- Early surgical decompression reduces the pressure of edematous tissues and allows prompt drainage with adequate specimens for biopsy and microbiological assays.
- Hydrotherapy in patients who are dehydrated with application of ***cold packs***.

Hence, we see that option 'b' and 'c' are correct while 'a' is not.

Ans.130. (b) Edentulous

Ref Killey's , 4th ed , pg 86

The dental splint originally described by ***Gunning*** in 1866 was a vulcanite overlay of the natural teeth which he used as a splint for the fractured mandible.

- The modern Gunning splint may be used when the patient is edentulous in one or both jaws.
- These splints take the form of modified dentures with bite blocks in place of the molar teeth and a space in incisor teeth for feeding.
- The upper splint is usually fixed using a 0.45mm soft SS wire while the lower by circumferential wiring (Obwegeser technique).
- These splints although widely used, are not efficient at immobilization and favor fungal growth, foul smell due to food stagnation.

Ans.131. (b) Battle sign

Ref http://en.wikipedia.org/wiki/Battle_sign

Battle's sign, also post**auricular ecchymosis**, is an indication of fracture of the base of the posterior portion of the skull and may suggest underlying brain trauma. It consists of bruising immediately behind the ears. This sign is named after William Henry Battle.

Another common bruising sign of a skull injury is ***raccoon eyes***, the purplish discoloration around the eyes following fracture of the frontal portion of the skull base.

Tinel's sign is a way to detect irritated nerves. It is performed by lightly banging (percussing) over the nerve to elicit a sensation of tingling or "pins and needles" in the distribution of the nerve.

The **Chvostek sign** (also Weiss sign) is one of the signs of tetany seen in hypocalcemia.

It refers to an abnormal reaction to the stimulation of the facial nerve. When the facial nerve is tapped at the angle of the jaw, the facial muscles on the same side of the face will contract momentarily (typically a twitch of the nose or lips) because of hypocalcaemia or hypomagnesia and hyperexcitability of nerves.

It was first described by František Chvostek, an Austrian physician in 1876, and later independently by Nathan Weiss in 1883.

Ans.132. (a) Risdon's wiring

Ref Neelima Malik, pg 308

Dental wiring techniques

- **Essig's wiring** – stabilize the dento-alveolar arch and anchoring IMF. Requires sufficient number of teeth on either side of fracture line for anchorage. The wire passes from the neck of at least 3 teeth (B to L and then L to B) on either side.
- **Gilmer's wiring** – direct wiring for IMF between maxillary and mandibular teeth. Most common, simple and practical method. 1 tooth anterior and 1 posterior to the segment in each arch is chosen and fixed. The main disadvantages are that wire has to be complete removed in emergency removal and that there is a risk of extrusion of the teeth.
- **Risdon's wiring** – common method for horizontal wire fixation. Usually, 2nd molar on either side are chosen for anchorage. A 26 gauge, 25cm long wire is passed around the 2nd molar on each side and the ends twisted to form a strong base wire. This is then brought to the midline. Additional small wires are passed interdentally and twisted along with the base wire. Thus offering s strong fixation.
- **Ivy Eyelet's wiring** – it consists of a loop that embraces two adjacent teeth. The free end passes through the interdental area and twisted together. The mandibular eyelets are secured to the maxillary eyelets by rubber bands or joining wires. The main advantage is that in case of breakage only that particular eyelet can be replaced without disturbing the main wire.
- **Col Stout's multiloop wiring** – the 4 posterior quadrants are used. It is desirable to use elastics for the same.

So while both option 'a' and 'b' are examples of Direct wiring, the Risdon's wiring technique is referred to as an "interdental wiring technique."

Ans.133. (c) Incomplete paralysis

Ref http://en.wikipedia.org/wiki/Paresis

Paresis is a condition typified by partial loss of movement, or impaired movement. When used without qualifiers, it usually refers to the limbs, but it also can be used to describe the muscles of the eyes. Neurologists use the term ***paresis to describe weakness,*** and ***plegia to describe paralysis*** [in which all movement is lost].

Subtypes

- **monoparesis** — one leg or one arm
- **paraparesis** — both legs or both arms
- **hemiparesis** — one arm and one leg on either side of the body
- **quadraparesis** — all four limbs
- **gastroparesis** — impaired stomach emptying

Ans.134. (d) Skin, superficial fascia, platysma, deep cervical fascia and masseter muscle

Ref Neelima Malik, pg 438.

The Risdon's incision (Submandibular incision)

- Sharp incision placed at least 2 cm below and parallel to the inferior and posterior surface of the mandible.
- Reflect the skin, subcutaneous tissue and the platysma muscle.
- The dissection plane is then taken deep to the investing fascia up to the lower border of mandible.
- The pterygomassetric sling is divided at the inferior border followed by sub periosteal reflection of the masseter muscle to expose the coronoid process, sigmoid notch and Condylar neck.

Hence, option'd' is correct.

Ans.135. (a) The depth at which the impacted tooth is located

Ref Neelima Malik, pg 118.

The position and depth of impacted teeth can be assessed during radiological examination , originally advocated by George Winter.

Three imaginary lines, known as the Winter's lines were advocated:

- **White line:** corresponds to the occlusal surfaces of first and second molar up till the third molar. It indicates the difference in occlusal level of 2nd and 3rd molar.
- **Amber line:** represents the bone level. Extends from the crest of interdental septum between 1st and 2nd molars extending to ascending ramus. This line denotes the amount of bone covering the impacted tooth.
- **Red line:** is drawn perpendicular from the amber line to an imaginary point of application of elevator. It indicates the difficulty encountered and the amount of bone required to be removed to extract the impacted teeth (the 'depth').

If the length of red line is ***>5mm***, then extraction is termed as ***'difficult'.***

Ans.136. (d) Surgical removal of root tip of an endodontically treated tooth

Explained Earlier refer A120

Ans.137. (d) Osteoradionecrosis

Ref http://en.wikipedia.org/wiki/Hyperbaric_oxygen_therapy

Hyperbaric oxygen therapy (HBOT) is the medical use of oxygen at a higher than atmospheric pressure. Oxygen transport by plasma is significantly increased under HBOT.

Several therapeutic principles are made use of in HBOT:

- Treatment of decompression sickness and air embolism.
- Certain non-healing wounds (post-surgical or diabetic).
- Radiation soft tissue necrosis and ***radiation osteonecrosis.***
- Chronic refractory Osteomyelitis.
- Necrotizing fasciitis (flesh eating bacteria).
- Carbon monoxide poisoning.

- Decompression sickness
- Acute arterial ischemia (crush injury, compartment syndrome, etc.)
- Compromised skin grafts or flaps.
- Severe infection by anaerobic bacteria (such as gas gangrene)
- Air or gas embolism.
- Severe uncorrected anemia when blood transfusion is not available (*e.g.*, in a Jehovah's Witness).
- Some sports injuries.

Ans.138. (b) Impacted mandibular 3rd molars'

Explained earlier, Please refer KCET-06 A126

Ans.139. (d) Temporal space infection

Ref Neelima Malik, pg 575-577

Temporal pouches are fascial spaces in relation to the Temporalis muscle. They are two in number.

- The superficial space- lies between the temporal fascia and temporalis muscle.
- The deep temporal space – lies between the temporal muscle and skull.

The two spaces are separated by the zygomatic arch and communicate with each other from below the arch and to the infra-temporal and pterygopalatine fossa. The space infection of temporal pouches is usually secondary form the above mentioned spaces.

It may present clinically as pain, trismus and swelling over the temporal region. The dumbbell shape is due to the swelling of the two spaces with the zygomatic arch dividing them in between. Extra-oral incision and drainage relieves the symptoms.

Ans.140. (b) Emissary veins

Explained earlier please refer KCET-07 A3

Ans.141. (b) No. 11

Explained earlier please refer KCET-06 A132

Ans.142. (d) a pre-prosthetic procedure

Ref Neelima Malik, pg 397

Visor osteotomy: is a pre-prosthetic surgical procedure aimed at increasing the height of mandibular ridge for denture support.

- It includes splitting the mandible arch in bucco-lingual dimension with superior positioning of the lingual segment.
- Cancellous bone graft material is placed on the outer cortex for improving the contour.
- The Modified Visor osteotomy comprises vertical splitting in posterior and horizontal in anterior mandible. The lingual segments are pushed superiorly and grafts placed.

PEDODONTICS

Ans.143. (c) Canine

Ref Bhalajhi, pg 57

Ugly duckling stage

- Transient self correcting anomaly in maxillary incisor region between ***8-9 yrs.***
- Coined by Broadbent, it is seen during eruption of canine.
- Erupting canine displaces the incisor root mesially and crowns distally.
- The midline spacing is corrected by itself once the canine erupts fully shifting the pressure from the roots to the distally tilted incisor crowns.

Ans.144. (b) Resorb more slowly than Normal

Ref Orbans, textbook of Dental Histology

The erupting successor is the prime force in the initiation of deciduous root resorption. when permanent teeth fail to erupt or are congenitally missing, this force is lacking and the deciduous tooth absorbs at a much slower rate than normal. Although the pulp of the teeth plays a role in root resorption, the role is predominantly passive and secondary.

Ans.145. (c) prophylactic odontotomy.

Ref Sturdevant pg 123

It is presented only as a historical concept characterized by minimally preparing and filling with amalgam, developmental, structural imperfections of the enamel, such as pit and fissures, to prevent caries originating in these sites. It is no longer advocated as a preventive measure. This has been replaced by pit and fissure sealants which have shown to be effective, to have long term retention, to cause regression of active lesions and to be superior to amalgam restoration in term of time requirements.

Indications for use of sealants:

(1) Prevent caries in newly erupted teeth.

(2) Arrest incipient caries.

(3) Prevent odontopathogenic bacterial growth in sealed fissures.

(4) Prevent infection of other sites.

These should be used on pit and fissures of patients with high caries activity as an alternative to restorations.

Ans.146. (a) Chromogenic bacteria.

Ref. Shafer's pg 522

In some people, mostly children, there is usually a heavy green stain especially prominent on the gingival third of the maxillary anterior teeth. It appears soft and furry and is difficult to remove, suggesting its association with enamel cuticle. Sometimes a green stain covers a decalcified area of enamel. It seems to be associated with chromogenic bacteria but no organism has been found as yet. It has also been suggested that coloration may be due to remnants of Nasmyth's membrane, possibly by blood pigments.

Other stains on teeth surface can be due to tobacco (yellowish- brown to black deposits), dental plaque (brown), or due to pigment producing microorganisms (orange stains).

Ans.147. (a) Acute herpetic gingivostomatitis.

Ref. Shafer's pg 468

- Herpetic stomatitis is a common oral disease transmitted by droplet spread or contact with the lesions.
- It affects the children and young adults. It rarely occurs before the age of six months, apparently because of the presence of circulating antibodies in the infant derived from the mother.
- It occurs in children with development of fever, irritability, headache, pain upon swallowing and regional lymphadenopathy.
- Within a few days, gingival becomes painful erythematous.
- The lip, tongue, buccal mucosa, palate, pharynx and tonsils may also be involved. Shortly, yellow fluid filled vesicles develop. These rupture and form shallow, ragged, extremely painful ulcers covered by gray membrane and surrounded by erythematous halo.
- These heal spontaneously in 7-14 days and leave no scar.

Ans.148. (b) Anxiety of being separated from parents.

Ref Shobha Tandon, pg 132.

FEAR

Fear is defined as an unpleasant emotion or effect consisting of psychological changes in response to realistic threat or danger to one's own experience.

Development of fear

- At birth like startle an grasp response.
- Pre-schooler (upto 5 yrs) – fear about failures, being left alone or abandoned by the parent.
- Early schooler (5-9 yrs)- fear of dark, ghosts.
- Late schooler- (+9 yrs) fear of bodily injury, like needles.
- Adolescents- fear of social rejection and performance.

Ans.149. (a) Formation of calcified bridge.

Ref Grossman pg 102-107

- Pulpotomy is the surgical removal of coronal pulp.
- Its objective is to preserve the vitality of the radicular pulp and relieve the pain in patients with acute pulpalgia.
- The materials usually used to promote healing of pulp are calcium hydroxide and zinc oxide and eugenol.

- Calcium hydroxide is used because of its predictability in bridge formation and maintenance of vitality of the residual pulp.
- In contrast. Zinc oxide- eugenol cement causes persistent chronic inflammatory response when applied directly to the pulp, with less likelihood of dentin bridge formation.
- Calcium hydroxide was introduced by Herman in 1930. It is available as dry powder, a paste mixed with sterile water or as a prepared paste such as pulpdent, dycal. A radiopaque material such as barium sulfate renders the mixture more visible in radiographs.
- Radiographic evidence of a calcific bridge formation is one criterion for success of pulpotomy.

Ans.150. (c) ¾ th of the root is completed.

Ref. Shobha tandon pg. 111

Transition from primary to the permanent dentition:

- Calcification of the permanent dentition begins between birth and three years of age. Second premolars may not begin calcification until five years of age.
- Eruptive movements do not begin before crown calcification is complete.
- Enamel calcification usually completed in three to four years before eruption into the oral cavity (mandibular incisors are exception).
- Crowns pierce the bony alveolar crest when approximately 2/3rd of the root development is complete.
- Teeth emerge into the oral cavity when approximately 3/4th of the root development is complete.
- Root development is complete in 2-3 years after eruption.

Ans.151. (c) primary teeth have marked cervical constriction.

Ref Shobha Tandon, pg 289

In primary dentition, the molars are more bulbous and are sharply constricted (bell-shaped) cervically. This, along with broader contacts, requires the operator to modify the conventional box type preparation. The gingival floor should be wide enough to place the margins in self-cleaning areas.

ORTHODONTICS

Ans.152. (a) 6-8years

Ref Bhalajhi, pg 10

Girls mature faster than boys (approx 2-3 yrs). Functional appliances are best given during the 'mixed dentition growth spurt' which is ***7-9yrs*** in girls and 8-11 yrs in boys (around the period of late-mixed dentition).

Hence, option 'a' is correct

The timings are different in boys and girls.

1. Just before birth
2. One year after birth
3. Mixed dentition growth spurt
   Boys : 8-11yrs
   Girls : 7-9 yrs
4. Pre-pubertal growth spurt
   Boys : 14-16 yrs
   Girls : 11-13 yrs

Ans.153. (c) Late mixed dentition

Refer previous answer

Ans.154. (b) Deflect the permanent tooth lingually

Ref Bhalajhi. pg 94

Prolonged retention of deciduous anteriors usually results in ***lingual or palatal*** eruption of their permanent successors. While in case of posterior teeth, the permanent successors are either deflected bucally/lingually or they become impacted.

Ans.155. (d) Incisor liability

Explained earlier KCET-06 A173

Ans.156. (d) Torsiversion

Ref Bhalajhi , pg 83

Lischer's modification of Angle's classification includes.

Transiversion – transposition of teeth.

Axiversion – abnormal axial inclination of teeth.

Torsiversion – rotation of teeth along its long axis.

Remember, Perversion – refers to impaction of teeth.

Ans.157. (a) Maxillary canine

Ref Neelima Malik, pg 113; Bhalajhi, pg 95

Frequency of impaction commonly seen-

- Mandibular third molars
- Maxillary third molars
- Maxillary canines
- Mandibular premolars
- Maxillary premolars
- Mandibular canine
- Maxillary incisors

Thus we see, that excluding the third molars, maxillary canine are the most frequently impacted teeth. The maxillary canine develops almost near the floor of the orbit and travel down to their final position in oral cavity. Thus they have a greater chance of perverted eruption.

Ans.158. (b) Leptoprosopic

Ref Bhalajhi, pg 126

Facial form:

- Mesoprosopic – average or normal face.
- Euryprosopic – face that is broad and short.
- Leptoprosopic – long and narrow face form.

Shape of head:

- Mesocephalic- average shape of head with normal dental arches.
- Dolicocephalic- long and narrow head with narrow arches.
- Brachycephalic- broad and short head with broad arches.

Ans.159. (c) Anterior open bite

http://ejo.oxfordjournals.org/cgi/reprint/22/5/463.pdf

Ref http://www.healthline.com/galecontent/lisping

Lisping **(sigmatism)** is a speech disorder characterized by the inability to pronounce the sounds of s or z, known as the sibilant consonants, correctly. Usually *th* sounds are substituted for the sibilants; the word "lisp," for example, would be pronounced "lithp" by someone with this speech disorder. Sometimes there are also problems with *sh* and *ch* sounds.

Many children lisp at certain stages of speech development, especially when they lose their front primary teeth. This frontal or interdental lisp, produced when the tongue protrudes through the front teeth, is the most familiar type of lisp. Sibilant production may be interfered with in a number of other ways as well. These are all classified as lisping and include excessive pressure by the tongue against the teeth; the tongue held too far back along the midline of the palate; and a "substitute hiss" produced in the throat.

Hence, we see that lisping is seen in conditions involving anterior spaces like anterior open bite, tongue thrust swallow, etc.

Ans.160. (a) 0 degree

Ref Bhalajhi, pg 155

Down's analysis: reference plane= FHP [Orbitale to porion]

PARAMETER	LOCATION	AVERAGE	RANGE	SIGNIFICANCE
Facial angle	N-Pog – F.H.P	87.8°	82-95°	↑ in Cl III ; ↓ in Cl II
Angle of convexity	N-A-Pog	0°	-8.5 - 10°	↑ in Cl II ; ↓ in Cl III
A-B plane angle	A-B and N-Pog	-4.6°	-9 - 0°	↑ in Cl III ; ↓ in Cl II
Mandibular plane (MP) angle	F.H.P – mandibular pl	21.9°	17-28°	↑ angle suggests vertical grower

Y- axis	S-Gn + FHP	59°	53-66°	↑ angle suggests vertical grower ↑ in Cl II ; ↓ Cl III
Cant of occlusal plane (OP)	OP - FHP	9.3°	1.5 - 14°	Gives the slope of OP
Inter-incisal	Long axis of upper-lower I	135.4°	130-150.5°	↓ in Cl I, II div 1 ↑ in Cl II div 2
Incisor occlusal plane angle	Long axis of lower I - MP	14.5°	3.5 – 20°	↓ angle mean ↑ lower I proclination
Incisor MP angle	Lower I - MP	1.4°	-8.5 – 7°	↑ angle mean ↓ lower I proclination
Upper I to A-Pog line	Linear unit from upper I – A-Pog line	2.7 mm	-1 to 5mm	↑ angle mean ↑ upper I proclination

Ans.161. (b) Skeletal maturity

Ref Bhalajhi, pg169

Leonard S. Fishman in 1982, proposed a system for evaluation of skeletal maturation

- Using hand-wrist radiographs with anatomical sites located on one thumb, third finger, 5th finger and radius.
- **11** discrete maturity indicators covering the entire adolescent period have been described.
- Used ***4 stages*** of bone maturation (Epi = diaphysis – appearance of adductor sesamoid- capping of epiphysis – fusion).

Ans.162. (c) Bolton analysis

Ref Bhalajhi , pg 181

According to Bolton, there exists a ratio between the mesio-distal widths of maxillary and mandibular teeth and that most of the malocclusion occur due to discrepancy between this ratio.

According to him,

Sum of mandibular 12 / Sum of maxillary 12 × 100 = **91.3** %

If the ratio is <91.3% = maxillary tooth excess

If the ratio is >91.3 % = mandibular tooth excess

Similarly,

Sum of mandibular anterior 6 / maxillary 6 × 100 = **77.2%**

Korkhaus analysis – is similar to Pont's , to determine the ideal arch width at the premolar and molar region.

Ans.163. (d) Rotation

Ref Bhalajhi, pg 380

Rotations are tooth movements around their long axis. It is often easy to treat but difficult to retain. In fact, rotations have a ***very high risk*** of relapse due to stretching of the supra-alveolar and trans-septal gingival fibers which adapt very slowly to their new position. *Pericision* with long term retention is often required for this purpose.

EXTRA EDGE

Remember, anterior teeth when rotated occupy less space and hence require additional space when de-rotated. The opposite is true for posterior teeth.

Ans.164. (d) Reciprocal anchorage

Explained earlier KCET-07 A159

Ans.165. (a) They are dependent on patient co-operation

Ref Bhalajhi, pg 274

Disadvantages of RPD

- As the appliance can be removed, patient cooperation is very important for the success of treatment.
- Treatment duration is prolonged when multiple movements are desired.
- Grater chances of patient misplacing or breaking the appliance.
- While all these are the disadvantages, the major ***limitation*** of using RPD is that it can be used for effecting tipping movements only.

Ans.166. (c) Nickel - Titanium

Explained earlier, please refer KCET-06 A35

Ans.167. (b) Inversely proportional to the cube of the length of the wire

Ref Bhalajhi , pg 284

Force exerted by wire varies as :-

$$F \propto \frac{D^4}{L^3} \text{ Where } = \begin{array}{l} D = \text{Diameter of wire} \\ L = \text{Length of the wire} \end{array}$$

Other factors influencing the forces exerted by the wire are material composition, heat/cold treatment it is subjected to, etc.

Ans.168. (b) Maxillary retrognathism

Ref Bhalajhi , pg 364

Face masks are basically reverse head gears for pulling the retracted maxilla forwards with respect to mandible. First used by Delaire and Hickam.

Recommendations: forces (450 gm/side) for 12-14 hrs/d with a15-20^0 downward pull.

Delaire face mask: uses the chin and forehead for support. The framework is a square.

Others include: Petit's, Hickam's, and Tubinger's model.

Ans.169. (c) Herbst appliance

Ref Bhalajhi , pg 349

Explained earlier please refer KCET-07 A162

Remember, advantages of Herbst's appliance

- Treatment may be completed in 6-8 months and hence can be used with patients in post-adolescent stage.
- Can be used in mouth-breathers unlike other functional appliances.
- As it is fixed, requires minimal patient cooperation.
- Indicated in treatment of Class II malocclusions.

Ans.170. (a) Stage I

Ref Bhalajhi, pg 311

Raymond Begg modified Angle's Ribbon arch technique and introduced the Begg's light wire differential force technique.

The Begg's therapy comprises of 3 stages:

- **1st stage**- alignment, correction of crowding, rotation correction, closure of anterior spaces, and achieving an edge to edge anterior bite.
- **2nd Stage**- closure of the extraction spaces while maintaining the previous corrections.
- **3rd stage:** uprighting and torquing is carried out to achieve normal axial inclination.

PROSTHODONTICS

Ans.171. (a) Behind the vibrating line

Explained earlier please refer KCET-07 A184

Ans.172. (b) Resistance against horizontal forces

Ref Nallaswamy, pg 64

Stability: is the ability of denture to resist *horizontal* forces. Factors affecting

- Vertical height of residual ridge.
- Quality of soft tissues covering the ridge.
- Quality of impression taken.
- Arrangement of teeth and their contour.

Support: refers to resistance to *vertical* forces of mastication, occlusal forces and other forces applied in a direction towards the denture-bearing area.

Ans.173. (b) The centric relation

Explained earlier please refer KCET-07 A176

Ans.174. (a) Reduces biting forces

Ref Nallaswamy, pg 148-150

When the interocclusal distance is decreased (by increasing the vertical dimension) there is premature contact of the teeth and hence resultant lower biting force.

Ans.175. (a) Less margin of error in posterior palatal seal

Ref Nallaswamy, pg 6

Major disadvantages of metallic bases are :-

- They are more expensive than resin based dentures.
- Require more time and expertise for fabrication.
- They cannot be relined/rebased.
- They require a refractory cast material.

However, metal bases can be used in thin sections which give excellent fit and are extremely light and comfortable for patient use. Also, heat transfer property enables patient's perception of taste and temperature.

Since these cannot be altered easily once made and due to the fact that metal undergoes considerable shrinkage, the margin of error in the PPS area is very less.

Ans.176. (a) Combined periodontal ligament area of the abutment tooth should equal or exceed that of tooth or teeth to be replaced.

Ref Nallaswamy, pg 750

Ante's law states that the combined pericemental area of all abutment teeth supporting a fixed partial denture should be equal to or greater than the tooth to be replaced. For removable prosthesis, the combined pericemental area of the teeth plus the mucosa area of denture base should be equal or be greater than those of missing teeth.

Crown Root ratio: for abutment teeth in FPD should always be 1. Ideally it should be 2:3 (0.66), acceptable ratio are up to 1:1.

Ans.177. (b) Point contact

Ref Nallaswamy, pg 511

PONTIC	FEATURES
Saddle pontic	Only buccal and lingual contact , least hygienic
Ridge lap pontic	Resembles natural tooth; ! esthetics but difficult to maintain hygiene
Modified ridge lap	• Reduced tissue contact (T-shaped) • Good esthetics + hygiene • Maxillary anterior and posterior areas; mandibular anterior
Spheroidal pontic	• Contacts the ridge without pressure • Not esthetic • Mandibular posterior area
Sanitary/hygienic/ fish belly pontic	• Zero tissue contact • Highly unaesthetic • At least 3mm gap between pontic and ridge • Mandibular area

Hence, we see that the pontic in maxillary posterior region should have a point contact (T end of the modified ridge lap).

Ans.178. (b) Covers whole of the clinical crown of a tooth

Ref Nallaswamy, pg 505

A full veneer crown is a type of retainer in FPD which covers all the surfaces of the natural tooth crown. They are the most retentive and resistant retainers of all.

EXTRA EDGE

Some FAQ about retainers

Condition	Type of retainer
Anterior teeth with intact facial surface	Partial veneer surface
Severely destructed , RCT treated posterior	Complete veneer + post and core
Endodontically treated anterior teeth	Reverse 3/4th crown
Lingually inclined mandibular molars	Metal ceramic crown
Posterior tilted abutments	One- half crowns
Posterior teeth with short/ unfavorable crowns	Complete veneer
Tooth with high caries activity	Complete veneer crown

Ans.179. (c) 6 months

Explained earlier please refer, KCET-07 A147

Ans.180. (c) 4 months

Explained earlier please refer, KCET-07 A147

Ans.181. (b) Shoulder.

Ref Nallaswamy pg 572

This finish line has a gingival finish wall perpendicular to the axial surfaces of the teeth. If the marginal wall is at 120 degrees to the axial wall, then it is termed as sloping shoulder. Generally, a shoulder finish line is preferred for all ceramic restoration where sufficient thickness of the margins is required for the structural durability. All anterior restorations are fabricated with a shoulder margin where aesthetics is the primary concern.

Characteristics

(A) it is the finish line of choice for all ceramic restoration and facial margins of metal ceramic restoration where aesthetics is more important.

(B) The wide ledge gives resistance.

(C) The sharp internal line angle may cause stress concentration and fracture of the tooth.

(D) Requires more tooth reduction.

Ans.182. (b) 1.5mm.

Ref. Nallaswamy, pg 575-576

All metal -full veneer crowns are usually given for posterior teeth.

- The principle of occlusal reduction is to achieve an occlusal clearance of ***1.5mm*** for the functional cusps and ***1.0mm*** for the non functional cusps. This provides adequate metal thickness to resist fracture under occlusal load.
- Fractured or malposed teeth may require lesser reduction.
- The depth orientation grooves and the tooth structure between the orientation groove are removed.
- A round end tapered diamond is used to place the grooves.
- The functional cusp bevel is placed using a round end tapered diamond on-

  The *buccal* inclines of mandibular *buccal* cusp.

  The *palatal* inclines of maxillary *palatal* cusp.

The angulation of bevel should be parallel to inner inclination of the opposing cusp.

- The occlusal clearance is verified by asking patient to close on a 2mm thick red utility wax.
- The insufficient clearance can be detected as a *thin spot* on the wax and it is reduced accordingly until there are no spots on wax. The occlusal reduction and the functional cusp bevel are smoothened with no. 171 bur.

Ans.183. (b) Class II lever principle.

Ref. Nallaswamy, pg 382

A ***lever*** is a long bar with a single support around which it rotates when a load is applied to any one of its ends. The support around which the lever rotates is called as the *fulcrum*. The lever can be of three types:

- **I order**: fulcrum is in the centre, resistance at one end and force or effort at other end. These are more efficient levers. This occurs in patients with ***distal extension partial dentures***. Direct retainers are the fulcrum, effort lies on the point where denture takes up the occlusal load; the load is the region of anterior end of the major connector. Using additional rest (indirect retainers) shifts the fulcrum line and prevents lever action in these dentures.
- **II order**: the fulcrum is at one end, effort is opposite and resistance or load is at centre. This occurs in ***indirect retention*** of removable partial denture. When a displacing force tends to lift the denture from one end, the anterior most point of the major connector will act as the axis of rotation, the intermediate zone of the denture which is lifted by the force will form the resistance of the lever.
- **III order**: fulcrum is at one end, resistance is opposite end and effort is at centre, *e.g.* Tweezers. This type ***does not occur*** in removable partial dentures.

Thus, adding an auxiliary rest anterior to the fulcrum prevents the lever action by acting as an indirect retainer. **When indirect retainers are given, the I order lever is converted into a II order lever** which is more beneficial for prosthesis.

Ans.184. (c) Horse shoe shaped.

Ref. Nallaswamy pg 332

As the name suggests this major connector is 'U' shaped running along the arch. It has thin metal band running along lingual surface of posterior teeth. Anteriorly it becomes more like a thin plate that covers the cingula of the teeth. The posterior border extends 6-8mm onto palatal tissues. The entire surface and the borders should be smooth and gently rounded.

Indications

- Used when any anterior teeth are to be replaced.
- Used in presence of tori extending to posterior border of the hard palate or a prominent median suture.
- Excessive vertical overlap of the anterior teeth.

Advantage

- Reasonably strong.
- Has moderate indirect retention and support.

Disadvantage

- When vertical forces are applied on either one or both ends it tends to straighten. Hence, it cannot be used for distal extension bases.
- Greater bulk is required to avoid flexing of the major connector. Increased thickness may cause patient discomfort.
- Because of lesser strength it is replaced by closed horse shoe or anterior posterior palatal strap where additional strength is due to l- beam effect and circular configuration is given by a strap of metal that extends between the two open ends of horse shoe.

Ans.185. (d) Ring clasp.

Ref. Nallaswamy pg 362

Back action clasp is a modification of the ***ring clasp***. Here the minor connector is connected to end of clasp arm and the occlusal rest is left unsupported.

Disadvantage

- Lack of support to the occlusal rest reduces its function.
- It has both biological and mechanical unsound principles.

COMMUNITY AND PREVENTIVE DENTISTRY

Ans.186. (c) Exposure and disease

Ref Park, 17th ed, pg 64

Bias is any systemic error in the determination of the association between the ***exposure and the disease***. It reflects some type of non-comparability between the study and the control groups.

Bias may be (case-control studies):

- **Memory/recall bias:** when control and cases are questioned about the past.
- Bias due to confounding – factor which is associated both with the disease and the exposure and is distributed unequally in the control or study groups. This may be avoided by matching.

- **Selection bias:** when the cases/controls are not representative of the general population. Best avoided by prevention of such selection.
- **Berkesonian bias:** arises due to different rate of admissions to hospitals for people with different disease.
- **Interviewer bias:** when the interviewer knows the hypothesis and the cases. Use of double-blinding studies avoids this.

Ans.187. (b) Switzerland

Ref Soben Peter, 2nd ed , pg 367

- Salt fluoridation has been limited to domestic salt.
- Since teeth are exposed only in the post-eruption stage, both topical and systemic actions are seen.
- First sold in Switzerland (1955).
- Fluoride concentration – 90-250 mg/kg of salt.
- Agents commonly used – CaF_2, NaF.

Remember, in milk – concentration of F = 5-15ppm.

Ans.188. (a) Filtration capacity

Ref Park, 17th ed , pg 494

WATER FILTERATION

Slow sand/Biological filters

- First used in Scotland in 1804 and later in London.
- Consists of a zone of supernatant water left to stand for about 3-12hrs.
- The sand bed is the most important part of about 1m with the sand particles measuring about 0.2-0.3 mm.
- The vital layer consists of a slimy growth known as '*Schmutzdecker*' consisting of threadlike algae, planktons and diatoms. This layer forms the "heart" of the slow filter and removes organic matter and bacteria and other nitrates.
- An under-drainage system allows the filtered water to seep through to the reservoir.
- The filter control consists of a ''Venturi meter'' which measures the bed resistance or "***loss of head***". When the resistance builds up , the regulator valve is opened to allow steady flow. Loss of head above 1.3 m (max 4 m) is uneconomical.
- The filter is normally cleaned by scrapping off the top layer when resistance increases.

Rapid sand/Mechanical filters

- First used in USA, in 1885. They are of two types – gravity (Paterson's) and pressure type (Candy's filter).
- The raw water is first treated with a coagulant like alum and later subjected to rapid mixing, flocculation and finally sedimentation processes.

- The filer bed usually is 80-90 m^3 with sand particles ranging form 0.4-0.7mm.
- As filtration proceeds, the alum-floc not removed by sedimentation is held back and forms a layer comparable to the slimy layer in slow sand filters.
- When the "loss of head" approaches 7-8 ft , filtration is stopped and' backwashing' is done
- Although it is less time consuming than slow filters, the efficiency is slightly less (98-99 % as compared to 99.99 % of the slow sand).

Ans.189. (b) 2.5-3.5 Gm . kg of body weight

Ref Soben Peter, 2nd ed, pg 343

The estimated lethal dose for a 15kg child is <u>500-1000mg</u> (0.5-1g)
Hence, for an adult (avg wt 70kgs), this value would be = 70 x (0.5-1) / 15
= <u>2.3 -4.6 g</u>
So, friends' option 'b' (2.5-3.5g) is the closest and hence the answer here
Also remember,
Molecular rate conversion ratio for

- NaF = 1 /2.2
- SnF2 = 1 / 4.1
- Na-monofluorophosphate = 1 /7.6

These should be multiplied by the conc of agent to get the % of F in it.
Death has been reported after accidental ingestion of *2.5-5.0 g*.
Now, friends looking at the question either it is incomplete or the choices are incorrectly framed. It *definitely* cannot by g/kg as mentioned.

Ans.190. (b) 0-32

Ref Soben Peter, 2nd ed ,pg 184

DMF index was originally given by <u>Klein, Palmer and Knutson</u> in 1938. Later WHO, modified this index in1986 which stated that-

- All third molars are to included.
- Temporary restorations are to be considered as 'D.'
- Only carious cavities (and not incipient, white chalky/ stained fissures) are to be considered as 'D.'

Hence, since even third molars are included in the index, the values of DMF can range form **0 -32.**

The DMF and DMFS (surface) index are the most commonly used <u>Caries indices</u> in practice. The 'def' index (Gruebbel, 1944) is an equivalent, but, for primary teeth only.

Ans.191. (b) Six point scale

Ref <u>http://en.wikipedia.org/wiki/Dental_fluorosis#Deans_index</u>

H.T. Dean's fluorosis index was developed in 1942 and is currently the most universally accepted classification system. An individual's fluorosis score is based on the most severe form of fluorosis found on two or more teeth.

Deans Index

Classification	Criteria – description of enamel
Normal	Smooth, glossy, pale creamy-white translucent surface
Questionable	A few white flecks or white spots
Very Mild	Small opaque, paper white areas covering less than 25% of the tooth surface
Mild	Opaque white areas covering less than 50% of the tooth surface
Moderate	All tooth surfaces affected; marked wear on biting surfaces; brown stain may be present
Severe	All tooth surfaces affected; discrete or confluent pitting; brown stain present

Ans.192. (a) Vital signs

Ref http://www.medscape.com/viewarticle/416686_5

NUTRITIONAL INDICATORS

The most basic, but critical, first step in the evaluation process is to obtain a baseline ***height and weight***. A series of patient weights recorded early in the disease may serve as a good baseline later. Along with actual weight, it is often useful to obtain information regarding usual weight, as well as weight at 6 months and 12 months previous to initial evaluation. Since weight can be affected by abnormalities in body composition, it is important to remember that weight measurements are a gross indicator of nutritional status.

Anthropometric Methods

Additional anthropometric measurements should be used to measure tissue fat stores and lean body mass. This assessment may include triceps/sub scapular ***skin fold measurements***, body-mass index calculations, bioelectrical impedance analysis (BIA), and dual-energy x-ray analysis (DEXA). The first 2 measurements are less useful because they are less likely to detect wasting and shifts in lean body composition. Furthermore, the standards used to indicate a normal or obese status with this method were established in healthy individuals. Presently, *BIA is the method of choice*, allowing for more reliable measurements of lean body mass in HIV-infected patients. This method is reliable, safe, noninvasive, fast, and inexpensive.

Laboratory Tests

Specific biochemical parameters useful for establishing current nutritional status and warning of potential OIs include albumin, prealbumin, cholesterol, triglycerides, renal panel, liver enzymes, hemoglobin, serum iron, magnesium, folate, vitamin B_{12}, and serum retinol (vitamin A). These are key indicators of visceral protein or specific nutrient status.

Albumin, in particular, is an excellent marker of nutritional status.

A level of **3.2 to 4.5g/dL** is considered normal, while 2.8 to 3.1g/dL indicates mild protein depletion, 2.1 to 2.7g/dL moderate depletion, and below 2.1g/dL severe depletion. However, albumin has a *half-life* of about 3 weeks, and readings can be skewed by variables such as hydration, blood loss, and liver disease. ***Prealbumin***, the precursor form of albumin, has a shorter half-life and is a more sensitive indicator of changes in protein metabolism.

Thus we see that vital signs like BP, pulse and temperature do not form a basis for nutritional assessment.

Ans.193. (b) Chronic disease

Ref http://www.sph.umich.edu/miih/papers/2figures.pdf

Primordial Prevention	Primary Prevention
Focus on Aspects of Social Organization	Focus on Groups of Individuals
Modifiy the conditions that generate and structure the unequal distribution of health damaging exposures, susceptibilities and health protective resources among the population	Modifiy the individual level behavioral, psychosocial and biological mediators that lead to increased CVD inidence
Prevent the appearance of the mediating risk factor in the population	Alter the mediating risk factor level after it appears in the population

Although both primordial and primary prevention aims at controlling the chronic diseases, primordial prevention is undertaken in communities without any pre-existing risk factors.

Ans.194. (d) The tooth is already calcified and cannot be altered in this fashion

Ref Soben Peter, 2nd ed , pg 341

Fluorosis is an endemic disease in geographic areas where the fluoride content exceeds 2 ppm. Enamel Fluorosis is a developmental phenomenon due to excessive ingestion during amelogenesis stage. Once the crowns of the teeth are formed, no further Fluorosis can be induced by additional intake or b post-eruptive topical application.

EXTRA EDGE

Also remember, frequency in which teeth are affected:

- Premolars
- 2nd molars
- Maxillary incisors
- Canines
- 1st molars
- Mandibular incisors

Ans.195. (d) Endodontically treated tooth should be considered

Ref Soben Peter,2nd ed,pg184

Friends lets consider all the options one by one.

(a) according to 1996 modification by WHO, even third molars are considered.

(b) Only those teeth lost due to caries are considered as 'M.'

(c) teeth lost due to ortho treatment, congenitally missing or impacted are not 'M.'

Option'd' is most probably incomplete. We cannot figure out whether option'd' means that endodontic tooth are considered in DMF or any sub-category.

So we see, that while all three are correct, option'd' is taken as answer of exclusion.

Ans.196. (d) 2% NaF application should be carried out at the age of 3, 7,12 & 18 yrs

Ref Soben Peter, 2nd ed, pg 310

Friends, the catch here is the age group.

Knutson's technique

- Neutral NaF solution is used in this method.
- Initial appointment – cleaning with pumice slurry, followed by isolation.
- 2% NaF solution is painted on dry-surfaces of teeth.
- Allowed to dry for 3-4 min and then repeated.
- 4 such applications at week's interval is recommended.
- This procedure recommended for age groups- ***3,7,11 and 13.***

Ans.197. (d) Four

Explained earlier KCET-06 A190

Ans.198. (a) Six

Ref Soben Peter, 2nd ed

PHP or Patient Hygiene Performance Index

- Given by Podshadley and Haley in 1968.
- Assess an individual's oral hygiene performance based on 6 index teeth.
- Teeth used 16,11,26,36,31,46
- After applying a disclosing agent, each tooth surface is evaluated in 5 sections.
- It is primarily used to document and motivate the patient and also evaluate the effectiveness of home care methods.

Ans.199. (d) Caries index

Explained above, please refer A190.

Ans.200. (d) Xylitol

Ref http://en.wikipedia.org/wiki/Xylitol#Dental_care

Xylitol, also called **wood sugar** or **birch sugar**, is a five-carbon sugar alcohol that is used as a sugar substitute.

- Xylitol is a naturally occurring sweetener found in the fibers of many fruits and vegetables.
- Xylitol is a "toothfriendly" sugar. In addition to not encouraging tooth decay (by replacing dietary sugars), xylitol may actively aid in repairing minor cavities caused by dental caries.
- Recent research confirms a plaque-reducing effect and suggests that the compound, having some chemical properties similar to sucrose, attracts and then "starves" harmful micro-organisms, allowing the mouth to remineralize damaged teeth with less interruption.

2004

Questions & Answers

4

KCET 2004

QUESTIONS

ANATOMY AND HISTOLOGY

1. The first brachial arch is called as.

(A) Maxillary arch
(B) Mandibular arch
(C) Hyoid arch
(D) None

2. When a patient is asked to say "ah", if the uvula is drawn upwards to the left, the cranial nerve likely to be damaged is

(A) Vagus
(B) Right accessory
(C) Left accessory
(D) Hypoglossal

3. All of the following are examples of fibrous joint except

(A) Symphysis
(B) Gomphosis
(C) Sutural
(D) Syndesmosis

4. First pharyngeal arch derivatives include which of the following structures?

(A) Hyoid bone
(B) Maxillary process
(C) Stapes
(D) Styloid process

5. Basal lamina consists of

(A) Type I collagen fibers
(B) Type II collagen fibers
(C) Type IV collagen fibers
(D) Type III collagen fibers

6. Secretion of salivary gland is

(A) Apocrine
(B) Holocrine
(C) Merocrine
(D) Endocrine

DENTAL ANATOMY AND HISTOLOGY

7. Congenital absence of teeth is most likely to affect the growth of
(A) Palate
(B) Maxillary sinus
(C) Upper lip
(D) Alveolus

8. Primary teeth begin to calcify at the age of
(A) 4 to 5 week of fetal life
(B) Between 4-6 months of fetal life
(C) At birth
(D) 2-4 months after birth

9. Deviation in which of the following stages of development of dentition result in supernumerary teeth
(A) Apposition.
(B) Morpho differentiation
(C) Initiation
(D) Multiplication

10. When the jaw is opened
(A) Condyles move upwards.
(B) Articular disc moves posteriorly
(C) Lateral pterygoids contract
(D) Condyles moves around vertical axis

11. Regarding teeth which statement is wrong?
(A) Enamel is harder than dentine
(B) Enamel has no cells
(C) Ameloblasts secrete enamel and dentine
(D) Odontoblast produce dentine

12. The crown formation of all permanent teeth except third molar is completed between
(A) Birth to 6 years
(B) Birth to 8 years
(C) Birth to 12 years
(D) 6 years to 12 years

13. The formation of which of the following does not represent normal physiological process of dentin formation
(A) Primary and secondary dentin
(B) Secondary dentin and circum pulpal dentin
(C) Tertiary dentin and sclerotic dentin
(D) All of the above

14. Which of the following has a nonfunctional cusp?
(A) Mandibular canine
(B) Maxillary second premolar
(C) Mandibular first premolar
(D) Maxillary canine

PHYSIOLOGY

15. Following are the features of cretinism, except
(A) Pot-belly
(B) Idiotic look
(C) Normal intelligence
(D) Stunted growth

16. The part of nephron "least permeable to water" is

(A) Proximal tubule
(B) Descending limb of loop of Henle
(C) Ascending limb of loop of Henle
(D) Collecting tubule

17. Hemophilia is due to deficiency of

(A) Factor V
(B) Factor VIII
(C) Ca ions
(D) Prothrombin

18. At neuromuscular junction following neurotransmitter is released

(A) Nor-adrenaline
(B) Glycine
(C) Serotonin
(D) Acetylcholine

19. Following are extra pyramidal tracts except

(A) Reticulospinal
(B) Corticospinal
(C) Rubrospinal
(D) Vestibulospinal

20. Liver cells cannot utilize ketone bodies as source of energy due to deficiency of ?

(A) Glucose 6 phospatase
(B) Thiophorase
(C) Thiolase
(D) Thiokinase

21. The hormone which exerts hypoglycemic effect is

(A) Insulin
(B) Glucagon
(C) Growth hormone
(D) Epinephrine

22. Scurvy is a deficiency disease of

(A) Pyridoxine
(B) Niacin
(C) Riboflavin
(D) Ascorbic acid

23. Urea synthesis takes place mainly in

(A) Muscle
(B) Liver
(C) Kidney
(D) Adipose tissue

24. Normal serum calcium level is.

(A) 5 to 7 mg%
(B) 7 to 9 mg%
(C) 9 to 11 mg%
(D) 11 to 13 mg%

MICROBIOLOGY

25. Which of the following provides best guarantee for sterilization in the heat sterilizer?'

(A) Using chemical indicator strip or pouch.
(B) Recording a temp/pressure readings from sterilizer gauge.
(C) Using a bacterial spore test.
(D) Determining the ability of a sterilizer to kill the hepatitis B virus.

26. Borrelia vincenti is a

(A) Mycoplasma
(B) Mycobacteria
(C) Spirochaete
(D) Chlamydia

27. Actinomycosis is a

(A) Bacterial infection
(B) Viral infection
(C) Fungal infection
(D) Parasitic infection

28. Teichoic acid is present in

(A) Cell wall of Gram-positive organisms
(B) Cytoplasm of Gram-positive organisms
(C) Cell wall of Gram-negative organisms
(D) Cytoplasm of Gram-negative organisms

29. EBV is responsible for all except

(A) Nasopharyngeal carcinoma
(B) Burkitt's lymphoma.
(C) Hepatoma
(D) Infectious mononulceosis

30. The most pronounced effect on the oral micro flora of a reduction in rate of salivary flow is a

(A) Significant increase in number of oral bacteria.
(B) Shift towards more acidogenic micro flora.
(C) Significant decrease in number of oral bacteria.
(D) Shift towards more aerobic micro flora.

31. Kaposi's sarcoma is more commonly seen inpatient with

(A) AIDS
(B) Amyloidosis
(C) Leukemia
(D) HSV infection.

32. All of the following lab tests can be used to distinguish Streptococcus mutans from other oral streptococci, except

(A) Gram staining.
(B) Fermentation of mannitol and sorbital.
(C) Production of intracellular and extra cellular adherent polysaccharide.
(D) Colony morphology on saliva agar.

33. Which of the following is not a characteristic of exotoxins?

(A) Produced in minute amounts
(B) Released from bacterial cell wall.
(C) Destroyed by proteolytic enzymes
(D) weakly antigenic

34. Which of the following are correctly matched?

(A) Transfer of antibody from mother to child is through colostrums and acquired passive immunity naturally.
(B) Injection of antibodies (hepatitis) is artificially acquired passive immunity.
(C) Antigenic stimulus given by vaccine (polio) is artificial active immunity.
(D) All of the above.

GENERAL PATHOLOGY

35. Essential granulation tissue constituents include all except

(A) Fibroblast
(B) Macrophages
(C) Polymorphs giant cells
(D) Budding blood vessels

36. Apoptosis is

(A) Single cell necrosis
(B) Intracytoplasmic accumulation
(D) Neoplastic change in the cell
(D) Degenerative change

37. In a 15-yr old type II collagen is present in

(A) Skin
(B) Bone
(C) Cartilage
(D) Basement membrane

38. Caisson disease refers to

(A) Amniotic fluid embolism
(B) Fat embolism
(C) Arterial embolism
(D) Gas embolism

39. All of the following malignancies metastasize except

(A) Basal cell carcinoma
(B) Adenocarcinoma
(C) Squamous cell carcinoma
(D) Melanoma

DENTAL MATERIALS

40. If two elements form an intermetallic compound the mechanical properties of this compound

(A) Are higher than those of either element
(B) Are lower than those of either element
(C) Fall between those of the elements
(D) Can not be predicted

41. The term "Chroma aspect" in selection of artificial teeth refers to

(A) Degree of saturation of hue
(B) Intensity of value
(C) Both value and hue
(D) None of the above

42. Advantage of minimum mercury technique or Eames technique is all except

(A) High strength
(B) Sets quickly
(C) Needs no squeezing of excess mercury
(D) Greater plasticity and adapts well to cavity walls

43. Gold with highest strength and can be used in stress bearing areas

(A) Gold foil.
(B) Mat gold
(C) Spherical gold
(D) Electralloy

44. When selecting a dental wire for its ability to withstand a certain stress without experiencing permanent deformation one should consult data tables for the property known as

(A) Elastic limit
(B) Fracture strength
(C) Modulus of elasticity
(D) Percent elongation

45. Inorganic phase of the composites aid in

(A) Increasing the mechanical strength
(B) Decreasing the coefficient of thermal expansion
(C) Reducing the polymerization shrinkage
(D) All of the above

46. The solder used for soldering two metal alloy parts should have fusion temperature

(A) below the fusion temperature of both the alloys
(B) Above the fusion temperature of both the alloys
(C) Equal to either or the alloys
(D) None of the above.

47. The main advantage exhibited by the porcelain compared to the tooth colored restorations

(A) Good marginal integrity
(B) High tensile strength
(C) Better color harmony
(D) highly insoluble

48. Knoop hardness number of the enamel is

(A) 68
(B) 110
(C) 343
(D) 450

49. Suck back porosity in the casting can be eliminated by

(A) Increasing the mould metal temperature difference
(B) Increasing the flow of molten metal
(C) Flaring the point of the sprue attachment
(D) None of the above

PHARMACOLOGY

50. Buprenorphine acts by following mechanism

(A) Mu receptor antagonist
(B) Kappa receptor antagonist
(C) Mu receptor partial agonist
(D) Kappa receptor partial agonist

51. Which of the following drugs undergoes "Hoffmann elimination"?

(A) d-tubercurarine
(B) Acetylcholine
(C) Atracurium
(D) Acetazolamide

52. Mention the drug causing gynecomastia, hirsuitism, menstrual disturbance on long-term use

(A) Hydrochlorothiazide
(B) Amiloride
(C) Spironolactone
(D) Acetazolamide

53. Magnesium tri-silicate should not be combine with

(A) Aluminum hydroxide gel
(B) Oxithazaine
(C) Sucralfate
(D) Ranitidine

54. INH induced neuropathy is treated with

(A) Thiamine
(B) Pyridoxine
(C) Niacin
(D) Riboflavin

55. Ibuprofen is contraindicated in

(A) Patients having fever
(B) Patients having asthma
(C) Patients having amoebic dysentery
(D) Patients having bronchitis

GENERAL MEDICINE

56. Which of the following tests will be abnormal in a patient with hemophilia?

(A) Bleeding time (B) PTT (partial thromboplastin time)

(C) PT (prothrombin time) (D) Platelet count

57. Confirmatory test for HIV infection is

(A) ELISA (B) Western blot

(C) RIA (D) None of the above

58. The most important investigation done in infective endocarditis is

(A) 2-D Echo cardiography (B) ECG

(C) Serial blood cultures (D) ASO titer

59. Which of the following is not correct about nephrotic syndrome?

(A) Proteinuria (B) Hypoalbuminemia

(C) Hypolipidemia (D) Lipiduria

60. Which of the following represents the serologic evidence of recent Hepatitis B virus infection during "window" period?

(A) HBs Ag (B) IgM anti-HBc

(C) Anti HBs (D) None of the above

61. Cryoprecipitate is a rich source of

(A) Factor V (B) Factor VII

(C) Factor VIII (D) Factor XII

62. Which of the following conditions causes transudative pleural effusion?

(A) Cirrhosis of liver (B) Tuberculosis

(C) Bronchogenic carcinoma (D) Rheumatoid arthritis

63. Hepatitis B infection spreads through all of the following routes except

(A) Blood transfusion (B) Sexual contact

(C) Faeco oral route (D) Perinatal transmission

64. Treatment of choice for Pneumocystis carinii pneumonia is

(A) Trimethoprim/sulfamethoxazole (B) Erythromycin

(C) Ofloxacin (D) Tetracycline

65. All of the following are bactericidal drugs against Mycobacterium tuberculosis except

(A) Rifampicin (B) Isoniazid

(C) Pyrazinamide (D) Tetracycline

66. What are the symptoms of diabetes mellitus?

(A) Poydipsia (B) Polyuria

(C) Polyphagia (D) All of the above

GENERAL SURGERY

67. Punched out edge is a characteristic of which type of ulcer

(A) Tuberculosis
(B) Rodent ulcer
(C) Syphilitic
(D) Non specific

68. Cystic hygroma is

(A) Lymphangiectasia
(B) Cavernous haemangioma
(C) Sebaceous cyst
(D) All of the above

69. Early postoperative complications of tracheostomy are all except

(A) Apnoea
(B) Hemorrhage
(C) Pneumomediastinum
(D) Tracheal stenosis

70. Treatment strategy in Ludwig's angina includes

(A) Amoxycilline plus metronidazole
(B) Decompression of both submandibular triangles
(C) Tracheostomy
(D) All of the above

71. Symptoms of hyperthyroidism are the following except

(A) Emotional liability
(B) Heat intolerance
(C) Weight gain
(D) Excessive appetite

72. Eighty percent of all salivary stones occur in

(A) Parotid
(B) Submandibular
(C) Sublingual
(D) Minor salivary glands

73. A lesion composed of microscopic vessels is called as

(A) Haemangioma
(B) Angioma
(C) None
(D) Haemangioma and Angioma

ORAL PATHOLOGY

74. The swollen degenerating epithelial cell due to acantholysis is

(A) Anitschow cell
(B) Tzank cell
(C) Ghost cell
(D) Prickle cell

75. The rate of malignant transformation is highest in

(A) Leukoplakia
(B) Oral submucous fibrosis
(C) Oral lichen planus
(D) Erythroplakia

76. Ackerman's tumor is an acronym for

(A) Fibrous dysplasia
(B) Pemphigoid
(C) Pemphigus
(D) Herpes zoster

77. Nikolsky's sign is positive in

(A) Herpes labialis
(B) Pemphigoid
(C) Pemphigus
(D) None of the above

78. Ghost cells are seen in

(A) Ghost teeth
(B) Pindborg's tumour
(C) Odontogenic keratocyst
(D) Calcifying odontogenic cyst

79. Oral hairy leukoplakia is a feature of

(A) White sponge nevus
(B) Hairy cell leukemia
(C) Speckled leukoplakia
(D) None of the above

80. Liquefaction degeneration of basal cell layer is a histological feature of

(A) Hairy leukoplakia
(B) White sponge nevus
(C) Oral lichen planus
(D) Herpes zoster

81. Areca nut chewing is etiological factor in

(A) Leukoedema
(B) Oral submucous fibrosis
(C) Erythema multiformae
(D) Oral lichen planus

82. Oral co-carcinogenesis concept was suggested by

(A) Thomas
(B) Goldhaber
(C) Shafer
(D) Pindborg

83. Which of following is not a oral precancerous

(A) Leukoplakia
(B) Leukoedema
(C) Verrucous hyperplasia
(D) Erythroplakia

84. The inheritance pattern of dentinogenesis imperfecta is

(A) Homozygous
(B) Autosomal dominant
(C) Recessive
(D) X-linked recessive

85. Three stages in progression of acute odontogenic infection are

(A) Periapical osteitis — cellulites —abscess
(B) Abscess— cellulites — periapical osteitis
(C) Cellulites— Abscess— periapical osteitis
(D) Periapical osteitis – abscess — cellulites

86. The common site in oral cavity for lesion of lymphogranuloma venereum.

(A) Gingiva
(B) Tongue
(C) Lips
(D) Palate

87. Chronic sinus tract present at the angle of lower jaw, yellow purulent granular discharge, is due to

(A) Tuberculosis
(B) Staphylococcal infection
(C) Actinomycosis
(D) Histoplasmosis

ORAL MEDICINE AND RADIOLOGY

88. Why an increased target-film distance is required in the paralleling techniques?

(A) To avoid image magnification (B) To avoid distortion
(C) To reduce scattered radiation (D) To improve film placement

89. Which of the following is not a type of particulate radiation?

(A) Alpha particles (B) Beta particles
(C) Protons (D) Nucleons

90. Thyroid dose from panoramic radiography is about

(A) 0.022 mGy (B) 0.034 mGy
(C) 0.051 mGy (D) 0.074 mGy

91. Of the following, which is the best projection to study the fracture of zygomatic arch

(A) Lateral oblique view (B) PA Caldwell view
(C) Submentovertex view (D) Lateral cephalometric view

92. Most commonly used color of the filter used in dark room safelight is

(A) Blue (B) Red
(C) Green (D) Yellow

93. A cyst can be differentiated from granuloma radiographically by injecting

(A) Radiopaque dyes (B) Polyacrylamide gel
(C) Sodium morrhuate (D) Corticosteroids

94. Grinspan syndrome is associated with

(A) Leukoplakia (B) Lichen planus
(C) Apthous ulcer (D) Oral submucous fibrosis

95. In hemophilia A there is deficiency of

(A) Factor VIII (B) Factor V
(C) Factor VI (D) Factor X

96. Puetz-Jegher syndrome is characterized by

(A) Deafness (B) Multiple supernumerary teeth
(C) Multiple intestinal polyps (D) Scleroderma

97. Cyst that has high recurrence rate is

(A) Incisive canal cyst (B) Periapical cyst
(C) Dentigerous cyst (D) Odontogenic Keratocyst

98. Routine assessment of jaw function does not consist of

(A) Palpation of TM joint (B) Determination of maximum opening'
(C) Observation of lateral deviation (D) Arthrography

99. Which is best for diagnosis of primary herpes simplex infection?

(A) Smear stained with Giemsa stain (B) Smear stained with Wrist's stain
(C) Fluorescent staining of cytology smears (D) Routine cytology

100. Normal bleeding time is

(A) 1 to 6 minutes
(B) 8 to 10 minutes
(C) 30 to 40 seconds
(D) 40 to 50 seconds

101. Most common tumor associated with AIDS is

(A) Carcinoma
(B) Kaposi's sarcoma
(C) Melanoma
(D) Ewing's sarcoma

102. In sickle cell anemia there is

(A) 75% to 100% hemoglobin S
(B) 10% to 20% haemoglobin S
(C) 20% to 30% haemoglobin S
(D) 50% to 60% haemoglobin S

PERIODONTICS

103. Dendritic cells located among keratinocytes at all suprabasal levels and belonging to reticuloendothelial system derived from bone marrow are

(A) Melanocytes
(B) Langerhans cells
(C) Lymphocytes
(D) Merkel cell

104. One of the following systemic diseases involving periodontal tissue is not a disorder of neutrophil function

(A) Agranulocytosis
(B) Chediak-Higashi syndrome
(C) Leukemia'
(D) Cyclic neutropenia

105. The predominant fiber groups affected in the early lesion of gingivitis are

(A) Circular and dento gingival
(B) Circular and horizontal
(C) Circular and alveolar crest
(D) Circular and trans septal

106. All of the following are biologic properties of IgG except.

(A) Passes the placental barrier
(B) Neutralizes bacterial toxins
(C) Binds with organisms enhancing phagocytosis
(D) Most efficient activator of complement system

107. The distance between the bottom of calculus and alveolar crest in human periodontal pocket is constant having an approximate length of.

(A) 0.97 mm
(B) 1.97 mm
(C) 2.97 mm
(D) 3.97 mm

108. Which of the following is not an instrument grasp during scaling procedure~?

(A) Pen grasp
(B) Thumb grasp
(C) Modified pen grasp
(D) Palm and thumb grasp

109. Gracey curettes have an offset blade placed to the shank of the instrument at an angle of.

(A) 180 degrees
(B) 100 degrees
(C) 70 degrees
(D) 50 degrees

110. The concept of calculus formation in which seeding agents induce small foci of calcification which enlarge and coalesce to form 'a calcified mass is termed as.

(A) Mineral precipitation (B) Calculus adaptation
(C) Heterogeneous nucleation (D) None of the above

111. Patient's exaggerated concept that something is mechanically wrong in his/her occlusion or jaw is termed as

(A) Bruxism (B) Skeletal malocclusion disharmony
(C) Phantom bite (D) Juvenile occlusal disharmony

112. The inorganic component of sub gingival plaue is derived from

(A) Saliva (B) Gingival crevicular fluid
(C) Inorganic matter of tooth (D) Food debris

113. Gingival fluid from diabetics contain a reduced level of cyclic adenosine mono-phosphate which may lead to

(A) Increased severity of gingival inflammation
(B) Decreased severity of gingival inflammation
(C) No response on gingiva
(D) Epithelial desuamation

114. The overall effect of HIV is to gradually impair the immune system by interference with

(A) Helper T lymphocytes (B) Natural killer cells
(C) Plasma cells (D) Macrophages

115. The region in which cementum formation is most rapid is

(A) Middle (B) Coronal
(C) Apical (D) Inter-radicular

116. Alveolar bone proper is also known as

(A) Lamina Lucida (B) Lamina densa
(C) Lamina propria (D) Lamina dura

117. One of the following drugs can slow the loss of alveolar bone in periodontitis

(A) Dexamethasone (B) Ibuprofen
(C) Penicillin (D) Calcium channel blockers

CONSERVATIVE DENTISTRY AND ENDODONTICS

118. In a pin retained amalgam restoration, use of pins

(A) Does not reinforce the tooth (B) Weakens the tooth
(C) Reinforces the amalgam structure (D) Improves retention of restoration

119. Mercury rich condition in a slow setting amalgam alloy system in a restoration results in

(A) Accelerated corrosion
(B) Fracture of the restoration
(C) Marginal damage
(D) All of the above

120. Ethoxy benzoic acid increases the strength and solubility of the cement

(A) Zinc oxide eugenol
(B) Polycarboxylate cement
(C) Zinc phosphate cement
(D) Silicate cement

121. A 15% solution of EDTA has a pH of

(A) 5.5
(B) 7.3
(C) 7.9
(D) 7

122. Percussion is a dental diagnostic procedure used in determining whether

(A) The tooth is vital
(B) A pulp is hyperemic
(C) A periodontitis exists
(D) The pulp is metaplastic

123. Glass bead endodontic sterilizer is operated at temperature range

(A) 425 - 475^{0}F
(B) 550 - 760^{0}F
(C) 285 - 330^{0}F
(D) 218 - 246^{0}F

124. Average length of maxillary cuspid is

(A) 26 mm
(B) 33 mm
(C) 21 mm
(D) 18 mm

125. Internal resorption is characterized by

(A) Pain on percussion
(B) Slow dull continuous pain
(C) No characteristic feature, symptom free
(D) Increased pulpal pain when lying down

126. Urethane dimethacrylate based composite resin is cured by

(A) Ultraviolet light
(B) Visible light
(C) Chemical means
(D) None of the above

127. A giromatic hand piece for endodontic instrumentation operates by

(A) Rotating motion
(B) Oscillating motion
(C) Zigzag motion
(D) All

128. Which of the following restorative material is most biocompatible to the pulp?

(A) Silver amalgam
(B) Composite resin
(C) GIC II
(D) Silicate cement

129. The rate of tarnish and corrosion of class II cast material having VHN 200 is

(A) 0%
(B) 2 to 3 %
(C) 5 to 10%
(D) Less than 1%

130. Effective conditioning of the tooth enamel for retention purpose prior to insertion of tooth colored resin restoration using aueous solution of phosphoric acid has the concentration

(A) 8 to 85%
(B) As low as 15%
(C) 35 to 50%
(D) None of the above

131. A dental bur cuts the tooth structure more effectively when rake angle of bur is
(A) Positive
(B) Negative
(C) Radial
(D) None of the above

ORAL AND MAXILLO-FACIAL SURGERY

132. Toxic effect of local anesthetic include
(A) Convulsions
(B) Asystole
(C) Methemoglobinemia
(D) All of the above

133. The weakest part of the mandible where fracture occurs is
(A) Neck of condyle
(B) Angle of mandible
(C) Canine fossa
(D) Symphysis

134. Foreign body aspirated during dental procedures can be retrieved by
(A) Bronchoscopy
(B) Gastroscopy
(C) Arthroscopy
(D) None of the above

135. Local reaction due to local anesthetic solution is
(A) Pain
(B) Local irritation
(C) Haematoma
(D) Dermatitis

136. In Jorgensen techniue on IV sedation for dental procedures drugs used are
(A) Pentobarbital
(B) Mepiridine
(C) Scopolamine
(D) All above

137. Pick out odd drugs for anesthetic emergencies are
(A) Aminophylline
(B) Epinephrine
(C) Atropine sulphate
(D) Amoxicillin

138. Nerves anaesthetized in incisive nerve block are
(A) Incisive nerve only
(B) Incisive and mental nerve
(C) Incisive and inferior alveolar nerve
(D) Mental and inferior alveolar nerve

139. Masticator space infection usually results from
(A) Infections of the last two lower molar
(B) Non aseptic techniue in local anesthesia
(C) External or internal trauma to the mandibular angle region
(D) All of the above

140. The horizontal fracture of maxilla is called as
(A) Le fort I fracture
(B) Floating jaw fracture of maxilla
(C) Both of above
(D) None of the above

141. Pre auricular pain, grating sensation and partial trismus are the symptoms of
(A) TM joint fibrous ankylosis
(B) TM joint bony ankylosis
(C) TM joint pain dysfunction syndrome
(D) Ear infection

142. Which of the following is not a surgery for anterior open bite
(A) Thomas trapezoid osteotomy
(B) Thomas' corticotomy
(C) Thomas Y osteotomy
(D) Limberg's osteotomy

143. Which one of the following is not a sign of recurrence of injured inferior alveolar nerve
(A) Prikling sensation
(B) Hyperesthesia
(C) Anesthesia
(D) Partial return of sensation

144. Which of the following is/are known for recurrence
(A) Keratocyst
(B) Ameloblastoma
(C) Both of them
(D) None of them

145. Spontaneous closure can be expected in
(A) Chronic oroantral fistula
(B) Acute oroantral fistula
(C) Both chronic and acute oroantral fistula
(D) None of the above

PEDODONTICS

146. "Fluoride syndrome" is a type of
(A) 'Enamel hypoplasia
(B) Dentin hypoplasia
(C) Dental caries
(D) Fluorosis.

147. It is essential that restoration involving the proximal surfaces of deciduous teeth, restore the original mesio-distal dimensions of teeth primarily to
(A) Maintain arch length
(B) Maintain esthetics
(C) Prevent food impaction
(D) Prevent secondary caries

148. Familiarization can be solution of child's behavior problem, in the clinic, if the basis of problem' is
(A) Pain
(B) Sibling rivalry
(C) Fear
(D) Parents

149. A mandibular lingual holding arch with loops mesial to each molar band used in children for
(A) Correction of rotation
(B) Regaining the space
(C) Space maintenance only
(D) Correction of distally tilted molar

150. When there is a large exposure of the pulp, in a vital tooth with immature apex the treatment of choice is
(A) Apexification
(B) Apexogenesis
(C) Pulpotomy
(D) Pulpectomy

151. When natal teeth are present the most common and preferable approach is to
(A) Extract the teeth
(B) Grind the sharp incisal edges
(C) Take radiograph and determine the status of adjacent unerupted tooth
(D) Retain the teeth if possible

152. The Snyder test is designed to
(A) Give a uantitative determination of acidogenic micro-organisms in the oral cavity
(B) Predict the acidity of the saliva
(C) Estimate the cariogenic potential of dental plaue
(D) Identify the organisms involved in the carious process

153. Prolonged use of antibiotics in children can result in
(A) Necrotizing ulcerative gingivitis
(B) Candidiasis
(C) Actinomycosis
(D) Apthous ulcers

154. During mixed dentition stage, which of the following appliance should be used as a space maintainer for missing primary molars in mandibular arch.
(A) Distal shoe
(B) Nance holding arch
(C) Passive lingual arch
(D) Removable functional acrylic

155. When the cry of child is characterized by a siren like vocabulary, it is called as?
(A) Compensatory
(B) Frightened
(C) Hurt
(D) Obstinate

ORTHODONTICS

156. Premature exfoliation of the primary mandibular canine is the most often the seuel of which of the following
(A) Caries
(B) Trauma
(C) Serial tooth extraction
(D) Arch length inadeqacy

157. Which of the following is a feature of Class I type 3 malocclusion?
(A) Posterior cross bite
(B) Anterior crossbite
(C) Mesial drifting of molars
(D) Protrusion of mandibular incisors

158. In occlusion the teeth have
(A) Cusp to cusp contact
(B) Edge to edge contact
(C) Marginal contact
(D) Surface to surface contact

159. The condition in which the occlusal plane of the teeth lies nearer the Frankfort plane than it does in normal occlusion is termed
(A) Distraction
(B) Contraction
(C) Attraction
(D) Retraction

160. All of the following are dental characteristic of a skeletal class III malocclusion, except
(A) Anterior cross bite
(B) Distocclusion
(C) Linguoversion of the mandibular molars
(D) Posterior cross bite

161. In orthodontic treatment, in order to avoid injuries to the tissues, the forces applied should not exceed the
(A) Arterial blood pressure
(B) Capillary blood pressure
(C) Masticatory forces
(D) Muscular forces of facial muscles

162. What is the most common skeletal finding in cephalometric radiographs in a patient with a history of cleft palate and anterior cross bite
(A) Maxillary retrusion
(B) mandibular protrusion
(C) Mandibular retrusion
(D) Maxillary protrusion

163. Orthodontic brackets attached directly to the tooth are retained by a
(A) Compressive force.
(B) Hydrostatic force
(C) Mechanical bond
(D) Chemical bond

164. Eruption of the permanent maxillary second molar prior to the maxillary second pre-molar is
(A) Normal and desirable
(B) Abnormal and undesirable
(C) Abnormal and desirable
(D) Normal and undesirable

165. Frankfort horizontal plane is drawn from
(A) Sella to nasion
(B) Orbitale to nasion
(C) Orbitale to porion
(D) Sub nasion to nasion

166. Head gear applied to maxillary molars can improve antero-posterior skeletal dysphasia by
(A) Maxillary growth redirection
(B) Bilateral expansion of the palate
(C) Anterior repositioning of the maxillary teeth
(D) Stimulating growth of the mandible

167. The type of resorption seen when light continuous orthodontic forces are applied
(A) Apical
(B) Frontal or direct
(C) Indirect or undermining
(D) No resorption is seen

168. After 6 years of age, the lengthening of mandible occurs mainly
(A) At the symphysis
(B) Between the canines
(C) Distal to first permanent molar
(D) Along the lower border

169. An early pre-pubertal growth spurt indicates
(A) Metabolic disturbance
(B) Fast maturing child
(C) Endocrine dysfunction
(D) Slow maturing child

170. "Grow spurt" refers to-
(A) Period uniform growth
(B) Period of sudden acceleration of growth
(C) Axis of increased growth extending from head towards the feet
(D) None of the above

171. Mechanism of bone growth is by
(A) Bone deposition and resorption
(B) Cortical drift
(C) Displacement
(D) All of the above

PROSTHODONTICS

172. Which type of RPD can best resist the forces, to which it is subjected
(A) Class I
(B) Class II
(C) Class III
(D) Class IV

173. How far should be the border of a maxillary major connector from the gingival crevices of the teeth?
(A) 1 mm
(B) 4-6 mm
(C) 1-2 mm
(D) 0 mm

174. When a large inoperable palatal torus is present, then the major connector of choice
(A) Palatal strap
(B) Antero-posterior palatal strap
(C) Antero-posterior palatal bar
(D) Complete palatal plate

175. Compared to resin, base the main disadvantage of a metallic denture base in distal extension situation is that, metal bases
(A) Are difficult to keep clean
(B) Transfer thermal changes uickly to mucosa
(C) Cannot be relined in event of ridge resorption
(D) Are subjected to distortion and breakage

176. In Distal extension base partial dentures the impression is recorded in
(A) Pressure impression techniue
(B) Mucostatic impression
(C) Physiologic impression techniue
(D) Minimum pressure impression techniue

177. Ante's law concerns the
(A) Degree of tipping allowable in the abutment tooth
(B) Amount of increase in retentive factor with a full crown versus a 3/4th crown
(C) Crown : Root ratio
(D) Ratio of combined pericemental root surface area of the abutment teeth and the pericemental root surface area's of the teeth to be replaced

178. Extra retention in abutment teeth is obtained by.
(A) Dovetail
(B) Screws, pins and grooves
(C) Outline form
(D) Increasing tooth reduction

179. Predictable compliment of optimum tooth preparation should satisfy

(A) Biological reuirement

(B) Esthetic reuirement

(C) Combination of compromises among the prevalence biological and mechanical considerations

(D) Biological, mechanical and esthetic reuirement

180. Tissue displacement commonly needed to obtain

(A) Adeuate access to prepared tooth

(B) To expose all necessary surfaces, both prepared and not prepared

(C) Both of the above

(D) None of the above

181. Post and core is indicated for

(A) Vital tooth with primary caries

(B) Badly damaged non-vital endodontically treated tooth

(C) Badly damaged vital tooth

(D) Tooth with fractured incisal third

182. When making complete denture the occlusal plane should be parallel to the

(A) Frankfort horizontal plane only
(B) Interpupillary line only

(C) Campers plane only
(D) Campers plane and interpupillary line

183. The primary function of the compensatory curve, incorporated in complete dentures is to provide

(A) Stability in centric relation

(B) Balanced occlusion, during lateral movements of mandible

(C) An esthetically pleasing dentures

(D) Balancing occlusal contacts, during protrusive movements

184. One of the major disadvantages to immediate denture treatment is

(A) Pain associated with treatment
(B) Difficulty in managing occlusions

(C) Need for reline
(D) No control over tooth placement and shape

185. Over dentures are indicated over retained roots instead of extracting them and making complete dentures because

(A) To preserve the alveolar bone

(B) To allow proprioception from the periodontium of remaining teeth

(C) Carrier for patient to adjust

(D) All of the above

186. The Gothic arch tracing device is used to record

(A) The vertical dimension of occlusion
(B) The centric relation

(C) The centric occlusion
(D) Vertical dimension at rest

COMMUNITY AND PREVENTIVE DENTISTRY

187. Any principal/Dean of recognized Dental College can become a member of Dental Council of India. The maximum members in such category can be

(A) Two (B) Three
(C) Four (D) Six

188. The priority program of WHO is

(A) Global eradication of small pox
(B) Immunization against common diseases of childhood
(C) Surveillance of communicable diseases
(D) Child nutrition

189. The headuarters of UNICEF is situated at

(A) Geneva (B) London
(C) New York (D) Washington

190. The branch of biostatistics which deals with the births, deaths and marriage is called as

(A) Health (B) Medical
(C) Demography (D) Vital

191. Awakening the fundamental desire to learn is known as

(A) Motivation (B) Interest
(C) Learning (D) Comprehension

192. "NALGONDA" techniue of defluoridation was developed at

(A) Chennai (B) Nagpur
(C) Nalgonda (D) Bangalore

193. In a path-finder survey, the examination carried out for various age groups in years are

(A) 5, 10, 15, 35-44, 65-74 (B) 6, 12, 15, 35-44, 64-74
(C) 6, 12, 15, 35-44, 65-74 (D) 5, 12, 15, 30-44, 65-74

194. When a circle is divided into different sectors corresponding to the freuencies of the' variable in the distribution, the diagram is known as

(A) Pie (B) Bar
(C) Histogram (D) Pictogram

195. In lake water, the highest fluoride value ever recorded is 2800 PPM. In which country this lake is situated?

(A) Japan (B) Kenya
(C) Libya (D) South Africa

196. According to WHO technical series published, CPITN probe is also known as

(A) 611 (B) 617
(C) 621 (D) 625

197. New Zealand type of school dental nurse can perform all of the following clinical duties except

(A) Prophylaxis
(B) Pulp capping
(C) Root canal treatment
(D) topical fluoride application

198. Sampling which involves grouping the population and then selecting the groups is known as

(A) Cluster
(B) uota
(C) Systematic
(D) Simple random

199. Dental auxiliaries are not in existence in

(A) America
(B) India
(C) Saudi-Arabia
(D) New Zealand

200. "No Tobacco Day" is celebrated every year by the world on

(A) 7th April
(B) 31st May
(C) 1st August
(D) 5th December

2004
ANSWERS & EXPLANATIONS

ANATOMY

Ans.1. (B) Mandibular arch

Ref BDC textbook of anatomy

- First arch – Mandibular arch
- SecoPapar-2005
- Third arch - Glossopharyngeal nerve
- Fourth and sixth arch – Vagus nerve (Sup. Laryngeal, Rec. laryngeal resp.)

Ans.2. (B) Right accessory

Ref BDC, 4th ed , vol 3 , pg 210

Uvula is a conical projection hat hangs from the middle of the inferior border of soft palate. Also as explained previously, all muscles of soft palate except tensor palati are supplied by pharyngeal plexus by *accessory nerve* through Vagus.

Now remember one important rule:- Rule Of 17

10 + 7	=	12 + 5
Opposite side		same side

Here, it is easy to remember that lesions of cranial nerve X (Vagus) and VII (Facial) , deviations are seen in opposite side while XII (hypoglossal) and V(Trigeminal) produce deviations in the same side.

Now, since the question mentions 'left deviation' the possible lesions could be located at

- Left hypoglossal
- Left trigeminal (mandibular nerve)
- Right facial
- Right accessory (Vagus)

So, from above uvula would be deviated to left by lesions in right Vagus/accessory.

Ans.3. (A) Symphysis

Ref http://en.wikipedia.org/wiki/Joints

JOINTS classification

Structural classification

Structural classification names and divides joints according to how the bones are connected to each other. There are three structural classifications of joints:

(A) Fibrous/Immovable: bones are connected by dense connective tissue, consisting mainly of collagen. The fibrous joints are further divided into three types:

Sutures are found between bones of the skull. In fetal skulls the sutures are wide to allow slight movement during birth. They later become rigid (synarthrodial).

- **Syndesmosis** are found between long bones of the body, such as the radius and ulna in forearm and the fibula and tibia in leg. Unlike other fibrous joints, syndesmoses are moveable (amphiarthrodial).
- **Gomphosis** is a joint between the root of a tooth and the sockets in the maxilla or mandible.

(B) Cartilaginous - bones are connected entirely by cartilage. Cartilaginous joints allow more movement between bones than a fibrous joint but less than the highly mobile synovial joint. An example would be the joints between the ribs and the sternum. Cartilaginous joints also form the growth regions of immature long bones and the intervertebral discs of the spinal column.

- **Primary cartilaginous joints** - Known as "synchondroses". Bones are connected by hyaline cartilage, typically between ossification centres. This cartilage may ossify with age. Examples in humans are the joint between the first rib and the manubrium of the sternum, and the "growth plates" between ossification centres in long bones. These joints do not allow movement.
- **Secondary cartilaginous joints** - Known as "symphyses". Fibrocartilaginous joints, usually occurring in the midline. Examples in human anatomy would be the intervertebral discs, and the pubic symphysis. These joints allow a little movement.

(C) Synovial - synovial joints have a space between the articulating bones for synovial fluid. This classification contains joints that are the most mobile of the three, and includes the knee and shoulder. These are further classified into ball and socket joints, condyloid joints, saddle joints, hinge joints, pivot joints, and gliding joints.

Functional classification

Joints can also be classified functionally, by the degree of mobility they allow.

(A) Synarthrosis permit little or no mobility. They can be categorized by how the two bones are joined together:

Synchondroses are joints where the two bones are connected by a piece of cartilage.

- *Synostoses* are where two bones that are initially separted eventually fuse together, essentially becoming one bone. In humans the plates of the cranium fuse together as a child approaches adulthood. Children whose craniums fuse too early may suffer deformities and brain damage as the skull does not expand properly to accommodate the growing brain, a condition known as craniostenosis. Most synarthrosis joints are fibrous.

(B) Amphiarthrosis - permit slight mobility. The two bone surfaces at the joint are both covered in hyaline cartilage and joined by strands of fibrocartilage. Most amphiarthrosis joints are cartilaginous.

(C) Diarthrosis - permit a variety of movements (*e.g.* flexion, adduction, pronation). Only synovial joints are diarthrodial. They can be divided into six classes:

- *Ball and Socket* - such as the shoulder or the hip and femur.
- *Hinge* - such as the elbow.

- *Pivot* - such as the radius and ulna.
- *Condyloid (or ellipsoidal)* - such as the wrist between radius and carpals, or knee
- *Saddle* - such as the joint between carpal thumbs and metacarpals.
- *Gliding* - such as between the carpals.

Ans.4. (B) Maxillary process

Ref http://en.wikipedia.org/wiki/Pharyngeal_arches

Pharyngeal arch	Muscular contributions	Skeletal contributions	Nerve and Artery
1st ("mandibular arch")	muscles of mastication (temporalis, masseter, medial) pterygoid), anterior belly of digastric, mylohyoid, tensor veli palatini	maxilla, mandible (only as a model for mandible not actual formation of mandible), the incus and malleus of the middle ear, also Mackel's cartilage	Trigeminal nerve (V2 and V3) Maxillary artery
2nd ("hyoid arch")	Muscles of facial expression, buccinator, platysma, stapedius, stylohyoid, digastric posterior belly	Stapes, styloid process, hyoid (lesser horn and Part of Body), Reichert's cartilage	Facial nerve (VII)
3rd	Stylopharyngeus	Hyoid (geater horn and part of Body)	Glossopharyngeal nerve (IX), Common carotid/Internal carotid
4th and 6th	Intrinsic muscles of larynx, pharynx; levator palati	thyroid cartilage, cricoid cartilage, epiglottic cartilage, arytenoid cartilages	Vagus nerve (X) Pulmonary artery

Ans.5. C) Type IV collagen fibers

Ref http://en.wikipedia.org/wiki/Basal lamina

The layers of the basal lamina ("BL") are described below:

Name	Features
lamina lucida / lamina rara interna	Electron-lucid layer containing the glycoprotein laminin
lamina densa	Electron-dense layer composed of type IV collagen
lamina lucida / lamina rara externa	Similar composition to lamina rara interna. Some sources do not consider this a distinct layer.
lamina reticularis	The three above layers of the basal lamina typically sit on top of the **reticular lamina**, which is synthesized by cells from the underlying connective tissue and contains fibronectin. The exception is when two epithelial layers abut one another as in the alveoli of the lungs and glomeruli of the kidneys, in which the basal lamina of one epithelial layer fuses with that of the other.

Anchoring fibers composed of ***type IV collagen*** extend from the basal lamina into the underlying reticular lamina and loop around collagen bundles. Although found beneath all basal laminae, they are especially numerous in stratified squamous cells of the skin.

These layers should not be confused with the lamina propria, which is found outside the basal lamina

Ans.6. (C) Merocrine

http://en.wikipedia.org/wiki/Exocrine_glands

Typical exocrine glands include sweat glands, salivary glands, mammary glands, and many glands of the digestive system.

There are multiple ways of classifying exocrine glands:

Structure

Exocrine glands contain a glandular portion and a duct portion, the structures of which can be used to classify the gland.

The duct portion may be branched (called *compound*) or unbranched (called *simple*).

The glandular portion may be tubular, acinar, or may be a mix of the two (called tubuloacinar). If the glandular portion branches, then the gland is called a branched gland.

Method of secretion

Exocrine glands are named apocrine, holocrine gland, or merocrine gland based on how their product is secreted.

Apocrine - bud their secretions off through the plasma membrane producing membrane bound vesicles in the lumen.

Examples of an apocrine gland include:

-the lactating mammary gland.

-cerumen ("wax") of the outer ear.

Holocrine

secretions are produced within the cell followed by the rupture of the plasma membrane, thus releasing the cellular contents into the lumen.

Examples of holocrine glands include the sebaceous glands of the skin and the meibomian glands of the eyelid.

- **Merocrine** (eccrine)- A cell is classified as merocrine if the secretions of that cell dump directly into the lumen. This is done by vesicles opening onto the surface of the cell, and the secretory product is discharged from the cell - normal exocytosis (*e.g.* salivary glands).
- Merocrine is the most common manner of secretion. The structures that are usually called "apocrine sweat glands" actually secrete in a merocrine fashion.

Product secreted

Serous cells secrete proteins, often enzymes. Examples include chief cells and Paneth cells.

Mucous cells secrete mucus. Examples include Brunner's glands, esophageal glands, and pyloric glands.

Mixed glands secrete both protein and mucus. Examples include the salivary glands, although parotid gland is predominantly serous, and sublingual gland is predominantly mucous.

DENTAL ANATOMY AND HISTOLOGY

Ans.7. (D) Alveolus

Ref Wheeler's, pg 330

The alveolar process is the part of jaw bones that develop with the eruption of teeth. The form and depth of each alveolus is determined by the roots of the teeth. These processes fail to develop when the teeth are congenitally missing.

After extraction of teeth, they are referred to as *residual alveolar ridge.*

Ans.8. (B) Between 4-6 months of fetal life

Ref Wheelers, pg 24

Both primary and permanent central incisors begin to calcify at 3-4 months of IU life and by 6 months all the deciduous teeth starts to calcify.

Ans.9. (C) Initiation

Ref Orbans textbook of histology

Anomaly	Stage
Initiation	Anodontia, supernumerary teeth, fusion , germination
Histo differentiation	Dentinogenesis imperfecta, corresponds to bell stage.
Morpho differentiation	Talon's cusp, dens in dente, macrodontia, Hutchinson's incisor, peg lateral
Apposition	Enamel hypoplasia, concrescence, intrinsic staining, hypo calcification.

Ans.10. (C) Lateral pterygoids contract

Ref Wheelers,6th ed pg 361

When the jaw is opened the condyles move downwards along the glenoid fossa. During protrusion the condyles make a pure hinge movement/rotation to about <u>20-25mm</u> (10-13 degree) and then translation. The rotation around vertical axis is seen during the lateral jaw movements.

The opening movement is primarily mediated by contraction of lateral pterygoid, digastric, mylohyoid and Geniohyoid muscle.

The articular disk provides an interface for the condyle as it glides across the temporal bone. The upper compartment has a volume of 1.2 mL and provides for gliding movement. The lower compartment has a volume of 0.9 mL and provides for the hinge movement of condyles.

Ans.11. (C) Ameloblasts secrete enamel and dentine

Ref Orbans, textbook of histology

It is quite obvious from the choices that option 'c' is incorrect. Ameloblasts are specialized cells that are involved with enamel formation only;

Ans.12. (B) Birth to 8 years

Please refer KCET-07 A10

Ans.13. (C) Tertiary dentin and sclerotic dentin

Ref Orbans textbook of histology

Predentin	• First formed dentin, not mineralized • Located adjacent to pulp • 2-6 um wide
Peritubular dentin	• Dentin surrounding tubules • Highly mineralized • 1um near CEJ • Outer dentin 0.75 ; inner 0.4 um
Intertubular dentin	• Main body of dentin • Located between tubules • 0.5 – 0.2 um
Mantle dentin (primary dentin)	• 1st formed dentin- clinical crown • Outermost layer of primary dentin
Circum pulpal dentin (primary dentin)	• Dentin formed prior to root completion • Forms the bulk of primary dentin • More mineralized than mantle
Secondary dentin	• Adventitious dentine • Forms after root completion • Tubules fewer in no. with a bend
Reparative dentin	• Tertiary dentin • Dentin formed in response to extensive abrasion, caries, and other insults • Fewer and more twisted tubules
Dead tracts	• Insults may result in empty tubules filled with air • Black in transmitted and white in reflected • Initial step in sclerosis
Sclerotic / transparent	• Protective mechanism • After an insult Cs gets deposited • Found mainly in elderly, roots • Light in transmitted, black in reflected
Interglobular dentin	• Hypo mineralized area, fail to fuse • Crowns of teeth in circumpulpal layer below mantle dentin

Pneumonic: Dead Tracts – (DT) appear Dark in Transmitted light
While sclerotic appear in reverse order.

Ans.14. (C) Mandibular first premolar

Please refer previous papers

PHYSIOLOGY

Ans.15. (C) Normal intelligence

Ref Ganong, 22nd ed, pg 328

Cretinism clinical features:

- Children that are hypothyroid from birth or before
- Dwarfed
- ***Mentally retarded***
- Potbellies
- Enlarged and protruding tongue
- If treatment is started before birth than degree of retardation is less severe.

Ans.16. (C) Ascending limb of loop of Henle

Ref Ganong , 22nd ed , pg 714

The descending loop of Henle is permeable to water but the thick ascending loop isn't. Na, K, and Cl are co-transported out of the ascending loop and hence the fluid in descending loop becomes hypertonic to the interstitial fluid. On the other hand, fluid in ascending loop becomes more hypotonic and this creates a counter-current mechanism.

Ans.17. (B) Factor VIII

Pleases refer KCET-07 A13

Ans.18. (D) Acetylcholine

Ref Ganong , 22nd ed , pg100

The principal neuro-transmitter at the NMJ is **acetylcholine.** It is enclosed in small, clear synaptic vessels. It is rapidly removed from the synapse if repolarization has to occur, by the enzyme acetylcholinestearse NMJ has nicotinic type of cholinergic receptors which are also found in autonomic ganglia and the CNS.

- Serotonin is present in highest concentration in blood platelets and GIT, it is converted to melatonin in the pineal gland.
- Noradrenaline is the chief transmitter at most sympathetic postganglionic nerve endings like adrenal medulla.

Ans.19. (B) Corticospinal

Ref http://www.csuchico.edu/~pmccaffrey//syllabi/CMSD%20320/images/Notes-UNIT10.html

Ganong, 22nd ed , pg 203

The fibers of the lateral corticospinal tract form the pyramids in the medulla; the pathways are referred to as pyramidal systems.

The rest of the descending brainstem and spinal pathways that do not pass through the pyramids and are concerned with postural control have been called as extra-pyramidal systems.

The Extrapyramidal Tract

This system is involved in automatic motor movements, and in gross rather than fine motor movement. It works with the autonomic nervous system to help with posture and muscle tone and has more influence over midline structures than over those in the periphery. **Facial expression** is one important communicative behavior that is mediated by the extrapyramidal tract. In contrast to pyramidal tract, the extrapyramidal tract is an indirect, multisynaptic tract.

Components of the extrapyramidal tract include the basal ganglia, the **red nucleus**, the **substancia nigra**, the **reticular formation** and the **cerebellum**. All of these structures send information to the lower motor neurons in an indirect fashion.

The basal ganglia act to inhibit the **release phenomenon**, or the rapid firing of motor neurons. It is aided in this function by the substancia nigra of the midbrain. The muscles most often affected by these inhibitory functions are those controlling the head, the hands, and the fingers.

The neurotransmitters involved in the inhibitory function of the basal ganglia include **dopamine**, which is produced by the substancia nigra, **acetylcholine**, and **GABA**, which is a glutamate. Dopamine is an especially powerful inhibitor.

Extrapyramidal Projections to Lower Motor Neurons

- The **rubrospinal tract** passes through the **red nucleus**. The cerebellum sends messages to the spinal nerves along this tract. Information flows from the superior cerebellar peduncle to the red nucleus and finally to the spinal nerves. This information is very important for somatic motor, or skeletal muscle control and the regulation of muscle tone for posture.
- The **reticulospinal tract** runs from the reticular nuclei of the pons and medulla to the spinal nerves. It is involved in somatic motor control like the rubrospinal tract and also plays an important role in the control of autonomic functions.
- The **tectospinal tract** has points of origin throughout the brain stem, but especially in the midbrain area, and ends in the spinal nerves. It is involved in the control of neck muscles and also in visual and auditory reflexes. So, when you jump after hearing a noise or duck when you see something coming toward you, this tract helps to mediate these reactions.
- The **vestibulospinal tract** runs from the vestibular nuclei located in the lower pons and medulla to the spinal nerves. It is involved in balance.

The Pyramidal Tract

- This group of fibers carries messages for voluntary motor movement to the lower motor neurons in the brain stem and spinal cord.
- Approximately 80% of the cell bodies of the pyramidal tract are located on the precentral gyrus of the frontal lobe, which is also known as the motor strip. Particularly large cells

located here whose axons are part of the pyramidal tract are called pyramidal cells. Approximately 20% of the pyramidal tract fibers also originate in the post-central gyrus of the parietal lobe, in Brodmann's areas 1, 2, and 3. Regardless of the location of their cell bodies, pyramidal tract fibers descend from the cortex inside the internal capsule.

- This tract is ***direct*** and ***monosynaptic***, meaning that the axons of its neurons do not synapse with other cells until they reach their final destination in the brain stem or spinal cord. These direct connections between the cortex and the lower motor neurons allow messages to be transmitted very rapidly from the central nervous system to the periphery.
- The fibers of the pyramidal tract that synapse with spinal nerves sending information about voluntary movement to the skeletal muscles form the **corticospinal tract**. These axons are among the longest in the central nervous system, as some of them travel all the way from the cortex to the inferior part of the spinal cord. As they descend through the brain, they form part of the **posterior limb** of the internal capsule.
- At the **pyramids** in the inferior part of the medulla, eighty-five to ninety percent of corticospinal fibers decussate, or cross to the other side of the brain. The remaining ten to fifteen percent continue to descend ipsilaterally. The fibers that decussate are called the **lateral corticospinal tract** or the **lateral pyramidal tract.** Because they descend along the sides of the spinal cord, the **uncrossed** or **direct** fibers that synapse with spinal nerves on the ipsilateral side of the body are called the **direct pyramidal tract**. They may also be referred to as the **ventral pyramidal tract** or the **anterior corticospinal tract** since they travel down the ventral aspect of the spinal cord.

Ans.20. (B) Thiophorase

Ref http://www.musc.edu/comsc/Knowledge/webpage/biochem/ketone.doc

KBs are synthesized in mitochondria of the liver and kidney when carbohydrates are lacking. The brain can use KB as a source of energy only in times of starvation or metabolic disturbance (diabetes).

Acetyl Coa →	Ketone Bodies	→ Energy
HMG CoA Synthase (Liver & Kidney Mitochondria)		Thiophorase (Not in Liver)

EXTRA EDGE

Ketone Body Synthesis

Confusing Points:

Acetyl CoA →	HMG CoA →	Cholesterol (reductase)
		Ketone Bodies (Synthase)

	EH Cytosol	EH Mito.	Liver Cytosol	Liver Mito.
HGM CoA Synthase	Yes	No	Yes	Yes
HMG CoA Reductase	Yes	No	Yes	No
HMG CoA Lyase	No	Yes	No	Yes
	Cholesterol	Nothing	Cholesterol	Ketone Bodies

Regulation

The availability of carbohydrates regulates ketogenesis and fatty acid oxidation. The key regulatory step is Malonyl CoA. In times when energy is high, and TCA is inhibited, carbohydrates could be said to be in excess. Therefore, Citrate would back up and leave the mitochondria from TCA. This would be broken down in to Acetyl CoA and finally Malonyl CoA in the cytoplasm.

Malonyl CoA directly inhibits the Carnitine shuttle. This would result in fewer fatty acids entering the mitochondria, and therefore slow B-Oxidation and Ketogenesis.

Remember, liver cells cannot utilize KB due to absence of enzyme Thiophorase while most of the extra-hepatic tissues cannot synthesize KB due to absence of mitochondrial HMG CoA Synthase.

Ans.21. (A) Insulin

Ref Ganong, 22nd ed , pg 350-352

- Insulin is glycogenic, *anti-gluconeogenic, anti-lipolytic, and anti-ketotic* in its action. Hence, it is known as the "hormone of energy storage".
- Glucogon, on the other hand is glycogenolytic, gluconeogenetic, lipolytic and ketogenic. It mobilizes energy stores and is a hormone of energy release.
- The catecholmines have a similar effect on glucose level by activating liver phosphorylase. They also increase FFA and decreases peripheral utilization of glucose.
- The effects of growth hormone are partly direct and partly mediated by IGF-1. it mobilizes FFA from adipose tissues and decreases glucose uptake in some tissues, increases hepatic glucose uptake and may decrease tissue binding of insulin.

Ans.22. (D) Ascorbic acid

Avitaminoses include

- vitamin A deficiency causes xerophthalmia or night blindness
- thiamine deficiency causes beriberi (dry/wet)
- niacin deficiency causes pellagra
- vitamin B12 deficiency leads to pernicious anemia
- vitamin C deficiency leads to scurvy
- vitamin D deficiency causes rickets
- vitamin K deficiency causes bleeding

Ans.23. (B) Liver

Ganong, 22nd ed, pg 294

Most of the NH_4 formed by deamination of amino acid in the liver is converted to urea, and the urea is excreted in the urine.

NH_4 → carbamoyl phosphate → ornithine → citrulline → arginine → urea + ornithine

Thus most of the urea is formed in the liver and in sever liver deficiency the BUN falls and urea rises.

Ans.24. (C) 9 to 11 mg%

Ref Ganong, 22nd ed , pg382

- The normal plasma concentration of calcium is 10 (9-11) mg/dL (5meq/L, 2.5mmol/L) is partially bound to protein and partly diffusible.
- The total calcium content of body = 1100 g (27.5 mol)
- Also, major site of resorption of Ca in kidneys is PCT (60%)

Also remember, Phosphorus level in plasma = 12 mg/dL

Total content in body = 500-800 g

MICROBIOLOGY

Ans.25. (C) Using a bacterial spore test

Explained earlier, please refer KCET-07 A19

Ans.26. (C) Spirochaete

Ref http://en.wikipedia.org/wiki/Borrelia

Borrelia is a genus of bacteria of the spirochete class. It is a zoonotic, vector-borne disease transmitted primarily by ticks and some by lice, depending on the species. There are 37 known species of borrelia.

Lyme Borreliosis

Of the 37 known species of Borrelia, 12 of these species are known to cause Lyme disease or borreliosis and are transmitted by ticks. The major borrelia species causing Lyme disease are *Borrelia burgdorferi*, *Borrelia afzelii*, *Borrelia garinii* and *Borrelia valaisiana*.

Relapsing Fever

Other *Borrelia* species cause relapsing fever such as *Borrelia recurrentis*, caused by human body louse. No animal reservoir exists. Lice that feed on infected humans acquire the *Borrelia* organisms that then multiply in the gut of the louse. When an infected louse feeds on an uninfected human, the organism gains access when the victim crushes the louse or scratches the area where the louse is feeding. *B. recurrentis* infects the person via mucous membranes and then invades the bloodstream.

Ans.27. (A) Bacterial infection

Please refer KCET-06 A95

Ans.28. (A) Cell wall of Gram-positive organisms

Ref http://en.wikipedia.org/wiki/Teichoic_acid

Teichoic acids

- Are polymers of glycerol or ribitol linked via phosphodiester bonds.
- These acids can be found in the cell wall of gram-positive bacteria, such as *Staphylococci, Streptococci, Bacillus, Clostridium, Corynebacterium* and *Listeria*, and appear to extend to the surface of the peptidoglycan layer.
- Teichoic acids are ***not found*** in the gram-negative bacteria. They can be either covalently bonded to N-acetylmuramic acid of the peptidoglycan layer or linked to the plasma membrane lipids found in the cytoplasmic membrane. The combined units comprised of teichoic acids and lipids are referred to as lipo-teichoic acids.
- Teichoic acids are negatively charged and therefore contribute to the negative charge of the gram-positive cell wall. They may also provide structural support for the cell wall and act as antigen.

Ans.29. (C) Hepatoma

Please refer KCET-07 A27

Ans.30. (B) Shift towards more acidogenic micro flora

Ref Shafer, 5th ed, pg 760.

The following lines from Shafer leave no doubt-

"The primary cause of radiation induced caries lies in alterations in the saliva induced by either direct or indirect radiation of the salivary glands. The radiation induces-xerostomia produces a pronounced shift in oral microbial population, with acidogenic caries-promoting microorganism gaining prominence at the expense of non-cariogenic ones."

Thus we see that there is an increase in acidogenic bacteria ***at the expense*** of other without overall increase in total bacterial count. Hence answer is 'b' and not 'a'.

Ans.31. (A) AIDS

Please refer KCET-07 A25

Ans.32. (A) Gram staining

Ref Paniker 7th ed, pg 216

Streptococcus is a genus of spherical shaped **Gram-positive bacteria**, belonging to the phylum Firmicutes and the lactic acid bacteria group.

[Thus ***all Streptococci are Gram +ve***]

- They test positive for oxidase and negative for catalase.
- Cellular division occurs along a single axis in these bacteria, and thus they grow in chains or pairs, thus the name—from Greek *streptos*, meaning easily bent or twisted, like a chain. Contrast this with staphylococci which divide along multiple axes and generate grape-like clusters of cells.

- Clinically, individual species of *Streptococcus* are classified primarily based on their hemolytic properties (breakdown of red blood cells in a laboratory)- alpha, beta and gamma.

Beta-hemolytic streptococci are further characterized via the **Lancefield serotyping** - based on specific carbohydrates in the bacterial cell wall. These are named Lancefield groups A to T, although some species, such as *S. pneumoniae*, do not express Lancefield antigens. Medically the most important groups are the alpha-hemolytic streptococci, *S. pneumoniae* and *Streptococcus* Viridans-group, and the beta-hemolytic streptococci of Lancefield groups A and B (also known as "Group A Strep" and "Group B Strep")

Alpha-Hemolytic Streptococci

- Pneumococci
- *S. pneumoniae*, a leading cause of bacterial pneumonia, otitis media and meningitis.
- Viridans and Others
- *S. mutans*, a contributor to dental caries.
- *S. viridans*, a cause of endocarditis and dental abscesses.
- *S. thermophilus*, used in the manufacture of some cheeses and yogurts.

Beta-Hemolytic Streptococci

- **Group A**

  S. pyogenes (also known as *GAS*) is the causative agent in Group A streptococcal infections, (*GAS*) including strep throat, acute rheumatic fever, scarlet fever, acute glomerulonephritis and necrotizing fasciitis. Human infections by non-*S. pyogenes* GAS strains (some *S. dysgalactiae* subsp. *equisimilis* and *S. anginosus* Group strains) appear to be uncommon.
- **Group B**

  S. agalactiae, or *GBS*, causes meningitis in neonates and the elderly, with increasing the risk for premature rupture of membranes and transmission to the infant.
- **Group C**

  Includes *S. equi* which causes strangles in horses, and *S. zooepidemicus* which causes infections in several species of mammals including cattle and horses. This can also cause death in chickens and moose.
- **Group D (Enterococci) *variable in hemolysis**

  Many former Group D streptococci have been reclassified and placed in the genus *Enterococcus* (includes *S. faecalis*, *S. faciem*, *S. durans*, and *S. avium*).

  For example, *Streptococcus faecalis* is now *Enterococcus faecalis*.

  The remaining non-enterococcal Group D strains include *S. bovis* and *S. suis*.

Non-Hemolytic Streptococci

Non-hemolytic streptococci rarely cause disease. However weakly hemolytic group D beta-hemolytic streptococci and *Listeria monocytogenes* should not be confused with non-hemolytic streptococci.

Ref http://en.wikipedia.org/wiki/Streptococci

INVESTIGATIONS

(1) Hemolysin production (blood agar plates-BAP; bright blood red):

- Important ingredients: red blood cells.
- This medium is a differential medium used to distinguish species of *Streptococcus* contains 5% sheep's blood.
- Some species produce proteins called hemolysins. These proteins can lyse erythrocytes (red blood cells), releasing hemoglobin.
- Inoculate the plate with a single streak and incubate at 35°C for 24 to 48 hours.
- **α-hemolysis**: only the hemoglobin in the RBC is broken down (partial or incomplete hemolysis). The medium surrounding the colony is cloudy and discolored, turns green, *e.g. S.pneumoniae, S. salivarius.*
- **α-hemolysis**: the RBC is completely broken down and there is a colorless, clear, sharply defined zone of hemolysis surrounding colonies. *e.g. S. pyogenes.*
- **α-hemolysis**: no affect on RBC, no lysis. *S. faecalis* is non-hemolytic after 24 hour incubation, but may become á-hemolytic after a longer incubation.

(2) MacConkey Agar (dark red agar plate, sometimes brownish red if plate is old)

- Important ingredients: crystal violet, bile salts, neutral red, lactose.
- This is a selective medium that contains crystal violet to inhibit gram positive organisms, although it sometimes inhibits poorly.
- It is primarily used as a differential medium by differentiating between bacteria that produce the enzyme galactosidase and subsequently ferment the glucose produced.
- Bile salts and the pH indicator neutral red react with acid fermentation products to produce a bright pink color. Inoculate the plate with a single streak and incubate at 35°C for 24 to 48 hours.
- Pink agar is therefore an indication that the organism is positive for lactose fermentation.
- Non-lactose fermenting organisms will produce white colonies and turn the agar yellow.

(3) Eosin Methylene Blue Agar (EMB plates, dark, purplish red):

- Important ingredients: eosin, methylene blue, lactose.
- EMB agar is both a differential medium and a selective medium. As a selective medium, it inhibits the growth of gram-positive organisms. As a differential medium, it gives lactose fermenting *E. coli* a greenish metallic sheen. Other lactose fermenting bacteria will appear pink and thick, or mucoid.
- Nonlactose-fermenting organisms are colorless on this medium, and may take on the color of the agar. This gives results similar to MacConkey agar.
- Inoculate the plate with a single streak and incubate at 35°C for 24 to 48 hours.

(4) Bile Esculin Agar - BEA (beige agar plate):

- These plates look like a regular nutrient agar plate like TSA, but contain bile, the glycoside esculin, and iron salts as an indicator.

- Group D *Streptococcus* sp. will convert the esculin to 6,7-dihydroxy-coumarin, which reacts with the iron salts, producing a black color in the agar.
- Non-Group D *Streptococcus* sp. do not produce the black color.

(5) 6.5% NaCl broth (purple broth):

- The Group D Streptococci can be separated into enterococci (*e.g. Enterococci faecalis*) and non-enterococci (*e.g. Streptococcus bovis*).
- Only the enterococci are able to grow in the presence of high salt. This high salt broth contains a pH indicator that will turn from purple to yellow if the microorganism can grow.

EXTRA EDGE

Algorithm for diagnosis of Streptococcus:

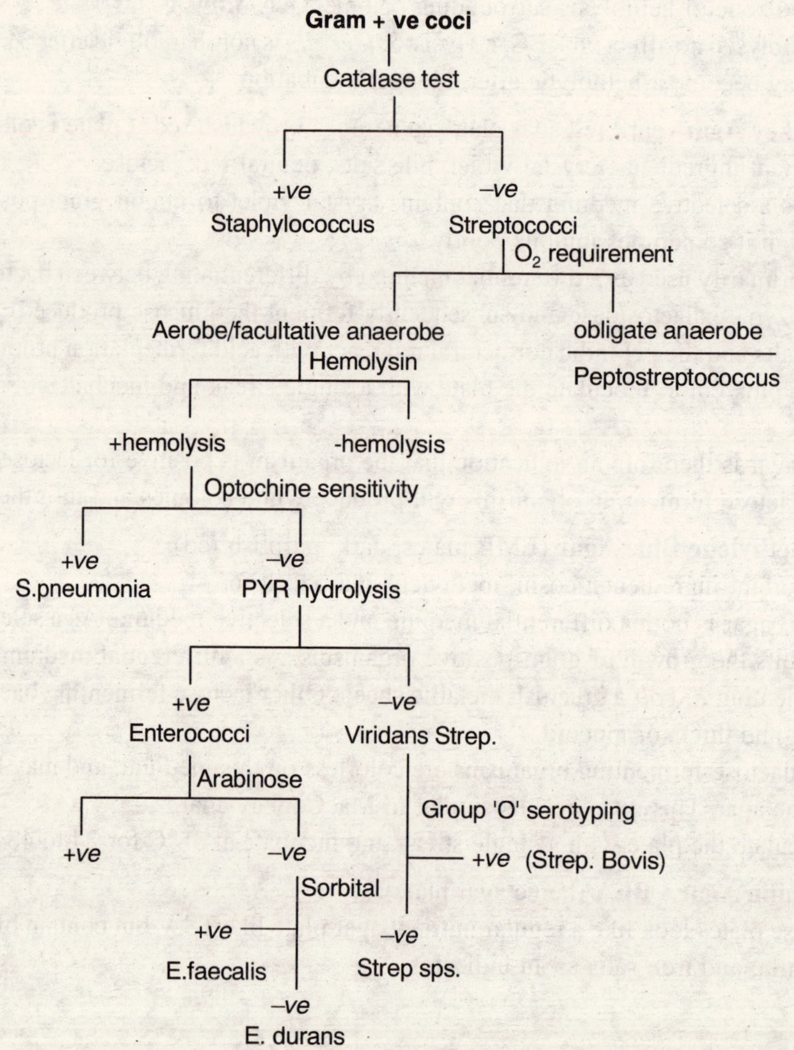

Ans.33. (D) Weakly antigenic

Ref http://en.wikipedia.org/wiki/Exotoxins

An **exotoxin** is a soluble chemical excreted by a microorganism, including bacteria, fungi, algae, and protozoa. An exotoxin is a ***protein*** which can cause damage to the host by destroying cells or disrupting normal cellular metabolism. Both gram negative and gram positive bacteria produce exotoxins. They are ***highly potent*** and can cause major damage to the host. Exotoxins may be secreted, or, similar to endotoxins, ***may be released during lysis of the cell.***

Most exotoxins can be destroyed by heating. They may exert their effect locally or produce systemic effects. (Nester, 2007). Well known exotoxins include the botulinum toxin produced by *Clostridium botulinum*, the *Corynebacterium diphtheriae* exotoxin which is produced during life threatening symptoms of diphtheria.

Exotoxins are susceptible to antibodies produced by the immune system, but many exotoxins are so toxic that they may be fatal to the host before the immune system has a chance to mount defenses against it.

EXTRA EDGE

Types:

There are three main types of exotoxins:

- ***toxins that act upon the extracellular matrix or connective tissue:*** this allows the further spread of bacteria and therefore the infection deeper into tissue regions. Examples are protease and endopeptidase.
- ***A-B type toxins:*** the 'B'-subunit attaches to target regions on cell membranes, the 'A'-subunit enters through the membrane and tends to possess enzymatic functions that affect internal cellular bio-mechanisms. The structure of these toxins allows for the development specific vaccines and treatments. Certain compounds can be attached to the B unit, which is not generally harmful, which the body learns to recognize, and which elicits an immune response. This allows the body to detect the harmful toxin if it is encountered later, and to eliminate it before it can cause harm to the host. Toxins of this type include cholera toxin, pertussis toxin, Shiga toxin and heat-labile enterotoxin from E. coli.
- ***Membrane damaging toxins:*** these toxins are designed primarily to puncture and disrupt the cellular membrane killing cells, a significant resulting example is that of Gangrene caused by *Clostridium perfringens*. Exotoxins that act on red blood cells and cause hemolysis.

Ans.34. (D) All of the above

Ref http://en.wikipedia.org/wiki/Vaccine

A **vaccine** is an antigenic preparation used to establish immunity to a disease. The term derives from ***Edward Jenner's*** use of cowpox ("vacca" means cow in Latin), which, when administered to humans, provided them protection against smallpox, which Pasteur and others perpetuated. Jenner realized that milkmaids who had contact with cowpox did not get smallpox. The process of distributing and administrating vaccines is referred to as vaccination.

Vaccines can be prophylactic (*e.g.* to prevent or ameliorate the effects of a future infection by any natural or "wild" pathogen), or therapeutic (*e.g.* vaccines against cancer are also being invest gated; see cancer vaccine.

Vaccines may be dead or inactivated organisms or purified products derived from them.

There are four types of traditional vaccines:

- ***Vaccines containing killed microorganisms:*** these are previously virulent micro-organisms that have been killed with chemicals or heat. Examples are vaccines against flu, cholera, bubonic plague, and hepatitis A.
- ***Vaccines containing live, attenuated microorganisms:*** these are live micro-organisms that have been cultivated under conditions that disable their virulent properties. They typically provoke more durable immunological responses and are the preferred type for healthy adults. Examples include yellow fever, measles, rubella, and mumps.
- ***Toxoids:*** these are inactivated toxic compounds from micro-organisms in cases where these (rather than the micro-organism itself) cause illness. Examples of toxoid-based vaccines include tetanus and diphtheria.
- ***Subunit:*** rather than introducing a whole inactivated or attenuated micro-organism to an immune system, a fragment of it can create an immune response. Characteristic examples include the subunit vaccine against HBV that is composed of only the surface proteins of the virus (produced in yeast) and the virus like particle (VLP) vaccine against Human Papillomavirus (HPV) that is composed of the viral major capsid protein.

The live tuberculosis vaccine is not the contagious strain, but a related strain called "BCG"; it is used in the United States very infrequently.

A number of innovative vaccines are also in development and in use:

- **Conjugate:** certain bacteria have polysaccharide outer coats that are poorly immunogenic. By linking these outer coats to proteins (*e.g.* toxins), the immune system can be led to recognize the polysaccharide as if it were a protein antigen. This approach is used in the *Haemophilus influenzae* type B vaccine.
- **Recombinant Vector:** by combining the physiology of one micro-organism and the DNA of the other, immunity can be created against diseases that have complex infection processes.
- **DNA vaccination:** in recent years a new type of vaccine, created from an infectious agent's DNA called *DNA vaccination*, has been developed. It works by insertion (and expression, triggering immune system recognition) into human or animal cells, of viral or bacterial DNA. Some cells of the immune system that recognize the proteins expressed will mount an attack against these proteins and cells expressing them.

GENERAL PATHOLOGY

Ans.35. (C) Polymorphs giant cells

Ref *http://en.wikipedia.org/wiki/Granulation_tissue*

Granulation tissue is the perfused, fibrous connective tissue that replaces a fibrin clot in healing wounds. Granulation tissue typically grows from the base of a wound and is able to fill wounds of almost any size.

Appearance

During the proliferative phase of wound healing, granulation tissue is:

- light red or dark pink in color,
- being perfused with new capillary loops or "buds";
- soft to the touch;
- moist; and
- bumpy (granular) in appearance.

Structure

Granulation tissue is comprised of tissue matrix supporting a variety of cell types, most of which can be associated with one of the following functions:

- extracellular matrix,
- immune system, or
- Vascularization.

Extracellular Matrix

The extracellular matrix of granulation tissue is created and modified by fibroblasts. Initially, it consists of a network of Type III collagen, a weaker form of the structural protein that can be produced rapidly. This is later replaced by the stronger, long-stranded Type I collagen, as evidenced in scar tissue.

Immunity

The main immune cells active in the tissue are macrophages and neutrophils, although other leukocytes are also present. These work to phagocytize old or damaged tissue, and protect the healing tissue from pathogenic insult. This is necessary both to aid the healing process and to protect against invading pathogens, as the wound often does not have an effective skin barrier to act as a first line of defense.

Vascularization

It is necessary for a network of blood vessels to be established as soon as possible to provide the growing tissue with nutrients, to take away cellular wastes, and transport new leukocytes to the area. Fibroblasts, the main cells that deposit granulation tissue, depend on oxygen to proliferate and lay down the new extracellular matrix. In vascularization, also called angiogenesis, endothelial cells quickly grow into the tissue from older, intact blood vessels. These branch out in a systematic way, forming anastomoses with other vessels

Ans.36. (A) Single cell necrosis

Ref *http://en.wikipedia.org/wiki/Apoptosis*

Ans. Apoptosis is a process of deliberate life relinquishment by a cell in a multicellular organism. It is one of the main types of programmed cell death (PCD).

In contrast to necrosis, which is a form of traumatic cell death that results from acute cellular injury, apoptosis is carried out in an orderly process that generally confers advantages during an organism's life cycle Apoptosis (Greek: *apo* - from, *ptosis* - falling) was distinguished from traumatic cell death in 1972 by Andrew H. Wyllie while studying tissues with electron microscopes.

EXTRA EDGE

A cell undergoing apoptosis shows a characteristic morphology that can be observed with a microscope:

- Cell shrinkage and rounding due to the breakdown of the proteinaceous cytoskeleton by caspases.
- The cytoplasm appears dense, and the organelles appear tightly packed.
- Chromatin undergoes condensation into compact patches against the nuclear envelope in a process known as ***pyknosis***, a hallmark of apoptosis.
- The nuclear envelope becomes discontinuous and the DNA inside it is fragmented in a process referred to as karyorrhexis. The nucleus breaks into several discrete *chromatin bodies* or *nucleosomal units* due to the degradation of DNA.
- The cell membrane shows irregular buds known as ***blebs***.
- The cell breaks apart into several vesicles called *apoptotic bodies*, which are then phagocytosed.

During karyorrhexis, endonuclease activation leaves short DNA fragments, regularly spaced in size. These give a characteristic "***laddered***" appearance on agar gel after electrophoresis. Tests for DNA laddering differentiate apoptosis from ischemic or toxic cell death.

Intracellular apoptotic signaling is a response initiated by a cell in response:

- To stress, and may ultimately result in cell suicide.
- The binding of nuclear receptors by glucocorticoids, heat, radiation, nutrient deprivation, viral infection and hypoxia are all factors which can lead to the release of intracellular apoptotic signals by a damaged cell.
- A number of cellular components, such as poly ADP ribose polymerase, may also help regulate apoptosis.
- **Cytochrome c** is also released from mitochondria due to increased permeability of the outer mitochondrial membrane, and serves a regulatory function as it precedes morphological change associated with apoptosis.
- Once cytochrome c is released it binds with ***Apaf-1*** and ATP, which then bind to *pro-caspase-9* to create a protein complex known as an apoptosome. The apoptosome cleaves the procaspase to its active form of caspase-9, which in turn activates the effector *caspase-3.*

Ans.37. (C) Cartilage

Ref Robbins, basic pathology, 6th ed

The various types of collagen found in human:

- **Type I Collagen** - The most abundant collagen in the body. Found in tendons, bones, skin and other tissues. Particularly abundant in the scar tissue.
- **Types II, IX, X, XI** - Cartilage
- **Type III** - Common in fast growing tissue, particularly at the early stages. (Phase 1) of wound repair. Much of it is replaced later by the type stronger and tougher type I collagen.
- **Type IV** - Basal lamina (filtration membrane of capillaries).
- **Type V, VI** - Generally found alongside type I.
- **Type VII** - Epithelia (lining of GI tract, urinary tract, etc.)
- **Type VIII** - Lining of blood vessels.
- **Type XII** - Found alongside and interacts with types I and III.

The most abundant types of collagen in the skin are I and III; their fibrils form the mesh largely responsible for the skin's mechanical properties. Other types of collagen in the skin are V, VI, and XII. They are found in much smaller amounts and appear to have a supportive role, whose details remain unclear.

Ans.38. (D) Gas embolism

Ref Robbins, 6th ed pg 74

Air embolism: is a condition wherein gas bubbles within the circulation obstructs vascular flow causing a distal ischemic injury. About **100 mL** of air is required for such an injury to take place.

A common form of gas embolism is the ***Decompression sickness*** when an individual is exposed to sudden changes in atmospheric pressure. Scuba and deep sea divers are particularly at risk. At high pressures, air (nitrogen in particular) is dissolved more rapidly in blood and tissues. If the diver ascends (de-pressurizes) too quickly the nitrogen expands in the tissues and bubbles out in blood forming emboli.

Bends and Chokes the rapid formation of gas bubbles in the skeletal muscles cause the painful bends. In lungs, these may cause respiratory distress – the chokes.

A more chronic form of decompression sickness is called *Caisson disease*, in which the persistence of gas emboli in the bone leads to multiple foci of ischemic injuries, particularly heads of femur, tibia and humerus.

Ans.39. (A) Basal cell carcinoma

Basal cell carcinoma is unique in that it shows only local invasion without distant metastasis. For this '***burrowing effect***', it is generally referred to as the rodent ulcer.

For details about other options, please refer **previous papers.**

DENTAL MATERIALS

Ans.40. (D) Can not be predicted

Ref http://www.ul.ie/~walshem/fyp/intermetallic%20compound.htm

Whilst some metal alloy systems exhibit total or partial solubility and others are insoluble in the solid state, a number of metals combine together to form an intermediate phase or intermediate compounds. There are two types of intermetallic compounds which are often encountered.

Electron compounds

These compounds are of definite chemical crystal structure and arise if the two alloying metals are of different crystal structure, valency, and if one of these metals is electro- positive with the other being electro- negative an example of this type of electron compound would be an alloy of the elements Magnesium and Tin which combine to form an intermetallic compound Mg_2SN. The composition of the compound is fixed and consists of two atoms of Magnesium combining with one atom of Tin. Metallic compounds form a crystal lattice with the atoms of the alloying metals taking up specific positions within the lattice. These compounds are usually hard and brittle.

Interstitial compounds

Interstitial compounds, as the name suggests form between metals, or metals and non- metallic elements, with atom sizes very similar to those that form interstitial solid solution. One set of atoms fit into the spaces, or interstices, between the larger atoms. Iron Carbide (Fe3C) or cementite which is important in the study of Iron-Carbon diagrams is an example of an interstitial compound.

While physical properties like melting range etc can be easily determined, the mechanical properties of such compound cannot be determined with accuracy.

Ans.41. (A) Degree of saturation of hue

Ref Vimal Sikri, pg 490

Color dimensions were described by Clark as:

- **Hue** – quality by which one color is distinguished from another. *e.g.* red, yellow.
- **Chroma** is the quality by which we distinguish a strong color from a weak one. It is the saturation or intensity of a hue.
- **Value** – it is the property by which we distinguish a light color from a dark color. It is related to the whiteness or blackness *i.e.* achromatic aspects of the color. For *e.g.* a color of high value is seen as light grey and that of low value as dark grey.

Remember, **Benzold Bruck effect** –is a phenomenon there is an increase in luminance or brightness of a color, there is an increase shift towards blue and yellow. *e.g.* a red yellow object appears yellowier than red with a rise in brightness levels.

Ans.42. (D) Greater plasticity and adapts well to cavity walls

Ref Vimal Sikri, pg 230

EAMES technique was developed in order to reduce the mercury content with minimum loss f mechanical properties. The adjusted level is around 45-50% and should not exceed **55%.** The reduce level of mercury ensures higher strength, shorter setting time, and low residual mercury with lower creep value. Even with this technique, mulling, or squeezing the mix is required.

However, the adaptation will not improve with lower mercury, as higher mercury ensures plasticity of the mass which aids in better adaptation/ and hence is the answer here.

Ans.43 (D) Electralloy

Ref Vimal Sikri, pg 328

Electra-alloy is an alloy of electrolytic gold and calcium. The calcium content is usually 0.1 0.5% by weight. The purpose is to produce stronger restorations by dispersion hardening.

Ans.44. (A) Elastic limit

Ref http://en.wikipedia.org/wiki/Elastic_limit

- The **elastic limit** is the maximum stress a material can undergo at which all strains are recoverable. (*i.e.*, the material will return to its original size after removal of the load).
- At stress levels below the elastic limit the material is said to be elastic.
- Once the material exceeds this limit, it is said to have undergone plastic deformation (also known as permanent deformation).
- When the stress is removed, some permanent strain will remain, and the material will be a different size.

The concept of elastic limit should not be confused with the ***proportional limit***, which is the stress above which the relationship between stress and strain is no longer linearly proportional.

Ordinarily, the elastic limit is greater than the proportional limit; however, for many materials (such as steel), the two are close enough to be identical for all practical purposes.

Ans.45. (D) All of the above

Ref Skinners, pg 218

The inorganic phase of composites comprises the filler particles which significantly improve the mechanical properties of composite resin. At the same time since the resin content decreases, the % shrinkage, water sorption and coefficient of thermal expansion are also less. Most composites have a filler particle concentration of 30-70% by vol or 50-85% by wt.

Ans.46. (A) Below the fusion temperature of both the alloys

Ref Skinners, 9th ed pg 530

Soldering is a technique wherein metal parts are joined together by melting a filler particle between them at a temperature below the solidus temp of each metal being joined and below 450°C.

Above 450°C, the procedure is referred to as brazing.

Remember, flux is a material which is used to prevent oxidation of parent metal and dissolves any oxides already present, *e.g.* includes borax, boric acid and fluoride fluxes. Whereas, anti-flux are materials used to limit the flow of solder *e.g.* graphite.

Ans.47. (C) Better color harmony

Ref Skinners, 9th ed pg 507-511

Dental porcelain has superior mechanical properties than other esthetic restorative materials. However, they are extremely brittle and hence are having low tensile strengths. Although they are themselves insoluble, the luting cement may dissolve causing failure. However, the most outstanding feature of porcelain is their ability to simulate adjacent teeth in color, and physical properties like translucency and hue. They are extremely color stable as compared to composite resins.

Ans.48. (C) 343

Ref http://www.lib.umich.edu/dentlib/Dental_tables/Knoophard.html

Enamel (human)	**KHN**
Etched	88-171
Softened	149-179
Sound	355-431

Other,

Calculus (on teeth)	86
Cementum	40
Dentin	68

Ans.49. (C) Flaring the point of the sprue attachment

Ref Skinners, 9th ed , pg 419

Suck-back porosity is a type of solidification shrinkage porosity wherein a ***'hot- spot'*** is created owing to faulty sprue direction. When the sprue is attached perpendicular to the casting surface, a point of heat concentration is created and the metal in this zone solidifies last. This results in a suck back of metal from the surrounding solidified zone to compensate for the metal shrinkage during solidification, leaving a void behind.

To avoid such porosity, the sprue should, ideally, be attached at an angle of 45° (flared) to the proximal casting surface.

PHARMACOLOGY

Ans.50. (C) Mu receptor partial agonist

Ref KDT pg 446

Buprenorphine is a synthetic drug that acts as a weak agonist of μ receptors.

- It is highly lipid soluble and about 25 times more potent than morphine.
- Action lasts about 6-8 hrs.
- Constipation is less marked than morphine.
- It is suitable for morphine substitution at low dependence levels but precipitates withdrawal symptoms at higher dependency reflecting its partial agonistic action.

- Sublingual route shows good efficacy and is excreted unchanged in bile.
- Nalaxone can partially reverse its effects.
- Dose = 0.3-0.6 mg i.m. or sc/ sublingually.

Ans.51. (C) Atracurium

Ref KDT, pg 154

Atracurium

- Is a competitive neuromuscular blocker, 4 times less potent than pancuronium and short acting.
- Unique feature is its inactivation in plasma by spontaneous non-enzymatic degradation or Hoffmann elimination in addition to that by cholinesterase.
- Hence, its dose need not be adjusted in patients with hepatic/renal insufficiency.
- Although it is neutral, histamine release may occur.

Ans.52. (C) Spironolactone

Ref KDT, pg 571

Important complications associated with the use of diuretics:

Spironolactone

- Drowsiness, confusion, abdominal upset.
- Hirsuitism, menstrual irregularities, impotence, gynecomastia.
- Most serious is Hypokalemia and acidosis especially in cirrhotics.

High ceiling and Thiazides

- Hypokalemia –
- Acute saline depletion and hyponatremia
- GIT and CNS disturbances – nausea, headache weaknes
- Hearing loss – ethacrynic acid
- Allergies
- Hyperuricaemia, hyperlipidemia and hypercalcaemia

Acetazolamide

- Acidosis, Hypokalemia, paresthesia, especially in COPD
- Hypersensitivity reaction
- Bone marrow depression
- It is C/I in patients with liver disease – may ppt hepatic coma

Ans.53. (C) Sucralfate

Ref KDT, pg 640

Non-systemic Antacids - are insoluble and poorly absorbed basic compounds react in stomach to form the corresponding chloride salt.

Magnesium salts–Mg trisilicate has low solubility and reactivity; 1 g can react with 10mEq acid. Silica produced by reaction with HCl is gelatinous. It is claimed to absorb and inactivate pepsin and to protect the ulcer base. All Mg compounds have laxative action. The soluble forms are used as osmotic purgatives.

Now considering the options-

- The use of Mg compds with Al is desirable as the purgative actions of Mg are balanced by the constipating effect of Al when in proper ratio.
- The use of antacids is additive to the actions of Proton pump and H2 blockers.
- However, the simultaneous use with Sucralfate reduces the efficiency of the latter, as Sucralfate (a basic aluminium salt of sulfated sucrose) requires a pH of <4 to polymerize. At this pH, it preferentially adheres to ulcer base and further precipitates protein to form a protective coat.

Antacids given concurrently reduce the efficacy of Sucralfate

Ans.54. (B) Pyridoxine

Ref KDT, pg 753

INH or Isoniazid is the drug of choice for most anti-tubercular regimes. Although well tolerated, peripheral neuritis along with other neurological manifestations (paresthesia, numbness, mental disturbances etc) are the most important dose dependent toxic effects.

These are due to interference with pyridoxine utilization and its increased excretion in urine.

Pyridoxine given prophylactically, (10mg/day) prevents neurotoxicity even with higher doses. Once developed, it is treated with 100mg/d of pyridoxine.

Other common side effects are hepatitis, rashes, fever, acne and arthralgia.

Ans.55. (B) Patients having asthma

Ref KDT, pg 460

Ibuprofen is a propionic acid derivative NSAID. Although better tolerated than aspirin, it has its share of adverse effects:

- Gastric discomfort and erosions and hence avoided in patients with peptic ulcers.
- Rashes, itching and other hypersensitivity may also precipitate aspirin induced asthma.
- Avoided in pregnant women as they cross placental barrier.
- They tend to decrease anti- hypertensive and diuretic action of thiazides, furosemide.
- They are generally avoided in patients on anti-coagulant therapy.

GENERAL MEDICINE

Ans.56. (B) PTT (partial thromboplastin time)

Please Refer KCET-07 A54

Ans.57. (B) Western blot

Ref http://en.wikipedia.org/wiki/Western_blot

Western blot (alternately, **immunoblot**) is a method to detect a specific protein in a given sample of tissue homogenate or extract.

- It uses gel electrophoresis to separate native or denatured proteins by the length of the polypeptide (denaturing conditions) or by the 3-D structure of the protein (native/ non-denaturing conditions). The proteins are then transferred to a membrane (typically nitrocellulose or PVDF), where they are probed (detected) using antibodies specific to the target protein.
- The method originated from the laboratory of George Stark at Stanford. The ***confirmatory HIV test*** employs a western blot to detect anti-HIV antibody in a human serum sample. Proteins from known HIV-infected cells are separated and blotted on a membrane as above. Then, the serum to be tested is applied in the primary antibody incubation step; free antibody is washed away, and a secondary anti-human antibody linked to an enzyme signal is added. The stained bands then indicate the proteins to which the patient's serum contains antibody.
- A Western blot is also used as the definitive test for Bovine spongiform encephalopathy (BSE, commonly referred to as 'mad cow disease').
  Some forms of Lyme disease testing employ Western blotting.

EXTRA EDGE

Remember, The name **western blot** was given to the technique by W. Neal Burnette

- Southern blot, a technique for DNA detection developed earlier by Edwin Southern.
- Detection of RNA is termed Northern blotting.

Ans.58. (C) Serial blood cultures

Ref http://www.bmj.com/cgi/reprint/333/7563/334.pdf

The incidence of infective endocarditis is approximately 1.7-6.2 cases per 100 000 patient years, although rates are higher in intravenous drug users. Men are more often affected than women (in a ratio of 2:1), and the incidence progressively increases with age. Underlying degenerative aortic and mitral valve disease now predominate over Rheumatic disease.

Clinical features:

- Up to 90% of patients present with a fever, often associated with systemic symptoms of chills, poor appetite, and weight loss.
- Heart murmurs are found in up to 85% of patients peripheral stigmata of infective endocarditis
- (Osler's nodes, Janeway lesions) are increasingly uncommon elsewhere, as patients generally present at an early stage of the disease.
- However, vasculitic phenomena such as splinter hemorrhages, Roth spots, and glomerulonephritis remain common, and emboli to brain, lung, or spleen occur in 30% of patients and are often the presenting feature.
- Mycotic aneurysms may result from systemic emboli and are seen more frequently in the developing world, where presentation is often delayed.
- Atypical presentation is common in elderly or immunocompromised patients, in whom fever is often absent.

Investigations

Given the need for prolonged antibiotic treatment in most patients with infective endocarditis, positive microbiological cultures and sensitivities are vitally important for successful management.

- ***Current guidelines recommend that three sets of blood cultures are drawn one hour apart before the introduction of antibiotic treatment***—the first two sets are positive in more than 90% of cases.
- Blood cultures are negative in 14% of cases of endocarditis, often delaying diagnosis and the start of treatment with profound impact on clinical outcome.
- Negative cultures are most commonly related to the previous administration of antibiotics, but they may also be associated with fastidious pathogens, including *Legionella, Coxiella*, the **HACEK group** (*Haemophilus* species, *Actinobacillus actinomycetemcomitans, Cardiobacterium hominis, Eikenella corrodens*, and *Kingella kingae*), and fungi such as *Candida, Histoplasma*, and *Aspergillus* species. Serological testing can be particularly useful for investigating the possibility of *Coxiella burnetti* (Q fever) and *Bartonella* infection and should be done in all patients who are initially culture negative.

Echocardiography

Transthoracic echocardiography is the initial technique of choice for investigating infective endocarditis.In low risk patients, a normal transthoracic echocardiogram provides confirmation that endocarditis is unlikely.

Modified Duke criteria

Pathological criteria

- Positive histology or microbiology of pathological material obtained at autopsy or cardiac surgery (valve tissue, vegetations, embolic fragments, or intracardiac abscess content).

Major criteria

- Two positive blood cultures showing typical organisms consistent with infective endocarditis, such as *Streptococcus viridans* and the HACEK group.

OR

- Persistent bacteraemia from two blood cultures taken > 12 hours apart or three or more positive blood cultures where the pathogen is less specific, such as *Staphylococcus aureus* and *Staph epidermidis* OR
- Positive serology for *Coxiella burnetti*, *Bartonella* species, or *Chlamydia psittaci* OR
- Positive molecular assays for specific gene targets.
- Positive echocardiogram showing oscillating structures, abscess formation, new valvular regurgitation, or dehiscence of prosthetic valves.

Minor criteria

- Predisposing heart disease.
- Fever > 38°C.
- Immunological phenomena such as glomerulonephritis, Osler's nodes, Roth spots, or positive rheumatoid factor.

- Microbiological evidence not fitting major criteria.
- Elevated C reactive protein or erythrocyte sedimentation rate.
- Vascular phenomena such as major emboli, splenomegaly, clubbing, splinter hemorrhages, petechiae, or purpura

Definite infective endocarditis

- Pathological criteria positive OR
- Two major criteria OR
- One major and two minor criteria OR
- Five minor criteria

Ans.59. (C) Hypolipidemia

Ref *http://en.wikipedia.org/wiki/Nephrotic_syndrome*

Nephrotic syndrome is a disorder where the kidneys have been damaged, causing them to leak protein from the blood into the urine. It is characterized by ***proteinuria*** (>3.5g/ day) hypoalbuminemia, and edema

The most common sign is excess fluid in the body. This may take several forms:

- Puffiness around the eyes, characteristically in the morning.
- Edema over the legs which is *pitting* (*i.e.* leaves a little pit when the fluid is pressed out, which resolves over a few seconds).
- Fluid in the pleural cavity causing pleural effusion. Fluid in the peritoneal cavity causing ascites.
- Hypertension (rarely).
- Some patients may notice foamy urine, due to a lowering of the specific gravity by the severe proteinuria. Actual urinary complaints such as hematuria or oliguria are uncommon, and are seen commonly in nephritic syndrome.
- May have features of underlying cause, such rash associated with SLE, or neuropathy with diabetes.

Examination should also exclude other causes of gross edema- especially the cardiovascular and hepatic system.

Investigations

The following are baseline, essential investigations:

- Urine sample shows Proteinuria. It is also examined for active casts; which is more a feature of active nephritis.
- Hypoalbuminemia: albumin levels in blood < 30g/L.
- High levels of cholesterol (hypercholesterolemia), specifically elevated LDL, usually with concomitantly elevated VLDL (hence ***hyperlipidemia***).
- Electrolytes, urea and creatinine (EUCs): to evaluate renal function.
  Further investigations are indicated if the cause is not clear.
  Biopsy of kidney (not usually done in children).
  Auto-immune markers (ANA, ASOT, C3, cryoglobulins, serum electrophoresis).

Ans.60. (B) IgM anti-HBc

Please Refer KCET-07 A20

Ans.61. (C) Factor VIII

Ref http://en.wikipedia.org/wiki/Cryoprecipitate

Cryoprecipitate is a blood product prepared from plasma. Each 15 mL unit contains about 100 U of factor VIII, 350 mg of fibrinogen, von Willebrand's factor, factor XIII, and fibronectin.

Indications for giving cryoprecipitate include:

- Hemophilia
- von Willebrand's disease
- hypofibrinogenaemia (low fibrinogen levels), as can occur with massive transfusions
- bleeding from excessive anticoagulation
- massive hemorrhage
- Disseminated intravascular coagulation

Ans.62. (A) Cirrhosis of liver

Please refer KCET-07 A61

Ans.63. (C) Faeco oral route

Please refer KCET-05 A51

Ans.64. (A) Trimethoprim/sulfamethoxazole

Ref http://www.walgreens.com/library/contents.jsp?doctype=1&docid=000671

This is an infection of the lungs caused by the fungus Pneumocystis carinii, now renamed Pneumocystis jiroveci.

Ans.lternative Names

Pneumocystosis; PCP; Pneumocystis jiroveci

Causes, incidence, and risk factors

PCP is a pneumonia caused by the fungal organism Pneumocystis carinii, which is widespread in the environment, and is not a pathogen (does not cause illness) in healthy individuals.

However, in individuals with weakened immune systems due to cancer, HIV/AIDS, solid organ and/or bone marrow transplantation, as well as individuals receiving chronic corticosteroids or other medications that affect the immune system, Pneumocystis carinii may lead to a lung infection.

Individuals with advanced AIDS are of particular interest, since PCP was a relatively rare infection prior to the AIDS epidemic.

PCP in the setting of AIDS usually develops slowly and is less severe—several weeks of cough, fevers, and progressive shortness of breath, especially with exertion. Individuals with PCP who do not have AIDS usually get sick faster and are more acutely ill.

Symptoms

- fever
- cough—often mild and dry

- shortness of breath—especially with exertion (activity)
- rapid breathing

Signs and tests

- X-ray of the chest may reveal lung abnormalities — yet up to 10% of individuals with PCP in the setting of AIDS may have a normal chest X-ray.
- Sputum induction: for special stains to detect Pneumocystis carinii.
- Bronchoscopy (with lavage) — if sputum induction is negative.
- Lung biopsy may rarely be needed if the above studies fail to yield a diagnosis.
- blood gases which may show decreased oxygen level in blood and helps in determining whether an individual might benefit from corticosteroids.

Treatment

- Trimethoprim-sulfamethoxazole is the ***drug of choice*** for PCP, and may be given orally or via the intravenous route depending on the severity of the illness.
- In individuals with low levels of oxygenation and moderate to severe PCP, *corticosteroids* are frequently used as well.
- Other antimicrobials used for the treatment of PCP include: pentamidine, trimethoprim-dapsone, clindamycin, primaquine, and atovaquone.

Ans.65. (D) Tetracycline

Ref KDT, pg 753

http://en.wikipedia.org/wiki/Tuberculosis_treatment#The_standard_regimen

Anti – tubercular drugs:

First line tuberculosis drugs		
3-letter	1-letter	Drug
EMB	E	ethambutol
INH	H	isoniazid
PZA	Z	pyrazinamide
RMP	R	rifampicin
STM	S	streptomycin
Second line tuberculosis drugs		
CIP	(none)	ciprofloxacin
MXF	(none)	moxifloxacin
PAS	P	*p*-aminosalicylic acid

There are six classes of second-line drugs (SLDs) used for the treatment of TB. A drug may be classed as second-line instead of first-line for one of two possible reasons: it may be less effective than the first-line drugs (*e.g.*, *p*-aminosalicylic acid); or, it may have toxic side-effects (*e.g.*, cycloserine); or it may be unavailable in many developing countries (*e.g.*, fluoroquinolones):

- aminoglycosides: *e.g.*, amikacin (AK), kanamycin;
- polypeptides: *e.g.*, capreomycin, viomycin, enviomycin;
- fluoroquinolones: *e.g.*, ciprofloxacin (CIP), moxifloxacin (MXF);
- thioamides: *e.g.* ethionamide, prothionamide.
- cycloserine (the only antibiotic in its class);

Other drugs that may be useful, but are not on the WHO list of SLDs:

- rifabutin
- macrolides: *e.g.*, clarithromycin (CLR);
- linezolid (LZD);
- thioacetazone (T);
- thioridazine;
- arginine; vitamin D; R207910

The rationale for using multiple drugs to treat TB is based on simple probability. The frequency of spontaneous mutations that confer resistance to an individual drug are well known: 1 in 10^7 for EMB, 1 in 10^8 for STM and INH, and 1 in 10^{10} for RMP

Drug Regimes

TB Category	Features	Drug regime	Duration
I	New cases: untreated, smear negative, sever forms (extra-pulmonary)	2HREZ/4HR$_3$	6 months
II	Smear positive, failure relapse and interrupted cases.	2HRZES + 1 HRZE /5 HRE$_3$	8 months
III	New cases of less	2HRZ/ 4 HR$_3$ Or 6 HE	6 months 8 months
IV	Chronic cases mostly multi-drug resistant (MDR)	RZE Or ZE + S/Etm + Cipro	12 months

Ans.66. (D) All of the above

Ref http://en.wikipedia.org/wiki/Diabetes#Signs_and_symptoms

The ***classical triad*** of diabetes symptoms is polyuria (frequent urination), polydipsia (increased thirst and consequent increased fluid intake), polyphagia (increased appetite).

- Weight loss may occur, particularly fast in type 1 (despite normal or increased eating) and irreducible fatigue.
- When the glucose concentration in the blood is high (*i.e.*, above the "renal threshold"), reabsorption of glucose in the proximal renal tubuli is incomplete, and part of the glucose remains in the urine (glycosuria). This increases the osmotic pressure of the urine and thus inhibits the resorption of water by the kidney, resulting in an increased urine production (polyuria) and an increased fluid loss. Lost blood volume will be replaced osmotically from water held in body cells, causing dehydration and increased thirst.
- Vision changes: Prolonged high blood glucose causes glucose absorption and so leads to changes in the shape of the lenses of the eyes, leading to. Blurred vision is a common

complaint leading to a diabetes diagnosis; type 1 should always be suspected in cases of rapid vision change.

- Diabetic ketoacidosis (DKA) (usually with type 1 diabetes)- an extreme state of metabolic dysregulation eventually characterized by the smell of acetone on the patient's breath, Kussmaul breathing (a rapid, deep breathing), polyuria, nausea, vomiting and abdominal pain, and any of many altered states of consciousness or arousal (*e.g.*, hostility and mania or, equally, confusion and lethargy). In severe DKA, coma (unconsciousness) may follow, progressing to death. In any form, DKA is a medical emergency and requires expert attention.
- Hyperosmolar nonketotic state, which is more common in type 2 diabetes, and is mainly the result of dehydration due to loss of body water. Often, the patient has been drinking extreme amounts of sugar-containing drinks, leading to a vicious circle in regard to the water loss.

GENERAL SURGERY

Ans.67. (C) Syphilitic

Ref http://www.similima.com/thesis25a.html

Syphilitic ulcers

- Hard chancre appears on the external genitalia 3-4 weeks after the infection in the first stage of disease. It is painless with ***punched out edges*** and is having an indurated base which feels like a button.. Lymph nodes are enlarged, mobile, firm, painless and discrete ***(shotty).*** Extra genital chancres seen in nipple, lip, tongue, and anal canal are not often indurated and may be slightly painful.
- Mucus patches and condylomas seen in secondary stage of syphilis. There is small round, superficial , transient erosions in the mouth which coalesce to form snail track ulcers.
- Gummatous ulcers-occur in tertiary syphilis. These ulcers are result of obliterative endarteritis, necrosis and fibrosis and are mostly seen over subcutaneous bones. The most characteristic feature is punched out indolent edge and yellowish gray gummatous tissue (***wash-leather slough***) in the floor. Pain and tenderness are totally absent.

EXTRA EDGE

Tuberculous ulcer

This mostly occurs from bursting of a caseous lymph node. This type of ulcer may develop when cold abscess from bone and joint tuberculosis breaks out on the surface. Usually seen in neck, axilla and groin. Edges are thin reddish blue and ***undermined***. Regional lymph nodes are enlarged non- tender and matted. The ulcer tends to be chronic.

Meleney's ulcer

These ulcers are seen in post operative wounds either after operation for perforated viscous or for drainage of empyema thoracis.

Bazin's disease: erythrocaynoid ulcer- these ulcers are associated with erythrocyanosis frigida. This is an exclusive disease of ***young women***. Abnormal amount of subcutaneous fat with thick ankles combined with an abnormally poor arterial supply are the predisposing factors. The patient finds that the ankle skin is abnormally sensitive to temperature changes. Small superficial painful nodules are formed which breakdown to form ulcers.

Martorell's ulcer: *hypertensive ulcer*- it is seen in old age and associated with atherosclerosis.A local patch of skin on the back or outer side of the calf suddenly necroses and sloughs away leaving a punched out ulcer extending down to the deep fascia. Characteristic severe pain is the prominent symptom.

Trophic ulcer or neurogenic ulcer

These ulcers have punched out edge with slough in the floor thus resembling a gummatous ulcer. Bedsore and perforating ulcers are typical examples of trophic ulcers. These ulcers develop as a result of repeated trauma to the insensitive part of the body. Commonly seen in the heel and the ball of the foot in ambulatory patients and on the buttock and on the back of the heel in non-ambulatory patients. These ulcers starts with callosity under which suppuration takes place, the pus comes out and the central hole forms the ulcer which gradually burrows through the muscles and tendons to the bone. The resulting is a callous ulcer with punched out corny edge. The surrounding skin has no sensation. The cause may be spinal or leprosy or peripheral nerve injury, diabetic neuropathy, tabes dorsalis, transverse myelitis or meningomyelocele.

Ans.68. (A) Lymphangiectasia

Please refer KCET-05 A61.

Ans.69. (D) Tracheal stenosis

Ref http://en.wikipedia.org/wiki/Tracheostomy

Tracheotomy or **tracheostomy** is a surgical procedure performed on the neck to open a direct airway through an incision in the trachea (the windpipe). (Technically, the former term, with the Greek root *tom-* meaning "to cut," refers to the procedure of cutting into the trachea, whereas the latter term, with the root *stom-* meaning "mouth," refers to the procedure of making a semi permanent or permanent opening. *Tracheostomy* can also refer to the result of the procedure, *i.e.* the opening itself.)

Complications

- **Immediate:** pneumothorax or pneumomediastinum, tracheoesophageal fistula, injury to great vessels or recurrent laryngeal nerves, bleeding, *e.g.* from divided thyroid isthmus.
- **Early:** secretions and mucus plugging, dislodged tube, respiratory arrest and post obstructive pulmonary edema (when tracheostomy is performed in a patient with longstanding upper airway obstruction, and is dependent on hypoxia drive for respiration).
- **Late:** bleeding from tracheoinnominate fistula (can be torrential), ***tracheal stenosis*** (from ischemia induced by a cuffed tracheostomy tube), tracheoesophageal fistula, tracheocutaneous fistula and cosmetic deformity must be considered upon decannulation.

Ans.70. (D) All of the above

Explained earlier, Please refer, KCET-05 A129

Ans.71. (C) Weight gain

Ref http://en.wikipedia.org/wiki/Hyperthyroidism#Signs_and_symptoms

Signs and symptoms- thyrotoxicosis

- Major clinical ***weight loss*** (often accompanied by a ravenous appetite).
- intolerance to heat, fatigue, weakness, hyperactivity, irritability, apathy.
- Depression, polyuria, and sweating.
- Additionally, patients may present with a variety of symptoms such as palpitations and arrhythmias (notably atrial fibrillation), shortness of breath (dyspnea), loss of libido, nausea, vomiting, and diarrhea.
- In the elderly, these classical symptoms may not be present and they may present only with fatigue and weight loss leading to apathetic hyperthyroidism.
- Neurological manifestations are tremor, chorea, myopathy, and periodic paralysis. Stroke of cardioembolic origin due to coexisting atrial fibrillation may be mentioned as one of the most serious complications of hyperthyroidism.
- As to other autoimmune disorders related with thyrotoxicosis, an association between thyroid disease and myasthenia gravis has been well recognized. Some very rare neurological manifestations that are reported to be dubiously associated with thyrotoxicosis are pseudotumor cerebri, amyotrophic lateral sclerosis and a Guillain-Barré-like syndrome.
- Minor ocular signs, which may be present in any type of hyperthyroidism, are eyelid retraction ("stare") and lid-lag. These "fear-like" eye-signs result from thyroid hormone's exacerbation of the action of norepinephrine.
- In hyperthyroid *stare* (***Dalrymple sign***) the eyelids are retracted upward more than normal (the normal position is at the superior corneoscleral limbus, where the "white" of the eye begins at the upper border of the iris).
- In lid-lag (***von Graefe's sign***), when the patient tracks an object downward with their eyes, the eyelid fails to follow the downward moving iris, and the same type of upper globe exposure which is seen with lid retraction occurs, temporarily.
- These signs disappear with treatment of the hyperthyroidism or treatment by certain anti-adrenergic drugs.

Neither of these ocular signs should be confused with exopthalmos (protrusion of the eyeball) which occurs in one thyroid-related disease (Graves' disease), but which is not caused by the hyperthyroid state in that disease, and is unrelated to it. Exopthalmos when present may exacerbate these signs.

So friends, we see that **weight loss and not gain** is associated with hyperthyroidism.

Ans.72. (B) Submandibular

Explained earlier, Please refer KCET-06 A96

Ans.73. (D) Haemangioma and Angioma

Ref http://en.wikipedia.org/wiki/Angioma

Angiomas are benign tumors that are made up of ***small blood vessels***. They usually appear at or near the surface of the skin. Angiomas may appear anywhere on the body, and aren't considered dangerous. However, they may be present as symptoms of another more serious disorder, such as cirrhosis. When they are removed, it is generally for cosmetic reasons.

Hemangioma is described as a congenital benign skin lesion consisting of dense, usually elevated masses of ***dilated blood vessels***". In most cases, hemangiomas will disappear over time. They are formed either during gestation or appear during the first few weeks of life and may present as a birthmark. Hemangiomas occur in approximately ten percent of Caucasians, and are less prevalent in other races. Females are three to five times more likely to have hemangiomas than males. Hemangiomas can be vivid superficial lesions, known as capillary hemangiomas (often referred to as "Strawberry Marks"), or they can be deep bluish swelling, known as cavernous hemangiomas. Sometimes they can be both superficial and deep. Approximately eighty percent are located on the face and neck, with the next most prevalent location being the liver. Although hemangiomas are benign, some serious complications can occur.

ORAL PATHOLOGY

Ans.74. (B) Tzank cell

Ref Shafer, 5th ed , pg 1128

Peri-vascular edema weakens the epithelial junction and the resultant clumps of epithelial cells are often found lying freely within these vascular spaces. These have been called the ***'Tanck cells'*** and are characterized by degenerative changes which include swelling of the nuclei and hyper chromatic staining. There is marked increase RNA content. These cells are found in freshly opened vesicles of Pemphigus, Herpes etc.

Ans.75. (D) Erythroplakia

Shafer, 5th ed , pg 133

"In contrast, to leukoplakia, erythroplakia is always associated with premalignant changes, and is therefore the most important precancerous lesion. The term was coined by Queyrat."

Ans.76. (C) Pemphigus

Ref http://www.dms.moph.go.th/inderm/Journal/Pediatric%20Dermatology/2003/vol20-no3-May/vol20-no3-p238.pdf

Paraneoplastic pemphigus (PNP) was first described in 1990 by ***Anhalt*** *et al.*

- The disease consists of cutaneous and mucocutaneous lesions, often with refractory stomatitis.
- Because it often has polymorphic features including papulosquamous, targetoid, blistering, and necrotic attributes, PNP can clinically resemble Erythema multiforme, Stevens–Johnson syndrome, lichen planus, and bullous pemphigoid.

- Histopathologically lesions demonstrate intraepithelial acantholysis, epidermal spongiosis, suprabasilar clefts, basal cell vacuolar change, and keratinocyte dyskeratosis resembling Pemphigus vulgaris.
- Biopsy from open resection of the tumor revealed an inflammatory myofibroblastic tumor. The tumor showed ***three*** diagnostic histologic patterns: a dense paucicellular fibrous tissue; a densely cellular mixed inflammatory cell infiltrate featuring lymphocytes and plasma cells with occasional organized lymphoid aggregates, a vascular stromal background, and plump spindle cells with prominent eosinophilic cytoplasm; and interweaving fascicles of spindle cells with eosinophilic cytoplasm and a vaguely myxoid stromal background.
- These features are diagnostic of inflammatory myofibroblastic tumor, which is synonymous with inflammatory fibrosarcoma according to the World Health Classification of soft tissue tumors and also known as ***inflammatory pseudotumor***. (Biopsy results rendered first by Dr. Louis Dehner from the Lauren V. **Ackerman** Laboratory of Surgical Pathology, Department of Pathology, Barnes.)

Review of previous biopsy material showed focal areas of acantholysis in oral mucosal tissue (strongly suggestive of Pemphigus).

Features of Paraneoplastic Pemphigus

Etiology	**Presence of underlying tumor**
Skin findings	Bullous, papulosquamous (Lichen planus-like), targetoid
Laboratory findings	Immunoprecipitation of specific 250, 230, 210, 190, and 170 kDa proteins Positive indirect immunofluorescence to rat bladder or monkey esophagus
Histopathology findings	Intraepithelial acantholysis, epidermal spongiosis, suprabasilar clefts, basal cell vacuolar changes, dyskeratotic keratinocytes
Associated findings	Bronchiolitis obliterans

Friends, I know this may not be very conclusive, but that's all I could gather about *Ackerman's tumor*. You may help us with a better reference!

Ans.77. (C) Pemphigus

Ref Shafer, 5th ed , pg 1126

Pemphigus vulgaris is characterized by rapid appearance of vesicles and bullae. When the bullae rupture they leave a raw, eroded, surface, similarly to when a lateral pressure is applied to relatively unaffected skin, the epithelium slides off. This is termed as ***Nikolsky's sign***, and is a characteristic sign of Pemphigus.

Remember, this is caused by Pemphigus antibodies formed against the desmoglein 1 and 3.

Ans.78. (D) Calcifying odontogenic cyst

Ref Shafer, 5th ed , pg 410

Ghost cells

- Contain nuclear remnants, cytoplasmic organelles and numerous tonofilaments.
- Larger and more vacuolated than normal keratotic squames.
- Intracellular edema with dilated degenerated organelles
- Seen in COC (Gorlin-Gold cyst), and odontomas, Ameloblastoma, ameloblastic fibro-odontoma and ameloblastic odontoma.

Ans.79. (D) None of the above

Explained earlier Please Refer KCET-06 A97

Ans.80. (C) Oral lichen planus

Explained earlier, please refer KCET-05 A88

Ans.81. (B) Oral submucous fibrosis

Ref http://www.emedicine.com/derm/topic653.htm

In 1952, Schwartz coined the term atrophica idiopathica mucosa oris to describe an oral fibrosing disease he discovered in 5 Indian women from Kenya. **Joshi** subsequently termed the condition oral submucous fibrosis (OSF) in **1953.**

- OSF is a chronic, debilitating disease of the oral cavity characterized by inflammation and progressive fibrosis of the submucosal tissues (lamina propria and deeper connective tissues). It results in marked rigidity and an eventual inability to open the mouth. The buccal mucosa is the most commonly involved site, but any part of the oral cavity can be involved, even the pharynx.
- The condition is well recognized for its malignant potential and is particularly associated with ***areca nut chewing***, the main component of betel quid. Betel quid chewing is a habit practiced predominately in Southeast Asia and India that dates back for thousands of years. The mixture of this quid, or chew, is a combination of the areca nut (fruit of the *Areca catechu* palm tree, erroneously termed betel nut) and betel leaf (from the *Piper betel,* a pepper shrub), tobacco, slaked lime (calcium hydroxide), and catechu (extract of the *Acacia catechu* tree) .Lime acts to keep the active ingredient in its freebase or alkaline form, enabling it to enter the bloodstream via sublingual absorption. Arecoline, an alkaloid found in the areca nut, promotes salivation, stains saliva red, and is a stimulant.

ETIOLOGY

The areca nut component of betel quid plays a major role in the pathogenesis of OSF. Smoking and alcohol consumption alone, habits common to areca nut chewers, have been found to have no effect in the development of OSF but their addition to areca nut chewing can be a risk for OSF. Commercially freeze-dried products such as pan masala, guthka, and mawa have higher concentrations of areca nut per chew and appear to cause OSF more rapidly than self-prepared conventional betel quid, which contains smaller amounts of areca nut.

Arecoline, an active alkaloid found in betel nuts, stimulates fibroblasts to increase production of collagen by 150%. In one study, arecoline was found to elevate the mRNA and protein expression of cystatin C, a nonglycosylated basic protein consistently up-regulated in a variety of fibrotic diseases, in a dose-dependent manner in persons with OSF. Apart from this, it has an effect of:

- Up regulation of Keratinocytes growth factor-1, insulin like growth factor-1, and interleukin 6 expressions, have all been implicated in tissue fibrogenesis.
- Arecoline is an **inhibitor of metalloproteinases** (particularly metalloproteinase-2) and a stimulator of tissue inhibitor of metalloproteinases, thus decreasing the overall breakdown of tissue collagen.
- Insertion/deletion 5A polymorphism in the promoter region of the matrix metalloproteinase-3 gene, which results in alteration of transcriptional activities.
- **Flavanoid, catechin, and tannin** in betel nuts cause collagen fibers to cross-link, making them less susceptible to collagenase degradation This results in increased fibrosis by causing both increased collagen production and decreased collagen breakdown. *OSF remains active even after cessation of the chewing habit*, suggesting that components of the areca nut initiate OSF and then affect gene expression in the fibroblasts, which then produce greater amounts of normal collagen. Chewing areca quid may also activate NF-kappaB expression, thereby stimulating collagen fibroblasts and leading to further fibrosis in persons with OSF.
- Areca nuts have also been shown to have a **high copper content**, and chewing areca nuts for 5-30 minutes significantly increases soluble copper levels in oral fluids. This increased level of soluble copper supports the hypothesis that copper acts as an initiating factor in persons with OSF by stimulating fibrogenesis through up-regulation of copper-dependent lysyl oxidase activity. Further, a significant gradual increase in serum copper levels from pre-cancer to cancer patients has been documented, which may have a role in oral fibrosis to cancer pathogenesis.

Ingestion of chilies

- A hypersensitivity reaction to chilies is believed to contribute to OSF.
- capsaicin in chilies stimulates widespread palatal fibrosis.

Genetic and immunologic processes

- A genetic component with increased frequency of HLA-A10, HLA-B7, and HLA-DR3.
- An immunologic process (Canniff, 1985). The increase in CD4 and cells with HLA-DR in OSF tissues suggests that most lymphocytes are activated and that the number of Langerhans cells is increased. These reactions may be the result either of direct stimulation from exogenous antigens, such as areca alkaloids, or of changes in tissue antigenicity that leads to an autoimmune response.
- Further, the major histocompatibility complex class I chain-related gene A (*MICA*) is expressed by keratinocytes and other epithelial cells and interacts with gamma/delta T-cells localized in the submucosa. The phenotype frequency of allele A6 of *MICA* in subjects with OSF was significantly higher and suggests a risk for OSF.
- Some authors have demonstrated increased levels of pro-inflammatory cytokines and reduced anti-fibrotic interferon gamma (IFN-gamma) in patients with OSF, which may be central to the pathogenesis of OSF.

Nutritional deficiencies

Iron deficiency anemia, vitamin B complex deficiency, and malnutrition are promoting factors that derange the repair of the inflamed oral mucosa, leading to defective healing and resultant scarring. The resulting atrophic oral mucosa is more susceptible to the effects of chilies and betel nuts.

Other significant factors

Some authors have found a high frequency of mutations in the *APC* gene and low expression of the wild-type *TP53* tumor-suppressor gene product in patients with OSF, providing some explanation for the increased risk of oral squamous cell carcinoma development in patients with OSF. Other studies have suggested that altered expression of retinoic acid receptor-beta may be related to the disease pathogenesis.

Ans.82. (B) Goldhaber

Sorry friends, no reference for this, I have searched in Shafer, Burket's, and even net but couldn't find a conclusive line. Need your help in this!

Ans.83. (B) Leukoedema

Explained earlier, please refer KCET-06 A89

Ans.84. (B) Autosomal dominant

Ref Shafer, 5th ed , pg75

Dentinogenesis imperfecta – features

- Autosomal dominant condition affects both dentition.
- Related to chromosome #4 encoding DSPP – dentin sialo phosphoprotein.
- Teeth are 'tulip' shaped and gray to yellowish-brown (amber) in color.
- Brandywine type presents with "shell teeth."

Ans.85. (A) Periapical osteitis — cellulites —abscess

Ref Shafer 5th ed , pg 669

Stages in peri-apical infection:

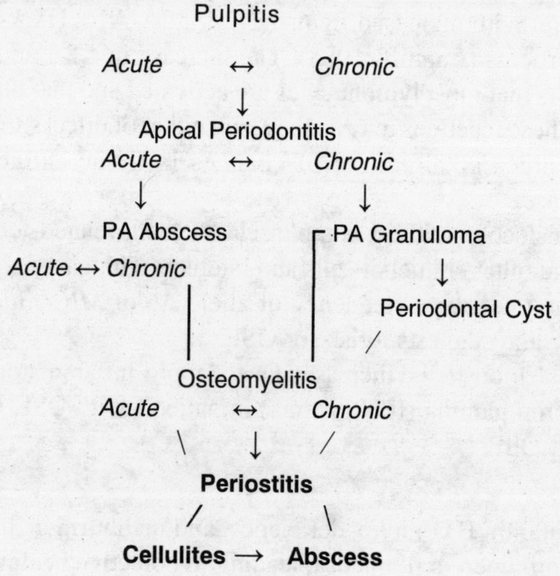

Pulpitis
Acute ↔ *Chronic*
↓
Apical Periodontitis
Acute ↔ *Chronic*
↓ ↓
PA Abscess — PA Granuloma
Acute ↔ *Chronic*
PA Granuloma ↓ Periodontal Cyst
Osteomyelitis
Acute ↔ *Chronic*
↓
Periostitis
/ \
Cellulites → Abscess

Ans.86. (B) Tongue

Ref http://en.wikipedia.org/wiki/Chlamydia

Lymphogranuloma venereum (LGV), also known as lymphopathia venerea, tropical bubo, climatic bubo, strumous bubo, poradenitis inguinales, Durand-Nicolas-Favre disease and lymphogranuloma inguinale, is a sexually transmitted disease caused by the invasive serovars L1, L2, or L3 of *Chlamydia trachomatis.*

The clinical manifestation of LGV depends on the site of entry of the infectious organism (the sex contact site) and the stage of disease progression.

- Inoculation at the mucous lining of external sex organs (penis and vagina) can lead to the **inguinal syndrome** named after the formation of buboes or abscesses in the groin (inguinal) region where draining lymph nodes are located.
- The **rectal syndrome** arises if the infection takes place via the rectal mucosa (through anal sex) and is mainly characterized by proctocolitis symptoms.
- The **pharyngeal syndrome** is rare, starts after infection of pharyngeal tissue and bubos in the neck region can occur. Intra- oral lesions are extremely rare and if present involve the tongue, buccal mucosa etc.

Ans.87. C) Actinomycosis

Please refer KCET-06 A95

ORAL MEDICINE AND RADIOLOGY

Ans.88. (A) To avoid image magnification

Ref White and Pharoah, 5th ed , pg 90

Paralleling technique is the preferred method for making intra-oral radiographs. The film is placed parallel to the long axis of the tooth. The procedure minimizes image distortion by placing the film towards the middle of the oral cavity, away from the teeth (and hence increasing object-film distance) . Since we know,

$$\text{Magnification} = \frac{\text{Object-film distance}}{\text{Focal spot- object distance}}$$

Hence there is some degree of magnification and unsharpness with this technique. To overcome this, the use of long cone (open ended cylinder) has been utilized to further increase the Fs-O Distance. This directs only the most central and parallel rays of the beam to the film and improves the sharpness of image.

Ans.89. (D) Nucleons

Ref White and Pharoah, 5th ed , pg 4

Radiation is the transmission of energy through space. It may occur in two forms:

(a) **Particulate:** atomic/sub-atomic particles moving at high velocity.

e.g. alpha (He^{+2}), beta particles, cathode rays (electrons), protons.

Remember, *LET (linear energy transfer)* refers to the loss of energy from a particle when it strikes matter. Alpha particles have a higher LET than beta but a lower penetration power. Also, beta particles are used for treatment of skin lesions.

(b) **Electromagnetic radiation:** when the velocity of an electrically charged particle is altered (in electric or magnetic fields) this type of radiation are produced. For *e.g.* Gamma rays, x-rays, U-V rays, visible light, infra-red rays, microwaves etc.

Remember, Gamma waves have high energy while U-V rays have high wavelengths.

Ans.90. (D) 0.074 mGy

Ref White and Pharoah, 5th ed , pg 53

Thyroid dose

From OPG – 0.074 mGy
From 21-film IOPA – 0.94 mGy
From x-ray chest – 0.01 mGy
From cervical spine x-ray – 5.5 mGy
Also remember,

Exposures

- Mean active bone marrow - 0.01 mSv for single OPG and 0.142 mSv for 21 IOPA
- Gonad dose - 0.001 mGy for both OPG and 21 IOPA

(1Sv = 1 Gy)

Ans.91. (C) Submentovertex view

Ref White and Pharoah, 5th ed , pg 224

AREA	BEST PROJECTION
Mandibular body	True lateral oblique, OPG
Coronoid process	Water's view, Lateral oblique (ramus)
Condyle (head , neck)	Reverse Towns
Nasal bones	Lateral Cephalogram
Zygomatic arch	**Sub-mento vertex (SMV)**
Sinus - - Maxillary - Frontal - Sphenoid	Water's view Laterla ceph, SMV Lateral ceph, PA
Zygoma	Water's
Orbit	PA view

Ans.92. (B) Red

Ref: White and Pharoah 5th ed pg 98-99.

Dark room processing procedures/equipment

- The room should be conveniently spaced with at least 4 x 5 feet in dimensions
- Light proofing: a light-tight door or a door less maze. Well ventilated, temperature control.
- Safelighting: room should have both white light and safelighting Safelight is a low intensity *illumination of relatively* ***long wavelength (red)*** that does not rapidly affects open film while permitting operator to see well enough. It is best to place one safelight above the work area on the wall behind the processing tank and somewhat right to the fixing tank. A 15-watt bulb mounted at least 4 feet above the surface is ideal to minimize fogging.
- x- ray films are very sensitive to blue-green region of visible spectrum and less sensitive to yellow and red wavelengths. Accordingly, a red GBX-2 filter is recommended as a safelight that transmits only light at red end of spectrum. The older ML-2 filters(yellow light) are seldom used now. Film handling under safelight should be limited to about 5 min.

Ans.93. (B) Polyacrylamide gel

Ref.http://translate.google.com

Often we are confronted with two pathologies, the *periapical cyst and chronic apical periodontitis* which manifest themselves in clinically similar ways, so that the value of complementary tests assume even greater importance. Tests of pulp vitality could be absolutely reliable if performed correctly, except in certain situations which the dentist should detect and avoid. However, if this is not possible, he should be able to evaluate the impact they have on the results of the test. The combination of thermal cold and electrical tests is the best way of detecting teeth with the pulp vitality still intact.

It is radio logically impossible to establish an absolute and objective differentiation between a periapical cyst and an apical granuloma. Some authors such as *Grossman or Wood* were daring enough to make an approximate radiographic diagnosis, indicating that the cyst presented more defined limits and was even bordered by a more sclerotic bone area, and therefore, showed a more radio opaque image. Other elements for this differentiation could be the separation of the root apexes caused by the pressure of the cyst liquid, or even the possibility of observing or palpating this fluctuation. It is also claimed that the larger the size, the higher the probability that the lesion had evolved, and therefore transformed itself from a primitive granuloma into a cyst through the proliferation of the Malassez rest and posterior lysis of part of this structure.

ADVANCED RADIOLOGY

In one study by Shrout in the University of Washington, they managed to find statistically significant differences between the radiometric analyses of these periapical lesions. More specifically, they found that the histogram of apical granulomas had a larger range of brown and less grey scale than cysts. This suggested the possibility of using digital analysis to differentiate between lesions that were radiographically indistinguishable to normal vision.

Other diagnostic techniques

Some authors, aware of the lack of efficient diagnostic alternatives to exploratory surgery and histopathological study of the lesion (the only test, on the other hand, that guarantees the diagnosis), investigated alternative forms of diagnosis such as the injection of contrast medium into the bone rarefaction, or the electrophoretic analysis of the liquid contained inside the lesion. This method consists of studying the liquid obtained by transdental aspiration using the technique of electrophoresis with ***poly-acrylamide gel***. When the result is a light blue colour it is considered as granulomas, but if the colour obtained is dark blue, intense or blackish, (due to proteins, generally albumin and gamma globulin), a cyst is identified.

Ans.94. (B) Lichen planus

Ref Shafer, 5th d , pg 1103

Grinspan's syndrome is a clinical triad involving lichen planus, hypertension and diabetes mellitus described by Grinspan.

Ans.95. (A) Factor VIII

Please refer KCET-07 A54

Ans.96. (C) Multiple intestinal polyps

Refhttp://www.emedicine.com/med/byname/peutz-jeghers-syndrome.htm

Peutz-Jeghers syndrome

- Autosomal dominant inherited disorder characterized by intestinal hamartomatous polyps in association with mucocutaneous melanocytic macules.
- Although the intestinal lesions are hamartomas, patients with Peutz-Jeghers syndrome have a 15-fold increased risk of developing intestinal cancer compared to that of the general population.
- Cancer location includes gastrointestinal and extraintestinal sites.
- The syndrome was described in 1921 by Peutz, who noted a relationship between the intestinal polyps and the mucocutaneous macules in a Dutch family.

Ans.97. (D) Odontogenic Keratocyst

Explained ahead, please refer A144

Ans.98. (D) Arthrography

Ref Burket's, 10th ed , pg 287

Physical examination of TMJ includes –

- **INSPECTION:** facial asymmetry, swelling, opening pattern- maximum opening and other mandibular range of motion.
- **PALPATION:** muscles, lymph nodes, joint.
- **PROVOCATION:** static pain test, tooth clenching test.
- **INTRA-ORAL examination:** signs of parafunction (lip bite, Bruxism, linea alba).

While arthrography forms an important tool in TMJ examination it is utilized only when clinical assessment suggests a progressive pathologic condition of TMJ or an inconclusive diagnosis is reached.

Ans.99. (C) Fluorescent staining of cytology smears

Ref http://www.postgradmed.com/issues/2000/03_00/nadelman.htm

Herpes simplex infection generally occurs in two phases: the initial, primary infection, followed by secondary, recurrent disease at the same site. In the first phase, the virus spreads by close person-to-person contact with lesions or mucosal secretions (*e.g.*, saliva, cervical discharge) as well as by respiratory droplets. Contrary to previous belief, the virus can be transmitted during asymptomatic periods, although the risk of transmission is higher during symptomatic reactivation.

Diagnosis

- Most cases of herpes simplex infection are recognized by the morphologic characteristics of the disease (small, grouped vesicles on erythematous bases, which then become pustules, umbilicate, and later crust).
- Diagnostic tests are used when vesicles appear in unusual sites and configurations. The Tzanck test is the most commonly used diagnostic tool for detecting a herpes infection. When viewed under the microscope, infected epithelial cells collected from herpetic vesicles demonstrate typical characteristics.
- Nuclear changes include centrally located eosinophilic masses surrounded by a clear halo (Cowdry type A bodies), and the cells have a perinuclear ground-glass appearance. Infected cells also fuse to become multinucleated giant cells, which are characteristic of herpes infection.
- These changes, however, are not unique to herpes simplex. Therefore, the Tzanck test cannot be used to differentiate HSV from varicella-zoster virus.
- ***Fluorescent staining of cytology smears is more sensitive*** (83%) than routine cytological smears using Giemsa , Wright's or Papanicolaou's stain.

  Ref Burkitt's,10th ed pg 53
- Direct immunofluorescence studies of biopsy specimens from skin, liver, or brain allow more specific detection of the virus. With indirect immunofluorescence, a fourfold rise in IgG titer in paired serum samples is needed to establish a diagnosis of primary herpes.
- Culture is the most definitive method for detecting herpes infection.

Ans.100. (A) 1 to 6 minutes

*Ref*http://www.healthatoz.com/healthatoz/Atoz/common/standard/transform.jsp?requestURI=/healthatoz/Atoz/ency/bleeding_time.jsp

Bleeding time is a crude test of hemostasis (the arrest or stopping of bleeding). It indicates how well platelets interact with blood vessel walls to form blood clots.

There are four methods to perform the bleeding test.

Methods

- The Ivy method – < 5 min (8 min according to some)
- Template - < 8 min
- Modified template - < 10 min
- Duke methods - <3 min

The Ivy method is the traditional format for this test, where a blood pressure cuff is placed on the upper arm and inflated to 40 mm Hg. A lancet or scalpel blade is used to make a stab wound on the underside of the forearm.

The template and modified template methods are variations of the Ivy method. For the Duke method, a nick is made in an ear lobe or a fingertip is pricked to cause bleeding. As in the Ivy method, the test is timed from the start of bleeding until bleeding is completely stopped.

Ans.101. (B) Kaposi's sarcoma

Please refer KCET-07 A91

Ans.102. (A) 75% to 100% hemoglobin S

Ref http://www.nlm.nih.gov/medlineplus/ency/article/003639.htm

Sickle-cell disease

- Group of genetic disorders caused by sickle hemoglobin (Hgb S or Hb S). In many forms of the disease, the red blood cells change shape, usually looking much like that of a banana, upon deoxygenation because of polymerization of the abnormal sickle haemoglobin.
- This process damages the red blood cell membrane, and can cause the cells to become stuck in blood vessels. This deprives the downstream tissues of oxygen and causes ischemia and infarction, which may cause organ damage, such as stroke. The disease is chronic and lifelong.

The term "disease" is applied here since the inherited abnormality causes a pathological condition that can lead to death and severe complications. Not all inherited variants of hemoglobin are detrimental, a concept known as genetic polymorphisms.

- Patients with sickle-cell anemia can have symptoms that vary in severity, with typical hemoglobin levels of ***6-9 g/dl***.
- Reticulocyte counts are elevated, reflecting new red blood cells replacing the rapidly destroyed older cells (red blood cell life span is markedly reduced in this disease).
- Often, the white blood cell and platelet counts are elevated, and these cells may contribute to vaso-occlusion. Because of its narrow vessels and function in clearing defective red blood cells, the spleen is frequently affected.
- It is usually infarcted before the end of childhood in individuals suffering from sickle-cell anemia. This *autosplenectomy* increases the risk of infection from encapsulated organisms; preventive antibiotics and vaccinations are recommended for those with such asplenia.
- Sickle-cell anemia is caused by a point mutation in the α-globin chain of haemoglobin, replacing the amino acid *glutamic acid* with the less polar amino acid *valine* at the sixth position of the â chain.
- The association of two wild-type α-globin subunits with two mutant α-globin subunits forms hemoglobin S, which polymerizes under low oxygen conditions causing distortion of red blood cells and a tendency for them to lose their elasticity.

http://en.wikipedia.org/wiki/Sickle_cell_disease

Many different types of hemoglobin (Hb) exist. The most common ones are HbA, HbA2, HbF, HbS, HbC, Hgb H, and Hgb M. Healthy adults only have significant levels of HbA and HbA2

In adults, these hemoglobin molecules make up the following percentages of total hemoglobin:

Hgb A1: 95% to 98%

Hgb A2: 2% to 3%

Hgb F: 0.8% to 2%

Hgb S: 0%

Hgb C: 0%

In infants and children, these hemoglobin molecules make up the following percentages of total hemoglobin:

Hgb F (newborn): 50% to 80%

Hgb F (6 months): 8%

Hgb F (over 6 months): 1% to 2%

In sickle cell disease 75 – 100 % of Hb is of S type
Whereas, in sickle cell trait it is only 20- 45 %

Refer Burket's, 10th ed, pg 433

PERIODONTICS

Ans.103. (B) Langerhans cells

Ref Carranza, pg10

Gingiva consists of two types of cells:

Keratinocytes: these are the principal cells found in basal and suprabasal layers which differentiate to form the keratinized layer of epithelium. They undergo progressive flattening ,production of keratohyaline granules and disappearance of nucleus.

Non-keratinocytes: these are 'clear cells' which include Langerhans cells, Merkel cells and melanocytes.

Now, the clear cells are either dendritic or non-dendritic. The word dendritic refers to cells involved in immune/ defence mechanism (antigen presenting cells).

- **Melanocytes:** are dendritic cells located in basal and spinous layers of epithelium. They contain tyrosinase and synthesize melanin. Melanin granules are phagocytosed and contained within cells called melanophores.
- **Langerhans cells:** are dendritic cells located among keratinocytes at all suprabasal levels. They belong to mononuclear phagocyte system (reticulo-endothelial system) and are derived from modified monocytes from the bone marrow. They are an important component in immune reaction as antigen-presenting cells for lymphocytes. They also contain g-specific granules (Birbeck's granules and have marked ATPase activity).
- **Merkel cells** are large oval cells found in the skin of vertebrates. They are non-dendritic cells associated with the sense of touch.

Ans.104. (C) Leukemia

Ref Shafer, 5th ed , pg 1064

Friends, the key word here is **"function of neutrophils"**. While all other conditions affect the functioning of neutrophils, Leukemia is a disorder mainly of lymphocytes and monocytes with erythrocyte and thrombocyte abnormality.

Chediak-Higashi Syndrome: described by Cezar in 1943, it is an Autosomal recessive immunodeficiency, wherein the CHS gene affects the secretary function of lysosomes of leukocytes, dense bodies of platelets, azurophilic granules of neutrophils and melanosomes of Melanocytes. The disease is often fatal in childhood with terminal infections(Staph, S.pyogenes,) and lymphomas,

Oral manifestations: include ulcerations and sever gingivitis, related to leucopenia. Birbeck granules and Dohle bodies in the leukocytes are the hallmark of this disorder. Pancytopenia ensues and child rarely reaches past 10 yrs of age.

In **cyclic neutropenia**, the 'cycle' commonly occurs every *three* weeks although it may be more in some. The blood count is near normal for first 4-5 days then falls rapidly for 2days and starts to rise in next 4-5 days.

Ans.105. (A) Circular and dento gingival

Ref Carranza, 9th ed , pg 264

Stage II or early lesion is characterized by increased collagen destruction. Around 70% of the collagen is destroyed around the cellular infiltrate. The main fibers affected are *circular* and the *dento-gingival* assemblies.

Ans.106. (D) Most efficient activator of complement system

Remember, IgM is a more potent activator of the complement system than IgG

For details, Pleases refer KCET-07 24

Ans.107. (B) 1.97 mm

Ref Carranza, 9th ed , pg 348

The distance between the apical end of calculus and the alveolar crest in human periodontal pockets is the most constant at **1.97 mm +/- 33.16%**.

The distance form the attached plaque and bone is always between 0.5 – 2.7mm.

Ans.108. (B) Thumb grasp

Ref Carranza, 9th ed , pg 597

INSTRUMENT GRASP

A proper grasp is essential for precise control of movements made during periodontal instrumentation. The various grasps are-

- **Standard pen grasp:** only thumb and index finger used while the side of the middle finger rests on the shank.
- **Modified pen grasp:** most effective and stable due to 'tripod effect'. The thumb, index finger and middle fingers are used. The thumb rests between the middle and index fingers. This enables the clinician to precisely control and roll the instrument and enhanced tactile sensitivity.

- **Palm and thumb grasp:** useful for stabilizing instruments during sharpening and for manipulating air and water syringes. Not recommended for periodontal instrumentation as it lacks maneuverability and tactile sensitivity.

Thus, thumb grasp has not been mentioned as an instrument grasp.

Ans.109. (C) 70 degrees

Although ideal is 60, it may be 60-70 degrees

For details Please refer KCET-05 A108

Ans.110. (C) Heterogeneous nucleation

Ref Carranza, 9th ed , pg187

Theories in mineralization of calculus:

1. Local rise in Ca and PO_4 ions concentration
   - Rise in pH of saliva that may attract Ca ion precipitation.
   - Colloidal proteins in saliva bind Ca and P ions.
   - Phosphatase form plaque, epithelial cells increases local PO_4 conc. and hence secondary Ca deposition.
2. Seeding agents induce small foci of calcification that coalesce to form a calcified mass. This is known as '***epitactic concept***' or ***heterogeneous nucleation***. This seeding agent usually is a carbo-protein complex.

Ans.111. (C) Phantom bite

Ref http://www.psy-world.com/news79.php

Some patients suffer from an uncomfortable sensation mainly affecting corrected dentition which is known as the **phantom bite syndrome**. Clinically there is no detectable abnormality, dental interventions are unsuccessful, and the condition is refractory to most treatments including psychotherapy. Tricyclic antidepressants can be effective, however their anticholinergic side-effects usually prevent the patients' compliance and the treatment is not followed correctly at the right doses.

Ans.112. (B) Gingival crevicular fluid

Ref Carranza, 9th ed , pg 185

Saliva is the source of mineralization of supra gingival plaque while the serum Transudate called gingival crevicular fluid (GCF) furnishes the minerals for sub-gingival. The salivary proteins present in supra gingival are lacking in the sub gingival.

Also remember, hydroxyapatite is the bulk of supragingival calculus detected most frequently followed by octa-calcium phosphate.

Brushite is more common in mandibular anterior region while magnesium whitlokite in the posterior areas.

Ans.113. (A) Increased severity of gingival inflammation

Ref http://www.thejcdp.com/issue018/gokhan/gokhan.pdf

Cyclic adenosine monophosphate (**cAMP**, **cyclic AMP** or 3'-5'-cyclic adenosine monophosphate) is a molecule that is important in many biological processes;

- It is derived from adenosine triphosphate (ATP).
- cAMP is a second messenger, used for intracellular signal transduction, such as transferring the effects of hormones like glucagons and adrenaline, which cannot get through the cell membrane.
- Its main purpose is the activation of protein kinases; it is also used to regulate the passage of Ca^{2+} through ion channels.

cAMP synthesis and decomposition

cAMP is synthesized from ATP by adenylate cyclase which is located at the cell membranes. Adenylate cyclase is activated by the hormones glucagon and adrenaline through the activation of adenylate cyclase stimulatory G (G_s)-coupled receptors and inhibited by agonists of adenylate cyclase inhibitory G (G_i)-protein coupled receptors. Liver adenylate cyclase responds more strongly to glucagon, and muscle adenylate cyclase responds more strongly to adrenaline.

cAMP decomposition into AMP is catalyzed by the enzyme phosphodiesterase.

Ref http://en.wikipedia.org/wiki/c-AMP

- The increased frequency of tooth loss in diabetics has been associated with periodontitis, its accompanying tooth mobility, and deep pocket formation.
- The effects of metabolic diabetes are multifaceted including plaque microbiology, vascular changes, and alterations in the metabolism of collagen tissues and in immunological responses.
- Compared to non-diabetic controls, glucose concentration in blood and gingival fluid in diabetics is higher; this results in qualitative changes in bacteria.
- ***The concentrations of the nucleotide, cAMP (adenosine 3',5'-cyclic monophosphate), in diabetics is reduced and cAMP suppresses inflammation***. Despite all these studies, the exact role of microorganisms in tooth loss is unknown.
- Studies in Type 2 diabetic patients with periodontal disease that have examined the leukocyte function have shown impairment in chemotaxis and phagocytic capabilities.
- These contribute to the development of periodontitis. Another finding in Type 2 diabetics with periodontitis is a significant increase in the concentration of immunoglobulins.
- Human leukocyte antigen complexes and cytokines also increase in periodontal diseases. The most important potential consequence of these alterations is the stimulation of osteoclastic resorption.
- Diabetes itself is not a direct cause of periodontal disease, but rather it facilitates the development of gingivitis and periodontitis through local pathological changes in the oral cavity.

Ans.114. (A) Helper T lymphocytes

Pleases refer previous papers

Ans.115. (C) Apical

Ref Carranza, 9th ed , pg 43

Cementum formation is a continuous process that varies throughout the life. It is most rapid in the apical regions, where it compensates for the tooth eruption.

Thickness- coronally – 16-60 μm

Apical third- 150-200 μm

Ans.116. (D) Lamina dura

Ref Carranza, 9th ed , pg 45

The alveolar process is the portion of maxilla and mandible that forms and supports the teeth. It consists of:

- An external plate of compact cortical bone.
- Inner socket wall called as the alveolar bone proper seen as ***lamina dura*** in the radiographs and histologically as ***Cribriform plate.***
- Interdental septum consists of cancellous supporting bone enclosed within compact border.

Ans.117. (B) Ibuprofen

ref http://www.walgreens.com/library/contents.jsp?doctype=10&docid=000024 Standard Nonsteroidal Anti-inflammatory Drugs (NSAIDs).

NSAIDs are agents that block factors that cause inflammation and pain.

- Over-the-counter NSAIDs include aspirin, ibuprofen (Motrin IB, Advil, Nuprin, Rufen), naproxen (Aleve), ketoprofen (Actron, Orudis KT).
- Prescription NSAIDs include ibuprofen (Motrin), naproxen (Naprosyn, Anaprox), diclofenac (Voltaren), tolmetin (Tolectin), ketoprofen (Orudis, Oruvail), indomethacin (Indocin).

The agents have been investigated not only for pain relief in periodontal disease but in slowing the disease process. NSAIDs block inflammatory enzymes triggered by cytokines, the important immune factors in periodontal disease. A number of NSAIDs have been investigated and have been shown to reduce gingivitis and slow progression of periodontal disease.

In one study, long-term use of oral flurbiprofen (Ansaid) resulted in significantly lower bone loss, although disease progression returned when the drug was stopped.

CONSERVATIVE DENTISTRY AND ENDODONTICS

Ans.118. (D) Improves retention of restoration

Ref Vimal Sikri, pg 290

Pins are used in restorative dentistry to provide support and materials and resist the dislodgment. They have been shown to improve the retention of the restorative material however same cannot be said about the resistance. Although, pin improves retention of amalgam, they tend to weaken it. (Markley, 1958)

Indications of pins

- Aid in retention in badly broken teeth.
- As foundations in full or partial ceramic crowns.
- In teeth with guarded prognosis, temporary restoration can be given.

Direct pins are generally 3 types – cemented, friction-lock (Goldstein, 1966), threaded pins (Going, 1966).

EXTRA EDGE

Remember certain ***Rules***,

- 1 pin per missing axial wall
- 1mm of sound dentin around the pin hole
- 0.5mm of distance form DEJ
- Pin should be parallel to the nearest external surface
- Ideal ratio of pin length in rest and dentin is 1:1
- A minimum of 2 mm inter-pin distance

Ans.119. (D) All of the above

Ref Skinner's, pg 342.

While certain amount of mercury is necessary to bind the mass together, excess (more than 55%) can be detrimental to the life of the amalgam restoration. Slow setting restorations develop their mechanical properties late as compared to conventional fast set. Hence, premature loading of these restorations with the masticatory forces, deteriorate the matrix and result in amalgam failure. Excess mercury also results in formation of corrosion products and subsequent loss of surface integrity. Thus, the incidence of marginal fracture is significantly higher in restorations with higher Hg content.

Ans.120. (A) Zinc oxide eugenol

Ref Skinner's, pg 465

Substitution of certain portion of eugenol with EBA in ZnO eugenol cement result in substantial increase in strength from 3-4 MPa to 50-55MPa.

Remember, ADA specification no. 30 addresses to ZnO eugenol.

Type I is used for temporary rest, whereas type II for permanent.

Ans.121. (B) 7.3

Explained earlier, please refer KCET-06 A120

Ans.122. (C) A periodontitis exists

Ref Grossman, pg 5

Percussion test enables one to evaluate the status of the periodontium surrounding a tooth. The tooth is struck with a quick, moderate, blow, initially with a low intensity first by the operator's fingers and later handle of the instrument.

A severe response indicates periodontitis but may be misleading if used alone. It is preferred to change the sequence to eliminate patient bias. It is used in conjunction with other tests like palpation, mobility and depressibilty.

Remember, this test is the indicator of periodontal involvement *with or without* pulpal infection. Hence, the tooth may still be vital and sensitive to percussion at the same time.

Ans.123. (A) 425 - 4750F

Ref Grossman, pg 139

Glass beads sterilizer is a modification of the original hot-salt sterilizer where the beads taken are less than 1mm diameter. Both function at the same temperature range of <u>218 – 246 ^{0}C (425-474 ^{0}F).</u>

Remember, that temp is higher on the outer rim and decreases progressively towards the center. At least ¼ inch of the instrument should be immersed beneath the salt.

RC instruments – 5sec while cotton pellets and points for 10sec.

Ans.124. (A) 26 mm

Ref Wheeler's, pg 155

The maxillary canine is the longest tooth in human arch and is roughly around 27mm (10 + 17). The mandibular canine also averages same at 27 mm (11 + 16).

Remember, Mandibular canine has a longer crown length than maxillary while the latter has a longer average root length.

Ans.125. (C) No characteristic feature, symptom free

Ref Grossman, pg 72

Internal resorption is a slow or fast progressive resorptive process occurring in the dentin of the pulp chamber or the root canals. It is a result of osteoclasts mediated resorption which may be filled by osteoid tissue. The patient may have a history of trauma and the condition is ***totally asymptomatic*** except for a reddish area called as "pink spot" in the crown. The treatment includes conventional pulp extirpation.

Ans.126. (A) Ultraviolet light

Please refer, KCET -07 A129

Ans.127. (B) Oscillating motion

Ref Grossman, pg 211.

Engine driven instruments may be used for opening root canals but not for canal preparation except as a last resort. Two engine-driven contra-angle hand pieces are available, namely, the Giromatic and the Racer.

The **<u>Giromatic hand piece</u>** activates a stainless steel barbed broach or reamer in the root canal through a 90 degree reciprocating arc at a speed up to 1000 cycles /min. this instrument may pack the dentinal shavings into the canal. It is also less effective for preparing root canals. The time taken was longer and large numbers of ledges were created.

<u>The Racer</u> uses a standard file and oscillates the file in the root canal. The instrument length can be adjusted to the working length. A major disadvantage of this instrument is that debris may be forced ahead of the instrument, with resultant clogging of the canal or pushing of debris into peri-apical tissues.

Remember, when engine-driven instruments are used, access to the apical foramen must always be made with hand reamers or files.

Ans.128. (C) GIC II

Ref Skinners, pg 449

Of the given choices, silver amalgam when used without a base causes marked pulpal reaction because of its metallic conduction of heat, and also by unreacted mercury that may leach out of restoration. The composite resin, too, should not be applied directly in deep cavities as the etched surface is open and the unreacted acid from the resin may cause pulp damage.

Silicate, by virtue of its extremely low pH (<3) is highly irritant to the dentin and pulp.

GIC type II, shows a far less pulpal response compared to above mentioned restorations.

Ans.129. (B) 2 to 3 %

Sorry friends, no reference! Need your help on this..!

Ans.130. (C) 35 to 50%

Ref Skinners, pg 237

Universally, used acid is phosphoric acid at a concentration between 37-50 %. Concentration greater than 50% results in formation of a monocalcium phosphate monohydrate that inhibits further dissolution. Similarly, a concentration of less than 37% results in formation of a dihydrate.

Remember, Time for etching is ideally <u>15 sec</u>. Resin tags reach a depth of <u>10-20 um</u>;. Bond strengths of etched enamel ranges from <u>16-22 MPa</u>.

Ans.131. (A) Positive

Ref Sturdevant, 4th ed, pg 335

The rake angle is the most important design characteristics of a bur blade. The more positive the rake angle the more is the cutting effectiveness of bur. However, the tool life reduces and clogging frequently occurs. The negative rake has a greater metal and hence used for cutting hard, brittle materials (thus high ***efficiency***).

Remember, positive rake angle refers to rake face trailing the radial line while a negative rake angle refers to the rake face ahead of radial line.

ORAL AND MAXILLO-FACIAL SURGERY

Ans.132. (D) All of the above

Ref Melamed 4th ed, pg 269

Methemoglobinemia is a condition in which a cyanosis like state develops n absence of cardiac or respiratory abnormalities. The commonly implicated LA for this are articaine and prilocaine. The condition is seen in individuals with the deficiency of enzyme *met hemoglobin reductase.*

Clinical symptoms arise when level of 1.5-3.0gm/dl is reached. Treatment usually includes 100% oxygen administration. Injecting methylene blue or ascorbic acid is also advocated.

Also Remember, levels of Lignocaine in blood and associated symptoms.

- 0.5 – 2.0 μg/ ml – normal level no features
- 0.5 – 4.0 μg /ml – Anticonvulsant action
- 4.5 – 7.0 μg /ml – CNS depression (excitation)
- 5.0 – 10.0 μg/ml – ECG alterations, myocardial depression
- 7.5 – 10.0 μg /ml – tonic-clonic seizures
- > 10.0 μg /ml – Generalized CNS depression, cardiac arrest, asystoles, massive peripheral vasodilatation.

Ans.133. (A) Neck of condyle

Ref Killey's, 4th ed, pg 10.

Forces of range **425 lbs** produce consistent fractures of condyle neck. This is regarded as a safety mechanism which protects the patient from serious injuries to middle fossa. Symphysial fracture required a force up to 800-900 lbs. Maxillary fractures occur at forces as low as 140 lbs.

Remember, the question referred to the ***weakest portion*** of mandible where fracture occurs. The most common site for fracture in recent world is the **angle area**.

Ans.134. (A) Bronchoscopy

Foreign bodies (endo instruments, tooth/parts of tooth,) may be aspirated by the patient inadvertently which may lodge themselves in the left or right lung. These can be visualized and retrieved using a bronchoscope.

An arthroscope is used to visualize closed spaces like TMJ joint while gastroscope is used for stomach inspection.

Ans.135. (B) Local irritation

Ref Malamed 4th ed , pg 247.; Neelima Malik , pg 702

Although pain following LA is common, a typical ***burning sensation*** resembling local irritation is far more common. This may be due to altered pH of the LA solution, or due to contamination of cartridge, or if the solution is injected rapidly.

The pH of LA solution is usually in the range of 5 but with addition of vasoconstrictor the pH falls to 3.

Other local complications:

- Pain on injection – careless technique, dull tip, rapid injection.
- Needle breakage – rare nowadays with disposable needles. Sudden unexpected movement of the patient is the most common cause. Use of proper gauge needles (25) and careful technique may help in avoiding this complications.
- Trismus – trauma/infection to muscles or blood vessels in the infra-temporal region; use of aseptic and careful technique may prevent this.
- Hematoma – arterial or venous puncture. sound knowledge of the anatomy, use of a short needle is advocated especially in PSA block. Remember, nicking an artery results in immediate Hematoma while vein/pterygoid plexus may take few days for the same.

- Infection/edema/soft tissue injury – poor technique by the dentist or self-induced injury by the patient due to anesthetic effect. Lip biting is usually seen in children.
- Post-anesthetic lesions – include herpetic and recurrent Apthous ulcers.

Ans.136. (D) All above

Ref http://www.llu.edu/llu/dentistry/journal/sum03/facultyprofile.html

Dr. Jorgensen was born in 1894 on the island of Fyn, in Denmark. To eliminate emotional barriers to dentistry, Dr. Leffingwell advocated the intravenous administration of barbiturate, the substitution of scopolamine for atropine, and the addition of the narcotic analgesic meperidine at a time when meperidine was not recommended for intravenous administration.

Dr. Leffingwell's credentials and reputation among medical anesthesiologists aided in the acceptance of the ***Loma Linda Technique (Dr. Jorgensen's preference), but better known as "The Jorgensen Technique***." In his studies he noted that time taken for 10 mg bolus of pentobarbital to travel from the Cubital Fossa to the brain is less than 20 seconds. Since 10 mg of pentobarbital (Nembutal) rarely had much sedative effect, by slowly and sequentially injecting increments of that amount while both observing and engaging the patient in "small talk," the injections could safely be carried to the first signs of sedation, designated as a baseline, and stopped. Varying widely among individuals, it is constant and reproducible for any one individual. Meperidine mixed with scopolamine was next administered intravenously.

Ans.137. (D) Amoxicillin

Ref KDT, pg 710.

While aminophylline , epinephrine and atropine are all considered emergency drugs , amoxicillin is an antibiotic that does not have any emergency potential. The t ½ of amoxicillin is 1hr.

Ans.138. (B) Incisive and mental nerve

Ref Malamed, 4th ed , pg 215

Mandibular nerve blocks

Nerve Block	Nerve anesthetized	Area anesthetized
1. Inferior alveolar	Inferior alveolar (IAN) , incisive, mental, lingual (commonly)	Mandibular teeth to midline; body of manible, buccal mucosa anterior to first molar , lingual soft tissues, ant 2/3rd of tongue
2. Buccal / long buccal nerve block	Buccal (branch of anterior div of mandibular)	Soft tissues and periosteum buccal to mandibular molar teeth
3.Mental block	Mental, a terminal branch of IAN	Buccal mucosa anterior to mental foramen to the midline; skin of lower lip and chin,
4. Incisive nerve block	Mental + incisive	Area by mental nerve + pulps of canine, premolars and incisors.

Remember,

Gow-gates: is a true 'mandibular' nerve block .it is an open-mouth technique and anesthetizes all divisions of V_3.

Vazarani-akinosi: is a closed mouth mandibular block technique. Its prime indication is cases with limited mouth opening. The needle passes at the height of muco gingival junction of *maxillary* third molars.

Ans.139. (D) All of the above

Ref http://www.utmb.edu/otoref/Grnds/Deep-Neck-Spaces-2002-04.htm

- The masticator space is formed by the superficial layer of the deep cervical fascia as it surrounds the masseter laterally and the pterygoid muscles medially.
- This space contains these muscles as well as the body and ramus of the mandible, the inferior alveolar nerves and vessels and the tendon of the temporalis muscle.
- Masticator spaces include- pterygomandibular, Submassetric, temporal and deep temporal spaces.
- The masticator space is in direct communication with the temporal space superiorly deep to the zygoma. The temporal space has as its lateral boundary the superficial layer of deep fascia as it attaches to the zygoma and temporal ridge and its medial boundary the periosteum of the temporal bone. It is subdivided into superficial and deep spaces by the body of the temporalis muscle. This space contains the internal maxillary artery and the mandibular nerve
- Masticator and temporal space infection most often arise from infections of the third molars, or from other sources of infection (trauma, surgery etc).
- Inflammation of the pterygoid muscles leads to marked trismus and pain. The posterior floor of mouth may become edematous and indurated. Externally, swelling occurs over the ramus of the mandible.

Ans.140. (C) Both of above

Ref Neelima Malik Pg 327

Rene Le Fort divided complex facial fractures into three types-

- Le Fort I – horizontal fracture or Guerin fracture, low-level fracture.
- Le Fort II – pyramidal or sub-zygomatic fracture.
- Le Fort III – supra-zygomatic, high level, cranio-facial disjunction.

Now friends, there is a confusion.

''Occasionally, there is a wide separation of the middle third of face from the skull base referred to as ''floating maxilla'' wherein there is II and III level fracture with additional level I fracture.''

-ref Killey's fractures of middle third of face 4th ed , pg 53

However Dr Neelima Malik is very clear on this fact-

"Le Fort I fracture is also called as *floating fracture* as there is separation of complete dento-alveolar part of the maxilla (pterygomaxillary disjunction) and the fractured segment is held only by the soft tissues and hence mobile.

Ans.141. (C) TM joint pain dysfunction syndrome

Ref Neelima Malik Pg 221

MPDS was first related to occlusal disharmony by Costen (Costen's syndrome). Schwartz later gave the etiology as muscular spasms and altered psychological make up.

Symptoms associated with MPDS –

- Pain or discomfort anywhere in head and neck region.
- Limitation of jaw movement.
- Joint noises – grating, clicking, snapping.
- Tenderness to palpation of the muscles of mastication.

Other symptoms may include- tingling, numbness, blurred vision. Fatigue, nausea, ear pain, tinnitus.

Ans.142. (D) Limberg's osteotomy

Refhttp://cpcj.allenpress.com/cpcjonline/?request=get-document&doi=10.1597%2F15451569(2000)037%3C0243:AMOUOF%3E2.3.CO%3B2

Limberg's osteotomy is a surgical procedure for the correction of ***unilateral complete cleft palate.***

A unilateral complete cleft palate has four significant features: (1) there is a cleft on the deformed side extending from the alveolar ridge to the uvula; (2) the size of the deformed side is smaller and its length shorter; (3) the position of the greater palatine foramen is more forward than that of the normal side; and (4) the horizontal plate of the palatine bone and the aponeurosis and musculature of the soft palate attaching to the bony plate of the deformed side are displaced anteriorly

The procedure consists of elevating a large arterial mucoperiosteal flap of the entire deformed side of the hard palate to close the hard palate cleft. Next, the posterio-medial wall of the greater palatine foramen has to be removed to free the greater palatine vessels and nerve that tether the mucoperiosteal flap to the palatal bone.

Friends, thus while Limberg procedure is for cleft palate surgeries, Thomas osteotomy procedure are primarily for open bite corrections.

Ans.143. (C) Anesthesia

Ref Malamed 4th ed, pg 249

The question is asking about the sensations that may be felt during post-traumatic nerve regeneration. Trauma to inferior alveolar nerve is very common malpractice and is generally manifested as prolonged paresthesia. Sometimes, *hyperesthesia* (increased sensitivity to noxious stimuli) and *dysesthesia* (painful sensation to non-noxious stimuli) may also occur. At other times, patient may feel tingling or 'electric shock' through the distribution of nerve if the nerve sheath is damaged during LA.

Remember, complete anesthesia is not a sign of recovery.

Ans.144. (C) Both of them

OKC coined by Philipsen (1956), has a pronounced tendency to recur, the recurrence rate may vary from 5-62 %. This may be attributed to:

- Presence of satellite cells.

- Tendency to multiplicity.
- Thin and fragile cystic lining.
- Syndromes like Basal cell nevoid.

Ref Neelima Malik Pg 404

The characteristic feature of multicystic Ameloblastoma is that is microscopically infiltrates bone beyond the tumor-bone interface seen in imaging. This accounts for their high recurrence (50 % for multi and 18-25% for unicystic types).

Ref Neelima Malik Pg 448

Ans.145. (B) Acute oroantral fistula

Ref Neelima Malik Pg 538

Treatment of acute OAF (oro-antral fistula): ideally immediate surgical closure with supportive measure (antibiotic, analgesics, nasal decongestants). Small fistula can be expected to close spontaneously after packing (Whitehead's varnish includes benzoin, iodoform, balsam of tolu, Storax).

The success of closure is more likely in acute as the risk of infection is less and it is easier to recover the lost fragment.

Treatment of delayed cases: here, usually the fistulous tract is well epithelialized and hence spontaneous closure is least expected. Adequate drainage of pus and infection along with supportive measures followed by surgical flap closure.

Types of surgical flaps in OAF treatment:

1. Buccal advancement flap – Rehrmann 1936.
2. Modified Rehrmann flap – with additional releasing incisions and a step for proper adaptation.
3. Rotational advancement flap – palatal flap.
4. Ashley's flap – island of palatal mucosa pedicled over the excised tract.
5. Caldwell-Luc – for removal of foreign bodies form the sinus.
6. Nasal antrostomy – form the inferior meatus.

PEDODONTICS

Ans.146. (C) Dental caries

Ref Shobha Tandon, pg 179.

"Fluoride syndrome" refers to hidden lesions that occur when pit and fissure enamel is exposed to high fluoride level and subsequently slows down the rate while the lesion continues in the dentin. This inner cavitated lesion masked by an outer intact enamel surface is known as *Fluoride bomb or syndrome*.

Ans.147. (A) Maintain arch length

Ref Shobha Tandon

It is very important that the original dimension and contours be replicated in the final restoration whether in deciduous or permanent teeth. However, in deciduous dentition the prime concern is to maintain the arch length for preventing any space deficit in the succeeding dentition.

Ans.148. (C) Fear

Ref Shobha Tandon

The basic cause of dental anxiety of a child is the *fear of unknown*. The main treatment modality used now days to overcome such fears and anxieties is the TSD approach. The child is familiarized with the various equipments inside the clinic which helps him to overcome his fear.

The maternal anxieties are also a major concern in child management but they require a systematic approach to manage both the child and the parent. Simple familiarization with the functioning of the clinic is not regarded sufficient.

Ans.149. (B) Regaining the space

Explained earlier please refer KCET-07 A152

Ans.150. (B) Apexogenesis

Ref Shobha Tandon,

Remember,		
Small pulp exposure in vital tooth	–	direct pulp capping / pulpotomy
Large pulp exposure in vital tooth with immature apex	–	Apexogenesis
Large pulp exposure in non-vital tooth with immature apex	–	Apexification
Pulp exposure with non-vital tooth	–	RCT/ Pulpectomy

Ans.151. (D) Retain the teeth if possible

Explained earlier, please refer, KCET-06 A84

Ans.152. (A) Give a quantitative determination of acidogenic micro-organisms in the oral cavity

Refhttp://jdr.iadrjournals.org/cgi/reprint/29/3/298

A SIMPLE colorimetric test for the estimation of numbers of lactobacilli in the saliva was described in 1940 by Snyder.

- The **Snyder Test** is used to determine a person's susceptibility to dental caries.
- The susceptibility is correlated with acid production that is assumed to result from fermentation by cariogenic *Lactobacillus* species on the teeth or in other areas of the mouth.
- The Snyder Test agar contains **2% glucose** and the pH indicator **brom cresol green.** The pH of the agar is ~ 4.8, which inhibits the growth of most organisms, but it is ideal for acidophiles such as *Lactobacillus* species.
- Saliva samples are inoculated into the tubes and allowed to incubate. If *Lactobacillus* is present in the saliva, it will ferment the glucose and produce lactic acid, causing the pH to

drop to ~ 4.4. This causes the brom cresol green to change from **green to yellow**. A culture demonstrating a yellow color indicates a person is susceptible to the formation of dental caries.

- Positive color change in 24 hours: marked caries activity.
- Positive color change in 48 hours: moderate (average) caries activity.
- Negative color change in 48 hours: slight caries activity.
- Negative color change in 72 hours: negative caries activity.

Ans.153. (B) Candidiasis

Ref Shafer, 5th ed , pg 506.

Candidiasis is the most common opportunistic infection in the world. Thrush or oral Candidiasis is the most common form occurring in debilitated, old and infants.

The other form, acute atrophic Candidiasis is also known as the antibiotic sore mouth. It is similar to thrush only that the white plaque is wiped off leaving a red erythematous area.

The chronic hyper plastic variety often resembles leukoplakia and is considered pre malignant.

Ans.154. (C) Passive lingual arch

Key word-'mandibular'. For details about Lingual arch please refer KCET-07 A152

Ans.155. (D) Obstinate

Ref Shobha Tandon, pg 131

Elsbach , 1963 classified crying of child in dental clinic into 4 types:

- **Obstinate cry:** loud, high-pitched, characterized as a siren- like wail. Represents child's external response to anxiety.
- **Frightened cry:** accompanied usually by tears, convulsive breath-catching snobs.
- **Hurt cry:** loud with a small whimper, a single tear rolling down without the child showing any resistance to treatment.
- **Compensated cry:** not a cry but an attempt to drown out the noise from the drill, slow and monotonic. It is a sort of coping mechanism.

ORTHODONTICS

Ans.156. (D) Arch length inadequacy

Well friends, we could not land up with a exact line stating the same, but it is quite obvious that in the event of crowding, the erupting premolars cause the deciduous canine to prematurely exfoliate. [Although, serial extraction procedures are also a cause of deciduous canine loss, they are by no means the most common cause].

Ans.157. (B) Anterior crossbite

Ref Bhalajhi, 2nd ed pg 82

Dewey proposed a modification of Angle's classification for malocclusion where he divided Class I into 5 and Class III into 3 subtypes:

Class I –Dewey's

- Type 1- Class I with crowded anterior teeth
- Type 2 – Class I with protruding anterior teeth
- Type 3 – Class I with anterior cross bite
- Type 4 – Class I with posterior cross bite
- Type 5 – mesial migration of first permanent molar

Class III

- Type 1 – as such each arch is normally sized with mandibular arch forwardly placed
- Type 2 – mandibular incisors are crowded and lingual to maxillary incisors
- Type 3 – maxillary incisors are crowded and n cross bite relation to mandibular

Ans.158. (D) Surface to surface contact

Well friends another question with no direct reference but easy to understand. In an ideal occlusion the upper teeth occlude in perfect harmony with the lower. While, in posterior teeth the cusps occlude with fossa and ridges, the lingual surfaces of upper anterior teeth closely adapt the labial surfaces of mandibular anteriors.

Looking at other options, cusp-cusp/ incisal edge-edge contact is highly undesirable as it leads to premature contacts with TMJ disorders.

Ans.159. (C) Attraction

Ref Bhalajhi , 2nd ed pg 84.

Simon classified occlusion into antero-posterior, transverse and vertical planes. It makes use of three craniometric planes – FHP, orbital and mid-saggital plane.

- **FHP**- when dental arch is closer to FHP- attraction.
  (Horizontal) When away from the FHP – abstraction.
- **Orbital plane** – when dental arch is away from orbital plane- protraction.
  (Vertical) When arch is closer to orbital plane - retraction.

Remember, ***Simon's law*** states that this plane should pass through the distal third of upper canine.

- **Mid-Saggital plane**- when the arch is away from this plane – distraction.
  (Transverse) When the arch is closer to this plane — contraction.

Ans.160. (B) Distocclusion

Ref Bhalajhi, 2nd ed pg 82.

In class III Angle's malocclusion, the mesio-buccal cusp of maxillary first molar occludes with the interdental space between the mandibular first and second molars.

The following features are associated –

- Excessively large mandible/ small sized maxilla.
- Forwardly placed mandible (mesio-occlusion).

- Lower incisors are lingually placed or in an edge to edge position (anterior cross bite). Hence we see that in Class III there is mesio-occlusion and not distocclusion.

Ans.161. (B) Capillary blood pressure

Pleases refer KCET-07 A160

Ans.162. (A) Maxillary retrusion

Ref Bhalajhi , pg 427; Shobha Tandon pg 580

Cleft deformity is associated with division, distortion and deficiency of oral tissue. The resultant defect produces both dental and skeletal effects.

- The maxillary arch is severely constricted producing anterior/posterior cross bite.
- Teeth are rotated, Ectopic eruption, impacted, and other aberrations.
- Anterior deep bite with protruding premaxilla (apparent).
- Palatal repair may inhibit the growth of maxilla and due to scar contracture , maxillary retrusion occurs.

Ans.163. (C) Mechanical bond

Ref Bhalajhi , pg 298

The method of fixing the brackets directly to the tooth surface is known as Bonding. After etching the surface of tooth (where bracket has to be applied) with 37% phosphoric acid bonding adhesive is applied and bracket pressed onto the surface. This is similar to resin tags formation where in micro-mechanical bonds are created involving the irregularities created by etching and the bonding agent.

Ans.164. (B) Abnormal and undesirable

Eruption of permanent second molar ahead of premolar is undesirable as it may result in encroachment of the space meant for eruption of second premolar and resultant Ectopic eruption/ impaction.

Ans.165. (C) Orbitale to porion

Please refer KCET-05 A160

Ans.166. (A) Maxillary growth redirection

Ref Bhalajhi , pg 360

Head gears are the most commonly used extra-oral orthopaedic appliances. They are used during the growth period to correct skeletal as well as dental malocclusions.

Types

- **Cervical:** anchorage from nape of neck . Extrude the maxillary molars increasing facial height and cause distal movement of maxilla.
- **Occipital:** anchorage from back of the head. Produces a distal and superior force on maxilla.

A force of 350-450 gms for 12-14hrs a day produces an orthopaedic effect on maxilla when the force is applied to the centre of resistance of maxilla *i.e.* above the roots of premolar teeth.

Ans.167. (B) Frontal or direct

Please refer KCET-07 A160

Ans.168. (C) Distal to first permanent molar

Ref Shobha Tandon, pg 73

Post –natal growth of mandible occurs chiefly in:

- Condylar cartilage (vertical growth).
- Posterior borders of ramus (horizontal + vertical growth).
- Alveolar ridges (vertical growth).

The ramus of mandible lengthens by periosteal bone formed at the posterior borders of the ramus. Thus, the ramus is translated posteriorly by the resorption of the anterior border and deposition at the posterior border, thus elongating the mandibular body.

The above lines, clearly state that growth in the ramus (distal to first molars) elongates the body of mandible providing at the same time adequate space for the permanent molars.

Ans.169. (B) Fast maturing child

Ref Bhalajhi, pg 10

Growth does not take place at a uniform rate but in 'spurts' or periods when a sudden increase in growth occurs.

The physiological alteration in hormonal balance is responsible for such accentuated growth. The timings are different in boys and girls.

1. Just before birth
2. one year after birth
3. mixed dentition growth spurt
   Boys : 8-11yrs
   Girls : 7-9 yrs
4. Pre-pubertal growth spurt
   Boys : 14-16 yrs
   Girls : 11-13 yrs

These timings are the ones commonly observed and small deviations may not necessarily indicate pathology. A pre-pubertal growth spurt may indicate a fast maturing child and not necessarily a hormonal imbalance.

Ans.170. (B) Period of sudden acceleration of growth

Refer above answer

Ans.171. (D) All of the above

Ref Bhalajhi, pg 16

Mechanism of bone growth:-

- **Deposition and resorption:** changes in shape and size by bone remodeling. These are basic mechanisms of bone changes.

- **Cortical Drift:** combination of above may result in movement of bone towards the deposition site. The thickness of bone remains the same.
- **Displacement** – movement of whole bone as a unit.
  1. ***Primary* displacement:** movement as a result of its own growth *e.g.* movement of maxilla by growth at tuberosity region against cranial base.
  2. ***Secondary* displacement:** bone gets displaced as a result of growth of adjacent bones. For *e.g.* deposition at cranial base causes the forward and downward displacement of maxilla.

PROSTHODONTICS

Ans.172. (C) Class III

Ref Nallaswamy, pg 381.

Tooth- tissue supported partial dentures (Kennedy's class I, II, IV) generally respond like an inclined plane or a lever when a force is applied to them. This is because these dentures derive their support from both the teeth and soft tissues and hence stress is precipitated in them owing to the different level of resiliencies of the tissues.

However, this is not the case with ***tooth supported dentures*** (Class III) wherein all the force is transmitted to the long axis of the abutment teeth and there is no fulcrum along which the denture can rotate.

Ans.173. (B) 4-6 mm

Please refer KCET-07, A181

Ans.174. (C) Antero-posterior palatal bar

Ref Nallaswamy, pg332

Cases with large inoperable tori are either surgically managed or an Antero-posterior (double palatal) bar type of major connector is advocated. It is a combination of anterior palatal strap and posterior palatal bar. It is very rigid because of the circular configuration but the support is less and additional support is derived from remaining teeth.

Other indications of double palatal bar –

- When anterior and posterior abutments teeth are widely separated.
- Patients who want to avoid complete palatal coverage.
- Long span Class II cases.
- Class IV cases.

Ans.175. (C) Cannot be relined in event of ridge resorption

Ref Nallaswamy, pg 6

Major disadvantages of metallic bases are:

- They are more expensive than resin based dentures.

- Require more time and expertise for fabrication.
- They cannot be relined/rebased.
- They require a refractory cast material.

However, metal bases can be used in thin sections and are extremely light and comfortable for patient use. Also, heat transfer property enables patient's perception of taste and temperature.

Ans.176. (C) Physiologic impression technique

Ref Nallaswamy, pg 409.

Anatomic form of the tissues is recorded with materials like ZnO Eugenol paste, Plaster of Paris etc. This type of denture will adapt well to tissues when at rest however when under occlusal load, a rotational force acts on the denture (due to tissue ward movement of the distal end tissues). In an anatomic form the forces are concentrated on the abutment teeth and are deleterious for the same. For this reason, anatomic impressions are avoided in a tooth-tissue supported denture (Distal extension). For such cases, a Functional Impression is preferred.

Functional impressions are recorded under functional load where the soft tissue are recorded in the compressed form and wouldn't exert additional forces on the abutment teeth. Remember, functional impressions are used to record the edentulous zone only while the teeth are recorded in the anatomic form. These dual impressions can be classified into:

- Physiological or functional /dual impressions-

McLean's, Hindle's, Functional relining, Fluid wax technique:

- Selective pressure impressions:

McLean's technique: two impressions are made. A functional impression of the edentulous area is made using a occlusal rim on a custom made impression tray. The second impression is made over this using alginate (Pick-up impression).

Hindle's technique: modified McLean's method. A special custom made tray with occlusal rim and provisions for finger space is constructed. The direct finger pressure ensures a functional load over the alginate and underlying tissues.

Functional relining: here, two anatomic casts are made. (Master and Refractory cast) the framework is constructed using the refractory cast and the master cast is then altered according to the functional impression made using the framework.

This technique differs from the selective pressure technique in that the later involves providing relief to the special tray overlying the relieving areas. Thus the denture applies forces only to the stress bearing areas and not other zones.

Ans.177. (D) Ratio of combined pericemental root surface area of the abutment teeth and the pericemental root surface area's of the teeth to be replaced.

Ref Nallaswamy, pg 750

Ante's law states that the combined pericemental area of all abutment teeth supporting a fixed partial denture should be equal to or greater than the tooth to be replaced. For removable prosthesis, the combined pericemental area of the teeth plus the mucosa area of denture base should be equal or be greater than those of missing teeth.

Crown Root ratio: for abutment teeth in FPD should always be 1. Ideally it should be 2:3 (0.66), acceptable ratio are up to 1:1.

Ans.178. (B) Screws, pins and grooves

Ref Nallaswamy, pg 569.

Retention in prepared teeth can be improved with internal features like proximal grooves, boxes and retention pinholes.

Indications-

- Over tapered preparations
- Partial veneer crowns
- Absence of two opposing walls (due to caries, etc)

Ans.179. (D) Biological, mechanical and esthetic requirement

Ref Nallaswamy, pg 567

In preparing teeth for FPD the characteristics that are incorporated into each are:

- Mechanical – includes retention, resistance form and structural integrity.
- Esthetics
- Biological –preservation of tooth structure, periodontium.

Table 1 Seven key principles of preparation (derived from Shillingberg[1])

Seven key principles	Functions
Conservation of tooth tissue	To avoid weakening the tooth uneccessarily To aovid compromisign the pulp
Resuistance form	to prevent dislodgement of a cemented restroration by apical or ovliquely-directed forces
Retention form	To prevent displacement of a cemented restoration a long any of its paths of insertion, including the long axis of the preparation
Structural durability	To provide enough space for a crown which is sufficiently thick to prevent fracture, distortion or perforation
Marginal integrity	To prepare a finish line to accommodate a robust margin with close adaptation to minimise microleakage
Preservation of the periodontium	To shape the preparation such taht the crown is not over contoured and its margin is accessible for optimal oral hygiene
Aesthetic considerations	To create sufficient space for aesthetic veneers where indicated

Ans.180. (C) Both of the above

Self- explanatory

Retraction procedures are explained in detail ahead, please ref KCET-03 A174

Ans.181. (B) Badly damaged non-vital endodontically treated tooth

Ref Nallaswamy, pg 555.

When an endodontically treated tooth is prepared for a full veneer crown, substantial amount of tooth is lost. In order to increase its resistance and support , a dowel core (post n core) can be inserted. The dowel is the screw inserted in the root canal and the core is the retentive component which behaves like a prepared crown.

Remember, the length of dowel core inside the canal should be at least 2/3rd the length of root canal.

Ans.182. (D) Campers plane and interpupillary line

Ref Nallaswamy, pg 120.

Orientation of the plane of occlusal rim.

While making a complete denture the occlusal rim should be parallel to the plane of maxilla. The plane of maxilla is determined.

Anteriorly: by the inter-pupillary line.

Posteriorly: by the Camper's line or the ala tragus line (line extending from the upper border of tragus of the ear to lower border of ala of nose).

The maxillary occlusal plane can be verified using a ***Fox's plane***. This device has an inner and an outer rim. The inner rim corresponds to the occlusal plane and the outer should correspond to the pupillary line anteriorly and Camper's line posteriorly.

Ans.183. (D) Balancing occlusal contacts, during protrusive movements

Ref Nallaswamy, pg 195

Curve of Spee is defined as, ''*Anatomic curvature of the occlusal alignment of teeth beginning at the tip of lower canine and following the buccal cusps of the premolars and molars continuing to the anterior border of ramus.*"

Thus, it is an imaginary curve that passes from canine to the head of condyle. It is seen in natural dentition and should be reproduced in CD. The **significance**, of this curve is that when the patient moves his mandible forward, the posterior teeth set on this curve will continue to remain in contact. When this curve is not included, there will be disocclusion during protrusive movements (*Christensen's phenomenon*)

Ans.184. (C) Need for reline

Ref Nallaswamy, pg 257

Immediate denture is defined as a denture constructed for use immediately after the extraction of teeth. There are two types-

- Interim – to be used for very short time , to ensure proper healing.
- Conventional – This can later be modified to serve as a permanent 1. Usually indicated in patients undergoing total extraction.

Advantages

- Psychological benefit to the patient.
- Muscle tone and vertical dimensions preserved.
- Less post-operative pain, better healing of socket.

- Teeth selection is easy and centric relations are easy to record.
- Easier for the patient to adapt to a permanent prosthesis.

Disadvantages

- Requires more chair side time.
- Need for relining every few months due to continuous changes in the socket.
- Try-in procedure is not possible. Hence, the dentist cannot have nay idea about the outcome of the denture.

Hence, out of the given choices , choice '*c*' is the most appropriate.

Ans.185. (D) All of the above

Ref Nallaswamy, pg 260

Over dentures are dental prosthesis that replaces missing teeth and their supporting structures and/or derive their support from the remaining modified natural teeth.

Advantages

- Maintains the integrity of the residual ridge.
- Improves retention and stability of the denture.
- Improved proprioception leads to better neuromuscular control.
- Psychological benefit of retaining natural teeth.
- Serves as a template for the patient and may be used as a complete denture in the event of abutment failure.

Disadvantages

- Frequent need for fluoride and diet counseling.
- High incidence of caries and periodontal disease around the abutment.
- More expensive than conventional dentures.
- Cannot be used in cases with reduced inter-arch distance.
- Periodontal condition of adjacent teeth may be compromised.

Ans.186. (B) The centric relation

Ref Nallaswamy pg 146

Gothic arch tracings are graphs or tracings used to record the centric relation. They may be either arrow point tracings or pantographs. The apex of the tracing gives the centric relation.

Remember, in extra-oral tracings the Central bearing plate is attached to the mandible rim while the centric bearing point (stylus) is attached to the maxillary rim. It is generally the opposite in the intra-oral tracings.

Other methods to record centric relations:

- *Physiologic methods* – tactile or interocclusal check record , pressure/ pressure less (nick and notch method).
- *Functional methods* – Needlehouse (metal styli attached to rim), Patterson (a trough filled with 1:1carborundum + plaster).
- Radiographic methods.

COMMUNITY AND PREVENTIVE DENTISTRY

Ans.187. (C) Four

Ref Soben Peter, 2nd ed , pg 707

The Dentist Act, 1948 was introduced on 29th march, 1948. The act contains 5 chapters-introduction, Dental Council of India, the state dental councils, the register and miscellaneous.

Composition of DCI

- 1 registered dentist with qualification from recognized college.
- 1 member elected from among themselves in MCI.
- Not more than 4 members elected from among themselves.
- Principals, Deans, Directors, Vice-Principals of Dental colleges in state with not more than 1 candidate from same college.
- Heads of dental wings of medical colleges in state.
- 1 member from each university established by law in states.
- 1 member to represent each state nominated by the Govt.
- 6members nominated by the Central Govt. with at least 1, a registered dentist in part A and 2 in part B.
- The Director general of health Services (ex-officio).

Ans.188. (B) Immunization against common diseases of childhood

Ref https://www.who.int/dg/lee/speeches/2003/londonschool_whopriorities/en/index.html Soben Peter, 2nd ed ,

The WHO was established by 61 countries in the year 1948 with its headquarters in Geneva, Switzerland and 7th April is celebrated as ''World's Health Day" every year.

The goals set by the United Nations Millennium Summit in the year 2000 include immunization/control of the major infectious diseases, and reducing child and maternal mortality. They also set targets for poverty reduction, education, gender equality and the environment.

Ans.189. (C) New York

Soben Peter, 2nd ed ,pg 734

UNICEF (United Nations International Children's Emergency Fund) was created in 1946

- Main purpose to meet emergency requirements of children around the world.
- The headquarters is located in New York with 9 other regional offices (inc India).
- Objectives include – child/maternal health, sanitation, education.

Ans.190. (D) Vital

Ref Soben Peter, 2nd ed , pg 838

Vital statistics is defined as the facts related to vital events like births, deaths etc collected systematically and numerically compiled.

Desmographic data comprises details of population size, distribution ethnic groups, socio-ecconomic factors and their trends over time.

Ans.191. (A) Motivation

Ref Soben Peter, 2nd ed , pg 542

Motivation is defined as the fundamental desire for learning in an individual. Primary motives are in-born while secondary motives are influenced by external forces.

Remember, in the Soil, Seed and Sower theory of health education – soil is represented by the patients/general public while the health facts form the seeds and the media used for spreading the information is the sower.

Ans.192. (B) Nagpur

Ref Soben Peter, 2nd ed , pg 364

Defluoridation of water was first performed in India by the National Environmental Engineering Research Institute (NEERI), at Nagpur in 1961. they adopted the Nalgonda Technique using sodium aluminate or lime, bleaching powder and filter alum.

Remember, Salt fluoridation requires – 90-250 mg /kg.

Milk fluoridation requires – 5-15 ppm.

Ans.193. (A) 5, 10, 15, 35-44, 65-74

Ref Soben Peter, 2nd ed , pg 618

Pathfinder surveys are pilot studies aimed at covering approx. 1% of the population.

The recommended ages are 5 years for primary teeth and 12, 15, 35-44 and 65-74 years.

At 5 years complete deciduous dentition can be examined.

At 12 years, it is most likely to find all permanent teeth erupted except third molars.

At 15 years, assessment of caries and periodontal diseases.

At 35-44 yrs , findings for adult group is standardized analyzing general effects on dentition.

At 65-74yrs, planning for care and maintenance for elderly becomes important.

Ans.194. (A) Pie

Ref Soben Peter, 2nd ed , pg 30

Pie diagrams are circle representations that are divided into different sectors corresponding to the frequencies of the variables in the distribution. They are commonly used for showing the percentage breakdown for qualitative data. However, this cannot be used to how two or more data.

Ans.195. (B) Kenya

Ref Soben Peter, 2nd ed , pg 285

In lake water, the highest fluoride level ever recorded is *2800 ppm* in lake Nakuru, located in the volcanic areas of Kenya. The soil in the lake shore contained about 5600 mg of F per kg.

Soil in Tennessee, USA contains F up to range 3800-8300 ppm.

Ans.196. (C) 621

Ref Soben Peter, 2nd ed , pg 174

The recommended probe for use with CPITN was first described by WHO (TRS 621 – 1978) the weight of this probe is 5gms. Ball tip diameter is 0.5mm and a black mark at 3.5-5.5mm reading. Probing force of 20gms or 7.5 N is recommended.

Remember, CPITN – E for epidemiological surveys has reading up till 5.5mm.

While CPITN-C for clinical surveys has an additional 8.5 - 11.5 mm reading.

Ans.197. (C) Root canal treatment

Ref Soben Peter, 2nd ed , pg 660

The School dental nurse program was started in Wellington, New Zealand in 1921 by TA Hunter. They are trained in both reversible and irreversible procedures, covering 450-700 school children, like

- Oral examination.
- Prophylaxis, topical F application.
- LA and extraction of primary teeth.
- Cavity preparation and amalgam restoration.
- Pulp capping and referral to specialist for complex treatment.

Hence, school nurses are not trained to perform root canal therapy.

Remember, in Britain these nurses were known as the 'New Cross Auxiliaries'.

Ans.198. (A) Cluster

Ref Soben Peter, 2nd ed , pg 27

Cluster sampling involves classification of population on the basis of natural groups or clusters like villages, wards et. Here, first a sample of the clusters is selected and then all the unit in each of the selected cluster is surveyed. Although the method is simpler and less time consuming, it gives a higher standard error.

Ans.199. (C) Saudi-Arabia

Ref Soben Peter, 2nd ed , pg 748

Well friends, I could not find a direct reference for this but it can be deduced while observing the data given in Soben Peter, While all other countries have a stratified layout of oral health care, EMRO (Eastern European Regional Office) countries like UAE and Saudi Arabia do not mention any auxiliaries. The dentist: population = 13: 100,000 (1990).

In India, dentist: population = 1:25,000.

Ans.200. (B) 31st May

Ref Soben Peter, 2nd ed , pg 736

Some important dates:

- 30th Jan – Anti-leprosy
- 7th April – World health day
- 31st May – World no-tobacco day
- 1st July – Doctor's day
- 11th July - World Population day
- 2nd Oct - Anti-drug addiction day
- 1st Dec – Anti – AIDS day
- 11th Dec – UNICEF day

2003

Questions & Answers

5

KCET 2003

QUESTIONS

ANATOMY

1. The only fixed cell of the Connective tissue

(a) Histiocyte.
(b) Lymphocyte.
(c) Polymorphs.
(d) Mast cell.

2. Mature bone is otherwise called as:

(a) Woven bone.
(b) Irregular bone.
(c) Lamellar bone.
(d) Resorbing bone.

3. The nerve supply of Buccinator:

(a) Facial nerve.
(b) Mandibular nerve.
(c) Maxillary nerve.
(d) Auriculo temporal nerve

4. The weakest part of Pharynx is:

(a) Sinus of Morgangni
(b) Between thyropharyngeus and cricopharyngeus
(c) Piriform fosa
(d) Pharyngeal recess.

5. Thyroid gland develops from:

(a) Laryngo tracheal diverticulum
(b) Rathke's pouch
(c) Buccinator muscle
(d) Orbicularis oris muscle

6. Oral diaphragm is formed by:

(a) Mylohyoid muscle
(b) Genioglossus muscle
(c) Buccinator muscle
(d) Orbicularis oris muslce

7. Supra-Meatal triangle externally represents:

(a) Transverse sinus (b) Promontory of middle car
(c) Internal acoustic meatus (d) Mastoid antrum.

8. Part of vertebral artery is related to:

(a) Superior cervical ganglion (b) Middle cervical ganglion
(c) Stellate ganglion (d) Ciliary ganglion

DENTAL ANATOMY AND HISTOLOGY

9. The transitory structure that is present in developing tooth germ:

(a) Enamel knot. (b) Stratum intermedium.
(c) Cervical coop. (d) All the above.

10. Secondary Cementum is generally confined to:

(a) Cervical third of the root. (b) Middle third of the root.
(c) Apical third of the root (d) No secondary cementum forms

11. The seuence of eruption of primary teeth is:

(a) ABCDE (b) ABDCE
(c) ACBDE (d) ADBCE

12. The most common teeth present at birth:

(a) Mandibular lateral incisors (b) Maxillary molars
(c) Maxillary central incisors (d) Mandibular central incisors.

13. The time taken for primary tooth root completion after eruption into oral cavity:

(a) 3 years (b) 1 year
(c) 2 years (d) 1 month

14. The first sign of future deciduous teeth, appears as a thickening of oral ectoderm at about:

(a) 25th day of intrauterine life (b) 34th day of intrauterine life
(c) 56th day of intrauterine life (d) 20 weeks of intrauterine life

15. The stage of relatively rapid eruption from the time a tooth first penetrates the gingiva until it reaches the occlusal level is called:

(a) Pre emergent spurt (b) Post emergent spurt
(c) occlusal euilibrium (d) Dilacerations

PHYSIOLOGY

16. Percentage of body water is greater in:

(a) Females than in male (b) Children than in adult
(c) Obese than in lean individuals (d) Old than in young objects.

17. Sensitivity to local anesthetics is greater in:
(a) Type B fibers
(b) Type C fibers
(c) Type A delta fibers
(d) Fibers supplying the muscle spindles.

18. Deficiency of Vit. K leads to decreased activity of:
(a) Platelets
(b) Coagulation factors II, V and VIII
(c) Coagulation factors VII, IX and X
(d) Fibrinolytic system.

19. At high altitude the following changes take place except:
(a) Increase in respiratory rate.
(b) Increase in depth of respiration.
(c) Increase in oxygen carrying capacity of blood.
(d) Increase in partial pressure of carbon dioxide.

20. Glucocorticoids have all the following actions except:
(a) Increase in blood glucose level
(b) Increase in protein catabolism
(c) Anti-insulin action in peripheral tissues
(d) Decrease in glucose uptake by the heart

21. Albumin is synthesized by:
(a) Liver
(c) Muscle
(b) Kidney
(d) Spleen

BIOCHEMISTRY

22. Coenzyme A contains which of the following Vitamins:
(a) Biotin
(b) Pyridoxine.
(c) Pantothenic acid
(d) Acetyl CoA

23. The Amino acid from which Niacin is synthesized is
(a) Tyrosine
(b) Threonine
(c) Tryptophan
(d) Glucuronic acid

24. Bilirubin is conjugated with which of the following?
(a) Glycine
(b) Glutamine
(c) Acetyl CoA
(d) Glucuronic acid

MICROBIOLOGY

25. Sterilization of liuid paraffin is done by:
(a) Autoclaving
(b) Hot air oven
(c) UV-Radiation
(d) Inspissations

26. Multiple drug resistance of bacteria depends on which of the following:
(a) Resistance transfer factor (RTF)
(b) Colicigenic factor (Col)
(c) Fertility factor (F +)
(d) All of the above

27. Both intranuclear and intracytoplasmic inclusions are present in which of the following viruses.

(a) Pox virus
(b) Measles virus
(c) Hepatitis B virus
(d) HIV

28. Afflatoxin's are produced by:

(a) Aspergillus niger.
(b) Aspergillus fumigatus
(c) Aspergillus flavus
(d) All of the above

29. Which of the following is enrichment medium?

(a) Blood agar.
(b) Selenite F Broth
(c) Mac'Conkey agar
(d) Nutrient broth

30. Which of the following organism predominant in early stage of plaue formation?

(a) Cocci
(b) Filamentous colony
(c) Actinomyces
(d) Spirochete

31. The most common organism related to Dental caries

(a) Borrelia Vincenti
(b) Streptococcus Mutans
(c) E-Coli
(d) Bacilli

32. Actinomycosis is a

(a) Bacterial infection
(b) Fungal infection
(c) Viral infection
(d) Parasitic infection

GENERAL PATHOLOGY

33. Caseating granuloma is commonly seen in:

(a) Viral infections
(b) Tuberculosis
(c) Typhoid
(d) Amoebiasis

34. The most definite feature of a malignant tumor is:

(a) Hemorrhage
(b) increased mitoses
(c) Metastasis
(d) Necrosis

35. Frozen sections can be used for the demonstration of:

(a) Fat
(b) Mucin
(c) Cartilage
(d) Iron

36. Increased proliferation of cells is called:

(a) Hypertrophy
(b) Atrophy
(c) Hyperplasia
(d) Metaplasia

37. 'Nutmeg liver' is a term used to denote:

(a) edema
(b) shock
(c) thrombosis
(d) chronic venous congestion

38. **The increase in size of individual cells is referred to as:**
(a) Hypertrophy ^ (b) Hyperplasia
(c) Hypodontia (d) Differentiation

DENTAL MATERIALS

39. **A uniform dispersion of minute droplets of one liuid within another liuid constitutes**
(a) Gels (b) Emulsions
(c) Sols (d) Osmosis

40. **When the two metals are completely miscible in the liuid state and they remain completely mixed on solidification, the alloy formed is called:**
(a) Solid solution (b) Eutectic mixture
(c) peritectic mixture (d) Intermetallic compounds

41. **The cleaning or etching solutions for acid etching are known as:-**
(a) Sealants (b) Bonding agents
(c) Preconditioning solutions (d) Cleansing agents

42. **The tin-mercury phase formed during amalgamation is**
(a) Gamma phase (b) Gamma -1 phase
(c) Gamma-2 phase (d) Lathe cut

43. **The ability of the base to resist occlusal forces and to support the restoration is affected by:-**
(a) Compressive strength (b) Tensile strength
(c) Young's modulus (d) Modulus of elasticity

44. **The strength of the gypsum specimen when the water in excess of that reuired for the hydrate of the hemihydrate is left in the specimen is called:**
(a) Dry strength (b) Green strength
(c) Water strength (d) Compressive strength

45. **The plasticizer used in poly ether impression materials is:**
(a) Poly ether polymer (b) Colloidal silica
(c) Glycol ether (d) Oi-vinyl poly (dimethyl siloxane)

46. **Porosity formed due to simultaneous nucleation of solid grains and gas bubbles at the first moment that the metal freezes at the mold walls is called:**
(a) Pinhole porosity (b) Gas inclusion porosity
(c) Microporosity (d) Subsurface porosity.

47. **Strengthening of Dental porcelain is done by:**
(a) Increasing the compressive stress
(b) Increasing the tensile stress
(c) By introduction of residual compressive stresses into the surface of the material
(d) By incorporating stress concentration

48. Austenite is an alloy of iron and carbon with the iron in:
(a) Alpha form
(b) Beta form
(c) Gamma form
(d) None of the above

PHARMACOLOGY

49. Ivermectin is indicated in:
(a) Scabies
(b) Intestinal nematode infection
(c) Filariasis
(d) All of the above

50. Dental procedures for which antibiotic of choice for the prophylaxis endocarditis in adults is?
[Note = patient is allergic to penicillin and He is not able to take oral medicine].
(a) Clarithromycin 500 mg. 1 Hour before dental procedures.
(b) Cephalaxin 2.g. 1 hour before dental procedures
(c) Cefadroxil 2.g 1 hour before dental procedures
(d) Clindamcin 600 mg. 30 min before dental procedures

51. INFLIXIMAB (systemic) is used in:
(a) Crohn's disease (treatment)
(b) To reduce the number of draining with enterocutaneous fistula (s) in patients fistulizing Crohn's disease.
(c) Rheumatoid arthritis (treatment)
(d) All of the above

52. Trifusal is a:
(a) Anti-inflammatory drug
(b) Antibiotic
(c) Anti-arthritic drug
(d) Anti platelet drug

53. Which of the benzodiazepines (BDZ) is comparatively safe in pregnancy
(a) alprozolam
(b) zolpidem
(c) lorazepam
(d) none of the above

54. What is a suitable alternative antibiotic when a child in sensitive to penicillin?
(a) Tetracycline
(b) Erythromycin
(c) Sulfanilamide
(d) Ampicillin

55. Which of the following drugs cannot reduce the salivary secretion?
(a) Amitriptyline
(b) Disopyrmide
(c) Antenolol
(d) Neostigmine

GENERAL MEDICINE

56. For diagnosis of Acute Rheumatic fever, essential feature is:
(a) prior h/o rheumatic fever
(b) recent sore throat infection

(c) 1 major and 2 minor criteria
(d) Erythema marginatum

57. Petechiae in Scurvy are due to:

(a) platelet dysfunction
(b) thrombocytopenia
(c) endothelial dysintegrity
(d) clotting factor deficiency

58. Infective endocarditis is lest likely to occur in

(a) VSD
(b) ASD
(c) Tetralogy of Fallot
(d) Coarctation of aorta

59. Cardiac massage is usually done in the:

(a) Middle of sternum
(b) Lower 1/3 of sternum
(c) Manubrium
(d) Xiphisternum

60. Most common opportunistic infection in AIDS is

(a) cryptococcosis
(b) tuberculosis
(c) Candidiasis
(d) aspergillosis

61. Bleeding time is prolonged in:

(a) Hemophilia
(b) Von willebrand's
(c) Henoch Schnolein purpura
(d) Telangiectasia

62. All of the following can be transmitted through blood transfusion except:

(a) Malaria
(b) Leukemia
(c) Hepatitis
(d) AIDS

63. Most important triad of symptoms in portal hypertension is:

(a) Splenomegaly, Hepatomegaly and Ascitis
(b) Splenomegaly, Oesophageal varices and Ascitis
(c) Piles, splenomegaly and general Anasarca
(d) Oesophageal varices, piles arid General Anasarc(a)

64. Bone changers in Hyperparathyroidism include:

(a) Generalized demineralization
(b) Brown tumors
(c) Cystic changes
(d) All of the above

65. In a case of hypoglycemic coma, induced by hypoglycemic drugs, which of the following may be tried if glucose for intravenous infusion is not available?

(a) Subcutaneous injection of 0.5 ml 1: 1000 Adrenaline.
(b) Subcutaneous injection of 1 mg. of Glucagon.
(c) Both of the above
(d) None of the above.

66. Serum Alkaline Phosphatase is elevated all except:

(a) Obstructive Jaundice
(b) heart disease
(c) Rickets
(d) Pregnancy

GENERAL SURGERY

67. All the following nerves may be injured while doing excision of submandibular salivary glands except:

(a) Lingual nerve (b) Spinal accessory nerve
(c) Mandibular branch of facial nerve (d) Hypoglassal nerve.

68. Sistrunk's operation is done for:

(a) Thyroglossal cyst (b) Thyroglossal fistula
(c) Both the above (d) None of the above.

69. The ideal time of repair of cleft lip is:

(a) at birth (b) between 3-6 months of age
(c) at 1 ½years of age (d) at 1 ½ to 2 years of age.

70. The ideal time of repair of cleft of hard palate is:

(a) at birth (b) between 3-6 months of age
(c) between 12-15 months of age (d) After 2 years of age

71. Lucid interval is characteristically seen in

(a) Extradural Haematoma (b) Subdural Haematoma
(c) Intracerebral haematoma (d) None of the above

72. FNAC (Fine Needle Aspiration Cytology) can diagnose all the following except

(a) papillary carcinoma of thyroid (b) follicular carcinoma of thyroid
(c) Anaplastic carcinoma of thyroid (d) Medullary carcinoma of thyroid

73. J.Cock's peculiar tumors is

(a) Infected suamous cell carcinoma (b) Infected basal cell carcinoma
(c) Infected, ulcerated sebaceous cyst (d) Infected ulcerated Dermoid cyst

74. Malignant pustule is referred to:

(a) Facio -cervical Actinomycosis (b) Cutaneous anthrax
(c) Infected suamous cell carcinoma (d) None of the above

75. Which of the following ace congenital cysts except

(a) External angular dermoid cyst (b) Sebaceous cyst
(c) Branchial cyst (d) Thyroglossal cyst

76. Scan used to preoperatively localize parathyroid adenoma is

(a) Thallium -Technetium scan (b) Radio -iodine scan
(c) Technetium scan (d) Metaliodobenzyl-guanidine (MIBG) scan

77. Extra oral sutures should be removed around the __ day.

(a) Seventh (b) Third
(c) Fourteenth (d) Tenth

78. Better healing of severely contused tissue occurs following

(a) Extensive debridement
(b) thorough trimming of wound edges
(c) Cleaning with strong antiseptics
(d) Minimum debridement

79. An example of a synthetic absorptive suture is:
(a) Chronic catgut
(b) Polyethylene
(c) Polyglyclic acid
(d) Polyamide

ORAL PATHOLOGY

80. There may be multiple supernumerary teeth in one of the following conditions:
(a) Mongolism
(b) Cleidocranial dysostosis
(c) Hypothyroidism
(d) Hypopituitarism

81. Bilateral symmetrical swelling of the mandible in a child is likely to be caused by:
(a) Acromegaly
(b) Paget's disease
(c) Cherubism
(d) Dental cyst

82. Which of the following sugar present in the human diet is considered the most caries promoting?
(a) Sucrose
(b) Fructose
(c) Lactose
(d) Glucose

83. Etiological factor for macro-glossia is:
(a) Atrophic glossitis
(b) Oral submucous fibrosis
(c) Syphilitic glossitis
(d) Hurler's syndrome

84. Not a type of lichen planus?
(a) Atrophic
(b) Reticular
(c) Verrucous
(d) Annular

85. Which clinical type of oral Candidiasis has got the feature of white plaues that are scrapable?
(a) Thrush
(b) Erythematous type
(c) Hyperplastic type
(d) None of the above

86. In which of the following type of tumor the HPV-6 can be detected?
(a) Papilloma
(b) CEOT
(c) Sarcoma
(d) Pyogenic Granuloma

87. Naso Labial cyst is thought to arise from
(a) Remnants of cell rests of Serre
(b) Remnants of cell rests of Mallassez
(c) Remnants of cell rests of embryonic lacrimal duct
(d) Maxillary sinus lining epithelium

88. The circulating auto antibodies against the intercellular attachments of suamous epithelia are seen in

(a) Scleroderma
(b) Rheumatoid arthritis
(c) Herpes Zoster
(d) Pemphigus vulgaris

89. The histiocytosis X is a spectrum of disorders which include the following condition

(a) Eosinophilic granuloma
(b) Hand Schuller -Christian disease
(c) Letterer -Siwe disease
(d) All of the above

90. Lisegang ring Calcifications are seen in the following lesion

(a) Amyloidosis
(b) Pindborg tumour
(c) Ossifying fibroma
(d) Fibrous dysplasia

91. Hypodontia is a feature seen in

(a) Gardner's syndrome
(b) Ectodermal dysplasia
(c) Paget's disease
(d) Browns tumor

92. Bell's palsy is triggered by

(a) Exposure to Cold
(b) Tooth extraction
(c) Local and systemic infection
(d) Any of the above

93. Storiform pattern of Fibrous tissue is seen in

(a) Fibrosarcoma
(b) Malignant fibrous histiocytoma
(c) Neruofibroma
(d) Ameloblastic fibroma

94. The following site is the common involvement in cases of Myositis ossificans

(a) Massetor
(b) Hyoglossus
(c) Stylohyoid
(d) Lateral pterygoid

95. The risk of development of cancer is highest in the following lesions

(a) Leukoplakia
(b) Erythroplakia
(c) Lichen planus
(d) Leukoedema

96. Lupus erythematosis is

(a) Reactive lesion
(b) Degenerative condition
(c) Auto immune disorder
(d) Neoplastic condition

ORAL MEDICINE AND RADIOLOGY

97. Nikolsky's sign is positive in:

(a) Pemphigus
(b) Recurrent Apthous stomatitis
(c) Lichen planus
(d) Erythema multiforme

98. Normal serum alkaline phosphatase level is:

(a) 100-400 Bodansky units
(b) 1000-4000 Bodansky units
(c) 0.1-0.4 Bodansky units
(d) 1-4 Bodansky units.

99. Non-Neoplastic non-specific enlargement of the salivary gland

(a) Sialadentis
(b) Sialosis
(c) Ptyalism
(d) Sialorrhea

100. Unusual extensibility of the tongue is a characteristic feature of:
(a) Epidermolysis bullosa (b) Syphilis
(c) Darier-While disease (d) Ehlers-Danlos syndrome

101. Ectopic sebaceous glands in the mouth are called:
(a) Linea alba buccalis (b) Heck's disease
(c) Lingual varices (d) Fordyce spots.

102. Which is not a feature of CREST of syndrome?
(a) Calcinosis (b) Endocrinopathies
(c) Raynand's phenomenon (d) Syndactyly.

103. Facial pain due to elongated Styloid process is called
(a) Cowden syndrome (b) Tic Dolorouex
(c) Eagle's syndrome (d) Reiter's syndrome.

104. Mathematical representation of inverse suare law is
(a) $I2 / I1 = (D2)^2 / (D1)^2$ (b) $I1 / I2 = (D2)^2 / (D1)^2$
(c) $I2 / I1 = D2 / D1$ (d) $I1 / I2 = D2 / D1$

105. X-rays are produced at:
(a) Anode (b) Cathode
(c) Glass wall (d) Molybdenum focusing cup.

106. Quality of the X-ray beam is governed by:
(a) KVp. (b) mA
(c) Filament current (d) Length of the X-ray tube

107. Which is not a property of X-rays?
(a) ionization (b) Action on photographic film
(c) Excitation (d) Collimation

108. Crimp marks in a radiograph are due to:
(a) Droplets of fixing solution (b) Droplets of developing solution
(c) Static electricity (d) Sharp bending of the film

PERIODONTICS

109. Plaque lodged inter proximally is best removed by:
(a) Tooth brush (b) Mouth wash
(c) Dental floss (d) Irrigation

110. The concept of Oral prophylaxis and prevention in periodontal therapy was developed by
(a) John W.Riggs (b) G.V. Black
(c) Berhard Gottilieb (d) J.LeonWiliiams

111. The basal cells of the junctional Epithelium show signs of proliferation and rete peg form in

(a) Stage I gingivitis (b) Stage II gingivitis
(c) Stage III gingivitis (d) Stage IV gingivitis

112. In periodontal disease, calculus is considered as:

(a) Contributing factor (b) Primary factor
(c) Etiological factor (d) Governing factor

113. Povidine iodine is the choice of mouth rinse in cases associated with AIDS because:

(a) It is a topical antimicrobial (b) It is a topical anesthetic
(c) Its ability to aid in blood coagulation (d) All the above

114. Reactive ingredient present in Tartar control tooth paste is:

(a) Pyrophosphate (b) Metaphosphate
(c) Carboxy methyl (d) Bi-carbonate

115. Computerized periodontal probe is:

(a) CPITN probe (b) Florida probe
(c) Michigan probe (d) Jeffcoat probe

116. The pattern of bone destruction in periodontitis is determined by:

(a) Depth of the pocket (b) Suppuration
(c) Pathway of inflammation (d) Composition of plaue

117. Instrumentation zone in periodontal therapy is:

(a) The portion of the tooth where calculus (or) attended cementum is found
(b) (C)E. Junction
(c) Exposed root surfaces
(d) epithelial lining of periodontal pocket

118. Periochip is a commercially available local drug delivery system containing:

(a) Doxycycline (b) Chlor hexidine
(c) Minocycline (d) Metronidazole

119. Lateral positioning of flap is done for:

(a) Gingival recession
(b) High frenal attachment
(c) Increasing the width of attached gingival
(d) Shallow vestibule

120. Bioglass is used in:

(a) Root biomodification (b) resective osseous surgery
(c) regenerative osseous surgery (d) mucogingival surgery

121. If an implant has lost some bone support, but bone loss is arrested, it is termed as

(a) Failed implant (b) Failing implant
(c) Ailing implant (d) Biointegration

122. Type of periodontitis which does not respond to therapy is:
(a) Refractory periodontitis (b) Juvenile periodontitis
(c) Rapidly progressive periodontitis (d) Chronic adult periodontitis

123. Bio-brane is a commercially available as:
(a) Root matrix protein (b) Biodegradable membrane
(c) Bone graft material (d) Non-bone graft material

CONSERVATIVE DENTISTRY AND ENDODONTICS

124. The ratio of 1.618 to 1 constant which is used as a guide for dental esthetics is
(a) Golden proportion (b) Geometric formula
(c) Fibonacci ratio (d) Youthful ratio

125. When dental bur is sterilized by autoclaving, chemical used for protection of bur?
(a) Sodium nitrate (b) Sodium nitrite
(c) Sliver nitrate (d) Silver nitrite

126. In non zinc containing dental amalgam alloy the percentage of zinc present is
(a) Less than 0.02% (b) Less than 0.1 %
(c) Less than 0.01 % (d) None of the above

127. In which of the condition "PIGGY BACK" wedging is indicated?
(a) Proximal caries with gingival recession (b) Tooth with fluted surface
(c) Class II with wide proximal box (d) Narrow class II Cavity

128. Which of the following is a caries detector dye?
(a) 1% basic fuschin in propylene glycol (b) 1% acid red in propylene glycol
(c) 1% basic fuschin in ethylene glycol (d) 1% acid red in ethylene glycol

129. The limit of urinary mercury in microgram/g of creatinine attributed to extensive amalgam rest is
(a) 1 microgram/g of creatinine (b) 3 microgram/g of creatinine
(c) 2 microgram/g of creatinine (d) 4 microgram/g of creatinine

130. Tick the odd one
(a) Degassing (b) Desorbing
(c) Annealing (d) Metalizing

131. Endo-Extractor kit is a modification of
(a) Endodontic plugger (b) Masserann kit
(c) Endo box (d) Rubber dam kit

132. Tail file is also known as
(a) Barbed broach (b) H file
(c) R file (d) Rat file

133. The color code for No.6 endodontic file is
(a) White
(b) Purple
(c) Grey
(d) Pink

134. Leubke -Ochsenbein flap for periapical surgery is known as
(a) Trapezoidal flap
(b) Rectangular flap with sulcular incision
(c) Submarginal flap
(d) Triangular flap

135. Thymosin is a type of
(a) Surgical curette
(b) Miniature hand piece
(c) Retrograde amalgam carrier
(d) Retrograde amalgam condenser

136. The Term Anamnesis is related to
(a) Diagnosis
(b) Prognosis
(c) Control
(d) Prevention

137. Tick the odd one out
(a) Abfraction
(b) Crazing
(c) Infraction
(d) Infarction

138. Ruddle's solution is used as irrigating solution in
(a) In non vital bleaching
(b) In vital bleaching
(c) As Irrigation solution
(d) For endo gram

139. For the balance of hand cutting instrument:
(a) Cutting edges of the working end should be centered over the long axis of the handle.
(b) The cutting edge centered on a line running at right angle to the long axis of the handle.
(c) It should have shorter, straighter shank.
(d) It should have solid handle.

ORAL AND MAXILLO-FACIAL SURGERY

140. The drug of choice in the management of life threatening allergic reaction is:
(a) Corticosteroids
(b) Antihistamines
(c) Adrenaline
(d) Diazepam

141. Walsham's forceps are used to:
(a) Remove teeth
(b) Remove root
(c) Clamp blood vessels
(d) Reduce nasal bone fractures

142. Inferior alveolar nerve block is absolutely contra indicated in patients suffering from one of the following diseases:
(a) Thrombocytopenia
(b) Hemophilia
(c) Hypoprothrombinaemia
(d) Von Willebrand's disease

143. Some of the causes for recurrent salivary gland swelling is:
(a) pleomorphic adenoma
(b) abscess
(c) punctate sialectasis
(d) Frey's syndrome

144. The American Heart Association recommendation for infective endocarditis prophylaxis before minor surgeries is:

(a) 2gms. of Amoxicillin
(b) 3 gms. of Amoxicillin.
(c) 3 gms. of Amoxicillin followed by 500mg after 6 hours.
(d) 2 gms. of Amoxicillin followed by 500 mg after 6 hours.

145. The fascial space that is divided by the styloid process into an anterior and posterior compartment is:

(a) Pterygomandibular
(b) Lateral pharyngeal
(c) Retropharyngeal
(d) Infratemporal.

146. An absolute contraindication for extraction of teeth is:

(a) hypertension
(b) Myocardial infarction
(c) Thyrotoxicosis
(d) Central haemangioma

147. The cyst is 'deroofed' and the surrounding periostem sutured to the margins of the cyst wall in

(a) Decortication
(b) Marsupialization
(c) Saucerization
(d) Enucleation

148. Bleeding from the ears is a sign of one of the following fractures

(a) Condylar
(b) Le fort I
(c) Le fort II
(d) Le fort III

149. Saggital split osteotomy is a procedure done in the mandibular:

(a) Ramus
(b) Body
(c) Symphysis
(d) Angle

150. Complication of Vincent's angina is:

(a) Actinomycosis
(b) Noma
(c) Systemic Candidiasis
(d) Cellulites

151. Endosseous implants are examples of ridge

(a) Preservation
(b) Extension
(c) Augmentation
(d) Reconstruction

152. After an extraction of teeth, ideally radiotherapy for oral cancer should be delayed for:

(a) Two weeks
(b) Six weeks
(c) One week
(d) Three weeks

PEDODONTICS

153. Which of the following level of fluorides in drinking water is associated with enamel Fluorosis?

(a) 0.2 ppm
(b) 0.7 ppm
(c) 2.5 ppm
(d) 1.2 ppm

154. In a case of rampant caries the ideal procedure to perform in the first visit is:
(a) Diet control instructions
(b) Topical fluoride application
(c) Gross excavation and restoration of teeth
(d) None of the above.

ORTHODONTICS

155. Primate spaces present in primary dentition are:
(a) Inter dental spaces present in Upper and Lower anteriors.
(b) Spaces present mesial to lower canine and distal to Upper canine.
(c) Space present distal to lower 1st molar and mesial to upper 1st molar.
(d) Space present distal to lower canine and mesial to upper canine.

156. In primary dentition the anatomic structure used to determine the molar relationship:
(a) Mesio buccal cusp of primary 2nd molar
(b) Distal plane of primary 1st molar
(c) Mesial surface plane of primary 1st molar
(d) Distal plane of primary 2nd molar.

157. Teeth present at birth are called
(a) Neonatal teeth (b) Primary teeth
(c) Natal teeth (d) Accessory teeth.

158. Midline diastema of Maxillary central Incisors at the age of 9 is indicative of
(a) Mesiodens (b) Ugly duckling stage
(c) Abnormal labial frenum (d) Any of the above

159. Cleft lip occurs due to non-union of:
(a) Maxillary and frontonasal process.
(b) Maxillary process and mandibular process.
(c) Maxillary process and palatine process.
(d) Frontonasal process and palatine process.

160. The holding of teeth in ideal aesthetic and functional positions is
(a) Ideal occlusion (b) Normal occlusion
(c) Retention (d) Functional occlusion

161. Apertognathia means:
(a) Anterior cross bite (b) Openbite
(c) Posterior crossbite (d) Prognathism

162. Serial extractions are indicated in patients who have:
(a) Class II molar relation (b) Excessive overbite
(c) Class I molar relation (d) Class III molar relation

163. Force maintained at some appreciable fraction of the original from one patient visit to the next is:

(a) Continuous force
(b) Intermittent force
(c) Interrupted force
(d) None of the above

164. The Adam's clasp is made of: 22 gauge wire or 0.7 mm or

(a) 24 mil wire
(b) 28 mil wire
(c) 23 mil wire
(d) 22 mil wire

165. Beta-titanium, an excellent choice for auxiliary springs in nothing but

(a) Nitinol
(b) TMA
(c) A-NiTi
(d) Sentinol

166. Ectopic eruption is most likely to occur in

(a) Eruption of maxillary first molars
(b) Mandibular canines
(c) Maxillary lateral incisors
(d) Maxillary canines.

167. The term orthodontics was coined by:

(a) Hunter
(b) Le felon of France
(c) Carabeli
(d) Norman Kingsley

168. The relative mesial or distal angulations of the crown and the root along the line of force is called:

(a) Torue
(b) Tip
(c) Offset
(d) Inclination of teeth

169. Possible indicator of pubertal growth spurt on hand wrist films is sought as:

(a) Ossification of adductor sesamoid
(b) Appearance of hook of hamate
(c) Ossification of all the carpal bones
(d) Ossification of pisiform

170. The point of intersection of dorsal contours of Mandibular processes and occipital bone is

(a) Supramentale
(b) Articulare
(c) Condylion
(d) Pterygomaxillary.

PROSTHODONTICS

171. A simplified pantograph measures the following components

(a) All the mandibular movements.
(b) Relationship of fossae in the Temporomandibular joint.
(c) Hinge axis.
(d) Condylar inclinations and mandibular side shift.

172. Indicated finish margin with porcelain fused to metal restoration is:

(a) Shoulder
(b) Labial Shoulder with chamfer lingually
(c) Heavy shoulder
(d) Heavy chamfer

173. A device known as Gothic arch tracer is used to record the mandibular movement in:
(a) vertical plane
(b) Horizontal plane
(c) Sagittal Plane
(d) Transverse plane

174. The process of achieving limited removal of epithelial tissue in the sulcus while creating chamfer finish margin is called:
(a) Rotary curettage
(b) Mechanico-surgical gingival retraction
(c) Electro surgery
(d) Periodontal curettage

175. The standard perforated tray for use with alginate impression materials may be brought to more customized contour by
(a) Utility wax
(b) Base plate wax
(c) Beading wax
(d) Boxing wax

176. The concept of lingualized occlusion was put forward by
(a) Gysi
(b) Mc Grane
(c) Sears
(d) Payne

177. The posterior speaking space was suggested by
(a) Pound
(b) Mc Grane
(c) Niswonger
(d) Silverman

178. Which of the following is an example of static method of recording centric relation?
(a) Intra oral records
(b) Needle house
(c) Patterson
(d) All of the above

179. The concept of Occlusion that maintained that the antero posterior plane of occlusion should be parallel with the denture foundation and not dictated by the horizontal condylar guidance is calle(d)
(a) Lingualised concept
(b) Balanced concept
(c) Neutrocentric concept
(d) Mutually protected concept

180. The use of selected initial roots in our denture therapy is called —
(a) Overlay denture therapy
(b) Biologic denture therapy
(c) Submucosal vital root retention
(d) Submerged denture therapy

181. Long span distal extension bases where rigidity is critical the major connector of choice is
(a) Palatal strap
(b) Antero posterior palatal bar
(c) Closed horse shoe
(d) Horse shoe

182. Ideally the depth of undercut on the proposed abutment teeth at the most desired location is
(a) 0.010 inch
(b) 0.015 inch
(c) 0.020 inch
(d) 0.030 inch

183. The Abutment teeth that are to have cast inlays are classified as
(a) Class I
(b) Class II
(c) Cass III
(d) Class IV

184. A ledge is created on the lingual surface of the full cost crown to accommodate the lingual clasp arm. The greatest advantage is that it provides for:
(a) Appropriate contact (b) Appropriate under cut
(c) Survey line (d) Guiding plane

185. The clasp most often used on the mandibular bicuspids when the most favorable retentive undercut is on the disto-buccal surface adjacent to edentulous area is
(a) Ring clasp (b) Reverse loop clasp
(c) Simple circlet clasp (d) Reverse approach circlet clasp

COMMUNITY AND PREVENTIVE DENTISTRY

186. A Gaussian distribution is:
(a) Normal distribution. (b) Log normal distribution.
(c) Poisson distribution. (d) Variant distribution.

187. The type II error is the acceptance of a null hypothesis as true when it is:
(a) True. (b) Nonexistent.
(c) Negative value (d) False.

188. Sensitivity is usually expressed in:
(a) Units. (b) Alphabets.
(c) Ascending order. (d) Percentage.

189. Secondary level of prevention includes:
(a) Health promotion. (b) Vaccination.
(c) Early diagnosis and prompt treatment. (d) Rehabilitation.

190. If the μ is outside the 95% confidence limits with Normal Deviate > 2 then P will be
(a) 0.05 (b) < 0.05.
(c) > 0.05. (d) None of these

191. The tooth brushing method least likely to remove plaue in the gingival margin is the:
(a) Sulcular method (b) Scrub method
(c) Modified still man (d) Roll stroke

192. Priority of five levels in relation to motivation was advocated by:
(a) Herzberg (b) F.W. Taylor
(c) Douglas McGregor. (d) A.H.Winslow

193. Hospital gives:
(a) Primary Health Care. (b) Comprehensive Health Care
(c) Specialized Services (d) Health Education

194. Waste water from kitchen is:
(a) Sullage (b) Sewage
(c) Waste water (d) Kitchen water

195. Residual chlorine of water should be:

(a) 1 mg/ltr. After 1 hour
(b) 1 mg/ltr. After 2hour
(c) 0.5 mg/ltr after 1 hour
(d) 0.5 mg/ltr after 2hour

196. Removal of bacteria is:

(a) Better with slow and filter
(b) between with rapid sand filter
(c) Eual with both
(d) Depends on hardness of water

197. A series may have all except:

(a) No mode
(b) One mode
(c) Many mode
(d) Negative mode

198. Correlation coefficient can range from

(a) 0 to + 1.
(b) 0 to 100
(c) -1 to +1.
(d) -1 to 100

199. When sample size increases standard deviation:

(a) Decreases
(b) Increases
(c) Remains the same
(d) May increase or decrease

200. In a 3 x 3 table, the number of degrees of freedom is:

(a) 4
(b) 9
(c) 3
(d) 6

2003
ANSWERS & EXPLANATIONS

ANATOMY

Ans.1. (a) Histiocyte

Ref http://en.wikipedia.org/wiki/Histiocyte

A **histiocyte** is a cell that is part of the human immune system; a tissue macrophage cell ("histo-" = "tissue", and "-cyte" = "cell".) Some sources also consider Langerhans cell derivatives to be histocytes.

- All categories of histiocytes are derived from the bone marrow by multiplication from a stem cell. The derived cells migrate from the bone marrow to the blood as monocytes. They circulate through the body and stop (and hence "***fixed***") in various organs where they undergo differentiation into histiocytes which are part of the mononuclear phagocytic system (MPS).
- Histiocytes have common histological and immunophenotypical characteristics (demonstrated by immunostains). Their cytoplasm is eosinophilic and contains variable amounts of lysosomes. They bear membrane receptors for opsonins, such as IgG and the fragment C3b of complement. They express LCAs (leucocyte common antigens) CD45, CD14, CD33 and CD4 (also expressed by T Helper Cells).
- These histiocytes are part of the immune system by way of two distinct functions: phagocytosis and antigen presentation. Phagocytosis is the main process of macrophages and antigen presentation the main property of dendritic cells (so called because of their star-like cytoplasmic processes).
- Macrophages and dendritic cells are derived from common bone marrow precursor cells that have undergone different differentiation (as histiocytes) under the influence of various environmental (tissue location) and growth factors such as GM-CSF, TNF and IL-4. The various categories of histocytes are distinguishable by their morphology, phenotype and size.
- Macrophages are highly variable in size and morphology, their cytoplasm contains numerous acid phosphatase laden lysosomes - in relation to their specialised phagocytic function. They express CD68.
- Dendritic cells have an indented (bean shaped) nucleus and cytoplasm with thin processes (dendritic). Their main activity is antigen presentation, they express Factor XIIIa, CD1c and Class II HLA antigens.
- A subset of cells differentiates into Langerhans cells; this maturation occurs in the squamous epithelium, lymph nodes, spleen, and bronchiolar epithelium. Langerhans cells are antigen presenting cells but have undergone further differentiation. Skin Langerhans cells express CD1a as do cortical thymocytes (cells of the cortex of the thymus gland). They also express S-100, and their nucleus contains tennis-racket like ultra-structural inclusions called Birbeck granules.

- Histiocytoses describe neoplasias where the proliferative cell is the histiocyte.

Ans.2. (c) Lamellar bone

Ref http://www.wheelessonline.com/ortho/microscopic_structure_of_bone

Bone in human and other mammal bodies is generally classified into two types (1) Cortical bone, also known as compact bone and (2) Trabecular bone, also known as cancellous or spongy bone. These two types are classified as on the basis of porosity and the unit microstructure. Cortical bone is much denser with a porosity ranging between 5% and 10%. Cortical bone is found primary is found in the shaft of long bones and forms the outer shell around cancellous bone at the end of joints and the vertebrae

BONE FACTS-

There are three types of cells intimately associated with bone:

osteocytes, osteoblasts, and osteoclasts;

- osteocytes dwell in small lacunae within the bone matrix;
    - they are oval in cross section, their longest diameter being roughly parallel to the lamellae of mature bone;

- **Woven Bone:** (primary bone)
    - forms embryonic skeleton, and is largely absent after age 4 yrs;
    - woven bone formation is seen in fracture callus in both children and adults;
    - woven bone does not contain lamellae, and rather has a relatively disorganized array of collagen and irregular mineralization pattern;

- **Lamellar Bone** (secondary bone):
    - layering of bone is the hallmark of mature bone;
    - it is in compact cortical bone of diaphysis that haversian systems are found;
    - nutrients pass thru haversian canals, which run in the direction of the long axis of the bone, to bone cells that lie buried in the thick cortex;
    - **Osteon:**
        - refers to the bone surrounding the haversian system;
        - the haversian canals are surrounded by concentric rings or lamellae, each about 5 micrometers thick;
        - histologically, these layers of bone will contrast with one another under polarized light because of the different orientations of collagen fibers in each layer;
        - **cement lines** surround the outer border of each osteon;
            - histologically they are seen as the demarcation between the point that bone resorption ceased, and bone formation began;
                - collagen fibers and canaliculi do not cross cement lines;
            - these lines do not bind adjacent lamellae but rather than separate them;
    - **canaliculi:**
        - w/in concentric lamellae of mature bone are small lacunae containing osteocytes;
        - from lacunae extend fine canaliculi that contain cell processes of osteocytes;

- these processes connect osteocytes to one another and to haversian canal, and are the pathways of nutrition from the canal to the bone cells;
- canaliculi connect osteocytes within one haversian system only;
  - they do not cross cement lines to other systems;
  - since canaliculi are much too small to permit passage of RBC's, osteocytes must depend on diffusion and cell pumping mechanisms for their supply of oxygen and nutrients;

Ans.3. (a) Facial nerve

Ref http://en.wikipedia.org/wiki/Buccal_branch_of_the_facial_nerve

The **facial nerve** is the seventh (VII) of twelve paired cranial nerves. It emerges from the brainstem between the pons and the medulla, and controls the muscles of facial expression, and taste to the anterior two-thirds of the tongue. It also supplies preganglionic parasympathetic fibers to several head and neck ganglia.

BRANCHES

Inside the facial canal

- Greater petrosal nerve - provides parasympathetic innervations to lacrimal gland, as well as special taste sensory fibers to the palate via the nerve of pterygoid canal.
- Nerve to stapedius - provides motor innervations for stapedius muscle in middle ear.
- Chorda tympani - provides parasympathetic innervations to submandibular and sublingual glands and special sensory taste fibers for the anterior 2/3 of the tongue.

Outside skull (distal to stylomastoid foramen)

- Posterior auricular nerve - controls movements of some of the scalp muscles around the ear
- Five major facial branches (in parotid gland) - from top to bottom:
- Temporal branch of the facial nerve
- Zygomatic branch of the facial nerve
- Buccal branch of the facial nerve
- Marginal mandibular branch of the facial nerve
- Cervical branch of the facial nerve
  (Two Zebras Bit My Cat)

The **Buccal Branches of the facial nerve** (infraorbital branches), of larger size than the rest of the branches, pass horizontally forward to be distributed below the orbit and around the mouth.

- The *superficial branches* run beneath the skin and above the superficial muscles of the face, which they supply: some are distributed to the Procerus, joining at the medial angle of the orbit with the infratrochlear and nasociliary branches of the ophthalmic.
- The *deep branches* pass beneath the Zygomaticus and the Quadratus labii superioris, supplying them and forming an infraorbital plexus with the infraorbital branch of the maxillary nerve. These branches also supply the small muscles of the nose.

- The *lower deep branches* supply the Buccinator and Orbicularis oris, and join with filaments of the buccinator branch of the mandibular nerve.

Remember, the sensory supply to buccinator is by buccal branch of the anterior division of mandibular nerve.

Ans.4. (b) Between thyropharyngeus and cricopharyngeus

Ref B.D.C textbook of anatomy, 4th ed, pg 223

Killian's dehiscence: in the posterior wall of pharynx, the thyropharyngeus muscle in the lower part exists as a single sheet not overlapped internally by superior and middle constrictors.

- This weak part lies below the level of vocal cords or upper border of cricoid lamina and is limited inferiorly by thick cricopharyngeal sphincter.
- Pharyngeal diverticula due to neuromuscular incoordination are frequent findings. If the cricopharyngeus fails to relax while the thyropharyngeus contract, the food bolus is pushed back forming a diverticulum.
- Remember, TP is supplied by pharyngeal plexus while CP by recurrent laryngeal nerve.

Ans.5. (a) Laryngo tracheal diverticulum

Ref B.D.C textbook of anatomy, 4th ed, pg 170

DEVELOPMENT OF THYROID GLAND

- Develops from median endodermal thyroid diverticulum which grows down in front of the neck from the floor of primitive pharynx, just caudal to tuberculum impar.
- While the lower end of this diverticulum enlarges to form the gland the rest remains narrow and is known as thyroglossal duct.
- This duct runs from foramen caecum of the tongue to the pyramidal lobe.
- The gland becomes functional during the third moth of development.

Ans.6. (a) Mylohyoid muscle

Ref B.D.C, 4th ed , Vol 3 , pg 158

- Mylohyoid are flat , triangular muscles that form the floor of mouth.
- It lies deep to anterior digastric and forms a diaphragm that separates the oral cavity from the structures in the neck.
- Fibers originate from the mylohyoid line in mandible and insert on the nody oh hyoid bone.
- Nerve to mylohyoid (branch of mandibular nerve) supplies the muscle.
- It elevates the floor of mouth, and helps in depressing the mandible to effect mouth opening.

Ans.7. (d) Mastoid antrum

Explained earlier please refer KCET-06 A7

Ans.8. (c) Stellate ganglion

Ref B.D.C 4th ed, pg 191

The **inferior cervical ganglion** (Stellate ganglion)

- Formed by fusion of 7th and 8th cervical ganglia.
- It is star shaped *(Stellate)* and often fused with 1st thoracic ganglion(cervicothoracic ganglion)
- Situated behind the transverse process of C7 , lies behind the vertebral artery and in front of ramus of C8.
- The vertebral branches forms a plexus around the vertebral artery.
- Subclavian branches form a plexus around the subclavian artery.

Also remember.

The **superior cervical ganglion** (SCG),

- The largest of the cervical ganglia (2.5 cm long), is placed opposite the second and third cervical vertebra.
- It contains neurons that supply sympathetic innervations to the face.
- It is of a reddish-gray color, and usually fusiform in shape; sometimes broad and flattened, and occasionally constricted at intervals; it is believed to be formed by the coalescence of four ganglia, corresponding to the upper four cervical nerves.
- It is in relation, in front, with the sheath of the internal carotid artery and internal jugular vein; behind, with the Longus capitis muscle.
- It receives input from the ciliospinal center.

DENTAL ANATOMY AND HISTOLOGY

Ans.9. (a) Enamel knot

Ref http://en.wikipedia.org/wiki/Enamel_knot

The **enamel knot** is a localization of cells on an enamel organ that appear thickened in the center of the inner enamel epithelium. The enamel knot is frequently associated with an enamel cord

The enamel knot is a signaling center of the tooth that provides positional information for tooth morphogenesis and regulates the growth of tooth cusps. The enamel knot produces a range of molecular signals from all the major signaling families, such as Fibroblast Growth Factors (FGF), Bone morphogenetic proteins (BMP), Hedgehog (Hh) and Wnt signals. These molecular signals direct the growth of the surrounding epithelium and mesenchyme.

Primary and secondary enamel knots

The primary enamel knot forms at the tip of the bud during the bud stage of tooth development. This primary enamel knot is removed by apoptosis. Later secondary enamel knots appear that regulate the formation of the future cusps of the teeth.

The **enamel cord**, also called **enamel septum**, is a localization of cells on an enamel organ that appear from the outer enamel epithelium to an enamel knot.

These are temporary structures that cease to exist once enamel starts to form

Ref Orbans , 10th ed, pg 34

Ans.10. (c) Apical third of the root

Ref http://en.wikipedia.org/wiki/Cementum

Acellular cementum: at the cemento-enamel junction the cementum lacks the cellular components, and covers approximately 1/3-1/2 of the root.

cellular cementen: The more permeable form of cementum, covers 1/3-1/2 of the root apex, where it binds to the dentin.

There is also a third type of cementum, afibrillar cementum, which sometimes extends onto the enamel of the tooth.

Cementum's chemical makeup of is similar to that of bone, but it lacks vascularization. Volumetrically, it is approximately 65% inorganic material (mainly hydroxyapatite), 23% organic material (mainly [[collagen] type1]) and 12% water. Although it is only found in the root of human

Ans.11. (b) ABDCE

Ref Wheeler, 6th ed, pg24

Primary Teeth Development Chart

Upper Teeth	Eruption	Exfoliation	Crown completed	Root completed
Central incisor	8 to 12 months	6 to 7 years	4 months	1 ½ - 2 years
Lateral incisor	9 to 13 months	7 to 8 years	5 months	1 ½ - 2 years
Canine (cuspid)	16 to 22 months	10 to 12 years	9 months	2 ½ - 3 years
First molar	13 to 19 months	9 to 11 years	6 months	2 – 2 ½ years
Second molar	25 to 33 months	10 to 12 years	10-12months	3 years
Lower Teeth				
Second molar	23 to 31 months	10 to 12 years	10-12 months	3 years
First molar	14 to 18 months	9 to 11 years	6 months	2 – 2 ½ years
Canine (cuspid)	17 to 23 months	9 to 12 years	9 months	2 ½ - 3 years
Lateral incisor	10 to 16 months	7 to 8 years	4 ½ months	1 ½ - 2 years
Central incisor	6 to 10 months	6 to 7 years	4 months	1 ½ - 2 years

Permanent Teeth Development Chart

Upper Teeth	Eruption	Crown completed	Root completed
Central incisor	7 to 8 years	4-5 years	10 years
Lateral incisor	8 to 9 years	4-5 years	11 years
Canine (cuspid)	11 to 12 years	6-7 years	13-15 years
First premolar (first bicuspid)	10 to 11 years	5-6 years	12-13 years
Second premolar (second bicuspid)	10 to 12 years	6-7 years	12-14 years
First molar	6 to 7 years	2 ½ - 3 years	9-10 years
Second molar	12 to 13 years	7-8 years	14-16 years
Third molar (wisdom teeth)	17 to 21 years	12-16 years	18-25 years

Lower Teeth			
Third molar (wisdom tooth)	17 to 21 years	12-16 years	18-25 years
Second molar	11 to 13 years	7-8 years	15-16 years
First molar 6 to 7 years	17 to 21 years	2 ½ - 3 years	9-10 years
Second premolar (second bicuspid)	11 to 12 years	6-7 years	13-14 years
First premolar (first bicuspid)	10 to 12 years	5-6 years	12-13 years
Canine (cuspid)	9 to 10 years	6-7 years	12-14 years
Lateral incisor	7 to 8 years	4-5 years	10 years
Central incisor	6 to 7 years	4-5 years	9 years

Ans.12. (d) Mandibular central incisors

Explained earlier please refer KCET-07 A84

Ans.13. (b) 1 year

Please refer A11

Ans.14. (c) 56th day of intrauterine life

Ref Orbans, 10th ed , pg 24

Development of teeth

- The bucco-pharyngeal membrane ruptures at 27th day IU which establishes a connection of primitive oral cavity with the foregut.
- 2-3 weeks later, (6 wks) certain areas of basal cells of oral ectoderm proliferate at more rapid rate than do cells of adjacent areas.
- This leads to formation of a horse-shoe shaped epithelial band- dental lamina
- The dental lamina serves as the primordium for the ectodermal portion of the deciduous teeth.
- The permanent molars arise directly from the distal extensions of this lamina.(4th month IU)
- The total activity of this lamina extends over a period of at least 5 years.

So friends, we see that around 6-7th week IU the epithelium forms. Thus choice (c) is the closest answer here.

Ans.15. (b) Post emergent spurt

Ref Orbans, 10th ed, pg 366

Physiologic tooth movement is described as consisting of the following –

- **Pre-operative tooth movement**-mainly bodily and eccentric movements of the tooth buds. Incisors /canines develop lingual to the deciduous tooth in the same bony crypt and later erupt. Premolars also develop lingually and then move in between the divergent roots of primary molars. First Molars differ in not having any predecessor. The maxillary molar develops in the tuberosity and swings forward. All these movements are linked to jaw growth.

- **Eruptive tooth movement** – from the position in their crypts to the occlusion plane. When the tooth breaks the mucosal barrier it continues to erupt until it contacts the antagonist tooth. A ***'gubernacular cord'*** is believed to guide eruption of the tooth.
- **Post-eruptive tooth movement**: these include movements that aim to correct the axial alignment of tooth and help it to compensate for the wear and tear. The purpose is to cope up with jaw growth primarily by deposition of cementum.

PHYSIOLOGY

Ans.16. (b) Children than in adult

Ref http://en.wikipedia.org/wiki/Body_water

In individuals of normal weight, water is abundant in most parts of the body, except in adipose tissue (fat). These calculations are for adults of average build, and are inappropriate for obese or overly muscular people. These proportions are very simplified and use round numbers for quick calculation.

In men about 55% of the body mass is water. This value is about 51% in women due to a higher proportion of body fat. This is the *total body water*.

Body water is broken down into the following *compartments:*

- Intracellular fluid (2/3 of Body Water)
- Extracellular fluid (1/3 of Body Water)
- Plasma (1/4 of Extracellular fluid)
- Interstitial fluid (3/4 of Extracellular fluid)
- Transcellular fluid (normally ignored in calculations)
- Contained inside organs, such as the gastrointestinal, cerebrospinal, and ocular fluids.

EXTRA EDGE

Measurement of body water Dilution and equilibration

Total body water can be determined using Flowing afterglow mass spectrometry FA-MS measurement of deuterium abundance in breath samples from individuals. A known dose of deuterated water (Heavy water, D2O) is ingested and allowed to equilibrate within the body water. The FA-MS instrument then measures the deuterium-to-hydrogen (D:H) ratio in the exhaled breath water vapour. The total body water is then accurately measured from the increase in breath deuterium content in relation to the volume of D2O ingested.

Different substances can be used to measure different fluid compartments:[2]

- total body water: tritiated water or deuterium
- extracellular fluid: inulin
- blood plasma: Evans blue

Ans.17. (b) Type C fibers

Ref Ganong, 22nd ed, pg 61

Stimuli	Most susceptible	moderate	Minimal
Hypoxia	B	A	C
Pressure	A	B	C
Local anesthetics	C	B	A

EXTRA EDGE

Also remember,

Fiber type	Function	Velocity (m/s)
A		
• α	Propioception	70-120
• β	Touch, pressure, motor	30-70
• γ	Motor to muscle spindles	15-30
• δ	Pain, cold, touch	12-30
B	Preganglionic autonomic	3-15
C		
• Dorsal root	Pain, temp, reflex response	0.5-2
• Sympathetic	Postganglionic sympathetic	0.7-2.3

Ans.18. (c) Coagulation factors VII, IX and X

Ref Ganong, 22nd ed

Specific Factors

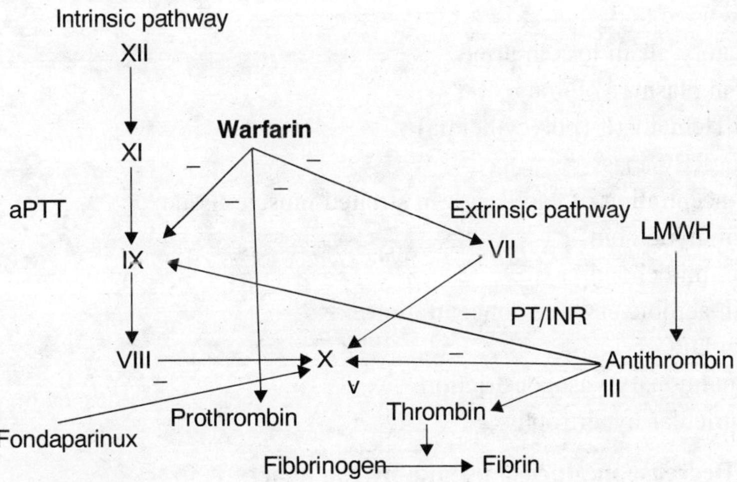

- prothrombin (factor II)
  - converts finbrinogen to fibrin
  - activates V, VIII & XIII (when bound to thrombomodulin)
  - activates protein C;

- Vit K dependent factors – II, VII ,IX,X
  factor VII: *part of factor VII/tissue factor complex that activates factor X and IX*
  factor IX: *acts w/ IXa /VIIIa /phos complex that activates factor X*
  factor X: *acts as Xa/Va phos complex that actives prothrombin;*
  also remember,

Ans.19. (d) Increase in partial pressure of carbon dioxide

Ref http://en.wikipedia.org/wiki/Effects_of_high_altitude_on_humans

There are several effects of **high altitude** on humans:

The percentage saturation of hemoglobin with oxygen determines the content of oxygen in our blood. After the body reaches around 7000 feet (2100 m) above sea level, the saturation of oxy-hemoglobin begins to plummet.

Effects

Altitude acclimatization, the physiological adaptations to altitude, can have immediate and long term effects.

Immediate effects

- Hyperventilation
- Fluid loss (due to a decreased thirst drive)
- Increase in heart rate (HR)
- Slightly lowered stroke volume

Longer term effects

- Lower lactate production (because reduced glucose breakdown decreases the amount of lactate formed).
- Compensatory alkali loss in urine
- Decrease in plasma volume
- Increased Hematocrit (polycythemia)
- Increase in RBC mass
- Higher concentration of capillaries in striated muscle tissue
- Increase in myoglobin
- Increase in mitochondria
- Increase in aerobic enzyme concentration
- Increase in DPG
- Hypoxic pulmonary vasoconstriction
- Right ventricular hypertrophy

Ans.20. (d) Decrease in glucose uptake by the heart

Ref http://en.wikipedia.org/wiki/Glucocorticoids#Mode_of_action

A variety of **synthetic glucocorticoids,** some far more potent than cortisol, have been created for therapeutic use. They differ in the pharmacokinetics (absorption factor, half-life, volume of distribution, clearance) and in pharmacodynamics (for example the capacity of mineralocorticoid activity: retention of sodium (Na^+) and water; see also: renal physiology). Because they absorb well through the intestines, they are primarily administered *per os* (by mouth), but also by other methods, such as topically on skin. More than 90 per cent of them bind different plasma proteins, however with a different binding specificity.

Endogenous glucocorticoids and some synthetic corticoids have high affinity to the protein transcortin (also called CBG, corticosteroid binding protein), while all of them bind albumin. In the liver, they quickly metabolize by conjugation with a sulfate or glucuronic acid and are secreted in the urine.

EXTRA EDGE

Glucocorticoid potency, duration of effect, and overlapping mineralocorticoid potency varies (Table).

Comparative steroid potencies

Name	Glucocorticoid potency	Mineralocorticoid potency	Duration of action ($t_{1/2}$ in hours)
Hydrocortisone (Cortisol)	1	1	8
Cortisone acetate	0.8	0.8	oral 8, intramuscular 18+
Prednisone	3.5-5	0.8	16-36
Prednisolone	4	0.8	16-36
Methylprednisolone	5-7.5	0.5	18-40
Dexamethasone	25-80	0	36-54
Betamethasone	25-30	0	36-54
Triamcinolone	5	0	12-36
Beclometasone	8 puffs 4 times a day equals 14 mg oral prednisone once a day	-	-
Fludrocortisone acetate	15	200	-
Deoxycorticosterone acetate (DOCA)	0	20	-
Aldosterone	0.3	200-1000	-

Ans.21. (a) Liver

Explained earlier please refer KCET-06 A64

BIOCHEMISTRY

Ans.22. (c) Pantothenic acid

Ref http://en.wikipedia.org/wiki/Coenzyme_A

Coenzyme A (CoA, CoASH, or HSCoA)

- is a coenzyme, notable for its role in the synthesis and oxidization of fatty acids, and the oxidation of pyruvate in the citric acid cycle.
- It is adapted from cysteamine, pantothenate and adenosine triphosphate.
- Since coenzyme A is chemically a thiol, it can react with carboxylic acids to form thioesters, thus functioning as an acyl group carrier.
- A molecule of coenzyme A carrying an acetyl group is also referred to as **acetyl-CoA**. When it is not attached to an acyl group it is usually referred to as 'CoASH' or 'HSCoA'.

List of coenzyme A activated acyl groups

- Acetyl-CoA
- Propionyl-CoA
- Acetoacetyl-CoA
- Coumaroyl-CoA (used in flavonoid and stilbenoid biosynthesis)
- Acyl derived from dicarboxylic acids
- Malonyl-CoA
- Succinyl-CoA
- Hydroxymethylglutaryl-CoA (used in isoprenoid biosynthesis)
- Pimelyl-CoA (used in biotin biosynthesis

Ans.23. (c) Tryptophan

Ref http://en.wikipedia.org/wiki/Niacin

Niacin, also known as **nicotinic acid** or **vitamin B$_3$**,

- is a water-soluble vitamin whose derivatives such as NADH, NAD, NAD$^+$, and NADP play essential roles in energy metabolism in the living cell and DNA repair.
- The designation *vitamin B$_3$* also includes the corresponding amide nicotinamide (or "niacinamide"), whose chemical formula is $C_6H_6N_2O$.
- The liver can synthesize niacin from the essential amino acid ***tryptophan*** (see below), but the synthesis is extremely inefficient;
- 60 mg of tryptophan are required to make one milligram of niacin.
- The 5-membered aromatic heterocycle of the essential amino acid, tryptophan, is cleaved and rearranged with the alpha amino group of tryptophan into the 6-membered aromatic heterocycle of niacin.

Ans.24. (d) Glucuronic acid

Ref Lippincott, pg 261

BILIRUBIN metabolism

- **Formation:** heme is degraded by microsomal enzyme *heme oxygenase* in presence of NADPH and oxygen, releasing ferric iron and CO_2- forming green pigment (biliverdin). This is the reduced to form a ***red-orange pigment*** known as Bilirubin.

- Bilirubin is only slightly soluble in plasma and is therefore transported to liver with albumin. In the hepatocytes, the Bilirubin binds to intracellular proteins (ligandin).
- **The solubility of Bilirubin is increased by addition of two molecules of glucuronic acid, by enzyme *Bilirubin glucoronyltransferase* using UDP-glucuronic acid.**
- This conjugated Bilirubin is now actively transported into the bile.
- This is then later hydrolyzed by gut bacteria into urobilinogen, a colorless compound.

MICROBIOLOGY

Ans.25. (b). Hot air oven

Explained earlier please refer KCET-07 A19

Ans.26. (a) Resistance transfer factor (RTF)

Ref http://www.kumc.edu/instruction//NURS325/Chemotherapy1/General%20Principles/conjugation

Conjugation is an important mechanism for single and multi-drug resistance development by allowing direct passage of resistance-conferring DNA between bacteria by way of a bridge.

- The transfer of genetic material requires two elements: an R-determinant plasmid which codes for the resistance itself and a resistance-transfer factor (RTF) plasmid which contains the genes required for bacterial conjugation. Sometimes both plasmid join to form a complete R factor.
- Some genes that confer resistance are located on transposons which can move from place to place in bacteria and plasmid genomes.
- **Conjugation-mediated resistance is prominent in gram-negative bacilli.**
- **Enterococci may contain plasmids that spread resistance among gram-positive organisms.**
- Conjugation appears to be the mechanism responsible for vancomycin resistance in entero coccal strains.
- Conjugation is associated with low efficiency. However, antibiotic-induced selection pressures have facilitated the elaboration of resistant strains.

R determinant - carries the resistance genes. The resistance genes are often parts of transposons.

Mode of action of resistance genes

(a) Modification (detoxification) of antibiotic - *e.g.* α-lactamase
(b) Alteration of target site - *e.g.* Streptomycin resistance
(c) Alteration of uptake - Tetracycline resistance
(d) Replacement of sensitive pathway - *e.g.* new folic acid pathway for resistance to sulfa drugs

Ans.27. (b) Measles virus

Ref ttp://www.health.gov.au/internet/wcms/Publishing.nsf/Content/cda-phlncd-measles.htm

Measles virus

- is a negative sense enveloped RNA virus that is a member of the Morbillivirus genus of the family Paramyxoviridae.
- Measles is highly infectious by the respiratory route presenting typically as cough, fever and conjunctivitis followed by a generalized maculopapular rash.
- Subacute sclerosing panencephalitis (SSPE) is a late complication of measles in about 1 in 25,00.
- Rapid diagnosis of measles by antigen detection can be achieved using smears made from nasopharyngeal or respiratory secretions stained with a monoclonal antibody(s) directed against virus structural proteins(Measles virus N protein).
- Although cytological appearances of giant cells or ***intranuclear (Cowdry A) or intracytoplasmic eosinophilic inclusions*** may be suggestive of measles infection a more positive identification is recommended. This cell, known as the Warthin-Finkeldey cell, is a multinucleated giant with eosinophilic cytoplasmic and nuclear inclusions.

Ans.28. (c) Aspergillus flavus

Ref http://en.wikipedia.org/wiki/Aflatoxin

Aflatoxins

- Naturally occurring mycotoxins that are produced by many species of *Aspergillus*, a fungus, most notably *Aspergillus flavus* and *Aspergillus parasiticus*. Aflatoxins are toxic and carcinogenic.
- After entering the body, aflatoxins are metabolized by the liver to a reactive intermediate, aflatoxin M_1, an epoxide.
- The native habitat of *Aspergillus* is in soil, decaying vegetation, hay, and grains undergoing microbiological deterioration and it invades all types of organic substrates whenever conditions are favorable for its growth.
- Virtually all sources of commercial peanut butter contain minute quantities of aflatoxin.

Ans.29. (b) Selenite F Broth

Ref Ananthnarayan Textbook of Microbiology, 7th ed, pg34-38

Culture media

1. **Simple media (Basal Broth)**
   - Nutrient broth
   - Nutrient agar
2. **Complex media**
   - Special ingredients for special purposes, for bringing out certain characteristics of an organism
3. **Synthetic or defined media**
   - Prepared from pure chemical substances and known composition
   - *e.g.*; Simple peptone water medium , 1% peptone with 0.5% NaCl in water

4. **Enriched media**
   - Substances like blood, serum or egg added to basal media
   - *e.g.* Blood Agar , Chocolate Agar , Egg media
5. **Enrichment media**
   - Substances added to media to inhibit growth of an organism
   - *e.g.* Tetrathionate broth , Selenite F broth
6. **Selective media**
   - *e.g.* deoxycholate citrate medium for dysentery bacilli
7. **Indicator media**
   - They have an indicator which changes color on growth of organism
   - *e.g.* Wilson and Blair Medium , McLeod medium for Diphtheria bacillus
8. **Differential media**
   - May also act as an indicator media
   - It has some substances incorporated in it which bring out different characteristics of a bacterium.
   - *e.g.* MacConkey's medium for Lactose fermenters
9. **Transport media**
   - *e.g.* Stuart media, Buffered glycerol saline

Ans.30. (a) Cocci

Explained earlier please refer KCET-06 A152

Ans.31. (b) Streptococcus Mutans

Explained earlier please refer KCET-06 A121

Ans.32. (a) Bacterial infection

Please refer KCET-06 A95

GENERAL PATHOLOGY

Ans.33. (b) Tuberculosis

Explained earlier please refer KCET-05 A26

Ans.34. (c) Metastasis

Explained elsewhere

Ans.35. (a) Fat

Ref http://en.wikipedia.org/wiki/Frozen_section_procedure

The **frozen section procedure** is a pathological laboratory procedure to perform rapid microscopic analysis of a specimen. It is used most often in oncological surgery. The technical name for this procedure is **cryosection.**

Uses

The principal use of the frozen section procedure is the examination of tissue while surgery is taking place. This may be for various reasons:

- If a tumor appears to have metastasized, a sample of the suspected metastasis is sent for cryosection to confirm its identity.
- If a tumor has been resected but it is unclear whether the surgical margin is free of tumor, an intraoperative consultation is requested to assess the need to make a further resection for clear margins.
- In a sentinel node procedure, a sentinel node containing tumor tissue prompts a further lymph node dissection, while a benign node will avoid such a procedure.
- If surgery is explorative, rapid examination of a lesion might help identify the possible cause of a patient's symptoms.
- Rarely, cryosections are used to detect the presence of substances lost in the traditional histology technique, for example ***lipids***. They can also be used to detect some antigens masked by formalin.

Ans.36. (c) Hyperplasia

Explained earlier please refer KCET-07 A32

Ans.37. (d) Chronic venous congestion

Explained earlier please refer KCET-05 A30

Ans.38. (a) Hypertrophy

Explained earlier please refer KCET-07 A32

DENTAL MATERIALS

Ans.39. (b) Emulsions

Ref Anusavice, Ch: Elastic Impression Materials, pg 108

When solute particles are dispersed in the solution media they represent colloids. When these solutes are large enough, they form a system termed either as a suspension or an emulsion.

When this comprises solids in liquid , it is known as *suspension*, while a liquids distributed in liquids forms an ***emulsion***.

Ans.40. (a) Solid solution

Ref Anusavice, Ch: Constitution of Alloys: 9th ed , pg 272

The metals, when completely soluble in the solid state are termed as ***solid solutions*** *.e.g.* Silver-palladium (Ag-Pd).

When these alloys exhibit complete liquid solubility, but limited solid solubility, they are known as ***eutectic*** alloys. *e.g.* Silver-copper (Ag-Cu).

When this limited solubility is accompanied by property of transformation (at a particular temp), the alloys are termed as ***peritectic alloys***. *e.g.* Silver-Tin (Ag-Sn).

EXTRA EDGE

The reactions in

- **Eutectic alloys :**Liquid → α-solid solution + β-solid solutions.
- **Peritectic alloys :** Liquid + β → α.
- **Hypo-peritectic:** Liquid + β → Liquid + α.

Ans.41. (c) Preconditioning solutions

Explained earlier please refer KCET-04 A130

Ans.42. (c) Gamma-2 phase

Explained earlier please refer KCET-05 A115

Ans.43. (a) Compressive strength

Ref Anusavice, Ch: Dental cements for restorations, 9th ed, pg 474

The cement base must have sufficient strength to withstand forces of condensation during the placement/condensation of restoration. It should also be able to resist the forces of mastication transmitted via the permanent filling.

Now we know, compressive strength refers to the crushing or shear strength where the material is subjected to vertical forces.

Compressive strengths at 7min interval is of particular interest as it coincides with the 'initial-set' period of most cements.

Ans.44. (b) Green strength

Ref Anusavice, 9th ed, Ch: Gypsum products, pg 84

The strength of gypsum investments is affected by the free water content and for this reason two strengths of gypsum products are recognized:-

- **Wet strength (green strength):** when water in excess of that required for the hydration of the hemi-hydrate is left in the specimen.
- **Dry strength:** strength measured when this excess water has evaporated.

Green strength ***should not be confused*** with the green shrinkage, seen in silicate bonded investments. (Volumetric contraction upon drying of the investment).

Ans.45. (c) Glycol ether

Ref Anusavice, Ch Elastomeric Impression Materials, 9th ed, pg 141

COMPOSITION

1. **Polyether** – 2 paste systems:
   - BASE- polyether polymer, colloidal silica (filler), glycol ether/phthalate (plasticizer)
   - ACCELERATOR- alkyl-aromatic sulfonate

2. **Condensation silicone**
   - BASE paste- silicone + colloidal silica (5-10 um) , micro-sized metal oxide.
3. **Addition silicone**
   - BASE – poly(methyl hydrogen siloxane) + fillers
   - CATALYST paste – platinum salt activator divinyl poly(dimethyl siloxane).
4. **Polysulphide**
   - BASE - Polysulphide polymer (mercaptan) +Fillers (lithopone, titanium dioxide) +Plasticizer (dibutyl phthalate) + 0.5 % sulfur.
   - ACCELERATOR- Lead dioxide (causes lengthening and cross-linking by oxidation of pendant –SH groups) + retarders (Oleic / Stearic acid).

Ans.46. (c) Microporosity

Explained earlier please refer KCET-05 A37

Ans.47. (c) By introduction of residual compressive stresses into the surface of the material

Ref Anusavice, Ch: Dental Ceramics, 9th ed , pg 510

Strengthening of Dental Porcelain:-

- **Introduction of Residual Compressive Stress**

  (1) **Ion Exchange method:** the sodium containing glass particles are subjected to ion exchange process with larger potassium ions (35%). This squeezing of larger K+ ions into previously occupied spaces by Na+ institutes a large compressive stress(700 Mpa) , known as chemical tempering.

  (2) **Thermal tempering:** *most common* method where quenching (rapid cooling) of hot, molten material produces a skin of rigid glass on the exterior. As the glass tends to shrink upon cooling, a stress is generated within.

  (3) **Thermal expansion Coefficient mismatch:** this process involves deliberate mismatch of the COTE of different layers of glass. As the inner layer (with higher COTE) tends to contract more than the outer layers, a stress is created which increases the strength of porcelain.
- **Interruption of Crack Propagation**

  (1) **Dispersion of a Crystalline Phase:** addition of a crystalline material like alumina to glass greatly improves the strength as any cracks that may develop, cannot penetrate the alumina particles as easily. *e.g.* Dicor Porcelain.

  (2) **Transformation Toughening:** a crystalline material is incorporated that is capable of undergoing a change in the crystal structure when placed under stress. ***Partially stabilized zirconia (PSZ)*** , utilizes the energy in such transformation, otherwise used to propagate the cracks through the porcelain. A major drawback is that PSZ scatters light as it passes through the porcelain and hence produces an opacifying effect.

Ans.48. (c) Gamma form

Explained earlier please refer KCET-07 A35

PHARMACOLOGY

Ans.49. (d) All of the above

http://en.wikipedia.org/wiki/Ivermectin

Ivermectin

- broad-spectrum antiparasitic agent.
- It is mainly used in humans in the treatment of onchocerciasis, but is also effective against other worm infestations (such as strongyloidiasis, ascariasis, trichuriasis and enterobiasis ***except tapeworms***).
- More recent evidence supports its off-label use in the treatment of mites such as scabies, usually limited to cases that prove resistant to topical treatments and/or who present in advanced state (such as Norwegian scabies).

Therapeutic dosage

Adults: Oral: 3 to 12 mg as a single dose per os (about 150 to 200 μg/kg bodyweight) for onchocerciasis and other parasitic infections. (Ex. 45 kg would be about 6.75 mg to 9 mg)

Children: Ivermectin is not given to children weighing less than 15 kg. The dose is 150 μg/kg bodyweight (in children weighing more).

Contraindications

Ivermectin is contraindicated in persons with an immediate hypersensitivity to the drug. It should not be given to mothers who are breast-feeding until the infant is at least three months old.

Ans.50. (d) Clindamcin 600 mg. 30 min before dental procedures

Explained earlier please refer KCET-06 A63

Ans.51. (d) All of the above

Ref http://en.wikipedia.org/wiki/Infliximab

Infliximab (brand name **Remicade→**) is a drug

- used to treat autoimmune disorders.
- Infliximab is known as a "chimeric monoclonal antibody" (the term "chimeric" refers to the use of both mouse (murine) and human components of the drug i.e. murine binding VK and VH domains and human constant Fc domains).
- The drug blocks the action of TNFα (tumour necrosis factor alpha) by binding to it and preventing it from signaling the receptors for TNFα on the surface of cells. TNFá is one of the key cytokines that triggers and sustains the inflammation response.
- Remicade is administered by intravenous infusion, typically at 2-month intervals, and at a clinic or hospital.
- It cannot be administered orally, because the digestive system would destroy the drug.

USES

- Ankylosing Spondylitis: 5mg per kg
- Crohn's disease: 5mg per kg

- Psoriatic Arthritis: 5mg per kg
- Rheumatoid Arthritis: 3mg per kg
- Psoriasis: 5mg per kg

This drug has been used for remission in the three variants of Crohn's disease: **stricturing** disease (which causes narrowing of the bowel), **penetrating** disease (which causes fistulae or abnormal connections of the bowel), and **inflammatory** disease (which causes primarily inflammation.

Ans.52. (d) Anti platelet drug

Ref http://www.kumc.edu/POL/ASP_Home/Meetings/Annual2000/Monday/view_abstract271.html

Trifusal, 2-acetoxy-4-trifluoromethylbenzoic acid, is a platelet antiaggregant drug. However, trifusal is considered a prodrug with its metabolite 2-hydroxy-4 trifluoromethylbenzoic acid (HTB) being the active form. Phototoxic processes have been frequently associated to Trifusal.

Ans.53. (a) alprozolam

Ref http://www.fetal-exposure.org/BENZOUPDATE.html

Friends, here is a divided opinion on this. Some say answer as Lorazepam and not Alprozolam. Now read the following text-

The **benzodiazepines** or **"benzos"** for short) are a class of psychoactive drugs considered as minor tranquilizers with varying hypnotic, sedative, anxiolytic, anticonvulsant, muscle relaxant and amnesic properties, which are brought on by slowing down the central nervous system.

Benzodiazepines (BZDs) are frequently prescribed during pregnancy to treat anxiety or panic disorder. They are well absorbed in the body and cross the placenta easily (Kanto, 1982); elimination half-lives for the BZDs range significantly (8-48 hours), with active metabolites often remaining in the body for longer periods of time (Gilman, 1990).

Initial concern regarding BZD exposure in pregnancy arose because they act upon GABA receptors; GABA is an amino acid neurotransmitter that may be related to palatal development (Kellogg, 1988). Early studies on Valium (diazepam), a commonly prescribed BZD, showed an increased risk for oral clefting in both animals (Zimmerman, 1984) and in retrospective and case-control studies in humans.

The investigated BZDs show the following result:-

Alprazolam	found no increased risk of malformations nor any pattern of the malformations described
Chlordiazepoxide	showed an increased frequency of malformations
Diazepam (Valium)	showed an increased risk of oral clefts
Lorazepam	shows an increase in respiratory distress, decreased APGARS, problems with temperature regulation and poor feeding
Oxazepam	associated with "fetal benzodiazepine syndrome" and neonatal withdrawal

Now at the same time-

'Lorazepam crosses the placenta more slowly than diazepam, and also has a short half life (12-16 hours). Lorazepam is not considered teratogenic in mice or rats, but human reproductive data is limited. Small prospective studies (N=30; N=112) have not shown an increase in pattern to the malformations observed in women exposed to lorazepam in the first trimester (Johnson et al., 1995; Ornoy, 1998). Much of the human information has reviewed use around labor, and (McElhatton, 1994).'

Therefore, although teratogenic potential of Lorazepam is low, it still can result in various fetal disoreders mentioned above. Hence, according to us Alprazolam is still safer in pregnancy when compared to other BZD's

Ans.54. (b) Erythromycin

Ref http://wellcaremc.com/drugs/mg/erythromycin.htm

DRUG CLASS

Macrolide antibiotic

Therapeutic actions

Bacteriostatic or bactericidal in susceptible bacteria; binds to cell membrane, causing change in protein function, leading to cell death.

Indications

Systemic administration

- Acute infections caused by sensitive strains of *Streptococcus pneumoniae, Mycoplasma pneumoniae, Listeria monocytogenes, Legionella pneumophila.*
- URIs, LRIs, skin and soft-tissue infections caused by group A beta-hemolytic streptococci when oral treatment is preferred to injectable benzathine penicillin.
- PID caused by *N. gonorrhoeae* in patients allergic to penicillin.
- In conjunction with sulfonamides in URIs caused by *Haemophilus influenzae.*
- As an adjunct to antitoxin in infections caused by *Corynebacterium diphtheriae* and *Corynebacterium minutissimum.*
- Prophylaxis against alpha-hemolytic streptococcal endocarditis before dental or other procedures in ***patients allergic to penicillin*** who have valvular heart disease.

Oral erythromycin

- Treatment of intestinal amebiasis caused by *Entamoeba histolytica*; infections in the newborn and in pregnancy that are caused by *Chlamydia trachomatis* and in adult chlamydial infections when tetracycline cannot be used; primary syphilis (*Treponema pallidum*) in penicillin-allergic patients; eliminating *Bordetella pertussis* organisms from the nasopharynx of infected individuals and as prophylaxis in exposed and susceptible individuals.
- Unlabeled uses: erythromycin base is used with neomycin before colorectal surgery to reduce wound infection; treatment of severe diarrhea associated with *Campylobacter* enteritis or enterocolitis; treatment of genital, inguinal, or anorectal lymphogranuloma venereum infection; treatment of *Haemophilus ducreyi* (chancroid).

Ophthalmic ointment

- Treatment of superficial ocular infections caused by susceptible strains of microorganisms; prophylaxis of ophthalmia neonatorum caused by *N. gonorrhoeae* or *C. trachomatis.*

Topical dermatologic solutions for acne

- Treatment of acne vulgaris.

Topical dermatologic ointment

- Prophylaxis against infection in minor skin abrasions.
- Treatment of skin infections caused by sensitive microorganisms.

Contraindications and cautions

Systemic administration

- Contraindicated with allergy to erythromycin.
- Use cautiously with hepatic dysfunction, lactation (secreted and may be concentrated in breast milk; may modify bowel flora of nursing infant and interfere with fever workups).

Ophthalmic ointment

- Contraindicated with allergy to erythromycin; viral, fungal, mycobacterial infections of the eye.

Ans.55. (d). Neostigmine

Ref KDT , pg 100

Neostigmine is a reversible anti-cholinesterase and prevents the breakdown of acetylcholine. This causes excess salivation rather than inhibiting it.

GENERAL MEDICINE

Ans.56. (c) 1 major and 2 minor criteria

Explained earlier please refer KCET-06 A65

Ans.57. (c) endothelial dysintegrity

Explained earlier please refer KCET-06 A100

Ans.58. (b) ASD

Explained earlier please refer KCET-06 A63

Ans.59. (b) Lower 1/3 of sternum

Ref http://www.answers.com/topic/cardiac-arrest?cat=health

Cardiopulmonary resuscitation (CPR) is an emergency first aid procedure for a victim of cardiac arrest or respiratory arrest. It is part of the chain of survival, which includes early access (to emergency medical services), early CPR, early defibrillation, and early advanced care.

The heart stops beating if the pacemaker-generated rhythm is halted, or if conduction of the electrical impulses is disrupted, sending the muscle of the ventricles — the heart's pumps — into the irregular and useless twitching state of fibrillation. If the instrument and the expertise are available, electric shocks are administered with a defibrillator, which may or may not restore a normal electrical rhythm and hence a regular beat. When this amenity is not at hand, or access to it is delayed, the first aid measure is *external cardiac massage*, consisting of rhythmic pressure on the chest, at the ***lower end of the sternum***. By squeezing the heart against the spinal column, this can temporarily restore circulation of the blood.

Ans.60. (c) Candidiasis

Ref http http://www.aids.org/factSheets/500-Opportunistic-Infections.html

The most common Opportunistic Infections are listed here, along with the disease they usually cause, and the CD4 cell count when the disease becomes active:

- **Candidiasis (Thrush)** is a fungal infection of the mouth, throat, or vagina. CD4 cell range: can occur even with fairly high CD4 cells. Fungus infection caused by Candida albicans. Candida is the most common HIV-related fungus infection. Other species causing candida are C. glabrata, C. parapsilosis, C. tropicalis, and C. krusei
- **Cytomegalovirus (CMV)** is a viral infection that causes eye disease that can lead to blindness.CD4 cell range: under 50.
- Herpes simplex viruses can cause oral herpes (cold sores) or genital herpes. These are fairly common infections, but if you have HIV, the outbreaks can be much more frequent and more severe. They can occur at any CD4 cell count.
- **Malaria** is common in the developing world. It is more common and more severe in people with HIV infection.
- **Mycobacterium avium complex (MAC or MAI)** is a bacterial infection that can cause recurring fevers, general sick feelings, problems with digestion, and serious weight loss. CD4 cell range: under 75.
- **Pneumocystis pneumonia (PCP)** is a fungal infection that can cause a fatal pneumonia. CD4 cell range: under 200. Unfortunately this is still a fairly common OI in people who have not been tested or treated for HIV. The US Centers For Disease Control considers PCP an *AIDS-defining* condition.
- **Toxoplasmosis (Toxo)** is a protozoal infection of the brain. T-cell range: under 100.
- **Tuberculosis (TB)** is a bacterial infection that attacks the lungs, and can cause meningitis. CD4 cell range: Everyone with HIV who tests positive for exposure to TB should be treated.

Ans.61. (b) Von Willebrand's

Explained earlier please refer KCET-06 A19

Ans.62. (b) Leukemia

Explained earlier please refer KCET-07 A34

Ans.63. (b) Splenomegaly, Oesophageal varices and Ascitis

Explained earlier please refer KCET-07 A58

Ans.64. (d) All of the above

Explained earlier please refer KCET-07 A58

Ans.65. (c) both of the above

Ref http://en.wikipedia.org/wiki/Diabetic_hypoglycemia#Treatment

TREATMENT

Oral intake of glucose

- The blood glucose can be raised to normal within minutes with 15-20 grams of carbohydrate in the form of food or drink if the person is conscious and able to swallow.
- This amount of carbohydrate is contained in about 3-4 ounces (100-120 ml) of orange, apple, or grape juice, about 4-5 ounces (120-150 ml) of regular (non-diet) soda), about one slice of bread, about 4 crackers, or about 1 serving of most starchy foods.
- Starch is quickly digested to glucose, but adding fat or protein retards digestion.
- Symptoms should begin to improve within 5 minutes, though full recovery may take 10-20 minutes.

Intravenous glucose

- If a person is suffering such severe effects of hypoglycemia that they cannot (due to combativeness) or should not (due to seizures or unconsciousness) be given anything by mouth, glucose can be given by intravenous infusion.
- Glucose is available for intravenous infusion in various concentrations. The highest is 50% dextrose (about 18 grams of glucose in 40 ml of fluid), but this should be given carefully as it is damaging to tissue if the infusion leaks from the vein.

Glucagon rescue

- Glucagon is a hormone that rapidly counters the metabolic effects of insulin in the liver, causing glycogenolysis and release of glucose into the blood.
- It can raise the glucose by 30-100 mg/dl within minutes in any form of hypoglycemia caused by insulin excess (including all types of diabetic hypoglycemia).
- It comes in a glucagon emergency rescue kit which includes tiny vials containing 1 mg, which is a standard adult dose.
- Glucagon works if given subcutaneously, but absorption and recovery are faster if it is injected deep into a muscle (usually the middle of the outside of the thigh). It has an even more rapid effect when given intravenously but this is rarely practicable.
- Side effects of glucagon can include nausea and headache, but these can also occur after severe hypoglycemia even when glucagon is not used.

Friends, the gluconeogenetic effect of adrenaline (α_2 agonist) has already been discussed before

Ans.66. (c) Rickets

Explained earlier please refer KCET-05A74

GENERAL SURGERY

Ans.67. (b) Spinal accessory nerve

Ref Manipal Manual of Surgery, pg 207-208

Excision of the Submandibular gland

- Incision is placed below the angle of the jaw. This should be about 2.5 cm below the angle to preserve the ***marginal mandibular branch of facial nerve*** passing postero-inferiorly.
- The gland is located in two planes (J-shape) by mylohyoid muscle and is in very close contact to the digastric muscle. Hence it is important to identify and retract the intermediate tendon of this muscle.
- Facial artery enters the gland poterolaterally and deeply grooves the gland. It should be ligated at this place during excision. It is ligated again, as it enters the face near the lower border of mandible.
- Wharton Duct arises from the deep part of the gland and opens on a papilla beside the frenum of the tongue.
- The middle part is related to the ***lingual and the hypoglossal nerves*** along with hyoglossus, styloglossus and submandibular ganglion.

A popular RULE OF 2 is followed while excising this gland

2 common indications – stone, radical neck dissection
2" long incision - curved incision over the swelling
Protect **2** superficial nerves – Cervical + mandibular branches of facial nerve
Protect **2** deep nerves – lingual and hypoglossal
Ligate facial artery **2** times – at deeper and superficial planes
Divide **2** muscles – platysma (superficially) mylohyoid (deep)
Remove **2** lobes – superficial and deep

Ans.68. (c) Both the above

Explained earlier please refer KCET-05A74

Ans.69. (b) between 3-6 months of age

Ref http://en.wikipedia.org/wiki/Cleft_palate#Treatment

CLEFT LIP

- Within the first *2-3 months* after birth, surgery is performed to close the cleft lip.
- preferred age is at approximately 10 weeks of age, following the "***rule of 10s***" coined by surgeons Wilhelmmesen and Musgrave in 1969 (*the child is at least 10 weeks of age; weighs at least 10 pounds, and has at least 10 g hemoglobin*).
- If the cleft is bilateral and extensive, two surgeries may be required to close the cleft, one side first, and the second side a few weeks later.

CLEFT PALATE: Often a cleft palate is temporarily closed using a palatal obturator. The obturator is a prosthetic device made to fit the roof of the mouth covering the gap.

- Cleft palate is corrected by surgery, usually performed between 9 and 18 months.
- Approximately 20-25% only requires one palatal surgery to achieve a competent velopharyngeal valve capable of producing normal, non-hypernasal speech. However, combinations of surgical methods and repeated surgeries are often necessary as the child grows.
- One of the new innovations of cleft lip and cleft palate repair is the ***Latham appliance***. The Latham is surgically inserted by use of pins during the child's 4th or 5th month. After it is in place, the doctor, or parents, turns a screw daily to bring the cleft together to assist with future lip and/or palate repair.

Ans.70. (c) Between 12-15 months of age

Explained above

Ans.71. (a) Extradural Haematoma

Ref http://en.wikipedia.org/wiki/Lucid_interval

A **lucid interval** is a temporary improvement in a patient's condition after a traumatic brain injury, after which the condition deteriorates. A lucid interval is especially indicative of an epidural hematoma. After the injury, the patient is momentarily dazed or knocked out, and then becomes relatively lucid for a period of time which can last minutes or hours. Thereafter there is rapid decline as the blood collects within the skull, causing a rise in intracranial pressure, which damages brain tissue. In addition, some patients may develop "pseudoaneurysms" after trauma which can eventually burst and bleed, a factor which might account for the delay in loss of consciousness.

Ans.72. (b) follicular carcinoma of thyroid

Explained earlier, please refer KCET-06 A67

Ans.73. (c) Infected, ulcerated sebaceous cyst

Ref Manipal Manual of Surgery , pg 153

Complications of Sebaceous Cysts (Epidermoid cyst)

Infection – due to an injury or scratch resulting in a abscess.

Sebaceous horn -slow drying of the cystic contents leaving a dry horny structure.

Cock's peculiar tumor- refers to an infected, ulcerated cyst of the scalp with pouting granulation tissue with everted edge resembling epithelioma.

Remember, ***Pott's puffy tumor*** refers to osteomyelitis of the frontal bone with edema of the scalp secondary to frontal sinusitis.

Ans.74. (b) Cutaneous anthrax

Ref http://www.odh.ohio.gov/pdf/IDCM/anthrax.pdf

ANTHRAX

(Malignant Edema, Malignant Pustule, Woolsorter's Disease, Charbon, Ragpicker's Disease)

AGENT

Bacillus anthracis, a gram-positive, encapsulated, spore-forming, non-motile rod. Thisorganism is found in a vegetative state in humans and animals. When exposed to air, it forms spores which are highly resistant to physical and chemical agents. The spores live for years in contaminated soils.

Clinical description

An illness with acute onset characterized by several distinct clinical forms, including the following:

- **Cutaneous:** a skin lesion evolving during a period of 2-6 days from a papule, through a vesicular stage, to a depressed black eschar.
- **Inhalation:** a brief prodrome resembling a viral respiratory illness followed development of hypoxia and dyspnea, with radiographic evidence of mediastinal widening.
- **Intestinal:** severe abdominal distress followed by fever and signs of septicemia.
- **Oropharyngeal:** mucosal lesion in the oral cavity or oropharynx, cervical adenopathy and edema, and fever.

Cutaneous anthrax is the most common form. The mortality rate is 5%-20% in untreated patients. Inhalation anthrax can present as respiratory distress with fever and shock. The mortality rate in inhalation anthrax is 80%-100%. Intestinal anthrax rarely occurs, but when it does, it usually manifests as explosive outbreaks of violent gastroenteritis with vomiting and bloody stools. The mortality rate is 25%-75%.

Ans.75. (b) Sebaceous cyst

Ref http://www.entcolumbia.org/neckcyst.htm

While all other are congenital cysts (present at birth) **Sebaceous Cysts** refers to lumps in or just under the skin. A sebaceous cyst is a catch-all term for a benign, harmless growth that occurs under the skin and tends to be smooth to the touch. Ranging in size, sebaceous cysts are usually found on the scalp, face, ears, and genitals. They are formed when the release of sebum, a medium-thick fluid produced by sebaceous glands in the skin, is blocked. Unless they become infected and painful or large, sebaceous cysts do not require medical attention or treatment, and they usually go away on their own. If they become infected, the physician may drain the fluid and cells that make up the cyst wall. Or, if the cyst causes irritation or cosmetic problems, it may be removed through a simple excision procedure.

Ans.76. (a) Thallium -Technetium scan

Ref http://www.utmb.edu/otoref/Grnds/Parathyroid-2002-03/Parathyroid-2002-03.htm

Preoperative localization studies have been found to decrease operative time, decrease total length of hospital stay, decrease the incidence of postoperative hypoparathyroidism, and decrease the incidence of reoperation.

The range of preoperative localization options include ultrasound, CT scan, fine needle aspiration (FNA), MRI, angiography with or without selective venous sampling, and Sestamibi scan.

- FNA confirms parathyroid lesions previously identified by imaging and can be useful prior to reoperation.
- MRI is best suited for finding ectopic parathyroid glands; because parathyroid tissue has an intensity similar to thyroid and fat, STIR images are most useful.
- Angiography can localize parathyroid tumor in 60% of cases, and has the advantage of allowing for the option of angioablation, which is particularly useful with mediastinal parathyroid glands. Angiography can be further enhanced and confirmed using selective venous sampling for PTH.
- Ultrasound is useful in distinguishing thyroid pathology from adenoma.
- MRI and CT scan are more commonly used to locate ectopic glands and arteriography is typically used in repeat operations.

The localization study of choice is the ***Sestamibi (Th-Tc) scan*** with a sensitivity of 80-90% and specificity approaching 100%. The first published report of Sestamibi identifying abnormal parathyroid tissue came in 1989.

- It is a cationic, lipophilic derivative of Technetium developed as an alternative cardiac imaging agent and was incidentally noted to have uptake and retention in abnormal parathyroid glands.
- With Sestamibi it is possible to perform 3-dimensional SPECT imaging, which allows for deep cervical and mediastinal parathyroid tissue.
- False positives can result in the presence of thyroid nodules, which is significant since 25% of patients have associated thyroid disease.
- This problem can be minimized by the use of iodine or pertechnetate subtraction techniques. False negatives are more of a problem and can occur with small adenomas and hyperplasia.
- Accuracy of Sestamibi scans may be reduced to 35% in the setting of multi-gland hyperplasia. In addition, radionuclide scans have the advantage of being inexpensive (comparable to ultrasound).

Ans.77. (a) Seventh

Ref http://en.wikipedia.org/wiki/Suture#Removal_of_sutures

Whilst some sutures are intended to be permanent, and others in specialized cases may be kept in place for an extended period of many weeks, as a rule sutures are a short term device to allow healing of a trauma or wound. According to article on nursing:

"Different parts of the body heal at different intervals. Common time to remove stitches will vary: facial wounds 3-5 days; scalp wound 7-10 days; limbs 10-14 days; joints 14 days; trunk of the body 7-10 days.

"Not all stitches must be removed. If a small area remains unhealed, notify the health care practitioner. Then if ordered, remove sutures from the healed area only."

Ans.78 (d). Minimum debridement

Ref http://connection.lww.com/Products/anderson3e/documents/PDFs/Ch06.pdf

Muscle contusions or bruises result from a direct compressive force sustained from a heavy blow. Such injuries vary in severity in accordance with the area and depth over which blood vessels are ruptured.

SIGNS AND SYMPTOMS OF CONTUSIONS

- History of acute onset.
- Mechanism is usually a compressive force.
- Pain is localized over the injury site.
- Ecchymosis may be present if hemorrhage is superficial.
- Range of motion may be limited because of swelling and hemorrhage.
- Swelling may compress nerves, leading to pain and temporary paralysis.
- If compressive force is great enough, injury also may occur in muscle tissue (strain).

Closed wound care focuses on immediately reducing inflammation, pain, and secondary hypoxia. Several initial steps should be followed by the athletic trainer in providing general acute care:

- Apply crushed ice packs directly to the skin as quickly as possible following the injury.
- Do not place a towel or elastic wrap (dry or wet) between the crushed ice pack and skin. This will reduce the effectiveness of the treatment.
- Apply the crushed ice-cold pack for 30 minutes (40 minutes for a large muscle mass such as the quadriceps).
  Elevate the body part at least 6 to 10 inches above the level of the heart.
- After the initial ice treatment, remove the ice pack, replace the compression wrap, and continue elevation.
- Reapply the crushed ice pack every 2 hours (every hour if the athlete is active between applications; for example, walking on crutches or showering) until the athlete goes to bed.

Contusions

For superficial contusions:

1. Pad with soft (open-celled) material next to the skin and denser (closed-cell) material as an external covering.
2. Cut a hole that matches the contused area in the soft material, or keep it solid.
3. Secure the pad with elastic athletic tape or an elastic wrap.
4. Following play, and periodically during the next few days, apply ice, compression, and elevation to the site.
5. Repeat until pain and swelling are gone.

For ***deep contusions***, determine disability after temporary paralysis subsides:

1. In moderate and severe cases, follow acute protocol for at least 24 hours with the muscle in a stretched position.
2. If an antalgic gait is present, fit for crutches and instruct the athlete to use a partial- or non–weight-bearing gait.
3. Seek medical advice for complications.

Ans.79. (c) Polyglyclic acid

Explained earlier, please refer KCET-07 A65

ORAL PATHOLOGY

Ans.80. (b) Cleidocranial dysostosis

Explained earlier, please refer KCET-07 A65

Ans.81. (c) Cherubism

Ref http://www.orpha.net/static/GB/cherubism.html

Cherubism

- Is a benign fibro-osseous disorder of childhood, limited to the lower half of the face, the maxilla and particularly the mandible.
- The prevalence is unknown, but probably lower than 1 in 10,000. The age at onset is between 6 and 10 years.
- With bilateral painless swelling of jaws (giving the so-called cherubic look) associated with multicystic bone tumors and eyes-to-heaven appearance.
- Dentition is also abnormal at the sites concerned: tooth agenesis, noneruption, displacement, root resorption and malocclusions are common.
- Radiology contributes greatly to the diagnosis. Radiographs show well-defined multilocular radiolucencies and with age, thick sclerotic borders. The bone lesions are generally symmetrical.
- The definitive diagnosis is established histologically with samples showing randomly distributed multinucleated giant cells and vascular spaces within a fibrous connective tissue stroma can be observed. Multinucleated giant cells are positive for osteoclastic specific markers.
- Cherubism is a hereditary, ***autosomal dominant disease***, with variable penetrance and expressivity. It can be caused by mutations in the *SH3BP2 gene*, which has been mapped to locus 4p16.3.
- Cherubism has also been associated with a range of other diseases such as Noonan syndrome and Noonan "like" syndrome (caused by mutations in the *PTPN11 gene*), Ramon syndrome associated with gingival fibromatosis and neurofibromatosis type I.
- Without treatment, cherubism might regress or, in rare cases, grow slowly. Conservative treatment is indicated. Nevertheless, surgical intervention (delayed until after puberty if possible) is suggested for improving maxilla mobility and the psychological status of the patients: curettage or surgical contouring may be proposed during the rapid growth of the lesions. Segmental mandibulectomy followed by reconstruction can be performed with good results in cases with extensive lesions and those at risk of pathologic fracture of the mandible.

Clinical signs

- Autosomal dominant inheritance
- Broad cheeks
- Enlargment of jaw

- High cheek bones
- Large face
- Anodontia/oligodontia
- Orbital region anomalies

Ans.82. (a) Sucrose

ref http://en.wikipedia.org/wiki/Dental_caries#Etiology

Bacteria in a person's mouth convert sugars (glucose and fructose, and most commonly sucrose - or table sugar) into acids such as lactic acid through a glycolytic process called fermentation.(for example *S.mutans* coverts sucrose into glucan with the help of an enzyme glycosyl-transferase, which forms plaque). If left in contact with the tooth, these acids may cause demineralization, which is the dissolution of its mineral content. The process is dynamic, however, as remineralization can also occur if the acid is neutralized; suitable minerals are available in the mouth from saliva and also from preventative aids such as fluoride toothpaste, dental varnish or mouthwash.

Ans.83. (d). Hurler's syndrome

Ref Shafer, 5th ed , pg 37

Macroglossia or tongue hypertrophy is commonly seen with

CONGENITAL

- Down syndrome (1 in 700 birth)
- Beckwith-Weidemann syndrome (0.07% / live birth)
- Haemangioma
- Lymphangioma
- Gland hypertrophy/ lingual thyroid
- Muco-polysaccharidosis

ACQUIRED

- Hypothyroidism /cretinism
- Syphilis / TB
- Pemphigus, Ludwig's angina
- Acromegaly
- Neurofibromatosis
- Neoplastic – carcinoma
- Amyloidosis/sarcoidosis

Ans.84. (c) Verrucous Oral

Ref Burket's, 10th ed pg 107

Lichen Planus are of following types

- Reticular – lace-like keratotic mucosal type
- Atrophic – keratotic types with mucosal erythema
- Erosive – pseudomembrane types + keratotic + erythema

- Bullous – vesico-bullous + reticular/erosive types

The erosive types is considered the most premalignnt

Ans.85. (a) Thrush

Explained earlier Please refer KCET-05 A72

Ans.86 (a) Papilloma

Explained earlier Please refer KCET-05 A85

Ans.87. (c) Remnants of cell rests of embryonic lacrimal duct

Explained earlier Please refer KCET-05 A80

Ans.88. (d) Pemphigus vulgaris

Explained earlier Please refer KCET-04 A77

Ans.89. (d) All of the above

Ref http://www.umm.edu/ency/article/000068.htm

Histiocytosis is a general name for a group of syndromes. These syndromes all include an abnormal increase in the number of certain immune cells, called histiocyte cells. Histiocyte cells include monocytes, macrophages, and dendritic cells.

There are 3 major classes of histiocytoses, but this article focuses on Langerhans cell histiocytosis, which is also called histiocytosis X.

The other 2 classes are non-Langerhans cell histiocytosis (also known as hemophagocytic syndrome) and malignant histiocytosis syndrome (now known as T-cell lymphoma).

Ans.lternative Names:

Eosinophilic granuloma; Pulmonary histiocytosis X; Nonlipid reticuloendotheliosis; Pulmonary Langerhans cell granulomatosis; Hand-Schuller-Christian disease; Letterer-Siwe disease; Langerhans cell histiocytosis

Causes, incidence, and risk factors

- Most cases of histiocytosis X affect children between ages 1 and 15 years old. The incidence peaks amongst children between 5 and 10. Histiocytosis X is thought to affect roughly 1 in 200,000 people each year.
- The extra immune cells may form tumors, which can affect various parts of the body. In children, histiocytosis X usually involves the bones (80%), and may affect one or more sites. The skull is frequently affected.
- The tumors produce a punched-out appearance on bone X-ray. Tumors in weight-bearing bones, such as the legs or spine, may cause the bones to fracture without apparent reason.
- There is often systemic (whole body) involvement as well, causing rashes, lung problems, gum problems, lymph gland swelling, hormonal problems, enlargement of the spleen and liver, and anemia . Not surprisingly, with a disease that affects so many systems and organs, histiocytosis can be deadly.

- Histiocytosis X has typically been thought of as a cancer-like condition, but more recently researchers have begun to suspect that it is actually an ***autoimmune*** phenomenon, in which rogue immune cells attack the body, rather than fight infections. Some forms of the disorder are genetic.

Another type of this disorder, pulmonary histiocytosis X, is characterized by inflammation of the small airways (bronchioles) and the small blood vessels in the lungs. It is most common in adults. The inflammation leads to stiffening (fibrosis) and destruction of the walls of the alveoli (parts of the lung). The cause is unknown. People 30 - 40 years old are affected most often. Cigarette smokers make up 90% of patients. Spontaneous pneumothorax occurs frequently in this condition.

Ans.90. (b) Pindborg tumor

Ref http://www.ajnr.org/cgi/content/full/21/2/343

CEOT is a benign neoplasm of unknown cause related to the odontogenic apparatus

- Pindborg, in 1958, first categorized it as a distinct histopathologic entity.

It is characterized by *three* different histologic hallmarks.

- The first structure comprises solid epithelial layers or islands with variable thickness and prominent borders. The polyhedral epithelial cells exhibit nuclear polymorphism and eosinophilic cytoplasm, but mitoses are rare.
- The second hallmark consists of an acellular hyalinized stromal bridge, interspersed with foci of an amyloid-like substance.
- The third hallmark comprises a variable amount of round, conglomerate, or concentric laminar (***Liesegang ring***) calcifications.
- Previously, uncertainty regarding the histologic characteristics of CEOT was reflected in the variety of terms for the disease, including unusual ameloblastoma, cystic odontoma, and adenoid adamantinoma.
- Association with adenomatoid odontogenic tumor and dentigerous cyst had been reported and suggests heterogeneity in histopathogenesis.
- CEOT occurs rarely, with a frequency ranging from 0.17% to 1.8% of all odontogenic tumors
- Both sexes are equally affected. The disease usually manifests between the ages of 20 and 60 years.
- Most of the patients are asymptomatic at the time of initial diagnosis. The slowly enlarging mass can result in mechanical effects.
- Although it is thought to be a benign tumor, local tissue invasion has been documented The reported recurrence rate ranges from 10% to 14%.
- Two thirds of CEOTs arise in the mandible, whereas one third arise in the maxilla The majority of recorded cases have been centrally located, mainly in the premolar-molar region of the mandible.

Ans.91 (b) Ectodermal dysplasia

Ref http://en.wikipedia.org/wiki/Ectodermal_dysplasia

Ectodermal dysplasia are described as "heritable conditions in which there are abnormalities of two or more ectodermal structures such as the hair, teeth, nails, sweat glands, cranial-facial structure, digits and other parts of the body.

CLINICAL FEATURES

Hair

- Individuals frequently have abnormalities of the hair follicles.
- Scalp and body hair may be thin, sparse, and very light in color, even though beard growth in affected males may be normal.
- The hair may be excessively brittle, curly, or even twisted.

Nails

- Fingernails and toenails may be thick, abnormally shaped, discolored, ridged, slow-growing, or brittle. The cuticles may be prone to infections.

Skin

- The skin may be lightly pigmented. In some cases, red or brown pigmentation may be present.
- Skin can be prone to rashes or infections and can be thick over the palms and soles. Care must be taken to prevent cracking, bleeding, and infection.

Sweat glands

Many individuals affected by ED syndromes cannot perspire. Their sweat glands may function abnormally or may not have developed at all. Without normal sweat production, the body cannot regulate temperature properly. Therefore, overheating is a common problem, especially during hot weather. Access to cool environments is important.

Teeth

- Abnormalities in the development of tooth buds usually result in ***missing teeth*** or in the growth of teeth that are peg-shaped or pointed.
- The enamel may also be defective. Dental treatment almost always is necessary and children may need dentures as early as two years of age. Multiple denture replacements are often needed as the child grows, and dental implants may be an option in adolescence. In other cases, teeth can be crowned. Orthodontic treatment also may be necessary.

Remember,

Gardner's syndrome

- is a genetic disorder characterized by the presence of multiple polyps in the colon together with tumors outside the colon. The extracolonic tumors may include osteomas of the skull, thyroid cancer, epidermoid cysts, fibromas and sebaceous cysts. The countless polyps in the colon predispose to the development of colon cancer.
- Gardner's syndrome is inherited in an autosomal dominant manner. Typically, one parent has Gardner's syndrome. Each of their children, male and female alike, are at 50% risk of inheriting the gene for Gardner's syndrome and manifesting it.

- Gardner's syndrome can be identified based on oral findings, including multiple impacted and supernumerary teeth, multiple jaw osteomas which give a "cotton-wool" appearance to the jaws, as well as multiple odontomas.

Ans.92. (d) Any of the above

Ref http://www.nlm.nih.gov/medlineplus/ency/article/000773.htm

Facial palsy; Idiopathic peripheral facial palsy.

Definition

Bell's palsy is a temporary form of **facial paralysis.** It results from damage to the nerve that controls movement of the muscles in the face.

Causes, incidence, and risk factors

Bell's palsy is a form of cranial mononeuropathy VII, and it is the most common type of this nerve damage. Bell's palsy affects about 2 in 10,000 people.

Bell's palsy involves damage to the seventh cranial (facial) nerve. This nerve controls the movement of the muscles of the face. The cause is often not clear, although herpes infections may be involved.

Bell's palsy is thought to be linked to inflammation of the nerve in the area where it travels through the bones of the skull. Other conditions, such as sarcoidosis, diabetes, and Lyme disease, are associated with Bell's palsy.

Attacks may often be triggered by trauma (tooth extractions), exposure to cold, systemic infections etc.

Symptoms

Symptoms usually start suddenly, and range from mild to severe. They may include:

- Twitching in face
- Weakness in face
- Face feels stiff or pulled to one side
- Droopy eyelid or corner of mouth
- Drooling due to inability to control facial muscles
- Facial paralysis of one side of the face, makes it hard to close one eye
- Change in facial expression (for example, grimacing)
- Dry eye or mouth
- Loss of sense of taste
- Difficulty with eating and drinking
- Pain behind or in front of the ear, may occur 1-2 days before muscle weakness
- Sensitivity to sound (hyperacusis) on the side of the face affected
- Headache

Signs and tests

Examination shows weakness in the upper and lower part of the face, usually on just one side. Weakness may affect the forehead, eyelid, or mouth. Blood pressure is normal.

Blood tests for sarcoidosis or Lyme disease may be considered. If there is no improvement in the facial paralysis after several weeks, an MRI is done to rule out other causes.

An EMG and nerve conduction studies may also be done to determine the severity of nerve damage.

Other causes of cranial mononeuropathy VII, such as head injury and tumor, need to be ruled out.

Treatment

In many cases, no treatment is necessary. The goal of treatment is to relieve the symptoms.

Corticosteroids or antiviral medications may reduce swelling and relieve pressure on the facial nerve. These drugs must be given early to be most effective (preferably within 24 hours of the symptoms starting).

Lubricating eye drops or eye ointments may be recommended to protect the eye if it cannot be closed completely.

Surgery to relieve pressure on the nerve (decompression surgery) is controversial and has not been shown to routinely benefit people with Bell's palsy.

Complications

- Disfigurement from loss of facial movement.
- Damage to the eye (corneal ulcers and infections).
- Chronic spasm of face muscles or eyelids.
- Chronic taste abnormalities.
- Synkinesis (abnormality in re-innervation of muscles resulting in tears when laughing or inappropriate salivation.

Ans.93. (b) Malignant fibrous histiocytoma

Ref Shafer, 5th ed , pg 224

Fibrous Histiocytoma

- Benign neoplasm exhibiting both fibrous + histiocytic differentiation.
- M/c seen in skin of extremities, but may present as submucosal nodule I/O spindle shaped fibroblast cells with pale oval nuclei are aggregated.
- Scattered foamy histiocytes- **Touton-type** MNGC with nuclei towards periphery are also seen. These contain phagocytosed lipid or hemosiderin.
- Dense collagenous tissue with interlacing fascicles from a central nidus intersecting with cells from adjacent aggregates , impart a '***storiform***' or criss-cross pattern in low power magnification.
- It is separated from overlying mucosa by a zone of fibro-vascular conective tissue (***Grenz zone***).
- Treated by wide excision.

Ans.94. (a) Massetor

Ref http://www.emedicine.com/ped/topic1538.htm

Myositis ossificans is a misnomer and the term fibrodysplasia ossificans progressiva (FOP), as used by McKusick, is preferred. It is a rare autosomal dominant disorder characterized by skeletal malformation and progressive, disabling heterotopic osteogenesis. The condition was first described by Guy Patin in 1692.

Pathophysiology: Myositis ossificans manifests in 2 forms.

Myositis ossificans circumscripta can develop either in response to soft tissue injury (*e.g.* blunt trauma, stab wound, fracture/dislocation, surgical incision) or can occur without known injury. Proposed mechanisms for atraumatic myositis ossificans include nondocumented trauma, repeated small mechanical injuries, and nonmechanical injuries caused by ischemia or inflammation.

- Recently Shore et al reported mapping FOP to chromosome 2q23-24 by linkage analysis. They have further identified an identical heterozygous mutation (617G?R206H) in the glycine-serine (GS) domain of the activin A receptor type I (*ACVR1*) gene, a bone morphogenic protein (BMP) type I receptor in all affected individuals thus fa Nonhereditary myositis ossificans.
  - Pain, tenderness, focal swelling, and joint/muscle contractions occur.
  - The condition can be asymptomatic and may be diagnosed incidentally.
  - The history of trauma causing the condition may be difficult to elicit.
  - Most (ie, 80%) ossifications arise in the thigh or arm. Other sites include intercostal spaces, erector spinae, pectoralis muscles, glutei, and the chest wall.
- FOP
  - The condition produces painful lumps and stiffness in the adjoining joint. Lumps decrease in a few weeks, but joint mobility reduction persists.
  - Exacerbating factors for ossifications at new sites includes sometimes very minor trauma, such as venipuncture, biopsy of lumps, IM injections, dental treatments, and excision of masses.
  - The most common sites are the sternocleidomastoid muscle, paraspinal muscles, the masticatory muscles (masseter) , and shoulder and pelvic girdle muscles. Spared are the abdominal muscles, extraocular muscles, and GI tract and tongue muscles.
  - Ossification progresses from proximal to distal and cranial to caudal.

Ans.95. (b) Erythroplakia

Explained earlier, please refer KCET-04 A75

Ans.96. (c) Auto immune disorder

Explained earlier, please refer KCET-07 A97

ORAL MEDICINE AND RADIOLOGY

Ans.97. (a) Pemphigus

Explained earlier Please refer KCET-04 A77

Ans.98. (c) . 0.1-0.4 Bodansky units

Explained earlier, please refer KCET-05 A74

Ans.99. (b) Sialosis

Explained earlier, please refer KCET-06 A90

Ans.100. (d) Ehlers-Danlos syndrome

Ref http://www.cda-adc.ca/jcda/vol-67/issue-6/Buithieu.html#Table%202

Ehlers-Danlos syndrome (EDS) is a hereditary collagen disease presenting primarily as dermatological and joint disorders. In 1901, Ehlers described the condition as a hyperelasticity of the skin and a strong tendency to bruising. It was not until 1934 that Pommeau-Delille and Soussie described the condition as Ehlers-Danlos syndrome. Other evocative terms such as "elastic man" (or woman) or "India rubber man" have been used.

Epidemiology and Diagnosis

The prevalence of the condition varies between 1:10,000 and 1:150,000. The diagnosis of EDS depends primarily on clinical findings and family history, as it is an autosomal dominant hereditary disorder which presents in several ways. Only 4 types of EDS, namely types IV, VI, VII and X can be confirmed by biochemical and molecular tests.

The differential diagnosis of EDS includes Marfan's syndrome, generalized familial joint hypermobility synd rome, cutis laxa, pseudoxanthoma elasticum and Larsen's syndrome.

Characteristics of EDS

The classic signs of EDS are joint hyper mobility; hyper elasticity of skin, which is soft, thin and fragile; the presence of dystrophic scars; and a tendency to excessive bleeding manifested by bruises, ecchymoses and hematomas. At least 15 phenotypes of the syndromes have been catalogued to date, with 2 having recently been reclassified.

Type I

- skin is *hyperelastic*.
- Bony prominences such as the forehead, chin, elbows, knees and ankles are constantly lacerated.
- Given the limited healing power of the skin with this condition, pigmented and atrophic scars ("***cigarette paper scar***") are frequently found in these areas.
- The patient usually has a mesomorphic appearance with hands and feet being slightly larger than average.
- Along with a generalized hypermobility of the joints there is usually an abnormal bleeding tendency. Occasionally the syndrome is accompanied by mitral valve prolapse.
- Over half of pregnant women with the condition give birth prematurely, following rupture of the fetal membranes.

Type II

Similar to type I, this form is ***less severe*** clinically. The scarring is less common, bleeding tendency is less pronounced and nodules are much smaller or totally absent. However, joint hypermobility is similar to that observed in type I and premature births are also a feature of type II, even if they are less common.

Type III

The patient with type III is usually tall and thin, as in *Marfan's syndrome*. The dominant features of this variation are joint hypermobility and hyperelasticity of the skin, which often feels velvety. Bruises and dystrophic scars are rarely observed.

Type IV

Type IV is characterized by

- ***marked fragility*** of the vascular system.
- The individual is usually smaller than average.
- The skin of the hands and of the back appears to age prematurely (acrogeria).
- The eyes are widely spaced, the nose is narrow, the ear lobes are atrophied and the hair is thin.
- Aneurysms of the large and medium-sized arteries (axillary, femoral and carotid) are common.
- Frequently scar tissue appears to be hemorrhagic. Rupture of internal organs is common even at a young age, and perforation of the intestinal tract can be a problem.
- Joint hypermobility is usually limited to the small articulations of the hand, with acro-osteolysis of the distal phalanges. Mitral valve prolapse can also be present.
- Rupture of arteries and hollow organs such as the uterus and the intestine explains the high mortality rate (51% before age 40). Type IV is consequently, the ***most serious*** form of EDS.

Type V

Women are only carriers of this rare form, similar to types I and II, because transmission is associated with the X chromosome.

Type VI

This form resembles type I except for an ocular involvement with detached retina being a common feature. Severe scoliosis and vascular rupture are also features.

Type VII

This is a rare phenotype characterized by joint hypermobility, bilateral dislocation of the hips and a small stature.

Clinical Manifestations of EDS

Oral examination can help diagnose EDS. Clinical manifestations of Ehler-Danlos syndrome,

Extraoral

The extraoral manifestations of EDS are the presence of scarring on the chin and forehead, a history of repeated luxations of the TMJ, epicanthus, hypertelorism, a narrow curved nose, sparse hair and hyperelasticity of the skin.

Intraoral

The classic intraoral signs of EDS can point to the eventual diagnosis of the condition.

Mucosa

- As fragile as the skin, the mucosa tears easily when touched by instruments. Sutures do not hold.

Periodontal Tissues

- The fragility of the gingiva can be detected following treatments such as prophylaxis, periodontal surgery or extraction. Hemorrhage may be difficult to control during surgical procedures. Early-onset generalized periodontitis is one of the most significant oral manifestations of the syndrome. This can lead to the premature loss of deciduous and permanent teeth.

The Teeth

- Hypoplasia of the enamel is commonly seen. Premolar and molar teeth can present with deep fissures and long cusps. The teeth seem to be fragile and microdontia is sometimes present. Radiographic examination often reveals pulp stones and roots that are short and deformed. One case of type III EDS with multiple supernumerary teeth has been reported in the literature.

The Tongue

- The tongue is very supple. Approximately 50% of those with the syndrome can touch the end of their nose with their tongue (**Gorlin's sign**), compared to 8-10% of the population.

The Palate

- The palate is commonly vaulted.

Clinical manifestations of Ehler-Danlos syndrome

Examination	Clinical Signs	Complications
Extraoral	Scarring of the forehead and chin Hypertelosirm and epicanthus Narrow curved nose Thin hair Deformed ears	Frequent luxations and subluxations of the TMJ Hyperelasticity of the skin
Intraoeral (soft tissues)	Supple tongue Gindival hyperplasia and fibrous nodules Bruising tendency	Buccal mucosa: Fragility Reduced healing capacity Priodontal tisues: Bleeding after Vulnerable to gingivitis and periodontal disease

Intraoral (hard tissues)	Vaulted palate Deep fissures and long cusps Microdontia Supernumeraries Pulp calcification Abnormal roots	Excessive post-extraction bleeding Teeth: Fragility Tendency to fracture

Ans.101. (d) Fordyce spots

Ref Shafer, 5th ed , pg 31

Fordyce's granules

- Developmental anomaly characterized by heterotopic collections of sebaceous glands at various intra-oral sites.
- Thought to be inclusions of ectoderm during development of face.
- Appear as yellow spots, projecting slightly above the tissue surface.
- M/C site is cheek mucosa opposite molar teeth, then lips, retromolar area, tongue etc.
- Unlike skin, these are not associated with hair follicles (except rarely).
- They are completely benign and seldom require any treatment.

Ans.102. (b) Endocrinopathies

Explained earlier, please refer KCET-05 A75

Ans.103. (c) Eagle's syndrome

Ref http://www.whonamedit.com/synd.cfm/3323.html

Eagle's syndrome (Watt Weems Eagle)

Description:

The elongation of the styloid process and stylohyoid ligament calcification. The tissues in the throat rub on the styloid process, which is a spike-like projection sticking off the base of the skull, during the act of swallowing with resulting pain along the glossopharyngeal nerve. There is also pain upon turning the head or extending the tongue. Other symptoms may include voice alteration, cough, dizziness, sinusitis or bloodshot eyes.

Ans.104. (b) I1 / I2 = (D2)^2 / (D1)^2

Ref http://zebu.uoregon.edu/2001/ph122/isq.html

The Inverse Square Law

The intensity of light observed from a source of constant intrinsic luminosity falls off as the square of the distance from the object. This is known as the *inverse square law* for light intensity.

Thus, if you double the distance to a light source the observed intensity is decreased to $(1/2)^2$ = 1/4 of its original value. Generally, the ratio of intensities at distances d_1 and d_2 are

$$\frac{I_1}{I_2} = \left(\frac{D_2}{D_1}\right)^2$$

Ans.105. (a) Anode

Explained earlier, please refer KCET-06 A103

Ans.106. (a) KVp

Explained earlier, please refer KCET-06 A104

Remember, while quality of X-ray depend upon the KVp , the quantity produced depends upon the mA (current).

Ans.107. (d) Collimation

Ref White and Pharoah, 5th ed , pg 58

Collimation

- is not a property of x-ray but it refers to the process of limiting the size of the x-ray beam reaching the patient to reduce the exposure from the same.
- This also results in increased image quality. With lesser mount of area exposed, lesser would be the scattered radiation. Thus film fog is decreased and the quality increase.
- Collimators may be of rectangular or round configuration. The standard size laid down by ADA is about 7cm diameter. A rectangular PID (position indicting device) having an exit of 3.5x4.4cms reduces the patient exposure by almost 60%.

Ans.108. (d) Sharp bending of the film

Ref http://www.dxis-net.com/downloads/usefuldocs/Successful%20Intraoral%20 Radiography.pdf

If film packets are bent forcefully, to conform with the patients mouth, the stress placed on the films emulsion can cause a white, crescent-shaped ***crimp mark*** to appear on the radiograph. These appear as White marks on the final radiograph.

Remember, static electricity produces a 'tree-like' effect on the film.

PERIODONTICS

Ans.109. (c) Dental floss

Explained earlier, please refer KCET-07 A113

Ans.110. (a) John W.Riggs

While M.L. Rhein of Ney York urged the dentists to teach their patients proper brushing habite and later coined the tem 'Oral hygiene' , it was about the turn of the Nineteenth century that J.Leon Williams stressed on the concept or oral hygiene and advocated the slogan ; a clean tooth never decays'

Ans.111. (b) Stage II gingivitis

Ref Carranza, pg 264

STAGES OF GINGIVITIS

Stage	Time (Days)	Predominant immune cells	Clinical finding
I. Initial lesion	2-4	PMNs	Gingival fluid flow
II. Early lesion	4-7	Lymphocytes	Erythema, bleeding on probing, *rete* peg formation with atrophic areas
III. Established lesion	14-21	Plasma cells	Changes in color, size, texture, severe than II
IV. Advanced lesion	25-40	Multinuclear osteoclasts, B-lymphocytes	Pocket formation, suppuration, tooth mobility

Ans.112. (a) Contributing factor

Ref Carranza , 9th ed, pg 187

Remember friends, contrary to the general perception, calculus is only a predisposing factor in the development of gingival inflammation. Read the following lines from Carranza,

"A positive correlation between the presence of calculus and prevalence of gingivitis occurs, but this correlation is not as great as seen with plaque. The non-mineralized plaque on the calculus surface is the principle irritant, but the underlying calcified portion may be a ***significant contributing factor****. It does not irritate the gingiva directly, but provides a nidus for the continuous accumulation of plaque and its retention in close proximity."*

Ans.113. (a) It is a topical antimicrobial

Ref http://www.oralhivlesions.com/adults.htm;http://home.intekom.com/pharm/cipla/dermadmw.html#INDICATIONS

A number of specific periodontal changes have been associated with HIV infection. Linear gingival erythema (LGE) is characterized by a profound erythema of the free gingival margin. In necrotizing ulcerative gingivitis (NUG), there is destruction of one or more interdental papilla with bleeding, ulceration, necrosis and sloughing. Tissue destruction is limited to the gingival tissues and does not involve alveolar bone.

Necrotizing ulcerative periodontitis (NUP) is characterized by advanced necrotic destruction of the periodontium. There is rapid loss of the periodontal attachment, destruction or sequestration of bone and teeth may become loose. It is accompanied by severe pain and halitosis. The disease process is thought to be caused by mixed aerobic and anaerobic bacterial flora, but severe cases are usually caused by gram-negative bacilli such as *Klebsiella pneumoniae* and *Enterobacter cloacae.*

Management is based on plaque reduction and thorough debridement. Patients should be encouraged to brush and floss meticulously to achieve a maximum level of oral health. A dental referral for a multi-step regimen of professional scaling, local debridement with subgingival irrigation, local and systemic antimicrobial therapy, immediate follow-up care and regular long-term maintenance is required.

Intervention is usually intensive curettage and debridement of all involved tissues. A regimen of topical antiseptic agents, such as povidone-iodine solution and 0.2% chlorhexidine gluconate mouth rinses is often initiated as adjunct therapy. This regimen should be continued until all the diseased hard and soft tissues are removed and the patient is no longer symptomatic. Povidone-iodine has ***disinfectant and antiseptic*** properties. It is active against bacteria, fungi, viruses, protozoa, cysts and spores. The germicidal activity is maintained in the presence of blood, pus, serum and necrotic tissue.

In severe cases topical antimicrobial therapy should be supplemented by a short course of systemic antimicrobial therapy, usually metronidazole. Clindamycin and amoxicillin are also recommended.

Ans.114. (a) Pyrophosphate

Explained earlier, please refer KCET-07 A194

Ans.115. (b) Florida probe

Ref Carranza, 9th ed, pg 490

Computerized Periodontal probes

1. **Florida:** automated probe having
   a. A probe handpiece, digital readout, foot switch, computer interface
   b. Tip diameter – 0.4 mm
   c. Coil springs provide constant probing force
   d. Mass storage possible
   e. However, they lack tactile sensitivitiy
   f. Inaccuracy may creep in as fixed force is applied to all parts
2. **Foster- Miller probe (Jeffcoat):** pocket depth measurement + detection of CEJ for calculation of clinical attachment levels.
3. **Toronto probe:**
   - Like Florida, uses occluso-incisal surfaces to measure relative clinical attachment levels
   - Diameter of probe (Ni-Ti wire) = 0.5 mm.
   - Air pressure controls the angulation by means of a mercury tilt sensor that limits the angulation within +/- 30 degrees.
   - Requires reproducible patient position and difficult for use in 2nd or 3rd molar region.

Also remember, the criteria by NIDCR for probe dimensions.

LIMITATION	Conventional probe	NIDCR -criteria
Precision	1 mm	0.1 mm
Range	12 mm	10 mm
Probing force	Non-standardized	Constant + standardized
Applicabilty	Non-invasive and easy	Non-invasive, light weight + easy to use
Reach	Easy to reach all teeth	Easy to access any portion
Angulation	Subjective	Guidance system ensuring proper angulation
Security	Easily sterilized	Complete sterilization + no bio-hazard from parts

Friends, I know option 'D' – Jeffcoat probe seems correct too, but I guess, it was just developed by him and not named , so Florida Probe is still the preferred answer here.

Ans.116. (c) Pathway of inflammation

Ref Carranza, 9th ed, pg 355

Read the following lines from Carranza, and the answer shall be clear.

"The most common cause of bone destruction in periodontal disease is the extension of inflammation from the marginal gingiva in to the supporting periodontal tissues. This marks he transition of gingivitis into periodontitis. This extension may be modified by the pathogenic potential of plaque or resistance of the host.

The pathway of the spread of inflammation is critical because it affects the pattern of bone destruction in periodontal disease."

Also know the various pathways of inflammation:

Interproximally

- from the gingiva into bone
- from bone into PDL
- from gingiva into PDL

Facial and lingually

- from gingiva along the outer periosteum

Ans.117. (a) The portion of the tooth where calculus (or) attended cementum is found

Ref Carranza, 9th ed, pg 633

Scaling is the process by which plaque and calculus are removed from both supra and sub-gingival tooth surfaces.

"Scaling and root planing strokes should be confined to the portion of tooth where calculus or altered cementum is found. This zone is known as the ***instrumentation zone."***

Ans.118. (b) Chlor hexidine

Ref Carranza, 9th ed, pg 683

Remember the following:

Product	Agent	Dosage + Form
Actisite	Tetracycline	12.7mg/9inches non-resorbable fiber
Perio Cline/ Dentamycin	Minocycline	2% solution in biodegradable mix-syringe
Atridox	Doxycycline	10% biodegradable gel – syringe
PerioChip	Chlorhexidine	0.12% -2.5 mg /chip biodegradable device
Elyzol	Metronidazole	25% gel

Ans.119. (a) Gingival recession

Ref Carranza, 9th ed , pg 863

Laterally positioned flap (horizontally displaced)

- originally described by Grupe and Warren 1956
- Used to cover isolated, denuded roots that have adequate tissue laterally and vestibular depth.
- A variant of this technique – the' double-papilla flap'' attempts to cover roots denuded by isolated gingival defects with a flap formed by contiguous halves of the adjacent interdental papillae.

Ans.120. (c) Regenerative osseous surgery

Ref Carranza, 9th ed , pg 819

Alloplasts – are synthetic materials that are used in regenerative osseous therapy.

The commonly used materials include-

1. **Plaster of Paris:** (calcium sulphate) is biocompatible and porous, allows fluid exchange preventing flap necrosis. Resorb completely in 1-2 weeks.
2. **Plastic materials:** like HTR polymer- non-resorbable, micro porous, biocompatible composite of poly-methylmethaacrylate and PHEM. Exhibited bone fill and attachment gain
3. **Calcium Phosphate:** biomaterials- with Ca:P of hydroxyapatite(1.67) and tricalcium phosphate(1.5). these are osteoconductive materials and do not elicit any foreign body response.
4. **Bioglass:**
   - Consists of sodium and calcium salts, phosphates and silicon dioxide.
   - Particle size about 90-170 um.
   - When in contact with tissue-fluid it absorbs hydroxycarbonateapatite with chondroitin sulphate and GAGs.
   - Attracts osteoblasts that rapidly form bone.
5. **Coral derived:** good results with pocket reduction, attachment gains and bone level gain but resorbs very slowly.

Ans.121. (c) Ailing implant

Ref Carranza, 9th ed, pg 930-933

Implant failures

- Failed implants- mobility + bone loss
- Failing implants – Bone loss without mobility
- Ailing implants – Bone loss arrested

Ans.122. (a) Refractory periodontitis

Ref Carranza, 9th ed, pg 404

Refractory periodontitis is defined as ''those patients who are unresponsive to any treatment provided, whatever the thoroughness or frequency.''

This should, however, not be confused with 'recurring periodontitis' where a complete remission occurs before the recurrence of symptoms.

Ans.123. (b) Biodegradable membrane

Ref Carranza, 9th ed, pg 810

GTR or Guided Tissue Regeneration: involves a material for prevention of epithelial migration along the cemental wall of the pocket. This material can be either non-absorbable (Gore-tex) or absorbable.

Absorbable GTR membranes- includes

- Rat/bovine collagen
- Cargile membranes form the cecum of an ox
- Polylactic acid (Guidor membranes, Atrisorb)
- Vicryl (polyglactin 910)
- ***Synthetic skin (Biobrane***)
- Freeze-dried duramater.

CONSERVATIVE DENTISTRY AND ENDODONTICS

Ans.124. (a) Golden proportion

Ref Sturdevant, pg 596

Anterior teeth, in addition to being asymmetric should be in a proper proportion to one another to achieve maximum esthetics.

- The quality of proportionality is relative and varies greatly depending on other factors (*e.g.* tooth position, tooth alignment, arch form, configuration of the smile).
- A theorem, ***Golden proportion***, originally formulated as one of the Euclid's elements advocates that- a smile, when viewed from the front, is considered to be esthetically pleasing if each tooth in that smile (starting from the midline) is approximately **60%** of the size of the tooth immediately mesial to it.
- The exact proportion of the smaller tooth to the larger tooth is **0.618**.
- These values are based on the apparent sizes of teeth when viewed straight on and not the actual sizes of teeth.
- In an esthetically pleasing smile, the teeth generally are in Golden proportion to one another.
- For achieving the proper proportion of teeth, accepted *width-length* ratio should be ***0.75-0.8***. This ratio represents the ideal proportions needed to optimize the esthetic results. (Remember, this is not the Golden proportion but the width: length ratio for individual teeth).

Ans.125. (b) Sodium nitrite

Ref Sturdevant pg 372

For autoclave sterilization, burs can be protected by keeping them submerged in a small amount of 2% sodium nitrite solution. Add 20g of nitrite to 1 L of pure water. The bur is placed in metal container containing this solution. Discard the solution after use.

Ans.126. (b) Less than 0.1 %

Ref Sturdevant, pg 152

Amalgam alloys with zinc (<0.1%) are termed as zinc-free alloys, while concentration above this are zinc-containing.

Originally zinc was added to conventional amalgam to suppress oxidation of key elements in the alloy.

A detrimental effect of residual zinc is that in the event of moisture contamination before setting, it converts to zinc oxide releasing hydrogen gas that causes the amalgam to expand (upto 400 μm after 3-5days) producing pain.

Ans.127. (a) Proximal caries with gingival recession

Ref Sturdevant, 4th ed

Wedge is a piece of soft material (wood, plastic) which is used to support and adapt the matrix against the tooth.
Wedging systems –

- **Single wedging:** placed more lingually if the contact is buccal or vice versa.
- **Horizontal wedging:** when gingiva is healthy, two wedges (buccally and lingually) are placed horizontally.
- **Piggy back wedging:** if gingival recession present then place a wedge with the base of triangle above and other wedge placed over it.
- **Double wedging:** if mesiodistal gap between two teeth is more than the width of one wedge then place two wedges crossing each other in horizontal direction.
- **Wedge –wedging:** when special consideration (as in mesial aspect of maxillary first premolar) is required for developmental depressions etc, one wedge in horizontal and the other vertically are placed.

Ans.128. (a) 1% basic fuschin in propylene glycol

Ref Vimal Sikri, pg 77

Dyes used in caries detection

(A) **Enamel caries**

- Procion dyes stain enamel lesions (irreversibly)
- Calcein dye makes a complex with Ca
- Zyglo ZL-22 fluorescent dye
- Brilliant Blue – enhances the diagnostic quality of FOTI (transillumination)

(B) **Dentinal caries**

- 0.5% Basic Fuchsin in propylene glycol - infected dentin was stained.
- Methylene Blue - however is slightly toxic
- Acid Red – is the current choice due to the toxic nature of above two dyes

Ans.129. (b) 3 microgram/g of creatinine

Ref http://www.flcv.com/adaabsr.html

Inorganic mercury is absorbed in small amounts from dental amalgam fillings. Exposure can be calculated by measuring the level of mercury in the blood or urine (u-Hg). The average u-Hg is approximately <u>*2-3 micrograms/g creatinine*</u> (approximately 1-2 nmol/mmol creatinine). Classic signs of mercury poisoning occur in a fraction of long-term exposed subjects with u-Hg > 100 micrograms/g creatinine (56 nmol/mmol creatinine). Subtle effects (*e.g.* enzymuria, altered selenium metabolism, and changes in tremor spectra) have been reported in humans at average levels of 20-35 micrograms/g creatinine (approximately 11-20 nmol/mmol creatinine).

Ans.130. (d) Metalizing

Ref Vimal Sikri, pg 328

<u>*Annealing/degassing or desorption*</u> refers to the removal of surface contaminants. The primary purpose is to produce an atomically clean surface and render the material cohesive and workable. Degassing is done to remove the protective ammonia film which had been placed over the surface to render it non-cohesive.

Alcohol flames or electric annealers may be used for the same.

Thus, metalizing is the odd one out, which refers to placing a metal layer over impressions.

Ans.131. (b) Masseram kit

Ref <u>http://www.roydent.com/spec_sheets/Endo_Extractor_lit.pdf</u>

Endo-Extractor System

The Endo-Extractor system is excellent for removal of separated files and silver points.

- Necessary tool for dental offices performing root canal therapy.
- The "Jacobs Chuck"-like device grabs the embedded article with equal force all the way around, requiring minimal pressure.
- Unique hollow trepan drill with an internal diameter of .80mm.
- Stainless steel.
- Sterilizable with autoclave, Chemiclave or dry heat sterilization.
- Available in complete kit or individual sizes.

Select appropriate size extractor. Holding the device by the handle, rotate the large, knurled ring counter-clockwise to open the jaws of the extractor. Carefully place the extractor over the imbedded article to be removed. Holding the extractor on the article by the small handle, rotate the knurled ring clockwise to engage the jaws of the extractor against the article. Tighten securely.

Thus, like the Masseram's kit , endo extractor is a vital system for retrieval of separated files and points.

Ans.132. (d) Rat file

Ref http://www.roydent.com/prod_endo/html/prod_endo_hra_ratt.htm

Rat Tail Files

- Extra sharp, flexible barbs
- Rounded tip to follow canal curve
- Available in 25 mm only

C-files

- Pre-applied silicone stops, color-coded by length: 21 mm - white, 25 mm - yellow
- Stiff, yet flexible
- Heat-tempered steel for stiffness
- Sharp edges twisted to the tip
- Non-cutting tip follows canal curve

Ans.133. (d) Pink

Ref Grossman, 11th ed, pg 195

Color code	Number	D1 diameter (mm)	D2 diameter (mm)
Pink	6	0.06	0.38
Gray	8	0.08	0.40
Purple	10	0.10	0.42
White	15	0.15	0.47
Yellow	20	0.20	0.52
Red	25	0.25	0.57
Blue	30	0.30	0.62
Green	35	0.35	0.67
Black	40	0.40	0.72
White	45	0.45	0.77
Yellow	50	0.50	0.82
Red	55	0.55	0.87
Blue	60	0.60	0.92
Green	70	0.70	1.02

A pneumonic- (PGP When You Run Balls Go Banging)
The color code and the number follow the same pattern thereafter.

Ans.134. (c) Submarginal flap

Ref http://www.stropko.com/ref/ref_pub1.html

A flap in endodontic surgery is designed to allow maximum manual and visual access to the operative site . the most common flaps are :-

- Semi lunar: when no underlying periodontal problems exist
- Trapezoidal
- Triangular
- Horizontally scalloped (Leubke- Ochsenbein)

The full sulcular flap: This design is used if there is little attached gingiva or there is a concern about the possibility of a dehiscence over the root of the tooth being operated on. The incision is made through the gingival crest, following the curvature around the cervical of the teeth involved in the surgical area. The operator should attempt to incise the tissue through the crest of gingival to the osseous crest of bone, leaving the healthy gingival attachment intact.

The SUB-MARGINAL Flap (Oshenbein-Leubke Flap): This flap is used only when there is an adequate amount of attached gingiva present and the periodontal probing is within normal limits. The incision design should have rounded scallops that generally follow the architecture of the teeth (Fig.3) and allow for easy repositioning upon completion of the apical microsurgical procedures.

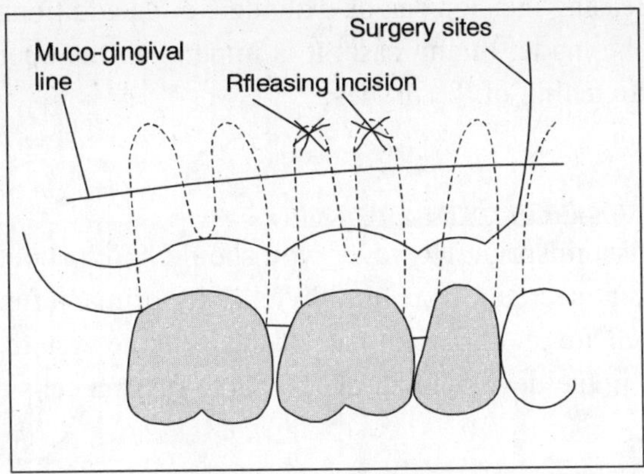

The releasing incision is made parallel to the long axis of the teeth. This is important because the blood supply to the area is also parallel to the long axis. If a "wide base" type flap is made, some of the blood supply to the coronal tissue is interrupted and healing is compromised.

The reflection of the flap is accomplished using either the Molt, Ruddle R, or Ruddle L (EIE) periosteal elevators. The working end of the instrument is gently inserted into the releasing incision, beneath the unattached gingival tissue and as far apically as the tissue will allow. The motion is a gentle "up-and-down" (apical-to-coronal) movement within the unattached gingival portion of the flap. Maintaining the same motion, the instrument is moved slowly toward the same apical position at the other extent of the flap. If done correctly, the attached gingival, or coronal portion of the flap, will gently release from the osseous surface. This atraumatic reflection of the flap is a major contributor to the rapid healing response normally observed only 24 hours post operatively. It is important the approximating surfaces of the flap are never touched after the incision is completed, so there are no crushing injuries to inhibit or retard the healing process. An instrument such as the old wax spatula shaped periosteal elevator has no place in the armamentarium of the endodontic microsurgeon.

Once the flap is gently and cleanly reflected, any "tissue tags" should be left intact as they will aid in the healing process. It is not necessary to clean the flap and exposed bone since these efforts are time consuming and can be traumatic to both the hard and soft tissue.

The retraction of the flap should be accomplished in a gentle and atraumatic manner. The most common cause of post-operative pain and swelling arises from impingement of the tissue during the retraction process. An effective way to achieve atraumatic retraction is to prepare a groove in the cortical plate of the bone, well apical to the surgery site. This allows a definite place for the retractor instrument to seat into and be definitely positioned without any slipping. A surgical length #8 round bur, on a high speed Innovator handpiece (EIE), is used for this purpose. In this way, there is a definite rest for the instrument and the flap doesn't get caught beneath it. A highspeed hand piece that has air escaping from the working end should never be used because of the danger of air embolism.

Retraction can be accomplished using either the Carr or Rubinstein Retractors. The specific retractor is chosen that will best maintain clear visibility to the surgical area. If there is any tension on the flap, the vertical releasing incision can be extended, or an additional releasing incision at the other side of the flap can be made. In any case, it is imperative the operator keeps in mind there should be no tension, or stretching of the tissues.

Ans.135.

Ref http://en.wikipedia.org/wiki/Thymosin

Most probably this was a misprint. However, you should know about it.

Thymosin is a hormone secreted from the thymus. Its primary function is to stimulate the production of T cells, which are an important part of the immune system.

Thymosin also assists in the development of B cells to plasma cells to produce antibodies

Ans.136. (a) Diagnosis

Ref http://www.ukrainebiz.com/technical/diagnosis_of_diseases.htm

First know what anamnesis is.

"Anamnesis is the recollection or remembrance of the past; *reminiscence*"

Diagnosis is and will be the most important problem of medicine, and the accuracy of diagnosis achieved in certain historical periods determines mainly the state-of-the-art in medical science. While examining a patient in modern diagnosis centers (anamnesis, physical examination, laboratory and instrument methods data, clinical data, etc.) a very large scope of initial data (more than 300 characteristics being measured mainly using numeral scales) is collected.

A diagnostic test, that does not result in information that supports decisions on interventions, i.e., treatment, non-treatment or prevention, including risk stratification and prognosis, is of limited value, even if the result is interesting from a research viewpoint. The most successful tests are those that provide a clear-cut basis for prevention, treatment alternatives or non-treatment

Ans.137. (d). Infarction

Ref http://www.dental1.org/care/dentalcondition20.cfm/33

An abfraction lesion ("lesion" refers to an area of tooth damage) is a loss of enamel or dentin (or both) from the tooth surface and is believed to be caused or produced by one or more of the following:

1. Erosion or corrosion: tooth surface loss (demineralization) caused by chemical action such as gastric acids involved with acid reflux disease, highly-acidic foods and beverages, or bulimia. Toothbrush abrasion can make erosion/corrosion worse.
2. Excessive chewing/biting forces, such as grinding (bruxism)
3. Clenching the teeth
4. Malocclusion (bite problems)
5. Tongue thrusting habits

Intraoral Exam:

- Inspecting each individual tooth for signs of crazing/stress lines, enamel fracture, restoration fracture, erosion/corrosion, abrasion and abfraction.
- Percussion: tapping on each tooth to determine if teeth are sensitive to percussion and to determine the sound of each tooth when tapped.
- Evaluating periodontal health and inspecting the tissues around the teeth for signs of recession that may be caused by toothbrush abrasion.
- Examining and evaluating occlusion (bite) to determine if the teeth are functioning properly or abnormally.
- Signs of abnormal wear on the teeth, such as wear facets, as well as signs of abnormal or excessive forces being placed on one or more teeth, known as occlusal trauma.
- Determine if any teeth are loose or mobile, or if any teeth have moved or migrated away from their original position, as this could be an indication of bite problems, where teeth may have improper or excessive chewing/biting forces continually placed on them. Teeth that are mobile or that have migrated may be a sign of occlusal trauma.
- Inspecting the jaw bone on the inside of the mouth for exostoses, which are areas of excess bone growth or bony protuberances that may indicate bruxism.
- Taking radiographs (X-rays) of the teeth and jaws to assess signs of traumatic occlusion and assess the bone support of each tooth.

  Infraction -Incomplete fracture (crack) of the enamel without loss of tooth structure

  infarction is the process resulting in a macroscopic area of necrotic tissue in some organ caused by loss of adequate blood supply.

So, friends we see that, while Abfraction, crazing and infraction, all point towards injury related events to the teeth, infarction is the odd one out.

Ans.138. (d) For endo gram

Ref http://www.endoruddle.com/solutiond.html

The Ruddle Solution

This solution has been patented, has undergone in vivo clinical trials, and is now awaiting FDA approval. The **endogram** will greatly enhance endodontic diagnostics.

The Ruddle Solution is a new intracanal irrigant which has been formulated to provide a breakthrough in clinical endodontic treatment and retreatment. This irrigant is a "cocktail" containing

- 5% sodium hypochlorite (NaOCl).
- Hypaque : water soluble, radiopaque, contrast solution which can be utilized to visualize root canal system anatomy, monitor the remaining wall thickness during preparation procedures, detect pathological defects and manage iatrogenic mishaps.
- 17% EDTA.

The composition of the Ruddle Solution simultaneously provides the "solvent action" of full-strength NaOCl, "visualization" as it is nearly as radiopaque as gutta percha, and improved "penetration" as the tensioactive agent lowers surface tension.

Clinically, the Ruddle Solution is passively injected into the root canal system once sufficient access has been made. The sodium hypochlorite portion of the composition will digest the pulp and eliminate the bacteria and related irritants which are harbored within the root canal system. The solvent action of this solution progressively clears out the contents of the root canal system thus enabling the iodine portion of the composition to flow into the vacated space.

- Useful for "visualizing pathological events" such as decay, certain fractures, missed canals and leaking restorations.
- Assists the diagnostician in managing internal resorption because the solution will map its location, size and extent.
- Shows promise in endodontic non-surgical re-treatment for improving diagnostics, treatment planning, and management of "iatrogenic events."
- Following disassembly procedures, helps clinicians visualize canals that may have been previously blocked, ledged, transported or perforated.
- Visualization assists dentists in determining the best course of action and in deciding whether to salvage or extract a tooth.

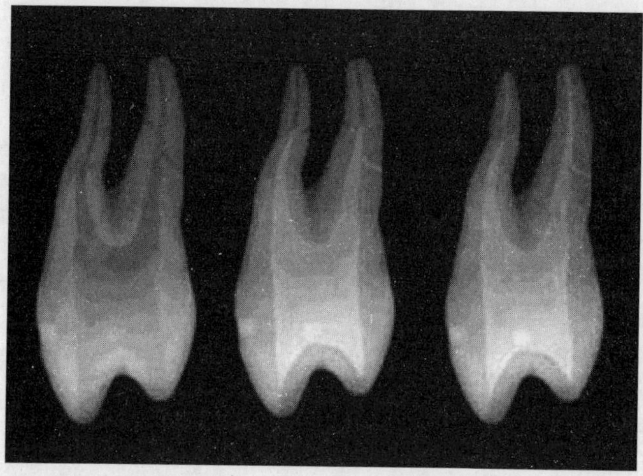

Ans.139. (a) Cutting edges of the working end should be centered over the long axis of the handle

Ref Sturdevant, 4th ed , pg 310

Most hand instruments regardless of use are composed of three parts: handle, shank and blade.

- Although, earlier hand instruments had large handles for a firm grip, these were not useful for delicate manipulations.
- Shanks are normally smooth, round, and tapered. Bends are given to avoid the twisting of instruments when in use.
- Balance in hand cutting instruments allows for the concentration of force onto the blade without causing rotation of the instruments in the grasp.
- Sharpness helps concentrate the force onto a small area of the edge, producing a high stress.

- Balance of instrument is achieved by designing the angles of shank so that the cutting edge of blade lies within the projected diameter of the handle (1-2mm) and nearly coincides with the projected axis of the handle.
  Hence, option 'a' is correct.

ORAL AND MAXILLO-FACIAL SURGERY

Ans.140. (c) Adrenaline

Ref http://www.bmj.com/cgi/content/full/316/7142/1442

Anaphylaxis is an acute systemic (multi-system) and severe Type I Hypersensitivity allergic reaction. The term comes from the Greek words 'ana' (against) and 'phylaxis' (protection). Anaphylaxis occurs when a person is exposed to a trigger substance, called an allergen, to which they have already become sensitized. Minute amounts of allergens may cause a life-threatening anaphylactic reaction. Anaphylaxis may occur after ingestion, inhalation (though this is rare), skin contact, or injection of an allergen.] The most severe type of anaphylaxis—anaphylactic shock—will usually lead to death in a matter of minutes if left untreated.

Features of anaphylaxis

- Erythema
- Pruritis (generalized)
- Urticaria
- Angio-oedema
- Laryngeal edema
- Asthma
- Rhinitis
- Conjunctivitis
- Itching of palate or external auditory meatus
- Nausea, vomiting, abdominal pain
- Palpitations
- Sense of impending doom
- Fainting, lightheadedness
- Collapse
- Loss of consciousness

Common causes of anaphylaxis

- Foods
- Bee and wasp stings
- Drugs
- Latex rubber

Foods commonly causing anaphylaxis

- Peanuts
- Tree nuts (*e.g.* brazil nut, almond, hazelnut)
- Fish
- Shellfish
- Egg
- Milk
- Sesame
- Pulses (other than peanuts)

Drugs causing anaphylaxis or anaphylactoid reactions

- Antibiotics (especially penicillin)
- Intravenous anesthetic drugs
- Aspirin
- Non-steroidal anti-inflammatory drugs
- Intravenous contrast media
- Opioid analgesics

Drug treatment of anaphylaxis in adults

- *Intramuscular* adrenaline 0.5 ml (500 μg), 1 in 1000 solution (1 mg/ml)
- Intramuscular or slow intravenous chlorpheniramine 10 mg
- Intramuscular or slow intravenous hydrocortisone 200 mg

EMERGENCY DRUG KIT

Mandatory drugs

Oxygen
Epinephrine
Nitroglycerin

Primary Support Drugs

Anticonvulsant
Analgesic
Vasopressin
Antihypoglycemic
Corticosteroids
Antihypertensive
Anticholinergic
Respiratory stimulant
Antihypoglycemic
Bronchodilator

DRUGS FOR ADVANCED CARDIAC LIFE SUPPORT

Supplementary Drugs

Narcotic antagonist
Benzodiazepine antogonist
Antiemergence delirium
Vasodilator

Ans.141. (d) Reduce nasal bone fractures

Ref Killey's pg 70

Nasal fractures may be reduced under LA or under GA with peroral endochondral tube. Walsham's and Asche's forceps are used for manipulating the fragment.

- **Walsham's forceps:** the unpadded blade is passed up the nostril and the nasal bone along with fragments of frontal process of maxilla between it and padded blade externally.
- **Asche's forceps:** the vomer and the perpendicular plate of the ethmoid are ironed out with these forceps, using one blade on each side. The finger pressure is used next to align the fragments properly.

Ans.142. (b) Hemophilia

As already explained previously, INV is contraindicated in patients suffering form hemophilia. (NOTE- the question in *KCET-06 Q131* stated a stable hemophiliac in which case, INV may be considered with local precautions).

Ans.143. (c) punctate sialectasis

Ref Shobha Tandon, pg 684

Chronic sialadenitis is the most common cause of the inflammation and swelling of the salivary glands in children and adults. Recurrent episodes of infection can result in acinar destruction and sialectasis. It may be obstructive or non-obstructive which may lead to stenosis, strictures or stones.

Remember while pleomorphic adenoma is the most common neoplasm affecting salivary glands, it is not the most common cause for 'recurrent' swelling of the glands.

Ans.144. (a) 2gms. of Amoxicillin

Explained earlier, please refer KCET-06 A63

Ans.145. (b) Lateral pharyngeal

Ref Neelima Malik, pg 579

The lateral Pharyngeal Space: it is a potential cone shaped space or cleft with its base uppermost at the base of skull and its apex at the greater cornu of hyoid bone. The space is divided into two by the styloid process as:

- **Anterior:** contains lymph node, ascending pharyngeal, facial artery, loose areolar connective tissue.
- **Posterior:** carotid sheath and contents, glossopharyngeal, spinal accessory, hypoglossal nerves, cervical sympathetic trunk.

These spaces separate the muscles of mastication from the muscles of deglutition.

The infection form this space can spread downwards into the carotid sheath towards mediastinum, a pathway called the "Lincoln's highway" (Mosher).

Ans.146. (d). Central haemangioma

Ref http://www.emedicine.com/derm/topic810.htm

Friends, there is no direct reference for this but it is very clear that of the choices given, the only absolute contraindication could be the presence of a central haemangioma as extraction wound in these patients may ex-sanguinate the patient to death. All others are relative contraindications. Now, have a look at the following statements:

Hemangiomas of the oral cavity are not common pathologic entities, but, among hemangiomas, the head and the neck are common sites. Most true hemangiomas involute with time, but certain small percentages do not, which may present with complications that require treatment.

- Although the mucosal and soft tissue lesions are readily suspected by their appearance, the intrabony lesions may be difficult to distinguish on sight alone.
  - Central jaw lesions can show hypermobility of the teeth and distortion of the arch form (Hayward, 1981).
  - Severe hemorrhage following dental extraction is not an uncommon presentation of central hemangiomas of the maxilla and the mandible (Yih, 1989).
  - Common clinical findings in central hemangiomas of the jaws include gingival bleeding, postextraction bleeding, swelling, pain, mobility of the teeth, and bony expansion (Yih, 1989).
  - Root resorption of the teeth has been reported in 30% of cases, but the vitality of the teeth is usually not affected (Hayward, 1981)

Ans.147. (b) Marsupialization

Ref Neelima Malik , pg 424

Partsch I procedure (decompression) or ***marsupialization*** refers to creating a surgical window (unroofing) in the wall of the cyst and evacuating the cystic contents. This process decreases the intra-cystic pressure and promotes shrinkage of the cyst and bone fill. The only portion removed is while window preparation. The cystic lining is then sutured to the oral epithelium or periosteum.

The modification Partsch II (Waldron's method) combines initial marsupialization and finally enucleation of the cyst.

Decortication: is a surgical procedure to removechronically infected lateral and inferior cortical plates of bone 1-2 cm beyond the area of involvement. This provides an access to the medullary cavity.

Saucerization: involves excision of margins of necrotic bone overlyng a focus of osteomyelitis. It is useful in chronic form, for removal of sequestra.

Ans.148. (a) Condylar

Ref Killey's. pg 26

In condylar fractures, there is swelling over the TMJ area and bleeding from ear on the side involved. Bleeding results from the laceration of the anterior wall of the external auditory meatus caused by violating movement of the condylar head against the skin in this region.

It is very essential to demarcate this from bleeding due to middle ear hemorrhage.

Ans.149. (a) Ramus

Ref Neelima Malik, pg 276

Bilateral Saggital Split Osteotomy (BSSO) is a very popular, most versatile procedure performed on the ***mandibular ramus and body***. First described by Trauner and Obwegeser and later modified by Dalpont, Hunsuck, and Epker. Since it is an intra-oral procedure, it is highly esthetic.

Obwegeser technique- involves a horizontal buccal and lingual cortical section.

Dalpont – modified this to a vertical cut on buccal cortex between first and second molar

Hunsuck – further modified the technique with a shorter, horizontal medial cut just posterior to the lingula (instead of posterior border) to minimize tissue damage.

Epker's modification include – minimal stripping of masseter muscle and limited medial dissection. This greatly decreased post-operative swelling, edema, hemorrhages etc.

Although, even option 'b' is correct, but friends the original procedure was devised for ramus correction.

Ans.150. (b) Noma

Ref http://en.wikipedia.org/wiki/Vincent%27s_angina

Trench mouth is a

- polymicrobial infection of the gums leading to inflammation, bleeding, deep ulceration and necrotic gum tissue; there may also be fever.
- It is also known as "Vincent's stomatitis", "Vincent's angina", or "acute necrotizing ulcerative gingivitis" (**ANUG**).
- Causative organisms include anaerobes such as *Bacteroides* and *Fusobacterium* as well as spirochetes (*Borrelia* and *Treponema* spp.).
- The common name was probably coined during World War I when many soldiers suffered from the condition. There are a number of other theories to the origin of the name.
- The condition is caused by an overpopulation of established mouth bacteria due to a number of interacting factors such as poor hygiene, poor diet, smoking, other infections.
- Treatment is by the simple reduction of the bacteria through improved oral cleaning and salt water or hydrogen peroxide-based rinses. Chlorhexidine or metronidazole can also be used in addition.
- Untreated, the infection may lead to *rapid destruction of the periodontium* and can spread, as necrotizing stomatitis, into neighboring tissues in the cheeks, lips or the bones of the jaw (NOMA). The condition can occur and be especially dangerous in people with weakened immune systems.

Ans.151. (a) Preservation

Ref Peterson, 4th ed, pg 409,

The four common implant anchorage devices are the miniplate, onplant, endosseus implant and miniscrew.

Osseointegrated endosseous implants are widely used for the rehabilitation of completely and partially edentulous patients, being the final prosthodontic treatment more predictable and the failures extremely infrequent.

These are placed into the alveolar and or basal bone of maxilla/mandible and transecting only one cortical plate. May be used for interim or definitive application.
Hence, these indicate that these are an attempt of ridge preservation.

Ref. Nallaswamy, pg 775.

Ans.152. (d) Three weeks

Ref Peterson, pg 409

Read the following lines from Peterson,

" *the dentist is in a race against time. It the extraction wound fails to heal, the radiotherapy will be delayed. If the radiation is delivered before the wound heals, healing will take months or years.*

*Traditionally, 7-14 days between tooth extraction and radiotherapy have been suggested. However, a **minimum of 3 weeks** interval should be retained if possible. This ensures that sufficient soft tissue healing has occurred."*

So friends, its clear that answer is 'd' 3 weeks.

PEDODONTICS

Ans.153. (c) 2.5 ppm

Ref Soben Peter, 2nd ed, pg 340

Fluoride level	Duration in drinking water	EFFECTS
0.7-1.2 ppm	depends upon temp of area	prevents dental caries; no dental/skeletal fluorosis
1.5 – 3.0 ppm	consumption for 5-10 yrs	mild dental fluorosis
3.0 – 8.0 ppm	consumption for 15-20 yrs	severe dental with mild skeletal fluorosis
8.0 ppm or higher	consumption for 5-10 yrs	severe dental + skeletal

Ans.154. (c) Gross excavation and restoration of teeth

Ref Shobha Tandon,, pg 206

MANAGEMENT of nursing-bottle/ rampant caries

Three steps are defined in the management of such cases

FIRST STAGE/ VISIT

- Gross excavation and temporary restoration.
- Indirect pulp capping or pulp therapy procedures when indicated.
- Drainage of any abscess and X-ray examination.
- Collection of saliva for assessing salivary flow and viscosity.
- Topical application of fluoride.
- Parent counseling on feeding habits, emotional condition, prepare a diet chart.

SECOND STAGE

- Analysis of diet chart and explanation of disease process.
- Isolate the sugar factors from the diet and control the sugar exposure.
- Reassess and redo the restorations already done/present.
- Caries activity tests are started and repeated at monthly intervals.

THIRD STAGE

- Restoring all teeth with permanent restoration.
- Endodontic treatment.
- Crowns for all grossly decayed and endodontically treated tooth.
- Review and recall after every 3 months.

ORTHODONTICS

Ans.155. (d). Space present distal to lower canine and mesial to upper canine

Ref Bhalajhi, 2nd ed, pg 51

Spacing seen mesial to maxillary canines and distal to mandibular canines during the deciduous dentition are physiologic spaces known as primate spaces / simian spaces or anthropoid spaces, as they are commonly seen in primates. These spaces help in placement of the canine cusps of the opposing arch.

Ans.156. (d) Distal plane of primary 2nd molar.

Explained earlier please refer KCET-07 A151

Ans.157. (c) Natal teeth

Explained earlier, please refer KCET-06 A84

Ans.158. (b) Ugly duckling stage

Explained earlier please refer. KCET-05 A143

Ans.159. (a) Maxillary and frontonasal process

Ref http://www.emedicine.com/ent/topic135.htm

Cleft lip is among the most common of congenital deformities. The condition is due to insufficient mesenchymal migration during primary palate formation in the fourth through seventh week of intrauterine life. This results in disfigurement and distortion of the upper lip and nose.

- Cleft lip may be associated with syndromes that include anomalies involving multiple organs.
- The most commonly recognized syndrome associated with clefts of the lip and palate is ***Van der Woude syndrome***. This syndrome is an autosomal dominant disorder characterized by clefts of the lip and/or palate and blind sinuses, or pits, of the lower lip.
- Combined cleft lip and palate is the most common presentation (50%), followed by isolated cleft palate (30%), and isolated cleft lip or cleft lip and alveolus (20%). Fewer than 10% of clefts are bilateral. Clefts of the secondary palate alone are far more likely to be associated with syndromes than are clefts involving the lip alone or the lip and palate. Most cases of lip clefts are nonsyndromic and believed to be either multifactorial in origin or the result of changes at a major single-gene locus.
- Development of the upper lip is characterized by ***fusion of the maxillary prominences with the lateral and medial nasal prominences***. This process starts during the fourth week of gestation and is completed by the seventh week. Failure of mesenchymal migration to unite one or both of the maxillary prominences with the medial nasal prominences results in a unilateral or bilateral cleft of the lip, respectively.

Ans.160. (c) Retention

Ref Bhalajhi, 2nd ed, pg 441

Teeth moved through bone have a tendency to return to their original positions. Stabilizing the treatment results by retention procedures is an integral part of orthodontic therapy. Moyer defined retention as maintaining newly moved teeth in position, long enough to aid in stabilizing their correction.

Relapse has been defined as loss of any correction achieved by orthodontic treatment.

Ans.161. (a) Anterior cross bite

Ref http://medical-dictionary.thefreedictionary.com/apertognathia

Apertognathia: A type of malocclusion characterized by the premature occlusion of posterior teeth and the absence of anterior occlusion. Also called *open bite.*

Ans.162. (c) Class I molar relation

Ref Bhalajhi, 2nd ed, pg 232

Serial Extraction is an interceptive procedure usually initiated in the early mixed dentition period when one can anticipate and recognize potential irregularities in the dento-facial complex.

- The procedure includes planned extraction of certain deciduous and permanent teeth in an orderly sequence to guide the erupting permanent teeth into a more favorable position.
- First used by Kjellgren (1929) and later by Nance.
- Indicated in Angle's Class I malocclusions with crowding, flaring of teeth or other features of arch length deficiency (5-7 mm)
- Contraindicated in Class II or III patients or those with spaced dentition.
- Dewel's method – $C_8/ D_9/ 4_{10}$
- Tweed's method – $D_8/ 4_9/ C_{10}$
- Nance method – similar to Tweed's

Ans.163. (a) Continuous force

Ref Bhalajhi , 2nd ed , pg 207

TYPES OF FORCES

Continuous forces: active orthodontic forces that decrease little in magnitude between appointment periods. *e.g.* Light wire appliances.- flexible + low forces.

Interrupted forces: force that decays to zero magnitude or nearly so prior to the next appointment. *e.g.* removable active plates – high stiffness + initial forces

Intermittent forces: force that is inactive for intervals of time between appointments. *e.g.* extra-oral orthopeadic appliances – heavy forces + long time

Ans.164. (b) 28 mil wire

Explained earlier, please refer KCET-07 A157

Ans.165. (a) Nitinol

Explained earlier, please refer KCET-06 A35

Ans.166. (a) Eruption of maxillary first molars

Ref http://dentistry.uic.edu/Depts/oralb/VariationInToothMorphology.htm

Disturbances in Eruption.

Ectopic eruption is a type of eruption disturbance; this occurs when a tooth cannot complete its eruption because it is blocked by an adjacent tooth or by a misplaced orthodontic band—usually on a first molar tooth.

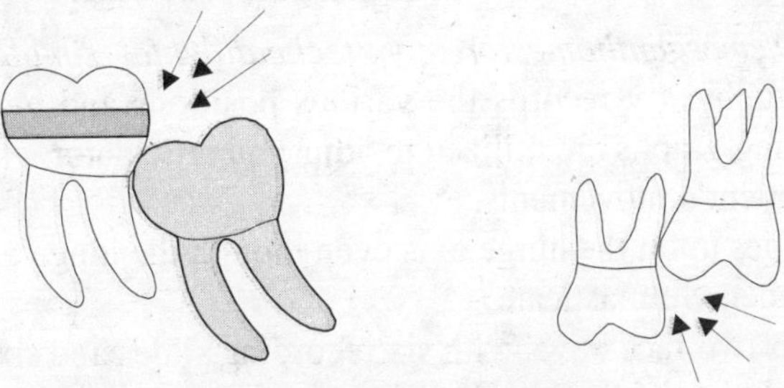

Ectopic Eruption of Motor

An iatrogenic disease or condition is one that is 'doctor-caused'. If a second molar is inadvertently impacted by a poorly placed molar band as shown in the diagram, it is an iatrogenic condition.

Ans.167. (b)Le felon of France

Ref Bhalajhi, 2nd ed , pg 1

The term Orthodontics was coined by ***Le Felon***.

<u>Jackson's triad</u> includes – functional efficiency, structural balance and esthetic harmony.

Ans.168. (b) Tip

Ref Bhalajhi, 9th ed, pg 204

Tipping is a simple type of tooth movement where a force applied to the crown results in movement of crown in the direction of force and the root in an opposite way.

Remember, Torquing is a bucco-lingual movement while, uprighting is a mesio-distal movement of the roots.

Ans.169. (a) Ossification of adductor sesamoid

Ref Bhalajhi, 2nd ed, pg 172

In most of the Skeletal Maturity Indicators, the pubertal growth spurt begins at the time of initial mineralization of ulnar ***sesamoid of thumb***. (Stage 4 – Bjork, Grave, Brown) ; (Stage 3 – Singer's method) ; (Hagg and Taranger method).

Ans.170. (b) Articulare

Ref Bhalajhi, 2nd ed, pg 148.

- **Articulare** – point at the junction of the posterior border of ramus and the inferior border of basilar part of occipital bone.
- **Condylion** – The most superior point on the head of condyle.
- **Supramentale** (Point B) deepest point in the midline between the alveolar crest of mandible and the mental process.
- **Ptm point** – intersection between the inferior border of foramen rotundum with the posterior wall of pterygomaxillary fissure.

PROSTHODONTICS

Ans.171. (d) Condylar inclinations and mandibular side shift

Ref http://www.emergenthomestore.com/techcat/dental_simulator.html

- The pantograph graphically records the various positions and movements of the mandible and then the resulting graphs are utilized to adjust an articulator which attempts to reproduce the paths of the patient's movements.
- The pantograph relies upon the hinge axis even though the hinge axis has control only along the border paths when we masticate.
- The pantograph has two face bows with six recording slides and six styli that scribe the paths of the centers of rotation of the mandible.
- The hinge axis is first located, and then an interocclusal record is taken at centric relation or centric occlusion. The pantograph then graphically records the movements of the jaw.
- In making these records, the clutches mounted to the pantograph have to be separated vertically so that there will be no tooth guidance during the registrations, and at the same time separated a minimum distance to reduce the error. After a record of the jaw movements has been registered and the orbital guide set, the arms of the pantograph are locked together and the entire assembly is removed intact from the patient and is transferred to the mounting frame or jig that holds the face bow in proper relation to the adjustable articular while the attaching stone sets.

DISADVANTAGES

- Pantographic tracings are not more accurate than the paths of movement that the operator records.

- Many pantographic errors result from failure to achieve a true terminal hinge condyle position during any part of the tracing.
- Further, there is the fear of recording a protrusive lateral path instead of the straight lateral border path.
- Another disadvantage of pantographic devices is that the tracings must be made at a considerably opened vertical dimension to make room for the clutches. It is essential that the terminal hinge axis be recorded precisely or the incorrect axis of the closure will introduce errors. It is also probable that in some mouths, at least, the border movements are different at the opened position from what they are at the correct vertical position.
- Errors in mounting of pantographic devices are common and easy to make. The slightest movement of either clutch produces a magnified error at the tracing Plate. Studies have shown that reproducibility of pantographic tracing is seldom achieved.

Mandibular movements are three-dimensional in character and have been found to be complex. The envelope of motion has anterior, posterior, and lateral limits, and there is a sequence of motion from one position to the other. Not only do the joints rotate in the vertical, horizontal, and saggital planes, but they are capable of bodily side shift (the Bennett movement) which adds another motion to the complexity of movement. When rotation and translation are combined, there is no constant axis of control. The axis that changes is called the instantaneous axis of rotation, and it is only in control for an instant and can only be located when motion is stopped. If the instantaneous centers cannot be located, there is no way of plotting the functional envelope of motion and the border paths of the complete envelope must be used. The task of duplicating such mandibular movements has been found to be lacking in these devices.

Ans.172. (b) Labial Shoulder with chamfer lingually

Refhttp://www.nature.com/cgi-taf/dynapage.taf?file=/bdj/journal/v192/n10/full/4801428a.html#table.1

Table 2. Suggested preparation features for posterior crowns

Crown type	Posterior crons–preparation features	
	Occiusal reduction*	**Finish line depth and configuration**
VMC	1 mm non-functional cusps 1.5 mm functional cusp	0–1.0 mm Chamfer, knife-edge, shoulder or shoulder with bevel
HSPC	2 mm non-functional cusps 2.5 mm functional cusps	0.8-1.0 mm Shoulder or heavy chamfer
PFM	As for VMC iof metal surface 2 mm non-functional cusps 2.5 mm functional cusps	1.2 mm labial shoulder[1] or chamfer 0.5 mm lingual chamfer

'Where tooth is tited or where vertical dimension is to be increased, the amont of occlusal reduction required will vary

'Too deep a reduction for diminutive teeth or for long clinical crowns where a metal coolar is preferable

Finish lines with marginal configurations for PFMs:

Crown type	Anterior crowns–preparation features	
	Occlusal reduction*	Finish line depth and configuration
PJC	2 mm incisally 1 mm lingual aspect	0.8-1.0 mm shoulder
RBPC	2 mm incisally 0.5-1.0 mm lingual aspect	> 0.4 mm chamfer
PFM	2 mm incisally 0.5-1.0 mm lingual aspect [porcelain guidance requires greater clearance]	1.2 mm labial shoulder[1] or heavy chamfer 0.5 mm lingual chamfer
*Where the vertical dimension is to be increased, the amount of occlusal reduction required will be less or non-existent *Too deep a reduction for diminutive teeth eg lower incisors or for long clinical crowns where a metal collar is preferable		

(PJC- Porcelain jacket crown; RBPC-Resin bonded; PFM-Porcelain fused metal)

Finish lines with marginal configurations for PFMs:

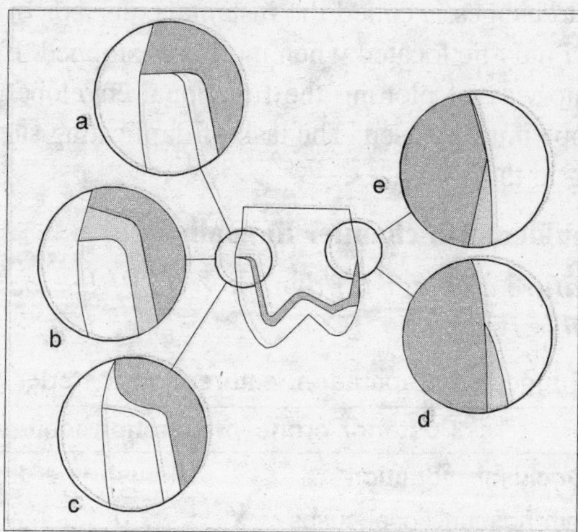

(a) Shoulder with porcelain butt fit; (b) Deep chamfer with metal collar; (c) Shoulder plus chamfer (bevel) with metal collar; (d) Knife edge with metal margin; and (e) Chamfer with metal margin.

Ans.173. (b) Horizontal plane

Explained earlier please refer KCET-07 A176

Remember, Jaw relations have 3 dimensions

Horizontal jaw relation (centric relation)

Vertical jaw relation

Orientation plane (Hinge axis)

Ans.174. (a). Rotary curettage

Refhttp://www.nature.com/bdj/journal/v192/n12/fig_tab/4801456t2.htm

Techniques for recording subgingival finish lines

Method	Description	Indications	Comments	Hazards
Retraction cord	Standard method using knitted/twisted cord	Gingival or subgingival finish lines	Two-cord technique shows better results where the smaller diameter cord is left in place during impression making	Trauma, recession, inflammation of gingival tissues
Chemical solutions	Retraction cords impregnated with epinephrine, alum, ferric sulphate	Twice as effective than plain cords with reduced bleeding	Ferric sulphate has better retractive, hemostatic properties	Concerns with 'epinephrine-syndrome' like raised BP, alum can cause necrosis, Fe sulphate –stain gums brown
Rotary curettage (*Gingettage*)	Use of chamfered diamond bur to remove epithelial lining while tooth prep.	For tooth preparations with healthy gingiva. Sulcus depth not to exceed 3mm and adequate width of keratinized gingiva.	Palatal tissues respond better than buccal tissues that are thin. Not suitable for cases where the probe can be seen through the gingiva	A slight deepening may result. Poor tactile sensation can result in damage and recession.
Electrosurgery	Controlled tissue destruction with current (frequency >1Mhz)	Used to widen sulcus for cord placement, removal of overgrown tissues.	3 types- troughing or gingivectomy coagulation.	Cardiac pacemakers, metallic objects restorations

Ans.175. (d). Boxing wax

Ref Nallaswamy, Pg 66

A perforated stock tray is preferred for making an impression with the alginate material.

- As these trays are of standard size, they may not fit the patient exactly. Hence the closest fitting tray is selected.
- A gap of 3 mm(1/8 inch) is recommended between the tray and the ridge.
- If the tray is short, soft, ***boxing wax*** is used to form an occlusal rim over the tray which would help in proper adaptation and protect the fragile border tissues.

Ans.176. (a) Gysi

Ref Nallaswamy, pg 198

LINGUALIZED OCCLUSION

- First proposed by Alfred Gysi in 1927.
- Involves the use of large upper palatal cusps against a wide lower central fossa.
- The buccal cusps do not contact each other; Clough reported superior chewing efficiency with such occlusion.
- ***Payne***'s modification includes the use of 30^0 anatomic teeth, later modified which had complete intercuspation without any deflective occlusal contacts.

Ans.177. (d) Silverman

Ref http://www.scielo.br/pdf/jaos/v13n4/27320.pdf

The phonetic method is one of the several techniques to determine vertical dimension of occlusion in dentate and edentate patients. This method was proposed by ***Silverman*** .and is based on sibilant sounds.

- He defined the closest distance of the mandible to the maxilla as the closest speaking space.
- Widely accepted, mainly because of the supposed stability of mandibular speaking positions, even after removal of teeth.
- Another advantage of this technique is the smaller variance of closest speaking space when compared to freeway space.
- According to Silverman, the sibilant sounds are the ones that most constantly bring the mandible to the closest speaking level.
- The sibilants are high-frequency sounds produced by a stream of air directed through a minimal incisal separation and an example of it is the /s/ sound. Its mandibular speaking position has been used for vertical dimension evaluation and also as a parameter for placing anterior artificial teeth. Tongue contacts the lingual portion of anterior teeth during /s/ sound and their position in a complete denture can affect emission quality.
- Speech movements can also be influenced by anatomo-functional factors such as incisor overlaps, face format and tongue movements.
- The average value is about 2-3 mm.

Ans.178. (a) Intra oral records

Explained earlier please refer KCET-07 A176

Ans.179. (c). Neutrocentric concept

Ref Nallaswamy, pg

Neutrocentric Concept of Occlusion: stated that the plane of occlusion should be flat and parallel to the residual alveolar ridge. The antero-posterior and bucco-lingual inclines are eliminated in order to direct the forces to the posterior teeth. The concept is similar to monoplane occlusion used to set non-anatomic teeth

Ans.180. (c) Submucosal vital root retention

Refhttp://translate.google.com/translate?sourceid=navclient&hl=en&u=http%3a%2f%2fwww%2eankara%2eedu%2etr%2fkutuphane% 2fDisHek%2f2005%5f32%5f2%2f09%2epdf

The presence of resorptive alveolar crest generally causes problems for fixed partial denture (FPD) applications. Early tooth loss and edentulousness for a long time are among the reasons of alveolar crest resorption. In these circumstances, when constructing FPD anteriorly the problems of oral hygiene and color match with the gingiva can be faced.

Vital root retention (VRR) contributes maintaining the alveolar bone height. In the cases of deficient inter-arch distance, VRR is an appropriate treatment approach to prevent esthetics and periodontal tissues in fixed prosthetic management.

Ans.181. (c) Closed horse shoe

Explained earlier, please refer KCET-05 A184

Ans.182. (a) 0.010 inch

Ref McCracken's 11th ed, pg 179

- To identify the location and magnitude of a retentive undercut, a surveyor is used.
- Undercuts may be measured with an *undercut gauge*, such as those provided with the Ney and Jelenko surveyors.
- The amount of undercut is measured in hundredths of an inch.
- The depth of an undercut/dimple should be verified with a tangent drawn to the height of the contour of the tooth.
- Although, theoretically the amount of undercut may be upto 0.03 inch, ideally, a **0.010"** deep undercut is considered sufficient.

Ans.183. (b) Class II

Ref McCracken's 11th ed, pg 255

CLASSIFICATION of abutment teeth

- **Class I**- those abutment teeth that require only minor modifications to their coronal portions.
- **Class II**- those that are to have restorations other than complete coverage crowns.
- **Class III**- those that are to have crowns (complete coverage).

So friends as mentioned in the question, abutment teeth with cast inlays -would fall in Class II category (*other than full coverage*).

Ans.184. (d) Guiding plane

Ref McCracken's 11th ed, pg 259

Consider the following lines, and the answer shall be clear…

''The crown ledge or shoulder, obtained on the crown restorations on abutment teeth provide for effective stabilization, reciprocation and indirect retention.

True reciprocation can only be produced by creating a path of placement for the reciprocal arm that is parallel to other guiding planes.

In this manner the reciprocal arm contacts the tooth surface before the retentive arm begins to flex, and the ledge, provides for a terminal stop for the reciprocal arm.

Thus, presence of a ledge enables the reciprocal arm to be placed parallel to the path of placement of the denture, augmenting the occlusal rest and providing indirect retention at the same time.

EXTRA EDGE

Spark Erosion: spark erosion is a highly advanced technology for producing the ultimate in precision fit of the reciprocal arm to the ledge on the casting. This system enables repositioning the casting with great accuracy and an electric discharge machine that is programmed to eròde minute metal particles through periodic spark intervals.

Ans.185. (d) Reverse approach circlet clasp

Ref Nallaswamy, pg 360

Reverse approach clasp

- Used when the retentive undercut on abutment tooth is located adjacent to the edentulous space.
- The clasp is designed to arise from the mesial side and end in a distal undercut in a distal extension denture base.
- Occlusal rest mesially means that the distal marginal ridge is unprotected and hence additional rest required.
- Poor esthetics and wedging of the clasp.

COMMUNITY AND PREVENTIVE DENTISTRY

Ans.186. (a) Normal distribution

Ref http://en.wikipedia.org/wiki/Gaussian_distribution

Gaussian distribution

The normal distribution, also called the Gaussian distribution, is an important family of continuous probability distributions, applicable in many fields. Each member of the family may be defined by two parameters, location and scale: the mean ("average") and standard deviation ("variability"), respectively. The standard normal distribution is the normal distribution with a mean of zero and a variance of one (the green curves in the plots to the right). Carl Friedrich Gauss became associated with this set of distributions when he analyzed astronomical data using them), and defined the equation of its probability density function. It is often called the bell curve because the graph of its probability density resembles a bell.

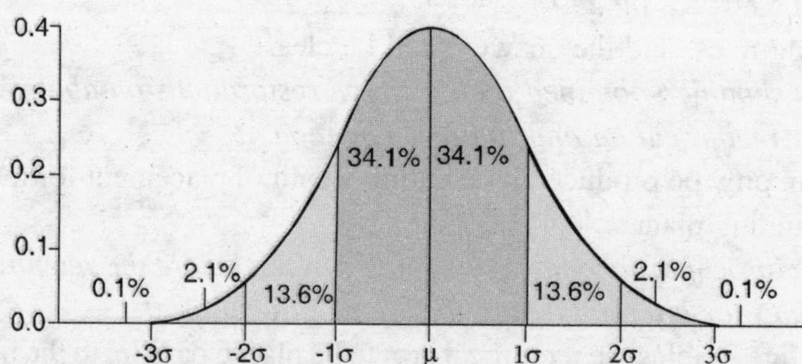

Standard deviation

Dark blue is less than one standard deviation from the mean. For the normal distribution, this (mu) accounts for about 68% of the set (dark blue) while two standard deviations from the mean (medium and dark blue) account for about 95% and three standard deviations (light, medium, and dark blue) account for about 99.7%.

About 68% of values drawn from a standard normal distribution are within 1 standard deviation away from the mean; about 95% of the values are within two standard deviations and about 99.7% lie within 3 standard deviations. This is known as the "**68-95-99.7 rule**" or the "**empirical rule**."

Ans.187. (d). False.

Ref http://en.wikipedia.org/wiki/Type_I_error

Type I error

Type I error, also known as an "error of the first kind", an ***á error***, or a "false positive": *the error of rejecting a null hypothesis when it is actually true*. In other words, this is the error of accepting an alternative hypothesis (the real hypothesis of interest) when the results can be attributed to chance. Plainly speaking, it occurs when we are observing a difference when in truth there is none (or more specifically - no statistically significant difference).

A false positive normally means that a test claims something to be positive, when that is not the case. For example, a test saying a woman is pregnant when she is actually not pregnant is an example of a false positive.

$$\frac{\text{Number of True Negative}}{\text{Number of True Negative + Number of False positive}}$$

Type II error

Type II error, also known as an "**error of the second kind**", a **â error**, or a "**false negative**": the error of accepting a null hypothesis when the alternative hypothesis is the true state of nature. In other words, this is the error of failing to observe a difference when in truth there is one. This type of error can only occur when the statistician accepts the null hypothesis

Ans.188. (d). Percentage

Ref http://en.wikipedia.org/wiki/Sensitivity-tests

Sensitivity, or **recall rate**, is a statistical measure of how well a binary classification test correctly identifies a condition

$$\text{sensitivity} = \frac{\text{number of True Positives}}{\text{number of True Positives + number of False Negatives}}$$

- A sensitivity of 100% means that the test recognizes all sick people as such.
- Sensitivity alone does not tell us how well the test predicts other classes (that is, about the negative cases).
- Sensitivity is not the same as the positive predictive value (ratio of true positives to combined true and false positives), which is as much a statement about the proportion of actual positives in the population being tested as it is about the
- A sensitive test will have fewer Type II errors

Specificity =

Remember,

- False positive rate (á) = FP / (FP + TN) = 1 - specificity
- False negative rate (â) = FN / (TP + FN)= 1 - sensitivity

Ans.189. (c) Early diagnosis and prompt treatment

EXPLAINED EARLIER

Ans.190. (b) < 0.05.

From the above explanation, we have seen that at mu level outside 95 % confidence limit occurs at 3 standard deviation (99.7 %) . this satisfies both conditions mentioned in the question (μ outside 95% with SD > 2) . hence, the P should be statistically significant at value <0.05.

Ans.191. (d) Roll stroke

EXPLAINED EARLIER

Ans.192. (a) Herzberg

Ref http://en.wikipedia.org/wiki/Motivation

Motivation refers to the initiation, direction, intensity and persistence of behavior (Geen, 1995). Motivation is a temporal and dynamic state that should not be confused with personality or emotion Motivation in the work situation can be measured in terms of 10 scales, and the basic logic derives from a synthesis of the best known need and process approaches to explaining what motivation is fundamentally all about. Its development can be traced from 3 main areas of research:

1. Adler, Maslow and ***Herzberg***'s work on self-actualisation;
2. Lewin, Vroom and Porter & Lawler's theories surrounding level of aspiration;
3. Murray, McClelland & Atkinson, Weiner, Rosenberg and Rotter's work relating to achievement motivation

1. Self-actualisation theory: The needs, listed from basic (lowest, earliest) to most complex (highest, latest) are as follows:

- Physiological
- Safety and security
- Social
- Self esteem
- Self actualization

Ans.193. (b) Comprehensive Health Care

Ref Park, pg 26

Levels of health care

- **Primary:** first level of contact where 'essential health care' is provided. PHC and their sub-centers provide care with the participation of the whole community
- **Secondary:** more complex problems comprising essentially curative services provided by district hospitals and community health centers. This constitutes 'first referral level' .

- **Tertiary:** provides super-specialty care by regional/center level institutions. Apart from health care, they provide management and teaching facilities.

Most hospitals provide comprehensive health care .This is a process of providing preventive, therapeutic and maintenance care necessary for function, aesthetics and integrity with balanced consideration to patient's physical, social, economic and psychosomatic status.

Although, specialized care is also a correct option, we shall take the most appropriate answer which is option 'b'.

Ans.194. (a) Sullage

Ref http://www.babylon.com/definition/sullage/

Greywater, sometimes spelled graywater, grey water or gray water and also known as ***sullage***, is non-industrial wastewater generated from domestic processes such as washing dishes, laundry and bathing. Greywater comprises 50-80% of residential wastewater. Greywater is distinct from blackwater in the amount and composition of its chemical and biological contaminants (from feces or toxic chemicals). Greywater gets its name from its cloudy appearance and from its status as being neither fresh (white water from groundwater or potable water), nor heavily polluted (blackwater). This generally excludes ***any solid*** wastes.

This should **not be confused** with 'sewage water'

Sewage is the mainly liquid waste containing *some solids* produced by humans which typically consists of washing water, faeces, urine, laundry waste and other material which goes down drains and toilets from households and industry. It is one type of wastewater, and is a major actual or potential source of pollution especially in urban areas

Ans.195. (c) 0.5 mg/ltr after 1 hour

Ref Park 17th ed, pg 498

The chlorine demand of water is the difference between the amount of chlorine added to the water ,and the amount of residual chlorine remaining at the end of a specific period of contact (usually 60 min) at a given temperature and pH of water. It is the amount of chlorine that is needed to destroy bacteria and to oxidize all the organic matter and ammoniacal substances present in the water. The point at which the chlorine demand of the water is met is termed as ***'break-point'***. Above this 'free-chlorine' (HOCl and OCl) begins to appear in water. The minimum recommended concentration of free chlorine is ***0.5 mg/L for 1hr***.

Ans.196. (a). Better with slow and filter

EXPLAINED EARLIER

Ans.197. (a) No mode

Ref http://en.wikipedia.org/wiki/Mode_%28statistics%29

Mode means the most frequent value assumed by a random variable, or occurring in a sampling of a random variable

- The mode is not necessarily unique, since the same maximum frequency may be attained at different values

- The mode of a discrete probability distribution is the value x at which its probability mass function takes its maximum value. In other words, it is the value that is most likely to be sampled.
- The mode of a continuous probability distribution is the value x at which its probability density function attains its maximum value, so, informally speaking, the mode is at the peak.
- When a probability density function has *multiple* local maxima, it is common to refer to all of the local maxima as modes of the distribution (even though the above definition implies that only global maxima are modes). Such a continuous distribution is called ***multimodal*** (as opposed to unimodal).
- In symmetric unimodal distributions, such as the normal (or Gaussian) distribution (the distribution whose density function, when graphed, gives the famous "bell curve"), the mean (if defined), median and mode all coincide.
- For a sample from a ***continuous distribution***, such as [0.935..., 1.211..., 2.430..., 3.668..., 3.874...], the concept is unusable in its raw form, since each value will occur precisely once. The usual practice is to discretize the data by assigning the values to equidistant intervals, as for making a histogram, effectively replacing the values by the midpoints of the intervals they are assigned to. The mode is then the value where the histogram reaches its peak
- Unlike mean and median, the concept of mode also makes sense for "***nominal data***" (i.e., not consisting of numerical values). For example, taking a sample of Korean family names, one might find that "Kim" occurs more often than any other name

Ans.198. (c) -1 to +1

Ref http://en.wikipedia.org/wiki/Correlation_coefficient

Correlation, also called **correlation coefficient**, indicates the strength and direction of a linear relationship between two random variables

A number of different coefficients are used for different situations. The best known is the *Pearson product-moment correlation coefficient*, which is obtained by dividing the covariance of the two variables by the product of their standard deviations. Despite its name, it was first introduced by Francis Galton

The correlation is defined only if both of the standard deviations are finite and both of them are nonzero. It is a corollary of the Cauchy-Schwarz inequality that the correlation **cannot exceed 1** in absolute value.

The correlation is 1 in the case of an increasing linear relationship, "1 in the case of a decreasing linear relationship, and some value in between in all other cases, indicating the degree of linear dependence between the variables. ***The closer the coefficient is to either "1 or 1, the stronger the correlation between the variables.***

If the variables are independent then the correlation is 0, but the converse is not true because the correlation coefficient detects only linear dependencies between two variables

Ans.199. (a) Decreases

Ref http://en.wikipedia.org/wiki/Standard_deviation

The **standard deviation** of a probability distribution, random variable, or population or multiset of values is a measure of the spread of its values. It is usually denoted with the letter ó (lower case sigma). It is defined as the ***square root of the variance***

Keep in mind, that variance is the *average* of the squared differences between data points and the mean. Variance is tabulated in units squared. Standard deviation, being the square root of that quantity, therefore measures the spread of data about the mean, measured in the same units as the data.

Said more formally, the standard deviation is the root mean square (RMS) deviation of values from their arithmetic mean i.e.

$$\sigma = \sqrt{\frac{1}{N}\sum_{i=1}^{N}(x_1\ \bar{x})^2}\ .$$

Where, N = sample size

Hence, we see that SD varies inversely with the sample size. So increasing the sample size would decrease the standard deviation.

Ans.200. (a) 4

Ref http://en.wikipedia.org/wiki/Degrees_of_freedom_%28statistics%29

In probability theory and statistics, the **chi-square distribution** (also **chi-squared** or $\div^2$ **distribution**) is one of the most widely used theoretical probability distributions in inferential statistics, i.e. in statistical significance tests.

It is useful because, under reasonable assumptions, easily calculated quantities can be proven to have distributions that approximate to the chi-square distribution if the null hypothesis is true.

The sum of the residuals (unlike the sum of the errors) is necessarily 0. If we have five numbers that must sum to zero, four of them, 5 – 1, can be arbitrarily chosen without violating the summing to zero constraint. That means the residuals are constrained to lie in a space of dimension *n* " 1. If we know the values of any *n* " 1 of the residuals, we can find the value of the last one. Thus, we say that **"there are *n* " 1 degrees of freedom for error"**

Hence, for a table of 3x3, the degree of freedom = (3-1) x (3-1) = 4.

1

Selftest 1

1. **Mandibular nerve does not supply:**
   (a) Buccinator (b) Masseter
   (c) Tensor tympani (d) Temporalis
2. **The enzyme used in polymerase chain reaction is:**
   (a) Thermostable enzyme (b) Enzyme stabilizer
   (c) Inorganic ion (d) Inorganic metal
3. **In familial hypercholesterolemia there is deficiency of:**
   (a) LDL receptor defect (b) Apo protein A
   (c) Apo protein C (d) Lipoprotein lipase
4. **Which process separates the fragments of DNA:**
   (a) Gel centrifugation (b) Paper chromatography
   (c) High speed centrifugation (d) Thin layer chromatography
5. **Specificity is related to:**
   (a) True positive (b) True negative
   (c) False positive (d) False negative
6. **Vitamin D is maximum in:**
   (a) Milk (b) Fish fat
   (c) Eggs (d) Cod liver oil
7. **Selye described a syndrome which has three stages; the syndrome is called the**
   (a) Selye syndromc (b) Specific alienation syndrome
   (c) General adaptation syndrome (d) Antistress syndrome
8. **Trickling filter is used in:**
   (a) Primary treatment of sewage (b) Secondary treatment of sewage
   (c) Oxygen ponds (d) Sewage farming
9. **Denominator in general fertility rate is:**
   (a) All women between 15-45 year age
   (b) All married women between 15-45 year age

(c) Total number of live births
(d) Total number of all births

10. In India, family planning is managed by:
(a) 100% sponsored by Central government only
(b) 100% by state government only
(c) 50% state and 50% central government
(d) Fully sponsored by central government with planning of state government

11. Morbidity detection in a community can be done by:
(a) Active surveillance
(b) Passive surveillance
(c) Sentinel surveillance
(d) Randon1 surveillance

12. In case control study of buccal carcinoma:
(a) CA is commoner in zarda pan users than non users
(b) Zarda pan is a cause of buccal CA
(c) Zarda pan is associated with buccal CA
(d) If use of zarda pan is stopped, number of cases will reduce

13. All are dihydrofolate reductase antagonists, except:
(a) Methotrexate
(b) Cytosine arabinoside
(c) Pentamidinc
(d) Pyrimethamine

14. A drug causing least physical dependence –
(a) Alprazolam
(b) Fluoxetine
(c) Dextroproxyphenc
(d) Pcntazocine

15. The Drug excretion through kidney depends on all,
(a) High blood flow in kidney
(b) Molecular weight of drug
(c) Lipid solubility of drug
(d) Plasma protein binding of drug

16. All are used for anaerobic streptococci except:
(a) Pcnicillin
(b) Carbenicillin
(c) Clindamycin
(d) Vancomycin

17. All occur' in botulism EXCEPT:
(a) Diplopia
(b) Diarrhoea
(c) Dysphagia
(d) Dysarthria

18. Most common tumor caused by virus is:
(a) Warts
(b) Carcinoma cervix
(c) Nasopharyngeal carcinoma
(d) Lymphoma

19. Macrophages are found in:
(a) Phase of scar formation
(b) Phase of repair
(c) Late phase of inflammation
(d) Early phase of inflammation

20. All arc the CNS findings in AIDS except:
(a) Vasculitis
(b) Perivascular infiltration in parenchyma
(c) Mesoglial nodules
(d) Spongiform changes in white matter

21. Prophylactic craniospinal irradiation is not recommended in:
(a) Gemistocytic astrocytoma (b) Posterior fossa ependymoma
(c) Meningioma (d) Medulloblastoma

22. Which of the changes occur in bone growth?
(a) Increased acid phosphatase (b) Increased urinary calcium
(c) Increased bone nucleotidase (d) Increased osteocalcin

23. Investigation of choice in case of a pt. with episodic hypertension, headache and thyroid nodule:
(a) Urinary HIAA
(b) Urinary catecholamine and aspiration of nodule
(c) Thyroid function test only
(d) Urinary basic amino *acid* metabolite

24. Which of the following graft is known as Wolf's graft:
(a) Split thickness graft (b) Full thickness graft
(c) Partial thickness graft (d) Myocutaneous graft

25. Which of the following is associated with cystic hygroma:
(a) Marfans syndrome (b) Turner's syndrome
(c) Own' s syndrome (d) Noonans's syndrome

26. A case of solitary thyroid nodule, investigation of choice is:
(a) T3, T4 estimation (b) Thyroid scan
(c) FNAC (d) Excision biopsy

27. Most common site for nasopharyngeal carcinoma
(a) Nasal septum (b) Fossa of rosenmuller
(c) Vault of nasopharynx (d) Antero-superior wall

28. Adenocarcinoma of ethmoid sinus associated with
(a) Wood workers (b) Nickel workers
(c) Coal workers (d) Chimney workers

29. A child's negative response to a dental drill is a
(a) Phobia (b) Fear
(c) Anxiety (d) Any of the above

30. Anesthetic agent causing hallucination is:
(a) Ketamine (b) Ether
(c) Nitrous oxide (d) Cyclopropane

31. Vasoconstriction is seen with
(a) Lignoeaine (b) Cocaine
(c) Idiotocaine (d) Bupivaeaine

32. Salick's maneuver is used
(a) To reduce dead space (b) To prevent alveolar collapse
(c) To prevent gastric aspiration (d) To facilitate assisted respiration

33. Delusion is a disorder of:
(a) Thinking (b) Memory
(c) Perception (d) Intellect

34. Which of the following is seen in osteoporosis'?
(a) Increased serum calcium (b) Increased serum phosphorus
(c) Normal serum phosphorus (d) Increased serum alkaline phosphates

35. Which of the cardiovascular conditions result in a medical emergency In the dental office causing substernal pain, facial pallor, and cold perspiration
(a) Angina pectoris (b) Congestive heart failure
(c) Hypertension (d) Patent ductus arteriosus

36. All the following are features of scurvy, except:
(a) Perifollicular hyperkeratotic papules (b) Purpura
(c) Hemarthrosis (d) Scorbutic rosary

37. All of the following arc features of tetanus except:
(a) Fracture can occur
(b) Survivors recover completely in 4 weeks
(c) Diagnosis is clinical and no microbiological tests are reuired
(d) Loss of consciousness occurs in moderately advanced cases

38. Ramu, 45-yrs-old patient, presents with odontogenic infection. He has had recurrent infections and weight loss in the recent past, has a good appetite with polydipsi(a) He should be investigated for:
(a) Chronic glomerulonephritis (b) Diabetes mellitus
(c) Malignancy (d) Infections mononucleosis

39. Hypercalcemia is seen in all, except:
(a) Chronic renal failure (b) Milk alkali syndrome
(c) Lithium therapy (d) Primary hyperparathyroidism

40. Impaired glucose tolerance can result in:
(a) Nephrotoxicity (b) Neurotoxicity
(c) Retinopathy (d) Ischemic heart disease

41. A 40-yrs-old female patient experiences severe throbbing headache of left craniofacial region. She also has nausea with paresthesia of right upper and lower lip. She may be suffering from:
(a) Cluster headache (b) Glossopharyngeal nerve neuralgia
(c) VII cranial nerve neuralgia (d) Migraine

42. Wide scars occur due to:
(a) Early suture removal (b) Excessive skin tension
(c) Use of subcutaneous absorbable sutures (d) Excessive undermining or skin edges

43. Tachycardia, nervousness, intolerance to heat and exophthalmos are seen in:
(a) Ilyperthyroidism (b) Hypothyroidism
(c) hyperparathyroidism (d) Hypoparathyroidism

44. Systolic pressure of 50 to 60 mm Hg is a striking feature of:

(a) Myxoedema (b) Agranulocytosis
(c) Egaloblastic anemia (d) Addison's disease

45. The most common tumor of bone seen in India is:

(a) Adamantinoma (b) Osteogenic sarcoma
(c) Suamous cell carcinoma (d) Osteoclastoma

46. Which of the following structures is not removed in radical neck dissections?

(a) Sternocleidomastoid muscle (b) Internal jugular vein
(c) Spinal accessory nerve (d) Phrenic nerve

47. Which of the following factors delay wound healing?

(a) Vitamin B-12 deficiency (b) Ascorbic acid deficiency
(c) Vitamin A deficiency (d) Infection

48. Which of the following is true for thyrotoxicosis

(a) In Graves disease antibodies are formed to TSH receptors which result in excessive thyroxin secretion
(b) Hashimoto's thyroiditis occurs in young males
(c) In primary hypothyroidism, decreased TSH levels are seen
(d) In Graves disease no antibodies arc formed to TSH receptors which result in decreased thyroxin secretion.

49. Which of the following is not a premalignant feature of suamous cell carcinoma of esophagus'!

(a) Achalasia (b) Barrett's esophagus
(c) Corrosive injury (d) Plummer· Vinson syndrome

50. A patient presents with suamous cell carcinoma of lip with invasion into the alveolus. The patient is edentulous appropriate treatment is.

(a) Segmental mandibulectomy (b) Resection mandibulectomy
(c) Hemi mandibulectomy (d) Commando operation

51. A patient with carcinoma of tongue has also an enlarged lymph node of lower neck. Treatment includes

(a) Suprahyoid neck dissection (b) Supraomohyoid neck dissection
(c) Radical neck dissection (d) None or the above

52. A patient has had goiter for the past 20 Years. It shows a sudden increase with hoarseness of voice Reason could be:

(a) Injection
(b) Cystic degeneration
(c) Malignant change to follicular carcinoma
(d) Malignant change to papillary carcinoma

53. Which of the following is a complication of tracheostomy?

(a) Surgical emphysema (b) Pneumothorax
(c) Carotid artery injury (d) Subglottic stenosis

54. Treatment of pleomorphic adenoma of parotid is

(a) Total parotidectomy
(b) Superficial parotidectomy
(c) Deep parotidectomy
(d) Radical parotidectomy

55. Which of the following factors is important in fluoride use in systemic fluoride supplement administered 10 a child?

(a) Age and Wight of child
(b) Average'~ temperature or the region where the child resides and the age or the child
(c) Weight of the child amount of fluoride level or the drinking water where the child resides
(d) Age of the child and the fluoride content of the drinking water where the child resides

56. Endemic dental Fluorosis occurs at what concentration of fluoride in the drinking water supply?

(a) 1 ppm
(b) 3 ppm
(c) 5ppm
(d) 7 ppm

57. Vomiting during impression moulding procedures may be prevented by:

(a) Sedating the patient
(b) Injecting local anesthetic
(c) Asking patient to come empty stomach
(d) Change the: impression material

58. In the development of balanced occlusion of a complete denture, during tooth arrangement, a steep condylar path is associated with a low degree of incisal guidance, this reuires that the compensating curve should be:

(a) Flat
(b) shallow
(c) prominent
(d) Reverse

59. The non-rigid connectors are used in the construction of FPD when the span is:

(a) Short, supplementing alveolar ridge reduction reuired
(b) Short, supplementing alveolar ridge reduction not reuired
(c) Long, supplementing alveolar ridge reduction
(d) Long supplementing alveolar ridge reduction not reuired

60. Post and core is preferred to a posterior crown abutment tooth as it is:

(a) Stronger
(b) Better esthetically
(c) Independent to the abutment tooth
(d) Less chair time fabrication

61. The correct comparison of amount of tooth reduction for metal ceramic crown and porcelain jacket crown is

(a) The racial tooth reduction
(b) The incisal reduction is the same for both
(c) There is more lingual reduction in metal ceramic
(d) There is less lingual reduction in metal ceramic

62. Biologically and mechanically acceptable solder joint of FPD is:

(a) It is thin occluso-gingivally and wide facio-lingually
(b) It extends to the entire interproximal space occluso-gingivally
(c) It is circular in form and occupies the region of contact area
(d) It extends into the facial margin or the retainer

63. It is better to reduce any occlusal deformities in the existing dentition before the fabrication of a FPD as:

(a) To prevent trauma to rest of the dentition

(b) To decrease the amount of adjustment reuired at the post insertion phase

(c) To prevent the duplication of the deflective occlusal contact in the new restoration

(d) To maintain a more accurate anatomical occlusal surface in the new restoration

64. A high occlusal contact occurs in the balancing position between the lingual cusps of maxillary 1sl molar and the buccal cusp of mandibular Ist molar. To eliminate this, which surface should be reduced?

(a) Lingual cusp of maxillary 1st molar or buccal cusp or mandibular 1" molar

(b) Either lingual cusp of maxillary I" molar or buccal cusp or mandibular Ist molar

(c) Lingual cusp of maxillary I" molar with milling paste at the time of denture insertion

(d) Lingual cusp of maxillary Isl molar in centric an

65. The distance between the teeth and the axis of rotation is shorter than the skull with the resultant loss of accuracy, the instrument which produces such type of replication is:

(a) Semi-adjustable articulator

(b) Hinge articulator

(c) Fully-adjustable articulator

(d) Face-how articulator

66. When establishing balanced occlusion, lingual cups of maxillary posterior teeth on the non-working side should contact:

(a) Facial inclines of the lingual cusp or mandibular posterior teeth

(b) The lingual incline of the lingual cusp of mandibular posterior teeth

(c) Lingual inclines of the facial cusp or mandibular posterior teeth

(d) Central fossae or mandibular posterior teeth

67. The secondary peripheral seal area of a mandibular complete denture is the

(a) labial border

(b) buccal border

(c) distolingual border

(d) Anterior lingual border.

68. For the preparation of the rest seat in the marginal ridge of a molar tooth which is reduced by 2 mm to achieve the coned width of thc rest scat. The marginal ridges are then rounded in order to:

(a) Reduce the chances of fracture of the metal rest

(b) Decrease food impaction

(c) For the better distribution or the vertical load

(d) Better clasp retention

69. The primary indication for precision attachment of RPD when the abutment teeth are well-supported when the patient is:

(a) Esthetically concerned

(b) Abutment teeth reuire restoration

(c) No posterior abutment teeth are present

(d) When teeth are present on both the ends of the edentulous area

70. The design of a maxillary cast RPD framework with a double bar (anterior posteriorly) type of major connectors is indicated when:

(a) Maximum palatal support is reuired
(b) High vault type of palate
(c) Acrylic plate for plate is to be used
(d) Where a single palatal bar connector would flex

71. The 1" step in the alteration of the abutment teeth contour in the natural tooth preparation for RPD is:

(a) Preparation of the occlusal rest scat
(b) Disking of the proximal surfaces, parallel to the path of insertion
(c) Cutting a retentive undercut in a dimple on the facial surface is needed
(d) Decreasing the height of contour to the gingival one-third on the abutment tooth.

72. To impart a hardening heat treatment to a dental gold alloy, the best method is to:

(a) Pickle the casting in a strong acid
(b) uench the hot casting in cold water
(c) Bench cool room casting temperature to room temperature
(d) Reheat the cooled casting to 450°C and cool uniformly to 250°C over a period of 15-30 min.

73. Polyacrylie acid is the parent compound of the:

(a) Zinc oxide-eugenol cements
(b) Zinc phosphate cements
(c) Cyanoacrylate cements
(d) Carboxylate cements

74. Commonly used acid for etching teeth in conjunction with pit and fissure sealant is:

(a) Hydrochloric acid
(b) Phosphoric acid
(c) Acetic acid
(d) Sulfuric acid

75. The radiographic appearance of a proximal carious lesion is:

(a) Larger than the actual lesion
(b) Smaller than the actual lesion
(c) An accurate reproduction of the size of the lesion
(d) Variable depending upon the exposure time and development process

76. The dental assistant must be comfortably seated on a stool which supports the back and legs and permits the feet to:

(a) Hang freely
(b) Rest on the floor
(c) Rest on a platform or ring approximately 8 in. off the floor
(d) Rest Oil a ring or platform approximately 4 in. off the floor

77. The reduction of cusps tends to decrease:

(a) Outline form
(b) Resistance form
(c) Retention form
(d) Convenience form

78. Compared to unfilled resins, composite resins have:

(a) Greater compressive strength
(b) Less solubility
(c) Greater working time
(d) Smoother finished surface

79. This of the following is not in and of itself a criterion for evaluation of what constitutes good medical or dental care'?

(a) Access
(b) Acceptability
(c) Uality
(d) Continuity

80. In modern epidemiology an epidemic is defined as:

(a) An acute outbreak of infectious disease
(b) An acute outbreak of chronic diseases
(c) A chronically present disease
(d) An occurrence of a disease clearly in excess of normal expectation

81. Which of the following is a properly expressed disease rate'?

(a) Population at risk cases of disease/ 100,000
(b) Total population/cases of disease/100,000
(c) Cases of disease/total population
(d) Cases of disease population at risk/ 100.000

82. The primary culprit in caries of the root surface of the tooth appears to be:

(a) Actinomyces
(b) Streptococcus
(c) Lactobacillus
(d) Pneumococcus

83. Which of the following statements best accounts for the effect of the fluorideion on tooth enamel? It makes tooth enamel:

(a) Harder
(b) Whiter
(c) More resistant to acid dissolution
(d) Basic in pH

84. Intervention in the disease process at a stage before the lesion occurs:

(a) Primary prevention
(b) Secondary prevention
(c) Tertiary prevention
(d) Preventive dentistry

85. Dental floss is useful in removing plaue from:

(a) Occlusal surfaces
(b) Facial and lingual surfaces
(c) Interproximal surfaces above contact point
(d) Interproximal surfaces below contact point

86. A removal partial denture is indicated over a fixed one when:

(a) The patient does not seem sufficiently motivated or capable of cleaning the fixed partial denture adeuately
(b) Supra erupted or submerged teeth have created an uneven plane of occlusion:
(c) The proposed abutment teeth are malaligned
(d) There are missing teeth on both sides of the arch

87. The onlay gains most of its retention from:

(a) The intracoronal portion
(b) The extracoronal portion
(c) Proximal contact
(d) The cementing agent

88. Over contoured crowns are most often the result of:

(a) The need for added retention
(b) Overbuilding by technicians
(c) Insufficient tooth reduction
(d) Periodontal considerations

89. What is the chief contraindication for using epinephrine impregnated retraction cord?

(a) It is chemically irritating to the tissue, causing sloughing.
(b) It produces systemic reactions affecting the cardiovascular system.
(c) It produces inadeuate retraction of the tissues.
(d) Its size makes it difficult to use where the gingival sulcus is shallow and the tissues firm.

90. Why is a custom impression tray used for polysulfide rubber base materials?

(a) The material is too fluid to be retained in a stock tray.
(b) The material needs the additional support afforded by a custom tray.
(c) A custom fit tray controls the thickness of the impression tray.
(d) custom fit tray is much easier to manipulate in the mouth.

91. The face-bow registration gives a record of the:

(a) Relationship of the maxillary arch to the temporomandibular joint
(b) Relationship between the maxillary and mandibular arches
(c) Relationship of the mandibular arch to the temporomandibular joint
(d) Condylar inclinations and the immediate side shift present:

92. At what temperature and for how long should the investment be heated when the hygroscopic techniue is used?

(a) 900°F for I hour
(b) I200°F for 30 min
(c) 1200°F for I hour
(d) 900°F for 30 min

93. If the retainers have a porcelain veneer, the best aesthetic results from the pontic will probably result from:

(a) Using a porcelain flatback facing
(b) Using a porcelain Trupontic
(c) Using an acrylic Truponitic
(d) Processing a porcelain-fused-to-metal pontic

94. The resistance to breakage of shoulder joint by occlusal forces is mostly determined by

(a) Buccolingual width of the joint
(b) Fineness of the solder used
(c) Type of retainer involved
(d) Occlusogingival thickness of the joint

95. How thick must the metal coping be to resist deformation under occlusal pressures?

(a) 0.1 - 0.3mm
(b) 0.3-0.5 mm
(c) 0.5 - 0.75 mm
(d) 0.75-1.1 mm

96. The chief advantage of zinc phosphate cement is its:
(a) Good compressive strength (b) Lack of irritation to the pulp
(c) Film thickness (d) Low solubility

97. The patient complains of sensitivity a few days after cementation of a fixed partial denture with polycarboxylate cement. What is the most likely cause?
(a) Irritation from the cement (b) A loose retainer
(c) Premature occlusion (d) An open margin

98. Aesthetics is an important consideration when deciding between a fixed and removable partial denture for which of the following Kennedy classification?
(a) Kennedy Class I (b) Kennedy Class II
(c) Kennedy Class III (d) Kennedy Class IV

99. As part of the preliminary oral rehabilitative phase of removable partial denture therapy,an isolated mandibular second premolar should ideally be:
(a) Extracted (b) Used for support only
(c) Used as a primary abutment (d) Splinted to a canine with a fixed prosthesis

100. The occlusal reuirements of a mandibular bilateral distal extension removable partial denture against a maxillary complete denture arc:
(a) Centric occlusion
(b) Centric occlusion and working contacts
(c) Centric occlusion and balancing contacts
(d) Centric occlusion, working contacts. and balancing contacts

101. Theoretically the best combination for a partial denture framework is:
(a) Chromium alloy for the clasps, gold alloy for frame work and connectors
(b) Gold alloy for the clasps and connectors, chromium alloy for the framework
(c) Chromium alloy for the clasps and connectors, gold alloy for the framework
(d) Gold alloy for the clasps, chromium alloy for' the framework and connectors.

102. When a patient needs a complete denture, preprosthetic surgery is generally not indicated when which of the following conditions exits?
(a) Pedunculated torus palatinus (b) Papillary hyperplasia
(c) Epulis fissuratum (d) Root tips embedded in mandibular bone

103. All of the following arc landmarks concerned with location of the posterior palatal seal except the:
(a) Fovea palatina (b) Hamular notch
(c) Anterior nasal spine (d) Posterior vibrating line

104. Centric relation must be accurately recorded so that the:
(a) Face-bow record can be accurately taken as the next step in denture construction:
(b) Centric occlusion can be developed in harmony with centric relation
(c) Vertical dimension of rest can be determined
(d) Degree of Bennet angle can be measure

105. In a completed monoplane denture arrangement:
(a) Maxillary anterior teeth may exhibit a small degree of vertical overlap in relation to the mandibular anterior teeth when an orthognathic ridge relationship exists.
(b) The degree of horizontal overlap of maxillary posterior teeth to mandibular teeth must be small regardless of ridge relationship
(c) Central fossae areas of maxillary molars arc always aligned over the mandibular crest of ridge line
(d) Inadeuate buccal overlap of maxillary posterior teeth in relation to mandibular posterior teeth may result in cheek biting.

106. All of the following procedures are carried out in preparation for the delivery appointment with the exception of:
(a) Preservation of face-bow record
(b) Construction of mounting casts
(c) Mounting of the mandibular denture
(d) Finishing and polishing of the restorations

107. Which of the following combinations of artificial teeth should not be used in complete maxillary and mandibular dentures?
(a) Anterior, plastic; posterior, porcelain
(b) Anterior, porcelain; posterior, plastic
(c) Anterior, plastic; posterior, plastic
(d) Anterior, porcelain; posterior, porcelain

108. A child's behavior problem in the dental office can be handled by familiarization if the basis of the problem is:
(a) The parent
(b) Pain
(c) Emotional
(d) Fear

109. The use of which of the following adjunctive aids is necessary to check the efficacy of oral prophylaxis for a young patient'!
(a) Disclosing solution
(b) Sandpaper strip
(c) Snyder test
(d) Unwaxed floss

110. Ectodermal dysplasia is characterized by:
(a) Marked salivary deficiency
(b) Missing deciduous teeth but normal number of permanent teeth:
(c) Missing deciduous and permanent teeth
(d) Moist skin

111. A corrected anterior cross bite is best retained by:
(a) The overbite achieved during treatment
(b) Over treatment and anticipated relapse
(c) Using an auxiliary Hawley's retainer for stabilization
(d) Using a mandibular acrylic guide plane

112. A 4-yrs-old child has severe, acute dental pain, so many teeth are carious that the determination of the offending tooth is difficult. The best diagnostic tool to be used is:
(a) Percussion
(b) Radiographs
(c) Electric pulp testing
(d) The patient's identification of the offending tooth

113. An 8-yr-old girl sustains injury to her maxillary left permanent central incisor. The fracture is well into the dentin. The tooth, however, is not sensitive'. A radiograph reveals no root damage. Immediate treatment should involve.

(a) Disking the roughened enamel margins
(b) Treating the exposed dentin with a stannous fluoride
(c) Advising the patient to return in 3 months
(d) Protecting the 100lh with a sedative treatment under a temporary covering,

114. During tooth preparation for a steel crown, the surface reuiring the least amount of reduction is the:

(a) Distal
(b) Buccal
(c) Mesial
(d) Lingual

115. A 2 ½ yrs-old child has an acute oral infection characterized by small reddish yellow vesicles on the buccal mucosa and on the hard palate. The temperature is 102 F, mouth is sore, and the child will not eat or drink.. The condition described is:

(a) Candidiasis
(b) infantile impetigo
(c) Acute herpetic stomatitis
(d) acute streptococcal infection

116. By what mechanism does the mandibular condyle grow?

(a) Subperiosteal surface addition
(b) Endosteal bone growth
(c) Appositional growth
(d) Endochondral bone formation

117. What is the response of alveolar bone to orthodontic forces ?

(a) Tooth movement stimulates jaw growth, thereby allowing arch expansion.
(b) Bone is deposited at pressure sites and resorbed at tension sites.
(c) Bone is deposited at tension sites and resorbed at pressure sites.
(d) Alveolar bone docs not respond to orthodontic forces unless the individual is growing,

118. Which of the following is not an example of intermaxillary anchorage?

(a) Criss-cross elastics to correct cross bites
(b) Class II elastics between maxillary incisors and mandibular molars
(c) Baker anchorage
(d) Retraction of maxillary incisors by tipping them lingually, using maxillary molars as anchorage

119. A patient presents with a history of cleft palate and anterior cross bite. What is the most likely skeletal cephalometric finding?

(a) Maxillary protrusion
(b) Maxillary retrusion
(c) Normal maxillary position
(d) Mandibular protrusion

120. How does the evaluation of posterior' arch length influence the management of intermediate segment deficiency'?

(a) Molar spacing or crowding can be ignored in the child and adolescent patient.
(b) Posterior crowding could eventually cause anterior crowding.
(c) Evaluation of the posterior segment may help determine bicuspid removal.
(d) Since mesial drift improves molar' positioning, the posterior segment should be observed but not treated in the mixed dentition.

121. A 7-yrs-old patient demonstrates unilateral buccal cross bite in centric occlusion, deviation of the mandibular midline, bilateral construction of the maxillary arch, and a lateral deviation from centric relation to centric occlusion. What is the most likely treatment for this?

(a) Unilateral cross-elastics to widen the constructed side
(b) Bilateral arch wire expansion
(c) Bilateral palatal expansion
(d) Reassess the malocclusion ill the permanent dentition,

122. The most common route for microorganisms and their toxic by-products to reach the pulp tissue is:

(a) Hematogenous anachoresis
(b) Direct extension through an open cavity or carious lesion
(c) Through exposed dentinal tubules following cavity preparation
(d) From the extension of periapical inflections from adjacent infected teeth.

123. A 24yr old male presents with continuous diffuse pain in the maxillary left canine region.. Upon visual examination the tissue in the mucobuccal vestibule appears inflamed and slightly swollen. Palpation reveals a tenderness over the apex of the lateral incisor and the canine. Both teeth arc slightly percussion sensitive.Radio graphically, no pathology is note(d) Further evaluation and the treatment should consist of:

(a) Initiating root canal therapy on both teeth because irreversible pulpal disease is present
(b) Further diagnostic testing, specifically thermal or electric pulp testing
(c) A test cavity on each of the two teeth
(d) Evaluation of pain of non dental origin

124. A 22-yrs-old male presents with continuous mild to moderate pain in the area of tooth #3. You ascertain the following information: history of rheumatic fever and hay fever, pain of 2 days duration, no caries or restorations, no abnormal visual or radiographic findings, a weakly positive percussion test, and a normal response to thermal and electric pulp tests. The most probable diagnosis is:

(a) Irreversible pulpal disease in #3
(b) Reversible pulpal disease in #3
(c) Sinusitis
(d) Referred pain

125. You have just completed root canal therapy on a patient whose lower left second molar had a pulpal periodontal disease. Prognosis for the endodontic therapy is good, but the periodontal prognosis is guarde(d) The tooth is missing the two buccal cusps and the distal marginal ridge due to caries. You want to begin restoration of the tooth next week Your treatment of choice is:

(a) Full cast crown
(b) Post-core with full porcelain to gold crown with margins above the gingival crest
(c) Pin amalgam core with full cast crown
(d) Amalgam build-up and reevaluation of periodontal status at a later date

126. The primary purpose of the endodontic access opening is to:
(a) Remove the coronal pulpal tissue
(b) Allow for removal of the canal contents
(c) Allow for the preparation of the dentinal walls
(d) Establish a straight line access to the apical foramen

127. Yesterday you did a pulpotomy on an emergency patient with pain on tooth #30 caused by irreversible inflammation of a vital pulp. Today the patient has called with moderate - severe pain. You should
(a) Prescribe antibiotics
(b) Prescribe antibiotics and analgesics
(c) Inform the patient it will probably go away
(d) Have patient return and perform complete pulpectomy

128. The normal color of gingiva (marginal, attached, and interproximal may best be described by which one of the following statements?
(a) Normal gingival color is described as coral pink.
(b) Normal gingival color is described as bright re(d)
(c) Normal gingival color is described as reddish blue.
(d) Normal gingival color is described as reddish pink.

129. The radiographic changes associated with gingivitis may best be described by which of the following statements?
(a) There is often a fuzziness or break in the crest of lamina dur(a)
(b) There is often an increase in the width of the periodontal ligament space
(c) There is often loss of alveolar bone height in the interdental septum.
(d) There arc no radiographic changes associated with gingivitis.

130. Occlusal analysis would not usually include examination for which one of the following parameters?
(a) The presence of para functional movements
(b) Soreness in the temporomandibular joint
(c) The presence of gingival inflammation
(d) The initial contact in retruded centric position

131. The predominant microorganisms in the first 24 hours of plaue formation arc:
(a) Vibrios
(b) Filaments
(c) Spirochetes and yibrios
(d) Rods and cocci

132. Which of the following statements is true of dental calculus?
(a) It is composed entirely of inorganic materials.
(b) It is the primary etiologic agent in periodontal disease,
(c) It is classified according to the degree of the inflammatory response it creates.
(d) It is dental plaue which has become mineralize

133. Which of the following statements regarding periodontal prognosis is true?

(a) The presence of a pseudo pocket makes the prognosis little more guarded than the presence of a true periodontal pocket.

(b) The pattern of bone loss does not affect the prognosis, while the amount of bone loss definitely does.

(c) A distal maxillary 1st molar furcation involvement has a poor prognosis because access for cleaning is poor.

(d) Generally the wider and broader the roots, of the tooth, the poorer the prognosis.

134. Which of the following statements is true of osseous surgery?

(a) Reshaping of the bone is referred to as ostectomy or osteoplasty.

(b) Implantation of bone is referred to as ostectomy or osteoplasty.

(c) Implantation procedures are utilized with increasingly greater freuency since the surgical results are reasonably predictable.

(d) Reshaping of bone should not be performed when supporting bone will have to be removed to eliminate the defect.

135. Which of the following is the most important aspect of tooth brushing?

(a) The design of the brush head

(b) The method of tooth brushing

(c) Thoroughness on the part of the patient

(d) The freuency

136. Which of the following statement about inflammatory periodontal disease is most accurate?

(a) The periodontal lesion does not usually reveal a straight line progression; many patients reveal periods of active disease and periods of remission.

(b) The inflammatory process is protective, but has destructive component.

(c) Plaue substances seem to activate various host defense mechanism

(d) All the above are correct.

137. The major portion of dental plaue consists of

(a) Mucin
(b) Levan
(c) Dextran
(d) Microorganisms

138. Experemetal evidence is accumulating that the primary organism responsible for initiation of dental caries is

(a) Staphylococcus
(b) I.actobacillus
(c) Mycobacterium
(d) Streptococcus

139. Blood borne seeding of bacteria into an area of previously damaged or irritated pulp with a resultant inflammation is known as:

(a) Bacterial endocarditis
(b) Koplik"s spots
(c) Chronic hyperplasic pulpitis
(d) Anachoretic pulpitis

140. Which of the following is normally characterized by pain'?

(a) Periapical dental granuloma
(b) Radicular cyst
(c) Periapical scar
(d) Acute periapical abscess

141. Hamartoma is best defined as:

(a) Overzealous repair process
(b) A true tumor, in that it has no apparent etiology
(c) An overproduction of tissue normal to a particular area
(d) *A* degenerative process of tissue normal to an area

142. Entities to be considered in the differential diagnosis of a white oral lesion suspected of being leukoplakia should not include:

(a) l.eukodema
(b) Lichen planus
(c) Lupus erythematosis
(d) Steven - Johnson syndrome

143. Teeth which exhibit a brownish gray discoloration and fluoresce bright yellow under ultra-violet light have probably been affected by

(a) Dcntinogenesis imperfecta
(b) Tetracycline staining
(c) Erylhroblastosis fetalis
(d) Porphyria

144. Which of the following oral lesions may show a striking unilateral distribution'?

(a) Herpes Zoster
(b) Lichen planus
(c) Acute necrotizing ulcerative gingivitis
(d) Primary herpetic gingivostomatitis

145. Pericoronitis in most cases is classified as

(a) Abscess
(b) Periodontal disease
(c) Granulomatous process
(d) Cellulites

146. Which of the following oral cysts would be expected to have the highest rate of recurrence?

(a) Radicular cyst
(b) Nasolabial cyst
(c) Keratocyst
(d) Incisive canal cyst

147. Of the following which is the commonly occurring complication seuel to tooth extraction!

(a) Condensing ostcitis
(b) Alveolar osteitis
(c) Osteomyelitis
(d) Pulmonary abscess

148. Which of the following lesions is characterized by inflammatory fibrous hyperplasia in the flange area of an ill-titling denture and is assumed to reuire surgical removal, as spontaneous regression is rare?

(a) Papillary hyperplasia
(b) Epulis fissurata
(c) Denture sore mouth
(d) Decubitus ulcer

149. Cyanosis of the lips is a common finding in all except:-

(a) Cardiac congestion
(b) Congenital heart defects
(c) Iron deficiency anemia
(d) Polycythemia

150. The most prominent oral sign of Gardener or Peutz - Jeghers syndrome is:

(a) The presence of numerous sl11all polyps on the buccal mucosa
(b) Small melanotic lesions on the lip and hard palate
(c) Numerous small petechiae on the buccal mucosa
(d) Ulcerations on the tongue

151. Minute yellow granules are readily detected on the buccal mucosa of approximately 80% of the population. These Fordyce's spots are one of the very few pathognomonic signs which enable a definitive diagnosis to be made because they are known to be:

(a) Aberrant tonsillar tissue
(b) Hyperkeratosis due to trauma
(c) Minor mucous glands
(d) Ectopic sebaceous gland

152. A 38 yr old brought her three teenaged children for initial examination. On the buccal mucosa of each were detected white, corrugated, firm, non-tender lesions. Although histological examination is necessary for definitive diagnosis, the strongest clinical suspicion to be entertained is that these lesions arc:

(a) Hyperkeratotic
(b) An atypical form of lichen planus
(c) Leukoedcma
(d) White sponge nevus

153. Leukoedema, occasionally observed on the buccal mucosa, is characterized by a clinically appearance of:

(a) Raised, white lesions with an annular configuration
(b) Erosions
(c) A milky white, translucent coloration of the mucosa with minute "hanging" folds of tissue.
(d) White lesions with a lacelike configuration

154. Redness and enlargement of minor salivary gland orifices in the palate arc clinical signs of

(a) Papillary inflammatory hyperplasia
(b) Nicotinic stomatitis
(c) Primary syphilis
(d) Secondary syphilis

155. Prolonged antibiotic administration is known to result in the presence of a:

(a) Crenated tongue
(b) Geographic tongue
(c) Black hairy tongue
(d) Median rhomboid glossitis

156. A 10-yrs-old female was brought in by her mother for restorative treatment. The history provided by the mother included a recent evaluation for emotional difficulties and problems with school work. She also reported that the girl had appeared rather listless for the past several years and that she was disposed to chew on her painted toys rather than play with them. Clinical examination disclosed pallor of the oral mucosa and a grayish blue discoloration of the gingiv(a) These findings arc most consistent with a clinical impression of:

(a) Cherubism
(b) Cretinism
(c) The Pierre Robin syndrome
(d) Plumbism

157. An 18-yrs-old female reuested aesthetic improvement of her "brown teeth." She reported that two of her four brother's teeth had a similar appearance. Some chipping of occlusal and incisal enamel, not attributable to caries .or trauma, was apparent. Radiographs demonstrated an absence of pulp chambers and canals of most teeth and unusually short tapering roots. These findings are characteristic of:

(a) Amelogenesis imperfecta (b) Dentinogenesis imperfecta
(c) Erythroblastosis fetalis (d) Fluorosis

158. Examination of a 4-yr.old male patient dentition revealed a pronounced yellow green discoloration of crowns of the entire dentition; The father reported multiple transfusions at the time of birth. These findings suggest that the most likely, although rare, cause of the patient's tooth discoloration is:

(a) Amelogenesis imperfecta (b) Dentinogenesis imperfecta
(c) Erythroblastosis fetalis (d) Fluorosis

159. A patient with Letterer-Siwe's disease is not apt to consult a dentist because:

(a) The primary symptoms relate to skeletal bon destruction
(b) The head and neck arc never involved
(c) This condition rarely occurs after the age of 2 years
(d) This condition invariably runs a rapid and fatal course

160. Most commonly associated with Trigeminal neuralgia

(a) tumor of the fifth cranial nerve
(b) Involvement of the left side of the face
(c) Its occurrence after the age of 30yrs
(d) The attacks are separated by longer time intervals as the condition progresses,

161. It is most likely for a male patient to have:

(a) Acute necrotizing ulcerative gingivitis (b) Chronic desuamative gingivitis
(c) Chronic gingivitis (d) Periodontitis

162. Female patients are known to be far more predisposed to develop:

(a) Dental caries
(b) Periapical cementifying fibroma (cementoma)
(c) Periapical abscesses
(d) Periodontitis

163. Ethnic background is a known predisposing factor in:

(a) Hemophilia (b) Iron deficiency anemia
(c) Pernicious anemia (d) Thalessemia

164. In the elicitation of the chief complaint and throughout the history taking procedure, it *is most* important for the examiner to:

(a) Appear to be concerned (b) Direct the uestioning
(c) Be unhurried (d) be seated

165. A low (below 70) voltage techniue is most advantageous in demonstrating:

(a) Alveolar crestal bone resorption
(b) Early or small carious lesions
(c) Periapical lesions
(d) A retained root

166. Greater object- film distances are reuired in (a) paralleling techniue than in a bisecting techniue. As a result the use of a long cone is indicated in order to :

(a) Reduce exposure lime
(b) Produce a radiograph of long gray scale contrast uality
(c) Minimize distortion
(d) Prevent loss of declination and/or detail

167. Definition and detail are terms which are often used synonymously. Technically, detail refers to:

(a) Image density
(b) Lack of image distortion
(c) Reproduction of very small objects
(d) Image sharpness

168. Production and use of faster film has been a major factor in reducing patient exposure'. However, the fastest film manufactured has not routinely used by clinicians because:-

(a) A long gray scale contrast cannot be obtained
(b) The image(s) are often distorted
(c) Images appear granular and lack definition
(d) It reuires more careful processing

169. A major advantage of the periapical radiograph as compared with a pantomograph is that:

(a) Distortion is totally absent
(b) Greater image sharpness can be obtained
(c) It is uicker and easier to produce
(d) Landmarks are never superimposed

170. Marked elongation because the vertical angulation was insufficient is most apt to result in:

(a) Burnout' structures of' minimum density
(b) Misinterpretation of actual alveolar crestal bone height as being less than actually is
(c) Misinterpretation or alveolar crestal bone height as being greater than it actually is
(d) Production of tooth images which suggest very short root length

171. Marked foreshortening because the vertical angulation was excessive is most apt to result in

(a) Misinterpretation of alveolar crestal bone height as being greater than it actually is
(b) Bum-out or structures of maximum density
(c) An appearance of osteoporosity of the trabecular pattern
(d) Misinterpretation of an abscess or granuloma

172. The wavelength of x-ray photons is determined bytill':

(a) Kilo voltage
(b) Mill amperage
(c) Amount of heat supplied to the filament
(d) uantity of electrons in the cathode stream,

173. Exposure time for. the maxillary molar region at an 8-in target-film distance is 30 impulses, using 10 ma and 60 kv, The exposure time for the same area using the same factors but increasing the target-film distance to 6-in would be:

(a) 15 impulses (b) 60 impulses
(c) 90 impulses (d) 120 impulses

174. Which of the following conditions is most likely if a radiograph shows a dense, diffuse radiopacity at the apex of the distal root of the mandibular left first molar having a filled root canal and widening of the periodontal space at the apex of the mesial root

(a) Osteoma (b) Ccmentoma
(c) Dental granuloma (d) Sclerosing osteitis

175. A patient, age 45, has pain in the mandible, On radiographic examination, several small, regular, distinct, radiolucent lesions are seen. The laboratory tests show Bence-Jones protein in the urine, The patient most probably has:

(a) Eosinophilic granuloma (b) Malignant melanoma
(c) Multiple myeloma (d) Metastatic carcinoma

176. The radiation protection guide advocates that the x-ray dose to operators of dental x-ray machines should not exceed:-

(a) 100 mill roentgens per week (b) 10 roentgens per week
(c) 100 roentgens per week (d) 300 roentgens per week

177. A patient has an extremely painful tooth which reuires extraction, Her BP is 170/100. The proper way to proceed would be to:

(a) send the patient to a physician but give her an analgesic prescription.
(b) Determine whether the patient is under treatment for hypertension, use anesthetic agents compatible with any drugs being taken, and remove the tooth
(c) Refer the patient to an oral surgeon because the patient should have a general anesthetic
(d) Use mild sedation, with local anesthetics compatible with patient's medication, and remove the tooth.

178. A patient reports that he had angina chest pills and that he has his own nitroglycerin tablets. He needs to have a single tooth extractc(d). Which of the following should the dentist do'?

(a) Simply remove the tooth under local anesthesia and send him on his way.
(b) Use supplemental oxygen and a tablet of nitroglycerin prior to the local anesthetic and then procee(d)
(c) Postpone all surgery until the physician gives permission
(d) Consult with physician, have oxygen available, use preoperative nitroglycerin tablets as indicates, use local anesthesi(a) and extract the tooth.

179. A sudden swelling of the lip which comes and goes without apparent cause is most likely:

(a) A mucocele (b) Angioneurotic edema
(c) A lymphangioma (d) A haemangioma

180. A 50-year-old man has a slow enlargement of his maxilla and a gradual loss of hearing and vision. A differential diagnosis should include

(a) Ossifying fibroma (b) Paget's disease
(c) Ameloblastoma (d) Eosinophilic granuloma

181. A patient dislocated her left mandibular condyle 12 hrs ago. Attempts to relocate are unsuccessful. Probably the major reason is a(n)

(a) Acute Spasm the masseter muscle
(b) Mechanical obstruction caused by an Articular eminence that is too large
(c) Acute spasm of the external pterygoid muscle
(d) Acute spasm or the internal pterygoid muscle

] 82. A closed fracture is one which is characterized by

(a) A lack of bone displacement
(b) An intact periosteum
(c) A lack of communication between (he fracture site and an external surface
(d) Communication between the fracture site and the oral cavity only

183. A horizontal fracture of the maxilla below the level of the orbits is classified as a:,

(a) Le Fort I fracture (b) Le Fort II fracture
(c) Le Fort III fracture (d) Zygomatico-maxillary complex fracture

184. Mandibular bone is best restored by

(a) Autogenous bone (b) Homogenous bone
(c) Freeze-dried bone (d) â-Iypholized bovine bone

185. To prevent inadvertent contamination hospital operating room protocol prescribes that when a sterile gowned surgeon and nurse need to pass each other, they should do so in which of the following manners?

(a) Back to back (b) Back to front
(c) Side to side (d) Front to front

186. Local anesthetics have both lipophilic and hydrophilic properties. These are used to:

(a) Limit force base and decrease diffusion into lipid-rich nerves
(b) Precipitate free base and increase diffusion into lipid-rich nerves
(c) Retard the solution's diffusion through interstitial tissues
(d) Increase the shelf life of the solution

187. Which of the following commonly used vasoconstrictors is most efficient when used with dental anesthetic solutions?

(a) Norepinephrine (b) Nordefrin hydrochloride
(c) Levonordefrin (d) Epinephrine

188. The minimal concentration of oxygen that should be Used with N_20 analgesia is:

(a) 10% (b) 20%
(c) 30% (d) 40%

189. Nasoendotracheal intubation is used freuently for moderate to long dental cases. The major' advantage of this procedure is that it

(a) Permits the dentist to operate without anesthetic euipment in the way
(b) Permits the anesthesiologist to monitor the patient without getting in the dentist's way
(c) Insures a patient's airway function at all times
(d) Prevents saliva from accumulating in the buccal vestibules

190. Hepatic or renal impairment during drug administration may produce drug:
(a) Allergy
(b) Cumulation
(c) Idiosyncrasy
(d) Tolerance

191. Some drugs do not produce any toxic effects because some drugs produce only one pharmacologic effect.
(a) Both statement and reason arc correct and related,
(b) Both statement and reason arc correct but not relate(d)
(c) The statement is correct, but the reason is not.
(d) Neither statement nor reason is correct.

192. The therapeutic index of a drug indicates the maximum effective dose of the drug because the therapeutic index compares therapeutic and lethal doses of a given drug to express its margin of safety.
(a) Both statement and reason are correct and relate(d)
(b) Both statement and reason arc correct but not relate(d)
(c) The statement is correct, but the reason is not.
(d) The statement is not correct. but the reason is an are accurate statement.

193. The chemical structure of a drug is critically important to its interaction with its receptor site because a drug and its receptor site chemically interact to alter physiologic processes.
(a) Both statement and reason are correct and relate(d)
(b) Both statement and reason are correct but not related
(c) The statement is correct, but the reason is not.
(d) The statement is not correct. but the reason is an accurate statement.

194. The principal site of biotransformation of a drug; is the:
(a) Plasma
(b) Spleen
(d) Liver
(c) Gastrointestinal tract

195. The combination of bactericidal and bacteriostatic antibiotics result in antagonism because bactericidal antibiotics affect only replicating microorganisms.
(a) Both statement and reason are correct and relate(d)
(b) Both statement and reason are correct but not relate(d)
(c) The statement is correct, but the reason is not.
(d) The statement is not correct. but the reason is an accurate statement.

196. Which of the following disease states is an absolute contraindication to the use of the sedative- hypnotic?
(a) Liver disease
(b) Renal impairment
(c) Angina pectoris
(d) Prophyrism

197. Which one of the following anticonvulsant drug is the agent of choice in terminating most tonic- clonic seizures?

(a) Primidone (b) Phenobarbital
(c) Phenytoin (d) Diazepam

198. Codeine is an effective analgesic for mild to moderate pain because codeine may induce serials narcotic drug dependence.

(a) Both statement and reason arc correct and relate(d)
(b) Both statement and reason are correct but nut relate(d)
(c) The statement is correct, but the reason is not.
(d) The statement is not correct, but the reason is an accurate statement.

199. The anti-inflammatory and antipyretic effects of aspirin arc related to its inhibition of the synthesis of:

(a) Adrcnocorticosteroids (b) Bradykinin
(c) Histamine (d) Prostaglandins

200. Which of the following drugs is used in the treatment of manic-depressive psychosis?

(a) Diazepam (b) Reserpine
(c) Phenytoin (d) Lithium carbonate

2

Selftest 2

1. The root growth theory of eruption proposes that eruption

(a) Proliferating periodontal ligament
(b) Elongating roots against the hammock ligament
(c) Elongating roots against the base of the alveolar crypt
(d) Expanding pulp in the root canals of tooth against the alveolar crypts

2. How soon after the eruption of a permanent tooth is the molar tooth apex usually fully developed?

(a) Immediately
(b) 3 months
(c) 2 or 3years
(d) 1 ½ yrs

3. In comparison with the mandibular permanent canine the maxillary permanent canine in the same mouth.

(a) Has a shorter root
(b) Is wider mesiodistally
(c) Is narrower mesiodistally
(d) has a less prominent cingulum

4. Cervical line contours are closely related to the attachment of the gingiva at the neck of the' tooth. The greatest contours of the cervical lines and gingival attachments occur on which of the following surfaces

(a) Distal surface of anterior teeth
(b) Distal surface of posterior teeth
(c) Mesial surface of anterior teeth
(d) Mesial surface of posterior teeth

5. Which of the following teeth arc most common ones in abnormal relation and contact with adjacent teeth in the same arch?

(a) Mandibular first premolars
(b) Maxillary canines
(c) Mandibular second molars
(d) Maxillary lateral incisors

6. The gingival sulcus (crevice) extends around the tooth is bounded by the:

(a) Surface of the tooth and the epithelium over the attached gingiva
(b) Free gingival groove and the junction of mucosa and the gingiva
(c) Epithelial covering of free gingiva and attached gingiva
(d) Epithelial covering over the free gingiva and the tooth surfaces

7. The muscle attached to coronoid process of mandible is
(a) Temporalis
(b) Hyoglossus
(c) Medial pterygoid
(d) Geniohyoid

8. Infraorbital nerve is a branch of:
(a) Maxillary division of V nerve
(b) Mandibular division of IV nerve
(c) Glossopharyngeal nerve
(d) Ophthalmic division of V nerve

9. Isthmus of thyroid gland overlies the:
(a) 1st tracheal cartilage
(b) 1st and 2nd tracheal cartilage
(c) 2nd, 3rd and 4th tracheal cartilage
(d) 3rd and 4th tracheal cartilage

10. All are branches of cerebral part of internal carotid artery. EXCEPT:
(a) Anterior choroidal artery
(b) Basilar artery
(c) middle cerebral artery
(d) Posterior communicating artery

11. Parotid dud opens into the:
(a) Vestibule of mouth at the leve1 of upper second molar tooth
(b) Vestibule of mouth at the level of upper third molar
(c) Oral cavil)' on sublingual fold
(d) Oral Cavity on the sublingual papilla

12. The initial. factor involved in the intrinsic coagulation pathway is:
(a) Factor VII
(b) Factor XII
(c) Factor II
(d) Factor XIII

13. When a person stands suddenly from lying down posture, there is
(a) Increased tone of capacitance vessels.
(b) Increase efferent discharge from IX cranial nerve
(c) decreased heart rate
(d) All of the above

14. Which of the following is not a function of somatostatin in human body:
(a) Inhibits growth hormone secretion
(b) Enhances insulin secretion
(c) Mediates cognitive effect
(d) None of the above

15. The mineral reuired to maintain normal parathyroid secretory response is:-
(a) Selenium
(b) Iodine
(c) Magnesium
(d) Fluorine

16. Which of the following cranial nerves is / are involved in the process of swallowing?
(a) Trigeminal
(b) Glossopharyngeal
(c) Facial
(d) All of above

17. The osmolal concentration of human plasma is:
(a) 250 mosm/L
(b) 270 mosm / L
(c) 290 mosm / L
(d) 310 mosm / L

18. Vitamin K dependent clotting factor are all, EXCEPT:
(a) II
(b) VII
(c) IX
(d) V

19. Protein synthesis occurs in:

(a) Rough endoplasmic reticulum
(b) Smooth endoplasmic reticulum
(c) Mitochondria
(d) Golgi apparatus

20. Fischer's lock and key theory' postulated that

(a) Active site in enzyme exists in proper conformation to the substrate molecule even in absence of substrate
(b) Active site during binding to substrate under goes conformational changes to fit
(c) There is absolute specificity in relation between enzyme and substrate
(d) Enzymes have catalytic power and accelerate reaction by reducing energy of activation.

21. Which of the following statement is not true about flavoproteins?

(a) Combine with Fe and Mo to form metalloflavoprotein
(b) these are active form of riboflavin
(c) Carotenoid is the prosthetic group in flavoproteins
(d) Cellular oxidation reduction protein.

22. Which of the following is true about primary structure of proteins?

(a) Linear seuence of amino acids held by peptide determine the primary structure.
(b) Primary structure is helical.
(c) Primary structure is stabilized by hydrogen and disulphide bonds.
(d) None of the above.

23. Which of the following is true about vitamin B12?

(a) Cobalt containing vitamin.
(b) Commercial preparation is cyanocobalamin.
(c) Not present in foods of vegetable origin.
(d) All of the above.

24. Which of the following immunoglobulin can cross the placenta?

(a) IgM
(b) IgD
(c) IgG
(d) IgA

25. Which of the following is not true about DNA?

(a) In viruses DNA is either single or double strande(d)
(b) DNA in homologous species is almost similar.
(c) Viruses contain only DNA and not RN(A)
(d) Besides in bacterial genome DNA is also present in episomes.

26. Which of the following is most virulent streptococci?

(a) Alpha haemolytic streptococci.
(b) Beta haemolytic streptococci.
(c) Gamma haemolytic streptococci.
(d) Group D streptococci.

27. All of the following virus contain souble stranded DNA EXCEPT?

(a) Parvo virus.
(b) Papilloma virus.
(c) Herpes virus.
(d) Pox virus.

28. Best method of sterilizing prosthetic culture plates is?
(a) Ethyleue oxide.. (b) Gamma irradiation.
(c) Moist heat. (d) Hot air.

29. Maurer's dot are seen in infection with?
(a) Plasmodium ovale. (b) Plasmodium falciparum.
(c) Plasmodium malariae. (d) Plasmodium vivax.

30. Most specific test for syphilis is?
(a) FTA-ABS. (b) TPH(A)
(c) TPI. (d) VDRL.

31. In acute hepatitis B infection which of the following is forst to appear in serum?
(a) HBsAg. (b) Anti HBs.
(c) HBeAg. (d) Anti HBe.

32. Botulinum toxin causes?
(a) Increase in smooth muscle activity. (b) Systemic manifestations.
(c) Parasympathomimeti(c) (d) Parasympatholyti(c)

33. Selective medium for Streptococcus pyogenes is?
(a) Chocolate agar. (b) Ludiam medium.
(c) Blood agar. (d) Pike's medium.

34. Which is not a cause of megaloblastic anemia?
(a) Phenytoin. (b) Aspirin.
(c) Folic acid deficiency. (d) Fish tapeworm.

35. Which of the folloeing type of pneumoconiosis is associated with tuberculosis?
(a) Bysinosis (b) Anthracosis
(c) Silicosis. (d) Asbestosis.

36. Which of the following feature differentiates carcinoma is?
(a) Cartwheel appearance of nucleus. (b) Pleomorphism.
(c) Increased mitotic activity. (d) Basement membrane invasion.

37. Commonest histological type of esophageal carcinoma is?
(a) Adenocarcinom(a) (b) Leiomyosarcoma
(c) Adeno-suamous carcinom(a) (d) Suamous cell carcinom(a)

38. All of the following chromosomal disorders are associated with advanced maternal age, EXCEPT?
(a) Down's syndrome. (b) Cri-du-chat syndrome.
(c) Edward's syndrome. (d) Patau's syndrome.

39. Characteristic histological feature of chronic graft rejection is?
(a) Necrotising vasculitis. (b) Fibrinoid necrosis.
(c) Arteriolar thrombosis. (d) Interstitial fibrosis.

40. All are feature of hemolytic anemia, EXCEPT?

(a) Raised serum haptoglobin.
(b) Unconjugated hyperbilirubinmei(a)
(c) Raised plasma LDH.
(d) Hemoglobinaemi(a)

41. Statement true about medullary carcinoma of thyroid is?

(a) Usually associated with MEN-1.
(b) Pro-Calcitonin is deposited as amyloi(d)
(c) Familial incidence.
(d) Histological pattern show Hurthle cells

42. Which of the following cephalosporin is active against Pseudomonas aeruginosa?

(a) Ceftriaxone.
(b) Cephalothin.
(c) Ceftazidime.
(d) Cefotaxime.

43. Which of the following antitubercular drug is contraindicated in pregnancy?

(a) Rifampicin.
(b) Ethambutol.
(c) Pyrazinamide.
(d) Streptomycin.

44. Which of the following is true about drugs useful in amoebiasis?

(a) Diloxanide furoate is useful in intestinal and extra intestinal amoebiasis.
(b) Emetine is tolerated well orally.
(c) Chlorouine is effective only in hepatic amoebiasis.
(d) Mepacrine is useful in chronic cyst passers.

45. Which of the following is not true about benzodiazepines?

(a) Acts on GABA receptor complex.
(b) Midazolam is shortness acting.
(c) Nitrazepam decreases REM sleep.
(d) Flumazenil is a specific antagonist.

46. Which of the following antitubercular drugs can be used in patients with hepatic dysfunction?

(a) Erythromycin.
(b) Cephalosporins.
(c) Chloramphenicol.
(d) Sulphonamides.

47. Pharmacogenerics is important in metabolism of?

(a) Rifampicin.
(b) Isoniazi(d)
(c) Digitalis.
(d) Propranolol.

48. Drug of choice in sore throat caused by Group A beta haemolytic streptococcus is?

(a) Sulphonamides.
(b) Erythromycin.
(c) Penincillin.
(d) Ceftriaxone.

49. Which of the following is not true about anti-fungal drugs?

(a) Amphotericin B is given only parenterally.
(b) Griseofulvin is effective orally.
(c) Ciclopirox olamine is effective in systemic mycoses.
(d) Fluconazole is effective orally as well as i.v.

50. Which of the following is not true about penicillin?

(a) Penicillin V is absorbed orally.

(b) Benzathine penicillin is short acing penicillin.

(c) Cloxacillin is â-lactamase and acid resistant.

(d) Ampicillin is not resistant to â-lactamases.

51. Absorption of a drug depends on all, EXCEPT?

(a) Half life.
(b) Concentration of drug.
(c) Route of absorption.
(d) Vascularity of absorbing surfaces.

52. The metabolism of a drug proceeding at a fixed rate regardless of any further increase in substrate concentration is?

(a) Zero order kinetics.
(b) First order kinetics.
(c) Second order kinetics.
(d) Third order kinetics.

53. All of the following drug causes photodermatitis, EXCEPT?

(a) Thiazides
(b) Phenytoin
(c) Phenothiazine
(d) Oral contraceptive.

54. Persons living at high altitude are more prone to develop which of the following chronic illness?

(a) Pulmonary oedema
(b) Kyphoscoliosis.
(c) Emphysema
(d) Pulmonary Hypertension.

55. To effect a weight reduction of 1Kg/month, the amount of calorie intake is to be reduced by?

(a) 250 kcal/day
(b) 350 kcal/day
(c) 450 kcal/day
(d) 550 kcal/day

56. Levels of creatine phosphokinase in serum are elevated in?

(a) Hypothyroidism
(b) Muscular dystrophy
(c) Acute MI
(d) All of the above

57. Ipsilateral third nerve palsy with cintralateral hemiplegia is called?

(a) Benedikt's syndrome
(b) Weber's syndrome
(c) Claude's syndrome
(d) None of the above

58. In status epilepticus, the drug of choice is?

(a) Phenytoin
(b) Phenobarbitone
(c) Lorazepam
(d) Primidone

59. Methemoglobinemia can be caused by?

(a) Dapsone
(b) Sulfonamides
(c) Primauine
(d) All of the above

60. Hyoid bone os removed to prevent the recurrence of?

(a) Thyroid adenoma
(b) Thyroglossal cyst.
(c) Ectopic thyroi(d)
(d) Papillary carcinoma

61. Which of the following is not an anterior mediastinal tumor?

(a) Thymic tumors
(b) Neurogenic tumors
(c) Pleuropericardial cyst
(d) Dermoid cyst

62. In carcinoid syndrome which of the following is excreted in urine?

(a) 5-HIAA
(b) 17-ketosteroids
(c) VMA
(d) Histamine

63. Which of the following statement is true about Vincent's angina?

(a) Caused by anaerobic, gram negative organisms
(b) Tonsillar infection occurs mainly
(c) Treatment is with penincillin and metronidazole
(d) All of the above

64. Which of the following swelling in the neck is brilliantly transilluminant?

(a) Ranula
(b) Thyroglossal cyst
(c) Cystic hygroma
(d) Sternomastoid tumour

65. False about adenoid cystic carcinoma is?

(a) Most commonly affects parotid gland
(b) Histology shows acidophilic cells as well as basophilic cells
(c) Neural invasion
(d) Tendency to recur

66. Internal opening of branchial fistula is located at?

(a) Fossil of tonsil
(b) Around 3rd molar tooth
(c) Behind palatopharyngeal arch
(d) Around 2nd premolar

67. Which of the following is a non absorbable suture material?

(a) Catgut
(b) Homopolymer of glycolide
(c) Homopolymer of polydioxanone
(d) Silk

68. All of the following are true about random pattern flap, EXCEPT?

(a) Vascular basis of flaps is the subdermal plexus of blood vessels
(b) Not suitable for use on face
(c) Many geometric designs are possible
(d) Rhomboid flap is most commonly used

69. Curling ulcer is seen in?

(a) Burns
(b) Head injury
(c) Corticosteroid intake
(d) Acute gastritis

70. Ketamine is contraindicated in?

(a) Hypertension
(b) Raised intracranial tension
(c) Raised intraocular tension
(d) All of the above.

71. Which of the following local anesthetic is sympathomimetic?

(a) Cocaine
(b) Procaine
(c) Lignocaine
(d) Tetracaine

72. Potency of anaesthetic agent can be estimated by?
(a) Molecular weight
(b) Lipid solubility
(c) Minimal alveolar concentration
(d) Boiling point

73. Capnography is?
(a) Monitoring of concentration 0f inhaled O2
(b) Monitoring of concentration of exhaled C02
(c) Monitoring of central venous pressure
(d) Monitoring of blood pressure during anaesthesia

74. Tachyarrhythmia's are least common with?
(a) Enflurancc
(b) Halothane
(c) Isoflurane
(d) Methoxyflurane

75. Which of the following statement about 'cadaveric spasm' is not true?
(a) It appears instantaneously after death
(b) All muscles of the body are involved
(c) Great force is reuired to overcome it
(d) It indicates the mode of death

76. In treatment of corrosive poisoning, Which of the following is not used?
(a) Gastric lavage
(b) Antacids
(c) Bland diet
(d) Intravenous fluids

77. Surest sign of death due to ante mortem hanging is?
(a) Cyanosis of face and lips
(b) Ligature mark around the neck
(c) Protruding tongue
(d) Trickling of saliva, down the angle of the mouth

78. Safe limit of fluorine in drinking water is?
(a) 0.1 – 0.3 mg/lit
(b) 1 – 1.5 mg/lit
(c) 0.5 – 0.8 mg/lit
(d) 3 – 3.5 mg/lit

79. Which of the following is not a live attenuated vaccine?
(a) Pertussis
(b) Measles
(c) Sabin polio vaccine
(d) BCG

80. Which of the following is not true about WHO standards recommended for drinking water?
(a) Hardness of water below 300 mg/litre
(b) Lead below 0.01 mg/litre
(c) Nitrates below 0.1 mg/litre
(d) Chlorination of Water

81. According to WHO, the oral rehydration solution (ORS) besides glucose 20g/lit, and sodium chloride 3.5g/lit, also contains?
(a) 3.5 g calcium chloride and 2.5 g potassium chloride
(b) 2.9 g sodium hydroxide and 1.5 g sodium acetate
(c) 2.5 g sodium bicarbonate and 1.5 g potassium chloride
(d) 1 g potassium hydroxide and 1.5 g potassium chloride

82. Which of the following is not true about chlorination of water?
(a) Contact period of at least 6 hours is essential
(b) Recommended residual free chlorine levels is 0.5 mg/litre for one hour
(c) Water should be free from turbidity
(d) Chlorine demand of water should be estimated

83. Protein content of rice is?
(a) 1.0 g % (b) 11.0 g %
(c) 7.0 g % (d) 7 g %

84. Which of the following insecticide is of plant origin?
(a) Paris green (b) Propoxur
(c) Malathion (d) Pyrethrum

85. Sewage is defined as?
(a) Discarded waste arising from man's activities
(b) Waste matter arising from preparation, cooking and consumption of food
(c) Waste water from community containing solid liuid excreta
(d) Waste water which does not contain human excreta

86. Screening is useful for?
(a) Disease which can be diagnosed at a latent stage
(b) Disease where early diagnosis and treatment favourably alters the natural history of the disease in a significant proportion
(c) Disease which is an important health problem
(d) All of the above

87. Which of the following is true about chi-suare test?
(a) Tests the significance or difference between two proportions
(b) Also be used when more than two groups are to be compared
(c) Both A and B
(d) None of the above

88. In a standard normal curve, mean ± 2 standard deviation covers?
(a) 60% (b) 65%
(c) 99% (d) 95%

89. The lateral spread of dental caries is facilitated most by the?
(a) Dentinoenamel junction (b) Selerotic dentin
(c) Striac or Retzius (d) Enamel spindles

90. The most widely accepted theory for the etiology or dental caries is the?
(a) Zonation theory (b) Proteolytic theory
(c) Proteolysis - chelation theory (d) Acidogenic theory

91. Chronic pulpitis is characterized microscopically by?
(a) Increased fibrosis (b) Decreased cellularity
(c) Presence cellularity (d) All or the above

92. The most constant microscopic feature in the periapical cyst is?
(a) Cholesterol slits (b) Foam cells
(c) Epithelium (d) Polymorphonuclear leukocytes

93. Facial nerve paralysis is a rather common finding associated with?
(a) Pleomorphic adenoma of the parotid (b) Epidermoid carcinoma of the parotid
(c) Warthin's tumor (d) Benign lymphoepithelial lesion

94. A large, double-crowned maxillary central incisor having a single root and canal is probably the result of?
(a) Fusion (b) Dentinal dysplasia
(c) Dens in dente (d) None of the above

95. A generalized widening of the periodontal ligaments is a findings associated with?
(a) Chronic discoid lupus erythematosus (b) Paget's disease
(c) Monostotic fibrous dysplasia (d) Seleroderma

96. Because of similarities in microscopic and radiographic appearances of the conditions, the dentist who receives a biopsy report diagnosis a central giant cell granuloma should take further steps to rule out?
(a) Fibrous dysplasia (b) Osteitis deformans
(c) Albright's syndrome (d) Hyperparathyroidism

97. The healing mechanism after tooth extraction is basically described as?
(a) Organization (b) Resolution
(c) Suppuration (d) Calcification

98. Of the following cysts, which is the most potentially aggressive and destructive?
(a) Dentigerous cyst (b) Globulomaxillary cyst
(c) Incisive canal cyst (d) Periapical cyst

99. Enlargement of the mandible in an adult resulting in prognathism and spacing of the teeth would be most characteristic of?
(a) Hyperparathyroidism (b) Addison's disease
(c) Hyperthyroidism (d) Hyperpituitarism

100. A young patient of yours has multiple areas of pigmentation on the lips and buccal mucos(a) His mother states that he freuently complains of the coli(c) You should suspect?
(a) Pierre Robin syndrome (b) Peutz- Jehgers syndrome
(c) Melkersson -Rosenthal syndrome (d) Gardner's syndrome

101. The most common cyst of the oral regions is the?
(a) Dermoid inclusion cyst (b) Dentigerous cyst
(c) Incisive canal cyst (d) Periapical cyst

102. Pulpal pain as a response to injury or disease is probably the result of?
(a) Increased pressure on nerve endings
(b) Irritation or nerve endings by toxic products of inflammation

(c) Crowding of odontoblasts by reparative denting
(d) Both 1 and 2

103. Ante's law concerns the?
(a) Degree of tipping allowable in an abutment tooth
(b) Amount of curvature acceptable in the plan of occlusion
(c) Amount or increase in retentive factors with a full crown versus a three-uarter crown
(d) None of the above

104. Chemo mechanical tissue retraction provides access primarily by?
(a) Displacing the gingival tissue away from the tooth
(b) Displacing the gingival tissue apically
(c) Tearing the gingival attachment slightly
(d) Removing the tissue on the inside or the sulcus

105. The hydrocolloid tray material is placed into a 115"F - 118'F tempering bath after boiling to?
(a) Make it less fluid so that it is easier to load and use
(b) Allow the necessary chemical reaction to occur
(c) Coo1 the material so that it will not burn the patient
(d) 1 and 3

106. Usually the biggest potential problem in pouring an impression is?
(a) Mixing the stone accurately
(b) Entrapment of an air bubble
(c) Achieving the proper thickness of the stone layer
(d) Placement of the die pins

107. Hygroscopic expansion of the investment material occurs because of?
(a) 900º F heat in the oven
(b) The water present when the investment is mixed
(c) The 100º F water bath which increases the setting expansion by releasing a gaseous component
(d) The 100º F water bath which allows the crystallization process to go to completion

108. Gold solders are classified in terms of their fineness. The lowest fineness gold solder that should be used is?
(a) 725 fineness
(b) 650 fineness
(c) 580 fineness
(d) 500 fineness

109. A high survey line that allows placement of' the retentive terminus of a clasp arm on the gingival one-third of the, abutment tooth indicates that?
(a) The angle of' cervical convergence is small
(b) The angle of cervical convergence is large
(c) The abutment tooth must be recontoured
(d) A bar clasp is the clasp design of choice

110. Which of the following treatment approaches should be considered for a severely extruded abutment tooth, the loss of which would create a distal extension area?

(a) Extraction
(b) Occlusal recontouring
(c) Endodontic therapy and cap placement
(d) Cast restoration

111. Which of the following maxillary partially edentulous arches docs not generally reuire record bases and occlusion rims (or framework) for an accurate face-bow records?

(a) Kennedy class I. modification I
(b) Kennedy class III, modification
(c) Kennedy class II
(d) Kennedy class II, modification 2

112. The final path of insertion may affect aesthetics by permitting?

(a) The most suitable size and shape of anterior tooth replacements
(b) Less clasp metal to be displayed
(c) Both of the above
(d) None of the above

113. According to the house classification of mental attitudes of complete denture patients, the least favourable prognosis is offered by the?

(a) Philosophical patient
(b) Exacting patient
(c) Indifferent patient
(d) Hysterical patient

114. The muscle responsible for elevating the floor of the mouth during swallowing and whose action may impart a characteristic S appearance to the lingual flange of a mandibular complete denture is the?

(a) Mylohyoid muscle
(b) Genioglossus muscle
(c) Superior constrictor muscle
(d) Digastric muscle

115. A face bow record in complete denture construction is used to?

(a) Orient the maxillary cast to the centric relation recor(d)
(b) Facilitate the mounting of the mandibular cast.
(c) Record the relation of the mandible to the opening and closing axis to the temporomandibular join.
(d) None of the above.

116. Which of the following pulpal cell types is a reservoir of multi potential cells capable of responding in an effective defensive manner following irritation?

(a) Polymorphonuclear leukocytes.
(b) Odontoblasts
(c) Lymphocytes
(d) Undifferentiated mesenchymal cells.

117. Although microorganisms possess specific virulence factors, the ultimate pathogenicity of a specific organism depends on?

(a) Ground substance spreading factors
(b) The ability of the organism to alter its metabolic activity
(c) The host-parasite relationship
(d) Antigen-antibody complex formation.

118. Effective root canal sterilization relies solely on the use of intra canal medicaments in the canal between appointments because long periods of medicament and root wall contact ensure total bacterial death and tissue neutralization?

(a) Both statement and reason are correct and relate
(b) Both statement and reason are correct but not related
(c) The statement is correct but the reason is not.
(d) Neither statement nor reason is correct.

119. An elderly male patient presents with a vague diffuse pain in the lower mandibular interior teeth. The pain comes and goes and has been present for 3 months. Although the medical history is non contributory, the patient has not had a physical exam in 5 years. You are unable to elicit any positive findings through diagnostic testing. Your next consideration should be to?

(a) Prescribe an analgesic and dismiss the patient
(b) Set up another appointment to re evaluate the situation in 2 weeks
(c) Refer the patient to a physician tor full examination and consultation prior to any further dental treatment
(d) Extract the teeth and replace them with a denture

120. During the preparation of tooth #31 to receive a MO amalgam you find that you have inadvertently created a mechanical exposure of the mesiobuccal pulp horn. The tooth had been properly isolated with a rubber dam and all the decay has been remove(d) The patient is 13 years old and has no history of symptoms with this tooth. The radiograph reveals no apparent pathology although the root apices are not fully forme(d) Treatment of choice consists of?

(a) An indirect pulp cap with calcium hydroxide followed by an amalgam restoration
(b) An indirect pulp cap with zinc oxide-eugenol followed by an amalgam restoration
(c) A direct pulp cap with calcium hydroxide followed by an amalgam restoration
(d) A direct pulp cap with zinc oxide-eugenol followed by an amalgam restoration

121. During the excavation of a very deep lesion on tooth #30 on an 8-yrs-old patient, you initially find large amounts of mushy, decayed tooth structure over a leathery, demineralised dentin. The tooth is asymptomatic and has given all signs that it is vital. Treatment contemplated should include?

(a) Total excavation; if no exposure is present. apply a base and restore
(b) Total excavation; if a pulp exposure is present, do a direct pulp cap
(c) Total excavation; if a pulp exposure is present, perform a pulpotomy
(d) Application of calcium hydroxide and/or zinc oxide-eugenol over the leathery dentin and restoration with amalgam

122. You have completed all the biomechanical preparation of the root canal of tooth #8. The patient returns in 24 hours with severe pain to biting on #8. You open the tooth and upon x-ray you find that your final file size (#55) is right at the radiographic apex. Treatment of choice is to?

(a) Enlarge the canal one or two sizes, irrigate, and close the tooth
(b) Trephinate at the apex
(c) Enlarge the canal two or three sizes to remove any pulpal remnants
(d) Decrease your working length. Open, irrigate. And close the tooth, reduce the occlusion, and prescribe analgesics

123. A patient is taking a coumarin drug and reuires the extraction of two teeth. This may be safely, performed when?
(a) The prothrombin time is three times the normal control
(b) The prothrombin time a week prior to surgery was two times the normal control
(c) The prothrombin time the day before surgery was two times the normal control
(d) The coumarin was discontinued an hour before surgery

124. Patients who have rheumatic or congenital valvular heart disease are given prophylactic antibiotics before oral surgery to?
(a) Prevent recurrent rheumatic fever
(b) Prevent subacute bacterial endocarditis
(c) Reduce circulating bacteria
(d) Prevent myocardial infarets

125. A patient's chief complaint is that a painless, soft lesion has been present on the mucous membrane side of the lower lip. It has varied in size and has slight blue colour to it. This describes an?
(a) Fibroma
(b) Hemangioma
(c) Mucocele
(d) Cystic carcinoma

126. A patient has an abscessed second mandibular molar with a firm swelling beneath the mandibular border, trismus, and a temperature of 102ºF, the infection has spread to the?
(a) Sublingual space
(b) Infratemporal space
(c) Submental space
(d) Submandibular space below the mylohyoid muscle

127. Radiographic examination is useful in diagnosis all but one of the following cysts?
(a) Globulomaxillary
(b) Nasoalveolar
(c) Traumatic bone
(d) Follicular

128. The Caldwell-Luc procedure is an approach to the?
(a) Masticator space
(b) Maxillary sinus
(c) Ethmoid sinus
(d) Mediastinum

129. A horizontal fracture of the maxilla below the level of the orbits is classified as a?
(a) Le Fort I fracture
(b) Le Fort II fracture
(c) Le fort III fracture
(d) Caldwell-Luc fracture

130. Astringent mouthwashes have the following effect on dental plaue?
(a) Do not effect the plaue significantly
(b) Remove the plaue to a large degree

(c) "Kill" the plaue, rendering it ineffective in producing disease
(d) None of the above

131. The proximal segment of an edentulous mandibular angle fracture is usually displaced?
(a) Posteriorly
(b) Inferiorly
(c) Anteriorly and inferiorly
(d) Anteriorly and superiorly

132. Proper treatment for post extraction alveolitis, "dry socket" should consist of?
(a) Thorough curettage of the socket
(b) Irrigation with Monsel's solution
(c) Gentle removal of debris, irrigation, and dressing of the socket with an obtundent
(d) Gentle anesthetization of the area and use of a bur to place holes in the socket and start fresh bleeding

133. A 20-yrs-old man has a true prognathous relationship between his maxilla and his mandible. Which of the following procedures could be helpful in restoring the arch relationship to normal?
(a) Le Fort I advancement
(b) Sagittal split ostcotomy of the mandible
(c) Bone graft to the molar eminences
(d) C advancement of the mandible

134. How much anaesthetic does 100 cc 2% lidocaine solution contain?
(a) 2 mg
(b) 20 mg
(c) 200 mg
(d) 2 g

135. Two minutes after an injection of a local anaesthetic with vasoconstrictor there is a total absence of pulse beat and respirations have stoppe(d) The patient has had?
(a) A syncopal attack
(b) An idiosyncratic reaction
(c) An anaphylactic reaction
(d) A toxic reaction

136. The minimum concentration of oxygen that should be used with N20 analgesia is?
(a) 10%
(b) 20%
(c) 30%
(d) 40%

137. Which of the following statements best describes the diagnostic information provided by a proper radiographic series?
(a) Radiographs provide a two dimensional visualization of the position of the septal bone.
(b) Radiographs provide information about the crown : root ratios.
(c) Radiographs provide information about the thickness of the periodontal ligament space.
(d) All of the above

138. Which of the following statements about the gingiva is not true?
(a) Normal gingiva is firm and resilient
(b) Normal gingival surface is either a keratinized or Para keratinized
(c) Gingival enlargement may cause a coronal positioning of the gingival margin
(d) Bleeding of the gingiva during tooth brushing usually is not considered an abnormal finding

139. The only accurate way to determine the presence or absence of a pocket is by?

(a) Radiographic examination
(b) Occlusal examination
(c) Pocket probing
(d) Visual examination for gingival enlargement

140. Para functional movements during bruxism or clenching have been described as potentially very destructive. This destruction may manifest itself by?

(a) Tooth mobility
(b) Excessive wear of teeth
(c) Muscle spasms
(d) All of the above

141. Predisposing factors have been described as those conditions which modify the host's response to plaue. Which of the following factors may not be considered a predisposing factor?

(a) Hormonal imbalance
(b) Gingival enlargement
(c) Temporomandibular joint disorders
(d) Blood dyscrasias

142. Which one of the following statements is not a correct sign or symptom of a periodontal abscess?

(a) There is a localized swelling of the gingiv(a)
(b) There is an abnormal response to electric and thermal pulp testing
(c) Pain in the area of the abscess
(d) Tooth or teeth very sensitive to pressure

143. Appearing almost immediately after the cleansing of a tooth, the film of salivary origin which coats the surface is called?

(a) Plaue
(b) Materia alba
(c) Pellicle
(d) Levans

144. Which of the following oral lesions may show a striking unilateral distribution?

(a) Herpes zoster
(b) Lichen planus
(c) Acute necrotizing ulcerative gingivitis
(d) Primary herpetic gingivostomatitis

145. Pericoronitis, in most cases, is classified as a

(a) Abscess
(b) Periodontal disease
(c) Granulomatous process
(d) Cellulitis

146. Which of the following oral cysts would be expected to have the highest rate of recurrence?

(a) Radicular cyst
(b) Nasolabial cyst
(c) Kemtocyst
(d) Incisive canal cyst

147. Of the following, which would be the most commonly occurring complication seuela to a tooth extraction?

(a) Condensing osteitis
(b) Alveolar osteitis
(c) Osteomyelitis
(d) Pulmonary abscess

148. Which of the following lesions is characterized by inflammatory fibrous hyperplasia in the flange area of an ill-fitting denture and is assumed to reuire surgical removal, as spontaneous regression is rare?

(a) Papillary hyperplasia
(b) Epulis fissurala
(c) Denture Sore mouth
(d) Decubitus ulcer

149. Cyanosis of the lips is a common finding in all except?

(a) Cardiac congestion
(b) Congenital heart defects
(c) Iron deficicncy anemia
(d) Polycythemia

150. The most prominent oral sign of Gardner's or Peutz-Jeghers syndrome is?

(a) The presence of numerous small polyps on the buccal mucosa
(b) Small melanotic lesions on the lip and hard palate
(c) Numerous small petechiae on the buccal mucosa
(d) Ulcerations on the tongue

151. Minute yellow granules arc readily detected on the buccal mucosa of approximately 80% of the population. There Fordyce's spots are one of the very few pathognomonic signs which enable a definitive diagnosis to be made because they are known to be?

(a) Aberrant tonsilar tissue
(b) Hyperkeratoses due to trauma
(c) Minor mucous glands
(d) Ectopic sebaccous glands

152. A 38 yrs-old female brought her three teen-aged children for initial examination. On the buccal mucosa of each were detected white, corrugated, firm, non tender lesions. Although histologic examination is necessary for definitive diagnosis, the strongest clinical suspicion to be entertained is that these lesions are?

(a) Hyperkeratotic
(b) An atypical form of lichen planus
(c) Leukoedema
(d) White sponge nevi

153. Leukoedema, occasionally observed on the buccal mucosa, is characterized by a clinically appearance of?

(a) Raised, white lesions with an annular configuration
(b) Erosions
(c) A milky white, translucent coloration of the mucosa with minute "hanging" folds of tissuc
(d) White lesions with a lace like configuration

154. Redness and enlargement of minor salivary gland orifices in the palate are clinical signs of early?

(a) Papillary inflammatory hyperplasia
(b) Nicotinic stomatitis
(c) Primary syphilis
(d) Secondary syphilis

155. Prolonged antibiotic administration is known to result in the presence of a?

(a) Crenated tongue
(b) Geographic tongue
(c) Black hairy tongue
(d) Median rhomboid glossitis

156. A 10-yrs-old female was brought in by her mother for restorative treatment. The history provided by the mother included a recent evaluation for emotional difficulties and problems with school work. She also reported that the girl had appeared rather listless for the past several years and that she was disposed to chew on her painted toys rather than play with them. Clinical examination disclosed pallor of the oral mucosa and a greyish blue discoloration of the gingiv(a) These findings are most consistent with a clinical impression of?

(a) Cherubism (b) Cretinism
(c) The Pierre Robin syndrome (d) Plumbism

157. An 18-yrs-old female reuested aesthetic improvement of her "brown teeth." She reported that two of her four brother's teeth had a similar appearance. Some chipping of occlusal and incisal enamel, not attributable to caries or trauma, was apparent. Radiographs demonstrated an absence of pulp chambers and canals of most teeth and unusually short tapering roots. These findings are characteristic of?

(a) Amelogenesis imperfecta (b) Dentinogenesis imperfecta
(c) Erythroblastosis fetalis (d) Fluorosis

158. Examination of a 4-yrs-old male patient's dentition revealed a pronounced yellow green discoloration of crowns of the entire dentition, The father reported multiple transfusions at the time of birth. These findings suggest that the most likely, although rare, cause of the patient's tooth discoloration is?

(a) Amelogenesis imperfecta (b) Dentinogenesis imperfecta
(c) Erythroblastosis fetalis (d) Fluorosis

159. A patient with letterer-Siwe's disease is not apt to consult a dentist because?

(a) The primary symptoms relate to skeletal bon destruction
(b) The head and neck are never involved
(c) This condition rarely occurs after the age of 2 years
(d) This condition invariably runs a rapid and fatal course

160. Most commonly associated with trigeminal neuralgia is?

(a) A tumour of the fifth cranial nerve
(b) Involvement of the left side of the face
(c) Its occurrence after the age of 30
(d) That attacks are separated by longer time intervals as the condition progresses

161. It is most rare for a male patient to have?

(a) Acute necrotizing ulcerative gingivitis (b) Chronic desuamative gingivitis
(c) Chronic gingivitis (d) Periodontitis

162. Female patients are known to be far more predisposed to develop?

(a) Dental caries
(b) Periapical cementifying fibromas (cementomas)
(c) Periapical abscesses
(d) Periodontitis

163. Ethnic background is a known predisposing factor in?

(a) Hemophilia
(b) Iron deficiency anaemia
(c) Pernicious anaemia
(d) Thalassemia

164. In the elicitation of the chief complaint and throughout the history-taking procedure, it is most important for the examiner to?

(a) Appear to be concerned
(b) Direct the uestioning
(c) Be unhurried
(d) Be seated

165. A low (below 70) kilo voltage techniue is most advantageous in demonstrating?

(a) Alveolar crestal bone resorption
(b) Early or small carious lesions
(c) Periapical lesions
(d) A retained root

166. Greater object- film distances are reuired in a paralleling techniue than in a bisecting techniue than in a bisecting techniue. As a result, the use of a long cone is Indicated in order to?

(a) Reduce exposure time
(b) Produce a radiograph of long gray scale contrast uality
(c) Minimize distortion
(d) Prevent loss of definition and/or detail

167. Definition and detail are terms which arc often used synonymously. Technically, detail refers to?

(a) Image density
(b) Lack of image distortion
(c) Reproduction of very small objects
(d) Image sharpness

168. Production and use of faster film has been a major factor in reducing patient exposure. However, the fastest film manufactured has not been used routinely by clinicians because?

(a) A long gray scale contrast cannot be obtained
(b) The image(s) arc often distorted
(c) Images appear granular and lack definition
(d) It reuires more careful processing

169. A major advantage of the periapical radiograph as compared wlth a pantomograph is that?

(a) Distortion is totally absent
(b) Greater image sharpness can be obtained
(c) It is uicker and easier to produce
(d) Landmarks are never superimposed

170. Marked elongation because the vertical angulation was insufficient is most apt to result in?

(a) Burn-out of structures of minimum density
(b) Misinterpretation of alveolar crestal bone height as being less than it actually is
(c) Misinterpretation of alveolar crestal bone height as being greater than it actually is
(d) Production of tooth images which suggest very short root length

171. Marked foreshortening because the vertical angulation was excessivc is most apt to result in?

(a) Misinterpretation of alveolar crestal bone height as being greater than it actually is
(b) Burn-out of structures of maximum density
(c) An appearance of osteoporosity of the trabecular pattern
(d) Misinterpretation of an abscess or granuloma

172. The wavelength of X-ray photons is determined by the?

(a) Kilo voltage (b) Milli ampere
(c) Amount of heat supplied to the filament (d) uantity of electrons in the cathode stream

173. Exposure time for the maxillary molar region at an 8-in target-film distance is 30 impulses, using 10 ma and 60 kv. The exposure time for the same area using the same factors but increasing the target-film distance to 16 in. would be?

(a) 15 impulses (b) 60 impulses
(c) 90 impulses (d) 120 impulses

174. Which of the following conditions is most likely if a radiograph shows a dense, diffuse radiopacity at the apex of the distal root of the mandibular left first molar having a filled root canal and widening of the periodontal space at the apex of the mesial root?

(a) Osteoma (b) Ccmentoma
(c) Dental granuloma (d) Selerosing osteitis

175. A patient, age 45, has pain in the mandible. On radiographic examination, several small, regular, distinct, radiolucent lesions are seen. The laboratory tests show Bence-Jones protein in the urine. The patient probably has?

(a) Eosinophilic granuloma (b) Malignant melanoma
(c) Multiple myeloma (d) Metastatic carcinoma

176. The radiation protection guide advocates that the X-ray dose to operators of dental x-ray machines should not exceed?

(a) 100 milliroentgens per week (b) 10 roentgens per week
(c) 100 roentgens per week (d) 300 roentgens per week

177. A patient has an extremely painful tooth which reuires extraction. Her BP is 170/100, the proper way to proceed would be to?

(a) Refer the patient to a physician but give her an analgesic prescription.
(b) Determine whether the patient is under treatment for hypertension, use anaesthetic agents compatible with any drugs being taken, and remove the tooth
(c) Refer the patient to an oral surgeon because the patient should have a general anaesthetic
(d) Use mild sedation, with local anaesthetics compatible with patient's medication, and remove the tooth

178. A patient reports that he had anginal chest pain and that he has his own nitroglycerin tablets. He needs to have a single tooth extracte(d) Which of the following should the dentist do?

(a) Simply remove the tooth under local anaesthesia and send him on his way.
(b) Use supplemental oxygen and a tablet of nitroglycerin prior to the local anaesthetic and then procee(d)
(c) Postpone all surgery until the physician gives permission
(d) Consult with physician, have oxygen available, use preoperative nitroglycerin tablets as indicates, use local anaesthesia, and extract the tooth

179. A sudden swelling of the lip which comes and goes without apparent cause is most likely?
(a) A Mucocele (b) Angioneurotic edema
(c) A lymphangioma (d) A hemangioma

180. A 50-year-old man has a slow enlargement of his maxilla and a gradual loss of hearing and vision. A differential diagnosis should include?
(a) Ossifying fibroma (b) Paget's disease
(c) Ameloblastoma (d) Eosinophilic granuloma

181. A patient dislocated her left mandibular condyle 12 hours ago. Attempts at reducing the dislocation are unsuccessful. Probably the major reason is a (n)
(a) Acute spasm of the masseter muscle
(b) Mechanical obstruction caused by an articular eminence that is too large
(c) Acute spasm of the external pterygoid muscle
(d) Acute spasm of the internal pterygoid muscle

182. A closed fracture is one which is characterized by?
(a) A lack of bone displacement
(b) An intact periosteum
(c) A lack of communication between the fracture site and an external surface
(d) Communication between the fracture site and the oral cavity only

183. A horizontal fracture of the maxilla below the level of the orbits is classified as a?
(a) Le Fort I fracture (b) Le Fort II fracture
(c) Le Fort III fracture (d) Zygomatico-maxillary complex fracture

184. Mandibular bone is best restored by?
(a) Autogenous bone (b) Homogenous bone
(c) Freeze-dried bone (d) â-lypholized bovine bone

185. To prevent inadvertent contamination hospital operating room protocol prescribes that when a sterilegowned surgeon and nurse need to pass each other, they should do so in which of the following manners?
(a) Back to back (b) Back to front
(c) Side to side (d) Front to front

186. Local anaesthetics have both lipophilic and hydrophilic properties. These are used to?
(a) Limit free base and decrease diffusion into lipid-rich nerves
(b) Precipitate free base and increase diffusion into lipid-rich nerves

(c) Retard the solution's diffusion through interstitial tissues
(d) Increase the shelf life of the solution

187. Which of the following commonly used vasoconstrictors is most efficient when used with dental anaesthetic solutions?
(a) Norepinephrine (b) Nordefrin hydrochloride
(c) Levonordefrin (d) Epinephrine

188. The minimal concentration of oxygen that should be used with N20 analgesia is?
(a) 10% (b) 20%
(c) 30% (d) 40%

189. Nasoendotracheal intubation is used freuently for moderate to long dental cases. The major advantage of this procedure is that it?
(a) Permits the dentist to operate without anaesthetic euipment in the way
(b) Permits the anaesthesiologist to monitor the patient without getting in the dentist's way
(c) Insures a patient's airway function at all times
(d) Prevents saliva from accumulating in the buccal vestibules

190. Hepatic or renal impairment during drug administration may produce drug?
(a) Allergy (b) Cumulation
(c) Idiosyncrasy (d) Tolerance

191. Some drugs do not produce any toxic effects because some drugs produce only one pharmacologic effect?
(a) Both statement and reason are correct and relate(d)
(b) Both statement and reason are correct but not relate(d)
(c) The statement is correct, but the reason is not.
(d) Neither statement nor reason, is correct

192. The therapeutic index of a drug indicates the maximum effective dose of the drug because the therapeutic index compares therapeutic and lethal doses of a given drug to express its margin of safety?
(a) Both statement and reason are correct and relate(d)
(b) Both statement and reason are correct but not relate(d)
(c) The statement is correct, but the reason is not.
(d) The statement is not correct, but the reason is an accurate statement.

193. The chemical structure of a drug is critically important to its interaction with its receptor site because a drug and its receptor site chemically interact to alter physio logic processes?
(a) Both statement and reason are correct and relate(d)
(b) Both statement and reason are correct but not relate(d)
(c) The statement is correct, but the reason is not.
(d) The statement is not correct, but the reason is an accurate statement.

194. The principal site of biotransformation of a drug is the?

(a) Plasma (b) Spleen
(c) Gastrointestinal tract (d) Liver

195. The combination of bactericidal and bacteriostatic antibiotics result in antagonism because bactericidal antibiotics affect only replicating microorganisms.

(a) Both statement and reason are correct and relate(d)
(b) Both statement and reason are correct but not relate(d)
(c) The statement is correct, but the reason is not.
(d) The statement is not correct, but the reason is an accurate statement.

196. Which of the following disease states is an absolute contraindication to the use of the sedative- hypnotic agents?

(a) Liver disease (b) Renal impairment
(c) Angina pectoris (d) prophyrism

197. Which one of the following anticonvulsant drugs is the agent of choice in terminating most tonic- clonic seizures?

(a) Primidone (b) Phenobarbital
(c) Phenytoin (d) Diazepam

198. Codeine is an effective analgesic for mild to moderate pain because codeine may induce serious narcotic drug dependence?

(a) Both statement and reason are correct and relate(d)
(b) Both statement and reason are correct but not relate(d)
(c) The statement is correct, but the reason is not.
(d) The statement is not correct, but the reason is an accurate statement.

199. The anti inflammatory and antipyretic effects of aspirin are related to its inhibition of the synthesis of?

(a) Adrenocorticosteroids (b) Bradykinin
(c) Histamine (d) Prostaglandins

200. Which of the following drugs is used in the treatment of manic-depressive psychosis?

(a) Diazepam (b) Reserpine
(c) Phenytoin (d) Lithium carbonate

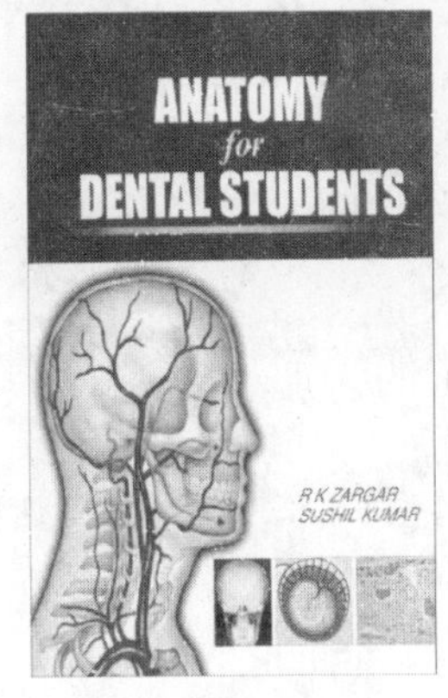
ANATOMY
for
DENTAL STUDENTS
R K ZARGAR
SUSHIL KUMAR

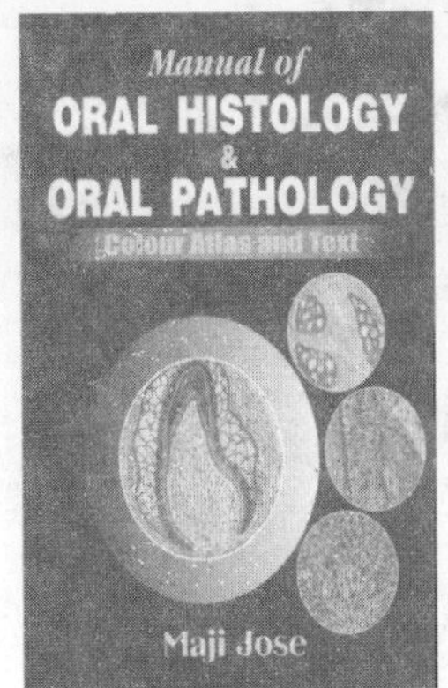
Manual of
ORAL HISTOLOGY
&
ORAL PATHOLOGY
Colour Atlas and Text
Maji Jose

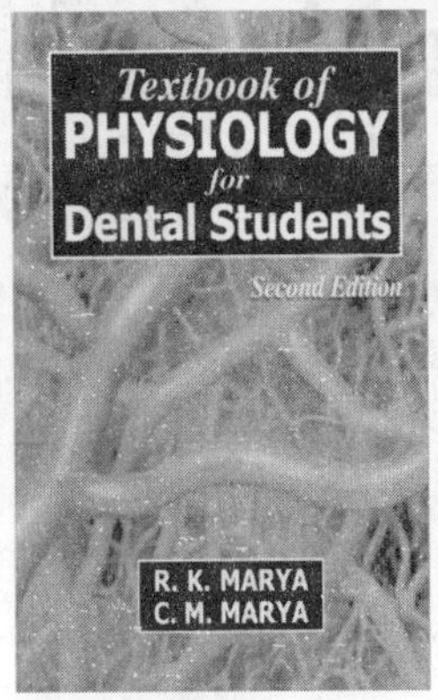
Textbook of
PHYSIOLOGY
for
Dental Students
Second Edition
R. K. MARYA
C. M. MARYA

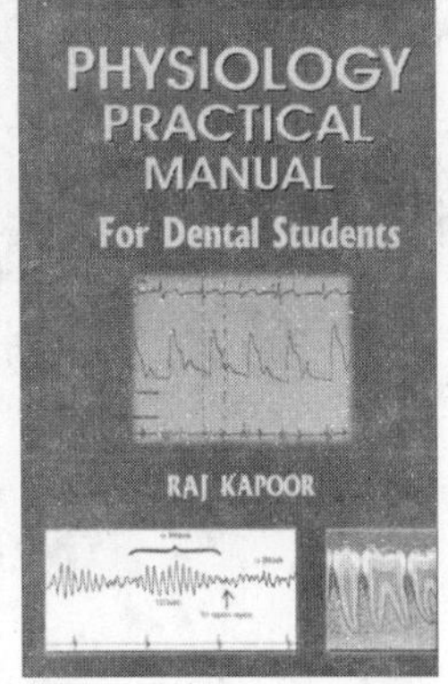
PHYSIOLOGY
PRACTICAL
MANUAL
For Dental Students
RAJ KAPOOR

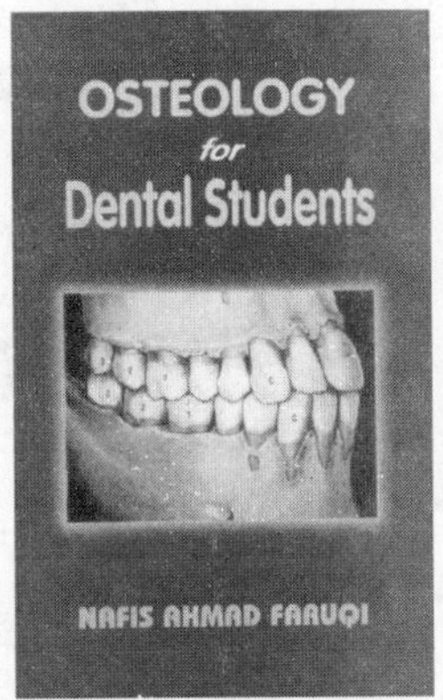
OSTEOLOGY
for
Dental Students
NAFIS AHMAD FARUQI

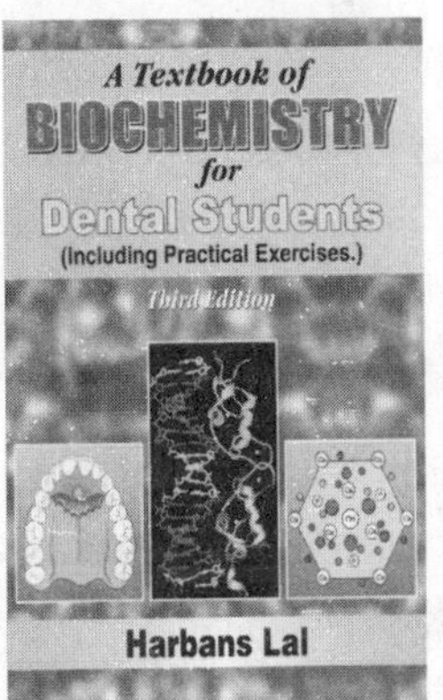
A Textbook of
BIOCHEMISTRY
for
Dental Students
(Including Practical Exercises.)
Third Edition
Harbans Lal

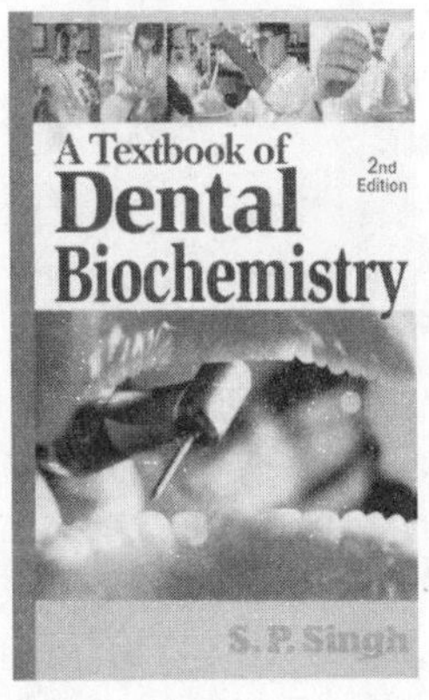
A Textbook of
2nd
Edition
Dental
Biochemistry
S. P. Singh

PRINCIPLES OF
DENTAL
PHARMACOLOGY
SECOND EDITION
Naresh Kumar Khanna

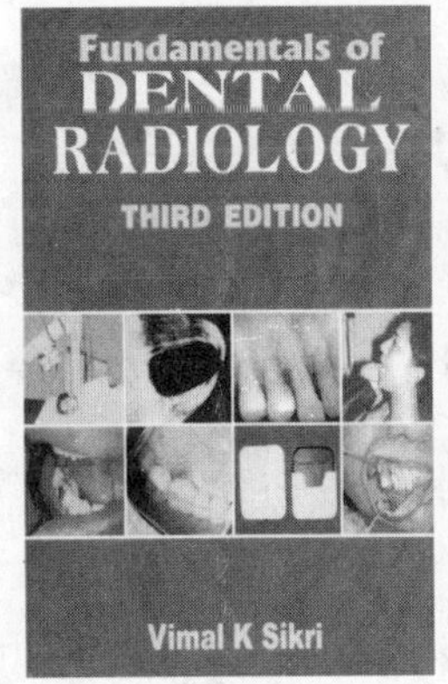
Fundamentals of
DENTAL
RADIOLOGY
THIRD EDITION
Vimal K Sikri

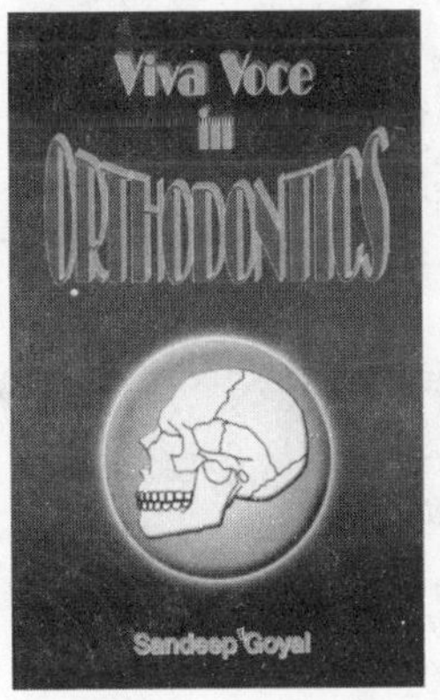
Viva Voce
in
ORTHODONTICS
Sandeep Goyal

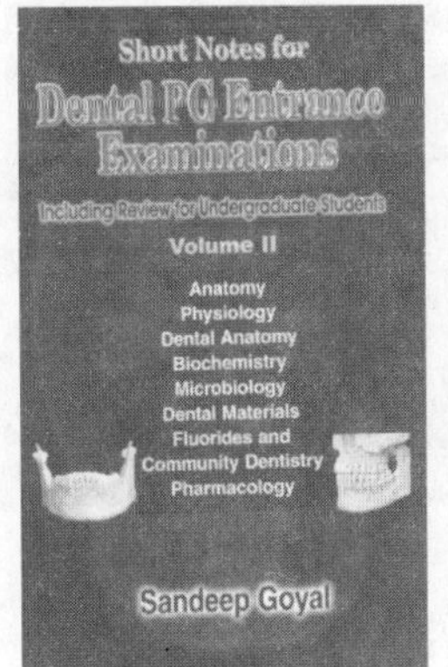
Short Notes for
Dental PG Entrance
Examinations
Including Review for Undergraduate Students
Volume II
Anatomy
Physiology
Dental Anatomy
Biochemistry
Microbiology
Dental Materials
Fluorides and
Community Dentistry
Pharmacology
Sandeep Goyal

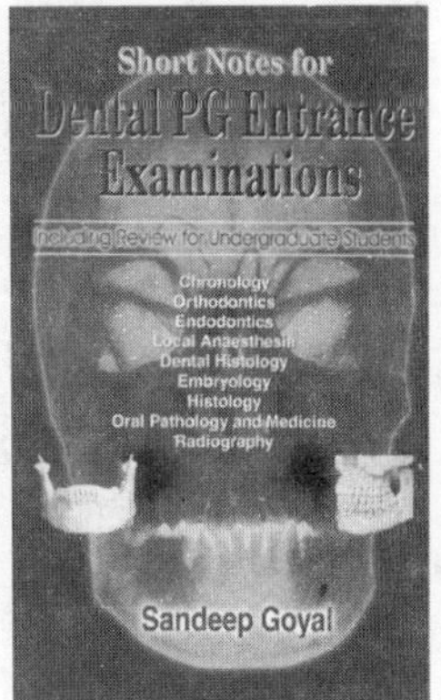
Short Notes for
Dental PG Entrance
Examinations
Including Review for Undergraduate Students
Chronology
Orthodontics
Endodontics
Local Anaesthesia
Dental Histology
Embryology
Histology
Oral Pathology and Medicine
Radiography
Sandeep Goyal

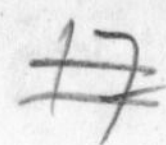

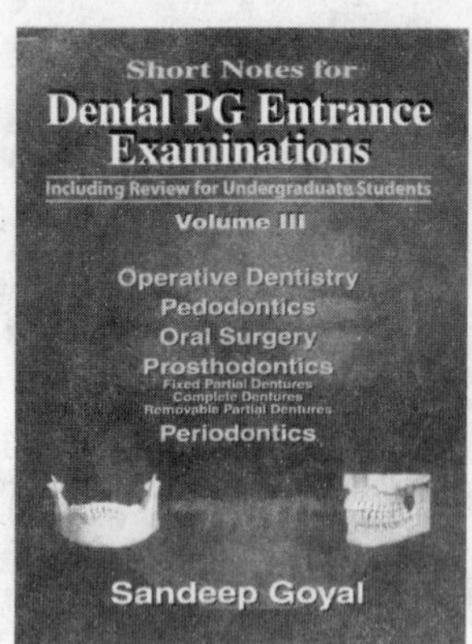

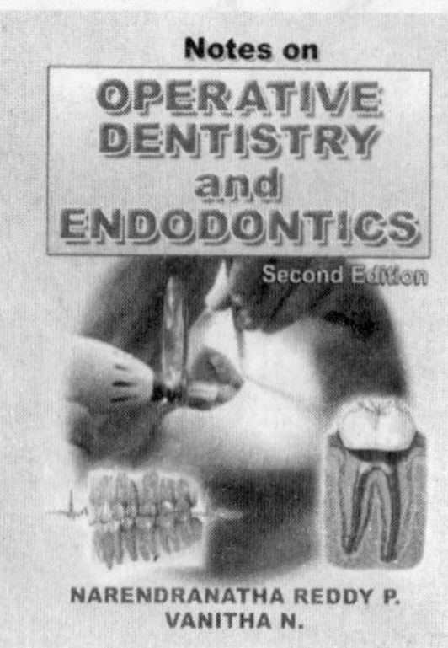

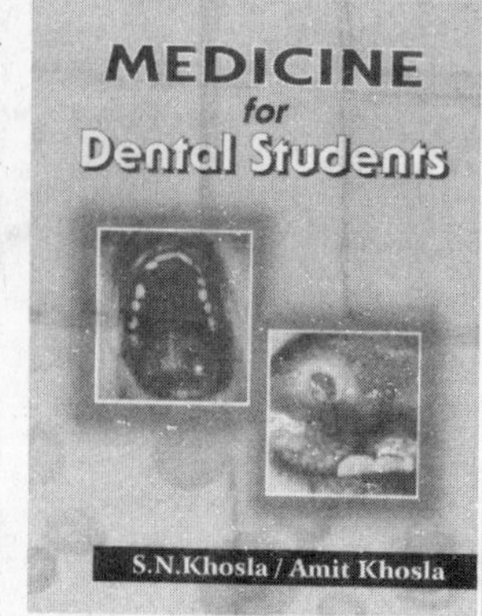

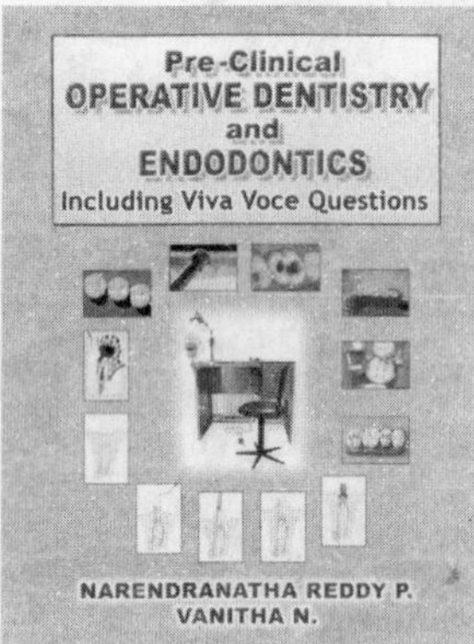

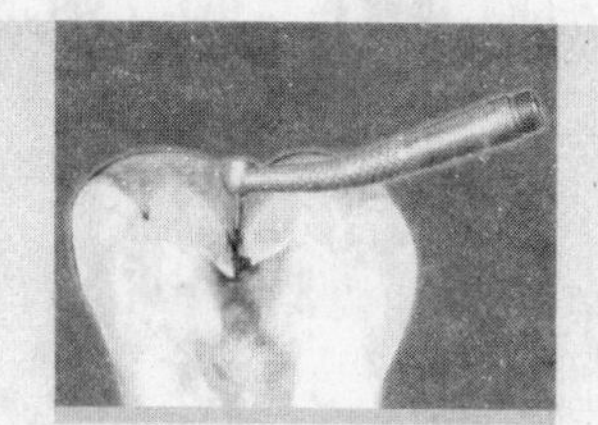

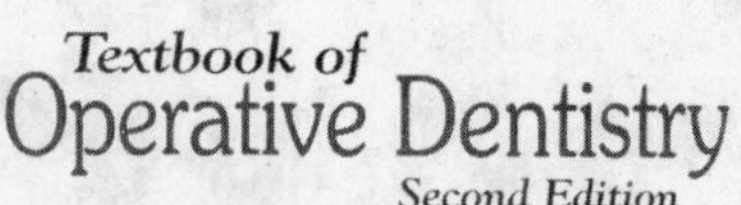

Vimal K Sikri

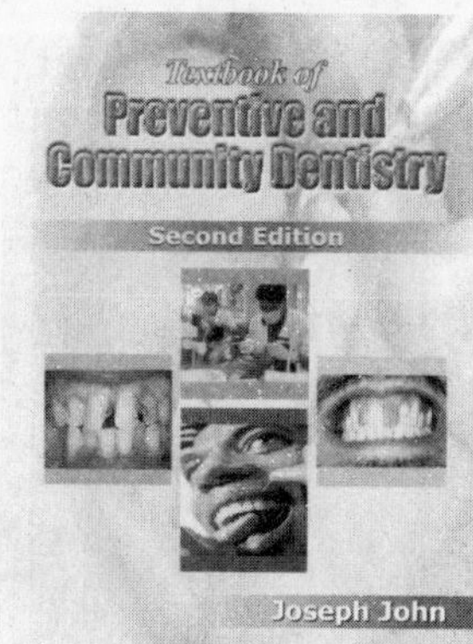

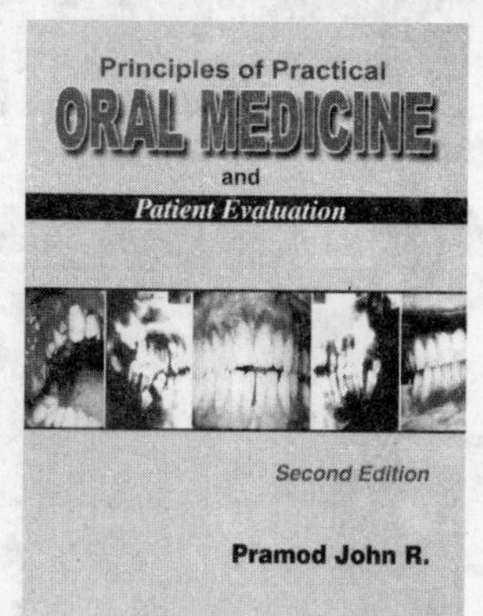

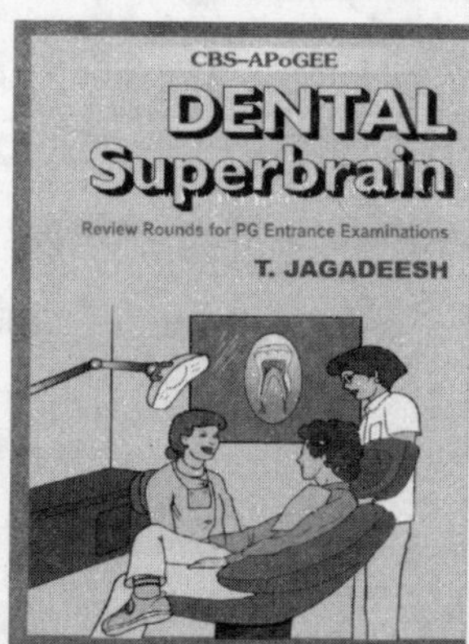